# THE LOEB CLASSICAL LIBRARY

FOUNDED BY JAMES LOEB

EDITED BY

## G. P. GOOLD

# GREEK LYRIC

# III

LCL 476

# GREEK LYRIC
# III

## STESICHORUS, IBYCUS,
## SIMONIDES, AND OTHERS

EDITED AND TRANSLATED BY

DAVID A. CAMPBELL

HARVARD UNIVERSITY PRESS
CAMBRIDGE, MASSACHUSETTS
LONDON, ENGLAND
1991

*Library of Congress Cataloging-in-Publication Data*

Greek lyric.
(The Loeb classical library)
Text in Greek with translation in English.
Includes index.
Bibliography.
Contents: v. 1. Sappho, Alcaeus — v. 2. Anacreon,
Anacreontea — v. 3. Stesichorus, Ibycus, Simonides,
and others
1. Greek poetry. 2. Greek poetry—Translations into
English. I. Campbell, David A. II. Title. III. Series.
PA3622.C3    1982         884'.01'08         82–17898
         ISBN 0–674–99157–5 (v. 1)
         ISBN 0–674–99158–3 (v. 2)
         ISBN 0–674–99525–2 (v. 3)
         ISBN 0–674–99508–2 (v. 4)

*Typeset by Chiron, Inc, Cambridge, Massachusetts.*
*Printed in Great Britain by St Edmundsbury Press Ltd,*
*Bury St Edmunds, Suffolk, on acid-free paper.*
*Bound by Hunter & Foulis Ltd, Edinburgh, Scotland.*

# CONTENTS

# CONTENTS

# PREFACE

This volume is devoted mainly to the poetry of Stesichorus, Ibycus and Simonides: Corinna, Bacchylides and other choral poets will follow in volume IV, and volume V will contain minor poets, drinking songs and other anonymous pieces.

It gives me pleasure to record my gratitude for Research Grants awarded by the University of Victoria and Research Time Stipends granted by the Social Sciences and Humanities Research Council of Canada. I wish also to thank Malcolm Davies, Michael Haslam, John Oleson and Martin West for their help, the Librarian and staff of the McPherson Library, University of Victoria, for obtaining rare books and periodicals, the Egypt Exploration Society for permission to include parts of P.Oxy. 3876 (Stesichorus 222B), Philippa Goold for her careful editing, and yet again Mrs. A. Nancy Nasser for typing the manuscript.

David A. Campbell

University of Victoria
January 1991

To my colleagues
in the
Department of Classics
of the
University of Victoria

*πολλοὶ πὰρ κρήτηρι φίλοι γίνονται ἑταῖροι,*
*ἐν δὲ σπουδαίῳ πρήγματι παυρότεροι.*

# INTRODUCTION

OUR earliest texts of choral poetry are from the Pelo-
ponnese: Eumelus, a Corinthian nobleman, wrote
his Delian processional song for the Messenians
*c.* 750 B.C.; Terpander, Thaletas and Polymnestus
made their homes in Sparta a century later; and
Alcman's poems were composed for Spartan choirs
in the last decades of the seventh century. In the
sixth century, however, the most important figures
belong to Sicily and south Italy.

## ARION

Arion, like Terpander, came to the Peloponnese
from Lesbos, but he provides a link with Western
Greece, since he made a successful tour of Sicily and
Italy as a cithara-singer. His professional career in
Corinth fell in the reign of the tyrant Periander
(*c.* 625–585: test. 3), and the dates offered by Euse-
bius and the *Suda* (testt. 1, 2) no doubt depend on
this synchronism. Some authorities regarded him
as a pupil of Alcman (test. 1), but he may have been
his contemporary. His contribution to choral poetry
lay in the development of the dithyramb, and the
names which he gave to his poems (test. 3) must

1

have indicated their various subjects, perhaps not all of them connected with Dionysus. Statements about his 'tragic style' (test. 1) or even his composition of tragedies (test. 6) must be due to scholars who, like Aristotle, believed that tragedy had its origin in the dithyramb. No scrap of his poetry survives.

## STESICHORUS

Stesichorus referred somewhere in his poetry to a predecessor, Xanthus, who composed an *Oresteia* which Stesichorus was said to have adapted, and this Xanthus may have been a western Greek. Stesichorus certainly was, although there was dispute about his birthplace and the place of his burial. Perhaps he was born in Metauron in the toe of Italy, but he was called 'the Himeraean' and must have spent some of his life at Himera on the north coast of Sicily: he mentioned the city and its river in his poetry (270). Anecdotes linked him with Locri (test. 17; cf. 19), and he may have lived there for part of his life. He seems to have been buried in Catana (testt. 1, 22) in east Sicily. It is possible that he spent some time in the Peloponnese: according to one report he was exiled from Pallantium in Arcadia (test. 1); he sets the story of Orestes in Sparta instead of Mycenae (216), possibly for the gratification of a Spartan audience; and if fr. S 166 ( = Ibycus 282A fr. 1) belongs to him rather than to

# INTRODUCTION

Ibycus, it too might be taken as evidence of his wish
to please the Spartans. The *Parian Marble* records
that he 'arrived in Greece' in 485/4 B.C. (test. 6), but
the date is far too late and the entry is of doubtful
value.

Stesichorus was known to have lived before
Simonides, who mentioned him in his poetry (Stes.
179 = Simon. 564), and this fact must account for
the dating of Stesichorus' death in the year in which
Simonides was born (testt. 1, 2). Likewise the year
of his birth was placed a conventional forty years
after the *floruit* of Alcman (27th Olympian, accord-
ing to *Suda*: Alcm. test. 1), who was believed to have
been earlier. But the resultant dates for Stesi-
chorus, *c.* 632–*c.* 556, fit reasonably well with other
indications of his life-span, the synchronism with
Sappho, Alcaeus and Pittacus (test. 4), with
Phalaris though not with Pythagoras (test. 5), and
with the dating of the poet's brother between Thales
and Pythagoras (test. 15). The date offered by the
*Parian Marble* (*c.* 485: test. 6) is clearly wrong, and
the 87 years attributed to the poet by 'Lucian' (test.
7) may be inaccurate. The tale which linked him to
the fighting between Locri and Croton would give a
later date if it is correctly placed *c.* 540 (test. 19
with n. 2); but the link is a very weak one, and the
date of the battle is uncertain. The eclipse which
Stesichorus mentioned (271) is likely to have been
that of 557 (see M. L. West, *Classical Quarterly* 21,
1971, 306). His active life belongs to the first half of

3

the sixth century.

His work was collected in 26 books, according to the *Suda* (test. 1): this is a very large figure in comparison with Sappho's 9, Alcaeus' probable 10, Ibycus' 7, Anacreon's probable 5 and Pindar's 17; since he was quoted not by the book number but by the titles of his poems, e.g. the *Scylla,* it is likely that it was 26 long poems that survived. We have titles for about half of them, and we know that the *Geryoneis* had at least 1300 lines and may have been considerably longer (P.Oxy. 2617 fr. 7 = S 27). His subjects were the Trojan War and its aftermath (*Helen, Wooden Horse, Sack of Troy, Homecomings, Oresteia* in two books), the Argonauts (*Funeral Games of Pelias*), the adventures of Heracles (*Geryoneis, Cycnus, Cerberus,* perhaps *Scylla*), the Theban story (*Eriphyle, Europia*), and Meleager and the Calydonian boar (*Boar-hunters*).

The discovery of fragments of his poems on papyrus has confirmed the testimony of ancient writers that he was 'most Homeric' (test. 39: cf. 24, 34, 36, 37, 41): he dealt with epic themes, his metres were mainly dactylic although not in continuous hexameters, and his amplitude and nobility of style could be called Homeric. The other side of the coin, his longwindedness (test. 41: cf. 24), is also attested by the papyrus fragments: in the *Geryoneis* the speech in which Geryon ponders his death (fr. S 11) is separated by nearly 400 lines from the account of his death (fr. S 15).

4

# INTRODUCTION

It has been universally assumed that Stesichorus was a choral poet: he was said to have acquired his name because he 'established choruses' (test. 1), and the triadic structure of his poems (test. 30) was taken to indicate choral performance. A strong case, however, has been made by M. L. West (*loc. cit.* 307 ff.) for regarding him as a singer, performing his own songs to his cithara accompaniment.

In comparison with the monodists and Alcman, Stesichorus attracted little scholarly attention. The Peripatetic writer Chamaeleon wrote a treatise on him *c.* 300 B.C., and in the Augustan age Tryphon will have drawn on him for his study of the dialect of Himera (test. 31).

## ECHEMBROTUS AND SACADAS

We know little about the lyric poetry of these Peloponnesian musicians: Echembrotus inscribed six short lines on the tripod with which he commemorated his Pythian victory in pipe-singing (586 B.C.), and he says that he sang 'songs and laments' at the festival; Sacadas was famous for his performances on the pipes, but 'Plutarch' speaks of a composition, the Three-part nome, which he describes as a choral work, and it is possible that Sacadas was the author of a *Sack of Troy* which listed the Greeks who hid in the wooden horse. He may have composed choral music for the Peloponnesian festivals with which he was associated (test. 2).

5

# INTRODUCTION

## IBYCUS

The testimonia for the life of Ibycus are few and usually difficult to interpret. His birthplace is likely to have been Rhegium, and he is certainly referred to as Ibycus the Rhegine, but a late source (test. 2) offers Messana as an alternative. A Hellenistic epigram (test. 6), which may be no more than 'a flight of fancy' (Gow-Page), celebrates Rhegium as his burial-place. Antipater of Sidon, who gives the earliest version of the much-repeated story of his murder by bandits, says that the circumstances of his death were revealed in Corinth (test. 5).

There was a story that he might have been tyrant, presumably in Rhegium, but left the city instead (test. 4). According to the emended text of the *Suda* (test. 1) he went from Rhegium to Samos when Polycrates' father ruled the island. That Ibycus arrived in the time of the tyrant's father is likely to be an inference from 282(a), part of a poem which Ibycus ends by promising everlasting fame to Polycrates: it was (and still is) possible to interpret the lines as meaning that his fame would be due to his beauty, in which case he was a youth and not yet tyrant. Anacreon likewise was said to have been fetched to Samos by Polycrates' father to tutor the boy in music (fr. 491).

The date of Ibycus' arrival in Samos is expressed in two ways in the *Suda*: it was 'in the time of Croesus' and it fell in the 54th Olympiad (564/560

# INTRODUCTION

B.C.). Croesus, who reigned in Sardis from *c.* 560 to *c.* 546, may have been mentioned by Ibycus in his poetry, or his name may be another way of indicating that Ibycus' arrival in Samos occurred before the maturity of Polycrates, who was tyrant in the days of Cambyses, son of Cyrus, the conqueror of Croesus. The 54th Olympiad is usually but not convincingly regarded as too early for Ibycus' arrival, and Mosshammer argues for 547/6 B.C., the year of Croesus' death. Eusebius' date for the poet's *floruit* is *c.* 540/539 (test. 3).

The remains of Ibycus' poetry add a little information about his life: it has been guessed from the allusions to Sicyonian myth (fr. 282(a). 40 ff., 308, 322) that he spent time in Sicyon, and frr. 282A(i) and (xi) and 339 may have been composed in Sparta. Fr. 282B(i) seems to commemorate an athlete from Leontini in Sicily; he sang of the mole built to connect Ortygia with the mainland (fr. 321), and an anecdote (fr. 343) mentions a journey from Catana to Himera. Schneidewin suggested that Ibycus' poetic career had two phases: an earlier period when he worked in the Greek west and wrote poems on mythological themes in the manner of Stesichorus, and a later period when he composed erotic verse to please his patron Polycrates; but it is sometimes difficult to separate the mythological and erotic themes (see especially 289, but also 282(a), 282B(v), 284, 309), and in any case there is no certainty that Ibycus stayed on in Samos after the murder of

7

Polycrates in 522: Anacreon is known to have left for Athens. The construction of the Syracusan mole to which Ibycus refers is dated *c.* 530 by Dunbabin (*The Western Greeks* 62). He may well have spent the last years of his life in the west.

His poetry was collected in seven books, on what principle we do not know. His love-poetry was what later generations particularly remembered, sometimes with distaste (testt. 11, 12); but he made extensive use of mythological themes, whether in lengthy Stesichorean-type poems or as part of his love-songs. We have allusions to the adventures of Heracles (282A (viii), (xii), 285, 298–300), Meleager (290) and the Argonauts (291, 301) and to the Trojan war and its sequel (especially 282(a), 282B(v), 293–297), all themes which Stesichorus had handled. He displays a marked interest in those myths which have erotic interest: the rivalry of Deiphobus and Idomeneus for Helen's love (297), the reunion of Menelaus and Helen in Troy (296), the rape of Ganymede and of Tithonus, mentioned in 'the song to Gorgias' (289), the beauty and death of Troilus (282(a), 282B(v)), Endymion (284); and the description of Talos as *erastes* of Rhadamanthys (309) shows that he played a part in what K. J. Dover calls 'the homosexualisation of mythology'.

The earliest epinician poetry has been accredited to Simonides, but recent papyrus finds suggest that Ibycus anticipated him: 282B(i) talks of boasts and success and athletics, and in 282B(ii), the title of which, 'Callias', is likely to be the name of the honorand, Ibycus speaks of his boasts and of possible criticism (cf. fr. 311) in tones reminiscent of Pindar's victory-odes.

LASUS

Lasus belonged to Hermione, a small city in the northeast Peloponnese, and he composed a hymn for Demeter of Hermione, but much of his life seems to have been spent in Athens: it was there that he came upon Onomacritus in the act of forgery (test. 2), and there also that he played a role in the development of the dithyramb (testt. 1, 3, 5); in one of his poems (fr. 705) he mentioned Buzyges, a hero of importance only in Attica. Like Anacreon and Simonides he must have enjoyed the patronage of Hipparchus. The date of his birth is given as 548/544 B.C., and his known activities are datable to the late sixth century (test. 1 with n. 5, testt. 2–4).

His importance in the history of the dithyramb is clear from the ancient testimony but difficult to assess. Some scholars made him rather than Arion the first to organise the circular chorus which sang the dithyramb (e.g. Arion test. 4). The *Suda* (unless Garrod's emendation of the text is accepted) says that he introduced dithyrambic competitions, while the *Parian Marble* reports that the first dithyrambs were performed in 509/8 B.C., when the obscure Hypodicus of Chalcis 'was the winner'. It may be that Lasus introduced competing dithyrambs for the City Dionysia in the time of the tyrants, who attached great importance to the festival, and that the date of the *Marble* is that of the first competition to be held under the democracy. That Lasus was believed in the fifth century to have taken part in dithyrambic competition is shown by Aristophanes' joke about the rival chorus-masters, Lasus and Simonides (test. 3).

The *Suda* says that he was the first to compose a study of music. This has been doubted as improbable in the sixth century, although the book on medicine written by Alcmaeon of Croton would be contemporary. His views on musical theory were cited by Aristoxenus and later writers (testt. 7, 8, test. 1 n. 4), but they may have been known only through oral tradition. As a poet he was remembered for his experiments in euphony (frr. 702(b), 704) and for the elaboration of his work (test. 9). Like Simonides he was regarded as a sophist before his time, interested in the manipulation of words and in eristic skill (testt. 1, 10, 11). Some classed him among the Seven Sages (test. 1), and examples of his wisdom were quoted (test. 12). The Peripatetics were the first to display a scholarly interest in him: Chamaeleon wrote an account of him (test. 10), and Aristoxenus is likely to have devoted space to him in his work *On the Dithyrambic Poets* as well as in his *Harmonics* (test. 7).

# INTRODUCTION

## PRATINAS

Pratinas, like Lasus, came to Athens from a small city in the northeast Peloponnese. His birthplace was Phlius, which is close to Corinth and Sicyon, and two of our fragments (709, 711) have Spartan allusions; but he competed in Athens for the tragic prize against the young Aeschylus and Choerilus just after 500 B.C. (test. 1). He is said to have been the first composer of satyr-plays (test. 1), and he is likely to have brought them to Athens from his native Phlius (test. 1 n. 2). Vase-paintings represent satyr-plays from 500 B.C. onwards in Athens and earlier in Corinth and the Peloponnese. The *Suda* attributes to him 32 satyr-plays and only 18 tragedies, which suggests that his satyr-plays were not only performed as sequels to tragic trilogies as was normal in fifth-century Athens. Pratinas must have died before 467 B.C. (test. 2 n. 1).

Our knowledge of his life and our fragments of his poetry come from late sources but must be derived ultimately from fourth-century writers, Glaucus of Rhegium and the Peripatetics, Chamaeleon and Aristoxenus, in addition to Heraclides of Pontus (see fr. 712). It is impossible to say with certainty to what genre of poetry our fragments belong: the longest, fr. 708, may be dramatic rather than lyric, and fr. 711 seems to be dramatic. He spoke of his music (fr. 712) and, it would seem, of the novelty of his poetry (fr. 710), and he named

11

earlier musicians and poets (fr. 713).

Simonides was born in Iulis on the island of Ceos, which lies some fifteen miles to the southeast of Attica. A famous epigram (test. 5) gives his age as 80 in the year 477/6, and the dates 556 and *c.* 467 (test. 8) are generally accepted for his birth and death.

Like Anacreon and Lasus he was in Athens in the time of the tyrant Hipparchus (527–514), who kept him there by means of generous fees and gifts (test. 10 with n. 2). His victory over Lasus in a dithyrambic contest, subject of a joke of Aristophanes (Lasus test. 3), will belong to these years, and his epinician for Glaucus (fr. 509) may be as early as 520 B.C. It is likely that on the death of Hipparchus Simonides spent some time with the Aleuadae, the Scopadae and other rulers of Thessaly (test. 13), and some of his most celebrated poems were composed for these patrons (frr. 510, 528, 542). Epinician poetry in honour of Eualcides of Eretria (fr. 518) belongs to the years before the Ionian revolt (499–494).

After the first Persian invasion he is said to have been acclaimed for his epitaph on the Athenians who died at Marathon (test. 15), and ten years later he honoured those who died at Thermopylae, Artemisium, Salamis and Plataea (frr. 532–6, eleg. 1–3, VI, VII, X–XIX, XXII–XXIV *F.G.E.*). He is said to have spent his last years in Sicily, where he was the friend of Hiero, tyrant of Syracuse (testt. 18–19, 23, 47(c), (d), (f)), and he was buried at Acragas (test. 21).

He was a successful poet in various genres and composed epinician odes, dirges, dithyrambs (test. 11) and other choral poetry, elegiacs and epigrams. His fame resulted in the attribution to him of scores of epigrams, scarcely any of which can be safely accepted as authentic. Wise sayings also were ascribed to him as to a sage: see test. 47. Many stories were told of his avarice, no doubt because he was a conspicuous example of a poet paid for his services by wealthy patrons.

Chamaeleon, the fourth-century Peripatetic, composed a work on Simonides (test. 30) as on Alcman, Sappho, Stesichorus, Lasus, Pindar, Anacreon and other poets. He was followed by one Palaephatus, perhaps c. 200 B.C., and by the Augustan scholar Tryphon, who wrote on his dialect (testt. 31–32).

# SELECT BIBLIOGRAPHY

Barron, J. P. 'Ibycus: to Polycrates', *Bulletin of the Institute of Classical Studies* 16 (1969) 119–49

Bergk, T. *Poetae Lyrici Graeci*[4], 3 vols., Leipzig 1882

Bowra, C. M. *Greek Lyric Poetry from Alcman to Simonides*[2], Oxford 1961 ( = *G.L.P.*)

Brussich, G. F. 'Laso d'Ermione, Testimonianze e frammenti', *Quaderni Triestini per il lessico della lirica corale greca* 3 (1975–6) 83–135

*Cambridge History of Classical Literature*, vol. i: *Greek Literature*, ed. P. E. Easterling and B. M. W. Knox, Cambridge 1985

Campbell, D. A. *Greek Lyric Poetry: A Selection of Early Greek Lyric, Elegiac and Iambic Poetry*, London 1967: repr. Bristol 1982; *The Golden Lyre: The Themes of the Greek Lyric Poets*, London 1983

Davison, J. A. *From Archilochus to Pindar*, London 1968

Diehl, E. *Anthologia Lyrica Graeca*, vol. ii[2], Leipzig 1942

Dunbabin, T. J. *The Western Greeks*, Oxford 1948

Edmonds, J. M. *Lyra Graeca*, vols. ii and iii, London 1924 and 1927

Fränkel, H. *Early Greek Poetry and Philosophy*, trans. by M. Hadas and J. Willis, Oxford 1975

Friedländer, P. (with H. B. Hoffleit) *Epigrammata: Greek Inscriptions in Verse from the Beginnings to the Persian Wars*, Berkeley and Los Angeles 1948

Gerber, D. *Euterpe: An Anthology of Early Greek Lyric, Elegiac and Iambic Poetry*, Amsterdam 1970

14

# BIBLIOGRAPHY

Hansen, P. A. *Carmina Epigraphica Graeca,* Berlin and New York 1983

Kirkwood, G. M. *Early Greek Monody,* Ithaca 1974

Page, D. L. *Poetae Melici Graeci,* Oxford 1962 (=*P.M.G.*); *Lyrica Graeca Selecta,* Oxford 1968 (=*L.G.S.*); *Supplementum Lyricis Graecis,* Oxford 1974 (=*S.L.G.*); *Epigrammata Selecta,* Oxford 1975; *Further Greek Epigrams,* Cambridge 1981 (=*F.G.E.*)

Parsons, P. 'The Lille Stesichorus', *Z.P.E.* 26 (1977) 7–36

Privitera, G. A. *Laso di Ermione,* Rome 1965

Vürtheim, J. *Stesichoros' Fragmente und Biographie,* Leiden 1919

West, M. L. 'Stesichorus', *Classical Quarterly* 21 (1971) 302–14; *Iambi et Elegi Graeci ante Alexandrum Cantati,* 2 vols., Oxford 1971 (=*I.E.G.*); *Greek Metre,* Oxford 1982; *Studies in Early Greek Elegy and Iambus,* Berlin and New York 1974

Wilamowitz-Moellendorff, U. von *Sappho und Simonides,* Berlin 1913 (=*S.u.S.*)

Woodbury, L. E. 'Ibycus and Polycrates', *Phoenix* 39 (1985)

# ARION

## TESTIMONIA VITAE ATQUE ARTIS

**1** *Sud.* A 3886 (i 351 Adler)

Ἀρίων, Μηθυμναῖος, λυρικός, Κυκλέως υἱός, γέγονε κατὰ τὴν λη′ Ὀλυμπιάδα. τινὲς δὲ καὶ μαθητὴν Ἀλκμᾶνος ἱστόρησαν αὐτόν. ἔγραψε δὲ ᾄσματα· προοίμια εἰς ἔπη β′. λέγεται καὶ τραγικοῦ τρόπου εὑρετὴς γενέσθαι καὶ πρῶτος χορὸν στῆσαι καὶ διθύραμβον ᾆσαι καὶ ὀνομάσαι τὸ ᾀδόμενον ὑπὸ τοῦ χοροῦ καὶ Σατύρους εἰσενεγκεῖν ἔμμετρα λέγοντας.

**2** Euseb. *Chron.* Ol. 40.2 (p. 97 Helm, ii 91 Schoene)

Arion Methymnaeus clarus habetur, qui a delfino in Taenarum dicitur transportatus.

# ARION

## LIFE AND WORK

**1** *Suda,* Arion

From Methymna,[1] lyric poet, son of Cycleus,[2] flourished in the 38th Olympiad (628/624 B.C.). Some said he was a pupil of Alcman. He wrote songs: preludes for epic poems in two books. He is also said to have been the inventor of the tragic style, and to have been the first[3] to organise a chorus, sing a dithyramb and give a title to what the chorus sang, and the first to introduce Satyrs speaking verses.

[1] Cf. Strabo 13. 2. 4. Arion was represented on coins of Methymna: see G. M. A. Richter, *Portraits of the Greeks* i 68 with figs. 269–70.  [2] The name has doubtless been derived from Arion's circular choruses: see testt. 4, 5.  [3] See test. 3.

**2** Eusebius, *Chronicle*

Olympiad 40.2 (619/618 B.C.)[1]: Arion of Methymna is regarded as famous. He is said to have been carried by a dolphin to Taenarum.[2]

[1] The Armenian version gives 610/609. For Eusebius' dating see A. A. Mosshammer, *The Chronicle of Eusebius* 226–33.  [2] See test. 3.

# GREEK LYRIC

3 Hdt. 1.23s.

ἐτυράννευε δὲ ὁ Περίανδρος Κορίνθου· τῷ δὴ λέγου-
σι Κορίνθιοι (ὁμολογέουσι δέ σφι Λέσβιοι) ἐν τῷ βίῳ
θῶμα μέγιστον παραστῆναι, Ἀρίονα τὸν Μηθυμναῖον
ἐπὶ δελφῖνος ἐξενειχθέντα ἐπὶ Ταίναρον, ἐόντα
κιθαρῳδὸν τῶν τότε ἐόντων οὐδενὸς δεύτερον, καὶ διθύ-
ραμβον πρῶτον ἀνθρώπων τῶν ἡμεῖς ἴδμεν ποιήσαντά
τε καὶ ὀνομάσαντα καὶ διδάξαντα ἐν Κορίνθῳ. τοῦτον
τὸν Ἀρίονα λέγουσι, τὸν πολλὸν τοῦ χρόνου διατρί-
βοντα παρὰ Περιάνδρῳ, ἐπιθυμῆσαι πλῶσαι ἐς Ἰτα-
λίην τε καὶ Σικελίην, ἐργασάμενον δὲ χρήματα μεγάλα
θελῆσαι ὀπίσω ἐς Κόρινθον ἀπικέσθαι. ὁρμᾶσθαι μέν
νυν ἐκ Τάραντος, πιστεύοντα δὲ οὐδαμοῖσι μᾶλλον ἢ
Κορινθίοισι μισθώσασθαι πλοῖον ἀνδρῶν Κορινθίων·
τοὺς δὲ ἐν τῷ πελάγει ἐπιβουλεύειν τὸν Ἀρίονα
ἐκβαλόντας ἔχειν τὰ χρήματα· τὸν δὲ συνέντα τοῦτο
λίσσεσθαι, χρήματα μέν σφι προϊέντα, ψυχὴν δὲ παραι-
τεόμενον. οὐκ ὦν δὴ πείθειν αὐτὸν τούτοισι, ἀλλὰ
κελεύειν τοὺς πορθμέας ἢ αὐτὸν διαχρᾶσθαί μιν, ὡς
ἂν ταφῆς ἐν γῇ τύχῃ, ἢ ἐκπηδᾶν ἐς τὴν θάλασσαν
τὴν ταχίστην. ἀπειληθέντα δὲ τὸν Ἀρίονα ἐς ἀπορίην
παραιτήσασθαι, ἐπειδή σφι οὕτω δοκέοι, περιιδεῖν
αὐτὸν ἐν τῇ σκευῇ πάσῃ στάντα ἐν τοῖσι ἐδωλίοισι ἀεῖ-
σαι· ἀείσας δὲ ὑπεδέκετο ἑωυτὸν κατεργάσεσθαι. καὶ
τοῖσι ἐσελθεῖν γὰρ ἡδονὴν εἰ μέλλοιεν ἀκούσεσθαι τοῦ
ἀρίστου ἀνθρώπων ἀοιδοῦ, ἀναχωρῆσαι ἐκ τῆς πρύμνης

---

[1] *C.* 625–585 B.C.        [2] Herodotus may have the Lesbian his-
torian Hellanicus in mind.        [3] The southernmost promontory
of the Peloponnese.        [4] Lucian *Dial. Mar.* 8 says that A. was

18

# ARION

**3** Herodotus, *The Histories*

Periander was tyrant[1] of Corinth. According to the Corinthians, with whom the Lesbians[2] agree in the matter, a most astonishing thing happened during his life: Arion of Methymna was carried safely to Taenarum[3] on the back of a dolphin. This Arion was the foremost cithara-singer of his time and the first man that we know of to compose a dithyramb, give it a title and produce it in Corinth.

He had spent the greater part of his life, they say, at the court of Periander when he felt the urge to sail to Italy and Sicily. After making a great fortune there, he decided to return to Corinth.[4] So he set out from Tarentum, chartering a Corinthian ship, since he had more confidence in Corinthians than in any others; but when they were on the open sea the crew plotted to throw Arion overboard and keep his money. When he realised what they were up to, he implored them to take the money but spare his life. It was no good: the sailors told him either to commit suicide and so get burial on land or to jump into the sea immediately. Seeing that their minds were made up, Arion at his wits' end asked permission to stand in full costume on the stern-benches and perform a song, promising to take his own life when he had done so. The crew were delighted at the chance of hearing the finest singer in the world and moved to the middle of the ship to make room for him in the

on his way home from Corinth to Methymna when the dolphin rescued him and carried him to Taenarum.

ἐς μέσην νέα. τὸν δὲ ἐνδύντα τε πᾶσαν τὴν σκευὴν καὶ
λαβόντα τὴν κιθάρην, στάντα ἐν τοῖσι ἑδωλίοισι δι-
εξελθεῖν νόμον τὸν ὄρθιον, τελευτῶντος δὲ τοῦ νόμου
ῥῖψαί μιν ἐς τὴν θάλασσαν ἑωυτὸν ὡς εἶχε σὺν τῇ
σκευῇ πάσῃ. καὶ τοὺς μὲν ἀποπλέειν ἐς Κόρινθον, τὸν
δὲ δελφῖνα λέγουσι ὑπολαβόντα ἐξενεῖκαι ἐπὶ Ταίνα-
ρον. ἀποβάντα δὲ αὐτὸν χωρέειν ἐς Κόρινθον σὺν τῇ
σκευῇ καὶ ἀπικόμενον ἀπηγέεσθαι πᾶν τὸ γεγονός.
Περίανδρον δὲ ὑπὸ ἀπιστίης Ἀρίονα μὲν ἐν φυλακῇ
ἔχειν οὐδαμῇ μετιέντα, ἀνακῶς δὲ ἔχειν τῶν πορθ-
μέων· ὡς δὲ ἄρα παρεῖναι αὐτούς, κληθέντας ἱστορέ-
εσθαι εἴ τι λέγοιεν περὶ Ἀρίονος. φαμένων δὲ ἐκείνων
ὡς εἴη τε σῶς περὶ Ἰταλίην καί μιν εὖ πρήσσοντα
λίποιεν ἐν Τάραντι, ἐπιφανῆναί σφι τὸν Ἀρίονα ὥσπερ
ἔχων ἐξεπήδησε· καὶ τοὺς ἐκπλαγέντας οὐκ ἔχειν ἔτι
ἐλεγχομένους ἀρνέεσθαι. ταῦτα μέν νυν Κορίνθιοί τε
καὶ Λέσβιοι λέγουσι, καὶ Ἀρίονος ἔστι ἀνάθημα χάλ-
κεον οὐ μέγα ἐπὶ Ταινάρῳ, ἐπὶ δελφῖνος ἐπεὼν ἄνθρω-
πος.

stern. He put on his full costume, took his cithara, stood on the stern-benches and sang the whole Orthian nome[5]; the performance over, he plunged into the sea just as he was, wearing full costume. The crew sailed on to Corinth; but a dolphin, they say, took Arion on its back and carried him safely to Taenarum. When he came ashore, he made his way to Corinth, still wearing his costume, and on his arrival told the whole story. Since Periander did not believe him, he kept him in strict confinement and waited eagerly for the sailors. When they arrived, they were summoned and asked if they had anything to say about Arion. They replied that he was safe and sound in Italy: they had left him doing well for himself in Tarentum; whereupon Arion himself appeared, looking exactly as he did when he jumped from the ship. The crew were thunderstruck and in no position to make further denials, now that they were shown to be liars.

This, then, is the account given by both the Corinthians and the Lesbians[6]; and there is also Arion's dedication at Taenarum, a small bronze figure of a man riding on a dolphin.[7]

---

[5] Attributed to Terpander: see Terp. testt. 13, 19 n. 2, fr. 2.     [6] Plutarch elaborates the story in *Sept. Sap. Conv.* 18f.; cf. 'Dio Chrys.' xxxvii (init.)., Tzetz. *chil.* 1. 396 ff.     [7] Pausanias (3. 25. 7: cf. 9. 30. 2) mentions the dedication, 'a bronze figure of Arion, the cithara-singer, on a dolphin'. Aelian (*N. A.* 12. 45) quotes the inscription on the figure (see Page *F.G.E.* 499), together with what he calls Arion's hymn of thanksgiving to Poseidon = fr. adesp. 939 *P.M.G.*, probably a work of the 4th c. B.C.

**4** Schol. Ar. *Av.* 1403 (p. 241 Dübner, p. 254 White)

τὸν κυκλιοδιδάσκαλον· ἀντὶ τοῦ διθυραμβοποιόν ...
'Αντίπατρος δὲ καὶ Εὐφρόνιος ἐν τοῖς ὑπομνήμασί φασι
τοὺς κυκλίους χοροὺς στῆσαι πρῶτον Λᾶσον τὸν Ἑρμι-
ονέα, οἱ δὲ ἀρχαιότεροι Ἑλλάνικος καὶ Δικαίαρχος
'Αρίονα τὸν Μηθυμναῖον, Δικαίαρχος μὲν ἐν τῷ περὶ
Διονυσιακῶν ἀγώνων (*F.H.G.* ii 249 fr. 45, fr. 75
Wehrli), Ἑλλάνικος δὲ ἐν τοῖς Καρνεονίκαις (*F.Gr.H.*
4 F86).

**5** Procl. *Chrest.* (ap. Phot. *Bibl.* p. 320a Bekker, v 160
Henry)

εὑρεθῆναι δὲ τὸν διθύραμβον Πίνδαρος ἐν Κορίνθῳ
λέγει· τὸν δὲ ἀρξάμενον τῆς ᾠδῆς 'Αριστοκλῆς (Rose:
codd. 'Αριστοτέλης) 'Αρίονά φησιν εἶναι, ὃς πρῶτος
τὸν κύκλιον ἤγαγε χορόν.

**6** Io. Diac. in Hermog. (Rabe, *Rh. Mus.* 63, 1908, 150) =
Solon 30a West

τῆς δὲ τραγῳδίας πρῶτον δρᾶμα 'Αρίων ὁ Μηθυ-
μναῖος εἰσήγαγεν, ὥσπερ Σόλων ἐν ταῖς ἐπιγραφομέ-
ναις 'Ελεγείαις ἐδίδαξε.

# ARION

**4** Scholiast on Aristophanes, *Birds* 1403

'Trainer of circular choruses' is used for 'dithy-rambic poet' ... Antipater[1] and Euphronius[2] say in their commentaries that Lasus of Hermione[3] was the first to organise circular choruses, but the older authorities, Hellanicus[4] and Dicaearchus,[5] say that it was Arion of Methymna,[6] Dicaearchus in his treatise *On the Dionysiac Contests,* Hellanicus in his *List of Carnean Victors.*

[1] Unknown.    [2] Alexandrian grammarian of 3rd c. B.C.
[3] See Lasus test. 5    [4] Historian from Lesbos, late 5th c.
[5] Peripatetic grammarian, late 4th c. B.C.    [6] So also schol. Pind. *Ol.* 13. 18 f.

**5** Proclus, *Chrestomathy*

Pindar says (*Ol.* 13. 18 f.) that the dithyramb was invented at Corinth; Aristocles[1] says that it was Arion who originated the song and that he was the first to introduce the circular chorus.

[1] Aristocles of Rhodes, grammarian of 1st c. B.C.

**6** John the Deacon, *Commentary on Hermogenes*

The first performance of drama was introduced by Arion of Methymna, as Solon stated in the poems entitled *Elegies.*[1]

[1] The passage is of doubtful value: see G. F. Else, *The Origin ... of Greek Tragedy* 17, West on Solon 30a.

**7** Luc. *Ver. Hist.* 2. 15 (i 109 Macleod) = fr. 276(b) *P.M.G.*

οἱ μὲν οὖν χοροὶ ἐκ παίδων εἰσὶν καὶ παρθένων·
ἐξάρχουσι δὲ καὶ συνᾴδουσιν Εὔνομός τε ὁ Λοκρὸς καὶ
Ἀρίων ὁ Λέσβιος καὶ Ἀνακρέων καὶ Στησίχορος· καὶ
γὰρ τοῦτον παρ᾽ αὐτοῖς ἐθεασάμην, ἤδη τῆς Ἑλένης
αὐτῷ διηλλαγμένης.

**7** Lucian, *A True Story*

The choirs[1] are of boys and girls, and they are led and accompanied by Eunomus of Locri, Arion of Lesbos, Anacreon and Stesichorus—yes, I saw him among them; Helen had by now made her peace with him.

[1] At banquets on the Island of the Blessed.

# XANTHUS

**699** Athen. 12. 512f–513a (iii 132 Kaibel)

τοῦτον οὖν (τὸν Ἡρακλέα), φησίν (ὁ Μεγακλείδης),
οἱ νέοι ποιηταὶ κατασκευάζουσιν ἐν λῃστοῦ σχήματι
μόνον περιπορευόμενον, ξύλον ἔχοντα καὶ λεοντῆν καὶ
τόξα. καὶ ταῦτα πλάσαι πρῶτον Στησίχορον τὸν Ἱμε-
ραῖον. καὶ Ξάνθος δ' ὁ μελοποιός, πρεσβύτερος ὢν
Στησιχόρου, ὡς καὶ αὐτὸς ὁ Στησίχορος μαρτυρεῖ (229
P.M.G.) ὥς φησιν ὁ Μεγακλείδης, οὐ ταύτην αὐτῷ
περιτίθησι τὴν στολὴν ἀλλὰ τὴν Ὁμηρικήν. πολλὰ δὲ
τῶν Ξάνθου παραπεποίηκεν ὁ Στησίχορος, ὥσπερ καὶ
τὴν Ὀρέστειαν καλουμένην.

**700** Ael. V. H. 4. 26 (p. 74 Dilts)

Ξάνθος ὁ ποιητὴς τῶν μελῶν (ἐγένετο δὲ οὗτος
πρεσβύτερος Στησιχόρου τοῦ Ἱμεραίου) λέγει τὴν
Ἠλέκτραν τοῦ Ἀγαμέμνονος οὐ τοῦτο ἔχειν τοὔνομα
πρῶτον ἀλλὰ Λαοδίκην. ἐπεὶ δὲ Ἀγαμέμνων ἀνῃρέ-
θη, τὴν δὲ Κλυταιμνήστραν ὁ Αἴγισθος ἔγημε καὶ ἐβα-
σίλευσεν, ἄλεκτρον οὖσαν καὶ καταγηρῶσαν παρθένον
Ἀργεῖοι Ἠλέκτραν ἐκάλεσαν διὰ τὸ ἀμοιρεῖν ἀνδρὸς
καὶ μὴ πεπειρᾶσθαι λέκτρου.

---

[1] Cf. *Iliad* 9. 145.　[2] The Doric form of her name, Alectra, is
here wrongly derived from ἀ-, 'without', and λέκτρον, 'marriage-bed'.

# XANTHUS

**699** Athenaeus, *Scholars at Dinner*

Heracles, says Megaclides,[1] is represented by the modern poets as travelling about alone in the guise of a bandit with club and lionskin and bow; and, he adds, it was Stesichorus of Himera who first thought this up. Xanthus, the lyric poet, who was earlier than Stesichorus, as Stesichorus himself testifies (229) according to Megaclides, does not give him this equipment but represents him as Homer did. Many of Xanthus' poems have been adapted by Stesichorus,[2] for example the one called *The Oresteia*.

[1] Homeric scholar, probably of 4th c. B.C.  [2] Lesky suggested that Xanthus, like Stesichorus, belonged to Magna Graecia.

**700** Aelian, *Historical Miscellanies*

Xanthus, the lyric poet, who was earlier than Stesichorus of Himera, says that Electra, daughter of Agamemnon, was originally called Laodice[1]; but after Agamemnon had been murdered and Aegisthus had married Clytemnestra and become king, Laodice, unwed and growing old in her virginity, was called Electra by the Argives since she had had no intercourse with any man and had no experience of the marriage-bed.[2]

# STESICHORUS

## TESTIMONIA VITAE ATQUE ARTIS

**1** *Sud.* Σ 1095 (iv 433 Adler)

Στησίχορος· Εὐφόρβου ἢ Εὐφήμου, ὡς δὲ ἄλλοι Εὐκλείδου ἢ Εὐέτους (Wilamowitz: Ὑέτους codd.) ἢ Ἡσιόδου. ἐκ πόλεως Ἰμέρας τῆς Σικελίας· καλεῖται γοῦν Ἰμεραῖος· οἱ δὲ ἀπὸ Ματαυρίας τῆς ἐν Ἰταλίᾳ· οἱ δὲ ἀπὸ Παλαντίου τῆς Ἀρκαδίας φυγόντα αὐτὸν ἐλθεῖν φασιν εἰς Κατάνην κἀκεῖ τελευτῆσαι καὶ ταφῆναι πρὸ τῆς πύλης, ἥτις ἐξ αὐτοῦ Στησιχόρειος προσηγόρευται. τοῖς δὲ χρόνοις ἦν νεώτερος Ἀλκμᾶνος τοῦ λυρικοῦ, ἐπὶ τῆς λζ΄ Ὀλυμπιάδος γεγονώς. ἐτελεύτησε δὲ ἐπὶ τῆς νε΄. εἶχε δὲ ἀδελφὸν γεωμετρίας ἔμπειρον Μαμερτῖνον καὶ ἕτερον Ἡλιάνακτα νομοθέτην. γέγονε δὲ λυρικός. καί ἐστιν αὐτοῦ τὰ ποιήματα Δωρίδι διαλέκτῳ ἐν βιβλίοις κϛ΄. φασὶ δὲ αὐτὸν γράψαντα ψόγον Ἑλένης τυφλωθῆναι, πάλιν δὲ γράψαντα Ἑλένης ἐγκώμιον ἐξ ὀνείρου, τὴν παλινῳδίαν, ἀναβλέψαι.

---

[1] For Euphemus cf. testt. 9, 13, for Euclides test. 14, for Hesiod, the famous poet, testt. 10–12; see also M. L. West, *C.Q.* 21 (1971) 303.   [2] See fr. 270, test. 8.   [3] See test. 9.   [4] W. G. Forrest, *A History of Sparta 950–192 B.C.,* 76 suggests that the exile was due to Tegeate disapproval of Stesichorus' support for a Spartan Orestes (fr. 216). See also fr. S 85 = 182 *P.M.G.*   [5] In Sicily, north of Syracuse.   [6] The Olympiad in which

# STESICHORUS

## BIOGRAPHY

**1** *Suda*, Stesichorus

Son of Euphorbus or Euphemus or according to others of Euclides or Euetes or Hesiod.[1] From the city of Himera[2] in Sicily: at any rate he is called the Himeraean; but some say he is from Matauria[3] in Italy. Others say that when exiled from Pallantium[4] in Arcadia he came to Catana[5] and that he died there and was buried in front of the gate which is called Stesichorean after him. In date he was later than the lyric poet Alcman, since he was born in the 37th Olympiad (632/28 B.C.). He died in the 56th Olympiad (556/2 B.C.).[6] He had a brother Mamertinus[7] who was an expert in geometry and a second brother Helianax, a law-giver. He was a lyric poet. His poems are in the Doric dialect[8] and in 26 books.[9] They say that he was blinded for writing abuse of Helen and recovered his sight after writing an encomium of Helen, the Palinode, as the result of a dream.[10] He was called Stesichorus

---

Simonides was born: cf. Sim. test. 1.     [7] See test. 15.
[8] Cf. frr. 261, 264, anon. elegiacs in schol. Pind. (i 10 Drachmann), and see West, *loc. cit.* 304 with n. 2.     [9] Probably 26 poems (e.g. *Geryoneis, Helen*) are meant.     [10] See fr. 192.

ἐκλήθη δὲ Στησίχορος ὅτι πρῶτος κιθαρῳδίᾳ χορὸν
ἔστησεν· ἐπεί τοι πρότερον Τισίας ἐκαλεῖτο.

2 Cic. *De Rep.* 2. 20 (p. 54 Ziegler)

quo [enim] ille (sc. Stesichorus) mor[tuus, e]odem
[est an]no na[tus Si]moni[des ol]ympia[de se]xta et
quin[quag]esima.

suppl. Niebuhr, Rohde

3 Euseb. *Chron.* (pp. 98, 102 Helm, ii 90s. Schoene)

(i) Ol. 42.2: Stesichorus poeta clarus habetur.
(ii) Ol. 55. 1: Stesichorus moritur.

4 *Sud.* Σ 107 (iv 322s. Adler)

Σαπφώ· . . . λυρική, γεγονυῖα κατὰ τὴν μβ′ Ὀλυμ-
πιάδα, ὅτε καὶ Ἀλκαῖος ἦν καὶ Στησίχορος καὶ Πιττα-
κός.

because he was the first to establish (*stēsai*) a chorus of singers to the cithara; his name was originally Tisias.

## CHRONOLOGY[1]

**2** Cicero, *On the Republic*[2]

For Stesichorus died in the year in which Simonides was born, in the 56th Olympiad (556/2 B.C.).[3]

[1] See also test. 1, fr. 271.          [2] The passage follows test. 12.
[3] Cicero's date goes back via Nepos to Apollodorus (see *F.Gr.H.* 244 F 337). See also Simon. test. 1.

**3** Eusebius, *Chronicle*

(i) Olympiad 42.2 (611/0 B.C.)[1]: the poet Stesichorus is regarded as famous.

(ii) Olympiad 55.1 (560/59 B.C.)[2]: death of Stesichorus.

[1] The Armenian version gives 608/7. For the Eusebian dates see A. A. Mosshammer, *The Chronicle of Eusebius* 218–21. Cyril also places the *floruit* of Stesichorus in the 42nd Olympiad along with that of Alcman and Pittacus.          [2] The Armenian version gives 558/7.

**4** *Suda,* Sappho (1st notice)[1]

Sappho: . . . a lyric poetess; flourished in the 42nd Olympiad (612/08 B.C.), when Alcaeus, Stesichorus and Pittacus were also alive.

[1] See Sa. test. 2 with n. 3 and vol. i p. xiii f.

**5** Tzetz. *Vit. Hes.* 18 (p. 38 Colonna)

ὁ δὲ Στησίχορος οὗτος σύγχρονος ἦν Πυθαγόρᾳ τῷ φιλοσόφῳ καὶ τῷ Ἀκραγαντίνῳ Φαλάριδι.

**6** *Marm. Par.* Ep. 50 (*F.Gr.H.* ii B 999)

ἀφ' οὗ Αἰσχύλος ὁ ποιητὴς τραγῳδίᾳ πρῶτον ἐνίκησε καὶ Εὐριπίδης ὁ ποιητὴς ἐγένετο καὶ Στησίχορος ὁ ποιητὴς εἰς τὴν Ἑλλάδα ἀφίκετο ἔτη ΗΗΔΔΙΙ, ἄρχοντος Ἀθήνησι Φιλοκράτους.

**7** [Luc.] *Macr.* 26 (i 81 Macleod)

Ἀνακρέων δὲ ὁ τῶν μελῶν ποιητὴς ἔζησεν ἔτη πέντε καὶ ὀγδοήκοντα, καὶ Στησίχορος δὲ ὁ μελοποιὸς ταῦτά, Σιμωνίδης δὲ ὁ Κεῖος ὑπὲρ τὰ ἐνενήκοντα.

**8** Schol. Pind. *Ol.* 12 (i 349 Drachmann)

Inscr. a: ἀπῆλθεν (sc. ὁ Ἐργοτέλης) εἰς Ἱμέραν πόλιν τῆς Σικελίας, ἐξ ἧς ἦν ὁ Στησίχορος ὁ μελοποιός.

Cf. inscr. c (i 350 Dr.)

---

[1] See also test. 1. Stesichorus is said to have sung the praises of Himera and to have spoken of its river (270); this may be why it came to be regarded as his birthplace. Cf. Ael. Arist. 32. 24. He was represented on 2nd c. B.C. coins of Himera: see G. M. Richter, *Portraits of the Greeks* i 68.

# STESICHORUS

**5** Tzetzes, *Life of Hesiod*[1]

This Stesichorus was a contemporary of the philosopher Pythagoras[2] and of Phalaris[3] of Acragas.

[1] The passage follows test. 10.    [2] Cf. test. 24; but Pythagoras' dates are *c.* 570–*c.* 490.    [3] See test. 16; he was tyrant from *c.* 570/65 to 554/49. Stesichorus is often mentioned in the so-called 'Letters of Phalaris' (2nd c. A.D.?).

**6** *Parian Marble*

From the time when the poet Aeschylus first won a victory with a tragedy and the poet Euripides was born and the poet Stesichorus arrived in Greece 222 years,[1] in the archonship of Philocrates.

[1] I.e. in 485/4 (or 486/5): see Cadoux, *J.H.S.* 68 (1948) 118. The date is a century too late for our Stesichorus (see test. 16 n. 3). The *Marble* dates the Athenian victory of 'the second Stesichorus of Himera' to 370/68: see *P.M.G.* 841.

**7** 'Lucian', *On Longevity*

The lyric poet Anacreon lived for 85 years, the lyric poet Stesichorus for the same number,[1] Simonides of Ceos for over 90.

[1] Cicero, *On Old Age* 7. 23 says that Stesichorus continued to compose in his old age, Hieronymus, *Epistles* 52. 3 that the poems written when he was near death were swan-like and sweeter than usual.

## BIRTHPLACE[1]

**8** Scholiast on Pindar *Ol.* 12 (for Ergoteles of Himera)

Ergoteles departed for the Sicilian city of Himera, from which came the lyric poet Stesichorus.

**9** Steph. Byz. s.v. Μάταυρος (p. 437 Meineke)

πόλις Σικελίας, Λοκρῶν κτίσμα· ὁ πολίτης Ματαυ-
ρῖνος. Στησίχορος Εὐφήμου παῖς Ματαυρῖνος γένος, ὁ
τῶν μελῶν ποιητής.

**10** Tzetz. *Vit. Hes.* 18 (p. 38 Colonna)

Ἀριστοτέλης γὰρ ὁ φιλόσοφος, μᾶλλον δὲ οἶμαι ὁ
τοὺς Πέπλους συντάξας, ἐν τῇ Ὀρχομενίων πολιτείᾳ
(fr. 565 Rose) Στησίχορον τὸν μελοποιὸν εἶναί φησιν
υἱὸν Ἡσιόδου ἐκ τῆς Κτιμένης αὐτῷ γεννηθέντα τῆς
Ἀμφιφάνους καὶ Γανύκτορος ἀδελφῆς, θυγατρὸς δὲ
Φηγέως· ὁ δὲ Στησίχορος οὗτος ... (v. test. 5).

**11** Schol. Procl. Hes. *Op.* 271a (p. 92 Pertusi)

ἰστέον δὲ ὅτι υἱὸς Ἡσιόδου †Μνασέας ἐστί· Φιλόχο-
ρος δὲ (*F.Gr.H.* 328 F213) Στησίχορόν φησι τὸν ἀπὸ
Κλυμένης· ἄλλοι δὲ Ἀρχιέπης.

# STESICHORUS

**9** Stephanus of Byzantium

Mataurus: a city in Sicily,[1] founded by the Locrians. The citizen is called Mataurine. The lyric poet Stesichorus, son of Euphemus, was Mataurine by birth.

[1] Metauron is actually in south Italy, north of Rhegium: see T. J. Dunbabin, *The Western Greeks* 147 (map), 168 f.

## FAMILY

**10** Tzetzes, *Life of Hesiod*

For Aristotle the philosopher—or rather, in my view, the composer of the *Robes*—says in his *Constitution of Orchomenus* that the lyric poet Stesichorus was the son of Hesiod[1] by Ctimene, sister of Amphiphanes and Ganyctor and daughter of Phegeus. But this Stesichorus . . .[2]

[1] Fantasy: Hesiod's working life is dated *c.* 700 B.C.　　[2] Continued at test. 5. Tzetzes goes on to say (p. 39 Colonna) that Hesiod was murdered by Ctimene's brothers for seducing her.

**11** Proclus on Hesiod, *Works and Days* 271 ('my son')

*N.B.* Hesiod's son is Mnaseas (?); but Philochorus[1] says he was Stesichorus, son of Clymene, and others say he was Archiepes.[2]

[1] Writer on Athenian history and history of literature, *c.* 345–259 B.C.　　[2] Cf. Tzetzes ad loc.

# GREEK LYRIC

**12** Cic. *De Rep.* 2. 20 (p. 54 Ziegler)

neque enim Stesichor]us ne[pos ei]us (sc. Hesiodi), ut di[xeru]nt quid[am, e]x filia. quo [enim] . . . (v. test. 2).

suppl. Niebuhr, Mommsen, Rohde

**13** Pl. *Phaedr.* 244a

ὃν δὲ μέλλω λέγειν (sc. λόγον) Στησιχόρου τοῦ Εὐφήμου, Ἱμεραίου.

**14** *I.G.* xiv 1213 (p. 318 Kaibel)

Σ]τησίχορ[ος Ε]ὐκλείδο[υ Ἱ]μεραῖο[ς

**15** Procl. in Euclid. Prolog. 2 (p. 65 Friedlein)

μετὰ δὲ τοῦτον (sc. Θαλῆν) Μάμερκος ὁ Στησιχόρου τοῦ ποιητοῦ ἀδελφὸς ὡς ἐφαψάμενος τῆς περὶ γεωμετρίαν σπουδῆς μνημονεύεται. καὶ Ἱππίας ὁ Ἠλεῖος (86 B 12 D.-K.) ἱστόρησεν ὡς ἐπὶ γεωμετρίᾳ δόξαν αὐτοῦ λαβόντος. ἐπὶ δὲ τούτοις Πυθαγόρας . . .

**12** Cicero, *On the Republic*

For Stesichorus is not, as some have alleged, Hesiod's grandson on his mother's side. For Stesichorus died . . .[1]

[1] Continued at test. 2.

**13** Plato, *Phaedrus*

But the words I am going to quote belong to Stesichorus, son of Euphemus,[1] from Himera.

[1] This name also in Steph. Byz. (test. 9) and anon. elegiacs in Schol. Pind. (i 10 Drachmann); see also test. 1. Plato perhaps finds significance in the names Euphemus ('uttering fine sounds') and Himera (cf. ἵμερος, 'desire').

**14** *Greek Inscriptions*[1]

Stesichorus of Himera, son of Euclides.[2]

[1] On a headless herm from Tivoli.    [2] See test. 1. Euclides was the name of one of the founders of Himera in 649 B.C. (Thuc. 6. 5. 1).

**15** Proclus, *Commentary on Euclid*

After Thales[1] Mamercus, brother of the poet Stesichorus, is remembered as having applied himself to the study of geometry; and Hippias of Elis[2] spoke of his fame as a geometer. After them, Pythagoras . . .[3]

[1] *Floruit* 585 B.C.    [2] Sophist, 5th c. B.C.    [3] Cf. Heron, *Definitions* 136. 1 (where the name is given as Mamertius). For the name see test. 1 and West, loc. cit. 303.

# GREEK LYRIC

**16** Ar. *Rhet.* 2. 20. 1393b (p. 136 Roemer, p. 115s. Kassel) = fr. 281(a) *P.M.G.*

λόγος δὲ οἷος ὁ Στησιχόρου περὶ Φαλάριδος . . . · Στησίχορος μὲν γὰρ ἑλομένων στρατηγὸν αὐτοκράτορα τῶν Ἱμεραίων Φάλαριν καὶ μελλόντων φυλακὴν διδόναι τοῦ σώματος τἄλλα διαλεχθεὶς εἶπεν αὐτοῖς λόγον, . . . · οὕτω δὲ καὶ ὑμεῖς, ἔφη, ὁρᾶτε μὴ βουλόμενοι τοὺς πολεμίους τιμωρήσασθαι ταὐτὸ πάθητε τῷ ἵππῳ· τὸν μὲν γὰρ χαλινὸν ἔχετε ἤδη, ἑλόμενοι στρατηγὸν αὐτοκράτορα· ἐὰν δὲ φυλακὴν δῶτε καὶ ἀναβῆναι ἐάσητε, δουλεύσετε ἤδη Φαλάριδι.

**17** Ar. *Rhet.* 2. 21. 1394b–95a (p. 140s. Roemer, p. 119 Kassel) = fr. 281(b) *P.M.G.*

ἁρμόττει δ᾽ ἐν τοῖς τοιούτοις . . . τὰ αἰνιγματώδη, οἷον εἴ τις λέγει ὅπερ Στησίχορος ἐν Λοκροῖς εἶπεν, ὅτι οὐ δεῖ ὑβριστὰς εἶναι, ὅπως μὴ οἱ τέττιγες χαμόθεν ᾄδωσιν.

cf. *Rhet.* 3. 11. 1412a

# STESICHORUS

## LIFE[1]

**16** Aristotle, *Rhetoric*

An example of the fable is that of Stesichorus about Phalaris[2] ... When the Himeraeans had chosen Phalaris as general with absolute power and were on the point of offering him a bodyguard, Stesichorus finished a speech by telling them a fable[3]: ... 'You too', he said, 'must take care lest in your eagerness for revenge on your enemies you find yourselves in the same plight as the horse: by choosing a general with absolute power you already wear the bridle, and if you give him a bodyguard and so allow him to mount you, you will at once be the slaves of Phalaris.'[4]

[1] See also Ibycus 343. [2] See test. 5 with n. 3, Dunbabin, loc. cit. 318 f. [3] A horse enlisted a man's help to clear his field of a stag but finished by being bridled, mounted and so enslaved by the man. [4] In the version of Conon, mythographer of the Augustan era, Stesichorus tells the fable in connection with Gelo, tyrant of Gela and Syracuse (491/0–478!) and victor over the Carthaginians at Himera (*F.Gr.H.* 26 F 1.42). For Phalaris and Stesichorus see also Tzetzes, *chil.* 1. 674 ff., 5. 927 ff.

**17** Aristotle, *Rhetoric*

In such cases enigmatic sayings are appropriate, for example the one used by Stesichorus to the Locrians: 'You must not be presumptuous, lest the cicadas sing from the ground.'[1]

[1] I.e. after the enemy (the Rhegines?) invade Locrian territory and cut down their trees.

**18** Philodem. *Mus.* 1. 30. 31ss. (p. 18 Kemke, p. 220ss. Rispoli) = Diog. Bab. fr. 85 Arnim (*S.V.F.* iii 232) = fr. 281(c) *P.M.G.*

καὶ περὶ Στησιχ[όρ]ου δ' ἱστορεῖται διότι τῶν [ἀστῶ]ν (suppl. Kemke) ἀν[τι]παρατεταγμένων [ἤδη] καταστὰς ἐν μέσοις [ᾖσέ τι παρα]κλητικὸν καὶ δια[λλάξ]α[ς] διὰ τοῦ μέλου[ς εἰς ἡσυχ]ίαν αὐτοὺς μετέσ[τησεν.

*Mus.* 4. 20. 7ss. (p. 87 Kemke, p. 65 Neubecker) = fr. 281(d) *P.M.G.*

ἀλλὰ μὴν καὶ τὸ μὲν κα[τ]ὰ Στησίχορον οὐκ ἀκρι[β]ῶ[ς] ἱστο[ρεῖ]ται . . .

**19** Paus. 3. 19. 11–13 (i 251s. Rocha-Pereira)

ὃν δὲ οἶδα λέγοντας Κροτωνιάτας περὶ Ἑλένης λόγον, ὁμολογοῦντας δέ σφισι καὶ Ἱμεραίους, ἐπιμνησθήσομαι καὶ τοῦδε. ἔστιν ἐν τῷ Εὐξείνῳ νῆσος κατὰ τοῦ Ἴστρου τὰς ἐκβολὰς Ἀχιλλέως ἱερά· ὄνομα μὲν τῇ νήσῳ Λευκή. . . . ἐς ταύτην πρῶτος ἐσπλεῦσαι λέγεται Κροτωνιάτης Λεώνυμος. πολέμου γὰρ Κροτωνιάταις συνεστηκότος πρὸς τοὺς ἐν Ἰταλίᾳ Λοκρούς, τῶν Λοκρῶν κατὰ οἰκειότητα πρὸς Ὀπουντίους Αἴαντα τὸν Ὀιλέως ἐς τὰς μάχας ἐπικαλουμένων, ὁ Λεώνυμος Κροτωνιάταις στρατηγῶν ἐπῄει τοῖς ἐναντίοις κατὰ τοῦτο ᾗ προτετάχθαι σφίσι τὸν Αἴαντα ἤκουε. τιτρώ-

---

[1] Actually off the estuary of the Dnieper.    [2] The battle at the river Sagra in which the Locrians beat off the Crotoniates is dated

# STESICHORUS

**18** Philodemus, *Music*[1]

(Book 1) About Stesichorus the story goes that when (the citizens?)[2] were drawn up to do battle with each other he at once took up his position between them and sang a song of exhortation, and reconciling them by his song restored the peace.[3]

(Book 4) But the story[4] about Stesichorus is inaccurate ...

[1] Arguing against the 2nd c. B.C. Stoic philosopher Diogenes of Babylon.     [2] The Locrians?     [3] A similar story was told of Terpander: see Terp. test. 9 with n. 1.     [4] I.e. the story told by Diogenes.

**19** Pausanias, *Description of Greece*

I shall tell the story about Helen which I know is told by the Crotoniates and in the same terms by the Himeraeans. In the Black Sea off the mouths of the Danube[1] there is an island called White Island which is sacred to Achilles ... The first man to sail to it is said to have been a Crotoniate called Leonymus. Croton was at war with the Italian Locrians,[2] and the Locrians because of their kinship with the Opuntian Locrians used to summon Ajax, son of Oileus, to help them in their battles. Leonymus, who was in command of the Crotoniates, attacked the enemy where he heard Ajax had taken up his position in their ranks. He was wounded in

by Dunbabin (loc. cit. 359, 486) c. 540 B.C., by P. Bicknell (*Phoenix* 20, 1966, 294 ff.) to 580 or 576.

σκεται δὴ τὸ στέρνον καί — ἔκαμνε γὰρ ὑπὸ τοῦ τραύ-
ματος — ἀφίκετο ἐς Δελφούς. ἐλθόντα δὲ ἡ Πυθία
Λεώνυμον ἀπέστελλεν ἐς νῆσον τὴν Λευκήν, ἐνταῦθα
εἰποῦσα αὐτῷ φανήσεσθαι τὸν Αἴαντα καὶ ἀκέσεσθαι τὸ
τραῦμα. χρόνῳ δὲ ὡς ὑγιάνας ἐπανῆλθεν ἐκ τῆς Λευ-
κῆς, ἰδεῖν μὲν ἔφασκεν Ἀχιλλέα, ἰδεῖν δὲ τὸν Ὀιλέως
καὶ τὸν Τελαμῶνος Αἴαντα, συνεῖναι δὲ καὶ Πάτροκλόν
σφισι καὶ Ἀντίλοχον· Ἑλένην δὲ Ἀχιλλεῖ μὲν συνοι-
κεῖν, προστάξαι δέ οἱ πλεύσαντι ἐς Ἱμέραν πρὸς Στη-
σίχορον ἀγγέλλειν ὡς ἡ διαφθορὰ τῶν ὀφθαλμῶν ἐξ
Ἑλένης γένοιτο αὐτῷ μηνίματος. Στησίχορος μὲν ἐπὶ
τούτῳ τὴν παλινῳδίαν ἐποίησεν.

**20** *Sud.* E 2681 (ii 386s. Adler)

ἐπιτήδευμα· ἄσκησις, μάθησις. Ἱκανὸς ὄνομα, λη-
στὴς τὸ ἐπιτήδευμα· ὃς ἀνεῖλεν Αἰσχύλον τὸν αὐλητὴν
καὶ Στησίχορον τὸν κιθαρῳδόν.

**21** Pollux 9. 100 (ii 175 Bethe)

καὶ μὴν καὶ Στησίχορος ἐκαλεῖτό τις παρὰ τοῖς
ἀστραγαλίζουσιν ἀριθμός, ὃς ἐδήλου τὰ ὀκτώ· τὸν γὰρ
ἐν Ἱμέρᾳ τοῦ ποιητοῦ τάφον ἐξ ὀκτὼ πάντων συντε-
θέντα πεποιηκέναι τὴν 'πάντ' ὀκτώ' φασι παροιμίαν.

the chest and, seriously ill, went to Delphi. There the Priestess told him to go to White Island: Ajax would appear to him there and heal his wound. Later, when he was cured and returned home from White Island, he claimed that he had seen Achilles and also Ajax, son of Oïleus, and Ajax, son of Telamon, and that Patroclus and Antilochus were with them; Helen, he said, was living with Achilles and had ordered him to sail to Himera and tell Stesichorus that his blindness was the result of Helen's anger. On hearing this Stesichorus composed the Palinode (192).[3]

[3] The story is told also by Conon, *F.Gr.H.* 26 F 1. 18, Hermias on Plato, *Phaedrus* 243a, *Suda* s.v. Φορμίων ; see West, loc. cit. 303 f.

## 20 *Suda*

ἐπιτήδευμα : 'profession, trade', as in 'Hicanus ( = 'competent') by name, robber by trade'; it was Hicanus who killed the piper Aeschylus and the cithara-singer Stesichorus.

## 21 Pollux, *Vocabulary*

What is more, among dice-players the throw which came to eight was called Stesichorus; for it is said that the poet's tomb in Himera, being built eight all ways, gave rise to the proverbial expression 'eight all'.[1]

[1] Cf. Eustathius *Il.* 1289. 59ss. = Suetonius, π. παιδιῶν (p. 67 Taillardat) = Schol. Plato *Lysis* 206e (p. 456 Greene).

**22** Phot. *Lex.* (i 52 Naber) = *Sud.* Π 225 (iv 23 Adler) = Apostol. xiii 93 (ii 601 Leutsch-Schneidewin)

πάντα ὀκτώ· οἱ μὲν Στησίχορόν φασιν ἐν Κατάνῃ ταφῆναι πολυτελῶς πρὸς ταῖς ἀπ᾽ αὐτοῦ Στησιχορείοις λεγομέναις πύλαις καὶ τοῦ μνημείου ἔχοντος ὀκτὼ κίονας καὶ ὀκτὼ βαθμοὺς καὶ ὀκτὼ γωνίας.

**23** Cic. *Verr.* 2. 2. 86

Himera deleta quos civis belli calamitas reliquos fecerat, ii se Thermis collocarant in isdem agri finibus neque longe ab oppido antiquo. his se patrum fortunam ac dignitatem recuperare arbitrabantur cum illa maiorum ornamenta in eorum oppido collocabantur. erant signa ex aere complura: in his eximia pulchritudine ipsa Himera in muliebrem figuram habitumque formata ex oppidi nomine et fluminis. erat etiam Stesichori poetae statua senilis incurva cum libro, summo ut putant artificio facta, qui fuit Himerae, sed et est et fuit tota Graecia summo propter ingenium honore et nomine. haec iste ad insaniam concupiverat.

---

[1] See test. 44, Richter, loc. cit. 68.     [2] By Carthage, 409 B.C.
[3] See R. Heidenreich, 'Eine Dresdener Mantelstatue', *A.A.* 87

**22** Photius, *Lexicon*

'Eight all': some say that Stesichorus was given an expensive burial at Catana near the gates called Stesichorean after him,[1] and that the monument had eight pillars, eight steps and eight corners.

[1] Cf. test. 1.

### PORTRAITS[1]

**23** Cicero, *Speech against Verres*

On the destruction of Himera[2] the survivors of the calamitous war had settled at Thermae in the same district, quite close to the ancient town; and they felt that they were regaining the prosperity and solid worth of their fathers when those objects of art which had adorned the city of their ancestors were set up in their new city. There were several bronze statues, including an exceptionally beautiful one of Himera herself in the form and dress of a woman, bearing the name of the town and river. There was also a statue of the poet Stesichorus, a bent old man holding a book, a masterpiece of art, so they believe[3]; Stesichorus belonged to Himera but enjoyed and still enjoys the highest honour and distinction throughout Greece for his poetic genius. Verres had conceived a madman's craving to possess these statues.

(1972) 570 ff. for a Roman copy of a 5th c. Greek statue of Stesichorus.

# GREEK LYRIC

**24** *Anth. Pal.* 7. 75 = Antipater of Thessalonica lxxiv Gow-Page

Στασίχορον ζαπληθὲς ἀμέτρητον στόμα Μούσας
ἐκτέρισεν Κατάνας αἰθαλόεν δάπεδον,
οὗ κατὰ Πυθαγόρεω φυσικὰν φάτιν ἁ πρὶν Ὁμήρου
ψυχὰ ἐνὶ στέρνοις δεύτερον ᾠκίσατο.

---

[1] Or perhaps Antipater of Sidon.　　[2] With reference to the volcanic ash of Mt. Etna.

**25** [Plut.] *Mus.* 3. 1132bc (p. 112 Lasserre, vi 3. 3 Ziegler)

οὐ λελυμένην δ᾽ εἶναι τῶν προειρημένων τὴν τῶν
ποιημάτων λέξιν καὶ μέτρον οὐκ ἔχουσαν ἀλλὰ καθά-
περ Στησιχόρου τε καὶ τῶν ἀρχαίων μελοποιῶν, οἳ ποι-
οῦντες ἔπη τούτοις μέλη περιετίθεσαν.

**26** [Plut.] *Mus.* 7. 1133ef (p. 114 Lasserre, vi 3. 7 Ziegler)

τὸν δὲ καλούμενον Ἁρμάτειον νόμον λέγεται ποιῆ-
σαι ὁ πρῶτος Ὄλυμπος, ὁ Μαρσύου μαθητής. . . . ὅτι
δ᾽ ἐστὶν Ὀλύμπου ὁ Ἁρμάτειος νόμος ἐκ τῆς Γλαύκου
συγγραφῆς τῆς ὑπὲρ τῶν ἀρχαίων ποιητῶν (fr. 3
Müller) μάθοι ἄν τις, καὶ ἔτι γνοίη ὅτι Στησίχορος ὁ
Ἱμεραῖος οὔτ᾽ Ὀρφέα οὔτε Τέρπανδρον οὔτ᾽ Ἀρχίλο-
χον οὔτε Θαλήταν ἐμιμήσατο ἀλλ᾽ Ὄλυμπον, χρησά-
μενος τῷ Ἁρματείῳ νόμῳ καὶ τῷ κατὰ δάκτυλον εἴδει,
ὅ τινες ἐξ Ὀρθίου νόμου φασὶν εἶναι.

---

[1] See Olymp. test. 3.　　[2] Glaucus of Rhegium, late 5th c. scholar: see G. Huxley, *G.R.B.S.* 9 (1968) 47 ff.　　[3] See West, loc. cit. 310 f.

# STESICHORUS

## 'EPITAPH'

**24** *Palatine Anthology*: Antipater of Thessalonica[1]

Stesichorus, the full and limitless voice of the Muse, was given burial by the sooty land[2] of Catana. In his breast, according to Pythagoras' words about man's nature, the soul that was once Homer's made its second home.

## MUSIC AND METRES[1]

**25** 'Plutarch', *On Music*

The work of the poets mentioned earlier, he said,[2] was not free and unmetrical but resembled that of Stesichorus and the ancient lyric poets, who composed lines of verse and set them to music.[3]

[1] For metres attributed to Stesichorus or named after him see 275(a).    [2] Heraclides Ponticus, 4th c. B.C. philosopher, referring to Amphion, Linus and other early cithara-singers. [3] Continued as Terp. test. 18.

**26** 'Plutarch', *On Music*

The so-called Chariot nome is said to have been composed by the first Olympus,[1] pupil of Marsyas.... That it is by him can be gathered from Glaucus,[2] *On the Ancient Poets,* where one can learn also that Stesichorus of Himera imitated not Orpheus nor Terpander nor Archilochus nor Thaletas but Olympus, using the Chariot nome and the dactylic rhythm,[3] which some say is derived from the Orthian nome.

**27** [Plut.] *Mus.* 12. 1135c (p. 116 Lasserre, vi 3. 11 Ziegler)

ἔστι δὲ <καὶ> τις Ἀλκμανικὴ καινοτομία καὶ Στησιχόρειος, καὶ αὗται οὐκ ἀφεστῶσαι τοῦ καλοῦ.

**28** Dion. Hal. *Comp.* 19 (vi 85 Usener-Radermacher)

οἱ μὲν οὖν ἀρχαῖοι μελοποιοί, λέγω δὲ Ἀλκαῖόν τε καὶ Σαπφώ, μικρὰς ἐποιοῦντο στροφάς, ὥστ' ἐν ὀλίγοις τοῖς κώλοις οὐ πολλὰς εἰσῆγον μεταβολάς, ἐπῳδοῖς τε πάνυ ἐχρῶντο ὀλίγοις. οἱ δὲ περὶ Στησίχορόν τε καὶ Πίνδαρον μείζους ἐργασάμενοι τὰς περιόδους εἰς πολλὰ μέτρα καὶ κῶλα διένειμαν αὐτὰς οὐκ ἄλλου τινὸς ἢ τῆς μεταβολῆς ἔρωτι.

**29** Tzetz. *Vit. Hes.* (p. 35s. Colonna)

καὶ γνωρίσματα μέν ἐστι λυρικῶν ποιητῶν τὸ πρὸς λύραν τὰ τούτων ᾄδεσθαι μέλη, ὡς τὰ τοῦ Πινδάρου καὶ Στησιχόρου καὶ Ἀνακρέοντος . . .

**30** *Sud.* T 943 (iv 586 Adler) = 275(b) *P.M.G.*

τρία Στησιχόρου· στροφήν, ἀντίστροφον, ἐπῳδόν· ἐπῳδικὴ γὰρ πᾶσα ἡ τοῦ Στησιχόρου ποίησις. καὶ τὸν τελέως ἄμουσόν τε καὶ ἀπαίδευτον λοιδοροῦντες ἔφασκον ἂν οὐδὲ τρία τὰ Στησιχόρου εἰδέναι.

---

[1] I.e. its metrical structure is triadic, based on these three stanza-forms; see West, loc. cit. 312 f.  [2] See Leutsch-Schneidewin, *Corp. Par. Gr.* i 288, M. Davies, *J.H.S.* 102 (1982) 206 ff. The original form of the proverb may have meant, 'You don't know even the

# STESICHORUS

**27** 'Plutarch', *On Music*

There is also a certain originality (sc. in metre) in Alcman (test. 21) and Stesichorus, although their innovations do not abandon the noble manner[1] either.

[1] I.e. the manner of Terpander. See Terp. test. 22.

**28** Dionysius of Halicarnassus, *On Literary Composition*

The ancient lyric poets, I mean Alcaeus and Sappho, made their stanzas short, so they did not introduce many variations in their few colons, and they used the 'epode' or shorter line very sparingly (Sa. test. 36). But Stesichorus, Pindar and the like made their periods longer and divided them into many metres and colons for the sheer love of variety.

**29** Tzetzes, *Life of Hesiod*

The distinguishing feature of lyric poets is that their songs are sung to the lyre, for example the songs of Pindar and Stesichorus and Anacreon. . . .

**30** *Suda*

'Three of Stesichorus': strophe, antistrophe, epode; for all the poetry of Stesichorus is epodic.[1] If someone was completely devoid of culture and education it was said by way of insult that he did not know even the three of Stesichorus.[2]

three of Stesichorus' lines', with reference to the three famous lines of the Palinode (192).

**31** Athen. 14. 620c (iii 367 Kaibel)

Χαμαιλέων δὲ ἐν τῷ περὶ Στησιχόρου (fr. 28 Wehrli) καὶ μελῳδηθῆναί φησιν οὐ μόνον τὰ Ὁμήρου ἀλλὰ καὶ τὰ Ἡσιόδου καὶ Ἀρχιλόχου, ἔτι δὲ Μιμνέρμου καὶ Φωκυλίδου.

**32** Athen. 4. 172e (i 388 Kaibel)

ὅτι δὲ τὸ ποίημα τοῦτο (sc. Ἆθλα ἐπὶ Πελίᾳ) Στησιχόρου ἐστὶν ἱκανώτατος μάρτυς Σιμωνίδης ὁ ποιητής, ὃς περὶ τοῦ Μελεάγρου τὸν λόγον ποιούμενός φησιν ·

ὃς δουρὶ πάντας
νίκασε νέους, δινάεντα βαλὼν
Ἄναυρον ὕπερ πολυβότρυος ἐξ Ἰωλκοῦ ·
οὕτω γὰρ Ὅμηρος ἠδὲ Στησίχορος ἄεισε λαοῖς.

**33** Athen. 14. 638e (iii 410 Kaibel) = 276(b) *P.M.G.*

καὶ ὁ τοὺς Εἵλωτας δὲ πεποιηκώς φησιν (fr. 148 K.-A.) ·
τὰ Στησιχόρου τε καὶ Ἀλκμᾶνος Σιμωνίδου τε
ἀρχαῖον ἀείδειν. ὁ δὲ Γνήσιππος ἔστ' ἀκούειν . . .

---

[1] Eupolis (5th c. comic poet); Gnesippus composed lovers' serenades. Eupolis also mentioned Stesichorus in his mockery of Socrates' behaviour at a party (fr. 395). See also fr. 274 for Stesichorus as old-fashioned in Aristophanes, *Clouds* 967. Aristophanes adapted S.'s *Oresteia* in *Peace*: see frr. 210–212. For Stesichorus

# STESICHORUS

## ANCIENT COMMENTARIES[1]

**31** Athenaeus, *Scholars at Dinner*

Chamaeleon in his treatise *On Stesichorus*[2] says that not only Homer's verses were set to music but those of Hesiod and Archilochus and also Mimnermus and Phocylides.

[1] Theon of Alexandria (1st c. B.C.) and Aristonicus (Augustan era) commented on the *Wooden Horse* (S 133a, 136). Tryphon (Augustan era) wrote on the dialect of Himera (*Suda* T 1115).     [2] See also 193, 274, Lamprocles 735.

## THE VERDICT OF ANTIQUITY[1]

**32** Athenaeus, *Scholars at Dinner*

That this poem (sc. *Funeral Games of Pelias*) is the work of Stesichorus (179) is adequately attested by the poet Simonides, who says in his account of Meleager (564), 'who defeated all the young men with his spear, hurling it from grape-rich Iolcus over the eddying Anaurus: for so Homer and Stesichorus sang to the peoples.'[2]

[1] Cf. testt. 23, 24, 30 n. 2.     [2] Our earliest reference to Stesichorus.

**33** Athenaeus, *Scholars at Dinner*

The author[1] of the *Helots* says, 'To sing the songs of Stesichorus and Alcman and Simonides is old-fashioned; but we can all hear Gnesippus . . .'

and Simonides sung at parties see fr. 276(b), schol. Ar. *Wasps* 1222, Arion test. 7.

**34** *Anth. Pal.* 9. 184. 3s. = anon. xxxvi (a), 1196s. *F.G.E.*

  . . . Ὁμηρικὸν ὅς τ᾽ ἀπὸ ῥεῦμα
ἔσπασας οἰκείοις, Στησίχορ᾽, ἐν καμάτοις.


**35** *Anth. Pal.* 9. 571. 3 = anon. xxxvi (b), 1206 *F.G.E.*

 λάμπει Στησίχορός τε καὶ Ἴβυκος . . .


**36** Hor. *Carm.* 4. 9. 5–8

 non, si priores Maeonius tenet
 sedes Homerus, Pindaricae latent
  Ceaeque et Alcaei minaces
   Stesichorive graves Camenae.


**37** Dion. Hal. *Comp.* 24 (vi 120s. Usener-Radermacher)

 ἡ δὲ τρίτη καὶ μέση τῶν εἰρημένων δυεῖν ἁρμονιῶν,
ἣν εὔκρατον καλῶ σπάνει κυρίου τε καὶ κρείττονος ὀνό-
ματος, σχῆμα μὲν ἴδιον οὐδὲν ἔχει, κεκέρασται δὲ ὡς ἐξ
ἐκείνων μετρίως καὶ ἔστιν ἐκλογή τις τῶν ἐν ἑκατέρᾳ
κρατίστων . . . κορυφὴ μὲν οὖν ἁπάντων καὶ σκοπός
. . . δικαίως ἂν Ὅμηρος λέγοιτο. πᾶς γὰρ αὐτῷ τόπος,
ὅτου τις ἂν ἅψηται, ταῖς τε αὐστηραῖς καὶ ταῖς γλαφυ-
ραῖς ἁρμονίαις εἰς ἄκρον διαπεποίκιλται. τῶν δ᾽
ἄλλων ὅσοι τὴν αὐτὴν μεσότητα ἐπετήδευσαν . . .
ἀξιοθέατοι, μελοποιῶν μὲν Στησίχορός τε καὶ Ἀλκαῖος
. . .

# STESICHORUS

**34** *Palatine Anthology*: anon. on the nine Lyric Poets

... and you, Stesichorus, who channeled the Homeric stream into your own works.

**35** *Palatine Anthology*: anon. on the nine Lyric Poets

Stesichorus shines and Ibycus too.

**36** Horace, *Odes*

Even if Maeonian Homer holds first place, the poetry of Pindar and Simonides, the threatening songs of Alcaeus and the grave songs[1] of Stesichorus are not hidden in obscurity.

[1] Cf. Dio Chrysostomus *Or.* 2. 28, 'fit for kings to sing', Statius *Silvae* 5. 3. 154, 'proud Stesichorus'. The Stoic Chrysippus (3rd c. B.C.) quoted Stesichorus (frr. 906 f. *S.V.F.*).

**37** Dionysius of Halicarnassus, *On Literary Composition*

The third type of structure, which for want of an appropriate and better name I call 'mixed', is intermediate to the other two; it has no individual character but is, as it were, a moderate blend of the others and a sort of selection from the best features of each ... As peak and high-point of all such writers ... one would justly mention Homer. Every passage, no matter where you take him up, has been elaborated to perfection from the austere and the elegant types. Of the others who used this intermediate style ... among lyric poets Stesichorus and Alcaeus deserve attention ...

**38** Dion. Hal. *Imit.* 2. 421 (vi 205 Usener-Radermacher)

ὅρα δὲ καὶ Στησίχορον ἔν τε τοῖς ἑκατέρων τῶν
προειρημένων (sc. Σιμωνίδου καὶ Πινδάρου) πλεονε-
κτήμασι κατορθοῦντα, οὐ μὴν ἀλλὰ καὶ ὧν ἐκεῖνοι λεί-
πονται κρατοῦντα· λέγω δὲ τῇ μεγαλοπρεπείᾳ τῶν
κατὰ τὰς ὑποθέσεις πραγμάτων, ἐν οἷς τὰ ἤθη καὶ τὰ
ἀξιώματα τῶν προσώπων τετήρηκεν.

**39** 'Longinus' *de subl.* 13. 3 (p. 19 Russell)

μόνος Ἡρόδοτος Ὁμηρικώτατος ἐγένετο; Στησί-
χορος ἔτι πρότερον ὅ τε Ἀρχίλοχος, πάντων δὲ τούτων
μάλιστα ὁ Πλάτων . . .

**40** Plin. *N.H.* 10. 82 (ii 243 Mayhoff) = 281(e) *P.M.G.*

breviterque omnia tam parvulis in faucibus quae
tot exquisitis tibiarum tormentis ars hominum exco-
gitavit, non ut sit dubium hanc suavitatem prae-
monstratam efficaci auspicio cum in ore Stesichori
cecinit infantis.

**41** Quint. *Inst.* 10. 1. 62 (ii 579s. Winterbottom)

novem vero lyricorum longe Pindarus prin-
ceps. . . . Stesichorum quam sit ingenio validus

---

[1] Quintilian assesses only two others of the nine, Alcaeus (test. 21)
and Simonides (test. 41).

# STESICHORUS

**38** Dionysius of Halicarnassus, *On Imitation*

Look at Stesichorus succeeding where both of these poets (Simonides and Pindar) show their excellence and in addition prevailing where they fall short, namely in the magnificence of the settings of his subject-matter; in them he has preserved the traits and reputations of his characters.

**39** 'Longinus', *On Sublimity*

Was Herodotus the only writer to be 'most Homeric'? No, earlier still there were Stesichorus[1] and Archilochus, and more Homeric than any of these was Plato . . .

[1] Cf. Aelian fr. 150 Hercher = *Suda* Θ 115, 'if it is right for the Himeraean to raise his eyes towards Homer', Dio Chrysostomus *Or.* 55. 6 7, Stes. fr. 203.

**40** Pliny, *Natural History* (on the nightingale)

To put it briefly, everything that human skill has devised in the elaborate modulations of the pipes can be found in this tiny throat; so it was undoubtedly a sure omen that Stesichorus would possess such sweetness when the nightingale sang on his infant lips.[1]

[1] Cf. test. 44.

**41** Quintilian, *Principles of Oratory*

Among the nine lyric poets[1] Pindar easily takes first place. . . . The greatness of Stesichorus' genius

materiae quoque ostendunt, maxima bella et claris-
simos canentem duces et epici carminis onera lyra
sustinentem. reddit enim personis in agendo simul
loquendoque debitam dignitatem, ac si tenuisset
modum videtur aemulari proximus Homerum
potuisse, sed redundat atque effunditur, quod ut est
reprehendendum, ita copiae vitium est.

**42** Hermog. *Id.* 2. 4 (p. 338s. Rabe)

ταῦτά τοι καὶ ὁ Στησίχορος σφόδρα ἡδὺς εἶναι δοκεῖ
διὰ τὸ πολλοῖς χρῆσθαι τοῖς ἐπιθέτοις.

**43** Amm. Marc. 28. 4. 15 (ii 80 Seyfarth)

... cum multa et varia pro amplitudine
gloriarum et generum lectitare deberent, audientes
destinatum poenae Socraten coniectumque in car-
cerem rogasse quendam scite lyrici carmen Stesi-
chori modulantem ut doceretur id agere dum liceret,
interroganteque musico quid ei poterit hoc prodesse
morituro postridie, respondisse, ut aliquid sciens
amplius e vita discedat.

is shown among other things by his subject-matter: he sings of the most important wars and the most famous commanders[2] and sustains on his lyre the weight of epic poetry. In both their actions and their speeches he gives due dignity to his characters, and if only he had shown restraint he could possibly have been regarded as a close rival of Homer; but he is redundant and diffuse, a fault to be sure but explained by the abundance of what he had to say.

[2] Cf. Synesius, *Insomn.* 156b.

**42** Hermogenes, *Kinds of Style*

That is why Stesichorus seems to give very great pleasure by his use of many epithets.

**43** Ammianus Marcellinus, *History*

They[1] ought to be studying many different works to match the distinction of their fame and families; they ought to learn that Socrates, condemned to death and thrown into prison, asked someone who was skilfully performing a song of the lyric poet Stesichorus to teach him to do it while there was still time; and when the musician asked of what use this could be when he was to die on the following day, Socrates replied, 'So that I may know something more when I depart from life.'[2]

[1] The Roman nobility in the reign of Gratian.  [2] Cf. Sappho test. 10.

**44** *Anth. Pal.* 2. 125ss. = 281(e) *P.M.G.*

Στησίχορον δ' ἐνόησα λιγύθροον, ὅν ποτε γαῖα
Σικελίη μὲν ἔφερβε, λύρης δ' ἐδίδαξεν ᾿Απόλλων
ἁρμονίην ἔτι μητρὸς ἐνὶ σπλάγχνοισιν ἐόντα.
τοῦ γὰρ τικτομένοιο καὶ ἐς φάος ἄρτι μολόντος
ἔκποθεν ἠερόφοιτος ἐπὶ στομάτεσσιν ἀηδὼν
λάθρη ἐφεζομένη λιγυρὴν ἀνεβάλλετο μολπήν.

**44** *Palatine Anthology*: Christodorus[1]

And I saw clear-voiced Stesichorus, whom once the land of Sicily nurtured, whom Apollo taught the tuning of the lyre while he was still in his mother's womb: for at his birth, when he had just reached the light of day, a nightingale,[2] travelling through the air from somewhere or other, perched unnoticed on his lips and struck up her clear song.

[1] From his description of the statues in the Baths of Zeuxippus in Constantinople.    [2] Cf. test. 40.

# STESICHORUS

## FRAGMENTA

## ΑΘΛΑ ΕΠΙ ΠΕΛΙΑΙ

**178** *Et. Mag.* 544. 54

Κύλλαρος· ἵππος Κάστορος. παρὰ τὸ κέλλειν, ὁ ταχύς. Στησίχορος ἐν τοῖς ἐπὶ Πελίᾳ Ἄθλοις τὸν μὲν Ἑρμῆν δεδωκέναι φησί·

**Φλόγεον \<τε\> καὶ Ἅρπαγον, ὠκέα τέκνα Ποδάργας,**

Ἥραν δὲ Ξάνθον καὶ Κύλλαρον.

cf. *Et. Gud.* 353. 22, Tertull. *de spect.* 9, Serv. et al. in Verg. *Geo.* 3. 89 (v. Alcm. 25) +

\<τε\> Hiller-Crusius: v. M. W. Haslam, *Q.U.C.C.* 17 (1974) 12. Hemsterhuys: δ' ἐξάλιθον vel sim. codd.

# STESICHORUS

## FRAGMENTS

*Frr. 178–222 together with S 7–150 are assigned to named poems (in Greek alphabetical order); 222A (the Lille papyrus) is concerned with Theban myth, 222B with several myths; 223–39 deal with various mythological figures, 240–1 refer to Stesichorus' poetic composition, 242–5 are phrases, 246–68 words (in alphabetical order) cited from Stesichorus, 269–73 contain references to the content of his poems, 274 is of disputed authorship, 275 gives information about the poet's metres, 276 provides testimonia about the types of poetry he composed, 277–80 are spurious, 281 gives the apophthegms.*

### FUNERAL GAMES OF PELIAS

**178** *Etymologicum Magnum*

Cyllarus: Castor's horse. Derived from κέλλειν ('to drive on'), the name means 'the swift one'.[1] Stesichorus in his *Funeral Games of Pelias* says that Hermes gave (the Dioscuri)[2]

Phlogeus and Harpagus, swift foals of Podarge,

while Hera gave them Xanthus and Cyllarus.[3]

[1] Impossible etymology; the name may mean Crab-legs.
[2] Castor and Pollux, who were competing in the chariot-race.
[3] Cf. Alcm. 25, *Il.* 16. 148 ff., 19. 400.

61

# GREEK LYRIC

**179** Athen. 4. 172de (i 387s. Kaibel)

(a) πεμμάτων δὲ πρῶτόν φησιν μνημονεῦσαι Πανύασσιν Σέλευ-
κος (*F.Gr.H.* 634 F2.2), ἐν οἷς περὶ τῆς παρ' Αἰγυπτίοις ἀνθρω-
ποθυσίας διηγεῖται, πολλὰ μὲν ἐπιθεῖναι λέγων πέμματα, πολλὰς
δὲ νοσσάδας ὄρνις (fr. 23 Davies), προτέρου Στησιχόρου ἢ Ἰβύκου
ἐν τοῖς Ἄθλοις ἐπιγραφομένοις εἰρηκότος φέρεσθαι τῇ παρθένῳ
δῶρα

σασαμίδας χόνδρον τε καὶ ἐγκρίδας
ἄλλα τε πέμματα καὶ μέλι χλωρόν.

(b) ὅτι δὲ τὸ ποίημα τοῦτο Στησιχόρου ἐστὶν ἱκανώτατος μάρ-
τυς Σιμωνίδης ὁ ποιητής, ὃς περὶ τοῦ Μελεάγρου τὸν λόγον ποιού-
μενός φησιν (564 *P.M.G.*). ὁ γὰρ Στησίχορος οὕτως εἴρηκεν ἐν τῷ
προκειμένῳ ᾄσματι ⟦τοῖς Ἄθλοις⟧·

θρῴσκων μὲν ἄρ' Ἀμφιάραος ἄκοντι δὲ
νίκασεν Μελέαγρος.

(a) cf. Athen. 14. 645e μνημονεύει αὐτῶν (sc. ἐγκρίδων) Στησίχορος διὰ
τούτων· χόνδρον — χλωρόν.
(b) Kleine: μὲν γὰρ codd.

**180** Zenob. vi 44 (i 173s. Leutsch-Schneidewin)

χειροβρῶτι δεσμῷ· τοῖς πυκτικοῖς ἱμᾶσι. διὰ τὸ τὰς σάρκας
διακόπτειν καὶ ἀναλίσκειν. βέλτιον δὲ τὸν δεσμὸν ἀκούειν τὸν ἀπο-
βιβρώσκοντα τὼ χεῖρε. ἐδέθη γὰρ ἔν τινι †πετραίῳ· Στησίχορος ἐν
ἀρχῇ τῶν ἐπὶ Πελίᾳ Ἄθλων.

cf. *Sud.*, Hesych. s.v. χειροβρῶτι.

# STESICHORUS

**179** Athenaeus, *Scholars at Dinner*

(a) Cakes, according to Seleucus,[1] were first mentioned by Panyassis[2] in his account of human sacrifice in Egypt, where he says that they placed (on the altar? on the victim?) many cakes and many young fowls; but Stesichorus or Ibycus had previously said in the poem entitled *Funeral Games* that the maiden[3] was offered gifts of

> sesame cakes and groats and oil-and-honey cakes and other cakes and yellow honey.

(b) That this poem is the work of Stesichorus is adequately attested by the poet Simonides, who says in his account of Meleager (564; Stes. test. 32), '. . . for so Homer and Stesichorus sang to the peoples.' For in the poem in question Stesichorus said,

> Amphiaraus won with his leap, Meleager with his javelin-throw.

[1] Alexandrian scholar, 1st c. A.D.    [2] 5th c. B.C. epic poet.
[3] Probably Alcestis, daughter of Pelias, whose marriage to Admetus, a competitor in the Games, Stesichorus seems to have described in this poem (Vürtheim 6).

**180** Zenobius, *Proverbs*

'arm-gnawing[1] bonds': boxing thongs, so called because they cut through and destroy the flesh; but it is preferable to interpret the words as 'the bonds that eat away the arms,'[2] for . . . was bound (in a rocky place?): so Stesichorus at the beginning of the *Funeral Games of Pelias*.[3]

[1] Or 'hand-gnawing'.    [2] Or 'hands'.    [3] In a description of a boxing match, or with reference to Prometheus, seen by the Argonauts on their journey (Vürtheim 9: cf. Ap. Rhod. 2. 1248 ff.)?

ΓΑΡΥΟΝΑΙΣ

S 7 = 184 *P.M.G.*   Str. 3. 2. 11 (i 228 Kramer)

ἐοίκασι δ᾽ οἱ παλαιοὶ καλεῖν τὸν Βαῖτιν Ταρτησσόν, τὰ δὲ Γά-
δειρα καὶ τὰς πρὸς αὐτὴν νήσους Ἐρύθειαν. διόπερ οὕτως εἰπεῖν
ὑπολαμβάνουσι Στησίχορον περὶ τοῦ Γηρυόνος βουκόλου διότι γεν-
νηθείη

    σχεδὸν ἀντιπέρας κλεινᾶς Ἐρυθείας

    <

                  > Ταρτησ-
    σοῦ ποταμοῦ παρὰ παγὰς ἀπείρονας ἀρ-
    γυρορίζους
5   ἐν κευθμῶνι πέτρας.

v. Haslam, loc. cit. 16    5 Hermann (et Kleine): κευθμώνων
codd.

S 8 P.Oxy. 2617 fr. 6

    διὰ] κ̣[ύ]μαθ᾽ ἁλὸς βαθέ̣ας ἀφίκον-
    το θ]ε̣ῶν περικαλλέ[α ν̣]ᾶσον
    τ]όθι Ἑσπερίδες π[αγχρ]ύσεα δώ-
    μα]τ̣᾽ ἔχοντι·
5   . . . . . . . .]. [ . ]ασσ̣ . . [ . . . . . . ]και
    . . . . . . κ]αλύκω̣[ν
    . . . . . . . .]λατ[

1 διὰ suppl. Page βαθέας legit Barrett        6 suppl. Barrett
cetera Lobel

---

[1] Perhaps the infant Eurytion and his mother Erytheia, who was
one of the Hesperides.    [2] Goddesses who guarded a tree of
golden apples on the western bank of Ocean.

# STESICHORUS

## GERYONEIS

*The publication of new fragments of the Geryoneis (P.Oxy. 2617) necessitated the reordering of the book-quotations (181–186 P.M.G.). The fragments are printed here in the following sequence, that of S.L.G.: S 7 = 184 P.M.G., S 8–16, the new 184A, S 17 = 185 P.M.G., S 18, S 19 = 181 P.M.G., the isolated words contained in S 20–84, S 85 = 182 P.M.G., S 86 = 183 P.M.G., S 87 = 186 P.M.G. See D. L. Page, J.H.S. 93 (1973) 138 ff. The poem dealt with Heracles' acquisition of the cattle of Geryon, a triple-bodied monster living on the Atlantic island of Erytheia.*

**S 7** = 184 *P.M.G.*　　Strabo, *Geography*

The ancient writers seem to call the Baetis[1] Tartessus, and Gadeira[2] and the nearby islands Erytheia. This, it is supposed, is why Stesichorus could say of Geryon's herdsman[3] that he was born

almost opposite famous Erytheia ... by the limit-less silver-rooted[4] waters of the river Tartessus in the hollow of a rock.

[1] River of southern Spain (now the Guadalquivir), flowing into the Atlantic just north of Cádiz.　　[2] Gades, now Cádiz, coastal city north-west of Gibraltar.　　[3] Eurytion.　　[4] With reference to the silver mined in the region.

**S 8** Papyrus of early 1st c. A.D.

... over the waves of the deep brine they[1] came to the beautiful island of the gods, where the Hesperides[2] have their homes of solid gold; ... (buds?) ...

# GREEK LYRIC

**S 9** P.Oxy. 2617 fr. 42(b)

κε]φαλάν·
ἰο]δόκα

]. ωρ ποκα[
]ἀνήρ· ουτ[
5    ]ν ἦτορ.[.].[

1 suppl. Lobel    2 e.g. Barrett (vel ἀιστο]δόκα)

**S 10** P.Oxy. 2617 fr. 25

[              ἀλ-
γινόεντος·
ἀλλ' ὦ φίλε ματ[έρα Καλλιρόαν
καὶ ἀρηίφιλο[ν
5 Χρ[υσά]ορα σ.[

1 suppl. Lobel, 3–5 Barrett

**S 11** P.Oxy. 2617 frr. 13+14+15

χηρσὶν δ[           · τὸν
δ' ἀπαμ[ειβόμενος
ποτέφα [κρατερὸς Χρυσάορος ἀ-
θανάτοιο [γόνος καὶ Καλλιρόας·

5 "μή μοι θά[νατον προφέρων κρυόεν-
τα δεδίσκ[ε' ἀγάνορα θυμόν,
μηδεμελ[
αἰ μὲν γὰ[ρ γένος ἀθάνατος πέλο-
μαι καὶ ἀγή[ραος ὥστε βίου πεδέχειν

66

# STESICHORUS

**S 9** Same papyrus

... head; ... quiver[1]; ... the man once ...; ... heart ...

[1] Carried by Heracles? Barrett suggests that Menoites, herdsman of Hades in that region, is describing Heracles to Geryon.

**S 10** Same papyrus

... painful ...; no, my friend, ... your mother Callirrhoe and Chrysaor, dear to Ares, ...[1]

[1] Menoites tells Geryon to remember his parents (Barrett).

**S 11** Same papyrus

... with his hands.... Answering him[1] the mighty son of immortal Chrysaor and Callirrhoe said, 'Do not with talk of chilling death try to frighten my manly heart, nor (beg me?) ...; for if I am by birth immortal and ageless, so that I shall

[1] Geryon answers Menoites (Barrett).

10    ἐν Ὀλύμπ[ωι,
    κρέσσον[               ἐ-
    λέγχεα δ[

    καὶ τ[
    κεραϊ[ζομένας ἐπιδῆν βόας ἁ-
15    μετέρω[ν ἀπόνοσφιν ἐπαύλων·
    αἰ δ' ὦ φί[λε χρὴ στυγερόν μ' ἐπὶ γή-
    ρας [ἱκ]έσθαι,
    ζώ[ει]ν τ' ἐν ἐ[φαμερίοις ἀπάνευ-
    θε θ[ε]ῶν μακάρω[ν,
20    νῦν μοι πολὺ κά[λλιόν ἐστι παθῆν
    ὅ τι μόρσιμ[ον ἢ θάνατον προφυγῆν

    καὶ ὀνείδε[α παισὶ φίλοισι
    καὶ παντὶ γέ[νει καταχευέμεν ἐξ-
    οπίσω Χρυσ[άο]ρο[ς υ]ἱόν·
25    μ]ὴ τοῦτο φ[ί]λον μακά[ρε]σσι θε[ο]ῖ-
    σι γ]ένοιτο
    ....].[.].κε[..].[.] περὶ βουσὶν ἐμαῖς
                           ]
                    ]κλέος.[

suppl. Lobel (2, 3 ἁ-, 5 θανατ-, 6 δεδίσκεο, 11 ἐ-, 14 ἁ-, 16 φίλε,
20 κάλλιον, 25s. μὴ — γένοιτο), Page (5 προφέρων, 8–10, 20 ἐστι π.),
Diggle (23 γένει), Führer (21 ἢ θ. π., 22 π.φ., 23 κ. ἐξ-), Snell (22
ὀνείδεα), cetera Barrett, qui frr. 13, 14, 15 coniunxit       7 μηδέ με
λ[ίσσεο e.g. Page         29 Ἡρα]κλέος ? Lobel

share in life on Olympus, then it is better (to endure?) the reproaches ... and ... to watch my cattle being driven off far from my stalls; but if, my friend, I must indeed reach hateful old age and spend my life among short-lived mortals far from the blessed gods, then it is much nobler for me to suffer what is fated than to avoid death and shower disgrace on my dear children and all my race hereafter — I am Chrysaor's son. May this not be the wish of the blessed gods ... concerning my cattle ... (Heracles?) ... '

# GREEK LYRIC

**S 12** P.Oxy. 2617 fr. 19

      πεφ[
  ο . αμ[ . . πε]φυλαγμε[
    πεν ἰ[δοῖσ]ά τε νισόμ[ενον ποτέφα·

  "νικᾶ[ι τὸ] κράτος ν[
 5 στυγε[ρ- . . ] . . . [
    γμ̣ατε . ν λευκ[
  πείθευ, τέκνον [
    σα γ . [
  κατα[             αἰ-
10  γιοχο[
  μεγα
    θησε[ῖ

  οὐκε[
    θανατ[
15 ἀλλ' ὑπ[
    . αντ[
    ασαπ . [
    χερὶ δ[

2 suppl. Lobel, 3 *l.* τε ν. Barrett, ποτέφα Führer, 4 Führer, 5 Barrett    7 Barrett: πειθου pap.    9 suppl. Lobel, 12 Page

# STESICHORUS

**S 12** Same papyrus

... guarded ... and seeing him coming she[1] addressed him: 'Strength wins victory ... hateful ... white.... Obey me, my child, ... aegis-bearing (Zeus) ... will set great ... not ... death ... but ... hand ...'

[1] Callirrhoe addresses her son Geryon (Barrett).

**S 13** P.Oxy. 2617 fr. 11

```
. . . . . . . ] ἐγὼν [μελέ]α καὶ ἀλασ-
      τοτόκος κ]αὶ ἄλ[ασ]τα παθοῖσα ·
   ἀλλά σε Γ]αρυόνα γωνάζομα[ι,
5    αἴ ποκ' ἐμ]όν τιν μαζ[ὸν] ἐ[πέσχεθον
. . . . . . . . ]ωμον γ[
. . . . . . . . . ]
   παρὰ ματρὶ] φίλαι γανυθ[εὶς
. . . . . . εὐφ]ροσύναις.'

10 ὣς φαῖσα θυώ]δεα πέπλ[ον
   ] . [ . . ]κλυ . . . . [
            ]ρευγων ·
            ]γον ελ[
```

2, 3 init. suppl. Barrett       4 ἀλλά σε tent. Page       5 init. suppl. Barrett    ἐπέσχεθον Page    8 π. μ., 9 Barrett,    10 e.g. Führer, θυώδεα e.g. Barrett       cetera Lobel

**S 14** P.Oxy. 2617 fr. 3

```
   οὐ γάρ τις ἔμ]ιμνε παραὶ Δία παμ-
      βασιλῆα ·]

   τόκα δὴ γλαυκ]ῶπις Ἀθάνα
   φάτ' εὐφραδέω]ς ποτὶ ὸν κρατερό-
5    φρονα πάτρω' ἰ]πποκέλευθον ·
   "ἄγ' ὑποσχέσιο]ς μεμναμένος ἄ[ν
      περ ὑπέστας]
   μὴ βούλεο Γαρυ]όναν θ[αν]άτου
```

1 tent. Barrett       2, 3 τόκα δὴ, 4 φάτ' suppl. Page,    εὐφρ. Barrett,    5 πάτρω', 6, 7 Page,    8 μὴ β. Barrett       cetera Lobel

72

# STESICHORUS

**S 13** Same papyrus

'... I, unhappy woman,[1] miserable in the child I bore, miserable in my sufferings; but I beseech you, Geryon, if ever I offered you my breast ... at your dear (mother's side,) gladdened ... by (your feasting).' (With these words she opened) her fragrant robe ...

[1] Callirrhoe continues her appeal to her son.

**S 14** Same papyrus

(For no-one) remained by the side of Zeus, king of all[1]; then grey-eyed Athena spoke eloquently to her stout-hearted uncle, driver of horses[2]: 'Come now, remember the promise you gave and (do not wish to save) Geryon from death ...'

[1] In an assembly of the gods.  [2] Poseidon, father of Chrysaor and so grand-father of Geryon.

# GREEK LYRIC

**S 15** P.Oxy. 2617 frr. 4 + 5

col. i

```
          ]ν[
          ]ναντ[
          ]αν δοιω . [
          ]
   5      ]τα νόωι διέλε[ν
          ]ν·
   ἐδοάσσατό οἱ ]πολὺ κέρδιον εἶν
          ]οντα λάθραι πολεμε[ῖν

          ἀνδρὶ] κραταιῶι·
   10         εὐρ]ὰ̣ξ κατεφράζετ[ό] οἱ
          πι]κρὸν ὄλεθρον·
   χὠ μὲν στέρνων ἔ]χεν ἀσπίδα πρόσ[θ',
          ὁ δὲ πέτρωι]
   κροτάφοιο καθίκ]ετο· τοῦ δ' ἀπὸ κρα-
   15     τὸς ἄφαρ μεγάλαι]
   καναχᾶι πέσεν ἱπ]πόκομος τρυφάλει'·
   ἁ δ' αὐτόθι μίμνεν] ἐπὶ ζαπέδωι·
```

*desunt vv. xiii*

col. ii

```
          φέρ]ων στυγε[ρ]οῦ
       θανάτοι]ο τέ[λος
   κ]ε̣φ[αλ]ᾶι πέρι [πότμον] ἔχων, πεφορυ-
   γ]μένος αἵματ[ι . . . . . ] . . [ . . ]ι τε χολᾶι,
```

col. i    7 suppl. Diggle,    9 Page,    10 εὐρὰξ Barrett,    12–14
Page,    15 ἁ. μ., 16 κ. π., 17 e.g. Page

col. ii    1 φέρων e.g. Barrett, Führer    2 τέλος, 3 πότμον suppl.
Barrett

# STESICHORUS

**S 15** Same papyrus

col. i      ... two ... in his mind he distinguished[1]
...; it seemed to him to be much better ... to fight
by stealth ... against the mighty man; ... (crouch-
ing?) on one side he devised for him ... bitter des-
truction; and he [Geryon] kept his shield in front of
(his chest, but the other struck his brow with a
stone?); and from his head (immediately with a
great clatter?) fell the helmet with its horse-hair
plume; (and it remained there) on the ground;

[*gap of 13 lines*]

col. ii      ... (bringing)[2] the end that is hateful
(death), having (doom) on its head, befouled with

---

[1] Heracles deliberated whether to kill Geryon by stealth or in open
fight.      [2] Seemingly  the  description  of  Heracles'  arrow.

5 ὀλεσάνορος αἰολοδε[ίρ]ου
 ὀδύναισιν Ὕδρας· σιγᾶι δ’ ὅ γ’ ἐπι-
 κλοπάδαν [ἐ]νέρεισε μετώπωι·
 διὰ δ’ ἔσχισε σάρκα [καὶ] ὀ[στ]έα δαί-
 μονος αἴσαι·
10 διὰ δ’ ἀντικρὺ σχέθεν οἰ[σ]τὸς ἐπ’ ἀ-
 κροτάταν κορυφάν,
 ἐμίαινε δ’ ἄρ’ αἵματι πορφ[υρέωι
 θώρακά τε καὶ βροτό̣εντ[α μέλεα·

 ἀπέκλινε δ’ ἄρ’ αὐχένα Γαρ[υόνας
15 ἐπικάρσιον, ὡς ὅκα μ[ά]κω[ν
 ἅτε καταισχύνοισ’ ἁπαλὸν [δέμας
 αἶψ’ ἀπὸ φύλλα βαλοῖσα ν[

8, 12–14, 16 Page          cetera Lobel


**S 16** P.Oxy. 2617 fr. 31

          ] . δε . μα̣[
 ὁ δὲ δεύτερ[ο-
 ρόπαλον κ̣[

2 suppl. Lobel


**184A** Paradox. Vat. 32 (Giannini, *Paradox. Graec. Rel.*
340)

 παρ’ Ὁμήρῳ Πρωτεὺς εἰς πάντα μετεμορφοῦτο, καθὰ Θέτις
(Rohde: καθατις cod.) παρὰ Πινδάρῳ καὶ Νηρεὺς παρὰ Στησιχόρῳ
καὶ Μήστρα (Rohde: μίστρα cod.) <παρ’ Ἡσιόδῳ add.
Wilamowitz>.

blood and with ... gall, the anguish of the dapple-necked Hydra, destroyer of men[3]; and in silence he thrust it cunningly into his brow, and it cut through the flesh and bones by divine dispensation; and the arrow held straight on the crown of his head, and it stained with gushing blood his breastplate and gory limbs; and Geryon drooped his neck to one side, like a poppy which spoiling its tender beauty suddenly sheds its petals and ...

[3] I.e. Heracles used an arrow poisoned with the blood and gall of the Hydra, which he had killed.

**S 16** Same papyrus

And he ... the second ... his club[1] ...

[1] Heracles used his club on Geryon's second head?

**184A** *Vatican Paradoxographer*

In Homer (*Od.* 4. 455 ff.) Proteus changed into all manner of shapes, just like Thetis in Pindar, Nereus in Stesichorus,[1] Mestra in Hesiod.[2]

[1] In the version of Panyassis (fr. 7A D.) Heracles got the Sun's cup from Nereus.  [2] Cf. fr. 43(c) M.-W.

# GREEK LYRIC

**S 17** = 185 *P.M.G.*     Athen. 11. 469e (iii 32 Kaibel)

ὅτι δὲ καὶ ὁ Ἥλιος ἐπὶ ποτηρίου διεκομίζετο ἐπὶ τὴν δύσιν Στησίχορος μὲν οὕτως φησίν·

   τᾶμος δ' Ὑπεριονίδα ἲς
   δέπας ἐσκατέβα <παγ>χρύσεον ὄ-
   φρα δι' Ὠκεανοῖο περάσαις
   ἀφίκοιθ' ἱαρᾶς ποτὶ βένθεα νυ-
5  κτὸς ἐρεμνᾶς
   ποτὶ ματέρα κουριδίαν τ' ἄλοχον
   παῖδας τε φίλους,
   ὁ δ' ἐς ἄλσος ἔβα δάφναισι κατά-
   σκιον †ποσὶν παῖς Διὸς† . . .

1 τᾶμος Barrett: ἅλιος codd.     -δα ἲς West: -δας codd.     2 West,
Führer: ἐσκατέβαινε χρύσεον codd.     3 -σαις Page: -σας codd.
4 -κοιθ' Blomfield: -κηθ' codd.     ἱαρ- Page: ἱερ- codd.

Athen. xi 781d (iii 16 Kaibel)

τὸν δὲ Ἥλιον ὁ Στησίχορος ποτηρίῳ διαπλεῖν φησι τὸν Ὠκεανόν, ᾧ καὶ τὸν Ἡρακλέα περαιωθῆναι ἐπὶ τὰς Γηρυόνου βόας ὁρμῶντα.

cf. Eust. *Od.* 1632. 23

**S 18** P.Oxy. 2617 fr. 21

   2 ]κρατος [   3 ]ᾳ τιμὰν[   5 ἐκπ]επέ-
ραντ[αι suppl. Haslam   6 ]και παντ[
8 ]ακουσο[   10 ἀ]δίκοισιν[ suppl. Barrett
11 Κρο]νίδα βα[σιλεῦ suppl. Barrett

# STESICHORUS

**S 17** = 185 *P.M.G.*   Athenaeus, *Scholars at Dinner*

That Helius too was conveyed to his setting in a cup Stesichorus tells us in the following words:

And then Hyperion's strong child[1] went down into the cup of solid gold, so that he might cross over Ocean and reach the depths of holy, dark night and his mother and wedded wife and dear children; while he[2] (Zeus' son?) went (on foot?) into the grove, shady with its laurels.

[1] Helius, the Sun.   [2] Heracles, who has reached Erytheia in the cup or, more probably, has travelled back to the mainland in it, now returns it to Helius. See Athen. 11. 470c for Pherecydes' version of the story.

Athenaeus, *Scholars at Dinner*

Stesichorus says that Helius sailed across Ocean in a cup and that Heracles also crossed over in it when travelling to get Geryon's cattle.

**S 18** Same papyrus as S 8–16

... strength ... honour ... has been accomplished ... every ... unjust ... son of Cronus, king[1] ...

[1] Geryon complains to Zeus of the theft of his cattle (Barrett)? If so, the fragment belongs between S 10 and S 11.

**S 19** = 181 *P.M.G.*    Athen. 11. 499ab (iii 100 Kaibel)

Στησίχορος δὲ τὸ παρὰ Φόλῳ τῷ Κενταύρῳ ποτήριον σκύφιον δέπας καλεῖ ἐν ἴσῳ τῷ σκυφοειδές. λέγει δ' ἐπὶ τοῦ Ἡρακλέους·

σκύφιον δὲ λαβὼν δέπας ἔμμετρον ὡς
      τριλάγυνον
πί' ἐπισχόμενος, τό ῥά οἱ παρέθη-
      κε Φόλος κεράσαις.

4 -σας codd.

**S 20** P.Oxy. 2617 fr. 46

col. i 3 ]αδικω[
col. ii 3 δῶκε[      4 ἐνθεν[      5 οἶνον . [
5s. πευ]|καλίμο[ισιν

5 suppl. Lobel, 6 Barrett

**S 21** P.Oxy. 2617 fr. 1

1   ]ν μεν[ ] . ρονες ὠκυπέτα[ι      2 ἐχοίσαι
3 ἐπ[τ]άξαν ἐπ[ὶ] χθόνα·      4 ]απε . η κεφαλὰ χαρ[

suppl. Lobel

**S 22** P.Oxy. 2617 fr. 17

1  φατὰ] κωὐ φατὰ θ . . [      2 ἀ]κάματος καὶ
ἀμ[      4 ]φύλοπις ἀργαλέα[      6s. μάχαι τ' ἀν-
δρο[κτασίαι | τε      7 δι]απρυσίοι· [      8 ]ος ἵππων [

1 tent. Page      cetera Lobel

# STESICHORUS

**S 19** = 181 *P.M.G.*  Athenaeus, *Scholars at Dinner*

Stesichorus calls the drinking vessel at the home of Pholus the Centaur σκύφιον δέπας (bowl-cup), giving σκύφιον the sense of σκυφοειδές (bowl-shaped). He says[1] of Heracles,

And taking the bowl-cup with the capacity of three flagons he drank it, holding it to his lips — the bowl-cup which Pholus[2] had mixed and handed to him.

[1] In the *Geryoneis* (Athen. 11. 499e).    [2] Pholus' cave was in Arcadia. Perhaps Heracles is on his way home to Tiryns.

*S 20–84 are from the same papyrus as S 8–16, 18.*

**S 20**

... unjust ... (he) gave ... whence ... wine[1] ... with shrewd (words? thoughts?) ...

[1] Cf. S 19.

**S 21**

... swift-flying ... having ... cowered on the earth ... head ...

**S 22**

... (things speakable) and things unspeakable ... untiring and un- ... painful strife ... battles and slaughterings of men ... piercing (cries?); ... of horses ...

**S 23** P.Oxy. 2617 fr. 24

1 ἀ]θανάτοις καταμαν[ύειν      2 ]πεδαμώνιον ε . [

1 ἀ] suppl. Lobel      κατ. tent. Page

**S 24** P.Oxy. 2617 fr. 18

1 ἐ]ν κονίαις[      3 φ]ύλοπιν α[ἰνὰν
4 (ἀπ)]ολωλότε[ς

1, 3 φυλ. suppl. Lobel      3 αἰνὰν vel ἀργαλέαν, 4 Page

**S 25** P.Oxy. 2617 fr. 70

1 ὣς ἦνε[πε      2 ἀπαμε[ιβ-

suppl. Lobel

**S 26** P.Oxy. 2617 fr. 2

2 μ]έγ' ἄριστοι [      3 ]νθεν ἐρ<ε>ικομένο[ι
5 ἐ]λίσσετο κυ-      [

2, 3 suppl. Lobel      5 tent. Page

**S 27** P.Oxy. 2617 fr. 7

col. i   2   ]φυγῆν ·      col. ii   6 marg. N̄

**S 28** P.Oxy. 2617 fr. 8

3 (ἀ)με]ίλιχον [

suppl. Lobel

**S 29** P.Oxy. 2617 fr. 10

3   ]νομῆα[

**S 23**

... to denounce to the immortals ... vain(ly) ...

**S 24**

... in the dust ... grim strife ... dead[1] ...

[1] Plural participle.

**S 25**

So he spoke ... in answer ...

**S 26**

... by far the greatest (warriors.) ... were -ed, being torn ... (he) prayed ...

**S 27**

to flee [1]

[1] The figure 1300 in the margin marks the 1300th line of the roll and presumably of the poem.

**S 28**

(un)kind

**S 29**

herdsman[1]

[1] Presumably Eurytion, Geryon's herdsman.

**S 30** P.Oxy. 2617 fr. 12

2 ]μοι φθιμενο[

**S 31** P.Oxy. 2617 fr. 13(b)

3 ἀθ]άνατον βίοτ̣[ον

tent. Page

**S 32** P.Oxy. 2617 fr. 20

4 χρυ[σ-    8 ῾Αφα[ιστ-

8 tent. Barrett

**S 37** P.Oxy. 2617 fr. 27

1 πέτετ̣[-    2 μαν̣ι̣α̣[

**S 39** P.Oxy. 2617 fr. 29

1 ο]ὐ̣κ ῎Αιδος οὐδ[    3 ]ρες ἠλύθον ε ̣[
4 εὐρ]υχορ[

1 tent. Page, 4 Lobel

**S 50** P.Oxy. 2617 fr. 41

2 ]επανταν̣[    3 ]εν ἱππο[
4 ( - )εκ]ν̣άμφθη[

4 suppl. Lobel

**S 53** P.Oxy. 2617 fr. 45

3 ]πτολε[μ-

**S 54** P.Oxy. 2617 fr. 47

1 ]ἔργα χερῶ[ν    3 ]τ̣ριπόδων ̣[

1 suppl. Lobel

**S 30**

dead

**S 31**

immortal life[1]

[1] Cf. S 11.

**S 32**

. . . gold . . . (Hephaestus?) . . .

**S 37**

. . . flies . . . (madness?) . . .

**S 39**

. . . not (of?) Hades nor . . . (they) came . . . (spacious?) . . .

---

**S 50**

. . . (all?) . . . horse(s) . . . was torn . . .

**S 53**

war

**S 54**

. . . the works of (his?) hands . . . tripods . . .

**S 55** P.Oxy. 2617 fr. 48
2 ῎Α]φαιστος ε ̣ [
suppl. Lobel

**S 56** P.Oxy. 2617 fr. 49
2 τ]ερπικερα[υν-
suppl. Lobel

**S 70** P.Oxy. 2617 fr. 63
4 Ϝαρυ[όν-
suppl. Lobel

**S 71** P.Oxy. 2617 fr. 64
2 ἐρ]ασιπλο[καμ-
tent. Lobel

**S 72** P.Oxy. 2617 fr. 65
1   ] ̣ ν θνα̣τ̣ο[

**S 75** P.Oxy. 2617 fr. 68
1   ]ἐ̣πὶ ῥηγ[μῖνι
tent. Lobel

**S 79**
1 κ]αὶ φυλο̣[πι-   2   ]ν ἰαίνη[
1 tent. Führer

**S 55**

Hephaestus


**S 56**

(Zeus,) wielder of the thunderbolt


**S 70**

Geryon


**S 71**

with lovely tresses

---

**S 72**

mortal

**S 75**

(on the beach?)


**S 79**

(battle-din?) . . . warm(s)

**S 85** = 182 *P.M.G.*     Paus. 8. 3. 2 (ii 224 Rocha-Pereira)

Παλλαντίου μὲν δὴ καὶ Στησίχορος ὁ Ἱμεραῖος ἐν Γηρυονηίδι ἐποιήσατο μνήμην.

**S 86** = 183 *P.M.G*     Schol. Ap. Rhod. 1. 211 (p. 26 Wendel)

Στησίχορος δὲ ἐν τῇ Γηρυονίδι καὶ νῆσόν τινα ἐν τῷ Ἀτλαντικῷ πελάγει Σαρπηδονίαν φησί.

**S 87** = 186 *P.M.G.*     Schol. Hes. *Theog.* 287 (p. 57 di Gregorio)

ἐστὶ δὲ ὁ Γηρυονεὺς ἐκ Καλλιρρόης τῆς Ὠκεανοῦ καὶ Χρυσάορος. Στησίχορος δὲ καὶ ἓξ χεῖρας ἔχειν φησὶ καὶ ἓξ πόδας καὶ ὑπόπτερον εἶναι.

## ΕΛΕΝΑ

**187** Athen. 3. 81d (i 189 Kaibel)

Κυδωνίων δὲ μήλων μνημονεύει Στησίχορος ἐν Ἑλένῃ οὕτως·

πολλὰ μὲν Κυδώνια μᾶλα ποτερρίπτουν ποτὶ δίφρον
 ἄνακτι,
πολλὰ δὲ μύρσινα φῦλλα
καὶ ῥοδίνους στεφάνους ἴων τε κορωνίδας οὔλας.

2 Schneidewin: μυρεινα, μύρρινα codd.

# STESICHORUS

**S 85** = 182 *P.M.G.*    Pausanias, *Description of Greece*

Pallantium[1] was mentioned by Stesichorus of Himera in his *Geryoneis*.

[1] In Arcadia; perhaps mentioned in connection with the cave of Pholus (see S 19 = 181 *P.M.G.*).


**S 86** = 183 *P.M.G.*    Scholiast on Apollonius of Rhodes ('the Sarpedonian rock' in Thrace)

Stesichorus in his *Geryoneis* calls an island in the Atlantic sea Sarpedonian.


**S 87** = 186 *P.M.G.*    Scholiast on Hesiod, *Theogony* ('Chrysaor begot three-headed Geryon')

Geryon is son of Callirrhoe, daughter of Oceanus, and Chrysaor. Stesichorus says he has six hands and six feet and is winged.


## HELEN[1]

**187** Athenaeus, *Scholars at Dinner*

Cydonian apples[2] are mentioned by Stesichorus in his *Helen* as follows:

Many Cydonian apples they threw on their lord's chariot,[3] many myrtle leaves and garlands of roses and twined wreaths of violets.

[1] P.Oxy. 2735 ( = Ibycus S 166–219) is ascribed by some scholars to the *Helen* of Stesichorus. See also fr. 223.    [2] Quinces; Cydonia is in north-west Crete.    [3] The lines probably describe the marriage of Menelaus and Helen.

89

# GREEK LYRIC

**188** Athen. 10. 451d (ii 481 Kaibel)

καὶ Στησίχορος δ᾽ ἐν Ἑλένῃ

λιθαργύρεον ποδανιπτῆρα

ἔφη.

**189** Argum. Theocr. 18 (p. 331 Wendel)

τοῦτο τὸ εἰδύλλιον ἐπιγράφεται Ἑλένης ἐπιθαλάμιος καὶ ἐν αὐτῷ τινα εἴληπται ἐκ τοῦ πρώτου Στησιχόρου Ἑλένης.

**190** Schol. A Hom. *Il.* 2. 339 (i 103 Dindorf)

τῶν ἐκ τῆς Ἑλλάδος ἀρίστων ἐπὶ μνηστείαν τῆς Ἑλένης παρόντων διὰ τὸ γένος καὶ τὸ κάλλος, Τυνδάρεως ὁ πατὴρ αὐτῆς, ὥς τινές φασι, φυλασσόμενος μή ποτε ἕνα αὐτῶν προκρίνας τοὺς ἄλλους ἐχθροὺς ποιήσηται, κοινὸν αὐτῶν ἔλαβεν ὅρκον ἦ μὴν τῷ ληψομένῳ τὴν παῖδα ἀδικουμένῳ περὶ αὐτὴν σφόδρα πάντας ἐπαμυνεῖν. διόπερ Μενελάῳ αὐτὴν ἐκδίδωσιν. καὶ μετ᾽ οὐ πολὺ ἁρπασθείσης αὐτῆς ὑπὸ Ἀλεξάνδρου ἐκοινώνησαν τῇ στρατείᾳ διὰ τοὺς γενομένους ὅρκους. ἡ ἱστορία παρὰ Στησιχόρῳ.

**191** Paus. 2. 22. 6 (i 158s. Rocha-Pereira)

πλησίον δὲ τῶν Ἀνάκτων Εἰληθυίας ἐστὶν ἱερὸν ἀνάθημα Ἑλένης, ὅτε σὺν Πειρίθῳ Θησέως ἀπελθόντος ἐς Θεσπρωτοὺς Ἄφιδνά τε ὑπὸ Διοσκούρων ἑάλω καὶ ἤγετο ἐς Λακεδαίμονα Ἑλένη. ἔχειν μὲν γὰρ αὐτὴν λέγουσιν ἐν γαστρί, τεκοῦσαν δὲ ἐν Ἄργει καὶ τῆς Εἰληθυίας ἱδρυσαμένην τὸ ἱερὸν τὴν μὲν παῖδα ἣν ἔτεκε Κλυταιμνήστρα δοῦναι, συνοικεῖν γὰρ ἤδη Κλυταιμνήστραν Ἀγαμέμνονι, αὐτὴν δὲ ὕστερον τούτων Μενελάῳ γήμασθαι. καὶ ἐπὶ τῷδε Εὐφορίων Χαλκιδεὺς (fr. 90 Powell) καὶ Πλευρώνιος Ἀλέξανδρος (fr. 12 Powell) ἔπη ποιήσαντες, πρότερον δὲ ἔτι Στησίχορος ὁ Ἱμε-

---

[1] Statues of the Dioscuri, Helen's brothers.     [2] Cf. Alcm. 21: Theseus had kidnapped Helen and taken her to Athens; Aphidna is in N. E. Attica.     [3] 3rd c. B.C. epic poet.     [4] Alexander Aetolus, tragic poet, 3rd c. B.C.

# STESICHORUS

**188** Athenaeus, *Scholars at Dinner*

Stesichorus in his *Helen* said

> footbath of litharge.[1]

[1] Lead monoxide, a by-product of the separation of silver from lead; see J. F. Healy, *Mining and Metallurgy* 179.

**189** Introduction to Theocritus 18

This idyll is called *Helen's Epithalamium,* and in it certain things have been taken from the first book of Stesichorus' *Helen.*

**190** Scholiast on *Iliad* ('our covenants and oaths', Nestor)

When the best men of Greece had come to woo Helen because of her lineage and beauty, her father Tyndareus, according to some authorities, was eager to avoid making enemies of the others by choosing one of them; so he made them all alike swear that if the successful suitor were ever wronged on her account they would all come energetically to his help. That is why he gave her to Menelaus. Not long afterwards, when she was carried off by Alexander, they took part in the expedition because of the oaths they had sworn. The story is in Stesichorus.

**191** Pausanias, *Description of Greece* (on Argos)

Near the Lords[1] is a sanctuary of Eileithyia, dedicated by Helen at the time when Theseus had gone with Pirithous to Thesprotia and Aphidna was captured by the Dioscuri[2] and Helen was being taken to Sparta. They say that she was pregnant and that after giving birth in Argos and founding the sanctuary of Eileithyia she gave her baby daughter to Clytemnestra, who was already the wife of Agamemnon, and later on married Menelaus. Euphorion[3] of Chalcis and Alexander[4] of Pleuron, who wrote poetry on this subject, and even earlier Stesichorus of Himera all

ραῖος, κατὰ ταὐτά φασιν ᾿Αργείοις Θησέως εἶναι θυγατέρα ᾿Ιφιγέ-
νειαν.

## ΕΛΕΝΑ : ΠΑΛΙΝΩΙΔΙΑΙ

**192** Plat. *Phaedr.* 243a

ἐστὶν δὲ τοῖς ἁμαρτάνουσι περὶ μυθολογίαν καθαρμὸς ἀρχαῖος,
ὃν ῞Ομηρος μὲν οὐκ ἤσθετο, Στησίχορος δέ· τῶν γὰρ ὀμμάτων στε-
ρηθεὶς διὰ τὴν ῾Ελένης κακηγορίαν οὐκ ἠγνόησεν ὥσπερ ῞Ομηρος,
ἀλλ᾿ ἅτε μουσικὸς ὢν ἔγνω τὴν αἰτίαν καὶ ποιεῖ εὐθύς·

οὐκ ἔστ᾿ ἔτυμος λόγος οὗτος,
οὐδ᾿ ἔβας ἐν νηυσὶν ἐϋσσέλμοις
οὐδ᾿ ἵκεο πέργαμα Τροίας,

καὶ ποιήσας δὴ πᾶσαν τὴν καλουμένην Παλινῳδίαν παραχρῆμα
ἀνέβλεψεν.

2 Blomfield: εὐσέλμοις codd.　　　εὐσέλμοις <ποκά> Haslam


Isocr. *Hel.* 64 (i 240 Benseler-Blass)

ἐνεδείξατο δὲ καὶ Στησιχόρῳ τῷ ποιητῇ τὴν αὑτῆς δύναμιν·
ὅτε μὲν γὰρ ἀρχόμενος τῆς ᾠδῆς ἐβλασφήμησέ τι περὶ αὐτῆς, ἀν-
έστη τῶν ὀφθαλμῶν ἐστερημένος, ἐπειδὴ δὲ γνοὺς τὴν αἰτίαν τῆς
συμφορᾶς τὴν καλουμένην Παλινῳδίαν ἐποίησε, πάλιν αὐτὸν εἰς
τὴν αὐτὴν φύσιν κατέστησε.

agree with the Argives that Iphigenia was Theseus' daughter.[5]

[5] Cf. 223.


### HELEN: PALINODES

**192** Plato, *Phaedrus*

For those who have sinned in their telling of myths there is an ancient purification, known not to Homer but to Stesichorus: when he was blinded because of his slander of Helen he was not unaware of the reason like Homer, but being devoted to the Muses recognised the cause and immediately wrote,

That story is not true, and you did not go on the well-benched ships and you did not reach the citadel of Troy;

and having composed all the Palinode, as it is called, he at once regained his sight.


Isocrates, *Helen*

She (Helen) displayed her power to the poet Stesichorus also: for when at the beginning of his song he uttered a blasphemy against her, he stood up deprived of his sight; but when he had realised the cause of his plight and had composed the Palinode, as it is called, she restored him to his original condition.

# GREEK LYRIC

Plat. *Resp.* 9. 586c

. . . ὥσπερ τὸ τῆς Ἑλένης εἴδωλον ὑπὸ τῶν ἐν Τροίᾳ Στησίχο‐
ρός φησι γενέσθαι περιμάχητον ἀγνοίᾳ τοῦ ἀληθοῦς.

Ael. Aristid. *Or.* 1. 128 (i 1. 53 Behr)

. . . ὥσπερ τῶν ποιητῶν φασί τινες τὸν Ἀλέξανδρον τῆς Ἑλέ‐
νης τὸ εἴδωλον λαβεῖν, αὐτὴν δὲ οὐ δυνηθῆναι,

ubi schol. AC (iii 150 Dindorf) Στησίχορος ἐν τῇ ποιήσει λέγει
ὡς ἡρπακὼς τὴν Ἑλένην Ἀλέξανδρος καὶ διὰ τῆς Φάρου ἐρχό‐
μενος ἀφῃρέθη μὲν ταύτην παρὰ Πρωτέως, ἔλαβε δὲ παρ' αὐτοῦ ἐν
πίνακι τὸ εἴδωλον αὐτῆς γεγραμμένον ἵνα ὁρῶν παραμυθοῖτο τὸν
αὑτοῦ ἔρωτα.

Ael. Aristid. *Or.* 2. 234 (i 2. 211 Behr)

. . . ὥσπερ οἱ Στησιχόρου Τρῶες οἱ τὸ τῆς Ἑλένης εἴδωλον
ἔχοντες ὡς αὐτήν.

Dio Chrys. *Or.* 11. 40s. (i 125s. Arnim)

οὕτως δέ, ἔφη, γελοίως ἀπὸ τούτων διακεῖσθε ὑμεῖς ὥστε ποιη‐
τὴν ἕτερον Ὁμήρῳ πεισθέντα καὶ ταῦτα πάντα ποιήσαντα περὶ
Ἑλένης, Στησίχορον ὡς οἶμαι, τυφλωθῆναί φατε ὑπὸ τῆς Ἑλένης
ὡς ψευσάμενον, αὖθις δὲ ἀναβλέψαι τἀναντία ποιήσαντα . . . καὶ
τὸν μὲν Στησίχορον ἐν τῇ ὕστερον ᾠδῇ λέγειν ὅτι τὸ παράπαν οὐδὲ
πλεύσειεν ἡ Ἑλένη οὐδαμόσε, ἄλλοι δέ τινες ὡς ἁρπασθείη μὲν
Ἑλένη ὑπὸ τοῦ Ἀλεξάνδρου, δεῦρο δὲ παρ' ἡμᾶς εἰς Αἴγυπτον ἀφί‐
κοιτο.

cf. testt. 1, 19, 30, Hor. *Epod.* 17. 42–4 + schol., Philostr. *Vit. Apoll.*
6. 11 (ἐναντίον τῷ προτέρῳ λόγῳ), Max. Tyr. 21. 1 (τὴν ἔμπροσθεν
ᾠδήν), Tzetz. ad Lycophr. 113, *Antehomerica* 149, cett. ap.
M. Davies, *Q.U.C.C.* 12 (1982) 7–16.

# STESICHORUS

Plato, *Republic*

. . . just as Helen's phantom, according to Stesichorus,[1] was fought over by the warriors at Troy in ignorance of the truth.

[1] Helen's phantom is said to have been first mentioned by Hesiod (fr. 358 M.-W.).

Aelius Aristides, *Orations*

. . . just as some of the poets say Alexander took Helen's phantom but was unable to take her.

Scholiast: Stesichorus in his poetry tells that when Alexander had seized Helen and was making his way through Pharos[1] he was robbed of her by Proteus and received from him her portrait painted on a panel, so that he could assuage his passion by looking at it.

[1] Island west of the Nile delta.

Aelius Aristides, *Orations*

. . . just like the Trojans of Stesichorus, who have Helen's phantom, believing it to be Helen herself.

Dio Chrysostom, *Discourses*

These men, he said,[1] have had such a ridiculous effect on you Greeks that you say that another poet who was persuaded by Homer and gave in full the same account of Helen—Stesichorus, I believe—was blinded by Helen for telling lies and got his sight back when he told the opposite story . . . Stesichorus, you allege, said in his later song that Helen never sailed anywhere, whereas others say[2] that Helen was carried off by Alexander but came here to us in Egypt.

[1] The speaker is an Egyptian priest.    [2] But see 193.

# GREEK LYRIC

**193** P.Oxy. 2506 fr. 26 col. i

. . . [μέμ]φεται τὸν Ὅμηρο[ν ὅτι Ἑλέ]νην ἐποίησεν ἐν Τ[ροίαι]
καὶ οὐ τὸ εἴδωλον αὐτῆ[ς, ἔν] τε τ[ῆι] ἑτέραι τὸν Ἡσίοδ[ον]
μέμ[φετ]αι· διτταὶ γάρ εἰσι παλινωιδ<ίαι δια>λλάττουσαι (corr.
Lobel)· καὶ ἔστιν τῆς μὲν ἡ (E. Fraenkel: ἔστιν ἡ μὲν pap.)
ἀρχή·

> δεῦρ' αὖτε θεὰ φιλόμολπε,

τῆς δέ·

> χρυσόπτερε παρθένε,

ὡς ἀνέγραφε Χαμαιλέων (fr. 29 Wehrli, fr. 35 Giordano).
αὐτὸ[ς δ]έ φησ[ιν ὁ] Στησίχορο[ς] τὸ μὲν ε[ἴδωλο]ν ἐλθεῖ[ν ἐς]
Τροίαν, τὴν δ' Ἑλένην π[αρὰ] τῶι Πρωτεῖ καταμεῖν[αι· οὕ]τως
δὴ ἐκ[α]ινοποίησε τ[ὰς] ἱστορί[ί]ας [ὥ]στε Δημοφῶντ[α] μὲν τ[ὸ]ν
Θησέως ἐν τ[ῶ]ι νόστωι με[τὰ] τῶν Θεσ[τια]δῶν [    ] ἀνενεχ[θῆ-
ναι λέγ]ειν [ἐ]ς [Αἴ]γυπτον, [γενέσθα]ι δὲ Θη[σεῖ] Δημοφῶ[ντα
μ]ὲν ἐξ Ἰό[πης] τῆς Ἰφικ[λέους, Ἀ]κάμαν[τα δὲ ἐκ] Φα[ίδρας],
ἐκ δὲ τῆς Ἀμ[αζόνος Ἱππο]λύτη[ς]  . . λη . [ . . . τῆς [Ἑ]λένης
. . . Ἀγαμέμ[ν- . . . Ἀ]μφίλοχον . . .

omnia suppl. Page nisi ut supra

## ΕΡΙΦΥΛΑ

**194** Sext. Emp. *adv. mathem.* 1. 261 (iii 65 Mau)

ὑπόθεσιν γὰρ ἑαυτοῖς ψευδῆ λαμβάνοντες οἱ ἱστορικοὶ τὸν ἀρχη-
γὸν ἡμῶν τῆς ἐπιστήμης Ἀσκληπιὸν κεκεραυνῶσθαι λέγουσιν, οὐκ
ἀρκούμενοι τῷ ψεύσματι ἐν ᾧ καὶ ποικίλως αὐτὸ μεταπλάττουσι,
Στησίχορος μὲν ἐν Ἐριφύλῃ εἰπὼν ὅτι τινὰς τῶν ἐπὶ Θήβαις πε-
σόντων ἀνιστᾷ, Πολύανθος δὲ . . .

---

[1] Sextus was a doctor.    [2] Five other alleged reasons are listed
for Zeus' killing of Asclepius.

# STESICHORUS

**193** Papyrus commentary on lyric poets (2nd c. A.D.)

... (in one Palinode) he blames Homer because he put Helen in Troy, not her phantom; and in the other he blames Hesiod: for there are two different Palinodes,[1] and the beginning of one is

> Hither again, goddess,[2] lover of song and dance,

and of the other

> Golden-winged maiden,[2]

as Chamaeleon[3] wrote. Stesichorus himself says that the phantom went to Troy while Helen remained with Proteus.

He made such innovations in his stories that he says[4] that Demophon, son of Theseus, was brought to Egypt with the Thestiadae[5] in the homecoming from Troy, and that Demophon was Theseus' son by Iope, daughter of Iphicles, Acamas his son by Phaedra, Hippolytus by the Amazon ... Helen ... Agamemnon ... Amphilochus[6] ...

---

[1] See also Conon, *F.Gr.H.* 26 F1 (18) ('Stesichorus composed hymns to Helen'), Hippolytus, *Contra Haer.* 6. 19. 3, Irenaeus, *Contra Haer.* 1. 23. 2 Migne (both speak of 'the Palinodes').  [2] Probably the Muse in each case.  [3] Peripatetic philosopher and grammarian, late 4th and early 3rd c. B.C.: see test. 31.  [4] Perhaps in the *Homecomings* : see 208–9.  [5] See fr. 222.  [6] Cf. 228.

## ERIPHYLE

**194** Sextus Empiricus, *Against the Professors*

For the historians, working on a false assumption, say that Asclepius, the founder of our science,[1] was killed by a thunderbolt; and not satisfied with this lie they make various changes to its content: Stesichorus in his *Eriphyle* says that he raised from the dead some of those who fell at Thebes, whereas Polyanthus ...[2]

Schol. Pind. *Pyth.* 3. 54 ( = 3. 96, ii 75 Drachmann)

λέγεται δὲ ὁ Ἀσκληπιὸς χρυσῷ δελεασθεὶς ἀναστῆσαι Ἱππόλυ-
τον τεθνηκότα. οἱ δὲ Τυνδάρεων, ἕτεροι Καπανέα, οἱ δὲ Γλαῦκον,
οἱ δὲ Ὀρφικοὶ Ὑμέναιον, Στησίχορος δὲ ἐπὶ Καπανεῖ καὶ Λυκούρ-
γῳ.

cf. schol. Eur. *Alc.* 1 (ii 216s. Schwartz), 'Apollod.' *Bibl.* 3. 121
(p. 141s. Wagner), Philodem. *de piet.* 1609V (p. 52 Gomperz +
A. Henrichs, *Cron. erc.* 5 (1975) 8ss.)

**S 148** P.Oxy. 2618 fr. 1

col. i    ] . μελα . . . [
       ] ὧδε ποτήνεπε κ[
   Ἄδρασ]τος ἥρως · Ἄλκμαον, πόσε δαι-
   τυμόν]ας τε λιπὼν καὶ ἄριστον ἀοιδὸν
  5       ] . ἀνέστας;

   ὣς ἔφα · τ]ὸν δ' ὧδ' ἀμειβόμενος ποτέει-
   πεν Ἄρηι] φ[ίλ]ος Ἀμφιαρητεΐδας ·
   σὺ μὲν φ]ίλε πῖνέ τε καὶ θαλίαις
   εὔφραιν]ε θυμόν · αὐτὰρ ἐγὼν ἐπὶ πρᾶ-
 10 γμα]

col. ii      ]κτοσθεπ[
        ]νεσαμον[
   εκα . . [ . ] . ιονα ονιμ[
  5 θ' ὅπως ἀπήναν ζεύ[ξασ(α)
   ναδ' ἔβα παράκοιτι[ν
   μναστεύσοισα μάτῃ[ρ

# STESICHORUS

Scholiast on Pindar

It is said that Asclepius was enticed by gold to raise up the dead Hippolytus; others say he raised Tyndareus, others Capaneus, others Glaucus, the Orphics Hymenaeus, while Stesichorus speaks of Capaneus and Lycurgus.[1]

[1] Son of Pronax, depicted along with Adrastus, Tydeus and Amphiaraus on the Amyclean throne (Paus. 3. 18. 12), rather than the Thracian king who opposed Dionysus. The scholiast goes on to give four other versions.

**S 148** Papyrus of 1st c. A.D.[1]

col. i

... the hero (Adrastus?[2] addressed him (tauntingly?) thus: 'Alcmaon, where have you risen to go, leaving the banqueters and our excellent bard?' So he spoke, and Amphiaraus' son, dear (to Ares), answered and spoke to him thus: 'My friend, drink for your part and gladden your heart with festivity; but I (must go) about (a matter?) ...'

col. ii

... how my (his?) mother,[3] yoking a mule-wagon, went to (some city) to find me (him?) a

[1] Attributed to *Eriphyle* since Alcma(e)on was son of Amphiaraus and Eriphyle.  [2] Brother of Eriphyle.  [3] Eriphyle?

παῖδ' Ἀναξάνδροιο . [      ὑπερ-
φιάλου γαμὲν ἔκγο[νον

col. i    2 κ[ερτομέων tent. Page      3 suppl. Lobel, 4 Page, 6 ὡς
Barrett, ἔφα τ]ὸν Page, 7 Page, 8 Barrett, 9 Lobel

col. ii    5 tent. Page      6–9 suppl. Lobel

**S 150**   P.Oxy. 2618 fr. 3

col. i   4 μεμιγμ]ένα δ' ἐσθλὰ κακ[οῖσ(ιν)
7   ]δύ' ἐμοί     11 ἄμφω

col. ii    5 τὰν[      6 καρπαλ[ιμ-     7 -τες ει . [
8 ἐρυσά[ρματες

col. i   4 tent. Lobel
col. ii   6 suppl. Lobel      8 tent. Führer


## ΕΥΡΩΠΕΙΑ

**195**   Schol. Eur. *Phoen.* 670 (i 318s. Schwartz)

ὁ μὲν Στησίχορος ἐν Εὐρωπείᾳ τὴν Ἀθηνᾶν ἐσπαρκέναι τοὺς
ὀδόντας φησίν.


## ΙΛΙΟΥ ΠΕΡΣΙΣ

**196**   Harp. s.v. καθελών (i 165s. Dindorf)

Δημοσθένης ἐν τῷ κατ' Ἀριστοκράτους (23. 53) φησίν· ἢ ἐν
ὁδῷ καθελών, ἀντὶ τοῦ ἀνελὼν ἢ ἀποκτείνας. ἐχρήσαντο δὲ οὕτω
τῷ ὀνόματι καὶ ἄλλοι, ὡς καὶ Στησίχορος ἐν Ἰλίου Πέρσιδι καὶ Σο-
φοκλῆς ἐν Εὐμήλῳ (fr. 205 Pearson, Radt).

cf. *Sud.* K 48, Phot. *Lex.* (p. 122 Porson), Zonar. *Lex.* 1165 s.v.

bride, the daughter of arrogant Anaxandrus[4] . . . to marry, the child . . .

[4] Unknown.

**S 150** Same papyrus

col. i . . . good things (mixed) with evil . . . two to me[1] . . . both . . .

col. ii . . . (her?) . . . swift(ly) . . . (carrying?) . . . chariot-drawing (horses) . . .[2]

[1] Mother speaking of two sons (Führer)?      [2] A departure? Cf. S 148 col. ii.

## EUROPIA

**195** Scholiast on Euripides, *Phoenissae* ('from the teeth the earth sent up' armed men)

Stesichorus in his *Europia* says that it was Athena who sowed the teeth.[1]

[1] In Euripides' version Cadmus (brother of Europa) sowed the dragon's teeth at Thebes on the prompting of Athena.

## SACK OF TROY

**196** Harpocration, *Lexicon of the Ten Attic Orators*

Demosthenes in his speech *Against Aristocrates* says,[1] 'or by destroying him on the highway', using καθελών in the sense of ἀνελών, 'making away with' or 'killing'. Others also used the word in this sense, e.g. Stesichorus in his *Sack of Troy* and Sophocles in his *Eumelus*.

[1] Quoting a legal text.

# GREEK LYRIC

**197** Paus. 10. 26. 1 (iii 150 Rocha-Pereira)

Κλυμένην μὲν οὖν Στησίχορος ἐν Ἰλίου Πέρσιδι κατηρίθμηκεν ἐν ταῖς αἰχμαλώτοις.

**198** Paus. 10. 27. 2 (iii 153 Rocha-Pereira)

ἐς δὲ Ἑκάβην Στησίχορος ἐν Ἰλίου Πέρσιδι ἐποίησεν, ἐς Λυκίαν ὑπὸ Ἀπόλλωνος αὐτὴν κομισθῆναι.

**199** Athen. 13. 610c (iii 346 Kaibel)

καὶ ἐὰν μέν τίς σου πύθηται τίνες ἦσαν οἱ εἰς τὸν δούρειον ἵππον ἐγκατακλεισθέντες, ἑνὸς καὶ δευτέρου ἴσως ἐρεῖς ὄνομα· καὶ οὐδὲ ταῦτ᾽ ἐκ τῶν Στησιχόρου, σχολῇ γάρ, ἀλλ᾽ ἐκ τῆς †σακατου† Ἀργείου Ἰλίου Πέρσιδος· οὗτος γὰρ παμπόλλους τινὰς κατέλεξεν.

Eust. *Od.* 1698. 2

φασὶ δὲ τοὺς εἰς αὐτὸν (sc. τὸν δούρειον ἵππον) καταβάντας τινὲς μὲν ὧν καὶ Στησίχορος ἑκατὸν εἶναι, ἕτεροι δὲ δώδεκα.

**200** Athen. 10. 456f–457a (ii 493 Kaibel)

ἀνακομίζοντος δ᾽ αὐτοῖς τὸ ὕδωρ ὄνου ὃν ἐκάλουν Ἐπειὸν διὰ τὸ μυθολογεῖσθαι τοῦτο δρᾶν ἐκεῖνον καὶ ἀναγεγράφθαι ἐν τῷ τοῦ Ἀπόλλωνος ἱερῷ τὸν Τρωικὸν μῦθον, ἐν ᾧ ὁ Ἐπειὸς ὑδροφορεῖ τοῖς Ἀτρείδαις, ὡς καὶ Στησίχορός φησιν·

> ᾤκτιρε γὰρ αὐτὸν ὕδωρ
> αἰεὶ φορέοντα Διὸς κούρα βασιλεῦσιν.

cf. Eust. *Il.* 1323. 55

1 ᾤκτειρε δ᾽ αὐτὸν Eust.　　2 κούροις Eust.

---

[1] Simonides and the chorus he was training at Carthaea in Ceos.　　[2] At Carthaea.　　[3] Athena, who suggested that he build the wooden horse (*Od.* 8. 493).

# STESICHORUS

**197** Pausanias, *Description of Greece* (on Polygnotus' painting of the fall of Troy in the Cnidian Lesche at Delphi)

Now Stesichorus in his *Sack of Troy* lists Clymene[1] among the captive women.[2]

[1] A captive named in the painting. She was Helen's attendant (*Il.* 3. 144).    [2] Continued at 208.

**198** Pausanias, *Description of Greece* (on the same painting)

With regard to Hecuba Stesichorus said in his *Sack of Troy* that she was taken to Lycia by Apollo.[1]

[1] In other accounts she was turned into a dog. See also 224.

**199** Athenaeus, *Scholars at Dinner*

And if someone asks you who the men were who were shut inside the wooden horse, you will perhaps offer one name or two, and even those will hardly come from the works of Stesichorus but from the *Sack of Troy* of (Hagias? Sacadas?) of Argos, since he listed a great number of men.

Eustathius on *Odyssey* 11. 522

Some, among them Stesichorus, say that the men who went into the wooden horse numbered one hundred, others say twelve.

**200** Athenaeus, *Scholars at Dinner*

As their water was being fetched up by an ass which they[1] called Epeius because of the story that he carried water and the record in Apollo's temple[2] of the Trojan story in which Epeius is water-carrier for the Atridae, as Stesichorus also says:

for the daughter of Zeus[3] pitied him always carrying water for the kings.

# GREEK LYRIC

**201** Schol. Eur. *Or.* 1287 (i 214 Schwartz)

ἆρα εἰς τὸ τῆς Ἑλένης κάλλος βλέψαντες οὐκ ἐχρήσαντο τοῖς ξίφεσιν; οἷόν τι καὶ Στησίχορος ὑπογράφει περὶ τῶν καταλεύειν αὐτὴν μελλόντων. φησὶ γὰρ ἅμα τῷ τὴν ὄψιν αὐτῆς ἰδεῖν αὐτοὺς ἀφεῖναι τοὺς λίθους ἐπὶ τὴν γῆν.

**202** Schol. Eur. *Andr.* 10 (ii 249 Schwartz)

φασὶν ὅτι <οὐκ ἐβούλετο Schwartz> ὁ Εὐριπίδης Ξάνθῳ προσέχειν περὶ τῶν Τρωικῶν μύθων, τοῖς δὲ χρησιμωτέροις καὶ ἀξιοπιστοτέροις. Στησίχορον μὲν γὰρ ἱστορεῖν ὅτι τεθνήκοι (sc. ὁ Ἀστυάναξ), καὶ τὸν τὴν Πέρσιδα συντεταχότα κυκλικὸν ποιητὴν (F 3 Davies) ὅτι καὶ ἀπὸ τοῦ τείχους ῥιφθείη· ᾧ ἠκολουθηκέναι Εὐριπίδην.

**203** Dio Chrys. 2. 33 (i 23 Arnim)

Στησιχόρου δὲ καὶ Πινδάρου ἐπεμνήσθη (sc. Ἀλέξανδρος), τοῦ μὲν ὅτι μιμητὴς Ὁμήρου γενέσθαι δοκεῖ καὶ τὴν ἅλωσιν οὐκ ἀναξίως ἐποίησε τῆς Τροίας, . . .

**201** Scholiast on Euripides, *Orestes* ('Before her beauty have their swords been blunted?')

I.e., after looking on Helen's beauty did they fail to use their swords? Stesichorus indicates something similar in connection with the men who are on the point of stoning her: he says that the moment they saw her face, they dropped their stones on the ground.[1]

[1] Cf. Ibyc. 296.

**202** Scholiast on Euripides, *Andromache* ('Astyanax thrown from the walls')

They say that in the matter of the Trojan stories Euripides (did not wish)[1] to heed Xanthus[2] but rather the more useful and trustworthy authorities: for Stesichorus said that Astyanax died, and the cyclic poet[3] who put together the *Sack of Troy* made the additional point that he was thrown from the wall; and Euripides followed him.

[1] Text uncertain.  [2] Contemporary of Herodotus and author of *Lydian History*; it would seem that in his version Astyanax survived the destruction of Troy.  [3] Probably Lesches in the *Little Iliad* (Homer O.C.T. v 134 f.): see M. J. Wiencke, *A.J.A.* 58 (1954) 288, P. Brize, *Die Geryoneis des S.* 22.

**203** Dio Chrysostom, *Discourses*

He[1] mentioned Stesichorus and Pindar, Stesichorus because he seems to have been an imitator of Homer and depicted the capture of Troy in a manner not unworthy of him, . . .

[1] Alexander the Great, admirer of Homer, in conversation with his father Philip.

**204** Paus. 10. 26. 9 (iii 152 Rocha-Pereira)

ἐφεξῆς δὲ τῇ Λαοδίκῃ ὑποστάτης τε λίθου καὶ λουτήριόν ἐστιν ἐπὶ τῷ ὑποστάτῃ χαλκοῦν, Μέδουσα δὲ κατέχουσα ταῖς χερσὶν ἀμφοτέραις τὸ ὑπόστατον ἐπὶ τοῦ ἐδάφους κάθηται· ἐν δὲ ταῖς Πριάμου θυγατράσιν ἀριθμήσαι τις ἂν καὶ ταύτην κατὰ τοῦ Ἱμεραίου τὴν ᾠδήν.

**205** Tabula Iliaca Capitolina (*I.G.* 14. 1284)

titulus: Ἰλίου Πέρσις κατὰ Στησίχορον : Τρωικός (sc. κύκλος)

# STESICHORUS

**204** Pausanias, *Description of Greece* (on Polygnotus' painting: see 197, 198)

Next to Laodice is a stone pedestal with a bronze washbasin on it; Medusa is sitting on the base, holding the pedestal in both hands; she too may be counted as one of Priam's daughters according to the song of the Himeraean.

**205** Roman monument (Augustan era)

The monument, found near Bovillae, 12 miles S.E. of Rome, and now in the Capitoline Museum, Rome (photograph in G. K. Galinsky, *Aeneas, Sicily and Rome*, fig. 85), has annotated illustrations in low relief of scenes from the fall of Troy and carries in its central panel under the scene of Aeneas' departure the inscription 'Sack of Troy according to Stesichorus'. Scholars have deduced the content of Stesichorus' poem from the illustrations, and Page, for example, believed that the stone represented the poem, although not exactly; other scholars are sceptical, e.g. Bowra, *G.L.P.* ² 104 ff., Galinsky, *loc. cit.* 106 ff., and above all N. M. Horsfall, *J.H.S.* 99 (1979) 26 ff., who writes (p. 43), 'to cite the more obscure Stesichorus in place of the conventional Arctinus as the author of an *Iliou Persis* was but to score a good point.' Scenes which are particularly hard to accept as Stesichorean are (i) the departure of Aeneas 'for Hesperia' in the company of a trumpet-bearing Misenus and an Anchises who carries 'the sacred objects' (Virgilian, surely) and (ii) Menelaus pursuing Helen with a sword (cf. Stes. 201, Ibyc. 296).

*S 88–132, papyrus fragments of c. 200 A.D., were attributed to the 'Sack of Troy' because of their subject-matter; but S 133–147, fragments of 1st c. B.C. published three years later, almost certainly contain a text of the same poem as S 88–132 — see S 105(b) — and S 133 carries the title 'Stesichorus' (Wooden) Horse', a title not previously attested for*

**S 88** P.Oxy. 2619 frr. 1 + 47 (coniunx. Barrett)

col. i    4   -]τε δ' ὅμως    6   ]ντι βίαι τε καὶ
αἰχμᾶι    7 πεποιθότες· ἀλλ' ἄγε δὴ    9 μαχή-
μ]ονες ἀγκυλοτόξοι    11 ] ͚ς διάσταν·
13 ]ραπασιν    15 ] Ἀχαιῶν  16s. τέλος εὐρύ-
ο[πα | Ζεύς]    18 π(τ)ολέμου [τε]λευτά[
19 ]͙ν πυκιν[άς] τε φρ[έ]νας
21 ]ρηξήνορα    22 ὦτρ]υνε μέγαν φρ[α]σὶν ἐν
24 μετέ]πρεπε καὶ πιν[υ]τᾶι    26 ]εργον
27 ]͙οπτολ[

col. ii
  5 τονδ[ . . ]εδακυκλ[          ]με[
    πρὸς ναὸν ἐς ἀκρ[όπο]λ[ι]ν σπεύδοντες [ἐπεσσυμέ-
          νως
    Τρῶες πολέες τ' ἐπίκ[ου]ροι
    ἔλθετε, μη[δ]ὲ λόγο[ις π]ειθώμεθ' ὅπ{π}ως π[
    τόνδε κα[   ]͙ν ἵπ[π]ον
 10 ἁγνὸν ἄ[γαλ]μα [θε]ᾶς αὐτεῖ καται-
    σχ]ύνωμε[ν ἀ]εικ[ελί]ως,
    μᾶ]νιν δὲ[          ]͙ ἁζώμεσθ' ἀνάσ[σας

 15 ὣς] φά[τ]ο, τοὶ [δ'
    φ[ρ]άζοντο δ[
    ἵπ[π]ον μέγα[ν
    ᾧ δ' [ἀ]πὸ φυλλοφ[ορ-
    πυκινα[ῖ]ς πτερ[ύγεσσι
 20 κίρκον τανυσίπ[τερον
    ψᾶ]ρες ἀνέκραγον[

col. i    9 tent. Page    16s. suppl. Page, 22 ὦτρυνε Page, φρασὶν
Barrett    cetera Lobel

# STESICHORUS

*Stesichorus. Either S 88–132 should be attributed to the
'Wooden Horse', or 'Wooden Horse' was an alternative title
for the 'Sack of Troy' or the title of part of it.*

**S 88** col. i

'... and yet ... trusting in might and the sword;
but come, ... (warriors?) with curving bows ...
stood apart; ... all ... of the Achaeans ... the out-
come far-seeing Zeus (controls?) ... the end of the
war ... shrewd mind ... breaker of armed ranks ...'
... (with these words) he urged the great (spirit) in
their mind ... was[1] distinguished for his (     )
and wisdom ... task ... (war?) ...

col. ii

'... go in haste to the temple on the acropolis, you
Trojans and your many allies, and let us not be per-
suaded by arguments so that we shamefully disho-
nour here this (     ) horse, the holy offering to the
goddess, but let us respect with awe the anger of our
lady ...' So he spoke, and they ... considered (how
to bring) the great horse ...; and as from a leafy
(bush) ... close-feathered wings ... (starlings see-
ing?) a long-winged hawk shriek ...[2]

---

[1] The speaker of the lines in col. ii (Thymoetes or Sinon?), answer-
ing the previous speaker (Capys?), who must have urged the rejec-
tion of the horse.      [2] Supplement uncertain: perhaps the lines
are not a simile but describe a portent; and 'leafy' may be 'gar-
landed', of the horse.

---

col. ii   6, 8, 9, 10 suppl. Barrett      10s. κατ- West      11
ἀεικ. Barrett      12 μᾶνιν West      ἁζώμεσθ' Page      ἀνάσσας Bar-
rett      15 init. Barrett      τοὶ δ' West      17, 18 init., 21
Barrett      cetera Lobel

**S 89** P.Oxy. 2619 frr. 15(b) + 30 + 31 (coniunx. Barrett)

2 θεατυ[
  παρθεν[
  ἱμείρει[
5 νῦν δ᾽ ἃ[σ]εν [χα]λεπῶς πα[ρὰ καλλιρόους
  δίνα[ς] Σιμόεντος ἀνὴρ [
  θ]εᾶς ἰ[ό]τατι δαεὶς σεμν[ᾶς Ἀθάνας
  μέτ[ρα] τε καὶ σοφίαν, τοῦ [
      ]ος ἀντὶ μάχα[ς
10 καὶ] φυ[λόπ]ιδος κλέο[ς] [
  εὐρυ]χόρ[ο]υ Τρο<ΐ>ας ἁλώσι[μον ἆμαρ
      ]ν ἔθηκεν
      ] . εσσι πόνοι[

5 χαλεπῶς suppl. Lobel,   6 δίνας West,   10 e.g. ἀ[ρείθ᾽ οὕνεκεν
West,   11 corr. West         cetera Barrett

**S 90** P.Oxy. 2619 fr. 15(a)

2 ]χρυσ[

**S 91** P.Oxy. 2619 fr. 2

3 μέγα χωσαμ[εν-

**S 92** P.Oxy. 2619 fr. 3

2 ἀ]ργαλεα[     3 κ]ούφως[

**S 94** P.Oxy. 2619 fr. 5

1 ]αγορα[     5 ]αγερθη[     6   ]ε λόγον
7 ἀν]αστάς

7 suppl. West

# STESICHORUS

**S 89**

'... maiden(ly) ... longs ...; but now by the (fair-flowing) eddies of the Simois a man[1] has grievously misled us, taught his measurements and skill by the will of the august goddess Athena, a man by whose (devices trickery?) instead of fighting and the battle-cry (will have) fame (that it) brought the capture day of spacious Troy ... hardships ...'

[1] Epeius; the speaker is a Trojan.

**S 90**

gold

**S 91**

greatly angered

**S 92**

grievous ... lightly ...

**S 94**

assembly ... was gathered ... speech ... he, standing up ...

GREEK LYRIC

**S 99** P.Oxy. 2619 fr. 10

4   ]ν 'Αχαιοί

**S 102** P.Oxy. 2619 fr. 13

1 Παλλ]ὰδ' ἐπώμοσε σεμ[νάν    3   ]εσθ', ἐγὼν δ'
αυ[    5   ]γον εἴμειν    8 φάος ἀελίου    10
γ]ὰρ [κ]ατ' αἶσαν

1 suppl. Barrett,    10 γὰρ West,    κατ' Lobel

**S 103** P.Oxy. 2619 fr. 14

1 ]οντ' ἰαραις . . [    2 ]ι τόνδε λόχον[
3 ]  ενα κυδαλέο[ν    4 ]ύν τ' ἐχόντων[
5 ξ]ανθὰ δ' ῾Ελένα Πρ[ιάμου    6 βα]σιλῆος
ἀοίδιμος . [    7 τ]αι δ' ἐκέλευσετ[    8 δ]αΐωι
πυρὶ καιομεν[    9 ἐμ]πρησαντασε . [

2, 4 suppl. Barrett,    3 Page,    6 ἀοίδιμος, 9 West,    7 Führer,
cetera Lobel

**S 104** P.Oxy. 2619 fr. 16

1 αἶψα    2 ἐ]ναργές    3 ἐτύμως    4 ἡ]μιό-
νους    5 ]υραν πρὼ<ι> πε[    6 Κ]υπρογενὴς
α[    7 ἁλιπόρφυρον ἀγν[    8 ]αι μὲν ἐγὼν
λέγω[    9s. ]ι ἀθανάτοι|σιν εἴκε]λον ῾Ερμιόναν
τε[    11 ἐ]γὼν ποθέω νύκτ[ας τε καὶ ἄματα
12 αἰ]γλοπόδαν    13 ὑφαρπάγιμον    14 σ]υρο-
μέναν κνακα[ῖς    16 κ]ορυφαῖσι νάπαις [τε (vel
κορυφαῖσιν ἄπαις)    17 ]ων στυγερὸν    18 ]δα
παῖδα φίλον . [    19 ] . ο λέγω μηδ[    20 ]ω .
προλίπω .    21 ]οντο γένοιτ . [

9–11, 14, 16 τε suppl. Page, 12 Diggle, cetera Lobel

112

# STESICHORUS

**S 99**

### Achaeans

**S 102**

... he[1] swore by august Pallas ... '... (you?) ...,
but I ... to be[2] ... the light of the sun ... for duly ...

[1] Sinon?  [2] Unusual Rhodian and Sicilian Doric form.

**S 103**

... holy ... this ambush ... glorious ... having
... auburn Helen, much-sung (daughter-in-law) of
king Priam ... and he ordered (her?) ... (Troy?)
being burned in blazing fire ... having kindled ...

**S 104**

... suddenly ... clear ... truly ... mules ... early
... Cyprus-born (Aphrodite) ... sea-purple holy ...
I say ... Hermione,[1] like the immortal goddesses, I
long for, night and day ... with her shining foot ...
stolen away ... dragged off by the tawny (horses) ...
peaks and glens (or 'peaks ... childless') ... hateful
... dear son[2] ... I say, nor ... I abandon ... might
happen ...

[1] Daughter of Helen and Menelaus, in which case Helen will be the
speaker; but Hermione was also a Syracusan name for Persephone,
and Demeter might be mourning the loss of her daughter, carried
off in Hades' chariot (Page, *P.C.P.S.* 19, 1973, 56).  [2] Obscure.

**S 105(b)** P.Oxy. 2619 fr. 18 + 2803 fr. 11 (coniunx. West, Führer)

1 ]τ' ἐπικουρ[     2 ] ˌδαρ     3 ]λιποῖσα
4s. ]ματα Κα[σ| σάνδρ-    6 γαι]αόχου
7 πίτνη πυρ[     9 Δα]ναοὶ μεμ[αότ]ες ἐκθόρον
ʔ̣[π]π̣[ου    10 Ἐ]ννοσίδας γαιάχος ἁγνὸς
ε[    11 γ]ὰρ Ἀπόλλων    12 ἱ]αρὰν οὐδ' Ἄρτα-
μις οὐδ' Ἀφροδίτα    14 Τρωῶν π[ό]λι̣ν̣ Ζεὺς
16 ]ου Τρῶας    17 ]ιν ἄμερσ̣[

4s. tent. Führer    6, 9 μεμ., ἵππου, 12 ἱαρὰν, 14 πόλιν (π[ ˌ ˌ ˌ ]νη
leg. Page) suppl. West, 11 Page    14 Τρωῶν, 17 ἄμερσ' leg.
Barrett     cetera Lobel

**S 107** P.Oxy. 2619 fr. 19

1 ἱμερτὸν πρ[     2 ὧδε δέ νιν π̣[οτέφα     3 πῶς
ἀγαπαζ̣[    4 δ]υσώνυμος̣[     7 ὡς φά]το· τὰν [δ'

2 suppl. Führer     3 leg. Barrett     4 suppl. Lobel, 7 Bar-
rett

**S 108** P.Oxy. 2619 fr. 20

1   κ̣λυτα̣[     3 θέ]μεθλα[

3 suppl. Lobel

**S 109** P.Oxy. 2619 fr. 21

3  ]πεδὰ Μυρμιδ[όνεσσι

suppl. Lobel

**S 111** P.Oxy. 2619 fr. 23

2 πέρσαντες     3 καλλαδαπα[     4 αὐτοὶ καταε̣[

# STESICHORUS

## S 105(b)[1]

... allies ... (Cassandra?) leaving ... Earth-holder[2] ... was spreading fire ... the Danaans leapt eagerly from the horse ... holy Earth-shaker, Earth-holder[2] ..., for Apollo ... neither Artemis nor Aphrodite (still guarded?) the holy (city) ... the city of the Trojans Zeus ... Trojans ... deprived ...

[1] Page did not accept the combination of fragments proposed independently by West and Führer.　[2] Poseidon, who opposed the Trojans in the war; Apollo, Artemis and Aphrodite had supported them.

## S 107

... desirable ...; and thus (she) addressed him[1] ...: 'How (can you) love (me who) bearing an evil name ...? So (she spoke), and (he answered) her ...

[1] West suggests that Helen is speaking to Menelaus.

## S 108

... famous ... foundations ...

## S 109

among the Myrmidons

## S 111

... (they,) having sacked ... beautifully(?) ... they themselves ...

**S 113** P.Oxy. 2619 fr. 25

2 πον]τοπόρου[     5s. κῦμα πολὺ| [φλοίσβου θα-
λάσσας

2 suppl. Lobel     5s. e.g. Barrett

**S 114** P.Oxy. 2619 fr. 26

4 βλο]συροῖς

suppl. Lobel

**S 115 + 116** P.Oxy. 2619 frr. 27 + 28 (coniunx. Barrett)

1 ]ώσας πόλ[ι]ν     2 τ]έκος Αἰακίδαν     4 περὶ
ἀστυ . . [     7 Σκ]αμάνδριον ἀ[νθεμοέντα

7 ἀνθ. Führer     cetera Lobel

**S 118** P.Oxy. 2619 fr. 32

2 ]υδε ῥέα̣[     4 βαρέα στ[εναχ-     6 Τ]ροΐα̣ς
κλεεννο[     7 (ἐκ)πέ]ρσαντες ἐυκτιμε[ν-     9 ἀ]ν-
θρώπους κλέο[ς

6 suppl. Page     cetera Lobel

**S 119** P.Oxy. 2619 fr. 33

2 ]νᾶας . [     3 (νόστου) γλυ]κεροῦ[

tent. West

**S 120** P.Oxy. 2619 fr. 34

1 πολ]έμωι βία[ι τε

suppl. Führer

**S 113**

. . . sea-faring . . . the wave (of the noisy sea?) . . .

**S 114**

shaggy

**S 115 + 116**

. . . (he, having destroyed?) the city . . . the child
the descendant of Aeacus[1] . . . round the town . . .
(the flowery meadow) of Scamander . . .

[1] Achilles?

**S 118**

. . . easily . . . groan(ing) heavily . . . having
sacked the well-built glorious (citadel) of Troy . . .
glory (among) mankind . . .

**S 119**

. . . ships . . . sweet (homecoming) . . .

**S 120**

in war and might

**S 123** P.Oxy. 2619 fr. 37

2 ]ας ἄλλοις[    3 ]οκριτον    4 ]ἑκάστωι
νυ[    5 ᾿Εννͅ]οσͅ[ί]γαιοͅς

5 tent. Führer

**S 127** P.Oxy. 2619 fr. 41

1    ]ευτροχ[

**S 133** P.Oxy. 2803 fr. 1

(a) col. i 6s.    ]ατα Κασ | [σάνδρα-

4 marg. καὶ Θέ(ων) προσώιχετο, ᾿Αρ(ιστό)νι(κος)

col. ii 9 marg. Α

i 6s. suppl. Barrett, 4 marg. interpr. Lobel

(b) versa papyro    Στη[σιχόρου] ῞Ιππ[ος δούρειος

**S 135** P.Oxy. 2803 fr. 3

3   -]θαλέας πα ͅ [    5   ] ͅαν Πολυξέ[ν-    8s.
ᾱͅρ | [ξε    9   δ]ρακοῖσα    [    10 ͅ.]χεν   α[ῖ]ς
ἀλόχ[οις

5 suppl. Page      cetera Lobel

**S 136** P.Oxy. 2803 fr. 4

7 marg.    ]καὶ Θέ(ων)

# STESICHORUS

**S 123**

... others ... each ... Earth-shaker ...

**S 127**

well-wheeled (chariot? horse?)

*S 133–147: see introduction to S 88–132.*

**S 133**

(a) col. i

Cassandra(?)

marginal scholiast: ... and Theon προσώιχετο, 'arrived',[1] Aristonicus ...

col. ii: at line 9 the 100th line of the roll and presumably of the poem is indicated.

[1] The text may have had the Doric form ποτώχετο.

(b) on the back of col. i an entry denoting the contents of the roll: 'Stesichorus' *(Wooden) Horse'*

**S 135**

... flourishing ... Polyxena(?)[1] ... ruled(?) ... (she,) seeing ... his (their?) wives ...

[1] Daughter of Priam, killed by Neoptolemus at Achilles' tomb; cf. S 137, Ibyc. 307.

**S 136**

marginal scholiast: ... and Theon[1] ...

[1] Cf. S 133(a).

**S 137** P.Oxy. 2803 fr. 5

3 ἥ]ρως    Ἀχιλλευ[    4 ]δ' ἀφελεστε[    6 ]ώσας
πόλιν[        7 ]ε δὲ τείχεος[        9 ]νας θρασὺν [
11  ]. θαυμα[

8 marg. schol. μελαθ[ρ-

suppl. Lobel

**S 138** P.Oxy. 2803 fr. 6

3  ].σ.ν τρίς[    4  ]..έβαν οπλ[    6 ]..ν
ἀριστ[

**S 139** P.Oxy. 2803 fr. 7

7  ]ἐπασσύτεροι    9  ]αιδα χάριν

6 marg. ]οβριμ[    ]τοξοτ.[

**S 143** P.Oxy. 2803 fr. 11: v. S 105(b)

## ΚΕΡΒΕΡΟΣ

**206** Pollux 10. 152 (ii 236 Bethe)

ἀρύβαλλος δὲ ἐπὶ τοῦ συσπάστου βαλαντίου ἐν Ἀντιφάνους
Αὑτοῦ ἐρῶντι (ii 31 Kock) καὶ ἐν Στησιχόρου Κερβέρῳ.

cf. *Sud.* A 3870 (i 350 Adler), *Anecd. Gr.* i 444. 23 Bekker

# STESICHORUS

**S 137**

... hero Achilles ... he (you?) took away ... (he, having destroyed?) the city ... and (      ) the wall ... bold ... wonder(ful) ...

marginal scholiast at v. 8: roof

**S 138**

... thrice ... they went (      ) armour ... best ...

**S 139**

... one after another ... grace (sake?) ...

marginal scholiast: fierce bowman (-men?)

**S 143:**  see S 105(b)

## CERBERUS[1]

**206** Pollux, *Vocabulary*

ἀρύβαλλος is used of a purse that can be pulled tight in the *Self-lover* of Antiphanes and in the *Cerberus* of Stesichorus.

[1] The poem must have dealt with Heracles' descent to the underworld to fetch Cerberus, watchdog of Hades.

# GREEK LYRIC

## ΚΥΚΝΟΣ

**207** Schol. A Pind. *Ol.* 10. 19 (i 315 Drachmann)

Κυκνέα μάχη· ὅτι τὸν Ἄρεος Κύκνον Ἡρακλῆς φυγὼν αὖτις ἀνεῖλε Στησίχορος ἐν τῷ ἐπιγραφομένῳ Κύκνῳ φησίν.

ad 10. 21 (i 316 Dr.) ὁ Κύκνος υἱὸς ὢν τοῦ Ἄρεος ἐν τῇ παρόδῳ τῆς Θεσσαλίας οἰκῶν τοὺς παριόντας ξένους ἐκαρατόμει, ἐκ τῶν κεφαλῶν ναὸν τῷ Φόβῳ (Dawe: Ἀπόλλωνι cod.) ποιῆσαι βουλόμενος. παριόντι τοίνυν τῷ Ἡρακλεῖ ἐπεβούλευσε καὶ συστάσης μάχης ἐτράπη εἰς φυγὴν ὁ Ἡρακλῆς συλλαβομένου τοῦ Ἄρεος ὡς παιδὶ τῷ Κύκνῳ. ἀλλὰ ὕστερον αὐτὸν μόνον γενόμενον ἐνίκησεν ὁ Ἡρακλῆς.

## ΝΟΣΤΟΙ[1]

**208** Paus. 10. 26. 1 (iii 150 Rocha-Pereira)

ὡσαύτως δὲ καὶ Ἀριστομάχην ἐποίησεν (sc. Στησίχορος) ἐν Νόστοις θυγατέρα μὲν Πριάμου, Κριτολάου δὲ γυναῖκα εἶναι τοῦ Ἱκετάονος.

[1] cf. Tzetz. *Posthom.* 750 (p. 173 Jacobs) Στησίχορος δ' ἐρέησιν ἑοῖς ἐπέεσσιν νόστον.

# STESICHORUS

## CYCNUS

**207** Scholiast on Pindar ('Even the mighty Heracles was routed by the fight against Cycnus')

The story that Cycnus, son of Ares, was killed by Heracles after the latter had fled from him is told by Stesichorus in the poem entitled *Cycnus*.

Cycnus, son of Ares, lived in the pass of Thessaly and beheaded strangers who came along in order to build a temple to Panic[1] from the skulls. He plotted against Heracles when he came along, and after a fight Heracles turned in flight, since Ares had helped Cycnus, his son; but later when he was alone Heracles defeated him.

[1] For Panic (Phobos), perhaps identified by Stesichorus with Ares, see R. D. Dawe, *P.C.P.S.* 18 (1972) 28 ff. See also R. Janko, *C.Q.* 36 (1986) 48 ff.

## HOMECOMINGS[1]

**208** Pausanias, *Description of Greece* (on Polygnotus' painting: see 197)

Likewise[2] Stesichorus in his *Homecomings* spoke of Aristomache[3] as daughter of Priam and wife of Critolaus, son of Hicetaon.

[1] The returns of the Greek warriors from Troy.  [2] The passage follows 197.  [3] Named in the painting as one of the captive Trojan women.

**209** P.Oxy. 2360

col. i  θε[ῖ]ον ἐ[ξ]αίφνας τέρας ἰδοῖσα νύμφα,
      ὧδε δ᾽ ἔ[ει]φ᾽ Ἑλένα φωνᾶι ποτ[ὶ] παῖδ᾽ Ὀδύ-
          σειο[ν·
     'Τηλέμαχ', [ἦ] τις ὅδ᾽ ἁμὶν ἄγγελ[ο]ς ὠρανόθεν
     δι᾽ αἰθέρο[ς ἀτ]ρυγέτας κατέπτατο, βᾶ δ[(ὲ)
 5             ]   φοινᾶι κεκλαγ⟦γ⟧ώ[ς
     ] ᾳ ἐς ὑμετέρους δόμους προφαν[εὶς Ὀδυσε]ὺς
         ] αν ᾳ υς ἀνὴρ
     βο]υλαῖς Ἀθάνας·

           ] ᾳ ηις αυτα λακέρυζα κορώνα
 10          ]μ᾽ οὐδ᾽ ἐγώ⟨ν⟩ σ᾽ ἐρύ[ξ]ω
     Παν]ελόπα σ᾽ ἰδοῖσα φίλου πατ[ρ]ὸς υἱὸν
         ]σο . [ . ] τέλος ἐσθλ[όν
           ] . [ . ]θειον μ[

col. ii  ἀργυρέαν τεπ[
     χρυσῶι ὕπερθε[
     ἐκ Δαρδανιδ . . [
     Πλεισθενίδας . . [
 5  καὶ τὰ μὲν εὐ . [
     συνθ . [
     χρυσ[

col. i  3 ἦ suppl. Lloyd-Jones     5, 10 corr. Page     7
μάντις leg. Peek     9 μὴ] φῆις· 'αὖτα λ. κ.' Peek, fort. ἀλλ᾽ ἵνα μὴ
τόδε] φῆις vel sim. metri causa     cetera Lobel

# STESICHORUS

**209** Papyrus (1st c. A.D.)[1]

col. i

... the young woman[2] (rejoiced?) on suddenly seeing the divine portent[3]; and Helen spoke aloud thus to the son of Odysseus: 'Telemachus, truly this is some messenger for us from heaven that flew down through the unharvested air and went ... screaming with murderous (voice?)[4] ... Odysseus having appeared at your family's house ... a man[5] ... by the plans of Athena; (but, lest you say?), "This woman is a chattering crow", ... nor shall I detain you; ... Penelope (will rejoice?) on seeing you, the son of a dear father ... good outcome ... (divine?) ...

col. ii

... silver[6] ... with gold on top ... from Dardanian (Priam?) ... Pleisthenidas[7] ...; and these things ... gold ...

[1] Probably part of a 'Homecoming' of Odysseus: cf. *Od.* 15. 43 ff. for Telemachus' departure from Menelaus and Helen.     [2] Helen.
[3] In *Od.* 15. 160 ff. the portent was an eagle clutching a goose; Helen interpreted it as an omen of Odysseus' return to Ithaca and vengeance on the suitors.     [4] Or 'from bloody (throat)'.
[5] Perhaps 'a seer': Helen may be saying, 'I understand this like a seer.'     [6] In *Od.* 15. 113 ff. Menelaus gives Telemachus a silver mixing-bowl with a gold rim.     [7] Menelaus.

## ΟΡΕΣΤΕΙΑ : Α΄ (?)

**210** Ar. *Pax* 775ss.

Μοῦσα σὺ μὲν πολέμους ἀπωσαμένη μετ' ἐμοῦ | τοῦ φίλου χόρευσον | κλείσουα θεῶν τε γάμους ἀνδρῶν τε δαῖτας | καὶ θαλίας μακάρων, ubi schol. (ii 2. 122 Holwerda) αὕτη <παρα>πλοκή (corr. Bergk) ἐστι καὶ ἔλαθεν. σφόδρα δὲ γλαφυρὸν εἴρηται καὶ ἔστι Στησιχόρειον.

ita fort. Stesichorus:

Μοῖσα σὺ μὲν πολέμους ἀπωσαμένα πεδ' ἐμεῦ
κλείοισα θεῶν τε γάμους ἀνδρῶν τε δαίτας
καὶ θαλίας μακάρων

1 πεδ' Lobel    ἐμεῦ Bergk

**211** Ar. *Pax* 800

ὅταν ἠρινὰ μὲν φωνῇ χελιδὼν ἡδομένη (Bergk: ἑζομένη codd.) κελαδῇ, ubi schol. (p. 125 Holwerda) καὶ αὕτη <παρα>πλοκὴ (corr. Bergk) Στησιχόρειος. φησὶ γὰρ οὕτως ·

ὅκα ἦρος
ὥρᾳ κελαδῇ χελιδών

1 Page: ὅταν codd.

**212** Ar. *Pax* 797ss.

τοιάδε χρὴ Χαρίτων δαμώματα καλλικόμων | τὸν σοφὸν ποιητὴν | ὑμνεῖν ὅταν ἠρινὰ μὲν ... (v. 211), ubi schol. (p. 125 Holwerda) ἔστι δὲ παρὰ τὰ Στησιχόρου ἐκ τῆς Ὀρεστείας ·

# STESICHORUS

## ORESTEIA[1]: BOOK 1 (?)

**210** Scholiast on Aristophanes, *Peace* ('Muse, thrust aside wars and dance with me, your friend, glorifying the marriages of gods and the banquets of men and the festivities of the blessed')

This is an interweaving (of quoted and original poetry), and it has gone unnoticed; but it is most elegantly expressed and is Stesichorean.[2]

Muse, thrust aside wars and glorifying with me the marriages of gods and the banquets of men and the festivities of the blessed . . .

[1] See also 229 (last sentence).    [2] Editors remove the Aristophanic addition and introduce Doric forms. Attributed to *Oresteia* as being in the same metre as 212, which Aristophanes adapts in the same song; presumably the opening lines of the poem.

**211** Scholiast on Aristophanes, *Peace* ('when the swallow babbles its spring songs with glad voice')

This also is an interweaving of Stesichorus, who says

when in springtime the swallow babbles

**212** Scholiast on Aristophanes, *Peace* ('Such public songs of the lovely-haired Graces must the clever poet sing, when the swallow . . .': see 211)

This is derived from the lines of Stesichorus in his *Oresteia*:

τοιάδε χρὴ Χαρίτων δαμώματα καλλικόμων
ὑμνεῖν Φρύγιον μέλος ἐξευρόντας ἁβρῶς
ἦρος ἐπερχομένου.

δαμώματα δὲ τὰ δημοσίᾳ ᾀδόμενα.

2 Kleine: -όντα codd.

## ΟΡΕΣΤΕΙΑΣ Β΄

**213** Schol. Vat. in Dion. Thrac. *Art.* 6 (p. 183 Hilgard)

Στησίχορος δὲ ἐν δευτέρῳ Ὀρεστείας καὶ Εὐριπίδης (fr. 578 Nauck²) τὸν Παλαμήδην φησὶν εὑρηκέναι (sc. τὰ στοιχεῖα).

cf. p. 190 Hilgard, *Anecd.* ii 783 Bekker, *Anecd. Oxon.* iv 318 Cramer

**214** Habron (?) ap. P.Oxy. 1087 ii 47s. (ii 224 Erbse)

τὸ λιθακός, ἔνθεν φη(σὶ) Στησίχορος ἐν Ὀρεστείας β΄

λιθακοῖς

## ΟΡΕΣΤΕΙΑΣ Α΄ vel Β΄

**215** Philodem. *Piet.* (p. 24 Gomperz)

Στη[σίχορο]ς δ' ἐν Ὀρεστεί[αι κατ]ακολουθήσας [ Ἡσιό]δωι (fr. 23 M.-W.) τὴν Ἀγαμέ[μνονος Ἰ]φιγένειαν εἶ[ναι τὴ]ν Ἑκάτην νῦν [ὀνομαζ]ομένην . . .

# STESICHORUS

Such public songs of the lovely-haired Graces must we sing, tenderly finding out a Phrygian melody at the approach of spring.

'Public songs' are songs sung in public.[1]

[1] As opposed to songs for noble houses?

## ORESTEIA: BOOK 2

**213** Scholiast on Dionysius of Thrace

According to Stesichorus in book 2 of his *Oresteia* and Euripides the alphabet was invented by Palamedes.

**214** Habron (?) in scholiast on *Iliad* 7. 76 (μάρτυρος)

λιθακός,[1] 'stone', used by Stesichorus in *Oresteia,* book 2:

### stones

[1] Given as an example of a 'paronymous' noun, the nominative of which (e.g. μάρτυρος, λιθακός) is the same as the genitive of a cognate form (μάρτυς, λίθαξ); see also Sim. eleg. 3.

## ORESTEIA (BOOK 1 or 2)

**215** Philodemus, *Piety*

Stesichorus in his *Oresteia* follows Hesiod and identifies Agamemnon's daughter Iphigenia with the goddess called Hecate.

129

# GREEK LYRIC

**216** Schol. Eur. *Or.* 46 (i 102 Schwartz)

φανερὸν ὅτι ἐν Ἄργει ἡ σκηνὴ τοῦ δράματος ὑπόκειται. Ὅμηρος δὲ ἐν Μυκήναις φησὶ τὰ βασίλεια Ἀγαμέμνονος, Στησίχορος δὲ καὶ Σιμωνίδης (549) ἐν Λακεδαίμονι.

**217** P.Oxy. 2506 fr. 26 col. ii

... ὅ τε Στη]σίχορος ἐχρήσατ[ο διη]γήμασιν, τῶν τε ἄλλ[ων ποι]ητῶν οἱ πλείονες τ[αῖς ἀφορ]μαῖς ταῖς τούτου· με[τὰ γὰρ] Ὅμηρον κα[ὶ] Ἡσίοδον [οὐδενὶ] μᾶλλον Στησιχόρου [συμ]φων[οῦσι]· Αἰσχύλο[ς μὲν γὰρ] Ὀρέστ<ε>[ια]ν ποιήσα[ς τριλο]γίαν [Ἀ]γαμέμνον[α Χ]οηφ[όρ]ους Εὐμεν[ίδας . . . . . .] τὸν ἀναγ[νω]ρισμὸ]ν διὰ τοῦ βοστρύχο[υ· Στ]ησιχόρωι γὰρ ἐστιν [ . . . . ] , Ε[ὐ]ριπίδης δὲ τὸ τ[όξον] τὸ Ὀρέστου ὅτι ἐστὶν δε[δομέ]νον αὐτῶι δῶρον πα[ρὰ τ]οῦ Ἀπόλλωνος· παρ' ὧι [μὲν γ]ὰρ λέγεται· δὸς τόξα μ[οι κ]ερουλκά, δῶρα Λοξίου, | [οἷς εἶπ'] Ἀπόλλων μ' ἐξαμύ[νασ]θαι [θ]εάς (Eur. *Or.* 268s.)· παρὰ δὲ Στησιχ[όρω]ι·

τό[ξα δέ τιν] τάδε δώσω
παλά[μα]ισιν ἐμαῖσι κεκασμένα [ . . ] . . [ἐ]πικρα-
τέως βάλλειν·

[Εὐριπίδ]ης δὲ καὶ τὴν Ἰφ[ιγένειαν ἐ]ποίησε γαμουμέ[νην Ἀχιλλεῖ] . . . σα[τ[ . ]ρ . [

post Lobel suppl. Page (vid. M. Zicherl, *Z.P.E.* 55, 1984, 9–12)

**218** Schol. Aes. *Cho.* 733 (i 35 Smith)

Κίλισσαν δέ φησι τὴν Ὀρέστου τροφόν, Πίνδαρος δὲ Ἀρσινόην (*Pyth.* 11. 17), Στησίχορος Λαοδάμειαν.

# STESICHORUS

**216** Scholiast on Euripides, *Orestes*

It is clear that the play is set in Argos. But Homer puts Agamemnon's palace in Mycenae, Stesichorus and Simonides (549) in Sparta.

**217** Papyrus commentary (2nd c. A.D.)

... Stesichorus used narratives (of Homer? and Hesiod?), and most of the other poets used *his* material; for after Homer and Hesiod they agree above all with Stesichorus. Aeschylus, for example, in composing his trilogy the *Oresteia* — *Agamemnon, Choephori, Eumenides* — managed the recognition[1] by means of the lock of hair: this is in Stesichorus. Euripides says of Orestes' bow that it had been given to him as a gift by Apollo: his lines are, 'Give me the horn-tipped bow, the gift of Loxias, with which Apollo told me to ward off the goddesses' (*Orestes* 268 f.)[2]; and in Stesichorus we find

and I shall give you this bow fitted (?) to my hands ... for shooting mightily.

And Euripides[3] made Iphigenia (come to Aulis) to marry Achilles ...

[1] Of Orestes by Electra: see *Cho.* 164 ff.   [2] The scholiast on Euripides also notes that he followed Stesichorus here.
[3] Clearly following Stesichorus here too.

**218** Scholiast on Aeschylus, *Choephori*

Aeschylus calls Orestes' nurse Cilissa, Pindar Arsinoe, Stesichorus Laodamia.

**219** Plut. *ser. num. vind.* 10. 555a (iii 412 Pohlenz-Sieveking)

ὥστε πρὸς τὰ γιγνόμενα καὶ πρὸς τὴν ἀλήθειαν ἀποπλάττεσθαι τὸ τῆς Κλυταιμνήστρας ἐνύπνιον τὸν Στησίχορον οὑτωσί πως λέγοντα·

τᾷ δὲ δράκων ἐδόκησε μολεῖν κάρα βεβροτωμένος ἄκρον,
ἐκ δ᾽ ἄρα τοῦ βασιλεὺς Πλεισθενίδας ἐφάνη.

## ΣΚΥΛΛΑ

**220** Schol. Ap. Rhod. 4. 825–31 (g) (p. 295 Wendel)

Στησίχορος δὲ ἐν τῇ Σκύλλῃ †εἶδός τινος† Λαμίας τὴν Σκύλλαν φησὶ θυγατέρα εἶναι.

cf. Eust. *Od.* 1714. 34, schol. *Od.* 12. 124 (ii 541 Dindorf) = *Anecd. Par.* iii 479 Cramer

εἶδός τινος L, om. P: τῆς Ποσειδῶνος (cf. Paus. 10. 12. 1, al.) Wendel    Εἰδοῦς τινες ut glossema del. Vürtheim    fort. Λιβυστίδος Lloyd-Jones

## ΣΥΟΘΗΡΑΙ

**221** Athen. 3. 95d (i 219 Kaibel)

Στησίχορός τε φησιν ἐν Συοθήραις·

κρύψε δὲ ῥύγχος ἄκρον
γᾶς ὑπένερθεν

Dindorf: κρύψαι codd.

# STESICHORUS

**219** Plutarch, *On the slow revenge of the deity*

So Stesichorus makes Clytemnestra's dream accord with reality and truth when he says something like the following:

And it seemed to her that a snake came, the top of its head bloodstained, and out of it appeared a Pleisthenid king.[1]

[1] The snake must be the murdered Agamemnon, the king who grew out of the snake Orestes, his son; Aegisthus was not to be succeeded on the throne by a son of his.

## SCYLLA[1]

**220** Scholiast on Apollonius of Rhodes ('the malignant Ausonian Scylla, child of Phorcys')

Stesichorus in his *Scylla* says that Scylla is the daughter of Lamia.[2]

[1] See also 275(ii). The author may have been the 4th c. Stesichorus: see M. L. West, *C.Q.* 20 (1970) 206.    [2] Text corrupt: perhaps 'Lamia, child of Poseidon' or 'Libyan Lamia'.

## BOAR-HUNTERS[1]

**221** Athenaeus, *Scholars at Dinner*

Stesichorus says in his *Boar-hunters,*

and buried the tip of his snout beneath the earth.[2]

[1] See fr. 222B n. 1.  [2] The boar is nosing a root out of the ground: see G. Huxley, *G.R.B.S.* 7 (1966) 319 f., R. Renehan, *Studies in Greek Texts* 38 ff.

133

**222** P.Oxy. 2359 fr. 1

col. i     Θεσ]τιάδαι ·

    πέντε γ]ὰρ ὀψιγόνοι τε καὶ ἀσπασί-
    οι μένο]ν ἐν μεγάρ[ο]ισιν · ἀτὰρ πόδας
    ἀνορέα]ν τ' ἀγαθοὶ Προκάων Κλυτί-
5     ος τε νεέ]σθαν ·
    ἀπὸ Λαρίσ]ας δὲ μόλ' [Ε]ὐρυτίων
             ]ς τανυπ[έ]πλου
             ]ας

    καὶ μένο]ς Εἰλατίδαο δαίφρονος

col. ii  ἔνθεν μὲν Λοκρ[οὶ
     ἵζανον αἰχματαὶ [
     τέκνα φίλα[           ἐρί-
     ηρες Ἀχαιοὶ[
5    καὶ ὑπερθύμοι [Φωκᾶες, ὅσοι
     θ' ἱαρὰν Βοιωτίδ[α ν]αίον [
     χθόνα πυροφόρ[ον ·

     ἔνθεν δ' αὖ Δρύοπ[ές] τε κα[ὶ Αἰτω-
     λοὶ μενεχάρμα[ι

col. i     2, 6 init., 9 tent. Barrett      4 suppl. Snell,     5 Page

col. ii    5 e.g. Page      cetera Lobel

**222** Papyrus (2nd c. A.D.)

col. i

. . . sons of Thestius; for (five?) sons, born late and
a joy to their parents, remained at home; but Pro-
caon and Clytius[1] went, excellent in running and in
manliness; and from (Larissa) came Eurytion,[2] (son
of   ?) with her trailing robes . . . and the (mighty)
wise son of Elatus[3] . . .

col. ii

On one side the Locrian warriors were taking up
their positions[4] . . . dear sons . . . steadfast Achaeans
and proud (Phocians?) and those who lived in the
holy wheat-bearing land of Boeotia. On the other
side the Dryopians and the Aetolians, staunch in
war, . . .

[1] Sons of Thestius (Schol. T on *Il.* 9. 567), killed by their nephew
Meleager after the death of the Calydonian boar.       [2] Killed
accidentally by Peleus at the boar-hunt.       [3] Caineus.
[4] Against the boar, at the nets? See A. A. Barrett, *Cl. Ph.* 67 (1972)
117 ff.

# GREEK LYRIC

## ΘΗΒΑΙΣ (?)

**222A** P. Lille 76 + 73 (ed. G. Ancher, C. Meillier, *C.R.I. P.E.L.* 4, 1977, 287ss.; v. etiam P. J. Parsons, *Z.P.E.* 26, 1977, 7ss.)

176 ]Κρονίδας μὲν     178 ]εος υἱός     180 ] ας ἐνθεῖν
184 ]αυτας          186 ] . . . πρὶν          188 μ]έγα νεῖκος
190 ] . εν εἴσω     192 ]παῖδας     197 ] ος ἔγειρεν
201     ἐπ᾽ ἄλγεσι μὴ χαλεπὰς ποίει μερίμνας
   μηδέ μοι ἐξοπίσω
      πρόφαινε ἐλπίδας βαρείας.


   οὔτε γὰρ αἰὲν ὁμῶς
205     θεοὶ θέσαν ἀθάνατοι κατ᾽ αἶαν ἱρὰν
   νεῖκος ἔμπεδον βροτοῖσιν
   οὐδέ γα μὰν φιλότατ᾽, ἐπὶ δ᾽ ἀμέραι ἐν νόον ἄλλον
   θεοὶ τιθεῖσι.
   μαντοσύνας δὲ τεὰς ἄναξ ἑκάεργος Ἀπόλλων
210 μὴ πάσας τέλεσσαι.


   αἰ δέ με παῖδας ἰδέσθαι ὑπ᾽ ἀλλάλοισ<ι> δαμέντας
   μόρσιμόν ἐστιν, ἐπεκλώσαν δὲ Μοίρα[ι],
   αὐτίκα μοι θανάτου τέλος στυγερο[ῖο] γέν[οιτο
   πρίν ποκα ταῦτ᾽ ἐσιδεῖν
215     ἄλγεσ<σ>ι πολύστονα δακρυόεντα [     ,
   παῖδας ἐνὶ μεγάροις
      θανόντας ἢ πόλιν ἁλοίσαν.

# STESICHORUS

## THEBAID (?)[1]

**222A** Papyrus (before 250 B.C.)

176–200[2] ... (Zeus), son of Cronus ... son ... to go ... them(?) ... (as?) before ... great strife ... within ... sons ... (he) roused ...

201–234[3] ... to our sorrows do not add harsh anxieties, and do not show me heavy hopes for the future. For the immortal gods did not for all time alike establish over the holy earth strife unending for mortals, no, nor friendship either, but the gods establish within one day a different mind. As for your prophecies, may the far-working lord Apollo not accomplish them all. But if it is destined that I see my sons slain each by the other and the Fates have spun it, may the end of hateful death at once be mine before ever I see these lamentable tearful things (added?) to my sorrows, my sons dead in the palace or the city captured.

---

[1] Or *Seven against Thebes*? No attested title suits the contents.
[2] The first 175 lines, now missing, will have dealt with the death or exile of Oedipus, the quarrel of his sons Eteocles and Polynices, and the intervention of Tiresias. Only line-endings of 176–200 are preserved. [3] The queen (Jocasta or Epicaste rather than Eurygania) is addressing Tiresias.

---

188 Parsons        207 dub. Parsons        211 Haslam, Parsons
214 West: τοκα pap.            215 -εντ' ἀ[λάστοις tent. Barrett, -εντ{α}
[ἔπ' ἄλγη Page        216 ενιμμεγαροις pap.

137

ἀλλ' ἄγε, παῖδες, ἐμοῖς μύθοις, φίλα [τέκνα, πίθεσθε·
τᾷδε γὰρ ὑμὶν ἐγὼν τέλος προφα[ίνω,
220 τὸν μὲν ἔχοντα δόμους ναίειν πα[ρὰ νάμασι Δίρκας,
τὸν δ' ἀπίμεν κτεάνη
    καὶ χρυσὸν ἔχοντα φίλου σύμπαντα [πατρός,
κλαροπαληδὸν ὃς ἂν
    πρᾶτος λάχηι ἕκατι Μοιρᾶν.


225 τοῦτο γὰρ ἂν δοκέω
    λυτήριον ὕμμι κακοῦ γένοιτο πότμο[υ
μάντιος φραδαῖσι θείου,
αἴ γ' ἐτεὸν Κρονίδας γένος τε καὶ ἄστυ [φυλάξει
Κάδμου ἄνακτος,
230 ἀμβάλλων κακότατα πολὺν χρόνον [ἃ βασιλείαι
πέπρωται γενέ[θ]λαι.'


ὣς φάτ[ο] δῖα γυνά, μύθοις ἀγ[α]νοῖς ἐνεποῖσα,
νείκεος ἐν μεγάροις π[αυο]ίσα παῖδας,
σὺν δ' ἅμα Τειρ[ε]σίας τ[ερασπό]λος, οἱ δ' [ἐ]πίθο[ντο
234 αὐ[τὰρ      236 τὸν [μὲν  ]Θηβᾶν      237 γαῖα[ν
238 καὶ  [      ]α         239 τὸν [δ' ἀπίμεν κτεάνη

218 Maltomini, West      220 τομμεν pap.      suppl. Barrett,
πα[τρίαις ἐνὶ Θήβαις Diggle,      πα[ρὰ ματέρι κεδνᾷ Maltomini
228 Lloyd-Jones, Barrett: αιτενεον pap.      suppl. Lloyd-Jones,
[σαώσει Barrett      230 Lloyd-Jones      231 Barrett, Lloyd-Jones
233 εμμεγαροις pap.      π[αυο]ίσα, ἐ[ργ](οίσα) sscr., Barrett
234 τερ., ἐπιθ.      Barrett      235 vel αὐ[τίκα Parsons      236 τομ[
pap.      239 Parsons

No, come, my sons, obey my words, my dear children; for thus do I reveal the outcome for you, that one of you have the palace and dwell (by the spring of Dirce?),[4] and the other have the flocks and all the gold of his dear father and depart—he who in the shaking of lots[5] is the first to obtain his portion, thanks to the Fates. For this, I think, might be your release from the evil doom in the warning of the holy seer, if truly the son of Cronus means to guard the family and city of lord Cadmus, putting off for a long time the misfortune which is fated for the royal family.' So said the noble lady, speaking with gentle words, checking her sons from strife in the palace, and along with her Tiresias, interpreter of portents; and her sons obeyed,

235–269[6] and (at once?) . . . that one (should live in) the land of Thebes . . . and . . . , and the other

---

[4] In Thebes.   [5] I.e. the brother whose lot jumps out first from the helmet will get the worse portion, exile from Thebes. [6] Mostly line-endings. 235 ff. may have recounted the sons' acceptance of the queen's proposal, 244 ff. may have told how they cast lots and Polynices lost.

χρ]υσόν τ' ἐρίτιμον ἔχοντα    240 παμ[     ἔντ]οσθ'
ἔνησαν       241 ἠδ' ὅσα[ κ]λυτὰ μᾶλα νέμοντο
243 εὐεθ]είρας ἵππους      247 χρη]σμοὺς ἀσάμους
249 ἐ]νὶ στήθεσσι φίλοισι    251 ]εος, ἂν δ' ἔθορ'
αὐτὸς        253 μ]ῦθον ἔειπε     254 ]ἄλλως
255 πέφρ]αδε βουλάν     257 μύθο]ις πιθήσας
260 ]ε πολλά γ' ἄθυμον

270              ἄν]υσιν θέντες μεγάλαις ἐπ[ὶ λύπαις
             Ἄρ]γος
             ἄ]γεν ἕλικας βόας ἠδὲ καὶ ἵπ[πους
             κα]τ' αἶσαν ·

.. [         ]τοι τὸ μόρσιμόν ἐστι γεν[έσθαι ·
275   [       δό]μον 'Αδράστοι' ἄνακτος,
ὁ[ς δέ σε δεξάμε]νος δώσει περικαλλέα κο[ύραν
 .[         ]α
 .[        ]τον δωσοῦντι δᾶμος
   κα[ὶ πόλις 'Ακρισί]ου
280 φραδαῖσιν 'Αδράστ]οι' ἄνακτος.

             ]ω διαμπερέως Ἐτεο[κλ-
           ] ἐν στήθεσσιν αἰνῶ[ς
θ.[        ἐθέλ]ων ἔχεν Πολυνείκεος [αἶσαν
ω.[        ]
285    τεύξ[ηι μεγάλαν ἀνά]ταν πόλει τε πάσαι

240 vel παλλ[     suppl. Page post Instone     241 init. leg.
Parsons    243 West    247 Meillier    251 leg. Lloyd-Jones
255 Barrett     257, 270 Parsons    271, 272 ἄ]γεν tent. Par-
sons    274 vel ]σοι    suppl. Lloyd-Jones    275 Haslam, Parsons
276 init. West    279, 280 e.g. Parsons    281 ἐνέπ]ω vel μελέτ]ω
δ' Ἐτεο[κλεῖ tent. Parsons    283 e.g. Parsons    285 Page

should have the flocks and precious gold and depart
..., (the treasure which the descendants of
Cadmus?) had heaped up within and all the splen-
did flocks they pastured ... horses with fine manes
... obscure oracles ... in his breast ..., and he him-
self[7] jumped up ... (and) spoke these words: '...
(otherwise?) ... (she?) has revealed (a good?) plan
... (you), obeying (her words?) ... many things ...
spiritless ...

270–303[8] ... (you brothers?), putting an end to
great griefs: (you, Polynices, must go to Argos?) ...
to take the crumpled-horned cattle and the horses
... in accordance with fate. (I tell you) what is des-
tined to happen: (you will reach) the house of lord
Adrastus,[9] and he will (welcome you and) give you
his beautiful daughter ... and the people (and city
of Acrisius) will give you ... (at the prompting?) of
lord (Adrastus). (And to) Eteocles (I say) straight
out ... (I am?) terribly (afraid?) at heart (that he,
wanting) to have (the portion) of Polynices ... may
fashion (great disaster) for the whole city and for his

[7] Tiresias? It is he who speaks 270 ff.     [8] Mostly more exten-
sive line-endings.     [9] King of Argos.

ματ[ρί τ' ἀμαχανί]αν
ἀεὶ πο[ταίνιόν τ]ε πένθος.


τοῦ[το ῥύοιτο κακ]όν,
  θεῶ[ν ὅτις εὔνο]ος ἦι μάλιστα παντῶν
290  το[ῖς οἰζυροῖς βρο]τοῖσιν.'
ὣς φάτ[ο Τειρεσίας ὀ]νομάκλυτος, αἶψα δ' ἄ[ποικος
δόμων [ὅ γ' ἥρως ]
ὤιχετ[ο· σὺν δ' ἄρ' ἕπο]ντο φίλωι Πολυνείκεï τ[αγοὶ
Θηβαίω[ν ἄριστοι].


295  ἐρχόμεν[ος δ' ἀν' ὁδ]ὸν στεῖχεν, μέγα τεῖχ[ος ἀμείψας
  ......[         ] . . ἅμ' αὐτῶι
πολλὰ[        ]εππο . . τ' ἴσαν ἄκρο[ν Ἀθηνᾶν
ἄνδρες[
  πομπα[ῖσι θεῶν· ταχέω]ς δ' ἵκοντο Ἰσθμόν
300  ποντίου [Ἐννοσίδα]
  κραιν. [         ] εὔχαις·


αὐτὰ[ρ ἔπειτ' ἀπέβαν ἐπ'] ἄστεα καλὰ Κορίνθου,
ῥίμφα δ' [ἐϋκτιμένας] Κλεωνὰς ἦνθον


286 ματρί Page    ἀμαχ. tent. Parsons        287 e.g. Parsons
288–90 tent. Parsons    290 βροτ. Haslam, West       291 init.
Parsons      291 fin.–294 Page    295 init., fin. e.g. Parsons
297 τ' ἴσαν leg. Barrett, ἄκρον Meillier        Ἀθ. : v. Parsons
299 init. Barrett, ταχ. Parsons    300 West    302 αὐτὰρ
West    cetera e.g. Parsons    303 Barrett    cetera ed. pr.

mother (perplexity and fresh) grief always. (May he ward off this evil, whoever) of all the gods is most (kindly to wretched) mortals.'

So spoke famous Tiresias, and at once (the hero left) the house and departed; (and with) their dear Polynices (went the best leaders) of the Thebans. Making his way he began his journey along the road, passing the great wall[10] ... (and with) him ... many ... the men came to the furthest point (of Athens)[11] under the escort (of the gods); and (soon) they reached the Isthmus of the sea-god,[12] (the earth-shaker,) ... (and were accomplishing their journey?) with prayers; and (then they departed for) the fair towns of Corinth, and quickly came to (well-built) Cleonae ...

[10] Of Thebes? Perhaps of Erythrae.    [11] Eleusis (at the western edge of Attica)?    [12] The marginal letter Γ marks v. 300 of the poem.

# GREEK LYRIC

**222B** P.Oxy. 3876 (suppl. ed. pr., M. W. Haslam)

fr. 1  1 π]ρὸ μὲν . . [     2 ]ἀλλά νιν α[
3 ]αὐτὸς Ἐννά[λιος     4 Τριτογενής [τ(ε)
5 ἱ]πποσόα πτολ[     6 ]μέγα δ' ἐν φρεσ]ὶ
7 ὄλ]βιος ὅστις τ . [

7 Τρ[ιτογένειαν ?


frr. 2 + 6(b) (coniunxit Barrett)

2  . . . . . . ]ις ἀπέδωκε[
   . . . . . . ] . ία δ' ἄρ' ὅπως[
   (-)ἔκλυ]εν ἀγγελιά[ων ·
5 προέ]πεμψε δέ νιν[
   Ἄρτα]μις ἰοχέαιρα[ . ] . . λυμ[
   θυγάτ]ηρ Διὸς ἀγρεσ[ι]θήρα
       . . . . ὅ]πως Κα[λυδ]ῶν' ἐρατὰν . [
       . . . . . ] . αι μέγ[α . . ( . )]μα περικλ[υτ

2 -ο]ις, -α]ις   3 Ἀλθ]αία?   6 -αιρ' ἀ[π]' Ὀλυμ[π-?
9 δέρ]μα (vel δῶ]μα) περικλ[υτόν


fr. 3     2 πρόσ]θεν πόλι[ος   3 Κ]άστορος vel
ἀλ]άστορος   4 ] . βρισομ[αχ-

fr. 4

   . . . . . ]άθαν μ[
   . . . . . ]λετομ[
   . . . . . ]ψάμενος . [
   . . . . . ] ποτέ[ει]πε θ[
5  . . . . . ] . εὐπατέρει-

144

# STESICHORUS

**222B** Papyrus (2nd c. A.D.)[1]

fr. 1 ... (previously?) ... but him Enyalius[2] himself and Tritogenes[3] ... horse-driving[4] ... city(-) ... greatly at heart ... Happy the man who ... (Tritogenia?) ...

---

[1] The scraps seem to come from more than one poem: fr. 4 and with it frr. 1–3, 5–24 may belong to the *Boar-hunters* (see *P.M.G.* 221–222); fr. 62 and with it frr. 61, 63–77 may be from the *Homecomings* (see *P.M.G.* 208–209).    [2] Ares.    [3] Athena.    [4] Artemis (see fr. 2)? Poseidon?

frr. 2 + 6(b) ... gave back to ... (heard?) the message; and Artemis the arrow-shooter, daughter of Zeus, animal-huntress, sent him/her[1] (from Olympus?) ... in order to ... lovely Calydon ... the great glorious (hide?)[2] ...

---

[1] The messenger to Althaea (see fr. 4)?    [2] The boar's hide, over which Meleager and his uncles fought? Or 'house'?

fr. 3 ... (before the city?) ... Castor[1] ... (prevailing in fight?) ...

---

[1] One of the boar-hunters; or 'avenger'?

fr. 4 ... (forgetfulness?) ... (he?)[1] addressed (her): 'Daughter[2] of a noble father, you will soon learn

---

[1] Text uncertain; the speaker need not be male.    [2] Althaea?

α, τ]άχ᾽ ἀγγελίας ἀμεγάρτου
πε]ύσεαι ἐμ μεγάροις · τεθνᾶσί τ[ο]ι̣
ἅμα]τι τῶιδε παρ᾽ αἶ-
σαν] ἀδελφ[εοί] · ἔκτανε δ᾽ αὐτοὺς
10 . . . . . ]φ[            ]
      . . . . . ] . σ[ . . . . . . , ἀ]μύμων
. . . . . . . . . . . . . . . φρέ̣να[

1 λ]άθαν ?      3 lect. dub.      5 Θεστιὰ]ς ?


fr. 5      1 ]θαρσαλε̣[      2 ]μά̣λ̣[      3 μέ]γ᾽ ἀγασθε̣ί̣ς
4 ὑπερ]φίαλον δέμας[      5 ]ν χαρί̣εντα δ̣[
6 εὐρυ]βίαν σταθε̣ . [

6 σταθερ[όν τε ?


fr. 11   (a) 3 ἄκο[ς] εὐ̣[ρέμεναι
(b) 2 ματρό[      3 ὀλέσα[ι vel ὀλέσα̣[ν      4 χα̣λε-
π[όν


fr. 19   2 βά]λ᾽ ῎Αρτ[αμις


fr. 25 (a) 2 ]ν ἀλκάν   (b) 2 λιπαρὰν πόλ[ιν vel Λιπά-
ραν πόλ[ιν      6 θυμ]ὸν ἀέξων      7 ὁμοφρο]σύναισι ?
8 δ]νοφέα στάσις


fr. 26 12 ]αν γὰρ ἤδ[η      14 ]ε κρά-      15 ] . Μοιρᾶν[
17 (-)αδ]ε̣λ̣φεοῖς α . [      18 ] . ν αὐτῶ̣ν[      23 ἐν
με]γάροις̣ · ποθεν[      24 ]ἄπασι λαοῖς      26 ὀκρι]ό-
εσσι πετρᾶ[ν      28 ]Κηρσσίν ω[      34 ὠ]ρανομακ[
46 θρ]ήνου ?


146

unenviable tidings in your house. On this (day)
your brothers lie dead in unseemly circumstances:
their killer was the blameless[3] . . . (heart?) . . .

[3] Meleager, 'your son'?

fr. 5 . . . bold(ly) . . . very much . . . (he) greatly
amazed . . . the noble frame[1] . . . delightful . . . vastly
strong[2] (and steadfast?) . . .

[1] Of the boar?    [2] Epithet of the boar at Bacch. 5. 104.

fr. 11 . . . (to find?) a remedy . . . mother . . .
destroy(ed) . . . difficult . . .

fr. 19 . . . (Artemis struck her down?)

fr. 25 . . . valour . . . gleaming city[1] . . . he, keeping
courage high . . . (unanimity?) . . . murky civil strife
. . . (he) got . . .

[1] Or 'the city of Lipara' in the Aeolian islands, home of Aeolus (see
fr. 62).

fr. 26 . . . for already . . . head(s) . . . Fates . . . broth-
ers . . . (of) them . . . (in the palace?). Whence . . . (to)
all the men . . . jagged (points?) of rocks . . . Death-
goddesses . . . heaven-high . . . (lamentation?) . . .

fr. 35 2 ὄρνιθα]ς (vel κύκνο]ς) ἀερσιπότας[     4 ἔρνεα
(vel ὄρνεᾳ)

8          ]ν πλοκάμοισιν ἀλεξίδα[μος (vel [μον)
           τέ]ρεν ἄκρον ἄνθος
10         ] ο Σείκελε · μήποκ᾽ ἄλλα[ν (vel [ς, [ι)
           ]εταν ὅ γα μησάμενος[ ] [
           στ]υγεράν τε ἰδὼν ἀνοή[μ]ον[ά τ᾽
           πο]λέων γὰρ ἀνδρῶν
           με]γάλως ἐπεμάσσατο [
15         πο]λέας δὲ πλέχθεν
           στ]εφάνους ἀπαλῶν τε σελ[ίνων
           ναρκίσσου] τε ἴου τε ῥόδων τεσαῦ [

2 ε sup. o scr., i.e. var. lect. -πέτας     14 ν sup. π scr., i.e. var.
lect. ἐνεμάσσατο     15 πλέχθεν · pap.     17 τε σαργα[νας ?
τ᾽ ἐς αὖτε[ ?

fr. 36 (schol.)     6 ]τι νίκη[     7 ]Πυθοῖ μ[

fr. 37 1 ]ας Ἀιδόσδε νιν     2 θ]εὸν ἄμβροτον

fr. 39     1 ] ἐσθλῶν (vel -ῷι)     10 (-)]μίσγετ᾽
ἀ[ . . . ]ς     11 ] ὡς τερπνὸν ἔθηκε [ ]φ [
12 ]ρνος ὥς     13 φάος] ἁγνὸν Ἀοῦς     14 ]το δὲ
πρὸς θεῶν     15 ]Κ[α]δμεῖοι ερ [ ] [
16 ] Κλωθώ     18 ἐνὶ φρασὶν     19 ] [
]τέρπετο     21 μ]είζω     22 ] ἄστυ λιγέ [
23 σ]ιδάρεον α     30 (schol.) Πτολ(εμαῖος) ηὑρίσκ [

148

fr. 35 ... high-soaring (birds?)[1] ... shoots[2] ... locks
... people-protecting[3] ... the (soft?) full flower (of
youth?) ... Sicelus![4] Let him never ... another ...
having devised ... and having seen both hateful and
foolish ...; for of many men ... (he) strove greatly
after ... were[5] woven many garlands of tender pars-
ley (and narcissus?) and violet ... and roses ...

[1] Or (swan?).    [2] Or 'birds'.    [3] Or proper name Alexidamus.
[4] Or 'Sicilian!'    [5] Text and translation of remainder very un-
certain.

fr. 36 (scholium) ... victory ... Pytho ...[1]

[1] The context is epinician; note the garlands of fr. 35.

fr. 37 ... him to the house of Hades ... immortal god
...[1]

[1] From the story of Memnon, whom Zeus made immortal after his
death? See fr. 56.

fr. 39 ... noble ... mingled ... how (he) made
delightful ... like a ... the holy (light) of Dawn ...
and from the gods ... Cadmeans[1] ... Clotho ... in
(his) heart ... (he) enjoyed ... (greater?) ... city
shrilly ... (iron?) ... (schol.) Ptolemaeus[2] reads ηὑρί-
σκο[ν(?), 'they found'

[1] The Thebans.    [2] A Ptolemaeus is known as a scholar from
Athen. 11. 481d etc. (see Alcm. 3, schol. n. 1, Bacch. test. 11 n. 1),
but there were other scholars of this name. Cf. fr. 70 below.

fr. 40     3 ]Διὸς ἀγρ[     10 (-)]έχησι θ[
12 (-)δ]όκιμος τρ[ι]παλαιγενὲς απα[

12 ἀπά[λαμόν τε ? ed. pr.    â πα[ ? ego (cf. *Od.* 22. 395)


fr. 41     4 εὐ]ώδεος α̣[     5 ]το δ' ὄνας[ιν
7 ]ν ὑστάτ[οι

fr. 42 (a) 5 ]ν · αἰθέρος ̣ [     7 Θαύμαντος κ̣[ ] ̣ [
(b) 3 ἔλευ[σε (vel κ]ἐ̣λευ[)   (c) 2 τέκος[
3 ὠκέα[ν (vel ὠκέα[)    4 δ' Ἀχιλ̣[ ?     5 αἴ
σφι ̣ ̣ [ (vel σφισ̣[ι)   6 Ζηνὸς ἐρισφα[ράγου
(vel -οιο)

fr. 43     ii 3 ὄφι ε[   5 δριο̣[ 6 (ἔ)|νερ[θα
8 σφυρ[     10 κεφ ̣ [

fr. 44     ] ̣ο̣ · θαυμα[

fr. 45 3 ]ε παρὲκ ν[όον ?    4 ]ν νέμεσις φ ̣ ̣ [
6 ] ̣ πασᾱ[ν

fr. 46 2 ] ̣ τεθαλ[    4 ]πέπλων

fr. 48 2 μολε[(ν) (vel Α̣ἰ̣ολε[)    3 ἐναλιγκ[
4 κειμεν[    5 ὠμοφαγ ̣ [


fr. 49 1 ]θυγατρὶ δ' οπ[

fr. 56 5 ]τε Μέμνων ?

fr. 40 ... of Zeus[1] ... (he/she) has ... well-esteemed, you who were born long years ago,[2] ...

[1] Perhaps 'Artemis, daughter of Zeus, animal-huntress' as in fr. 2.    [2] Addressed to a man or a woman?

fr. 41 ... sweet-scented ... advantage ... last ...

fr. 42 ... (sky?) ... (daughter)[1] of Thaumas ... brought[2] ... child ... ocean[3] ... (Achilles?) ... who to them ... (of) loud-thundering Zeus ...

[1] Iris.    [2] Or 'order(ed)'.    [3] Or 'swift (Iris?)'.

fr. 43 ... (by a snake?) ... copse ... below ... ankle ... (head?) ...

fr. 44 ... wonder(ful)[1] ...

[1] Or Thaumas again?

fr. 45 ... (foolishly?) ... anger ... of all ...

fr. 46 ... (sea?)[1] ... -robed ...

[1] Or 'flourish(ing)'.

fr. 48 ... (he/she) went[1] ... like ... lying ... flesh-eating ...

[1] Or 'Aeolus'?

fr. 49 ... (to) the daughter ...

fr. 56 ... Memnon ...

# GREEK LYRIC

frr. 61–62 : 61.5 ῥ]όπαλον[ . . ]χε          7 ] . [ ] . κύ-
μασι . [          8 (ἁλὸς) π]ολιᾶς, ὅθεν[          9 ]ἁλὶ κλυ-
ζο[μεν-          10 ]γαίας λα . [          11 ]βροτοῖσι . [

61.12          ἀλλ' ὕδατ]ί τ' ἐλ[ο]έσσ[αν
62.1     εὖ λιαρῶι καὶ ἐχ]ρι-
          σαν ἀ]λείφ[ατι] νεκταρε[ό]δμωι·
          . . . ] δα . [ . ] . τ ν
          ἐστόλισεν μέ[γ]α φᾶρος ἀνέψιος
     5   Αἰόλου Ἱπ[π]οτάδα· καθ[αρ]αῖς δ' ἐτά-
          νυσσ<εν> ἐπ' αἰ[ό]νεσ-
          σι· πυρὰν δ' ὅ [γ]α μέμβλε[τ]ο νεκρῶι
          ποιεῖ]σθαι περιμάκεας ὄζους
          ναήσαις μ]ελίας τ' ἐριδα[νούς
     10  . . . . . . . αἰ]θέρ' αθ . . . [
          . . . . . . . . . ] . τι . . [

fr. 63  1 γλυκεραν θ . [          2 ἐλπίδ' ὅπως[
3 ]φίλοις θανα[τ-

fr. 64  (a) 1 (ἔκ)| τοθεν αρ . [          2 ζακότου[
3 ἐρασιπτο[λ          4 ἔθαλες[          5 ἀγαθ[
(b) 1 ]μαχα[
     2 μέ]γα γὰρ πόλις αὐ[ξάνεται
          ὁπ[ό]κ' ἐσθλὰ θεὸς δ[ώηι (vel δ[ιδοῖ),
          οὐδέ τις ἐστ' ἀρετὰ[(τιμά τε) βρο-
     5   τῶν παρὰ δα[ί]μον[ος αἶσαν
          καὶ Λάχεσιν· τ[ὸ] δὲ σᾶ[μα
          μά]λ' ἀριφραδέ[s
          πολ]έμου τε . [

# STESICHORUS

frr. 61–62 ... (club?)[1] ... waves ... the grey sea,
whence ... dashed by the sea ... land ... mortals
...; (but they?) washed him[2] (well with warm water
and) anointed him with nectar-scented oil; and ...
the cousin[3] of Aeolus, son of Hippotes, dressed him
in a great robe and stretched him out on clean
cloaks; and he took care to make a pyre for the
corpse, heaping up long branches and dry ash-trees
... (sky?) ...

[1] Heracles' club?    [2] End of fr. 61.    [3] Unknown. The
corpse may have been Misenus, whom Virgil calls 'son of Aeolus'
(*Aen.* 6. 164): Strabo makes him a companion not of Aeneas but of
Odysseus in his western travels (1. 2. 18, 5. 4. 6), so that the pas-
sage might be from Stesichorus' *Homecomings* or from a poem
about Odysseus. See Haslam in *Ox. Pap.* 57 pp. 42 f.

fr. 63 ... sweet ... hope that ... (to his) friends ...
death ...

fr. 64[1] ... thence[2] ... very angry ... war-loving[3] ...
you flourished ... good ... battle ...; for a city is
greatly (exalted) when god (grants) blessings, nor
is there any excellence (and honour?) (of mortals)
contrary to the deity's (dispensation) and Lachesis;
(and this mound, very) conspicuous, ... war ...

[1] From an address to the corpse of fr. 62? Cf. fr. 65.    [2] Or
'outside'.    [3] Or 'city-loving'.

fr. 65 i 3 ]ν φυγον&#817;&#807;&#807;    ii 5 χαῖρ[ε    6 κλει[τ-
7 μακα[ρ-

fr. 66 i 6 (κα]τ)ᾶρχε (vel -άρχε) καὶ τερ&#807;    7 ]νεχεν
8 θερά]ποντα πάν[|[τα ?    9 ]&#807;ον ἀνδρί·

fr. 67 (a) 2 ἅμα&#807;&#807; [    3 &#807;&#807;εφερο[    4 δαιτὸς
ἐ[ίσης?    5 ζακοτον[    6 κρατερο[
(b) 2 ]&#807;εραταν    3 ]&#807;φι βρότε[ι-    4 ἀργ]υ-
ρέων κ&#807;[    5 ]υς&#807; περὶ χρ[υσ-    6 ]τηλόθε χαλ[κ-
7 ]ς&#807; σέλας&#807;&#807; [    8 ]&#807;εισαλος ὦρτο[    10 (schol.)
]&#807;οντας ἰδόντ[ας

fr. 69 2 Ἀπόλλ]ωνα κλ[υτότοξον?    3 ]ασπιδο[
4 ]χαλκ&#807;[

fr. 70 (schol.) 3 Πτολ(εμαῖος)

fr. 72 2 ]αἴτᾱχθο[&#807;&#807; ]&#807; [    3 ]τόσαι (vel -τος α]ἰ)
ἀλκα(-)[ ]&#807;    7 χ]ρυσοτρ[ιαί]ναι&#807;&#807;·    9 ]&#807; ἀμ-
βροσι&#807;[&#807;&#807;] τε&#807; [

2 λ]αῖτα χθο[ν- ? (cf. Hsch. ληῖτη· ἱέρεια)

fr. 73 2 καὶ καλῶ&#807;[

fr. 74 2 ι&#807;· Αιολιδ&#807;&#807;&#807;&#807;[    4 ]Στροφα&#807;[

---

[1] Or Drifting Isles, sometimes identified with the Aeolian Isles
(Dion. Perieg. 465). Aeolus lived on a floating island (*Od.* 10. 3).
Cf. fr. 25 n. 1.

fr. 65 ... fled ... Greetings![1] ... famous ... blessed ...

[1] Or 'Farewell!' (to the corpse?).

fr. 66 ... (he/she) began[1] ... (he/she) had[2] ... (every servant?) ... to the man ...

[1] Or 'begin!'    [2] Or 'to have'.

fr. 67 ... at the same time[1] ... brought ... banquet (with fair contributions?) ... very angry ... strong ... lovely ... mortal ... silver ... (gold?) ... from afar (bronze?) ... brightness ... sea-swell[2] rose[3] ... (them) having seen ...

[1] The sequence of the words is not certain: 'at the same time' may have been followed by 'lovely', 'brought' by 'mortal', and so on. [2] Or 'the sea's'.    [3] Or 'rushed'.

fr. 69 ... (Apollo, famed for his bow?) ... shield ... bronze ...

fr. 70 (schol.) ... Ptolemaeus[1] ...

[1] Cf. fr. 39 n. 2.

fr. 72 ... (priestess of underworld divinities?) ... valour ... (to) (Poseidon) of the gold trident ... ambrosia(l) ...

fr. 73 ... and beautiful(ly) ...

fr. 74 ... (Aeolian?) ... the Strophades[1] ...

# GREEK LYRIC

## INCERTI LOCI

**223** Schol. Eur. *Or.* 249 (i 123 Schwartz)

Στησίχορός φησιν ὡς θύων τοῖς θεοῖς Τυνδάρεως Ἀφροδίτης ἐπελάθετο. διὸ ὀργισθεῖσαν τὴν θεὸν διγάμους τε καὶ τριγάμους καὶ λειψάνδρους αὐτοῦ τὰς θυγατέρας ποιῆσαι. ἔχει δὲ ἡ χρῆσις οὕτως·

οὕνεκα Τυνδάρεος
ῥέζων ποκὰ πᾶσι θεοῖς μόνας λάθετ᾽ ἠπιοδώρου
Κύπριδος· κείνα δὲ Τυνδαρέου κόρας
χολωσαμένα διγάμους τε καὶ τριγάμους ἐτίθει
καὶ λιπεσάνορας.

1s. Suchfort: ποτε post οὕνεκά codd.        ποκα Schneidewin
3 Sitzler: κούρας, κόραις, κούραις, κούρου codd.        4 West: τίθησι
codd.

**224** Schol. Lycophr. *Alex.* 265 (ii 115 Scheer)

Στησίχορος δὲ καὶ Εὐφορίων (fr. 56 Powell) τὸν Ἕκτορά φασιν εἶναι υἱὸν τοῦ Ἀπόλλωνος καὶ Ἀλέξανδρος ὁ Αἰτωλῶν ποιητής (fr. 13 Powell).

cf. schol. T *Il.* 24. 258 (v 568 Erbse)

**225** Plut. *sollert. anim.* 36 (vi 1. 74 Hubert)

ἡ δ᾽ Ὀδυσσέως ἀσπὶς ὅτι μὲν ἐπίσημον εἶχε δελφῖνα καὶ Στησίχορος ἱστόρηκεν.

cf. schol. Lycophr. *Alex.* 658 (ii 219 Scheer)

# STESICHORUS

*The remaining fragments are not assigned to named poems.*

**223** Scholiast on Euripides, *Orestes* ('Tyndareus fathered a family of daughters conspicuous for blame and of bad repute throughout Greece')

Stesichorus says that when Tyndareus was sacrificing to the gods he forgot Aphrodite: the goddess was angered and made his daughters twice-wed and thrice-wed and husband-deserters. The passage runs as follows:

because Tyndareus when sacrificing one day to all the gods forgot the Cyprian only, kindly in her giving; and she in anger made the daughters of Tyndareus twice-wed and thrice-wed and husband-deserters.[1]

[1] Helen's partners were Theseus (cf. 191), Menelaus and Paris and perhaps Deiphobus, Clytemnestra's Agamemnon and Aegisthus and perhaps Tantalus, Timandra's Echemus and Phyleus; cf. Hesiod fr. 176 M.-W. From the *Helen* or *Oresteia* or *Sack of Troy*.

**224** Scholiast on Lycophron, *Alexandra* (Hector, 'son of Ptoan Apollo')

Stesichorus and Euphorion say that Hector is Apollo's son, as does the poet Alexander the Aetolian.[1]

[1] See also 198, Ibyc. 295.

**225** Plutarch, *Whether sea or land animals are cleverer*

We are told by Stesichorus[1] that the shield of Odysseus had a dolphin emblazoned on it.[2]

[1] In *Sack of Troy* or *Homecomings*? See also Euphorion fr. 67 Powell.     [2] According to the Zacynthians, a dolphin had saved the child Telemachus from drowning.

# GREEK LYRIC

**226** Schol. T Hom. *Il.* 15. 336 (d) (iv 83 Erbse)

τὸν Ὀιλέα Ζηνόδοτος ἑπόμενος Ἡσιόδῳ (fr. 235. 1 M.-W.) καὶ Στησιχόρῳ χωρὶς τοῦ ο ὀνομάζει Ἰλέα, τὸ δὲ ο ἄρθρον φησίν.

cf. Eust. *Il.* 277. 2, 1018. 58

**227** 'Apollod.' *Bibl.* 3. 117 (p. 140 Wagner)

Κυνόρτου δὲ Περιήρης (sc. υἱὸς ἦν), ὃς γαμεῖ Γοργοφόνην τὴν Περσέως, καθάπερ Στησίχορός φησι, καὶ τίκτει Τυνδάρεων Ἰκάριον Ἀφαρέα Λεύκιππον.

cf. Tzetz. in Lycophr. *Alex.* 511 (ii 184 Scheer)

**228** Eust. *Il.* 316. 16 (i 491 van der Valk)

Πίνδαρος δὲ (e.g. *Ol.* 6. 77) οὐκ ἀδελφοὺς ἀλλὰ γονέας μητρὸς μάτρωας ἔφη. Στησίχορος δὲ πάτρωα τὸν κατὰ πατέρα πρόγονον εἶπεν, ἔνθα παρ' αὐτῷ Ἀμφίλοχος ἔφη τὸ

πάτρω' ἐμὸν ἀντίθεον Μελάμποδα·

Μελάμπους γὰρ οὗ Ἀντιφάτης οὗ Ὀικλῆς οὗ Ἀμφιάραος ὅθεν Ἀμφίλοχος.

cf. Ar. Byz. frr. 229, 230 Slater

# STESICHORUS

**226** Scholiast on *Iliad*

Zenodotus[1] follows Hesiod and Stesichorus and calls Oïleus[2] Ileus without the 'o', explaining that letter as the article (ὁ Ἰλεύς).

[1] Alexandrian Homeric scholar, 3rd c. B.C.   [2] Father of Locrian Ajax. From *Sack of Troy* or *Homecomings*? According to Eustathius, Stesichorus used both forms of the name.

**227** 'Apollodorus', *Library*

Cynortes' son was Perieres, who married Perseus' daughter Gorgophone, according to Stesichorus, and was father of Tyndareus,[1] Icarius, Aphareus and Leucippus.

[1] Cf. 223.

**228** Eustathius on *Iliad* 2. 662 (μήτρωα, 'mother's brother')

Pindar used the term μάτρωες not for a mother's brothers but for a mother's ancestors; and Stesichorus used πάτρως for an ancestor on the father's side when he made Amphilochus say,[1]

> my ancestor, godlike Melampus;

for the line of descent is Melampus — Antiphates — Oïcles — Amphiaraus — Amphilochus.

[1] In the *Eriphyle*? Cf. 'Apollodorus', *Library* 3. 86, 'Some say Alcmaeon and his brother Amphilochus killed [their mother] Eriphyle together, others that Alcmaeon did it alone.'

**229** Athen. 12. 512e–513a (iii 131s. Kaibel)

διόπερ καὶ Μεγακλείδης ἐπιτιμᾷ τοῖς μεθ' Ὅμηρον καὶ Ἡσίοδον ποιηταῖς ὅσοι περὶ Ἡρακλέους εἰρήκασιν ὡς στρατοπέδων ἡγεῖτο καὶ πόλεις ᾕρει . . . τοῦτον οὖν, φησίν, οἱ νέοι ποιηταὶ κατασκευάζουσιν ἐν λῃστοῦ σχήματι μόνον περιπορευόμενον, ξύλον ἔχοντα καὶ λεοντῆν καὶ τόξα· καὶ ταῦτα πλάσαι πρῶτον Στησίχορον τὸν Ἱμεραῖον. καὶ Ξάνθος δ' ὁ μελοποιός, πρεσβύτερος ὢν Στησιχόρου, ὡς καὶ αὐτὸς ὁ Στησίχορος μαρτυρεῖ, ὥς φησιν ὁ Μεγακλείδης, οὐ ταύτην αὐτῷ περιτίθησι τὴν στολὴν ἀλλὰ τὴν Ὁμηρικήν. πολλὰ δὲ τῶν Ξάνθου παραπεποίηκεν ὁ Στησίχορος, ὥσπερ καὶ τὴν Ὀρέστειαν καλουμένην.

cf. Eust. *Il.* 1279. 8

**230** Paus. 9. 11. 2 (iii 20 Rocha-Pereira)

ἐπιδεικνύουσι δὲ (sc. οἱ Θηβαῖοι) Ἡρακλέους τῶν παίδων τῶν ἐκ Μεγάρας μνῆμα, οὐδέν τι ἀλλοίως τὰ ἐς τὸν θάνατον λέγοντες ἢ Στησίχορος ὁ Ἱμεραῖος καὶ Πανύασσις (fr. 20 Davies) ἐν τοῖς ἔπεσιν ἐποίησαν. Θηβαῖοι δὲ καὶ τάδε ἐπιλέγουσιν, ὡς Ἡρακλῆς ὑπὸ τῆς μανίας καὶ Ἀμφιτρύωνα ἔμελλεν ἀποκτιννύναι, πρότερον δὲ ἄρα ὕπνος ἐπέλαβεν αὐτὸν ὑπὸ τοῦ λίθου τῆς πληγῆς· Ἀθηνᾶν δὲ εἶναι τὴν ἐπαφεῖσάν οἱ τὸν λίθον τοῦτον, ὅντινα σωφρονιστῆρα ὀνομάζουσιν.

**231** Plut. *de malign. Herod.* 14, 857ef (v 2. 2. 14 Hässler)

καίτοι τῶν παλαιῶν καὶ λογίων ἀνδρῶν οὐχ Ὅμηρος οὐχ Ἡσίοδος οὐκ Ἀρχίλοχος οὐ Πείσανδρος οὐ Στησίχορος οὐκ Ἀλκμὰν οὐ Πίνδαρος Αἰγυπτίου ἔσχον λόγον Ἡρακλέους ἢ Φοίνικος, ἀλλ' ἕνα τοῦτον ἴσασι πάντες Ἡρακλέα τὸν Βοιώτιον ὁμοῦ καὶ Ἀργεῖον.

---

[1] See Hdt. 2. 43 f.  [2] Prince of Tiryns (near Argos) but born in Thebes in Boeotia.

# STESICHORUS

**229** Athenaeus, *Scholars at Dinner*[1]

This too is why Megaclides[2] finds fault with those successors of Homer and Hesiod who have said of Heracles that he led expeditions and captured cities ... So, says Megaclides, Heracles is represented by the modern poets as travelling about alone in the guise of a bandit with club and lionskin and bow; and, he adds, it was Stesichorus of Himera who first thought this up.[3] Xanthus, the lyric poet, who was earlier than Stesichorus, as Stesichorus himself testifies according to Megaclides, does not give him this equipment but represents him as Homer did. Many of Xanthus' poems have been adapted by Stesichorus, for example the one called *The Oresteia.*

[1] See Xanthus 699.   [2] Homeric scholar, probably of 4th c. B.C.   [3] Strabo 15. 1. 9 says that the new guise of Heracles is due to Pisander of Rhodes, 7th or 6th c. epic poet.

**230** Pausanias, *Description of Greece*

The Thebans point out a memorial to the children Heracles had by Megara, and their account of the death[1] is exactly that given by Stesichorus of Himera and Panyassis in their verses. The Thebans add that Heracles in his madness intended to kill Amphitryon[2] too, but fell asleep first on being struck by the stone; it was Athena, they say, who aimed this stone, which they call 'the chastiser'.

[1] They were killed by Heracles in a fit of madness.   [2] His father. See Eur. *Heracles* 1001 ff.

**231** Plutarch, *On the malice of Herodotus*

And yet among the story-tellers of ancient times neither Homer nor Hesiod nor Archilochus nor Pisander nor Stesichorus nor Alcman nor Pindar made any mention of an Egyptian or Phoenician Heracles[1]: they all know this single Heracles, who is both Boeotian and Argive.[2]

**232** Plut. *de E apud Delph.* 21 (iii 24 Pohlenz-Sieveking)

εἰκότως οὖν ὁ Εὐριπίδης εἶπε (*Suppl.* 974b ss.) . . . καὶ πρότερος ἔτι τούτου ὁ Στησίχορος·

&lt;χορεύ&gt;ματά τοι μάλιστα<br>παιγμοσύνας &lt;τε&gt; φιλεῖ μολπάς τ' Ἀπόλλων,<br>κήδεα δὲ στοναχάς τ' Ἀΐδας ἔλαχε.

1 Wilamowitz: μάλα τοι codd.        2 τε suppl. Blomfield
3 Blomfield: κήδεα τε codd.

**233** P.Oxy. 2260 col. ii 18ss.

παρὰ δὲ Στησιχόρωι [κα]τὰ τὴν γένεσιν·

. . . τε]ύχεσι λαμπομέν[α<br>Παλλὰ]ς ὄρουσεν ἐπ' εὐρεῖαν χθ[ό]να.

2 Παλλὰς suppl. Merkelbach        cetera Lobel

Schol. Ap. Rhod. 4. 1310 (p. 313 Wendel)

πρῶτος Στησίχορος ἔφη σὺν ὅπλοις ἐκ τῆς τοῦ Διὸς κεφαλῆς ἀναπηδῆσαι τὴν Ἀθηνᾶν.

**234** Schol. AB Hom. *Il.* 23. 92 (ii 251, iv 309 Dindorf)

Διόνυσος Ἥφαιστον γενόμενον ἐν Νάξῳ μιᾷ τῶν Κυκλάδων ξενίσας ἔλαβε παρ' αὐτοῦ δῶρον χρύσεον ἀμφορέα. διωχθεὶς δὲ ὕστερον ὑπὸ Λυκούργου καὶ καταφυγὼν εἰς θάλασσαν, φιλοφρόνως αὐτὸν ὑποδεξαμένης Θέτιδος ἔδωκεν αὐτῇ τὸν ἡφαιστότευκτον ἀμφορέα. ἡ δὲ τῷ παιδὶ ἐχαρίσατο ὅπως μετὰ θάνατον ἐν αὐτῷ ἀποτεθῇ τὰ ὀστᾶ αὐτοῦ. ἱστορεῖ Στησίχορος.

**235** Schol. T Hom. *Il.* 6. 507 (c) (ii 217 Erbse)

Στησίχορος

κοιλωνύχων ἵππων πρύτανιν

τὸν Ποσειδῶνά φησιν.

# STESICHORUS

**232** Plutarch, *On the E at Delphi*

So it was appropriate for Euripides to say (*Suppliants* 974b ff.); and still earlier Stesichorus said,

Apollo loves dancing most of all and merriment and songs, but mourning and wailing are the portion of Hades.

**233** Papyrus commentary on a poetic text (2nd c. A.D.)

And in Stesichorus (Athena is described) at her birth:

. . . shining in armour Pallas leaped to the broad earth.

Scholiast on Apollonius of Rhodes ('Athena, when she leaped all shining from her father's head')

Stesichorus was the first to say that Athena sprang armed from the head of Zeus.

**234** Scholiast on *Iliad* 23. 92 ('the golden urn which your lady mother gave you')

When Dionysus had entertained Hephaestus on his arrival in Naxos, one of the Cyclades, he received from him the gift of a golden urn. Later, when he was pursued by Lycurgus and took refuge in the sea, Thetis gave him a kindly welcome, and he gave her the amphora, Hephaestus' handiwork. She gave it to her son,[1] so that when he died his bones might be put in it. The story is told by Stesichorus.

[1] Achilles.

**235** Scholiast on *Iliad* 6. 507 ('as a horse runs clattering over the plain')

Stesichorus calls Poseidon

lord of hollow-hoofed horses.

# GREEK LYRIC

**236** Paus. 9. 2. 3 (iii 3s. Rocha-Pereira)

τοῖς δὲ ἐκ Μεγάρων ἰοῦσι πηγή τέ ἐστιν ἐν δεξιᾷ καὶ προελθοῦ-
σιν ὀλίγον πέτρα· καλοῦσι δὲ τὴν μὲν Ἀκταίωνος κοίτην, ἐπὶ
ταύτῃ καθεύδειν φάμενοι τῇ πέτρᾳ τὸν Ἀκταίωνα ὁπότε κάμοι θη-
ρεύων, ἐς δὲ τὴν πηγὴν ἐνιδεῖν λέγουσιν αὐτὸν λουομένης Ἀρτέμι-
δος ἐν τῇ πηγῇ. Στησίχορος δὲ ὁ Ἱμεραῖος ἔγραψεν ἐλάφου περι-
βαλεῖν δέρμα Ἀκταίωνι τὴν θεόν, παρασκευάζουσάν οἱ τὸν ἐκ τῶν
κυνῶν θάνατον ἵνα δὴ μὴ γυναῖκα Σεμέλην λάβοι.

**237** Str. 1. 2. 34 (i 64 Kramer)

Ἡσίοδος δ' ἐν Καταλόγῳ (fr. 137 M.-W.) φησί· καὶ κούρην
Ἀράβοιο τὸν Ἑρμάων ἀκάκητα | γείνατο καὶ Θρονίη κούρη Βήλοιο
ἄνακτος. οὕτω δὲ καὶ Στησίχορος λέγει. εἰκάζειν οὖν ἔστιν ὅτι ἀπὸ
τούτου καὶ ἡ χώρα Ἀραβία ἤδη τότε ὠνομάζετο· κατὰ δὲ τοὺς
ἥρωας τυχὸν ἴσως οὔπω.

**238** Schol. Ap. Rhod. 1. 230–3 (p. 28 Wendel)

ὁ γὰρ Μινύας πολλὰς εἶχεν θυγατέρας. καὶ γὰρ ὁ Ἰάσων Ἀλκι-
μέδης ἐστὶ τῆς Κλυμένης τῆς Μινύου θυγατρός. Στησίχορος δὲ
Ἐτεοκλυμένης φησίν, Φερεκύδης δὲ (F.Gr.H. 3 F 104b) Ἀλκιμέ-
δης τῆς Φυλάκου.

# STESICHORUS

**236** Pausanias, *Description of Greece*

Travellers from Megara (to Plataea) have a spring on their right and, a little further on, a rock. They call the rock the bed of Actaeon, explaining that Actaeon used to sleep on it when exhausted from hunting; and they say that he looked into this spring when Artemis was bathing in it. Stesichorus of Himera wrote[1] that the goddess wrapped a deerskin round Actaeon,[2] ensuring that his hounds would kill him to prevent his marriage with Semele.[3]

[1] Perhaps in the *Europia*.      [2] H. J. Rose, *Mnemos.* 59 (1931) 431 f., took these words to mean that Actaeon was actually changed into a stag, as in Ovid's version (*Met.* 3. 131 ff.); so G. Nagy, *H.S.C.P.* 77 (1973) 179 f.      [3] Semele, daughter of Cadmus, Europa's brother, was reserved for Zeus.

**237** Strabo, *Geography* (on the name Arabia)

Hesiod says in the *Catalogue,* 'and the daughter of Arabus, son of guileless Hermaon[1] and Thronia, lord Belus' daughter'. Stesichorus says the same thing. So one might guess that by their day the country was called Arabia after Arabus, although it perhaps did not yet have that name at the time of the heroes.[2]

[1] Hermes.      [2] Strabo is arguing that Homer's form 'Erembians' (*Od.* 4. 84) need not be altered to 'Arabians'.

**238** Scholiast on Apollonius of Rhodes (most of the Argonauts 'claimed to be of the blood of the daughters of Minyas')

Minyas had many daughters: Jason himself is son of Alcimede, daughter of Minyas' daughter Clymene. Stesichorus[1] calls the latter Eteoclymene; Pherecydes makes him son of Alcimede, Phylacus' daughter.

[1] Perhaps in *Funeral Games of Pelias.*

**239** *Et. Gen.* (p. 44 Calame)

Τυφωέα· Ἡσίοδος (*Theog.* 821) Γῆς γενεαλογεῖ, Στησίχορος δὲ Ἥρας μόνης κατὰ μνησικακίαν Διὸς τεκούσης αὐτόν.

cf. *Et. Mag.* 772. 49, *Et. Sym.* cod. V ibid. Gaisford

**240** Eust. *Il.* 9. 43 (i 16 van der Valk)

οὐ μόνον γὰρ Ἡσίοδος ἐκ τῆς τῶν Μουσῶν ἐπικλήσεως ἄρχεται (*Theog.* 1ss., *Op.* 1ss.) . . . ἀλλὰ καὶ Στησίχορος ἐν τῷ

δεῦρ' ἄγε, Καλλιόπεια λίγεια.

cf. 10. 7

**241** Ael. Arist. *Or.* 33. 2 (ii 228 Keil)

καὶ ταῦτα μὲν δὴ ταῦτα. μέτειμι δ' ἐφ' ἕτερον προοίμιον κατὰ Στησίχορον.

**242** Athen. 4. 154f (i 349s. Kaibel)

ὁπότε δὲ παροξύνεται, τὸ μάχεσθαι ῥῆμα περιέχει, ὡς ἐν τῷ πυγμάχος, ναυμάχος,

αὐτόν σε πυλαιμάχε πρῶτον

παρὰ Στησιχόρῳ.

cf. schol. A Hom. *Il.* 5. 31 (ii 7 Erbse) τειχεσιπλῆτα· . . . ἐστὶν ἐπίθετον ἀνάλογον τῷ παρὰ Στησιχόρῳ πυλαιμάχῳ.

Blomfield: πυλα- Athen.    πυλε- schol. Hom.

**243** Schol. Ap. Rhod. 3. 106 (p. 220 Wendel)

ῥαδινῆς· . . . Στησίχορος (sc. ἔταξε τὸ ῥαδινὸν) ἐπὶ τοῦ εὐτόνου·

ῥαδινοὺς δ' ἐπέπεμπον ἄκοντας.

ἔπεμπον codd. PH

# STESICHORUS

**239** *Etymologicum Genuinum*

Typhoeus: Hesiod makes him son of Gaia (Earth), Stesichorus son of Hera, who bore him without a father in order to spite Zeus.[1]

[1] Zeus had given birth to Athena (233): cf. *h. Apoll.* 305 ff.

**240** Eustathius on *Iliad* 1. 1 ('Tell, Muse . . .')

For not only Hesiod begins with his invocation of the Muses: . . . Stesichorus does so too with his

> Come hither, clear-voiced Calliopia.

**241** Aristides, *Orations*

So much for that; and I shall turn to another prelude in the manner of Stesichorus.

**242** Athenaeus, *Scholars at Dinner*

But when the word ending in -μαχος is accented on the second-last syllable, it is a compound of the verb μάχομαι, 'fight',[1] as in πυγμάχος, 'fist-fighter', ναυμάχος, 'ship-fighter'; so πυλαιμάχος, 'gate fighter', in Stesichorus:

> yourself first, you fighter at the gate.[2]

[1] Not of the noun μαχή, 'fight', which gives e.g. σύμμαχος.
[2] Perhaps of Ares, like Homer's τειχεσιπλῆτα, 'wall-stormer'.

**243** Scholiast on Apollonius of Rhodes (ῥαδινῆς, 'slender')

Stesichorus used the word in the sense of 'vigorous'[1]:

> and they hurled slender javelins.

[1] An improbable statement: see also Anacr. 456, Ibyc. 336.

**244** Stob. 4. 56. 15 (v 1126 Hense) (παρηγορικά)

Στησιχόρου·

ἀτέλεστά τε γὰρ καὶ ἀμάχανα τοὺς θανόντας
κλαίειν.

cf. Apostol. *cent.* iv 23h (ii 316 Leutsch-Schneidewin)

1 Ahrens: ἀτελέστατα γὰρ, ἀτέλεστα γὰρ codd.          Schneidewin:
ἀμήχ- codd.

**245** Stob. 4. 58. 5 (ὅτι τῶν πλείστων μετὰ θάνατον ἡ μνήμη
διαρρεῖ ταχέως)

Στησιχόρου·

θανόντος ἀνδρὸς πᾶσα †πολιὰ† ποτ᾽ ἀνθρώπων χάρις.

cf. Arsen. 29. 73 = Apostol. cent. viii 83d (ii 455 Leutsch): θ. ἀ. πᾶσ᾽
†ὄλυτ᾽† ἀ. χ.

πᾶσ᾽ ἀπόλλυταί ποτ᾽ ἀ. χ. Kleine post Scaliger      πᾶσ᾽ ἀπώλ<ετ᾽> ἀ
ποτ᾽ ( = ποτὶ) ἀ. χ. Page      ἀπώλετο πᾶσα ποτ᾽ ἀ. χ. West

**246** *Et. Gud.* (i 34. 6 de Stefani)

Ἄιος· ὄνομα παρὰ τῷ Στησιχόρῳ.

cf. Choerob. ap. *Anecd. Oxon.* ii 171 Cramer, Cyrill. *lex.* in Cod.
Bodl. Auct. T. II (11) f. 90a

**247** Ptolem. Chennus *Nov. Hist.* 3. 10 (p. 24 Chatzis) ap.
Phot. *Bibl.* 148a. 31s. (iii 56 Henry)

περὶ τῶν παρὰ Στησιχόρῳ ζητουμένων

ἀκεσταλίων

ὀρνίθων.

# STESICHORUS

**244** Stobaeus, *Anthology* (words of consolation)

Stesichorus:

for it is futile and pointless to weep for the dead.

**245** Stobaeus, *Anthology* (the remembrance of most men fades quickly after their death)

Stesichorus:

When a man dies, all the goodwill from men perishes.

**246** *Etymologicum Gudianum*

Aïus[1]:

a name in Stesichorus.

[1] Vürtheim notes *Il.* 15. 365 ἦιε Φοῖβε, where Apollo has the epithet *eïos*, i.e. 'worshipped with the cry, e, e!'

**247** Ptolemaeus the Quail, *New History* (excerpted in Photius, *Library*)

On the unexplained

'acestalian' birds[1]

in Stesichorus.

[1] Still unexplained.

**248** Aristot. *Hist. Anim.* 5. 9. 542b 24 (p. 162s. Dittmeyer)

πάντων δὲ σπανιώτατον ἰδεῖν ἀλκυόνα ἐστίν· σχεδὸν γὰρ περὶ
Πλειάδος δύσιν καὶ τροπὰς ὁρᾶται μόνον καὶ ἐν τοῖς ὑφόρμοις ὅσον
περιπταμένη περὶ τὸ πλοῖον ἀφανίζεται εὐθύς. διὸ καὶ Στησίχορος
τοῦτον τὸν τρόπον ἐμνήσθη περὶ αὐτῆς.

**249** *Epim. Hom.* (i 74 Dyck) = Hdn. π. παθ. 194 (ii 239
Lentz)

ὡς δὲ παρὰ τὸ ἴξω ἴξαλος . . . κονίσω κονίσαλος, οὕτως καὶ ἴψω
ἴψαλος, ἀφ' οὗ παρὰ Στησιχόρῳ

> ἀνίψαλον παῖδα,

τὸν ἀβλαβῆ.

cf. *Anecd. Oxon.* i 205 Cramer, *Et. Mag.* 110. 45 + *Et. Sym.*, Hsch. A
5223 ἀνίψανον· οὐ βεβλαμμένον, οἱ δὲ ἡλικίας τάξιν.

ἀνίψανον *Et. Mag.* cod. D, *Et. Sym.*, Hsch.     ἀνίψαλλον *Et. Mag.* rell.

**250** Athen. 5. 180e (i 414 Kaibel)

καλεῖ δὲ Στησίχορος μὲν τὴν Μοῦσαν

> ἀρχεσίμολπον.

cf. Eust. *Od.* 1480. 22

fort. ἀρχεσίμολπε θεά West

**251** *Et. Gud.* s.v. (i 225 de Stefani)

> ἄτερπνος·

οὕτως ὁ ἄγρυπνος παρὰ Ῥηγίνοις, ὡς καὶ παρ' Ἰβύκῳ καὶ Στησι-
χόρῳ. . . . ἐστὶ γὰρ κατ' ἐντέλειαν ἀτέρυπνος, ὁ χωρὶς ὢν ὕπνου.

cf. *Et. Mag.* 163. 8, *Anecd. Par.* iv 61. 22 Cramer

# STESICHORUS

**248** Aristotle, *Account of Animals*

It is the most uncommon thing of all to see a halcyon: the bird is hardly ever observed except at the setting of the Pleiads[1] and at the winter solstice,[2] and then in anchorages it flies around the ship for a brief moment and immediately disappears. Stesichorus mentioned this characteristic.

[1] In late October.      [2] When there were fourteen 'halcyon' days of calm (Simon. 508).

**249** *Homeric Parsings* = Herodian, *On the Modification of Words*

As ἴξω,[1] 'come', gives ἴξαλος, 'bounding', ... and κονίσω,[1] 'make dusty', gives κονίσαλος, 'dust cloud', so ἴψω,[1] 'harm', gives ἴψαλος, 'harmed', whence Stesichorus' ἀνίψαλος, 'unharmed':

> unharmed child.

[1] Future tenses.

**250** Athenaeus, *Scholars at Dinner*

Stesichorus calls the Muse

> beginner of song and dance.

**251** *Etymologicum Gudianum*

ἄτερπνος: the Rhegine term for

> sleepless,

as in Ibycus (328) and Stesichorus.... In full it is ἀτέρυπνος, 'without sleep'.

171

**252** Schol. in Dion. Thrac. *Art.* 19 (p. 278 Hilgard) = *Anecd. Gr.* ii 945. 25 Bekker

οἷον ἔνδοθεν,

ἔξοθεν

παρὰ Στησιχόρῳ, πρόσσοθεν παρ᾽ Ὁμήρῳ (*Il.* 23. 533).


**253** *Et. Mag.* 100. 47 (cf. *Et. Sym.* cod. V ibid.), *Et. Parv.* A 50 (p. 9 Pintaudi), *Et. Gud.* (i 135 de Stefani)

ἀνασφῆλαι· ἀναρρωσθῆναι, σφῆλον γὰρ τὸ ἰσχυρόν· Στησίχορος

ἐρίσφηλον

ἔφη τὸν Ἡρακλέα, ἴσον τῷ ἐρισθενῆ.

cf. *Et. Gen.* A, Hsch. A 7967 (i 270 Latte) s.v. ἄσφηλοι, Zonar. s.v. ἀνασφήλας.

**254** *Et. Mag.* 427. 48

Στησίχορος δὲ Τάρταρον

ἠλίβατον

τὸν βαθὺν λέγει.

ita Phot. *Lex.* s.v. (i 258 Naber), Hsch. H 352 (ii 279 Latte), schol. Lucian. *Apol.* (p. 236 Rabe)

**255** Schol. BT Hom. *Il.* 21. 575 (b) (v 256 Erbse) = *Hdn. Iliac. Prosod.* (ii 118s. Lentz)

Ἀρίσταρχός τινάς φησι γράφειν κυνυλαγμόν· καὶ Στησίχορος δὲ ἔοικεν οὕτως ἀνεγνωκέναι. φησὶ γοῦν

ἀπειρεσίοιο κυνυλαγμοῖο.

cf. Eust. *Il.* 1251. 61

-οι -οί schol. B (fort. recte)     -ου κυνηλαγμοῦ Eust.

# STESICHORUS

**252** Scholiast on Dionysius of Thrace (on the accent of words in -οθεν)

For example ἔνδοθεν, '(from) inside', ἔξοθεν in Stesichorus,[1]

> (from) outside,

πρόσσοθεν, 'before', in Homer.

[1] Found in Ibyc. 330. 1.

**253** *Etymologicum Magnum* +

ἀνα-σφῆλαι: 'to recover one's strength', since σφῆλος means 'strong'. Stesichorus called Heracles ἐρί-σφηλος,

> very strong,

the equivalent of ἐρι-σθενής, 'very mighty'.

**254** *Etymologicum Magnum*

Stesichorus calls Tartarus

> steep,

in the sense of 'deep'.

**255** Scholiast and Herodian on *Iliad* 21. 575 (ἐπεί κεν ὑλαγμὸν ἀκούσῃ, 'when it hears barking')

Aristarchus says that some write κυνυλαγμόν, 'the barking of dogs'. Stesichorus seems to have read this; at any rate he says

> unending barking of dogs.

**256** Eust. *Il.* 524. 28 (ii 27 van der Valk)

καὶ γὰρ

λεύκιππος

λέγεται παρὰ Στησιχόρῳ ἐπιθετικῶς.

**257** *Et. Gen.* (p. 36 Calame)

μάτην· ἐστὶ γὰρ παρὰ τὸ ἡ μάτη θηλυκόν. Στησίχορος

μάτας εἰπών.

εἶτα ἡ αἰτιατικὴ εἰς ἐπιρρηματικὴν σύνταξιν.

cf. Zonar. 1338 Στησίχορος· μάτας εἰπών

*Et. Gen.* cod. B εἶπες (test. Alpers)

**258** Hsch. B 1226 (i 350 Latte)

βρυαλίκται· πολεμικοὶ ὀρχησταί·

<βρυαλίκται> μενέδουποι

Ἴβυκος (335) καὶ (ἢ Edmonds) Στησίχορος.

Hermann: ωρχηται μεναιδοιπου cod.

**259** *Anecd. Gr.* iii 1397 Bekker (Choerob. *in Theodos.*) = Hdn. (i 45, ii 743 Lentz)

Μεσόνυξ,

(gen.) Μεσόνυχος· εἷς τῶν ἑπτὰ πλανήτων παρὰ τοῖς Πυθαγορείοις ὀνομάζεται. μέμνηται Στησίχορος.

**256** Eustathius on *Iliad* 5. 77

In Stesichorus[1] we find λεύκιππος,

> white-horsed,

as an adjective.[2]

[1] Cf. Ibyc. 285. 1    [2] Not as a proper name.

**257** *Etymologicum Genuinum* on μάτην, 'in vain, foolishly'

The word is derived from the feminine noun μάτη, 'folly'. Stesichorus uses the plural:

> speaking foolish things.[1]

The accusative singular comes to be used adverbially.

[1] Text uncertain: perhaps 'you spoke foolish things'.

**258** Hesychius, *Lexicon*

βρυαλίκται: war-dancers:

> war-dancers steadfast in battle

in Ibycus (335) and Stesichorus.[1]

[1] It is not clear whether they used both the noun 'war-dancers' and the adjective 'steadfast in battle', and it is unlikely that both poets used such a rare phrase: perhaps 'Ibycus or Stesichorus' as in 179.

**259** Choeroboscus and Herodian

> Midnight-star:

the Pythagorean name for one of the seven planets.[1] Stesichorus mentions it.

[1] Mars, or less probably Jupiter or Saturn: see P. J. Bicknell, *Apeiron* 2 (1968) 10 ff.

# GREEK LYRIC

**260** Schol. Ap. Rhod. 4. 973 (p. 300 Wendel)

ὀρείχαλκος·

εἶδος χαλκοῦ. . . . μνημονεύει καὶ Στησίχορος καὶ Βακχυλίδης (fr. 51 Snell).

cf. Didym. Chalc. fr. 34a Schmidt, Ar. Byz. fr. 413 Slater

**261** Phot. *Lex.* (ii 76 Naber)

πέποσχα·

Δωριέων τινὲς τούτῳ κέχρηνται ὧν καὶ Στησίχορός ἐστιν.

**262** Schol. Ar. *Av.* 1302 (p. 239 White)

ὁ

πηνέλοψ

νήττῃ μέν ἐστιν ὅμοιον, περιστερᾶς δὲ μέγεθος· μέμνηται δὲ αὐτοῦ Στησίχορος καὶ Ἴβυκος (317. 3).

**263** Str. 8. 3. 31 (ii 141 Kramer)

Στησίχορον δὲ καλεῖν πόλιν τὴν χώραν Πίσαν λεγομένην ὡς ὁ ποιητὴς τὴν Λέσβον Μάκαρος πόλιν, Εὐριπίδης δ' ἐν Ἴωνι (294)· Εὔβοι' Ἀθήναις ἐστί τις γείτων πόλις.

# STESICHORUS

**260** Scholiast on Apollonius of Rhodes

### orichalc,[1]

a kind of copper. It is mentioned by Stesichorus[2] and Bacchylides.

[1] 'Mountain-copper'.     [2] It is in Ibyc. 282(a) 42 f.

**261** Photius, *Lexicon*

### I have suffered:

some of the Doric writers use this form (πέποσχα for Attic πέπονθα), among them Stesichorus.

**262** Scholiast on Aristophanes, *Birds*

The penelops,

### widgeon,

is a bird like a duck but dove-sized; it is mentioned by Stesichorus and Ibycus (317).[1]

[1] Also by Alcaeus 345.

**263** Strabo, *Geography*

Stesichorus, they say, calls the district known as Pisa[1] a city (πόλις) just as Homer calls Lesbos 'the city of Macar'[2] and Euripides in his *Ion* has 'Euboea is a neighbouring city to Athens.'

[1] The region around Olympia in N. W. Peloponnese.     [2] But in *Il*. 24. 544 the expression is 'the seat of Macar'.

**264** *Epim. Hom.* (*Anecd. Oxon.* i 191s. Cramer) = Hdn. π. παθ. 480 (ii 316 Lentz)

Δωριεῖς γὰρ τὸ ἐφοίτα ἐφοίτη λέγουσι καὶ τὸ ἐσύλα ἐσύλη καὶ τὸ ηὗδα ηὗδη. ὁ γοῦν Στησίχορός φησι

ποταύδη

ὃ λέγει ὁ ποιητὴς προσηύδα.

**265** Eust. *Il.* 772. 3 (ii 789 van der Valk)

ἡ δὲ παροιμία τοὺς φθονεροὺς καὶ ψογεροὺς Τελχῖνας ὡς ἐκ τῶν εἰρημένων καλεῖ. Στησίχορος δέ, φασί, τὰς Κῆρας καὶ τὰς σκοτώσεις

Τελχῖνας

προσηγόρευσε.

**266** Eust. *Od.* 1441. 16 = Philoxenus fr. 339b Theodoridis

Στησίχορος δὲ

ὑπερθυμέστατον ἀνδρῶν.

**267** Schol. Pind. *Ol.* 9. 129 (i 297 Drachmann)

ἔπειτα χάρμα· νῦν ἀντὶ τοῦ χαρά· Ὅμηρος δὲ ἐπὶ τῆς μάχης, οἱ δὲ περὶ Ἴβυκον (340) καὶ Στησίχορον

χάρμην

τὴν ἐπιδορατίδα φασίν.

# STESICHORUS

**264** *Homeric Parsings* = Herodian (on *Il.* 1. 92 ηὔδα, 'spoke')

Doric writers use ἐφοίτη for ἐφοίτα, ἐσύλη for ἐσύλα, ηὔδη for ηὔδα; at any rate Stesichorus has ποταύδη,

addressed,

where Homer has προσηύδα.

**265** Eustathius on *Iliad* 9. 525

The proverb calls spiteful and fault-finding people Telchines, as fits what has been said above; but Stesichorus, they say, used the term

Telchines

of death-spirits and darkenings.[1]

[1] Eclipses (cf. 271)? Killings?

**266** Eustathius on *Odyssey* 2. 190 (ἀνιηρέστερον)

Stesichorus has ὑπερθυμέστατος[1]:

most high-minded of men.

[1] For ὑπερθυμότατος.

**267** Scholiast on Pindar, *Olympian* 9. 86 (χάρμαι, 'joyous victories')

Here χάρμα is the equivalent of χαρά, 'joy'. But Homer uses χάρμη of 'battle', and Ibycus (340) and Stesichorus[1] use it of the

spear-point.

[1] Also Pindar, fr. 70c. 13 Snell.

# GREEK LYRIC

**268** Schol. Eur. *Rhes.* 5 (ii 326 Schwartz)

οἱ ἀρχαῖοι εἰς τρεῖς φυλακὰς νέμουσι τὴν νύκτα. Ὅμηρος ...
(*Od.* 14. 483). Στησίχορος δὲ καὶ Σιμωνίδης (644) πενταφύλα-
λόν φασιν ⟦ὑποτίθεσθαι τὴν νύκτα⟧.

Schwartz: στησί (superscr. χρ) δὲ ὁ σιμ. π. φησιν ὑ. τ. ν. cod. A
Στησίχορον δὲ ὁ Σιμ. π. φησιν ὑ. τ. ν. Vater

**269** Argum. in [Hes.] *Scut.* (*O.C.T.* p. 86 Solmsen)

καὶ Στησίχορος δέ φησιν Ἡσιόδου εἶναι τὸ ποίημα.

**270** Vibius Sequester *de fluminibus fontibus etc.* (p. 15 Gelsomino)

Himera oppido Thermitanorum dedit nomen Himerae.
hoc flumen in duas partes findi ait Stesichorus, unam in
Tyrrhenum mare, aliam in Libycum decurrere.

Himer. *Or.* 27. 27 (p. 126s. Colonna)

κοσμεῖ μὲν γὰρ Ἀνακρέων τὴν Τηίων πόλιν τοῖς μέλεσι (490),
... τὴν δὲ Ἱμέραν τὴν Σικελικὴν οὐκ ἐλευθέραν ποιεῖ μόνον τῶν
τυράννων ἀλλὰ καὶ λόγοις κοσμεῖ Στησίχορος.

# STESICHORUS

**268** Scholiast on Euripides, *Rhesus* ('the fourth watch of the night')

The ancients divide the night into three watches, e.g. Homer (*Od.* 14. 483); but Stesichorus and Simonides (644)[1] speak of

> night with its five watches.[2]

[1] Text uncertain: perhaps 'but according to Simonides Stesichorus assumes a night of five watches'.    [2] So Euripides in *Rhesus* 562.

**269** Introduction to 'Hesiod', *Shield of Heracles*

Stesichorus also says that the poem[1] is by Hesiod.[2]

[1] The *Shield*, in its present form a work of early 6th c. B.C., tells in 57 ff., 325 ff., of Heracles' fight with Cycnus (see Stes. 207). [2] S. may have named Hesiod, e.g. in his *Cycnus* (207), as he named Xanthus (229); see R. Janko, *C.Q.* 36 (1986) 41 f.

**270** Vibius Sequester, *On rivers, springs etc.*

The river Himera gave its name to Himera, the town of the Thermitani.[1] Stesichorus says it forks into two streams, one flowing (north) into the Tyrrhenian Sea, the other (south) into the Libyan Sea.[2]

[1] In 409 B.C. Carthage destroyed the original Himera and a year later founded Thermae Himeraeae nearby.    [2] There are two rivers, the North and the South Himera.

Himerius, *Orations*[1]

For Anacreon adorns the city of Teos in his songs, ... and Stesichorus not only frees Sicilian Himera from tyrants[2] but adorns it with words.

[1] Cf. Alc. test. 1 n. 1, Anacr. 490, Simon. 621, Bacch. fr. 43.
[2] See test. 16.

Sil. Ital. 14. 232ss.

litora Thermarum prisca dotata Camena
armavere suos qua mergitur Himera ponto
Aeolico.

**271** Plin. *N. H.* 2. 54 (i 143 Mayhoff)

viri ingentes supraque mortalia, tantorum numinum
lege deprehensa et misera hominum mente iam soluta, in
defectibus scelera aut mortem aliquam siderum pavente —
quo in metu fuisse Stesichori et Pindari vatum sublimia
ora palam est deliquio solis . . .

Plut. *de fac. in orbe lun.* 19. 931e (v 3. 57 Hubert-Pohlenz)

εἰ δὲ μή, Θέων ἡμῖν οὗτος τὸν Μίμνερμον (fr. 20 West) ἐπάξει
καὶ τὸν Κυδίαν (fr. 715 *P.M.G.*) καὶ τὸν Ἀρχίλοχον (fr. 122
West), πρὸς δὲ τούτοις τὸν Στησίχορον καὶ τὸν Πίνδαρον ἐν ταῖς
ἐκλείψεσιν ὀλοφυρομένους, 'ἄστρον φανερώτατον κλεπτόμενον'
(cf. Pind. *Pae.* 9. 2s.) καὶ

μέσῳ ἄματι νύκτα γινομέναν

καὶ τὴν ἀκτῖνα τοῦ ἡλίου 'σκότους ἀτραπὸν <ἐσσυμέναν>' (cf.
Pind. *Pae.* 9. 1, 5) φάσκοντας.

**272** Hsch. N 122 (ii 698 Latte)

ναυκληρώσιμοι στεγαί· τὰ πανδοκεῖα· †ἐπεὶ ἔνιοι ἐμπορεῖα λέ-
γουσιν. ὡς καὶ Στησίχορος

ἐμπορικὸν οἶκον

φησιν.†

---

[1] An obscure entry, presumably corrupt, from this point onwards.
Stesichorus is unlikely to have used the prosaic word ἐμπορικός.

# STESICHORUS

Silius Italicus, *Punic War*

The shore of Thermae, richly endowed by the ancient Muse, armed its men, where the Himera flows into the Aeolian Sea.

**271** Pliny, *Natural History* (on Thales and Hipparchus, who predicted eclipses)

O mighty heroes, more than mortal, who grasped the law of those great divinities (sc. sun and moon) and released from terror the wretched mind of men, who at eclipses of the stars feared crimes or some death — those sublime singers Stesichorus[1] and Pindar clearly felt such fear at an eclipse of the sun ...

[1] Probably in 557 B.C.: see M. L. West, *C.Q.* 21 (1971) 306.

Plutarch, *The Face on the Moon*

If you do not (remember the recent eclipse of the sun), Theon here will quote us Mimnermus and Cydias and Archilochus and in addition Stesichorus[1] and Pindar lamenting during eclipses and speaking of 'the most conspicuous star stolen away' and of

### night falling at mid-day

and of the sun's beam 'racing along the path of darkness'.

[1] The first and third quotations are inaccurate versions of Pindar, *Paean* 9. 1–5; the second is presumably from Stesichorus.

**272** Hesychius, *Lexicon*

Rooms to let: inns; since[1] some say 'trading-stations': Stesichorus, for example, has

### house of commerce.

**273** Schol. Hom. *Il.* 21. 65ss. ap. P.Oxy. 221 col. ii

ηὔξηκ[εν ὁ Λυκάων τὴν δέησ]ιν· εὐλόγως, [ὅπως συγγνώμης τύχηι·] καὶ ἄλλως δὲ [ἅπαντες οἱ μέλλον]τες τελευτᾶν [μακρολόγοι, ὅπως τοσοῦ]τόν γε χρόνο[ν κερδαίνωσι· καὶ παρὰ] Στησιχόρωι [

suppl. Wilamowitz e schol. Hom. BT (vid. v 82 Erbse)

**274** = Lamprocles 735

P.Oxy. 1611 frr. 5 + 43

ταις Φ[ρύ]ν[ιχος] ... ἀφηγο[ύ]μεν[ος] ... ῾Πα[λ]λά[δα] περ[σέπολιν κλήιζ]ω π[ολεμαδόκο]ν ἁγνὰν π[αῖδα Διὸς] μεγάλου δ[αμάσιπ]πον.' οὕτω παρα[ποιεῖ ?]· διαποροῦσι γὰρ ο[ὐκ ὀ]λίγοι π[ε]ρὶ τ[ού]των κα[θ]άπερ Χαμαιλέων (fr. 29c Wehrli) πότερόν ποτε Στη[σι]χόρου ἐστὶν ἢ Λαμπροκλ[έο]υς, κ[αίπ]ερ τοῦ Φρυν[ίχου Λαμ]προκλεῖ μα[θη<τῆι ?> Μίδωνος ?] προσνέμον[τος· καὶ ᾽Α]ριστοφάνης [δὲ? παραπ]οιεῖ λέγων· [Παλλάδα] π[ε]ρσέ[π]ο(λιν)

Schol. RV Ar. *Nub.* 967 (I 3. 1. 186 Holwerda)

Παλλάδα περσέπολιν δεινάν·

ἀρχὴ ἄσματος Στησιχόρου (van Leeuwen: Φρυνίχου cod. R), ὡς ᾽Ερατοσθένης φησίν. Φρύνιχος δὲ αὐτοῦ τούτου τοῦ ἄσματος μνημονεύει ὡς Λαμπροκλέους ὄντος· Παλλάδα περσέπτολιν κλήιζω πολεμαδόκον ἁγνὰν παῖδα Διὸς μεγάλου.

cf. schol. EMNp (185s. Holwerda), ubi Π. π. δ. θεὸν ἐγρεκύδοιμον

# STESICHORUS

**273** Scholiast on *Iliad* 21. 73 ff.

Lycaon has prolonged his plea — and with good reason, in order to win sympathy[1]; and in any case those who are on the point of dying all talk at great length, in order to gain so much time at least; for example, in Stesichorus[2] . . .

[1] From Achilles.    [2] Perhaps the reference is to Geryon: cf. S 11.

**274** = Lamprocles 735

Papyrus (early 3rd c. A.D.) containing literary criticism

. . . Phrynichus . . . telling . . . 'Pallas, sacker of cities, I summon, the warlike, the pure, the child of great Zeus, horse-tamer': he[1] takes the words over in this form. For many scholars, Chamaeleon[2] among them, are vexed over these lines: were they by Stesichorus or by Lamprocles[3]? Yet Phrynichus attributes them to Lamprocles, pupil of Midon. Aristophanes also takes them over, saying 'Pallas, sacker of cities, the grim'.

[1] Phrynichus, presumably the 5th c. comic poet.    [2] Peripatetic grammarian, *c*. 350–after 281 B.C.: see test. 31.    [3] Athenian poet, early 5th c.

Scholiast (RV) on Aristophanes, *Clouds* 967

Pallas, sacker of cities, the grim[1]:

the beginning of a song of Stesichorus,[2] as Eratosthenes[3] says. Phrynichus mentions this same song as being by Lamprocles: 'Pallas, sacker of cities, I summon, the warlike, the pure, child of great Zeus.'

[1] Used by Aristophanes as a sample of traditional song taught in the old-style education.    [2] So van Leeuwen: the mss. have 'Phrynichus'.    [3] Geographer and literary critic of Alexandria, 3rd c. B.C.

# GREEK LYRIC

Schol. Aristid. *Or.* 46. 162 = 3. 155 Behr (iii 538 Dindorf)

Παλλάδα περσέπτολιν· . . . τὸν δὲ ποιητὴν αὐτοῦ Ῥοῦφος καὶ Διονύσιος ἱστοροῦσιν ἐν τῇ Μουσικῇ Φρύνιχόν τινα, ἄλλοι δέ φασι Λαμπροκλέα ἢ Στησίχορον. τὸ δὲ δεινὰν γελοίως ἀντίκειται <παρὰ τῷ κωμικῷ add. cod. Oxon.>· τὸ γὰρ ᾆσμα οὕτως ἔχει· Παλλάδα περσέπολιν κλεισοπολεμοδόκον . . .

cf. Tzetz. *chil.* 1. 686 (p. 31 Leone), schol. ad loc. (p. 553 Leone), Dion. Chrys. *Or.* 13. 19 (i 184 von Arnim), *Sud.* T 490 (iv 539 Adler)

**274A** Philodem. *de piet.* 1088 III (p. 39 Gomperz)

κατ' Ἀπολλων[ί]δη (*Tr.G.F.* i 308, F 3 Snell) καὶ κατὰ [Ἡσίο]δον καὶ κα[τὰ Στη]σίχορον ἐν [Ὀρεστεί]αι καὶ παρ' ἃ [πρὶν ἔ]φην, τὸν [Κρόνον δι'] αὐτοῦ ταρ[ταροῦσθ]α̣[ι .

usque ad ἐν Ὀρεστείαι suppl. Bücheler, ἐν [Γηρυονί]δι Bergk cetera Philippson (*Hermes* 55, 1920, 250)

**275** artis metricae scriptorum testimonia

(a) (i) Diomed. *ars gramm.* 3 (i 512 Keil)

angelicum metrum celeritate nuntiis aptum Stesichorus invenit. unam enim ultimam syllabam detraxit hexametro et fecit tale:

> optima Calliope miranda poematibus

---

[1] For analysis see M. W. Haslam, *Q.U.C.C.* 17 (1974) 13 f.

# STESICHORUS

Scholiast on Aelius Aristides ('Pallas, sacker of cities')

... the composer of this song, according to Rufus[1] and Dionysius[2] in their *Music,* was a certain Phrynichus, but according to others it was Lamprocles or Stesichorus.[3] The word 'grim' is a comic substitution in Aristophanes, for the song runs 'Pallas, sacker of cities, I summon...'

[1] Scholar of Greek literature, date unknown (*R.E.* Rufus 17).  [2] D. of Halicarnassus, Greek literary critic of Hadrian's time.  [3] The testimonia are badly confused: the truth may be that there were poems by Stesichorus and by Lamprocles (a century later), both of which began 'Pallas, sacker of cities'; that Stesichorus continued with 'the grim goddess, rouser of war' (the fuller text in other scholia on Aristophanes), the text from which Aristophanes quoted three words; and that Aristophanes' contemporary Phrynichus quoted 'Pallas, sacker of cities, I summon... of great Zeus', naming Lamprocles as author. See K. J. Dover on *Clouds* 967, D. L. Page at *P.M.G.* 735.

## 274A Philodemus, *Piety*

... according to Apollonides[1] and Hesiod and Stesichorus in his (*Oresteia*?) and contrary to what I said before, that Cronus was thrown into Tartarus by him.[2]

[1] Tragedian, 2nd c. B.C.   [2] His son Zeus? Text very uncertain.

## 275 Writers on metre[1]

### (a) (i) Diomedes, *Grammar*

The 'angelic' metre, which is suited by its rapidity to messengers (ἄγγελοι), was invented by Stesichorus: he removed one syllable, the last, from the hexameter and produced the following:

$$-\cup\cup-\cup\cup---\cup\cup-\cup\cup-{}^2$$

[2] West suggests that the Latin words selected to show the rhythm are a translation of Stesichorus, e.g. 'Excellent Calliope, admired for your poetry and songs' (*Z.P.E.* 4, 1969, 137).

(ii) Fr. Bob. (vi 623 Keil)

octametrum catalecticum, quo usus est Stesichorus in Sicilia ('in Scilla' West):

> audiat haec nostri mela carminis et tunc per tua rura
>   volabit

(iii) Serv. *cent. metr.* (iv 461 Keil)

(dact.) stesichoreum constat pentametro catalectico, ut est hoc:

> Marsya cede deo, tua carmina flebis

(iv) Serv. *ibid.* (iv 461 Keil)

stesichoreum constat (dact.) heptametro catalectico, ut est hoc:

Aeacides iuvenis trahit Hectora, plangite Pergama Troes

*ibid.* (iv 462 Keil)

stesichoreum constat (anap.) trimetro acatalecto, ut est hoc:

> iacet in thalamo tibi virgo decens Veneris specie

Caes. Bass. *metr.* 2 (vi 256 Keil)

archebuleus (Stesichorus ... et Ibycus et Pindarus et Simonides usi sunt eo, sed passim et promiscue): exemplum,

> tibi nascitur omne pecus, tibi crescit herba

## (ii) Bobbio fragment on metres

The (dactylic) octameter catalectic, which Stesichorus used in Sicily[1]:

$$-\cup\cup--\cup\cup-\cup\cup\,||\;---\cup\cup-\cup\cup-\underline{\cup}$$

[1] West reads 'in his *Scylla*' (*C.Q.* 20, 1970, 206): see fr. 220.

## (iii) Servius, *Hundred Metres*

The stesichorean[1] is a (dactylic) pentameter catalectic:

$$-\cup\cup-\cup\cup-\cup\cup-\cup\cup-\underline{\cup}$$

[1] The term is also applied by the scholiast on Pindar to the trochaic trimeter and dimeter acatalectic (i 348, iii 196 Drachmann), units which are at home in dactylo-epitrites.

## (iv) Servius, *Hundred Metres*

dactylic heptameter catalectic (stesichorean):

$$-\cup\cup-\cup\cup-\cup\cup-\cup\cup-\cup\cup-\underline{\cup}$$

(e.g. S 148. 3–4)

anapaestic trimeter acatalectic (stesichorean):

$$\cup\cup-\cup\cup-\cup\cup-\cup\cup-\cup\cup-$$

(e.g. S 15 col. ii 10–11)

Caesius Bassus, *Metres*

archebulean, used by Stesichorus etc.:

$$\cup\cup-\cup\cup-\cup\cup-\cup\cup-\cup-\underline{\cup}$$

(e.g. 244. 1)

GREEK LYRIC

M. Plot. Sacerd. 3. 11 (vi 543s. Keil)

encomiologicum stesichoreum:
            mollibus in pueris aut in puellis

(b) = test. 30

MISCELLANEA

**276** (a) Athen. 13. 601a (iii 324s. Kaibel)

καὶ Στησίχορος δ' οὐ μετρίως ἐρωτικὸς γενόμενος συνέστησε καὶ τοῦτον τὸν τρόπον τῶν ᾀσμάτων, ἃ δὴ καὶ τὸ παλαιὸν ἐκαλεῖτο παίδεια καὶ παιδικά.

(b) Eupol. fr. 148 K.-A. = test. 33

Luc. *Ver. Hist.* 2. 15 = Arion test. 7

Athen. 6. 250b (ii 58 Kaibel) = Timaeus F 32 Jacoby

μετὰ τὸ δεῖπνον ἐκεῖνοι μὲν τῶν Φρυνίχου καὶ Στησιχόρου, ἔτι δὲ Πινδάρου παιάνων τῶν ναυτῶν τινας ἀνειληφότες ᾖδον.

# STESICHORUS

Plotius Sacerdos, *Grammar*

encomiologicum stesichoreum:

$$-\cup\cup-\cup\cup---\cup--$$

(e.g. 232. 2)

(b) = test. 30

## MISCELLANEOUS

**276** (a) Athenaeus, *Scholars at Dinner*[1]

Stesichorus also, who was immoderately amorous, composed songs of this kind (viz. love-songs)[2] too; in ancient times they were called boy-songs.[3]

[1] The passage follows Alcman 59: Chamaeleon may be the authority for this statement also. [2] None survives, but see the spurious *Rhadine* (fr. 278). [3] Pindar, *Isthm.* 2. 3, Bacch. fr. 4. 80.

(b) Eupolis fr. 148 = test. 33

Lucian, *A True Story* = Arion test. 7

Athenaeus, *Scholars at Dinner* (quoting Timaeus)

After dinner they[1] got some of the sailors and sang selections from the paeans of Phrynichus and Stesichorus[2] and Pindar too.

[1] Ambassadors of Dionysius II, tyrant of Syracuse (367–344 B.C.). The speaker is the flatterer Democles, who said he preferred to sing paeans composed by Dionysius. [2] The paeans of Phrynichus and Stesichorus are not attested elsewhere; perhaps 'selections from Phrynichus and Stesichorus and Pindar's paeans too'.

# GREEK LYRIC

(c) Clem. Alex. *Strom.* 1. 16. 78. 5 (ii 51 Stählin)

μέλος τε αὖ πρῶτος περιέθηκε τοῖς ποιήμασι καὶ τοὺς Λακεδαι-
μονίων νόμους ἐμελοποίησε Τέρπανδρος ὁ Ἀντισσαῖος, διθύραμβον
δὲ ἐπενόησεν Λᾶσος ὁ Ἑρμονεύς, ὕμνον Στησίχορος Ἱμεραῖος,
χορείαν Ἀλκμάν, κτλ.

SPURIA

## 277 ΚΑΛΥΚΗ

Athen. 14. 619de (iii 366 Kaibel)

Ἀριστόξενος δὲ ἐν τετάρτῳ περὶ Μουσικῆς (fr. 89 Wehrli)
ᾖδον, φησίν, αἱ ἀρχαῖαι γυναῖκες Καλύκην τινὰ ᾠδήν. Στησιχόρου
δ᾽ ἦν ποίημα, ἐν ᾧ Καλύκη τις ὄνομα ἐρῶσα Εὐάθλου νεανίσκου
εὔχεται τῇ Ἀφροδίτῃ γαμηθῆναι αὐτῷ. ἐπεὶ δὲ ὑπερεῖδεν ὁ νεανί-
σκος, κατεκρήμνισεν ἑαυτήν. ἐγένετο δὲ τὸ πάθος περὶ Λευκάδα.
σωφρονικὸν δὲ πάνυ κατεσκεύασεν ὁ ποιητὴς τὸ τῆς παρθένου ἦθος,
οὐκ ἐκ παντὸς τρόπου θελούσης συγγενέσθαι τῷ νεανίσκῳ, ἀλλ᾽ εὐ-
χομένης εἰ δύναιτο γυνὴ τοῦ Εὐάθλου γενέσθαι κουριδία, ἢ εἰ τοῦτο
μὴ δυνατὸν ἀπαλλαγῆναι τοῦ βίου.

cf. Eust. *Il.* 1236. 61

# STESICHORUS

(c) Clement of Alexandria, *Miscellanies*

Terpander of Antissa was the first to supply melody for his poems, and he set the laws of the Spartans to music, Lasus of Hermione invented the dithyramb, Stesichorus of Himera the hymn, Alcman choral song . . .

## SPURIOUS WORKS

**277**                     CALYCE[1]

Athenaeus, *Scholars at Dinner*

Aristoxenus in book 4 of his treatise *On Music* says that in time gone by women used to sing[2] a song called *Calyce,* the work of Stesichorus. In it a girl called Calyce loves a youth Euathlus and prays to Aphrodite that she be married to him. When the youth scorned her, she threw herself from a cliff; this took place near Leucas.[3] The poet represented the girl's character as very chaste, since she did not want to have intercourse with the youth by hook or by crook, but prayed to be Euathlus' wedded wife if she could, and to die if that were impossible.[4]

[1] See H. J. Rose, *C.Q.* 26 (1932) 92. L. Lehnus, *S.C.O.* 24 (1975) 191 ff., argues for Stesichorean authorship of *Calyce, Rhadine* and *Daphnis.*     [2] The song seems to have been lost by the time of Aristoxenus (4th c. B.C.).     [3] See Sappho test. 23.     [4] Hesiod made Aethlius and Calyce parents of Endymion (fr. 245 M.-W.).

278                                PAΔINH

Str. 8. 3. 20 (ii 125s. Kramer)

καὶ πεδίον δ᾽ αὐτόθι καλεῖται Σαμικόν· ἐξ οὗ πλέον ἄν τις
τεκμαίροιτο ὑπάρξαι ποτὲ πόλιν τὴν Σάμον. καὶ ἡ Ῥαδίνη δὲ ἦν
Στησίχορος ποιῆσαι δοκεῖ, ἧς ἀρχὴ

    ἄγε Μοῦσα λίγει᾽ ἄρξον ἀοιδᾶς ἐρατωνύμου
    Σαμίων περὶ παίδων ἐρατᾶ φθεγγομένα λύρᾳ,

ἐντεῦθεν λέγει τοὺς παῖδας. ἐκδοθεῖσαν γὰρ τὴν Ῥαδίνην εἰς Κό-
ρινθον τυράννῳ φησὶν ἐκ τῆς Σάμου πλεῦσαι πνέοντος Ζεφύρου, οὐ
δήπουθεν τῆς Ἰωνικῆς Σάμου· τῷ δ᾽ αὐτῷ ἀνέμῳ καὶ ἀρχιθέωρον
εἰς Δελφοὺς τὸν ἀδελφὸν αὐτῆς ἐλθεῖν, καὶ τὸν ἀνεψιὸν ἐρῶντα αὐ-
τῆς ἅρματι εἰς Κόρινθον ἐξορμῆσαι παρ᾽ αὐτήν· ὅ τε τύραννος
κτείνας ἀμφοτέρους ἅρματι ἀποπέμπει τὰ σώματα, μεταγνοὺς δ᾽
ἀνακαλεῖ καὶ θάπτει.

cf. Paus. 7. 5. 13 (ii 159 Rocha-Pereira)

1 Bergk: ἐρατῶν ὕμνους codd.

279                                ΔΑΦΝΙΣ

Aelian. V.H. 10. 18 (p. 118s. Dilts)

βουκολῶν δὲ κατὰ τὴν Σικελίαν ὁ Δάφνις, ἠράσθη αὐτοῦ νύμφη
μία καὶ ὡμίλησε καλῷ ὄντι . . . συνθήκας δὲ ἐποίησε μηδεμιᾷ ἄλλῃ
πλησιάσαι αὐτὸν καὶ ἐπηπείλησεν ὅτι πεπρωμένον ἐστὶν αὐτὸν
στερηθῆναι τῆς ὄψεως ἐὰν παραβῇ. καὶ εἶχον ὑπὲρ τούτων ῥήτραν

# STESICHORUS

RHADINE[1]

Strabo, *Geography* (on southern Elis)

A plain there is called the Samic plain, and one might
regard that as a stronger indication that there was once a
city called Samus. Moreover, the *Rhadine,* which seems to
be the work of Stesichorus and begins

Come, clear-voiced Muse, begin your song of lovely
repute about the Samian children, singing to your lovely
lyre,

says the children were from this Samus: for it tells how
when Rhadine had been given in marriage to a tyrant of
Corinth, she sailed there from Samus when the west wind
was blowing, so that it was clearly not the Ionian Samos.[2]
The same wind carried her brother to Delphi in charge of a
mission; and her cousin who was in love with her set out by
chariot to find her in Corinth; the tyrant killed both of
them and sent off the bodies in a chariot, but later
repented, called it back and gave them burial.

[1] H. J. Rose, *C.Q.* 26 (1932) 89 ff., argued from subject-matter and
metre (asclepiad) that the poem was not by Stesichorus. It may
have been by 'the second Stesichorus' (see test. 6 n. 1).        [2] But
Pausanias says that the tomb of Rhadine and Leontichus is on the
island of Samos.


DAPHNIS

Aelian, *Historical Miscellanies*

While Daphnis was tending his cattle in Sicily, a
nymph fell in love with him and had intercourse with him
since he was handsome ... She made an agreement with
him that he must not make love to any other girl, and
threatened that his fate was to be blinded if he broke it;

πρὸς ἀλλήλους. χρόνῳ δὲ ὕστερον βασιλέως θυγατρὸς ἐρασθείσης αὐτοῦ οἰνωθεὶς ἔλυσε τὴν ὁμολογίαν καὶ ἐπλησίασε τῇ κόρῃ. ἐκ δὲ τούτου τὰ βουκολικὰ μέλη πρῶτον ᾔσθη καὶ εἶχεν ὑπόθεσιν τὸ πάθος τὸ κατὰ τοὺς ὀφθαλμοὺς αὐτοῦ. καὶ Στησίχορόν γε τὸν Ἱμεραῖον τῆς τοιαύτης μελοποιίας ὑπάρξασθαι.

**280** Aelian, *N. A.* 17. 37 (i 428s. Hercher)

ἀμῶντες ἄνθρωποι τὸν ἀριθμὸν ἑκκαίδεκα τοῦ ἡλίου καταφλέγοντος δίψει πιεζόμενοι ἕνα ἑαυτῶν ἀπέστειλαν ἐκ πηγῆς γειτνιώσης κομίσαι ὕδωρ. οὐκοῦν ὁ ἀπιὼν τὸ μὲν δρέπανον τὸ ἀμητικὸν διὰ χειρὸς εἶχε, τὸ δὲ ἀρυστικὸν ἀγγεῖον κατὰ τοῦ ὤμου ἔφερεν. ἐλθὼν δὲ καταλαμβάνει ἀετὸν ὑπό τινος ὄφεως ἐγκρατῶς τε καὶ εὐλαβῶς περιπλακέντα. ἔτυχε δὲ ἄρα καταπτὰς μὲν ἐπ' αὐτὸν ὁ ἀετός, οὐ μὴν τῆς ἐπιβουλῆς ἐγκρατὴς ἐγένετο, οὐδέ, τοῦτο δὴ τὸ Ὁμηρικόν, τοῖς ἑαυτοῦ τέκνοις τὴν δαῖτα ἐκόμισεν, ἀλλὰ τοῖς ἐκείνου περιπεσὼν ἕρμασιν ἔμελλεν οὐ μὰ Δί' ἀπολεῖν ἀλλ' ἀπολεῖσθαι. εἰδὼς οὖν ὁ γεωργὸς τὸν μὲν εἶναι Διὸς ἄγγελον καὶ ὑπηρέτην, εἰδώς γε μὴν κακὸν θηρίον τὸν ὄφιν, τῷ δρεπάνῳ τῷ προειρημένῳ διακόπτει τὸν θῆρα, καὶ μέντοι καὶ τῶν ἀφύκτων ἐκείνων εἱργμῶν τε καὶ δεσμῶν τὸν ἀετὸν ἀπολύει. ὁδοῦ μέντοι πάρεργον τῷ ἀνδρὶ ταῦτα καὶ δὴ διεπέπρακτο, ἀρυσάμενος δὲ τὸ ὕδωρ ἧκε καὶ πρὸς τὸν οἶνον κεράσας ὤρεξε πᾶσιν, οἱ δὲ ἄρα ἔπιον καὶ ἀμυστὶ καὶ πολλὰς ἐπὶ τῷ ἀρίστῳ. ἔμελλε δὲ καὶ αὐτὸς ἐπ' ἐκείνοις πίεσθαι· ἔτυχε γάρ πως ὑπηρέτης κατ' ἐκεῖνο τοῦ καιροῦ ἀλλ' οὐ συμπότης ὤν. ἐπεὶ δὲ τοῖς χείλεσι τὴν κύλικα προσῆγεν, ὁ σωθεὶς ἀετὸς ζωάγρια ἐκτίνων οἱ καὶ κατὰ τύχην ἀγαθὴν ἐκείνου ἔτι διατρίβων περὶ τὸν χῶρον ἐμπίπτει τῇ κύλικι καὶ ἐκταράττει αὐτὴν καὶ ἐκχεῖ τὸ ποτόν. ὁ δὲ ἠγανάκτησεν, καὶ γὰρ ἔτυχε διψῶν, καὶ λέγει· εἶτα μέντοι σὺ ἐκεῖ

and they kept this bargain. But later on a king's daughter fell in love with him, and in a drunken state he broke the agreement and had intercourse with the girl. From that time onwards herdsmen's songs[1] were sung, having as their theme the story of his blinding. Stesichorus of Himera, they say, first composed this kind of song.[2]

[1] I.e. bucolic songs.     [2] Again, perhaps 'the second Stesichorus' (test. 6 n. 1): see M. L. West, *C.Q.* 20 (1970) 206. Daphnis was associated with Himera in Theocr. 7. 74 f.

**280** Aelian, *On the Nature of Animals*

Some men, sixteen in all, while reaping under a blazing sun were distressed by thirst and sent one of their number to fetch water from a nearby spring; and the man who went had his reaper's sickle in his hand and carried the pitcher on his shoulder. When he got there, he found an eagle held firmly and carefully in the coils of a snake: it had swooped down on the snake but failed to carry out its intention and carried no banquet to its young—the expression is Homer's (*Iliad* 12. 222); instead, it was caught in the snake's coils and far from killing looked like being killed. Now the countryman knew that the eagle was the messenger and servant of Zeus and the snake an evil creature, so he cut the snake in two with his sickle and freed the eagle from the prison from which there had been no escape.

So the man performed this extra task on his errand, then drew the water, went back, mixed it with the wine and handed it to all his companions, who drank many cups in great gulps over their lunch. He intended to drink after them—he happened on that occasion to be the serving-man, not their fellow-drinker. But when he put the cup to his lips, the eagle he had saved—luckily for him it was still around—repaid him for its life by swooping on the cup, knocking it from his hand and spilling the drink. He was furious, for he was a thirsty man, and said, 'So it is you

νος ὤν——καὶ γὰρ τὸν ὄρνιν ἐγνώρισε——τοιαύτας ἀποδίδως τοῖς σω-
τῆρσι τὰς χάριτας; ἀλλὰ πῶς ἔτι ταῦτα καλά; πῶς δ' ἂν καὶ ἄλλος
σπουδὴν καταθέσθαι θελήσειεν ἔς τινα αἰδοῖ Διὸς χαρίτων ἐφόρου τε
καὶ ἐπόπτου; καὶ τῷ μὲν ταῦτα εἴρητο, καὶ ἐφρύγετο· ὁρᾷ δὲ ἐπι-
στραφεὶς τοὺς πιόντας ἀσπαίροντάς τε καὶ ἀποθνῄσκοντας. ἦν δὲ
ἄρα ὡς συμβαλεῖν ἐμημεκὼς ἐς τὴν πηγὴν ὁ ὄφις καὶ κεράσας αὐ-
τὴν τῷ ἰῷ. ὁ μὲν οὖν ἀετὸς τῷ σώσαντι ἰσότιμον τῆς σωτηρίας
ἀπέδωκε τὸν μισθόν. λέγει δὲ Κράτης ὁ Περγαμηνὸς ὑπὲρ τούτων
καὶ τὸν Στησίχορον ᾄδειν ἔν τινι ποιήματι οὐκ ἐκφοιτήσαντί που ἐς
πολλοὺς σεμνόν τε καὶ ἀρχαῖον ὥς γε κρίνειν ἐμὲ τὸν μάρτυρα ἐσ-
άγων.

**281**          APOPHTHEGMATA

(a) = test. 16
(b) = test. 17
(c), (d) = test. 18
(e) = testt. 40, 44

again'—he had recognised it—'and this is how you repay the one who saved you? How can such good deeds seem attractive after this? How will anyone else be ready to exert himself on another's behalf, out of respect for Zeus, the overseer and superintendent of gratitude?' Those were his words, and he was becoming parched; but he turned round and saw the men who had drunk gasping and at death's door. The snake, it would seem, had vomited into the spring and polluted it with its venom. And so the eagle repaid the man who had saved its life by saving his life in turn.

Crates[1] of Pergamum says that Stesichorus sings of this in one of his poems which is not widely known, and Stesichorus in my view is an impressive and ancient authority for him to cite.

[1] Librarian and scholar, 1st half of 2nd c. B.C.

**281**     APOPHTHEGMS

(a) = test. 16

(b) = test. 17

(c), (d) = test. 18

(e) = testt. 40, 44

# ECHEMBROTUS

Paus. 10. 7. 4–6 (iii 101 Rocha-Pereira)

τῆς δὲ τεσσαρακοστῆς ὀλυμπιάδος καὶ ὀγδόης, ἣν Γλαυκίας ὁ
Κροτωνιάτης ἐνίκησε, ταύτης ἔτει τρίτῳ ἆθλα ἔθεσαν οἱ Ἀμφικτύ-
ονες κιθαρῳδίας μὲν καθὰ καὶ ἐξ ἀρχῆς, προσέθεσαν δὲ καὶ αὐλῳ-
δίας ἀγώνισμα καὶ αὐλῶν· ἀνηγορεύθησαν δὲ νικῶντες Κεφαλλήν
τε Μελάμπους (Boeckh: ὃς λάμποι, ὁ λάμπου codd.) κιθαρῳδίᾳ,
καὶ αὐλῳδὸς Ἀρκὰς Ἐχέμβροτος, Σακάδας δὲ Ἀργεῖος ἐπὶ τοῖς
αὐλοῖς· ἀνείλετο δὲ ὁ Σακάδας οὗτος καὶ ἄλλας δύο τὰς ἐφεξῆς
ταύτης πυθιάδας . . . · δευτέρᾳ δὲ πυθιάδι . . . αὐλῳδίαν τε κατέλυ-
σαν, καταγνόντες οὐκ εἶναι τὸ ἄκουσμα εὔφημον· ἡ γὰρ αὐλῳδία
μέλη τε ἦν αὐλῶν τὰ σκυθρωπότατα καὶ ἐλεγεῖα [[θρῆνοι]] προσ-
ᾳδόμενα τοῖς αὐλοῖς. μαρτυρεῖ δέ μοι καὶ τοῦ Ἐχεμβρότου τὸ ἀνά-
θημα, τρίπους χαλκοῦς ἀνατεθεὶς τῷ Ἡρακλεῖ τῷ ἐν Θήβαις· ἐπί-
γραμμα δὲ ὁ τρίπους εἶχεν·

> Ἐχέμβροτος Ἀρκὰς
> θῆκε τῷ Ἡρακλεῖ
> νικήσας τόδ' ἄγαλμα
> Ἀμφικτυόνων ἐν ἄθλοις,
> 5 Ἕλλησι δ' ἀείδων
> μέλεα καὶ ἐλέγους.

v. M. L. West, *Studies* 4ss., *Greek Metre* 34.

6 μέλεά τ' ἐλέγους τε? West

200

# ECHEMBROTUS

Pausanias, *Description of Greece* (on the Pythian Games)

In the third year of the 48th Olympiad,[1] in which Glaucias of Croton was victorious, the Amphictions[2] offered prizes in cithara-singing, as they had from the beginning, and added competitions in pipe-singing and pipe-playing. The winners they proclaimed were Melampus of Cephallenia in cithara-song, Echembrotus of Arcadia in pipe-song, Sacadas of Argos in pipe-playing; and this Sacadas went on to win at the next two Pythian Games ... But at the second Pythian Games ... they abolished the pipe-singing, judging its sound inauspicious: for pipe-singing consisted of the gloomiest pipe-music and elegiacs[3] sung to the pipes. My evidence for this is the offering of Echembrotus, a bronze tripod dedicated to the Theban Heracles, which carried this inscription:

Echembrotus the Arcadian dedicated this gift to the glory of Heracles, having been victorious at the contests of the Amphictions, where he sang songs and laments to the Greeks.

[1] I.e. in 586.  [2] Organisers of the Pythian Games at Delphi.
[3] But the word used by Echembrotus (ἔλεγοι) means 'laments', not 'elegiac couplets'.

# SACADAS

## TESTIMONIA VITAE ATQUE ARTIS

**1** [Plut.] *Mus.* 8. 1134ab (p. 114s. Lasserre, vi 3. 7s. Ziegler)

γέγονε δὲ καὶ Σακάδας <ὁ> Ἀργεῖος ποιητὴς μελῶν τε καὶ ἐλεγείων μεμελοποιημένων· ὁ δ᾽ αὐτὸς καὶ αὐλητὴς (Wyttenbach: ποιητὴς codd.) ἀγαθὸς καὶ τὰ Πύθια τρὶς νενικηκὼς ἀναγέγραπται· τούτου καὶ Πίνδαρος μνημονεύει (fr. 269)· τόνων γοῦν τριῶν ὄντων κατὰ Πολύμνηστον καὶ Σακάδαν, τοῦ τε Δωρίου καὶ Φρυγίου καὶ Λυδίου, ἐν ἑκάστῳ τῶν εἰρημένων τόνων στροφὴν ποιήσαντά φασι τὸν Σακάδαν διδάξαι ᾄδειν τὸν χορὸν Δωριστὶ μὲν τὴν πρώτην, Φρυγιστὶ δὲ τὴν δευτέραν, Λυδιστὶ δὲ τὴν τρίτην· καλεῖσθαι δὲ Τριμερῆ (Τριμελῆ Xylander) τὸν νόμον τοῦτον διὰ τὴν μεταβολήν. ἐν δὲ τῇ ἐν Σικυῶνι ἀναγραφῇ τῇ περὶ τῶν ποιητῶν (*F.Gr.H.* 550 F 2) Κλονᾶς εὑρετὴς ἀναγέγραπται τοῦ Τριμεροῦς νόμου.

# SACADAS

## LIFE AND WORKS[1]

**1** 'Plutarch', *On Music*

Sacadas of Argos also was a composer of songs and of elegiacs set to music. In addition he was a fine piper and is on record as having won the Pythian contest three times.[2] Pindar mentions him[3]: there were three tuning-systems at the time of Polymnestus and Sacadas,[4] the Dorian, the Phrygian and the Lydian, and they say that Sacadas composed a strophe in each and taught his chorus to sing the first in the Dorian, the second in the Phrygian, the third in the Lydian; this nome, they say, was called the Three-part[5] because of its modulation. In the record of the poets at Sicyon, however, Clonas is given as the inventor of the Three-part.

[1] For the *Sack of Troy* doubtfully attributed to him see Stesichorus 199.   [2] In 586, 582 and 578: see the entry above on Echembrotus and Paus. 6. 14. 9 f.   [3] See test. 6.   [4] See Polymnestus test. 3: P. (also mentioned by Pindar) lived some two generations before Sacadas.   [5] Perhaps 'the Three-tune'.

**2** [Plut.] *Mus.* 9. 1134bc (p. 115 Lasserre, vi 3. 8 Ziegler)

τῆς δὲ δευτέρας (sc. καταστάσεως) Θαλήτας τε ὁ
Γορτύνιος καὶ Ξενόδαμος ὁ Κυθήριος καὶ Ξενόκριτος
ὁ Λοκρὸς καὶ Πολύμνηστος ὁ Κολοφώνιος καὶ Σακάδας ὁ
Ἀργεῖος μάλιστα αἰτίαν ἔχουσιν ἡγεμόνες γενέσθαι·
τούτων γὰρ εἰσηγησαμένων τὰ περὶ τὰς Γυμνοπαιδίας
τὰς ἐν Λακεδαίμονι λέγεται κατασταθῆναι <καὶ> τὰ
περὶ τὰς Ἀποδείξεις τὰς ἐν Ἀρκαδίᾳ τῶν τε ἐν Ἄργει
τὰ Ἐνδυμάτια καλούμενα. ἦσαν δὲ ... οἱ δὲ περὶ
Σακάδαν ἐλεγείων (sc. ποιηταί).

**3** [Plut.] *Mus.* 12. 1135c (p. 116 Lasserre, vi 3. 10s.
Ziegler)

Πολύμνηστος δὲ μετὰ τὸν Τερπάνδρειον τρόπον
καινῷ ἐχρήσατο, καὶ αὐτὸς μέντοι ἐχόμενος τοῦ καλοῦ
τύπου, ὡσαύτως δὲ καὶ Θαλήτας καὶ Σακάδας· καὶ
γὰρ οὗτοι κατά γε τὰς ῥυθμοποιίας καινοί, οὐκ ἐκβαί-
νοντες μέν<τοι> τοῦ καλοῦ τύπου.

**4** Poll. 4. 78 (i 224 Bethe)

ὁ δὲ Σακάδα νόμος Πυθικός.

**2** 'Plutarch', *On Music*

Credit for the second organisation (of music) is best given to Thaletas of Gortyn, Xenodamus of Cythera, Xenocritus of Locri, Polymnestus of Colophon and Sacadas of Argos[1]: for it is said that it was on their suggestion that the festivals of the Gymnopaediae at Sparta, the Apodeixeis (Exhibitions) in Arcadia and the so-called Endymatia (Robings) at Argos were instituted ... Sacadas composed elegiacs.

[1] For the passage in full see Thaletas test. 7 with n. 3, Polymnestus test. 4.

**3** 'Plutarch', *On Music*[1]

Polymnestus, after the introduction of this Terpandrean style, used a new one, although he too kept to the noble manner, as did Thaletas and Sacadas, who were innovators at least in rhythmic composition, but did not depart from the noble style.

[1] See Terpander test. 22.

**4** Pollux, *Vocabulary*

The nome of Sacadas was the Pythian.[1]

[1] His Pythian nome in five movements, in which he represented on the double pipe the fight of Apollo against the Python, is variously described at Pollux 4. 78, Strabo 9. 3. 10, Pindar *Pyth.* hypothesis (ii 2 Drachmann).

GREEK LYRIC

**5** Paus. 2. 22. 8 (i 159 Rocha-Pereira)

ὀλίγον δὲ τῆς ἐπὶ Κυλάραβιν καὶ τὴν ταύτῃ πύλην
ἀποτραπεῖσι Σακάδα μνῆμά ἐστιν, ὃς τὸ αὔλημα τὸ
Πυθικὸν πρῶτος ηὔλησεν ἐν Δελφοῖς· καὶ τὸ ἔχθος τὸ
Ἀπόλλωνι διαμένον ἐς τοὺς αὐλητὰς ἔτι ἀπὸ Μαρσύου
καὶ τῆς ἁμίλλης τοῦ Σιληνοῦ παυθῆναι διὰ τοῦτον
δοκεῖ τὸν Σακάδαν.

**6** Paus. 9. 30. 2 (iii 56 Rocha-Pereira)

ποιητὰς δὲ ἢ καὶ ἄλλως ἐπιφανεῖς ἐπὶ μουσικῇ,
τοσῶν<δε> εἰκόνας ἀνέθεσαν· Θάμυριν μὲν.... ὁ δὲ
Σακάδα τοῦ Ἀργείου τὸν ἀνδριάντα πλάσας, οὐ συνεὶς
Πινδάρου τὸ ἐς αὐτὸν προοίμιον (fr. 269), ἐποίησεν οὐ-
δὲν ἐς τὸ μῆκος τοῦ σώματος εἶναι τῶν αὐλῶν μείζονα
τὸν αὐλητήν.

**7** Paus. 4. 27. 7 (i 334 Rocha-Pereira)

εἰργάζοντο δὲ καὶ ὑπὸ μουσικῆς ἄλλης μὲν οὐδε-
μιᾶς, αὐλῶν δὲ Βοιωτίων καὶ Ἀργείων· τά τε Σακάδα
καὶ Προνόμου μέλη τότε δὴ προήχθη μάλιστα ἐς ἅμιλ-
λαν.

**8** Hsch. (iv 3 Schmidt)

Σακάδειον· εἶδος μουσικοῦ ὀργάνου.

206

# SACADAS

**5** Pausanias, *Description of Greece* (on Argos)

If you turn off a short distance from the road to the gymnasium Cylarabis and the gate there, you reach the memorial of Sacadas, who was the first to play the Pythian pipe-tune at Delphi. It seems that the hatred felt by Apollo for pipers ever since Marsyas and the contest with that silenus was brought to an end thanks to this Sacadas.

**6** Pausanias, *Description of Greece* (on Mount Helicon)

Of poets or men otherwise distinguished in music they have set up likenesses of the following[1] ... But the sculptor of the statue of Sacadas of Argos, misunderstanding Pindar's prelude on him, has made the piper's body no longer than his pipes.

[1] Paus. lists Thamyris, Arion, Sacadas, Hesiod, Orpheus.

**7** Pausanias, *Description of Greece* (on the building of Messene by Epaminondas, 369 B.C.)

They worked to no music other than Boeotian and Argive pipes: at that time there was the keenest rivalry between the tunes of Sacadas and those of Pronomus.[1]

[1] 5th c. Theban piper.

**8** Hesychius, *Lexicon*

Sacadion: a type of musical instrument.

# IBYCUS

## TESTIMONIA VITAE ATQUE ARTIS

**1** *Sud.* I 80 (ii 607 Adler)

Ἴβυκος, Φυτίου, οἱ δὲ Πολυζήλου τοῦ Μεσσηνίου
ἱστοριογράφου, οἱ δὲ Κέρδαντος· γένει Ῥηγῖνος. ἐν-
θένδε εἰς Σάμον ἦλθεν, ὅτε αὐτῆς ἦρχεν ὁ Πολυκράτους
(Schmid: -κράτης codd.) τοῦ τυράννου πατήρ. χρόνος
δὲ οὗτος ὁ ἐπὶ Κροίσου, ὀλυμπιὰς νδ'. γέγονε δὲ ἐρω-
τομανέστατος περὶ μειράκια, καὶ πρῶτος εὗρε τὴν
καλουμένην σαμβύκην· εἶδος δέ ἐστι κιθάρας τριγώ-
νου. ἔστι δὲ αὐτοῦ τὰ βιβλία ζ' τῇ Δωρίδι διαλέκτῳ.
συλληφθεὶς δὲ ὑπὸ λῃστῶν ἐπὶ ἐρημίας ἔφη κἂν τὰς
γεράνους, ἃς ἔτυχεν ὑπερίπτασθαι, ἐκδίκους γενέσθαι.
καὶ αὐτὸς μὲν ἀνῃρέθη. μετὰ δὲ ταῦτα τῶν λῃστῶν εἷς
ἐν τῇ πόλει θεασάμενος γεράνους ἔφη· ἴδε, αἱ Ἰβύκου
ἔκδικοι. ἀκούσαντος δέ τινος καὶ ἐπεξελθόντος τῷ
εἰρημένῳ, τό τε γεγονὸς ὡμολογήθη καὶ δίκας ἔδωκαν

---

[1] Cf. 'Eudocia', *Violarium* p. 247 Flach, Constantine Lascaris, *On Greek Writers of Calabria* 20 *P.G.* 161. [2] A lawgiver of Rhegium named Phytius appears in the list of early Pythagoreans in Iamblichus, *Vit. Pyth.* 267, but the early 6th c. is too early for a Pythagorean. [3] There were no historians in early 6th c. [4] Perhaps a comic name, suggesting financial gain and foxy cunning; see test. 2. [5] See test. 2. [6] Aeaces (Hdt. 3. 39); cf. Anacr. 491 and see J. Labarbe, *Ant. Cl.* 31 (1962) 153 ff., J. P. Barron, *C.Q.*

208

# IBYCUS

## BIOGRAPHY

**1** *Suda*[1]

Ibycus: son of Phytius[2]; but some say son of the historian[3] Polyzelus of Messana, others son of Cerdas[4]; of Rhegium[5] by birth. From there he went to Samos when it was ruled by the father[6] of the tyrant Polycrates. This was in the time of Croesus, in the 54th Olympiad (564/560 B.C.).[7] He was completely crazed with love for boys,[8] and he was the inventor of the so-called *sambyke*,[9] a kind of triangular cithara. His works are in seven books[10] in the Doric dialect.[11] Captured by bandits in a deserted place he declared that the cranes which happened to be flying overhead would be his avengers; he was murdered, but afterwards one of the bandits saw some cranes in the city and exclaimed, 'Look, the avengers of Ibycus!' Someone overheard and followed up his words: the crime was confessed and the

---

14 (1964) 210 ff., A. A. Mosshammer, *The Chronicle of Eusebius* 290 ff.   [7] Croesus ruled *c.* 560–546.   [8] An inference from e.g. frr. 282A, 282C, 286–289.   [9] So Athenaeus 4. 175de, where the 3rd c. historian Neanthes of Cyzicus is cited as the authority, *Sud.* Σ 73 s.v. σαμβύκαι.   [10] Frr. 283–4 are from book 1, fr. 285 from book 5. [11] See D. L. Page, *Aegyptus* 31 (1951) 162–4.

οἱ λῃσταί· ὡς ἐκ τούτου καὶ παροιμίαν γενέσθαι, αἱ
Ἰβύκου γέρανοι.

**2** εἰς τοὺς ἐννέα λυρικούς 9s. (Schol. Pind. i 10 Drachmann)

Ἴβυκος Ἰταλός <ἐστ´> ἐκ Ῥηγίου ἠὲ Μεσήνης
†Ἡελίδαν τοῦ† πατρός, Δωρίδα δ᾽ ἡρμόσατο.

9 suppl. Wilamowitz      10 PQ: Ἡελίδα τοῦ E     Κέρδαντος Gallo

**3** Euseb. *Chron.* Ol. 60. 1 (p. 103 Helm, ii 99 Schoene)

Ibycus carminum scriptor agnoscitur.

bandits paid the penalty; whence the proverbial expression, 'the cranes of Ibycus'.[12]

[12] The association of Ibycus with birds may be due to the derivation of his name from the bird ἴβυξ (*Et. Mag., Et. Gud.*); the story of the cranes need not have been told of Ibycus originally: see Iamblichus, *Vit. Pyth.* 126, Wilamowitz, *S.u.S.* 243 f.; it is found in Antipater of Sidon ( = test. 5), Plutarch, *Garrul.* 509e–510a, Ausonius, *Technop.* 10. 12, Nemesius, *Nat. Hom.* 42, Diogenian 1. 35, Photius, *Bibl.* 148b.

## BIRTHPLACE[1]

**2** *On the Nine Lyric Poets* (quoted by Scholiast on Pindar)

Ibycus, an Italian from Rhegium or Messana; his father was (Eelides? Cerdas?), and he tuned his lyre in the Dorian style.

[1] Cf. testt. 1, 6, 7, 12; Constantine Lascaris (loc. cit.) says he was born in Messana but his father was from Rhegium.

## CHRONOLOGY[1]

**3** Eusebius, *Chronicle*

Olympiad 60.1 (540/539 B.C.)[2]: Ibycus, writer of songs, is known.

[1] Cf. test. 1.     [2] Or Ol. 59.3 or 60.3, 542/541 or 538/537, acc. to other mss.: see Mosshammer 301 f. Cyril puts Ibycus in Ol. 59 (544/540 B.C.) (Migne, *P.G.* 76, 13b).

**4** Diogen. 2. 71 (i 207 Leutsch-Schneidewin)

ἀρχαιότερος Ἰβύκου· ἐπὶ τῶν εὐηθῶν. οὗτος γὰρ
τυραννεῖν δυνάμενος ἀπεδήμησεν (εἰς Ἰωνίαν add. B).

cf. 5. 12 (i 251) ἀνοητότερος Ἰβύκου.

**5** *Anth. Pal.* 7. 745 = Antipater of Sidon xix Gow-Page

Ἴβυκε, λῃσταί σε κατέκτανον ἔκ ποτε νηός
βάντ᾽ ἐς ἐρημαίην ἄστιβον ἠιόνα,
ἀλλ᾽ ἐπιβωσάμενον γεράνων νέφος αἵ τοι ἵκοντο
μάρτυρες ἄλγιστον ὀλλυμένῳ θάνατον·
5 οὐδὲ μάτην ἰάχησας ἐπεὶ ποινῆτις Ἐρινύς
τῶνδε διὰ κλαγγὴν τίσατο σεῖο φόνον
Σισυφίην κατὰ γαῖαν. ἰὼ φιλοκερδέα φῦλα
λῃστέων, τί θεῶν οὐ πεφόβησθε χόλον;
οὐδὲ γὰρ ὁ προπάροιθε κανὼν Αἴγισθος ἀοιδόν
10 ὄμμα μελαμπέπλων ἔκφυγεν Εὐμενίδων.

1 Jacobs: νήσου codd.

212

# IBYCUS

## LIFE[1]

**4** Diogenian, *Proverbs*

'More antiquated than Ibycus': used of stupid people.[2] For Ibycus could have ruled as tyrant but went abroad to Ionia.[3]

[1] See also fr. 343.    [2] Elsewhere Diogenian gives 'sillier than Ibycus'.    [3] To Samos, presumably.

**5** *Palatine Anthology*: Antipater of Sidon

Ibycus, robbers murdered you when one day you came from the ship[1] to a desolate trackless beach, but only after you had cried out to a cloud of cranes which came as witnesses to your grievous death. Nor did you shout in vain, for thanks to their screams an avenging Fury exacted the penalty for your killing in the land of Sisyphus.[2] O greedy robber-bands, why do you not fear the anger of the gods? Even Aegisthus who in olden days murdered the bard[3] did not escape the eye of the black-robed Eumenides.

[1] 'From the island', acc. to the mss.; perhaps 'when you landed on the beach of the island'.    [2] Corinth.    [3] *Od*. 3. 267 ff.

**6** *Anth. Pal.* 7. 714 = anon. lii Gow-Page, *H.E.*

Ῥήγιον Ἰταλίης τεναγώδεος ἄκρον ἀείδω
αἰεὶ Θρινακίου γευομένην ὕδατος
οὕνεκα τὸν φιλέοντα λύρην φιλέοντα δὲ παῖδας
Ἴβυκον εὐφύλλῳ θῆκεν ὑπὸ πτελέῃ
5 ἡδέα πολλὰ παθόντα, πολὺν δ' ἐπὶ σήματι κισσόν
χεύατο καὶ λευκοῦ φυταλιὴν καλάμου.

**7** *I.G.* xiv 1167

Ἴβυκος] Φυτίου Ῥηγῖνος

**8** *I.G.* xiv 2485

Εἴβυκος. Πραξιτέλης ἐποίε[ι

**9** *Sud.* I 79 (ii 607 Adler)

ἰβύκινον· μουσικὸν ὄργανον, ἀπὸ Ἰβύκου.

# IBYCUS

**6** *Palatine Anthology*: anonymous poem from Meleager's *Garland*

I sing of Rhegium at the tip of Italy with its shallows, the city which always tastes the water of Sicily, because it placed under a leafy elm Ibycus, lover of the lyre, lover of boys, after he had enjoyed many pleasures, and shed much ivy and a bed of white reeds over his tomb.

## PORTRAITS

**7** Inscription on herm[1]

(Ibycus), son of Phytius, of Rhegium

[1] From Tivoli; now lost.

**8** Inscription on statue[1]

Ibycus: the work of Praxiteles

[1] From Crest (France); now lost. The statue represented an elderly bearded man.

## MUSIC AND METRES[1]

**9** *Suda*

ibycinon: a musical instrument named after Ibycus.[2]

[1] For metres named after Ibycus see fr. 345, West, *Greek Metre* 51.　　[2] See test. 1 for the sambyke.

**10** Ar. *Thesm.* 159ss.

ἄλλως τ' ἄμουσόν ἐστι ποιητὴν ἰδεῖν
ἀγρεῖον ὄντα καὶ δασύν. σκέψαι δ' ὅτι
Ἴβυκος ἐκεῖνος κἀνακρέων ὁ Τήιος
κἀλκαῖος, οἵπερ ἁρμονίαν ἐχύμισαν,
ἐμιτροφόρουν τε κἀχλίδων Ἰωνικῶς.

**11** Philodem. *Mus.* 4. col. xiv 8ss. (p. 57 Neubecker)

οὐδὲ τοὺς νέους τοῖς μέλεσι διαφθ[ε]ίροντας
παρέδειξεν τὸν Ἴβυκον καὶ τὸν Ἀνακρέοντα καὶ τοὺς
ὁμοίους, ἀλλὰ τοῖς διανοήμασι.

**12** Cic. *Tusc.* 4. 71

quid denique homines doctissimi et summi poe-
tae de se ipsis et carminibus edunt et cantibus?
fortis vir in sua re publica cognitus quae de iuvenum
amore scribit Alcaeus! nam Anacreontis quidem
tota poesis est amatoria. maxume vero omnium
flagrasse amore Reginum Ibycum apparet ex
scriptis. atque horum omnium lubidinosos esse
amores videmus.

# IBYCUS

## VERDICT OF ANTIQUITY[1]

**10** Aristophanes, *Thesmophoriazusae*

Agathon: Besides it's uncultured for a poet to look wild and shaggy. Consider the great Ibycus and Anacreon of Teos and Alcaeus, who made their music so succulent: they wore the headband and lived in Ionian luxury.

[1] See also Stes. test. 35.

**11** Philodemus, *On Music*

And he[1] did not show that Ibycus, Anacreon and the like corrupted young men by their melodies but rather by their ideas.

[1] The Stoic Diogenes, whom Philodemus is attacking.

**12** Cicero, *Tusculan Disputations*

Finally, what revelations do the greatest scholars and finest poets make about themselves in their poems and songs? Alcaeus was recognised as a valiant hero in his city, but look at what he writes about love for youths! Anacreon's poetry, of course, is all erotic. More than any of them Ibycus of Rhegium was ablaze with love, as his writings demonstrate. And we see that the love of all of these is lustful.

**13** *Anth. Pal.* 9. 184. 5s. = anon. xxxvi(a), 1198s. Page, *F.G.E.*

. . . ἡδύ τε Πειθοῦς
Ἴβυκε καὶ παίδων ἄνθος ἀμησάμενε.

**14** Stat. *Silv.* 5. 3. 146ss. (p. 121 Marastoni)

generosaque pubes
te monitore . . . discere . . .
. . . qua lege recurrat
Pindaricae vox flexa lyrae volucrumque precator
Ibycus . . .

**15** Schol. Pind. *Isthm.* 2. 1b (iii 213 Drachmann)

ταῦτα δὲ τείνει καὶ εἰς τοὺς περὶ Ἀλκαῖον καὶ Ἴβυ-
κον καὶ Ἀνακρέοντα καὶ εἴ τινες τῶν πρὸ αὐτοῦ δο-
κοῦσι περὶ τὰ παιδικὰ ἠσχολῆσθαι· οὗτοι γὰρ παλαι-
ότεροι Πινδάρου.

# IBYCUS

**13** *Palatine Anthology*: anon. on the nine Lyric Poets

... and you, Ibycus, who harvested the sweet blossoms of Persuasion and of boys.

**14** Statius, *Silvae*

... and noble youths under your guidance[1] learned the rules which govern the recurrent rhythms of Pindar's lyre with its winding utterance, of Ibycus, who prayed to the birds ...[2]

[1] Statius' father, who died in 19 A.D., was *grammaticus* of a school in Naples.　　[2] Statius also mentions Alcman, Stesichorus and Sappho.

**15** Scholiast on Pindar, *Isthmians*

This refers to Alcaeus and Ibycus and Anacreon and anyone else before Pindar who may have devoted his attention to his favourite boy: for these writers were older than Pindar.

# IBYCUS

## FRAGMENTA

**282** (a) = S 151    P.Oxy. 1790 frr. 1–3, 10, 12 + 2081(f)

. . .]αι Δαρδανίδα Πριάμοιο μέ-
γ᾽ ἄσ]τυ περικλεὲς ὄλβιον ἠνάρον
Ἄργ]οθεν ὀρνυμένοι
Ζη]νὸς μεγάλοιο βουλαῖς

5  ξα]νθᾶς Ἑλένας περὶ εἴδει
δῆ]ριν πολύυμνον ἔχ[ο]ντες
πό]λεμον κατὰ [δ]ακρ[υό]εντα,
Πέρ]γαμον δ᾽ ἀνέ[β]α ταλαπείριο[ν ἄ]τα
χρυ]σοέθειραν δ[ι]ὰ Κύπριδα.

10  νῦ]ν δέ μοι οὔτε ξειναπάτ[α]ν Π[άρι]ν
ἦν] ἐπιθύμιον οὔτε τανί[σφ]υρ[ον
ὑμ]νῆν Κασσάνδραν
Πρι]άμοιό τε παῖδας ἄλλου[ς

Τρο]ίας θ᾽ ὑψιπύλοιο ἁλώσι[μο]ν
15  ἆμ]αρ ἀνώνυμον, οὐδ᾽ ἐπ[ελεύσομαι
ἡρ]ώων ἀρετὰν
ὑπ]εράφανον οὕς τε κοίλα[ι

220

# IBYCUS

## FRAGMENTS

*Frr. 282–282C are papyrus finds; 283–5 come from num-*
*bered books (1 and 5), 286–9 are erotic fragments, 290–309*
*deal with mythology, 310–21 are other fragments with con-*
*secutive words, 322–5 give information about the content of*
*poems, 326–41 are words and forms used by Ibycus, 342–4*
*are miscellaneous, 345 gives metrical testimonia.*

**282** (a) = S 151     Oxyrhynchus papyrus (*c.* 130 B.C.)

. . . destroyed the great, glorious, blessed city of
Priam, son of Dardanus, setting off from Argos by
the plans of great Zeus, enduring much-sung strife
over the beauty of auburn Helen in tearful war; and
ruin mounted long-suffering Pergamum thanks to
the golden-haired Cyprian[1]; but now it was not my
heart's wish to sing of Paris, deceiver of his host, or
of slim-ankled Cassandra and Priam's other chil-
dren and the unmentionable day of the capture of
high-gated Troy, nor shall I recount the proud
valour of the heroes whom hollow, many-bolted

[1] Aphrodite, who brought about the war by prompting the abduc-
tion of Helen by Paris.

---

suppl. Hunt praeter     14 ἀλώσι[μο]ν Maas     15 ἆμ]αρ Wila-
mowitz     ἐπ[ανέρχομαι Hunt     οὐδὲ π[εδέρχομαι Handley

νᾶες] πολυγόμφοι ἐλεύσα[ν
Τροί]αι κακόν, ἥρωας ἐσθ[λούς·
20 τῶν] μὲν κρείων Ἀγαμέ[μνων
ἆρχε Πλεισθ[ενί]δας βασιλ[εὺ]ς ἀγὸς ἀνδρῶν
Ἀτρέος ἐσ[θλὸς π]άις ἔκγ[ο]νος.

καὶ τὰ μὲ[ν ἂν] Μοίσαι σεσοφι[σ]μέναι
εὖ Ἑλικωνίδ[ες] ἐμβαίεν λόγω[ι·
25 †θνατ[ὸ]ς δ' οὔ κ[ε]ν ἀνὴρ
διερὸς [ . . . . . . ]† τὰ ἔκαστα εἴποι,

ναῶν ὄ[σσος ἀρι]θμὸς ἀπ' Αὐλίδος
Αἰγαῖον διὰ [πό]ντον ἀπ' Ἄργεος
ἠλύθο[ν ἐς Τροία]ν
30 ἱπποτρόφο[ν, ἐν δ]ὲ φῶτες

χ]αλκάσπ[ιδες, υἷ]ες Ἀχα[ι]ῶν·
τ]ῶν μὲν πρ[οφ]ερέστατος α[ἰ]χμᾶι
ἷξε]ν πόδ[ας ὠ]κὺς Ἀχιλλεὺς
καὶ μέ]γας Τ[ελαμ]ώνιος ἄλκι[μος Αἴας
35 . . . . . . ] . . . [ . . . . . . ]λο[ . ] πυρός.

. . . . . . . . κάλλι]στος ἀπ' Ἄργεος
. . . . . . . . Κυάνι]ππ[ο]ς ἐς Ἴλιον
. . . . . . . . . . . . . ]
. . . . . . . . . . . . . ] . . [ . ] . . .

ships brought to be an evil to Troy, fine heroes: they were commanded by lord Agamemnon, Pleisthenid[2] king, leader of men, fine son born to Atreus. On these themes the skilled Muses of Helicon might embark in story, but no mortal man (untaught?) could tell each detail, the great number of ships that came from Aulis across the Aegean sea from Argos to horse-rearing Troy, with bronze-shielded warriors on board, sons of the Achaeans; among them foremost with the spear went swift-footed Achilles and great valiant Telamonian Ajax (who threw strong fire on Troy?); (with them also went) from Argos to Ilium Cyanippus,[3] the most handsome man, (descendant of Adrastus), (and Zeuxippus,[4]

---

[2] In Hesiod Pleisthenes was son of Atreus and father of Agamemnon (frr. 194–5 M.-W.); Ibycus follows Homer in making Agamemnon son of Atreus.  [3] Son of Adrastus, king of Argos ('Apollodorus' *Bibl.* 1. 9. 13) or son of Aegialeus and so grandson of Adrastus (Paus. 2. 18. 4); Paus. 2. 30. 10 implies that he was only a boy when the war began. For Homer Nireus of Syme was the most handsome Greek warrior at Troy except for Achilles (*Il.* 2. 673 f.).  [4] King of Sicyon (Paus. 2. 6. 7).

---

19 ἐσθ[λούς Lobel    22 ἐσ[θλὸς Barron    ἐσ[θλοῦ Hunt    ἔκ-γ[ο]νος Barron    25 θνατὸς secl. Barron, qui tent. 25 οὐκ ἀδάης δέ κ' ἀνὴρ    26 δ. τὰ ἔ. εἴποι αὐτὸς West    27, 30 Barron 33 βαίν]ε[ι, χωρ]ε[ῖ, ἱξε]ν Hunt    35, 36, 37 Barron, qui tent. 36 τοῖς δ' ἅμα καὶ κ. ἀπ' Ἄ.    37 ἦλθεν ἀνὴρ Κ. ἐς Ἴ.    38 Ἀδράστοιο γένος    39 Ζεύξιππος ἴδ' ὅν τ]ε Ναὶς

223

# GREEK LYRIC

40 . . . . . . . . . . . . . . ]α χρυσόστροφος
    Ὕλλις ἐγήνατο, τῶι δ᾿ [ἄ]ρα Τρωίλον
    ὡσεὶ χρυσὸν ὀρει-
    χάλκωι τρὶς ἄπεφθο[ν] ἤδη

    Τρῶες Δ[α]ναοί τ᾿ ἐρό[ε]σσαν
45 μορφὰν μάλ᾿ ἐΐσκον ὅμοιον.
    τοῖς μὲν πέδα κάλλεος αἰέν·
    καὶ σύ, Πολύκρατες, κλέος ἄφθιτον ἑξεῖς
    ὡς κατ᾿ ἀοιδὰν καὶ ἐμὸν κλέος.

schol. ad v. 37s. (suppl. e.g. Barron) . . . . ]ίμαχος ἐν τῶι περὶ
. . . . ρου φησί· τὸν [Ἄδραστο]ν [πάππο]ν τοῦ Κυανίππου· οὕτω
λέγε<ι> τὸν π[οιητὴν ἐ]σχά[τως α]ὑτοῦ τὴν γένεσιν ταύτην ἀνα-
πεπλ[ακέν]αι ὡς [ἀφίη]σι Αἰγιαλέα τοῦ Ἀδρά[σ]του γενόμε[νον,
ὃς ἐπ]εστρά[τευσε] τοῖς ελα[ . ] . . . . . . . . . α̣

v. J. P. Barron, *B.I.C.S.* 16 (1969) 119ss.

40 Φοίβωι κυσαμέν]α̣ χ.


**282** (b)(c) = S 152–165        P.Oxy. 1790 frr. 4, 5, 7 +
2081(f) fr. 4

(i)    4 νυσσον[        5 ἀσπιδα[        6 τοὶ δ᾿ αὖ λα̣
7 τυπτ[

(ii)   1 δασε[        3 ἴ]χνια[        4 αιθόια̣[
5 αιτελυ̣[

(iii)   3 κι]νητῆρι γα[ί]ας        6 τάμνω̣[

(iv)   5 ἀ̣γήτορ᾿ ἴχ[ν-

(ii) suppl. Hunt, (iii) Marcovigi, (iv) Barron


224

# IBYCUS

whom the Naiad,) golden-girdled Hyllis,[5] (conceived and) bore (to Phoebus); and to him Trojans and Greeks likened Troilus[6] as gold already thrice-refined to orichalc, judging him very similar in loveliness of form. These have a share in beauty always: you too, Polycrates, will have undying fame[7] as song and my fame can give it.[8]

Scholium on vv. 37–9 (added *c.* 1st c. A.D.)

]imachus in his work *On -rus* says: Adrastus is grand-father of Cyanippus; thus he says the poet has utterly refashioned this genealogy of his, allowing Aegialeus to be son of Adrastus,[9] who marched against ...

[5] Daughter of Hyllus, son of Heracles.     [6] Son of Priam; an exemplar of youth and beauty, especially on 6th c. vases (M. Robertson, *B.I.C.S.* 17, 1970, 12).     [7] Less probably, with change of punctuation, 'Among them, for beauty always you too, Polycrates, will have undying fame'.     [8] End of poem.     [9] See n. 3 above.

**282** (b)(c) = S 152–165     Fragments of same papyrus[1]

(i) ... stabbed the shield(s) ..., but the others for their part struck ...

(ii) ... shaggy ... tracks ...

(iii) ... steersman ... (mover of earth?) ... cleave ...

(iv) ... leader ... tracks ...

[1] Not necessarily from the poem to Polycrates, 282(a).

# GREEK LYRIC

**282A** = S 166–219     P.Oxy. 2735

(i) fr. 1 (S 166)

```
            ]τερεν . [
              ]εαπα[
        ]δ[  ]αριω[
         ]  δακτον ἔχω[
5     ὑπ᾽ α]ὐλητῆρος ἀείδο[ν
        ] ἀβρὰ π[α]ντῶς [
      πό]θος οἷά τ᾽ ἔρωτος [

        -ο]ιο κατ᾽ αἶσαν ὤ . [
          ]ατον τέλος ἀσφ[
10    ]α δύνασις· κράτ[ος
      ]ύνοι μέγα δαί-
      μονες] πολὺν ὄλβον ἐδώ[καν
      οἷς κ᾽ ἐθ]έλωσιν ἔχεν, τοῖς δ᾽ α[ὐ
      βουλα]ῖσι Μοιρᾶν.

15        ] Τυνδαρίδ[αι]σι λαγε[τ
         ] . ι σάλπιγγος ὄκ᾽ ἐν κε[
      Κάστορί] θ᾽ ἱπποδάμωι καὶ π[ὺξ ἀγαθῶι Πολυδεύκει
         ]ες ἀντιθέοι
         ]νοπάονες· οἷσιν εσ . [
20       ]εῖ μεγάλα χρύσαιγις [
```

suppl. Lobel praeter 4 leg. West   5 ὑπ᾽, ἀείδο[ν West   6 West
11 leg. West   13, 14 Page et West   19 ]ν ὀπ- vel συ]νοπ- Page

226

# IBYCUS

**282A** = S 166–219    Oxyrhynchus papyrus[1] (2nd c. A.D.)

(i) ... (they) sang to the piper's accompaniment ...
luxurious assuredly ... (desire?) like love's ...
rightly ... end (secure?) ... power; ... great
strength ... the gods give much prosperity to those
whom they wish to have it, but for the others (they
destroy it?) by the plans of the Fates; ... (to)
the sons of Tyndareus[2] ... leader(s) of the people ...
when in ... the trumpet's ... to Castor the horse-
tamer and to Polydeuces, excellent boxer, ... god-
like (heroes?) ... henchmen; to whom great
(Athena?) of the golden aegis ... (free?) of cares.

[1] Ascribed to Stesichorus by Lobel, hesitantly to Stesichorus' *Helen*
by West, more convincingly to Ibycus by Page. Not all of the frag-
ments come from the same poem.       [2] Castor and Polydeuces.

      ]ϟαδέα.

   καὶ τὸ] μὲν οὐ φατόν ἐστιν ε[
       ]ων τεκέεσσι· σὲ δ᾽ αὖ[
   οὐρανόθ]εν καταδέρκεται ἀ[έλιος
25     ]τα κάλλιστον ἐπιχθ[ονίων
   ἀθανάτ]οις ἐναλ[ί]γκιον εἶδο[ς
       ]ς ἄλλος οὕτῶς
   οὔτ᾽] ἀν᾽ Ἰάονας οὔτ . [


       κ]υδιάνειραν α[ἲ]ἐν[
30  Λακ]ϵδαίμονα ναίο[υσι(ν)
       ] ς τε χοροῖς ἵππο[ισί τε
       ]ᾶν βαθὺν Εὐ-
   ρώταν, περ]ί τ᾽ ἀμφί τε θαῦμα[
       ] ἄλσεα λαχνάεντ᾽ ἐλ[ατᾶν
35  κά]πους·

   ἔνθα παλαι]μοσύναι τε καὶ δρ[όμωι
       ταχ]υτᾶτ᾽ ἐς ἀγῶν᾽ ἐπας[κ
       ]ν πατέρων ἰδήρα[τ-
       ]νια
40     ]γε θεῶν [π]άρ᾽, ἔστι δὲ [
       ] ἐσσα[μένα] Θέμις κα[
                 ]

v. D. L. Page, *P.C.P.S.* 15 (1969) 69ss., M. L. West, *Z.P.E.* 4 (1969) 142ss., R. Führer, *Z.P.E.* 5 (1970) 15s., M. L. Haslam, *Q.U.C.C.* 17 (1974) 48s.

22 West   28, 29 Page et West   30 fin. ego   31, 33, 34, 35, 36 ἔνθα, 37, 40, 41 West

## IBYCUS

(And that) is not to be spoken ... (by) the children
...; but upon you on the other hand (the sun) looks
down (from the heaven) as upon the most handsome
of earth-dwellers, like the immortals in form; (no)
other (is) so (beautiful?), (either) among Ionians or
(among) ... (those who) dwell in Lacedaemon famed
for its men, always ... with choruses and horses ...
deep (Eurotas?), round about a wonder ... shaggy
groves (of firs?) ... (orchards?); (there) in wrestling
and running ... (practised?) speed for the contest
... beautiful ... of fathers ... from the gods; and
there is ... Themis clad ...

(ii) fr. 2 (S 167)

3 ]μεγιστ[ -      6 φοινίοισι      8 ἁδινοῖς  βελέεσσ[ι
9 ἀργυροπέζου      10 ]εγεντο

(iii) fr. 4 (S 169)

1 ]δακεθυμ[      2 ] ας παιδῶ[ν

(iv) fr. 6 (S 171)

2 ]θ’ ἐπὶ φρένας      3 ἀειδεν      4 λέγεν
5 στ]ομυλλίων

(v) fr. 8 (S 173)

3 ]εα · περὶ ἀνδρὶ δα[      4 ] ον · εὖτέ κεν
ὄρκον[      5 ]ιδων ἕλιγμα παιδ [      7 κάλ-
λ]ιστε παιδῶν[

(vi) fr. 9 (S 174)

2 εὐπ]ατέρεια θ[      3 ποταιν[ι-      5 ] κωι
ἐρευθ[      6 κελαδηι [      7 ] ετε τέκνα[
10 ]αιδ’ ἐρατ[

(vii) fr. 10 (S 175)

3 ’Αφρο]δίτας

(viii) fr. 11 (S 176)

ἡ]μιθέων ὄθ[
σ]τάδιον δρομ[
πάντας ἀπλάτ [
χαλεπὰ δέ τις α [

(ii) ... greatest ... bloody ... dense spears ...
silver-footed (goddess?) ... was born ...

(iii) ... heart-biting ... of boys ...

(iv) ... to the mind ... to sing (sang?) ... to tell
(told?) ... (chattering?)

(v) ... about the man ... whenever ... an oath ...
curl(?) of boys ... you most beautiful of boys ...

(vi) ... (daughter) of noble father ... fresh ... red ...
babbles ... children ... lovely (child?)

(vii) ... Aphrodite (?) ...

(viii) ... of demigods ... race of one course ...
(defeated?) all with unapproachable ...; and a

5 ἅτε σιδάρεος ἔπ[λετ(ο)
Ἡ]ρακλέος γᾶμεν  [
δ]ν ὑφ' ἅρμασι τε[            ἵπποι ἐ-
ν]ικάσαν τρεχο[ίσαι
τ]ὰς Ἰόλαος ἀρήιον[

10 ἐ]πιβάντα δεδε  [
Π]ηλεὺ[ϛ] δεπαλα  [
κ]ῦδος ὑπέρτερον [
δ]αμὲν οὐ δυν[α
τ]ὰν ἀνίκατο[ν

15 ὁ δὲ καὶ με  [
  ]αι κρατε  [
χρυσάορος[
Γαρυόναν γ[
ἔ]κτανεν  [

20   ]με  [
     ]αι  [

v. D. L. Page, *P.C.P.S.* 17 (1971) 89ss.

suppl. Lobel praeter 5, 7, 8 τρεχο[ίσαι, 9, 13 δ]αμὲν?, 15, 17
Page    19 Führer

(ix) fr. 13 (S 178)

1    ]αν πόλιν [

(x) fr. 14 (S 179)

2    ] ὅτ' ὀϊστὸς [

harsh (fate?) ... which was an iron (bond) ... (befell Euphemus[1]?) (who once) married (the sister) of Heracles; (Euphemus) whom horses harnessed to their chariots defeated running, (mares) which Iolaus[2] (drove, accepting) warlike (Heracles) who had mounted (the chariot); but Peleus in wrestling ... greater glory ... was not able to subdue ... that invincible girl[3] ...; and he also ... strong ... killed Geryon,[4] (son) of Chrysaor ...

[1] Charioteer who won the two-horse race at the Funeral Games of Pelias (Paus. 5. 17. 9); perhaps he was the defeated rival of Iolaus in the four-horse race (Page). For the Games see Stes. frr. 178–180.    [2] Charioteer of Heracles and winner of four-horse chariot race at the Games (Paus. 5. 17. 11).    [3] Atalanta, who defeated Peleus in wrestling at the Games ('Apollodorus', *Bibl.* 3. 9. 2).    [4] Killed by Heracles: see Stes. fr. 181 ff.

(ix) ... city ...

(x) ... arrow ...

(xi) fr. 16 (S 181)

3 ε]ὐχετάασθα[ι      8 ]βαινε . . [      10 περικα]λλέ'
ἐραστ̣[άν

schol. ad v. 2 Πρ]οκλέα κ(αὶ) Εὐρυσθένη . [

3, 10 init. suppl. Lobel      10 fin. Page


(xii) fr. 17 (S 182)

4  Ἐσ]περίδω[ν      5 χ]ρύσεα[ (μᾶλα)      7 ]χθών ·
8 ] . ἐλεφαντ[ -

4, 5 suppl. Lobel      8 leg. Page


(xiii) fr. 27 (S 192)

2 ]μάχαι γίγαντες[   3 ]μεν ἀρήονες ἀλκὰ[ν   4 γε-
νέσθ[αι   5 ]των νοον [   6 σ]υμφοραῖς[   9 ] ρόδε[
10 κά]λυκες . [      11 ]ἀεξὸμ[      13 ]ως δ' αὖ [
14 ]ἀγερώχοι · [   15 ]ο̣κρατὴς θαν̣[ατ-

suppl. Lobel praeter 10 Page


(xiv) fr. 33 (S 198)

2 β]ρο̣το̣ῖς[


(xv) fr. 34 (S 199)

2  ]δολοπ[λόκ-      5  ] . ν μελέων . [      6 ἐ]πι-
κρατέως[      7 τεμ]ενοῦχος . [      8  ]ν γάρ νιν
αν[      9  ]ήνατο π[ο]τν[ι-      10  ]ας κορυ-
φ[ας      12  ἀ̣θανάτα[

suppl. Lobel


234

# IBYCUS

(xi) . . . to pray (profess?) . . . went . . . very handsome lover . . .

Scholiast on v. 2: Procles and Eurysthenes[1]

[1] Twin brothers, descendants of Heracles, who founded the two lines of Spartan kings, Eurypontid and Agiad.

(xii) . . . golden (apples of the Hesperides?) . . . earth . . . ivory . . .

(xiii) . . . giants . . . in battle . . . better in valour . . . to become . . . mind . . . circumstances . . . rose- . . . (buds?) . . . growing . . . proud men . . . (all-)powerful death . . .

(xiv) . . . mortals . . .

(xv) . . . guile-weaving . . . limbs . . . overwhelmingly . . . (demesne-holding deity?) . . . For . . . lady (goddess) . . . head(s)[1] . . . immortal goddess(es) . . .

[1] Or peak(s).

(xvi) fr. 36 (S 201)

6 ἁ]γναν[

(xvii) fr. 42 (S 207)

6 ἀ]φίκον[ | το

tent. Page

(xviii) fr. 50 (S 215)

2 ὑπ]ερδέα

tent. Page (v. *Il*. 17. 330)

**282B** = S 220–257     P.Oxy. 2637

(i) fr. 1 (a) 1–31 (S 220)

. . . ν]ύμφα· οἷον χωρ[ . . . ] ͺ ε ταῖς νύ[μ]φαις . . .

] ͺ αι Κρονίου πτυχαι· φα[ . . . Κ]ρόνιον ἐν Λεοντίνοις [ . . .
πυ]κνῶς ἔρχεσθαι τὸν [ . . . ]τ. ποτὲ μὲν κυνηγε[ . . . ] ἐπιδείξαντα
τοῖς[ . . . ]χωρα καὶ τα[ . . .

] ͺ ν χαλεπὸν[ . . . ε]ὔκολόν φησιν . . . πλεῖον . . . δυσά[ρεστ- ?
. . .

αὔχα γλυκερὰ [ . . . ]σα ἰδίως ἀν[ . . . ]τις ἐλπὶς του[ . . . γ]λυ-
κερά. αὐ[χ]εῖ· καυχ[ᾶται . . . ἐ]λπίς· ἢ οὕτως· γλυκερὰ γίν[εται
ἡ καύχη]σις ἐὰν ἐπιτύχηι.

αἶπερ [ . . . ]ν ποδῶν· ὥσπερ καὶ ο ͺ [ . . . πόδ]ας ἐν τῆι
ἀθλ[ή]σει . . . ὁ γὰρ νικ[ . . . ]πονουδι[ . . . ] ἀναγινω[σκ- . . . ]νας
ἀδηλ[ . . . ]τεύων α ͺ [ . . . πο]λὺͺν γεͺνέͺσ[θαι . . . ] ἵν' οὕτωͺς
δεκα[ . . . ἀγα]θὸς γίνεται οπ[ . . . ἐ]πιτύχηι.

suppl. Lobel

# IBYCUS

(xvi) ... pure ...

(xvii) ... (they) arrived ...

(xviii) ... (very inferior?) ...

**282B** = S220–257    Oxyrhynchus papyrus (c. 150 A.D.)

*Fragments of commentary on lyric poetry: S 220–226 and possibly 227 deal with lines of Ibycus, 228–257 with unidentified poets.*

(i)
... **nymph:** i.e. (a place?) ... (to) the nymphs ...

... **glen(s) of Cronion** ...: Cronion[1] at Leontini ... that (he) often went to ...; once when hunting ... displaying it to ...

... **harsh**[2]: ... he says (he is not) good-tempered ... more ... un(pleasing?) ...

**sweet boast:** ... peculiarly ... hope ... sweet; αὐχεῖ means 'boasts' ... hope; or as follows: the boast turns out sweet if he succeeds;

**as ... (of) feet:** just as ... feet in the athletic contest ...; since the winner ... (toil?) ... read(s) ... unclear ... much ... to turn out ... so that in this way ... shows himself good ... succeeds.

[1] Hill or place of Cronus; Leontini is in Sicily, northwest of Syracuse.    [2] Not certainly part of a quotation.

(ii) fr. 1 (a) 32–42 (S 221)

Καλλ[ί]ας

αἰὲν ἐμοὶ πόνος οὗτος εἴη · | αἰ δέ τις βροτῶν μ᾽
ἐνίπτει | νόσφιν · οἷον χωρ[ὶ]ς καὶ λάθρα · [εἴ τ]ις ἐπιπλήσσει
μοι πάντα καλῶ[ς οἶ]δα ·

ἐγὼν δ᾽ ἔτι μ[είζο]ν᾽ αὔχαν | τίθεμαι περὶ τούτων ·
[οἷον εἴ] με αἰτιῶνται μείζονα [... καύχ]ησιν τίθεμ[αι
.]. ειρ. μαν[

ἰόεντα · μέ[λανα

omnia suppl. Lobel excepto καλῶς οἶδα (Treu et Page)

v. D. L. Page, *P.C.P.S.* 16 (1970) 93ss.

(iii) fr. 1 (b) (S 222)

ῥοπαλο[ ... ἀπὸ ῥοπ[αλ-
οὐδέ κεν Οἰδιπόδα καταεσσά[με] | νος δνοφέοις ἀχέεσ-
σιν Ἰ | νοῦ[ς τ᾽ ἀφαι]ρέοιτ[ο θ]υμόν · οὐδὲ γὰρ ἄν, φησ[ί,
δέηι ἔ]χειν τὰς τοῦ Οἰδίποδος πανουρ[γίας,] οὐδ᾽ εἰ τοῖς τῆς Ἰνοῦς
παθήμα[σι] κατέχοιτ[ο, ἀπο]στήσεται τοῦ [ἔ]ρωτος τού[του.

... τον ἔρ[ωτ- ? ... ]δισφυρω[
πολε]μίων λόχο[ν ... ὁ εἰσε . [... ἐ]νέδραν πολεμ[ί- ...
θεωρησα. [

suppl. Lobel praeter δνοφέοις (-οισιν pap.), τ᾽ ἀφαι-, δέηι ἔ- Page
τού[του Snell

v. D. L. Page, *P.C.P.S.* 16 (1970) 91s.

(iv) fr. 5 col. ii (S 223(a))

... Ἰ]βυκος ἐτέρω[θι ...

# IBYCUS

(ii)                    *Callias*[1]

Let this labour[2] always be mine; and if some mortal
upbraids me apart: i.e. away from me and secretly; if
someone reproves me I am well aware of it all;

(and?) I make a still greater boast about these
things: i.e. if they accuse me, I make a greater claim . . .;

violet-coloured: black . . .

[1] Presumably the name of the man or boy honoured, used as title of
the poem.    [2] The task of praising Callias.


(iii)

club: . . . from the club . . .

not even if clad in the murky woes of Oedipus or
Ino[1] would he rid himself of his passion: he says that
not even if he has to have the crimes[2] of Oedipus or were
gripped by the sufferings of Ino will he give up (this?) pas-
sion.[3]

. . . (the love?) . . . (ankles?)[4] . . .

the enemy's ambush: . . . the enemy's lying in wait . . .
(watched?) . . .

[1] 'Proverbial types of misery' (Page).    [2] The commentator
should have said 'misfortunes' (Page).    [3] Or 'his passion for
(the boy?)'.    [4] Is the subject still Oedipus? Perhaps
'hammers'.

(iv) (a)

. . . Ibycus elsewhere (says) . . .

# GREEK LYRIC

ἀ]πὸ χθονὸς ἐς . . ] . [ . . ]ạν βαθ[ὺν ἀ]έρα τάμνων·
Ἀ[κέ]σạνδρος ἐ[ν    ] περὶ Κυρήνης τὸν πε[ρὶ] τοῦ τρ[ικ]ẹφάλου
μῦθον ἀναιρῷ[ν] φησιν [α]ὐτὸν ἐπὶ τεθρίππου ὀχ[ε]ῖσθαι μ[ετ]ὰ δύο
παραβατῶν ι[ . . . ]νον, Τίμαιος δὲ [ . . . ] εἶναι, Θεόδω[ρος . . . ]s
ἀλλήλοις . . .

] . . ες χθ[όν]α . . .
ἀελ]λοπόδαν ο[ . . . ]  φησιν δεδαμάσθαι[ . . . ] τὸν Πήγασον
ο[ . . . Δο]ῦρις ἐν γ′ περὶ Ἀγαθ[οκλέα] . . . ὀνομάζọν[ται].
Πίν[δαρος Ὀ]λυμπιονίκ[αις] Κοριν[θ-

col. iii

. . . Ἀλẹξανδ[ρ- . . . ]κος Ποσει[δ-

suppl. Lobel praeter ἑτέρω[θι Marcovigi

v. D. L. Page, *P.C.P.S.* 16 (1970) 93s., G. Marcovigi, *S.I.F.C.* 43
(1971) 65ss.


S 223 (b) Schol. Ar. *Av.* 192 (p. 52 White)

χάους ἀντὶ τοῦ ἀέρος νῦν, ὡς Ἴβυκος·

   ποτάται δ᾽ ἐν ἀλλοτρίῳ χάει.

cf. *Sud.* X (iv 786 Adler)

v. Marcovigi l.c.


(v) fr. 12 (S 224)

. . . Τρ]ωίλου εκ . . [ . . . ]ọς τὸν φόνον . . . ] . αι ἐπιτηρήσας

παῖδα] θẹοῖς ἴκ[ελον τὸ]ν περγάμων ἔκτοσθεν Ἰλίο[υ

from earth to . . . , cleaving[1] the deep air[2];

Acesander[3] in book . . . of his *History of Cyrene,* explaining away the tale of the three-headed one,[4] says he[4] travelled on a four-horse chariot with two fellow-riders . . .; Timaeus[5] says they were . . . , Theodorus[6] that . . . each other.

. . . earth:

storm-footed[7] . . .: he says that Pegasus was subdued . . .; Duris[8] in book 3 of his *History of Agathocles* . . . are named. Pindar in his *Olympians*[9] says . . . Corinth . . .

. . . Alexander . . . Poseidon . . .

[1] Of Pegasus (see below)? Or the eagle that carried off Ganymede (fr. 289)? Or Geryon (see below), whom Stes. represented as winged (fr. 186)?    [2] Or 'mist'.    [3] Historian, 4th c. B.C.(?)    [4] Geryon.    [5] Historian of Sicily, c. 356–260 B.C. Perhaps he spoke of triplets.    [6] Probably the rhetorician from Gadara, 1st c. B.C.    [7] Of a horse? Cf. Simon. 515.    [8] Tyrant of Samos, historian, c. 340–260 B.C.    [9] In *Ol.* 13 Pindar used the myth of the Corinthian Bellerophon and the winged horse Pegasus.

(b) Scholiast on Aristophanes, *Birds*

He uses χάος ('void') instead of 'air' here, as does Ibycus[1]:

(he) flies in the alien void.[2]

[1] So also Bacch. 5. 27.    [2] Of Bellerophon? The attribution to Ibycus was accepted by Bergk but not by Diehl nor by Page in *P.M.G.*; Edmonds and Bowra saw reference to Ganymede's eagle: see n. 1 to (iv)(a) above.

(v)

. . . Troilus . . . the murder . . . after watching for him.

the boy, patterned on the gods, whom he slew out-

κτάνε·] ἀνεῖλεν τὸν Τρωίλον ἐκτ[ὸς τῆς πό]λεως ἐν τῶι τοῦ
Θυμβραίου ἱ[ερῶι· οὕτ]ῳ οὖν παῖδα θεοῖς ὅμοιον θε[οὶ οἱ ἐ]κτὸς
Ἰλίου ἱδρυμένοι το[ . . . ˏνω διατα[ . . . ]ᾳ προειρ[η- . . . ] ἀδελφὴ
[ . . . Ἕ]κτορος ˏ] ˏι Τρωίλ[ -

]κασι ˏ [ . . . ]ἀδελ[φ -

suppl. Lobel praeter Τρ]ωίλου Page, τὸ]ν Snell, κτάνε, οὕτ]ω, οἱ,
προειρ[η Page

(vi) fr. 14 (S 225)

. . . Ἰ]βυκο ˏ [ . . . ]ν λέγεινα[

(vii) fr. 32 (S 226)

Γοργια[

(viii) fr. 7 (S 227)

] Χαλκιδέων[ . . . προηγη[ . . . ] ἀποικίας [ . . . ] ὅρκια
πο[ . . . ]νως κυμ[ . . . ἐ]πὶ τοῖς ὅμμ[ασι . . . κ]ορύσσεται δε[ . . .
κορθ]ύεται· με[τ]εω[ρίζεται . . . ]ος ὁ πόθος ˏ [ . . . ] φησὶν ο ˏ[

suppl. Lobel

(ix) fr. 8 (S 228)

. . . ]ˏς γαληνοῖς ˏ [ . . . βέ]λτειον δεπια[ . . . κ]αλύμμασιν[ . . . ]ον
σὺν γενικῷ[ι . . . ν]έκυς ἔλλι[π]ε ιτ[ . . . ] χαλκοῦ μιˏς[ . . . σιδ]ήρου
δισκ[ . . .

suppl. Lobel praeter ἔλλι[π]ε ? Page

(x) fr. 11 (S 229)

. . . ]νοῦθον[ . . . ]ποσὶ τύπτῳ[ . . . ] ˏων ποσὶν α[ . . . ] ˏορος ἁβρὰ
β[αιν- ?

side the citadel of Ilium: he[1] killed Troilus outside the
city in the temple of Thymbraean Apollo; so in this way the
gods who were established (outside?) Ilium (abandoned?)
the godlike boy ... foretold(?) ... sister[2] ... of Hector ...
Troilus ...

sister[3] ...: ... sister[3] ...

[1] Achilles.     [2] Polyxena (sister of Hector and Troilus)? Vase-
painters depict Achilles' ambush of Troilus and Polyxena at a
fountain.     [3] Or 'brother'.

(vi)

... Ibycus ... say(s) ...

(vii)

... Gorgias[1] ...

[1] Cf. fr. 289.

(viii)

... Chalcidians[1] ... lead(er) ... of colony ... oaths ...
'wave' ... 'on the eyes' ... is given a crest ...; 'crests': rises
into the air ... desire ... (he) says ...

[1] Rhegium was a colony of Chalcis.

(ix)

'calm' ... better ... 'veils' ... with genitive ... 'corpse left'
... bronze ... (iron ... discus?) ...

(x)

... 'stamping' ... strike with the feet ... with the feet ...
'(step) delicately' ...

(xi) fr. 13 (S 230)

... ν]οήσῃ<ι> νεκτ[α]ρε- ...] νοήσῃι τὸ νέκταρ[...] τοιο[ῦ]τον
εὐπειθῆ [...]ς ἰοῦσιν· καὶ γὰρ [ αισ]ιον· καὶ γὰρ αυ[...] ˌ νεναι-
σιον ...

(xii) fr. 30 (S 232)

... Μναμος[

(xiii) fr. 33 (S 233)

...]π' ὠκεανο[...]ἐν γ' τονικ[ῶν ... ὠ]κεαν[-

τονικ[ῶν suppl. Lobel., ὠ]κεαν[ Page

(xiv) fr. 10 (S 240)

]ώς Φιλοστ[έφανος ἐν τῶι περὶ τῶν παραδόξων πο]ταμῶν τ[...]
Ἐρενίου ζ[...] πυθμένα[... ἐ]κ κυρίω[ν ...]αι· οἷον πυ[θμ-

suppl. Lobel

(xv) fr. 15 (S 241)

...]αδων γυν[αικῶν ... Σι]κελικὰ γε ˌ [... Σι]κελία ...

suppl. Lobel

(xvi) fr. 34 (S 255)

...]ωιδαριωι[...] ˌ μουσικη[...]νχαριν[...

**282C** P.Oxy. 3538

(i) fr. 1 col. i

         ]ιρο[ν εἴ]βην
         ]
5       ] δέ σ' ὕμνοι
  συμποτᾶν ˌ ] ἐπηράτοισιν, ὦ Χά-

(xi)

... 'thinks nectar': thinks the nectar ... such ... tempting ... for those going; 'for ... fitting' ...

(xii)

... 'Mnemosyne' ...

(xiii)

... 'ocean' ... in book 3 of his *Rules for Accentuation* ... ocean ...

(xiv)

... as Philostephanus[1] in his work, *On Incredible Rivers* .... Herennius[2] ... 'depth' ... from proper names ... i.e. depth ...

[1] Writer from Cyrene, 3rd c. B.C.   [2] Philo of Byblos, writer on verb-forms, synonyms, Phoenician religion, 64–141 A.D.

(xv)

... of women from ... Sicilian ... Sicily ...

(xvi)

... song ... music ... grace ...

**282C** Oxyrhynchus papyrus (*c.* 100 A.D.)

(i) col. i

... to drip ... and the songs (of fellow-drinkers?)

ρις, ῥόδων ἔ]θρεψας αὐτὸν ἐν κάλυξιν
Ἀφροδίτας] ἀμφὶ ναόν·
στέφαν]ον εὐώδη με δεῖ
10 λέγην, ὅσω]ν ἔχρ[ι]σε θωπά-
ζοισα παιδ]ίσκον· τέρεν δὲ
κάλλος ὠ]πάσαν θεαί.
ἀλλ' ἔφευγε] μὰν Δίκα θε-
ᾶν χορόν· β]αρύνομαι δὲ γυῖα,
15 πολλὰ δ' ἀ]γρύπνο[υ]ς ἰαύων
νύκτας ὀρμ]αίνω φρε[νί.

schol. ad v. 7 τ(ὸν) παῖδα

suppl. Lobel praeter 3, 6–11, 12 κάλλος, 13, 14 init., 15 init., 16
West    16 ]αινωιφρ̣ [ pap., em. West

v. M. L. West, Z.P.E. 57 (1984) 23ss.

col. ii

. . .]κλεος[ . . . ]μαινο[ . . . ]δᾶγμα[ . . .

(ii) fr. 2

. . . ]αιγλαι [ . . . μέ]γα νίκας[ . . . ]ισί τε Νικαγό-
ρα[ . . . ἐλ]κεσιπέπλων[ . . . ] ̣τιμᾶ[

μέ]γα suppl. West, ἐλ]κ. Lobel

(iii) fr. 3

. . .]σινου· [δ]έκ' ἄν σ' ὁ[πλίτας
ἐκ φάλαγγος ἑλκύ]σαιθ' ὑπεκφέρω[ν.

suppl. West

246

# IBYCUS

(praise) you. Among lovely buds (of roses), Charis,[1] you nurtured him[2] about the temple (of Aphrodite). I must (call the garland) fragrant, (all the flowers from which) she tinged the boy, flattering him. And the goddesses bestowed tender (beauty). But Justice (fled from the choir) of goddesses, and my limbs are weighed down, and passing sleepless (nights) I ponder (many things) in my heart.

[1] Goddess representing grace and charm.　　[2] 'The boy' (scholiast).

col. ii

... glory ... mad ... the sting[1] ...

[1] Of love?

(ii)

... (radiance?) ... great ... victory ... Nicagora[1] ... (women) of the trailing robes ... honour ...

[1] Or the male name Nicagoras; there is word-play with *nike*, 'victory'.

(iii)

... he would drag ten (hoplites out of the battle-line) in rescuing you.

(iv) fr. 6

. . . ]ς αἴαι ·


(v) fr. 11

]μητ᾽ ἂν ἔρωτ[

leg. West

(vi) fr. 17

αἰ]γιοχ[

leg. West

(vii) fr. 21

. . . ] ̣ο φευγω[ . . . ]ων κελη[ . . . ]ς̣ δεμ[ . . .

(viii) fr. 22

. . . ] ̣ς φλεγε[ . . . ] ̣ ελαύνων . . . ]υποπτερα[ . . .

(ix) fr. 23

. . . γ]λυκύς[ . . .

(x) fr. 24

. . . ο]μαλικος[ . . .

(συν-)ο]μ. suppl. Lobel

(xi) fr. 25

. . . ]παρθενικᾶι ξα[νθᾶι . . .

suppl. West

# IBYCUS

(iv)

... land[1] ...

[1] Perhaps Aea, the land of the Golden Fleece (West); for Jason and Medea cf. frr. 301, 291.

(v)

... would not ... love ...

(vi)

... aegis-bearing ...

(vii)

... flee(ing) ... steed(?) ... form(?) ...

(viii)

... blaze ... driving ... winged ...

(ix)

... sweet ...

(x)

... comrade ...

(xi)

... (to) the auburn girl ...

(xii) fr. 26

    . . . ] ̣ ολεσθαι[ . . . ] ̣ σω νοσω[ . . . ] ̣ το φαρμ[ακ-
. . . β]ροτοῖσιν ̣ [ . . . ]ε̣θηκε δ[ . . . ]ες θηρα[ . . .
μ]έγαν σπευ[

φαρμ[ακ, μ]έγαν suppl. Lobel       β]ροτοῖσιν . . . δ[αίμων? ego


(xiii) fr. 27

. . . αὐλ[ὸ]ς ἐσφ[ . . . ποικίλος ὕ[μνος . . . Μοισᾶν
Πιε[ρίδων . . . ἐν τῶι παιδ[α . . . ὑμνήσω τ[ . . .
ὀ]φθαλμο[ . . . δ]άσκια θ[ . . . κ]εκλιμέ[ν- . . . ἆμος
λευ[κοπάραος . . . Ἀὼς εἰσαν[ίηι . . . ἠριγένεια . . .
κ[αὶ θεοῖς α[ . . .

suppl. Lobel praeter ἐν τῶι παιδ[α, δ]άσκια, λευ[κοπάραος, εἰσαν[ίηι
West

v. M. L. West, *Z.P.E.* 57 (1984) 28s.


(xiv) frr. 29 + 31 (coniunx. West)

    . . . ]κα παρθ[εν-
    αἶ] μή τι κόρα̣[ς θάλ]αμον κα[ταβάς ποκα
    πά]μπαν ἀνεχ[ρίσθ]η τα̣κερᾶι φρεν[ὶ
    ματ]ρὸς ἐπιστ[α]μένας πά[ρ]α δῶρο[ν ἐ-
5   φίμ]ερον · ἀσπ[ά]σιος δ᾽ ὁ φέρων χά̣[ριν
    . . . . ]οϲα̣ιτ[᾽ ἀδ]ελφεᾶς παῖς

suppl. West praeter 6 ἀδ]ελφεᾶς Lobel

v. M. L. West, *Z.P.E.* 57 (1984) 29ss.

# IBYCUS

(xii)

... to perish(?) ... disease(s) ... remedy ... (for mortals?) ... (god?) established ... (wild beast?) ... great ... (hasten?) ...

(xiii)

... pipe ... A complex song of the Pierian Muses ... in which I shall sing of a boy ... his eyes ... shaggy[1] ... reclining ... when white(-cheeked?) Dawn climbs (the heavens), early-born, ... and to gods[2] ...

[1] Presumably of cheeks not yet 'shaggy' (West). [2] 'Bringing light both to mortals and to gods' (West).

(xiv)

... girl ... unless he,[1] going down (once) to the girl's room, had his melting heart completely tinged by his skilled mother with her gift of desire. Glad[2] is he who brings (favour?) ... (whether it is?) (her?) sister's son (or?) ...

[1] Presumably Eros, child of Aphrodite, fell in love with the girl (West). [2] Or 'welcome'.

(xv) fr. 30

... ε]τυχον χα[ρι ... νεκυοσ]τόλα· τυμ[β- ...
δ]ώματ' ἀλάμ[πετα ... ]ων· τοδεσ[ ... ]ασανέμο[ ...
μέ]γ̣', ὦ φί̣λε̣[ ...

τυμ[β-, δ]ώματ' ἀλάμ[πετα suppl. Lobel, cetera West

(xvi) fr. 32

... α]ῦτ' Ἔρω[ς ... ι]ππ[ ...

suppl. West (α]ῦτ' vel δη]ῦτ')

**283** Hdn. π. μον. λέξ. β' 36 (ii 941 Lentz: cf. i 392)

ὁπότε δὲ ἐπὶ τῆς ἐκπλήξεως παραλαμβάνεται, γένος ἐπιδέχε-
ται τὸ οὐδέτερον (sc. τάφος)·
ἡ δ' ἄνεω δὴν ἧστο, τάφος δέ οἱ ἦτορ ἵκανε (Od. 23. 93)·
ἀλλ' ἴσως τοῦτο ἀμφίβολον. ὁ μέντοι Ἴβυκος διέστειλε τὸ γένος ἐν
τῷ πρώτῳ, σχεδὸν τὸν Ὁμηρικὸν μεταλαβών· φησὶ γάρ·

δαρὸν †δάραοι† χρόνον ἧστο τάφει πεπαγώς·

οὕτω γὰρ ἔκλινεν ὡς βέλει.

δάραοι secl. Lehrs: παρά οἱ Hermann: ἄνεω Nauck        τάφεις cod.,
corr. Bloch        πεπηγώς cod.

**284** Schol. Ap. Rhod. 4. 57s (p. 264 Wendel)

Ἴβυκος δὲ ἐν α' Ἤλιδος αὐτὸν (sc. τὸν Ἐνδυμίωνα) βασιλεῦσαί
φησι.

# IBYCUS

(xv)

... chanced ... (corpse-bearing?) ... tomb ... unlit halls[1] ... (great?), my friend, ...

[1] Of Hades.


(xvi)

... once again Love ... (horse?)[1] ...

[1] Cf. fr. 287; or a proper name e.g. in -ippus.


**283** Herodian, *On Anomalous Words*

When τάφος is used in the sense of 'astonishment' it admits the neuter gender: cf. 'and she sat for a long time in silence, for amazement had come over her heart' (*Od.* 23. 93); but perhaps that example is ambiguous; Ibycus, however, made the gender clear in book 1, where he pretty well took over the Homeric line:

for a long time he sat (beside him? beside her?) frozen in amazement.

He declined the noun like τὸ βέλος.


**284** Scholiast on Apollonius of Rhodes

Ibycus in book 1 says Endymion[1] was king of Elis.

[1] Handsome young man beloved by Selene (the Moon).


253

# GREEK LYRIC

**285** Athen. 2. 57f–58a (i 135 Kaibel)

Ἴβυκος δὲ ἐν πέμπτῳ μελῶν περὶ Μολιονιδῶν φησι·

τούς τε λευκίππους κόρους
τέκνα Μολιόνας κτάνον,
ἅλικας ἰσοκεφάλους ἐνιγυίους
ἀμφοτέρους γεγαῶτας ἐν ὠέῳ
5 ἀργυρέῳ.

cf. Eust. *Od.* 1686. 45

1 Dindorf: κούρους codd.    2 κτάνεν ci. Hartung    5 ἀργυ-
φέῳ ci. West

**286** Athen. 13. 601b (iii 325 Kaibel)

καὶ ὁ Ῥηγῖνος δὲ Ἴβυκος βοᾷ καὶ κέκραγεν·

ἦρι μὲν αἵ τε Κυδώνιαι
μηλίδες ἀρδόμεναι ῥοᾶν
ἐκ ποταμῶν, ἵνα Παρθένων
κῆπος ἀκήρατος, αἵ τ' οἰνανθίδες
5 αὐξόμεναι σκιεροῖσιν ὑφ' ἕρνεσιν
οἰναρέοις θαλέθοισιν· ἐμοὶ δ' ἔρος
    οὐδεμίαν κατάκοιτος ὥραν·
ἀλλ' ἅθ' ὑπὸ στεροπᾶς φλέγων
Θρηίκιος Βορέας ἀίσ-
10 σων παρὰ Κύπριδος ἀζαλέαις μανί-
αισιν ἐρεμνὸς ἀθαμβὴς
    ἐγκρατέως πεδόθεν †φυλάσσει†
ἡμετέρας φρένας.

8 ἀλλ' ἅθ' ὑπὸ Mehlhorn: τε ὑπὸ codd.    11s. Schweighaeuser,
Hermann: ἀθάμβησεν κραταιῶς codd.    12 Naeke: παιδ' ὅθεν
codd.    τινάσσει Naeke: λαφύσσει West

254

# IBYCUS

**285** Athenaeus, *Scholars at Dinner*

Ibycus in book 5 of his *Songs* says of the Molionids

and I[1] killed those white-horsed[2] youths, the children of Molione,[3] like-aged, equal-headed, single-bodied, both born in a silver egg.

[1] Heracles.     [2] Cf. Stes. 256.     [3] In the *Iliad* (2. 621, 11. 709, 750 ff., 23. 638 ff.) they are Cteatus and Eurytus, twin sons of Poseidon, not Siamese twins (as here and in Hesiod fr. 18 M.-W.) but normal warriors from Elis who fought against Nestor.

**286** Athenaeus, *Scholars at Dinner*[1]

And the man of Rhegium, Ibycus, shouts and screams,

In the spring flourish Cydonian quince-trees, watered from flowing rivers where stands the inviolate garden of the Maidens, and vine-blossoms growing under the shady vine-branches; but for me love rests at no season: like the Thracian north wind blazing with lightning rushing from the Cyprian[2] with parching fits of madness, dark and shameless, it powerfully shakes[3] my heart from the roots.

[1] The passage follows Alcman 59 and Stes. 276(a): Chamaeleon (quoting Archytas) may be the speaker's authority here too.     [2] Aphrodite, mother of Eros (Love).     [3] Verb uncertain: perhaps 'devours my heart completely'.

# GREEK LYRIC

**287** Plato *Parmen.* 137a

καίτοι δοκῶ μοι τὸ τοῦ Ἰβυκείου ἵππου πεπονθέναι ᾧ ἐκεῖνος ἀθλητῇ ὄντι καὶ πρεσβυτέρῳ ὑφ' ἅρματι μέλλοντι ἀγωνιεῖσθαι καὶ δι' ἐμπειρίαν τρέμοντι τὸ μέλλον ἑαυτὸν ἀπεικάζων ἄκων ἔφη καὶ αὐτὸς οὕτω πρεσβευτὴς ὢν εἰς τὸν ἔρωτα ἀναγκάζεσθαι ἰέναι.

schol. ad loc. (p. 49 Greene): τὸ τοῦ μελοποιοῦ Ἰβύκου ῥητόν·

Ἔρος αὖτέ με κυανέοισιν ὑπὸ
    βλεφάροις τακέρ' ὄμμασι δερκόμενος
κηλήμασι παντοδαποῖς ἐς ἄπει-
    ρα δίκτυα Κύπριδος ἐσβάλλει·
5 ἦ μὰν τρομέω νιν ἐπερχόμενον,
ὥστε φερέζυγος ἵππος ἀεθλοφόρος ποτὶ γήρᾳ
ἀέκων σὺν ὄχεσφι θοοῖς ἐς ἅμιλλαν ἔβα.

cf. Procl. in Plat. *Parmen.* v 316 Cousin

3s. ἀπείρονα ci. Schneidewin, Hecker      4 Clemm (εἰσ-): βάλλει codd.


**288** Athen. 13. 564f (iii 245 Kaibel)

τυφλὸς ὁ ἔπαινος καὶ κατ' οὐδὲν ὅμοιος τῷ Ἰβυκείῳ ἐκείνῳ·

Εὐρύαλε γλαυκέων Χαρίτων θάλος, ‹Ὡρᾶν›
καλλικόμων μελέδημα, σὲ μὲν Κύπρις
ἅ τ' ἀγανοβλέφαρος Πει-
    θὼ ῥοδέοισιν ἐν ἄνθεσι θρέψαν.

cf. Eust. *Od.* 1558. 17

1 γλυκέων ci. Jacobs, Fiorillo      suppl. Page post Bergk

# IBYCUS

**287** Plato, *Parmenides*

Yet I[1] find myself in the same plight as Ibycus' horse, a champion and in his old age about to compete in the chariot race and trembling at the prospect since he has been through it before: Ibycus compared himself to the horse and declared that in his advanced years he was being forced to fall in love against his will.

Scholiast: the words of the lyric poet Ibycus are as follows:

Again Love, looking at me meltingly from under his dark eyelids, hurls me with his manifold enchantments into the boundless nets of the Cyprian. How I fear his onset, as a prize-winning horse still bearing the yoke in his old age goes unwillingly with swift chariot to the race.

[1] Parmenides, reluctant to embark on a lengthy exposition.

**288** Athenaeus, *Scholars at Dinner*

This praise[1] is blind and not in the least like the famous words of Ibycus:

Euryalus, offshoot of the blue-eyed Graces, darling of the lovely-haired (Seasons),[2] the Cyprian and soft-lidded Persuasion nursed you among rose-blossoms.

[1] I.e. Philoxenus of Cythera fr. 821 *P.M.G.*    [2] Cf. Hesiod, *W. and D.* 73 ff., Menander Rhetor, $\pi$. $\grave{\epsilon}\pi\iota\delta$. 149 (quoted at Alcaeus 308(a)).

# GREEK LYRIC

**289** Schol. Ap. Rhod. 3. 114–17b (p. 220 Wendel)

διὰ τούτων τῶν στίχων παραγράφει τὰ εἰρημένα ὑπὸ Ἰβύκου ἐν
οἷς περὶ τῆς Γανυμήδους ἁρπαγῆς εἶπεν ἐν τῇ εἰς Γοργίαν ᾠδῇ·
καὶ ἐπιφέρει περὶ τῆς Ἠοῦς ὡς ἥρπασε Τιθωνόν.

**290** Diomed. *ars gramm.* i (i 323 Keil)

patronymica sunt quae a patre sumuntur, ut Pelides
Priamides. abusive saepe etiam a matre fiunt, ut Latous
Apollo ... aut ab avo ... aut ab avia ... aut a fratribus ...
aut a maioribus, ut Belides Palamedes, aut a maritis, ut
Helena Menelais, aut a filiis, ut Althaea Meleagris

(Ἀλθαία Μελεαγρίς),

sicut Ibycus Graecus rettulit.

**291** Schol. Ap. Rhod. 4. 814–15a (p. 293 Wendel)

ὅτι δὲ Ἀχιλλεὺς εἰς τὸ Ἠλύσιον πεδίον παραγενόμενος ἔγημε
Μήδειαν πρῶτος Ἴβυκος εἴρηκε, μεθ' ὃν Σιμωνίδης (fr. 558).

**292** Philodem. *Piet.* (p. 18 Gomperz)

Αἰσχύλος δ[ . . . . . . . . ] καὶ Εὔβ[υκος καὶ Τε]λέστης (fr. 812)
[ . . . . . . . . . ] τὰς Ἁρπ[υίας ...

ποιοῦσιν] τὰς Ἁρπ[υίας θνησκ]ούσας ὑπ[ὸ τῶν Βορέου παί]δων suppl.
Gomperz    v. Aes. *Phineus* F 260 Radt

258

# IBYCUS

**289** Scholiast on Apollonius of Rhodes[1]

In these lines Apollonius takes over what Ibycus said in his account of the rape of Ganymede[2] in his song to Gorgias; Ibycus tells also how Dawn carried off Tithonus.

[1] Wilamowitz transferred the scholium from v. 158 to vv. 114–17.    [2] I.e. that he was carried off by a love-smitten Zeus, not by 'the gods' 'to be wine-pourer to Zeus' as in *Il.* 20. 234.

**290** Diomedes, *Grammar*

Patronymics are epithets based on the father's name, e.g. Pelides (son of Peleus) and Priamides (son of Priam). They are often formed irregularly from the mother's name, e.g. Latoan Apollo ... or a grandfather's ... or grandmother's ... or brothers' ... or ancestors' names, e.g. Belides Palamedes,[1] or husbands' names, e.g. Menelaid Helen,[2] or sons' names, e.g.

### Meleagrid Althaea,

as in Ibycus the Greek.

[1] See Virgil, *Aen.* 2. 82.    [2] This example too may be taken from Ibycus.

**291** Scholiast on Apollonius of Rhodes

Ibycus was the first to say that Achilles married Medea when he reached the Elysian plain, and Simonides followed him.

**292** Philodemus, *Piety*

Aeschylus ... and Ibycus and Telestes (represent) the Harpies (as being killed by the sons of Boreas?).

# GREEK LYRIC

**293** *Et. Gen.* (p. 17 Calame) = *Et. Mag.* 171. 7

αὔσιον· καὶ ὁ μὲν Ἴβυκος αὔσιον λέγει, οἷον·

οὐ γὰρ αὔσιον πάις Τυδέος,

ὁ δὲ Ἀλκμὰν ταυσία (fr. 112), ὁ δὲ ποιητὴς κατὰ διάστασιν καὶ τροπὴν τοῦ α εἰς η, οἷον· τηΰσίην ὁδόν (*Od.* 3. 316)· οὐδεὶς γὰρ τὸν σχηματισμὸν αὐτοῦ κατώρθωσεν. ἐγὼ δὲ ἡγοῦμαι ὅτι πρῶτον τὸ παρ᾽ Ἰβύκῳ, δεύτερον τὸ παρὰ Ἀλκμᾶνι, τρίτον τὸ παρὰ Ὁμήρῳ κατὰ διάστασιν. οὕτως Ἡρωδιανὸς περὶ Παθῶν (ii 176 Lentz).

πάις an παῖς incertum        Τυδέως codd.

**294** Schol. Pind. *Nem.* 10. 12a (iii 167s. Drachmann)

Διομήδεα δ᾽ ἄμβροτον ξανθά ποτε γλαυκῶπις ἔθηκε θεόν· καὶ οὗτος Ἀργεῖος, ὃς δι᾽ ἀρετὴν ἀπηθανατίσθη· καὶ ἔστι περὶ τὸν Ἀδρίαν Διομήδεια νῆσος ἱερά, ἐν ᾗ τιμᾶται ὡς θεός. καὶ Ἴβυκος οὕτω. τὴν Ἑρμιόνην γήμας ὁ Διομήδης ἀπηθανατίσθη σὺν τοῖς Διοσκούροις· καὶ γὰρ συνδιαιτᾶται αὐτοῖς. καὶ Πολέμων ἱστορεῖ (fr. 23 Müller, *F.H.G.* iii 122)· ἐν μὲν γὰρ Ἀργυρίπποις ἅγιόν ἐστιν αὐτοῦ ἱερόν. καὶ ἐν Μεταποντίῳ δὲ διὰ πολλῆς αὐτὸν αἴρεσθαι τιμῆς ὡς θεόν, καὶ ἐν Θουρίοις εἰκόνας αὐτοῦ καθιδρύσθαι ὡς θεοῦ.

post Ἴβυκος οὕτω lacunam indicavit Boeckh

**295** Schol. A Hom. *Il.* 3. 314 (i 157 Dindorf)

Πορφύριος ἐν τοῖς παραλελειμμένοις φησὶν ὅτι τὸν Ἕκτορα Ἀπόλλωνος υἱὸν παραδίδωσιν Ἴβυκος, Ἀλέξανδρος (fr. 13 Powell), Εὐφορίων (fr. 56 Powell), Λυκόφρων (*Alex.* 265).

---

[1] 3rd c. A.D. scholar.
Euphorion and Lycophron.

[2] A. of Aetolia, 3rd c. B.C. poet like
[3] Cf. Stes. 224.

# IBYCUS

**293** *Etymologicum Genuinum*

αὐσίον ('vain'): Ibycus uses αὔσιον:

> For not in vain (did) the son of Tydeus[1] . . .

Alcman has ταυσία (fr. 112). Homer has it with diaeresis and α changed to η: τηϋσίην ὁδόν ('vain journey', *Od.* 3. 316) — no-one has corrected his form of the word. I think that Ibycus' was the original form, Alcman's next, Homer's with diaeresis third. So Herodian, *On Inflexions.*

[1] Diomedes.

**294** Scholiast on Pindar, *Nemean* 10 ('And Diomedes once was made an immortal god by auburn, grey-eyed Athena')

He too was from Argos, and was immortalised for his valour. Off the Adriatic coast there is a holy island called Diomedia, on which he is honoured as a god. So in Ibycus.[1] Diomedes after marrying Hermione[2] was immortalised along with the Dioscuri; indeed he lives with them. Polemon[3] tells the story: in Argyrippa[4] there is a sanctuary which is sacred to him; in Metapontium also he is exalted as a god with much honour, and in Thurii statues of him are set up as if he were a god.

[1] Perhaps a quotation is lost. It is not clear whether the following sentence refers to Ibycus' account. [2] Daughter of Menelaus and Helen, who in other versions married Orestes; the Dioscuri were Helen's brothers. [3] Geographer from Ilium, 2nd c. B.C. [4] Arpi; all three cities are in S. Italy, Diomedia (mod. San Domenico) is off the east coast of Italy.

**295** Scholiast on *Iliad* ('Hector, son of Priam')

Porphyry[1] in his *Omissions* says that Hector is Apollo's son in the versions of Ibycus, Alexander,[2] Euphorion and Lycophron.[3]

**296** Schol. Eur. *Andr.* 631 (ii 293 Schwartz)

προδότιν αἰκάλλων κύνα· ἡττηθεὶς τοῖς ἀφροδισίοις. ἄμεινον ᾠκονόμηται τοῖς περὶ Ἴβυκον· εἰς γὰρ Ἀφροδίτης ναὸν καταφεύγει ἡ Ἑλένη κἀκεῖθεν διαλέγεται τῷ Μενελάῳ, ὁ δ' ὑπ' ἔρωτος ἀφίησι τὸ ξίφος. τὰ παραπλήσια <τούτοις καὶ Ἴβυκος ὁ suppl. Schwartz> Ῥηγῖνος ἐν διθυράμβῳ φησίν.

cf. scholl. Ar. *Vesp.* 714, *Lys.* 155

**297** Schol. T Hom. *Il.* 13. 516 (iii 500 Erbse)

ἀκόντισε Δηΐφοβος· ὡς ἀντεραστὴς Ἑλένης, ὡς μαρτυρεῖ Ἴβυκος καὶ Σιμωνίδης (fr. 561). ἀλλ' οὔτε ἦρα μεσαιπόλιος (*Il.* 13. 361) οὔτε τὸ παρὰ Ἰβύκῳ ἀληθές· ἀλλὰ διὰ τοὺς πεσόντας.

cf. Eust. *Il.* 944. 43 (iii 507 van der Valk)

**298** P.Oxy. 2260 col. ii 23ss.

καὶ ὁμοίως κατὰ τὸν Ἴβυκον· τὸν γὰρ Ἡρακλ[έ]α

π[ρ]όμαχον

γενέσθαι φ[ησὶ τ]οῦ Διὸς Δ[ιὸς

σ]ὺν ἀριστ[οπάτραι
καὶ κρατ]ερόφρονι Παλλάδι·
[τὰ]ν γὰρ ἔτικτ' αὐτός, κορυφᾶς δέ οἱ ἐξανέπαλτο.

v. D. L. Page, *C.R.* 3 (1953) 1s., R. Merkelbach, *Arch. f. Pap.* 16 (1956) 116, M. L. West, *C.Q.* 25 (1975) 308

suppl. Lobel praeter φ[ησὶ Merkelbach, τ]οῦ Διὸς σ]ὺν ἀριστ[οπάτραι Page

**299** Schol. Ap. Rhod. 2. 777–9 (p. 187 Wendel)

ἀκολούθως τῷ μύθῳ πεζὸν τὸν Ἡρακλέα φησὶν ἐπὶ τὸν ζωστῆρα τῆς Ἱππολύτης ἀπελθεῖν ... πολλοὶ δὲ λόγοι περὶ τοῦ ζωστῆρός εἰσιν. τινὲς μὲν γὰρ Ἱππολύτης, ἄλλοι δὲ Δηϊλύκης.

# IBYCUS

**296** Scholiast on Euripides, *Andromache*

'fawning on the treacherous bitch'[1]: overcome by sexual desire. The incident is better handled by Ibycus[2]; in his version Helen takes refuge in the temple of Aphrodite and speaks from there with Menelaus, who is overcome by love and drops his sword. Ibycus of Rhegium in a dithyramb gives a version similar to this.[3]

[1] Peleus reproaches Menelaus for not killing Helen after the fall of Troy.    [2] Cf. Stes. 201.    [3] This sentence seems to be an alternative scholium.

**297** Scholiast on *Iliad*

'Deiphobus threw his javelin (at Idomeneus)': since he was his rival for the love of Helen, according to Ibycus and Simonides; but Idomeneus was going grey (*Il.* 13. 361) and was not in love, and Ibycus' story is false; Deiphobus threw his javelin because of the Trojans that had fallen at the hands of Idomeneus.

**298** Papyrus commentary on a poetic text (2nd c. A.D.)[1]

Likewise in Ibycus: for he says that Heracles was Zeus' champion,[2] along with stout-hearted Pallas, child of an excellent father: for he himself bore her, and she leapt forth from his head ...

[1] The passage follows Stes. 233. The topic is the birth of Athena from the head of Zeus.    [2] He and Athena fought for Zeus against the Giants.

**299** Scholiast on Apollonius of Rhodes

It fits the story when Apollonius says Heracles went off on foot to fetch the girdle of Hippolyta ... There are many stories about the girdle: some say it belonged to Hippolyta,

Ἴβυκος δὲ ἰδίως ἱστορῶν Ὀιολύκης τῆς Βριάρεω θυγατρός φησιν.

(Ὀιολύκα, Βριάρηο κόρα Bergk)

cf. *Et. Mag.* 213. 23 Βριάρηο· οἷον Βριάρηο κόρα

## 300 Schol. Ar. *Nub.* 1051 (p. 200 Holwerda)

Ἡράκλεια λουτρά· Ἴβυκός φησι τὸν Ἥφαιστον κατὰ δωρεὰν ἀναδοῦναι τῷ Ἡρακλεῖ θερμῶν ὑδάτων λουτρά. ἐξ ὧν τὰ θερμά τινές φασιν Ἡράκλεια λέγεσθαι.

cf. *Sud.* H 460 (ii 581 Adler)

## 301 Schol. Ap. Rhod. 1. 287 (p. 33 Wendel)

ᾧ ἔπι μούνῳ· ἄρρενι μόνῳ. εἶχεν γὰρ (sc. ὁ Ἰάσων) ἀδελφὴν Ἱππολύτην, ὥς φησιν Ἴβυκος.

## 302 *Epim. Hom.* (*Anecd. Oxon.* i 255 Cramer)

ὥσπερ παρὰ τὸ Δάρδανος ἐκπίπτει πατρωνυμικὸν εἰς -ις Δαρδανίς, ... οὕτως ἔδει καὶ παρὰ τὸ Κάδμος Καδμίς· τὸ ἄρα Καδμηίς ἐπλεόνασε τὸ η. ὅτε οὖν φησιν ὁ Ἴβυκος

παρελέξατο Καδμίδι κούρᾳ,

τὸ ὀφειλόμενον ἀπέδωκεν.

cf. Hdn. ii 231, i 85 Lentz

## 303 'Hdn.' *Fig.* (*Rhet. Gr.* viii 605s. Walz)

τὸ δὲ Ἰβύκειον καὶ λέξεως καὶ συντάξεώς ἐστι, γίνεται δὲ ἐν τοῖς ὑποτακτικοῖς τρίτοις προσώποις τῶν ῥημάτων κατὰ πρόσθεσιν τῆς -σι συλλαβῆς ... καλεῖται δὲ Ἰβύκειον, οὐχ ὅτι πρῶτος Ἴβυκος

others to Deïlyca. Ibycus is alone in saying that it belonged to

Oeolyca, daughter of Briareus.

**300** Scholiast on Aristophanes, *Clouds* ('Heraclean baths')

Ibycus says Hephaestus sent up baths of hot waters as a gift to Heracles. Some say that is why hot springs are called Heraclean.

**301** Scholiast on Apollonius of Rhodes

'for whom alone'[1]: the adjective 'alone' is masculine, for according to Ibycus Jason had a sister Hippolyta.

[1] Alcimede speaks of Jason as her only child; Ap. does not follow Ibycus: the scholiast is muddled.

**302** *Homeric Parsings*

Just as *Dardanus* gives the patronymic *Dardanis* in *-is,* ... *Cadmus* should give *Cadmis*; the form *Cadmeïs* has a pleonastic 'e'. So when Ibycus says,

he lay with the daughter of Cadmus,[1]

he used the correct form, *Cadmis*.

[1] With reference to Semele and Zeus or Ino and Athamas or Agave and Echion or Autonoe and Aristaeus.

**303** 'Herodian', *On Figures of Speech*

The Ibycean figure belongs to both diction and syntax and occurs in 3rd person subjunctive forms of verbs through the addition of the syllable -σι ... It is called Iby-

αὐτῷ ἐχρήσατο, δέδεικται γὰρ καὶ παρ' Ὁμήρῳ πρότερον, ἀλλ' ἐπεὶ πολὺ καὶ κατακορὲς παρ' αὐτῷ. καὶ γάρ·

(a) γλαυκώπιδα Κασσάνδραν
ἐρασιπλόκαμον Πριάμοιο κόραν
φᾶμις ἔχησι βροτῶν.

καὶ δι' ἑτέρων·

(b) ἆμος ἄυπνος κλυτὸς ὄρθρος ἐγείρησιν ἀηδόνας,

ἀντὶ τοῦ ἐγείρῃ.

cf. *Et. Mag.* 440. 53, *Et. Gen.* (p. 29 Calame), schol. A Hom. *Il.* 5. 6 (ii 2 Erbse), *Il.* 22. 23 (v 266 Erbse), Lesbonact. ap. Ammon. 166 Valckenaer, Eust. *Od.* 1576. 56, *Et. Mag.* 650. 56

(a) 2 Page: κόραν Πριάμοιο, κόρην Πριάμου codd.
(b) Bergk: τᾶμος codd.      ἀύπνους ci. Schneidewin, ἀύπνος (accus.) Mucke      ἔγρησιν ci. Page

**304** Schol. Ap. Rhod. 1. 146–9 (p. 19 Wendel)

εἰκότως αὐτὴν (sc. Λήδαν) Αἰτωλίδα εἶπεν, ἐπεὶ Αἰτωλὸς ὁ Θέστιος. καὶ εἴρηκεν ἀπὸ τῆς χώρας, ὡς ἐάν τις τὸν Συρακόσιον Σικελὸν λέγῃ ἢ τὸν Ῥωμαῖον Ἰταλόν. ὁ δὲ Ἴβυκος αὐτὴν Πλευρωνίαν φησίν, Ἑλλάνικος δὲ (fr. 119 Jacoby) Καλυδωνίαν.

**305** Diomed. *ars gramm.* i (i 321 Keil)

his etiam unum accedit, agnomen ex aliqua virtute forinsecus quaesitum, quod ἐπιγέννητον Graeci dicunt, quo cognomina discriminantur, ut est Ulixi agnomen polytlas. nam praenomen est, ut ait Ibycus, Olixes, nomen Arcisiades, cognomen Odyseus, et ordinantur sic, Olixes Arcisiades Odyseus polytlas.

(ἐκαλεῖτο δ' Ὀλυσσεὺς (vel Ὀλιξεὺς)
Ἀρκεισιάδας Ὀδυσεὺς ὁ πολύτλας ci. Bergk)

cean not because Ibycus was the first to use it — instances
from Homer have been given above — but because he uses
it frequently, indeed *ad nauseam,* e.g.

(a) grey-eyed Cassandra of the lovely locks,
daughter of Priam, is held in the speech of mortals;

(b) when sleepless glorious daybreak rouses the
nightingales,[1]

where he uses ἐγείρησι(ν) for ἐγείρῃ.

[1] Perhaps 'the sleepless nightingales'.

---

**304** Scholiast on Apollonius of Rhodes ('Aetolian Leda')

It is reasonable for him to call her Aetolian, since Thes-
tius[1] was Aetolian. He gives her country, as if one were to
call a Syracusan Sicilian or a Roman Italian. Ibycus says
she was from Pleuron,[2] Hellanicus from Calydon.[2]

[1] Her father.    [2] City of Aetolia.

---

**305** Diomedes, *Grammar*

To these names is added one other, the agnomen ('addi-
tional name'), which is derived from outside the family and
is called ἐπιγέννητον by the Greeks: it serves to distinguish
one cognomen ('surname') from another; for example, the
agnomen of Ulysses is *polytlas* ('much-enduring'), since, as
Ibycus says, the praenomen ('personal name') is Olixes, the
nomen ('gentile name') is Arcisiades[1] and the cognomen is
Odyseus, and they are given in the following order: Olixes
Arcisiades Odyseus polytlas.[2]

[1] Arcisius was grandfather of Odysseus.    [2] Ibycus may have
said, 'and Olixes was called Arcisiades, Odysseus the much-
enduring'. The Latin system of nomenclature has no relevance to
Greek poetry.

# GREEK LYRIC

**306** Prisc. *inst.* vi 92 (ii 276 Keil) ( = Hdn. i 14 Lentz)

pro Φυλεύς Φύλης, pro Ὀρφεύς Ὄρφης et Ὄρφην dicunt (sc. Dores), pro Τυδεύς Τύδης. sic Antimachus in i Thebaidos (fr. 6 Wyss) . . . similiter Ibycus

$$\dot{o}νομάκλυτον\ \text{'}Ορφήν$$

dixit.

-κλυτος Ὄρφη (voc.) Schneidewin, -κλυτος Ὀρφήν (nom.) Bergk (cl. Arcad. 8. 15)

**307** Schol. Eur. *Hec.* 41 (i 17 Schwartz)

ὑπὸ Νεοπτολέμου φασὶν αὐτὴν (sc. Πολυξένην) σφαγιασθῆναι Εὐριπίδης καὶ Ἴβυκος.

**308** Paus. 2. 6. 5 (i 121 Rocha-Pereira)

Σικυῶνα δὲ οὐ Μαραθῶνος τοῦ Ἐπωπέως, Μητίονος δὲ εἶναι τοῦ Ἐρεχθέως φασίν. ὁμολογεῖ δέ σφισι καὶ Ἄσιος (fr. 11 Davies), ἐπεὶ Ἡσίοδός γε καὶ Ἴβυκος, ὁ μὲν ἐποίησεν (fr. 224 M.-W.) ὡς Ἐρεχθέως εἴη Σικυών, Ἴβυκος δὲ εἶναι Πέλοπός φησιν αὐτόν.

**309** Athen. 13. 603d (iii 330 Kaibel)

Ῥαδαμάνθυος δὲ τοῦ δικαίου Ἴβυκος ἐραστήν φησι γενέσθαι Τάλων.

**310** Plut. *Qu. Conv.* 748c, ix 15. 2 (iv 335 Hubert)

ἀλλ' οὐδὲν οὕτως τὸ νῦν ἀπολέλαυκε τῆς κακομουσίας ὡς ἡ ὄρχησις. διὸ καὶ πέπονθεν ὁ φοβηθεὶς Ἴβυκος ἐποίησε·

268

# IBYCUS

**306** Priscian, *Grammar*

The Dorians say Phyles instead of Phyleus, Orphes and Orphen instead of Orpheus, Tydes instead of Tydeus. So Antimachus in book 1 of his *Thebaid* ...; and similarly Ibycus said

## famous Orphes.[1]

[1] Perhaps 'Orphen'.

**307** Scholiast on Euripides, *Hecuba*

Euripides and Ibycus say that Polyxena was killed as a sacrifice by Neoptolemus.

**308** Pausanias, *Description of Greece*

They (i.e. the Sicyonians) say that the father of Sicyon was not Marathon, son of Epopeus,[1] but Metion, son of Erechtheus. Asius[2] agrees with them, but in Hesiod's poem Sicyon was the son of Erechtheus, while Ibycus says he is the son of Pelops.[3]

[1] As Eumelus of Corinth said (Paus. 2. 1. 1).   [2] Epic poet of Samos, 6th or 5th c. B.C.   [3] And so not Athenian (Erechtheus was king of Athens); see C. M. Bowra, *G.L.P.* 246 f., J. P. Barron, *C.Q.* 58 (1964) 224.

**309** Athenaeus, *Scholars at Dinner*

Rhadamanthys the just, according to Ibycus, was loved by Talos.

**310** Plutarch, *Table-talk*

But nothing at the present day has reaped the rewards of the low state of culture more than dancing. As a result it has experienced what Ibycus feared when he wrote:

δέδοικα μή τι πὰρ θεοῖς
ἀμβλακὼν τιμὰν πρὸς ἀνθρώπων ἀμείψω.

cf. Plat. *Phaedr.* 242cd, Synes. *ep.* 105 (*P.G.* 66. 1481c), Marin. *vit. Procl.* 1 (p. 14 Oikonomides), *Sud.* A 1654, I 78, M 994 (i 146s., ii 607, iii 390 Adler)

1 Mehlhorn: παρὰ codd.

**311** Porph. *comment. in Ptolem. harmon.* iv (p. 79 Düring)

ταχέως γὰρ ἄν τις τῶν ἀπείρων μὲν μουσικῆς καὶ τῶν τοιούτων θεωρημάτων ἃ νῦν ψηλαφῶμεν ἡμεῖς, ἐν δὲ τοῖς σοφιστικοῖς λόγοις καλινδουμένων

Ἐριδός ποτε μάργον ἔχων στόμα,

<ὥς> φησί που Ἴβυκος,

ἀντία δῆριν ἐμοὶ κορύσσοι.

1 ποτὶ Ursinus, Stephanus     <τάχα κέν τις ἀνὴρ> ante Ἐριδος Bergk     2 Nauck: ἐνιοικορ. codd.

**312** Galen. *comment. in Hippocr. epidem.* vi 1. 29 (*Corp. Med. Gr.* 5, 10, 2, 2, p. 47 Wenkebach-Pfaff)

ἐπὶ δὲ τοῦ νέφους δοκεῖ τετάχθαι (sc. πέμφιξ) κατὰ τόδε τὸ ἔπος ἐν Σαλμωνεῖ σατύροις παρὰ Σοφοκλεῖ (fr. 539 Pearson, Radt)· καὶ παρ' Ἰβύκῳ·

πυκινὰς πέμφιγας πιόμενοι·

λέλεκται δὲ οὗτος ὁ λόγος αὐτῷ κατά τινα παραβολὴν ἐπὶ χειμαζομένων εἰρημένην. διὸ καὶ τῶν γραμματικῶν (Wenkebach: προγνωστικῶν cod.) οἱ πλεῖστοι ἐπὶ τῶν κατὰ τοὺς ὄμβρους σταγόνων εἰρῆσθαί φασι τὰς πέμφιγας.

v. S. Radt ad Soph. fr. 337

# IBYCUS

I am afraid it may be in exchange for some sin before the gods that I get honour from men.

**311** Porphyry, *On the Harmonics of Ptolemy*

Perhaps among those who have no knowledge of music and such theories as we are now investigating but wallow nevertheless in sophistic arguments someone, as Ibycus says somewhere,

with the gluttonous mouth of Strife will one day arm for battle against me.

**312** Galen, *On Hippocrates' Epidemics* (on πέμφιξ, 'pustule')[1]

The word seems to be applied to cloud, according to this line from Sophocles' satyr-play *Salmoneus* (fr. 539) and in Ibycus:

about to drink dense clouds,

where he has followed a proverb about people caught in a storm; that is why most of the grammarians say the word is used of raindrops.

[1] The word has various meanings: bubble, gust of wind, ray of light, etc. (see Pearson on Soph. fr. 337).

**313** Chrysipp. π. ἀποφ. 14 (*S.V.F.* ii 55s. Arnim)

. . . Ἴβυκος ὁ ποιητὴς οὕτως ἀπεφαίνετο·

οὐκ ἔστιν ἀποφθιμένοις ζωᾶς ἔτι φάρμακον εὑρεῖν.

**314** Theon Smyrn. *Math.* (p. 146 Hiller)

κοινῶς τε γάρ, φησὶν ὁ Ἄδραστος, πάντας τοὺς ἀστέρας οἱ ποιηταὶ σειρίους καλοῦσιν, ὡς Ἴβυκος·

φλεγέθων ἅπερ διὰ νύκτα μακρὰν
σείρια παμφανόωντα

cf. Phot. *lex.* (ii 156 Naber), Hsch. Σ 346 (iv 17 Schmidt), *Sud.* Σ 285 (iv 347 Adler)

Martin: ἅπερ, ἅπερ codd.

**315** Athen. 15. 680f–681a (iii 506 Kaibel)

μνημονεύει αὐτοῦ (sc. τοῦ ἑλιχρύσου) Ἀλκμὰν ἐν τούτοις (fr. 60) καὶ Ἴβυκος·

μύρτα τε καὶ ἴα καὶ ἑλίχρυσος
μᾶλά τε καὶ ῥόδα καὶ τέρεινα δάφνα

2 Canter: τερινα δάφηα codd.

**316** *Et. Gen.* (p. 42 Calame) = *Et. Mag.* 703. 27 = *Et. Vat. gr.* 1708 = *Et. Gud.* 492. 18 = Zonar. 1608 = Hdn. (ii 577 Lentz)

ὅτι δὲ ῥαγεῖς ἔλεγον τοὺς βαφεῖς καὶ ῥέγος τὸ βάμμα σαφὲς Ἀνακρέων ποιεῖ (fr. 447)· καὶ παρ' Ἰβύκῳ·

ποικίλα ῥέγματα <καὶ> καλύπτρας
περόνας τ' ἀναλυσαμένα

1 καὶ add. Bergk     2 -λυσάμενα *Et. Gen.* B -λυσόμενα *Et. Gen.* A -λυσαμέναι ci. Edmonds

# IBYCUS

**313** Chrysippus, *Negatives*

. . . the poet Ibycus declared:

the dead cannot now find a remedy to restore life.

**314** Theon of Smyrna, *On Mathematical Questions arising in Plato*

The poets, according to Adrastus, use the word σείριος, *sirius*,[1] of all the stars in common, e.g. Ibycus,

blazing as through long night the brilliant sparklers.

[1] Perhaps originally an adjective meaning 'sparkling'.

**315** Athenaeus, *Scholars at Dinner*

Alcman mentions the gold-flower (fr. 60); so does Ibycus:

myrtles and violets and gold-flower and apple-blossoms and roses and soft bay-leaves.

**316** *Etymologicum Genuinum*

They called dyers ῥαγεῖς and dye ῥέγος, as Anacreon shows (fr. 447); Ibycus has ῥέγματα, 'dyed garments':

she, loosening her[1] many-coloured garments and veils and pins, . . .

[1] Perhaps 'they, . . . their'.

**317** Athen. 9. 388e (ii 347 Kaibel)

Ἴβυκος δέ τινας λαθιπορφυρίδας (Schweighaeuser: λαθιπόρφυρας cod.) ὀνομάζει διὰ τούτων·

(a) τοῦ μὲν πετάλοισιν ἐπ᾽ ἀκροτάτοις
    ἱζάνοισι ποικίλαι αἰολόδειροι
    πανέλοπες λαθιπορφυρίδες <τε> καὶ
    ἀλκυόνες τανυσίπτεροι.

ἐν ἄλλοις δέ φησιν·

(b) αἰεί μ᾽ ὦ φίλε θυμὲ τανύπτερος ὡς ὄκα πορφυρίς

cf. schol. Ar. *Av.* 1302 = Stes. fr. 262

(a) 1s. Wilamowitz: ἀκροτάτοισι ξανθοῖσι cod.       2s. ποικ. πανέλ. αἰολόδ. cod., transpos. Hermann       3 Schweighaeuser: αδοιπορφ cod.       <τε> suppl. Bergk
(b) Valckenaer: οὔμε cod.

**318** Hdn. π. μον. λέξ. β´ 32 (ii 938 Lentz: cf. i 391)

οὐδὲν εἰς -ωρ λῆγον οὐδέτερον ὑπὲρ μίαν συλλαβὴν ἔχει συμπλοκὴν δύο συμφώνων πρὸ τοῦ ω·... ἔλωρ (*Il.* 5. 684)..., νίκωρ (Sophr. fr. 133 Kaibel)..., ὕδωρ, ἔλδωρ· οὐ γὰρ συμπλοκὴ ἐνθάδε ἀλλὰ διάστασις. ὁ δὲ Ἴβυκος ἔσθ᾽ ὅτε καὶ θηλυκῶς προφέρεται·

(a) οὔτι κατὰ σφετερὰν ἐελδώ

καὶ

(b) †ἐσθλὸν προδεδεγμένον ἐέλδωρ†

(a) Schneidewin: ἐέλδωρ cod.
(b) ἐσθλὰν ποτιδεγμένων ἐελδώ ci. Schneidewin, ἐσθλὰν προδεδεγμένος ἐλδώ Edmonds, ἐσθλὸν προδεδεγμένον ἔλδωρ Bergk

# IBYCUS

**317** Athenaeus, *Scholars at Dinner*

Ibycus calls certain birds *lathi-porphyrides* ('hidden-purplebirds')[1] in these lines:

(a) on its topmost leaves sit many-coloured dapple-necked widgeon[2] and hidden-purplebirds and long-winged halcyons.

Elsewhere he says:

(b) always, my dear heart, as the long-winged purplebird . . .

[1] Not identified: see D'A. W. Thompson, *A Glossary of Greek Birds* 46, 251.  [2] Cf. Alc. 345, Stes. 262.

**318** Herodian, *On Anomalous Words*

No neuter noun ending in -ωρ, if it has more than one syllable, has a combination of two consonants before the ω: e.g. ἔλωρ, νίκωρ, ὕδωρ, ἔλδωρ ('desire'). This last shows not combination[1] but separation of consonants, ἔλ-δωρ. Ibycus sometimes uses a feminine form:

(a) not at all according to their desire,

and

(b) the noble desire (of those waiting?)[2]

[1] Unlike τέ-κμωρ, the form under discussion.  [2] Text uncertain. It is not clear whether Herodian is giving two examples of the fem. form or one fem., one neuter.

**319** Schol. Pind. *Isthm.* 8. 92 (iii 275 Drachmann)

νεικέων πέταλα δὶς ἐγγυαλιζέτω· ἀντὶ τοῦ τῶν φιλονεικιῶν τὰ φύλλα. τροπικώτερον δὲ τῶν φιλονεικιῶν τὰς στάσεις ἢ τὰ νείκη, ὡς Ἴβυκος·

κλάδον Ἐνυαλίου,

καὶ Ὅμηρος· ὄζον Ἄρηος.

**320** *Et. Gen.* (p. 35 Calame) = *Et. Mag.* 542. 51

Κυάρης· Ἴβυκος·

οὐδὲ Κυάρας ὁ Μηδείων στρατηγός.

τινὲς λέγουσιν, ἀπὸ τοῦ Κυαξάρης γέγονε κατὰ συγκοπήν· ἄλλοι δὲ ἀπὸ τοῦ †κυρά† (κυάραν *Et. Gen. B*)· ἐὰν οὖν ᾖ ἀπὸ τοῦ Κυαξάρας συγκεκομμένον (Bergk: συγκριτικὸν *Et. Gen. B*) οὐ πλεονάζει τὸ α, ἐὰν δὲ ἀπὸ τοῦ †κυάρα† πλεονασμῷ τοῦ α οὐ συγ<κεκομμένον> (suppl. Bergk).

στραταγός Bergk

**321** Schol. Pind. *Nem.* 1. 1 (iii 7s. Drachmann)

ἡ δὲ Ὀρτυγία πρότερον μὲν οὖσα νῆσος εἶτα προσχωσθεῖσα χερρόνησος γέγονεν, ὡς καὶ Ἴβυκος ἱστορεῖ·

†παρὰ χέρσον λίθινον
τῶν† παλάμαις βροτῶν·
πρόσθεν νιν πεδ' ἀναριτᾶν
ἰχθύες ὠμοφάγοι νέμοντο.

1 πὰρ ci. Boeckh        1s. λίθινον <πετρῶν | ἐκλεκ>τῶν Page (coll. Str.)        3 Schneidewin: παῖδα νήριτον codd.: πεδὰ νηριτᾶν ci. Boeckh

Str. 1. 3. 18 (i 89 Kramer)

. . . ἐπὶ τῆς πρὸς Συρακούσαις νήσου νῦν μὲν γέφυρά ἐστιν ἡ

# IBYCUS

**319** Scholiast on Pindar, *Isthmian* 8 ('place twice in our hands the foliage of feuds')

He uses this expression for 'the leaves of quarrels', as a more figurative way of saying 'the discords of quarrels' or 'feuds'; so Ibycus says

shoot of Enyalius,[1]

and Homer 'branch of Ares'.

[1] Either of Ascalaphus, son of Ares, or of any warrior, as Homer's phrase.

**320** *Etymologicum Genuinum*

Cyares: Ibycus has

nor Cyaras,[1] that commander of the Medians.

Some say it is a shortened form of Cyaxares, others that it is from (Cyra?): now if it is shortened from Cyaxaras, the (first) *a* is not redundant; but if it is from (Cyra?) with redundant *a* it is not a shortened form.

[1] Probably Cyrus, Ibycus' contemporary, rather than the earlier king Cyaxares.

**321** Scholiast on Pindar, *Nemean* ('Ortygia, scion of famous Syracuse')

Ortygia was once an island, but later it was joined to the mainland and it is now a peninsula, as Ibycus tells:

alongside stone land of boulders selected by the hands of mortals; previously it was the home of flesh-eating fish in company with sea-snails.

Strabo, *Geography*

. . . on the island off Syracuse there is now a bridge link-

συνάπτουσα αὐτὴν πρὸς τὴν ἤπειρον, πρότερον δὲ χῶμα, ὥς φησιν Ἴβυκος, λογαίου λίθου, ὃν καλεῖ ἐκλεκτόν.

Athen. 3. 86b (i 199 Kaibel)

τοῦ δ᾽ ἀναρίτου (μέμνηται) Ἴβυκος.

**322** Str. 6. 2. 4 (i 432 Kramer)

Ἴβυκος δὲ τὸν ἐν Σικυῶνι Ἀσωπὸν ἐκ Φρυγίας ῥεῖν φησι.

**323** Schol. Theocr. 1. 117 (p. 67s. Wendel)

Ἀρέθοισα· κρήνη ἐν Συρακούσαις. φασὶ διὰ πελάγους Ἀλφειὸν ἥκειν <　　　　>, ὥς φησιν Ἴβυκος παριστορῶν περὶ τῆς Ὀλυμπιακῆς φιάλης.

**324** Schol. Ap. Rhod. 3. 26 (p. 216 Wendel)

Ἀπολλώνιος μὲν Ἀφροδίτης τὸν Ἔρωτα γενεαλογεῖ, Σαπφὼ δὲ Γῆς καὶ Οὐρανοῦ (fr. 198), Σιμωνίδης δὲ Ἀφροδίτης καὶ Ἄρεως (fr. 575), Ἴβυκος <. . . . . . . >, ὁ δὲ Ἡσίοδος ἐκ Χάους λέγει τὸν Ἔρωτα (Theog. 116ss.).

Ἴβυκος καὶ Ἡσίοδος cod. P　　<δὲ Ἀφροδίτης καὶ Ἡφαίστου> suppl. Wilamowitz

ing it to the mainland, whereas there was previously a mole, as Ibycus says, made of chosen stone which he calls 'selected'.

Athenaeus, *Scholars at Dinner*

Ibycus mentions the sea-snail.

### 322 Strabo, *Geography*[1]

And Ibycus says that the Sicyonian Asopus flows from Phrygia.[2]

[1] Str. is mocking the belief that rivers (e.g. the Alpheus: see fr. 323) flow for long distances under the sea. [2] Bowra (*G.L.P.* 247) sees here another link between Sicyon and the Phrygian Pelops: cf. fr. 308.

### 323 Scholiast on Theocritus

Arethusa: a spring in Syracuse. They say that Alpheus came through the sea[1] ..., as Ibycus says when speaking incidentally about the cup of Olympia.[2]

[1] In pursuit of the nymph Arethusa. [2] The cup was said to have been thrown into the river Alpheus at Olympia and to have surfaced in the fountain of Arethusa (e.g. Strabo 6. 2. 4, Servius and schol. Dan. on Virg. *Ecl.* 10. 4).

### 324 Scholiast on Apollonius of Rhodes

Apollonius makes Eros child of Aphrodite, Sappho makes him child of Earth and Heaven (fr. 198), Simonides child of Aphrodite and Ares (fr. 575), Ibycus ...,[1] and Hesiod says Eros came from Chaos ('Void': see *Theog.* 116 ff.).

[1] Ibycus' version is missing: Wilamowitz proposed 'child of Aphrodite and Hephaestus'.

# GREEK LYRIC

**325** Athen. 2. 39b (i 90 Kaibel)

Ἴβυκος δέ φησι τὴν ἀμβροσίαν τοῦ μέλιτος κατ' ἐπίτασιν
ἐννεαπλασίαν ἔχειν γλυκύτητα, τὸ μέλι λέγων ἔνατον εἶναι μέρος
τῆς ἀμβροσίας κατὰ τὴν ἡδονήν.

cf. Eust. *Od.* 1633. 11

**326** Cod. Sorb. ap. *Et. Mag.* 387. 42

ὁ δὲ Ἡρωδιανὸς συντίθεται πρώτῳ Ἐτυμολογιῶν οὕτως λέ-
γων· τὸ παρ' Ὁμήρῳ ἐτώσιον τινὲς οἴονται παρὰ τὸ ἐτῶν ἐτώσιον·
ἀλλὰ μάχεται ὁ νοῦς. οἱ δὲ οὕτως· ἀητῶν ἀητώσιος, συστολῇ

### ἀετώσιον

παρ' Ἰβύκῳ· τοῦτο ἀφαιρέσει ἐτώσιον. ἢ οὕτως· ἐτός ἄετος ἀέτων
ἀετώσιος, ὁ μὴ ἀληθὴς ἀλλὰ μάταιος.

cf. *Et. Gud.* s.v. ἐτώσιον (p. 550s. de Stefani)

**327** Choerob. in Theodos. (i 267 Hilgard)

εἶτα αὕτη ἡ αἰτιατική, φημὶ δὴ ἡ ἴκτινον, κατὰ μεταπλασμὸν
γέγονεν ἴκτινα, ὡς παρὰ Ἀριστοφάνει (fr. 637 K.-A.), ὥσπερ ἀλί-
τροχον

### ἀλίτροχα

παρ' Ἰβύκῳ καὶ διθύραμβον διθύραμβα παρὰ Πινδάρῳ (fr. 86).

cf. *Anecd. Oxon.* (i 270 Cramer) = Hdn. (ii 626 Lentz)

**327A** = S 258   Hdn. π. καθ. προσῳδ. (v. H. Hunger,
*Jahrb. der Oesterreich. Byz. Gesellschaft* 16, 1967, pp. 5,
19)

### ἀμεριμναῖος·

Ἴβυκος.

# IBYCUS

**325** Athenaeus, *Scholars at Dinner*

Ibycus says with exaggeration that ambrosia has nine times the sweetness of honey, when he states that honey has a ninth of the sweetness of ambrosia.

**326** Codex Sorbonicus (in *Etymologicum Magnum*)

Herodian agrees, giving the following account in book 1 of his *Etymologies*: some believe that the Homeric ἐτώσιος, 'fruitless', is derived from ἐτῶν, 'years', but the meaning is against it. Others give the following account: ἀητῶν, 'gales', whence ἀητώσιος, shortened in Ibycus to ἀετώσιος,

### fruitless,

then by removal of the first syllable ἐτώσιος. Or again, ἐτός, 'true', ἄετος, 'untrue', gen. pl. ἀέτων, whence ἀετώσιος, of what is not true but idle.

**327** Choeroboscus on Theodosius

Then this accusative, ἴκτινον, becomes ἴκτινα by metaplasm, as in Aristophanes, just as ἀλίτροχον becomes ἀλίτροχα,

### sea-racing,[1]

in Ibycus, and διθύραμβον becomes διθύραμβα in Pindar.

[1] Masc. accus. sing. adjective.

**327A** = S 258 Herodian, *General Accentuation*[1] (on adjectives in -αῖος)

Ibycus has ἀμεριμναῖος (?)

### unworried

[1] On adjectives in -αῖος derived from nouns in -ή; but μέριμνα does not belong to this class.

# GREEK LYRIC

**328** *Et. Gud.* s.v. (i 225 de Stefani)

ἄτερπνος·

οὕτως ὁ ἄγρυπνος παρὰ Ῥηγίνοις, ὡς καὶ παρ' Ἰβύκῳ καὶ Στησιχόρῳ. . . . ἐστὶ γὰρ κατ' ἐντέλειαν ἀτέρυπνος, ὁ χωρὶς ὢν ὕπνου.

cf. *Et. Mag.* 163. 8, *Anecd. Par.* iv 61. 22 Cramer

**329** *Et. Gen.* (p. 23 Calame) = *Et. Mag.* 273. 24 = Hdn. (ii 385 Lentz)

διέφρασαι

παρ' Ἰβύκῳ· ἔστιν ἔφθαρσαι καὶ κατὰ πάθος ἔφαρσαι καὶ καθ' ὑπερβιβασμὸν ἔφρασαι καὶ διέφρασαι· οὕτως Ἡρωδιανός.

**330** Schol. Hom. *Il.* 23. 533 (cod. Ven. 458) (v. Erbse v 449s.)

πρόσσοθεν· συνέσταλται τὸ ω καὶ ἔστιν ὅμοιον τῷ παρ' Ἰβύκῳ

κύματος ἔξοθεν ἄκρου
πᾶσα κάλως ἀσινής.

v. T. W. Allen, *C.R.* 14 (1900) 244, Schol. Gr. in Hom. *Il.* (v 449s. Erbse)

1 ἔξωθεν cod.    2 καλῶς cod.

**331** Schol. in Basil. *orat. περὶ γενέσεως* (*Anecd. Oxon.* iii 413 Cramer)

ὁ δὲ αὐτὸς ἑωσφόρος καὶ ἕσπερος. καίτοι γε τὸ παλαιὸν ἄλλος ἐδόκει εἶναι ὁ ἑωσφόρος καὶ ἄλλος ὁ ἕσπερος. πρῶτος δὲ Ἴβυκος ὁ Ῥηγῖνος συνήγαγε τὰς προσηγορίας.

cf. Achill. Tat. *in Arat. isagog.* 17 (*comm. in Arat. rel.* 43 Maass)

**328** *Etymologicum Gudianum*

ἄτερπνος: the Rhegine term for

sleepless,

as in Ibycus and Stesichorus (251) ... In full it is ἀτέρ-
υπνος, 'without sleep'.

**329** *Etymologicum Genuinum*

διέφρασαι,

you are destroyed,

in Ibycus. There is ἔφθαρσαι, which is modified to ἔφαρσαι,
which by transposition of letters gives ἔφρασαι, whence διέ-
φρασαι. So Herodian.

**330** Scholiast on *Iliad* 23. 533 (πρόσσοθεν, 'before')

The ω (of πρόσωθεν) is shortened, and the form resem-
bles ἔξοθεν, 'outside, beyond', in Ibycus[1]:

beyond the crest of the wave the rope is all undamaged.

[1] Cf. Stes. 252.

**331** Scholiast on Basil, *Genesis*

The Dawn-bringer (Morning-star) and Hesperus
(Evening-star) are one and the same, although in ancient
times they were thought to be different. Ibycus of Rhe-
gium was the first to equate the titles.

**332** *Et. Gen.* (p. 28 Calame) = *Et. Mag.* 428. 28 = Hdn. (ii 242 Lentz)

ἤλσατο· Ἴβυκος

ἤλσατο βοῦς·

παρὰ τὸ ἠλάσατο, ἤλσατο.

v. M. L. West, *Studies* 179

**333** *Epim. Hom.* (*Anecd. Oxon.* i 65 Cramer) = Hdn. (ii 205 Lentz)

τῇ κλαγγῇ δοτικῇ εἶπεν ὁ Ἴβυκος

κλαγγί.

κλαγγίϊ cod.

**334** Hdn. π. μον. λέξ. βʹ 38 (ii 943 Lentz)

Λεβυαφιγενής· ἡ διὰ τοῦ φι ἐπέκτασις οὐδέποτε θέλει κατ' ἀρχὴν συντίθεσθαι, μόνῳ δὲ παρηκολούθησεν ἐν ἐπιρρήματι τῷ ἶφι τὸ τοιοῦτο· Ἰφιγένεια Ἰφικλῆς Ἰφιάνασσα καὶ ὅσα ἄλλα ἐστὶ τοιαῦτα. πεπλάνηται οὖν Ἴβυκος εἰπών

Λεβυαφιγενής.

**335** Hsch. B 1226 (i 350 Latte)

βρυαλίκται· πολεμικοὶ ὀρχησταί·

<βρυαλίκται> μενέδουποι

Ἴβυκος καὶ (ἢ Edmonds) Στησίχορος (258).

Hermann: ωρχηται μεναιδοιπου cod.

# IBYCUS

**332** *Etymologicum Genuinum*

(he) drove the cattle[1];

so Ibycus, using ἤλσατο ('drove'), which comes from ἠλάσατο.

[1] Translation doubtful, since the aorist should come from εἴλω, 'coop up', not ἐλαύνω, 'drive'; perhaps 'penned in his cattle' or 'the ox drew itself in' (West).

**333** *Homeric Parsings* (on *Il.* 1. 3 Ἄϊδι)

For the dative κλαγγῇ Ibycus said κλαγγί,

with noise.

**334** Herodian, *On Anomalous Words*

The lengthening with -φι never occurs at the beginning of a compound; the only exception is with the adverb ἶφι, 'mightily', in Iphigenia, Iphicles, Iphianassa and the like. So Ibycus has gone astray with his Λεβυαφιγενής,

Libya-born.

**335** Hesychius, *Lexicon*

βρυαλίκται: war-dancers:

war-dancers steadfast in battle

in Ibycus and Stesichorus (258).[1]

[1] See note there.

# GREEK LYRIC

**336** Schol. Ap. Rhod. 3. 106 (p. 220 Wendel)

ῥαδινῆς· ... Ἴβυκος δὲ (sc. ἔταξε τὸ ῥαδινὸν) ἐπὶ τῶν τὸν οὐρανὸν βασταζόντων κιόνων, εὐμεγέθεις λέγων.

**337** Schol. Ap. Rhod. 4. 1348 (p. 314 Wendel)

στέρφεσι· τοῖς δέρμασιν. ἔνθεν καὶ στερφῶσαι. Ἴβυκος δὲ

### στερφωτῆρα στρατὸν

εἴρηκε τὸν ἔχοντα δέρματα.

**338** *Et. Gen.* (p. 44 Calame, p. 284 Miller) + *Et. Mag.* 763. 41

τραπεζίτης· διὰ τοῦ ι σημαίνει τὸν ἐν τῇ συνηθείᾳ λεγόμενον τραπεζίτην, ἀπὸ τοῦ τράπεζα. διὰ δὲ τῆς ει διφθόγγου σημαίνει τὸν ἐν τῇ τραπέζῃ παριστάμενον, ὡς παρ' Ὁμήρῳ· τραπεζῆες κύνες· ἀπὸ τοῦ τραπεζεύς ἐστι. τὸ δὲ παρ' Ἰβύκῳ διὰ τοῦ η λεγόμενον, οἷον

### τραπεζήταν κύνα·

ἢ δωρικῇ τροπῇ ὡς πλείων πλήων, ἢ παραγώγως ὡς πρύμνα πρυμνήτης καὶ κομήτης.

κύνα *Et. Gen.* B    κύναν *Et. Gen.* A    κυνῶν *Et. Mag.*    -τᾶν κυνῶν Bergk

cf. *Anecd. Oxon.* (ii 45 Cramer) = Hdn. (i 77, ii 356, 436, 593 Lentz), *Anecd. Gr.* iii 1424 Bekker, *Et. Gud.* 533. 42, 534. 14, Eust. *Il.* 1257. 25, *Sud.* T 906 (iv 583 Adler), Poll. 3. 84

286

# IBYCUS

**336** Scholiast on Apollonius of Rhodes (ῥαδινῆς, slender')

Ibycus used the word

### slender

of the pillars that support heaven. He meant 'of great size'.[1]

[1] An improbable statement: see also Anacr. 456, Stes. 243.

**337** Scholiast on Apollonius of Rhodes

στέρφεσι: 'skins'; whence στερφῶσαι, 'to cover with hide'. Ibycus has στερφωτήρ,

### a hide-clad army,

meaning an army wearing skins.

**338** *Etymologicum Genuinum* +

τραπεζίτης with the ι is the everyday term for 'banker', from τράπεζα, 'banker's table'; τραπεζείτης with the diphthong ει means 'standing by the table' in the same sense as Homer's τραπεζῆες κύνες, 'table dogs', where τραπεζῆες comes from τραπεζεύς. The form in Ibycus is τραπεζήτης with η,

### table dog,[1]

either Doric, as πλήων for πλείων, or derived from τράπεζα as πρυμνητής from πρύμνα, κομήτης (from κόμη).

[1] Perhaps gen. pl., 'table dogs'.

# GREEK LYRIC

**339** Plut. *comp. Lyc. et Num.* 25 (3) (iii 2. 89 Ziegler)

ἔτι δὲ μᾶλλον ἡ περὶ τὰς παρθένους φυλακὴ κατέσταλται τῷ Νομᾷ πρὸς τὸ θῆλυ καὶ κόσμιον· ἡ δὲ τοῦ Λυκούργου παντάπασιν ἀναπεπταμένη καὶ ἄθηλυς οὖσα τοῖς ποιηταῖς λόγον παρέσχηκε·

### φαινομηρίδας

τε γὰρ αὐτὰς ἀποκαλοῦσιν, ὡς Ἴβυκος, καὶ ἀνδρομανεῖς λοιδοροῦσιν, ὡς Εὐριπίδης λέγων (*Androm.* 597s.).

cf. Poll. 2. 187, 7. 55 (φανο-), schol. Clem. Alex. (iv 128 Klotz) (φανο-)

**340** Schol. Pind. *Ol.* 9. 129 (i 297 Drachmann)

ἔπειτα χάρμα· νῦν ἀντὶ τοῦ χαρά· Ὅμηρος δὲ ἐπὶ τῆς μάχης, οἱ δὲ περὶ Ἴβυκον καὶ Στησίχορον (267)

### χάρμην

τὴν ἐπιδορατίδα φασίν.

**341** (a) Schol. Lond. Dion. Thrac. 12 (p. 542 Hilgard) = *Anecd. Oxon.* iv 329 Cramer (cf. i 162)

ὁ μὲν διὰ τοῦ -ωσιος Ῥηγίνων ἐστίν, ἐπεὶ συνεχὴς παρ' αὐτοῖς ἀπὸ γενικῆς γίνεται· ἀνάκων ἀνακώσιος, χαρίτων χαριτώσιος.

(b) Hdn. π. καθ. προσ. 19 (i 508 Lentz) = *Anecd. Gr.* iii 1347 Bekker

τὰ εἰς -ιν ἐπιρρήματα ἐκ πλεονασμοῦ ἔχει τὸ ν, οἷον αὖθι αὖθιν· οὕτω γὰρ λέγεται παρὰ Ῥηγίνοις.

# IBYCUS

**339** Plutarch, *Comparison of Lycurgus and Numa*

Moreover the arrangements made by Numa for the protection of girls aimed at femininity and decency, whereas those of Lycurgus by their complete absence of restraint and lack of femininity have given the poets something to write about: they call them[1]

### thigh-showing,

as Ibycus does, or berate them as man-mad, as Euripides (*Androm.* 597 f.).

[1] I.e. Spartan girls.


**340** Scholiast on Pindar, *Olympian* 9. 86 (χάρμαι, 'joyous victories')

Here χάρμα is the equivalent of χαρά, 'joy'. But Homer uses χάρμη of 'battle', and Ibycus and Stesichorus (267)[1] use it of the

### spear-point.

[1] Also Pindar, fr. 70c. 13 Snell.


**341**[1] (a) Scholiast on Dionysius Thrax

The adjectival form in -ωσιος belongs to Rhegium: the inhabitants often form the adjective from a genitive, e.g. ἀνακώσιος, 'lordly', from ἀνάκων, 'lords', χαριτώσιος, 'graceful', from χαρίτων, 'graces'.

(b) Herodian, *Universal Prosody*

The ν in adverbs in -ιν is pleonastic; cf. αὖθι and αὖθιν, 'again', the form used in Rhegium.

[1] These forms may have been found in Ibycus.

# GREEK LYRIC

**342** Aelian. *N.A.* 6. 51 (ii 72 Scholfield)

δεῖ δὲ καὶ μῦθον τῷδε τῷ ζῴῳ ἐπᾶσαί με ὅνπερ οὖν ἀκούσας οἶδα, ὡς ἂν μὴ δοκοίην ἀμαθῶς ἔχειν αὐτοῦ. τὸν Προμηθέα κλέψαι τὸ πῦρ ἡ φήμη φησί, καὶ τὸν Δία ἀγανακτῆσαι ὁ μῦθος λέγει καὶ τοῖς καταμηνύσασι τὴν κλοπὴν δοῦναι φάρμακον γήρως ἀμυντήριον. τοῦτο οὖν ἐπὶ ὄνῳ θεῖναι τοὺς λαβόντας πέπυσμαι. καὶ τὸν μὲν προϊέναι τὸ ἄχθος φέροντα, εἶναι δὲ ὥραν θέρειον, καὶ διψῶντα τὸν ὄνον ἐπί τινα κρήνην κατὰ τὴν τοῦ ποτοῦ χρείαν ἐλθεῖν. τὸν οὖν ὄφιν τὸν φυλάττοντα ἀναστέλλειν αὐτὸν καὶ ἀπελαύνειν, καὶ ἐκεῖνον στρεβλούμενον μισθὸν οἱ τῆς φιλοτησίας δοῦναι ὅπερ οὖν ἔτυχε φέρων φάρμακον. οὐκοῦν ἀντίδοσις γίνεται, καὶ ὁ μὲν πίνει, ὁ δὲ τὸ γῆρας ἀποδύεται, προσεπιλαβὼν ὡς λόγος τὸ τοῦ ὄνου δίψος. τί οὖν; ἐγὼ τοῦ μύθου ποιητής; ἀλλ' οὐκ ἂν εἴποιμι, ἐπεὶ καὶ πρὸ ἐμοῦ Σοφοκλῆς ὁ τῆς τραγῳδίας ποιητὴς (fr. 362 Pearson, Radt) καὶ Δεινόλοχος ὁ ἀνταγωνιστὴς Ἐπιχάρμου (fr. 8 Kaibel) καὶ Ἴβυκος ὁ Ῥηγῖνος καὶ Ἀριστίας (9 F 8 Snell) καὶ Ἀπολλοφάνης (fr. 9 Kock) ποιηταὶ κωμῳδίας ᾄδουσιν αὐτόν.

**343** Himer. *Or.* 69. 35 (p. 244 Colonna)

ἥρμοσε μὲν καὶ Ἀνακρέων μετὰ τὴν νόσον τὴν λύραν καὶ τοὺς φίλους Ἔρωτας αὖθις διὰ μέλους ἠσπάζετο, ἥρμοσε δὲ καὶ Στησίχορος μετὰ τὸ πάθος τὴν φόρμιγγα· Ἴβυκον δὲ κατέχει λόγος ἀπολισθεῖν μὲν ἐξ ἅρματος ἐς Ἱμέραν ἀπὸ Κατάνης ὀχούμενον· συντριβείσης δὲ αὐτῷ τῆς χειρὸς συχνόν τινα χρόνον ἀπῳδὸν γενέσθαι, τὴν λύραν δὲ ἀναθεῖναι Ἀπόλλωνι.

**344** Zenob. ii 45 (i 44 Leutsch-Schneidewin)

ἀγὼν πρόφασιν οὐκ ἐπιδέχεται οὔτε φιλία. ὁ Μύλων ὁ παροιμιογράφος Ἰβύκειον τὴν παροιμίαν ταύτην φησὶν ὡς πρώτου χρησαμένου τοῦ Ἰβύκου.

# IBYCUS

**342** Aelian, *On the Nature of Animals*

I must charm this creature[1] with a tale which I know
from hearing it, in case I give the impression of being
ignorant of it. The story goes that Prometheus stole the
fire and Zeus in a rage rewarded those who reported the
theft with a drug to ward off old age. I am told that those
who got it put it on the back of an ass, who went on ahead
with his load. It was summertime, and the ass was thirsty
and went to a spring in his need for the water. Now the
snake that was guarding the spring tried to stop him and
drive him off; so since he was tortured by his thirst he gave
the snake as payment for the loving-cup the drug he hap-
pened to be carrying. So an exchange took place: the ass
got his drink and the snake sloughed off his old age — but
also, so the story goes, got the ass's thirst. Now then, did I
invent the tale? Not a bit of it: it was told before me by the
tragedian Sophocles, by Dinolochus, the rival of Epi-
charmus, by Ibycus of Rhegium and by the comic poets
Aristias and Apollophanes.

[1] The snake called *dipsas,* whose bite caused intense thirst.

---

**343** Himerius, *Orations*

Anacreon tuned his lyre after his illness and greeted
his dear Loves again in song; Stesichorus also tuned his
phorminx after his mishap; but the story goes that when
Ibycus slipped from his chariot while riding from Catana to
Himera his hand was crushed and for some considerable
time he gave up his music and dedicated his lyre to Apollo.

**344** Zenobius, *Proverbs*

'No excuse is allowed by a contest or by a friendship':
Mylon, the collector of proverbs, calls this one Ibycean,
since Ibycus was the first to use it.

**345** (a) Serv. *Cent. Metr.* de dactylicis (iv 461 Keil)

ibycium constat hexametro acatalecto, ut est hoc:
>    sidera pallida diffugiunt face territa luminis.

ibycium constat heptametro acatalecto, ut est hoc:
carmina docta Thalia canit, properantius huc ades, o puer.

ibycium constat heptametro hypercatalecto, ut est hoc:
versiculos tibi dactylicos cecini, puer optime, quos facias.

(b) Aphth. ( = 'Mar. Vict.', vi 126 Keil)

   hic versus ab Archebulo archebulius dictus est, non ipso auctore editus sed ab eo frequenter usurpatus: nam et Ibycus et Pindarus et Simonides hoc versu longe ante usi ostenduntur.

cf. Caes. Bass. vi 256 Keil

# IBYCUS

**345** (on the metres of Ibycus) (a) Servius, *Hundred Metres*

The ibycean consists of a dactylic hexameter acatalectic[1]:

$$-\cup\cup \mid -\cup\cup \mid -\cup\cup \mid -\cup\cup \mid -\cup\cup \mid -\cup\cup$$

The ibycean consists of a dactylic heptameter acatalectic:

$$-\cup\cup \mid -\cup\cup \mid -\cup\cup \mid -\cup\cup \mid -\cup\cup \mid -\cup\cup \mid -\cup\cup$$

The ibycean consists of a dactylic heptameter hyper-catalectic:

$$-\cup\cup \mid -\cup\cup \mid -\cup\cup \mid -\cup\cup \mid -\cup\cup \mid -\cup\cup \mid -\cup\cup \mid -$$

[1] E.g. fr. 317(b).

(b) Aphthonius, *On all the metres*

This line[1] is called archebulean after Archebulus,[2] who used it often, although he was not its originator: Ibycus, Pindar and Simonides can be shown to have used it long before him.

[1] $\underset{\smile}{\smile} - \cup\cup - \cup\cup - \cup\cup - \cup - -$ ; 282(a). 3 f. is similar.     [2] Hellenistic poet, 3rd c. B.C..

(c) The term 'ibycean' is used also for the unit

$$-\cup\cup-\cup\cup-\cup-,$$

e.g. fr. 286. 1.

# APOLLODORUS

## TESTIMONIUM VITAE

Eust. *prooem. Pind.* 27 (iii 299s. Drachmann)

εἰς ποιητικὴν ἐτράπη (sc. ὁ Πίνδαρος) καθηγησα-
μένων αὐτῷ τοῦ μαθεῖν ἢ τοῦ Λάσου, ὡς εἴρηται, ἢ
τοῦ Ἀθηναίου Ἀγαθοκλέους ἢ Ἀπολλοδώρου, ὅν φασι
καὶ προϊστάμενον κυκλίων χορῶν καὶ ἀποδημοῦντα
πιστεῦσαι τὴν διδασκαλίαν Πινδάρῳ παιδὶ ὄντι· τὸν δὲ
εὖ τὸ πιστευθὲν διακοσμήσαντα περιβοηθῆναι.

## FRAGMENTUM

**701** Erotian. in Hipp. *Mul.* 2. 125 (p. 87 Nachmanson)

τὸ τέρθρον τοῦ πάθους ἀντὶ τοῦ τὸ τέλος· . . . καὶ Ἀπολλόδω-
ρος ὁ τοὺς ὕμνους γράψας φησί·

τίς τοιῇδ᾽ ἐν ὥρῃ
ἦλθεν ἐπὶ τέρθρον θυράων;

1 Meineke: τοι ἧδε ὥρη sim. codd.

# APOLLODORUS

## LIFE AND WORK

Eustathius, *Introduction to Pindar*

Pindar then turned to poetry and was taught the art either by Lasus, as I mentioned earlier, or by the Athenian Agathocles or by Apollodorus. They say that Apollodorus was in charge of circular choruses[1] and that when he was out of the city he entrusted their training to Pindar, who was still only a boy[2]; Pindar handled his assignment well and became the talk of the town.

[1] For the performance of dithyrambs.  [2] Pindar was born in 518 B.C.


## FRAGMENT

**701** Erotian, *Glossary to Hippocrates*

Hippocrates says 'the extremity' of the disease instead of 'the crisis'; ... so Apollodorus who wrote the hymns says:

Who came to the extremity of my doorway at such an hour?

# LASUS

## TESTIMONIA VITAE ATQUE ARTIS

**1** *Suda* Λ 139 (iii 236 Adler)

Λάσος, Χαρβίνου, Ἑρμιονεύς, πόλεως τῆς Ἀχαίας, γεγονὼς κατὰ τὴν νη′ Ὀλυμπιάδα, ὅτε Δαρεῖος ὁ Ὑστάσπου. τινὲς δὲ τοῦτον συναριθμοῦσι τοῖς ζ′ σοφοῖς ἀντὶ Περιάνδρου. πρῶτος δὲ οὗτος περὶ μουσικῆς λόγον ἔγραψε καὶ διθύραμβον εἰς ἀγῶνα (διθυραμβώδεις ἀγωγὰς Garrod) εἰσήγαγε καὶ τοὺς ἐριστικοὺς εἰσηγήσατο λόγους.

# LASUS

## LIFE AND WORK

**1** *Suda,* Lasus

Son of Charbinus[1]; from Hermione, a city of Achaea; born in the 58th Olympiad (548/544 B.C.), when Darius, son of Hystaspes, was born.[2] Some number him among the Seven Wise Men in place of Periander.[3] He was the first to write a treatise on music,[4] to make the dithyramb competitive[5] and to introduce wrangling arguments.[6]

[1] Diogenes Laertius 1. 42 says 'son of Charmantides or of Sisymbrinus or, according to Aristoxenus (fr. 86 Wehrli), of Chabrinus'. [2] Hdt. 1. 209 implies that Darius was born c. 549, Ctesias implies 557. [3] See Diog. Laert., *loc. cit.,* who cites Hermippus' list of 17 sages who at various times were included in the list. [4] Martianus Capella 9. 352 says L. 'made public' his views on the tripartite division of music; it is possible that the division into sound, rhythm and words goes back to L. [5] *Suda* K 2646 says L. was the first to establish the circular choruses (of the dithyramb); see also testt. 3, 5. Acc. to the *Parian Marble* the first dithyrambs were sung (in Athens) by a chorus of men in 509/8 B.C., the victor being Hypodicus of Chalcis. With Garrod's emendation of the text there is no mention of competition: 'L. introduced dithyramb-style rhythms.' [6] See testt. 10, 11.

**2** Hdt. 7. 6

ἐξηλάσθη γὰρ ὑπὸ Ἱππάρχου τοῦ Πεισιστράτου ὁ
Ὀνομάκριτος ἐξ Ἀθηνέων, ἐπ' αὐτοφώρῳ ἁλοὺς ὑπὸ
Λάσου τοῦ Ἑρμιονέος ἐμποιέων ἐς τὰ Μουσαίου χρησ-
μὸν ὡς αἱ ἐπὶ Λήμνῳ ἐπικείμεναι νῆσοι ἀφανιζοίατο
κατὰ τῆς θαλάσσης.

**3** Ar. Vesp. 1411s.

(Φι.)  Λᾶσός ποτ' ἀντεδίδασκε καὶ Σιμωνίδης·
ἔπειθ' ὁ Λᾶσος εἶπεν, 'ὀλίγον μοι μέλει.'

**4** Schol. Pind. (i 4 Drachmann) (Vita Thomana)

ἡ δὲ Μυρτὼ ἐγαμήθη Σκοπελίνῳ τῷ αὐλητῇ, ὃς τὴν
αὐλητικὴν διδάσκων τὸν Πίνδαρον, ἐπεὶ εἶδε μείζονος
ἕξεως ὄντα, παρέδωκε Λάσῳ τῷ Ἑρμιονεῖ μελοποιῷ,
παρ' ᾧ τὴν λυρικὴν ἐπαιδεύθη.

# LASUS

**2** Herodotus, *Histories*

Onomacritus[1] had been driven out of Athens by Hipparchus,[2] son of Pisistratus, after being caught red-handed by Lasus of Hermione in the act of inserting into the verses of Musaeus an oracle to the effect that the islands off Lemnos would vanish beneath the sea.

[1] Athenian editor of oracles.    [2] I.e. between the death of Pisistratus in 527 and the murder of Hipparchus in 514.

**3** Aristophanes, *Wasps* (Philocleon to the Bread-seller)

Lasus was once competing as chorus-director[1] against Simonides; and then[2] Lasus said, 'I couldn't care less.'

[1] Presumably in a dithyrambic contest.    [2] When he lost? The remark is Philocleon's insult to the Bread-seller.

**4** Thomas Magister, *Life of Pindar*

Myrto was the wife of Scopelinus the aulete, who taught pipe-playing to Pindar and on seeing that he had unusual skill handed him over to the lyric poet Lasus of Hermione, who taught him the lyre.[1]

[1] See also Apollodorus test.

# GREEK LYRIC

**5** Schol. Pind. *Ol.* 13. 26b (i 361s. Drachmann)

Χάριτες διθυράμβῳ· οὕτως ἀκουστέον· αἱ τοῦ Διο-
νύσου διθυράμβων ἐν Κορίνθῳ ἐφάνησαν χάριτες, του-
τέστι τὸ σπουδαιότατον τῶν Διονύσου διθυράμβων ἐν
Κορίνθῳ πρῶτον ἐφάνη· ἐκεῖ γὰρ ὡράθη ὁ χορὸς ὀρχού-
μενος· ἔστησε δὲ αὐτὸν πρῶτος Ἀρίων ὁ Μηθυμναῖος,
εἶτα Λάσος ὁ Ἑρμιονεύς.

**6** [Plut.] *Mus.* 29. 1141c (p. 124 Lasserre, vi 3. 24 Ziegler)

Λάσος δ' ὁ Ἑρμιονεὺς εἰς τὴν διθυραμβικὴν
ἀγωγὴν μεταστήσας τοὺς ῥυθμοὺς καὶ τῇ τῶν αὐλῶν
πολυφωνίᾳ κατακολουθήσας, πλείοσί τε φθόγγοις
καὶ διερριμμένοις χρησάμενος, εἰς μετάθεσιν τὴν
προϋπάρχουσαν ἤγαγε μουσικήν.

**7** Aristox. *Harm.* (p. 3 Meibom, p. 7 da Rios)

οὐ πάνυ ῥάδιον εἰπεῖν περὶ φθόγγου τί ποτ' ἐστίν.
ἀναγκαῖον δὲ τὸν βουλόμενον μὴ πάσχειν ὅπερ Λάσος
τε καὶ τῶν Ἐπιγονείων τινὲς ἔπαθον, πλάτος αὐτὸν
οἰηθέντες ἔχειν, εἰπεῖν περὶ αὐτοῦ μικρὸν ἀκριβέστε-
ρον.

# LASUS

**5** Scholiast on Pindar ('Whence came to light the glories of Dionysus along with the ox-driving dithyramb?')

To be taken as follows: the glories of Dionysus' dithyrambs appeared in Corinth, i.e. the most serious element in Dionysus' dithyrambs first appeared in Corinth; for it was there that the chorus was seen dancing. The first to organise it was Arion of Methymna, and next was Lasus of Hermione.[1]

[1] See also Arion test. 4, Clement of Alexandria, *Strom* 1. 16. 78. 5 (p. 51 Stählin), Tzetzes, *Prol. Lycophron* (ii 2 Scheer).

**6** 'Plutarch', *On Music*

Lasus of Hermione transferred the rhythms to the movement of the dithyramb[1] and imitated the polyphony[2] of pipes by using (sc. on the cithara) more numerous, scattered[3] notes, and thus he changed the existing system of music.

[1] Not clear, but 'the rhythms' may be the prosodiac, the choree and the bacchius which the writer has just mentioned; see Olympus test. 8.    [2] I.e. the variety of notes produced by the auloi.
[3] Presumably the melodic line jumped over wide intervals.

**7** Aristoxenus, *Harmonics*

It is not at all easy to say what a sound[1] is; but anyone who does not wish to make the same blunder as Lasus and some of the school of Epigonus,[2] who thought a sound had breadth, must tackle the question with a little more precision.

[1] Or 'a note'.    [2] Epigonus of Ambracia, 6th c. citharist and musical theorist.

# GREEK LYRIC

**8** Theon Smyrn. *Math.* (p. 59 Hiller)

ταύτας δὲ τὰς συμφωνίας οἱ μὲν ἀπὸ βαρῶν ἠξίουν λαμβάνειν, οἱ δὲ ἀπὸ μηκῶν (Bullialdus: μεγεθῶν codd.), οἱ δὲ ἀπὸ κινήσεων καὶ ἀριθμῶν, οἱ δὲ ἀπὸ ἀγγείων καὶ μεγεθῶν. Λᾶσος δὲ ὁ Ἑρμιονεύς, ὥς φασι, καὶ οἱ περὶ τὸν Μεταποντῖνον Ἵππασον Πυθαγορικὸν ἄνδρα συνέπεσθαι τῶν κινήσεων τὰ τάχη καὶ τὰς βραδυτῆτας δι' ὧν αἱ συμφωνίαι < . . . . . . . . . > ἐν ἀριθμοῖς ἡγούμενος λόγους τοιούτους ἐλάμβανεν ἐπ' ἀγγείων.

**9** Philodem. *Poem.* = Pap. Herc. 994 col. 37. 8–11, ed. F. Sbordone, *Rendic. Accad. Napoli* 30 (1955) 45

οὐδὲ <τὰ> Λάσου μάλιστα τοια<ῦτα> πεποικιλμένα ποιεῖ[ν τ]οιοῦτον

# LASUS

**8** Theon of Smyrna, *On Mathematical Questions arising in Plato*

These consonances[1] some claimed to establish by means of weights, others by lengths (sc. of strings), others by movements[2] and numbers, others by vessels and sizes. Lasus of Hermione, they say, and the school of the Pythagorean Hippasus[3] of Metapontum paid attention to the quickness and slowness of movements[2] through which the consonances (were created) . . . . . . . . . (he),[4] thinking (the consonances were to be found) in numbers, tried to establish such calculations by means of vessels.

[1] I.e. octave, fifth, fourth.     [2] I.e. displacements of resonant masses of air. Lasus seems to have linked these 'movements' with numbers.     [3] Early 5th c. B.C.     [4] The lacuna in the text makes interpretation uncertain, but it may have been Lasus who experimented with vessels, perhaps also with two strings and with the syrinx.

**9** Philodemus, *On Poems*

. . . nor does he[1] maintain that the poems of Lasus for all their elaboration[2] have this effect (sc. appeal to the ear alone).

[1] An unidentified critic.     [2] The context shows that the poems were regarded by critics of 2nd c. B.C. as models of euphony.

**10** Athen. 8. 338b (ii 243 Kaibel)

οἶδα δὲ καὶ ἃ ὁ Ἑρμιονεὺς Λᾶσος ἔπαιξε περὶ
ἰχθύων, ἅπερ Χαμαιλέων ἀνέγραψεν ὁ Ἡρακλεώτης ἐν
τῷ περὶ αὐτοῦ [τοῦ Λάσου] συγγράμματι λέγων ὧδε
(fr. 30 Wehrli) . . .

**11** Hsch. Λ 372 (ii 574 Latte)

Λασίσματα· ὡς σοφιστοῦ τοῦ Λάσου καὶ πολυ-
πλόκου.

**12** Stob. *Flor.* 3. 29. 70 (iii 641 Wachsmuth-Hense)

ἐκ τῶν Ἀριστοτέλους Χρειῶν· Λᾶσος <ὁ> Ἑρμιο-
νεὺς ἐρωτηθεὶς τί εἴη σοφώτατον 'ἡ πεῖρα' ἔφη.

# LASUS

**10** Athenaeus, *Scholars at Dinner*

I know also the jokes made about fish by Lasus of Hermione: Chamaeleon of Heraclea recorded them in his account of Lasus.[1]

[1] The gist of the first was that the fish is both raw and cooked (ὀπτός, which also means 'visible'); the second is a quibble about a fish Lasus stole and gave to a bystander: he swore that he neither had it nor knew that anyone else had taken it. Plutarch, *Vit. Pud.* 5 reports an exchange between Lasus and Xenophanes (*c.* 570–*c.* 478 B.C.): L. called X. a coward when he refused to play dice with him, and X. answered that he was indeed a coward when it came to disgraceful matters.

**11** Hesychius, *Lexicon*

Lasisms[1]: so-called because of Lasus' sophistry and verbal trickery.

[1] For Chamaeleon's examples see test. 10.

**12** Stobaeus, *Anthology*

From the *Maxims* of Aristotle: Lasus of Hermione on being asked what was the wisest thing answered, 'Experience.'[1]

[1] Cf. Alcman 125, Simonides 645.

# LASUS

## FRAGMENTA

**702  ΥΜΝΟΣ ΕΙΣ ΔΗΜΗΤΡΑ ΤΗΝ ΕΝ ΕΡΜΙΟΝΗΙ**

(a) Athen. 14. 624ef (iii 377s. Kaibel)

τὸ δὲ τῶν Αἰολέων ἦθος ἔχει τὸ γαῦρον καὶ ὀγκῶδες, ἔτι δὲ
ὑπόχαυνον· ὁμολογεῖ δὲ ταῦτα ταῖς ἱπποτροφίαις αὐτῶν καὶ ξενο-
δοχίαις· οὐ πανοῦργον δέ, ἀλλὰ ἐξηρμένον καὶ τεθαρρηκός. διὸ καὶ
οἰκεῖόν ἐστ' αὐτοῖς ἡ φιλοποσία καὶ τὰ ἐρωτικὰ καὶ πᾶσα ἡ περὶ
τὴν δίαιταν ἄνεσις. διόπερ ἔχουσι τὸ τῆς ὑποδωρίου καλουμένης
ἁρμονίας ἦθος. αὕτη γάρ ἐστι, φησὶν ὁ Ἡρακλείδης (fr. 163
Wehrli), ἣν ἐκάλουν Αἰολίδα, ὡς καὶ Λᾶσος ὁ Ἑρμιονεὺς ἐν τῷ εἰς
τὴν ἐν Ἑρμιόνι Δήμητρα ὕμνῳ λέγων οὕτως·

> Δάματρα μέλπω Κόραν τε Κλυμένοι' ἄλοχον
> μελιβόαν ὕμνον ἀναγνέων
> Αἰολίδ' ἀμ βαρύβρομον ἁρμονίαν.

ταῦτα δ' ἄδουσιν πάντες ὑποδώρια τὰ μέλη. ἐπεὶ οὖν τὸ μέλος
ἐστὶν ὑποδώριον [[τὰ μέλη del. Casaubon]], εἰκότως Αἰολίδα
φησὶν εἶναι τὴν ἁρμονίαν ὁ Λᾶσος.

1 fort. τε <τὰν> Page      2 Hartung: μελίβοιαν codd.      Bergk:
ἀναγνῶν codd.      3 Edmonds: ἅμα codd.

# LASUS

## FRAGMENTS

**702**   HYMN TO DEMETER OF HERMIONE[1]

(a) Athenaeus, *Scholars at Dinner*

The character of the Aeolians contains the elements of haughtiness and turgidity, even conceitedness, which are in keeping with their horse-breeding and their entertainment of strangers; it is not so much wicked as lofty and self-confident. This explains their fondness for drinking and love-making and every aspect of the relaxed way of life. It is why they have the character of the so-called Hypodorian *harmonia,* which according to Heraclides[2] is the one they used to call Aeolian, as Lasus of Hermione does in his hymn to Demeter of Hermion, when he says,

I sing of Demeter and the Maiden,[3] wife of Clymenus,[4] raising the honied shout of a hymn in the deep-sounding Aeolian *harmonia.*[5]

Everyone sings these lyrics Hypodorian; so since the melody is Hypodorian, Lasus quite naturally calls the *harmonia* Aeolian.

[1] For Demeter's worship in Hermione see Paus. 2. 35. 3. L. may have set the rape of Persephone there: cf. 'Apollodorus' 1. 5. 1.
[2] H. of Pontus, 4th c. B.C. philosopher.   [3] Persephone, daughter of Demeter.   [4] Hades, 'the famous'. See Paus. 2. 35. 5, Callim. fr. 285, Philicus in Page, *Select Papyri* iii 402 ff.   [5] I.e. the Aeolian tuning of the lyre, together with its musical idiom. Heraclides confuses it with the hypodorian octave-species.

(b) Athen. 10. 455cd (ii 490 Kaibel)

καὶ ὁ εἰς τὴν Δήμητρα δὲ τὴν ἐν Ἑρμιόνῃ ποιηθεὶς τῷ Λάσῳ ὕμνος ἄσιγμός ἐστιν, ὥς φησιν Ἡρακλείδης ὁ Ποντικὸς ἐν τρίτῳ περὶ μουσικῆς (fr. 161 Wehrli), οὗ ἐστιν ἀρχή·

Δάματρα μέλπω Κόραν τε Κλυμένοι' ἄλοχον.

**703** ΔΙΘΥΡΑΜΒΟΙ

Aelian. *N.A.* 7. 47 (ii 162 Scholfield)

ἔοικε δὲ καὶ τὰ τῶν λυγκῶν ἔκγονα ὁμοίως (sc. σκύμνοι) ὀνομά- ζεσθαι· ἐν γοῦν τοῖς Λάσου λεγομένοις Διθυράμβοις οὕτως εὑρίσκε- ται ⟦σκύμνος del. Hercher⟧ εἰρημένον τὸ βρέφος τὸ τῆς λυγκός.

v. Ar. Byz. fr. 175 Slater

**704** ΚΕΝΤΑΥΡΟΙ

Athen. 10. 455c (ii 490 Kaibel)

ταῦτα (sc. Pind. fr. 70b. 1–3 Snell) σημειώσαιτ' ἄν τις πρὸς τοὺς νοθεύοντας Λάσου τοῦ Ἑρμιονέως τὴν ἄσιγμον ᾠδὴν ἥτις ἐπιγράφεται Κένταυροι.

# LASUS

## (b) Athenaeus, *Scholars at Dinner*[1]

The hymn to Demeter of Hermione composed by Lasus is also asigmatic,[2] as Heraclides of Pontus reports in Book 3 of his treatise, *On Music*[3]; it begins

## I sing of Demeter and the Maiden, wife of Clymenus.

[1] This passage follows fr. 704.    [2] It avoids the letter s (sigma); see also fr. 704. Aristoxenus (fr. 87 Wehrli) said that sigma was unsuited to pipe-music.    [3] So also Eustathius on *Il.* 24. 1 (p. 1335. 52).

### 703    DITHYRAMBS[1]

Aelian, *On the Nature of Animals*

The young of lynxes also seem to be called σκύμνοι ('cubs'); at any rate in the so-called[2] Dithyrambs of Lasus we find the baby lynx[3] given this name.

[1] See also testt. 1, 3, 5, 6, Arion test. 4.    [2] Aristophanes of Byzantium, from whom Aelian draws this material, throws doubt on their authenticity.    [3] The animal was associated with Dionysus.

### 704    THE CENTAURS

Athenaeus, *Scholars at Dinner*

One might point out these lines (sc. Pindar's Dithyramb for the Thebans 1–3[1]) to those who reject as spurious the asigmatic[2] ode of Lasus of Hermione entitled 'The Centaurs'.

[1] Pindar spoke of 'the impure *san*', the Doric equivalent of sigma.
[2] See 702(b) n. 2.

**705** P.Oxy. 1367 fr. 1 col. ii 53–55 (Hermippi περὶ νομοθετῶν ii epitoma ab Heraclide Lembo facta)

] Βουζύγης νομο[θετῆ]σαι· μέμνηται δ' α[ὐτοῦ] καὶ Λᾶσος ὁ ποιη[τής.

**706** Aelian. *V.H.* 12. 36 (p. 141 Dilts)

ἐοίκασιν οἱ ἀρχαῖοι ὑπὲρ τοῦ ἀριθμοῦ τῶν τῆς Νιόβης παίδων μὴ συνᾴδειν ἀλλήλοις. Ὅμηρος μὲν ἓξ λέγει <ἄρρενας> καὶ τοσαύτας κόρας, Λᾶσος δὲ δὶς ἑπτὰ λέγει . . .

**706A** Natalis Comes, *Myth.* 9. 18 (p. 1018 ed. Francof. 1581)

fuit autem Sphinx Echidnae Typhonisque filia, ut scribit Lasus Hermioneus.

# LASUS

**705** Oxyrhynchus papyrus (2nd c. A.D.) (Heraclides Lembus, Epitome of Hermippus, *On Lawgivers*)

... Buzyges[1] (is said) to have been a lawgiver; the poet Lasus mentions him.

[1] Attic hero, mythical ancestor of an Athenian priestly family; said to have invented ploughing and instituted various moral observances.

**706** Aelian, *Historical Miscellanies*

The ancients seem to have been at loggerheads over the number of Niobe's children. Homer says six males and six females (*Il.* 24. 603), Lasus says twice seven ...[1]

[1] Continued at Alcman 75; see also Sappho 205, Telesilla 721. The Attic dramatists followed Lasus.

**706A** Natale Conti, *Mythology*[1]

The Sphinx was daughter of Echidna and Typhon,[2] according to Lasus of Hermione.

[1] Of little value: Conti was not above attaching the name of an ancient author to material he found in his sources, in this case schol. Eur. *Phoen.* 1020, 'Apollodorus' 3. 5. 8.    [2] Hesiod, *Theog.* 326 f. made her parents Chimaera (or Echidna) and Orthos: see West ad loc.

# TYNNICHUS

**707** Plat. *Ion* 534d

μέγιστον δὲ τεκμήριον τῷ λόγῳ Τύννιχος ὁ Χαλκιδεύς, ὃς ἄλλο μὲν οὐδὲν πώποτε ἐποίησε ποίημα ὅτου τις ἂν ἀξιώσειεν μνησθῆναι, τὸν δὲ παιῶνα ὃν πάντες ᾄδουσι, σχεδόν τι πάντων μελῶν κάλλιστον, ἀτεχνῶς, ὅπερ αὐτὸς λέγει,

εὕρημά τι Μοισᾶν.

Porph. *de abst.* 2. 18 (p. 148 Nauck)

τὸν γοῦν Αἰσχύλον φασὶ τῶν Δελφῶν ἀξιούντων εἰς τὸν θεὸν γράψαι παιᾶνα εἰπεῖν ὅτι βέλτιστα Τυννίχῳ πεποίηται· παραβαλλόμενον δὲ τὸν αὐτοῦ πρὸς τὸν ἐκείνου ταὐτὸ πείσεσθαι τοῖς ἀγάλμασιν τοῖς καινοῖς πρὸς τὰ ἀρχαῖα.

# TYNNICHUS[1]

**707** Plato, *Ion*

My argument is well supported by the case of Tynnichus of Chalcis: he never composed any poem worth remembering with the exception of the paean which everyone sings, almost the most beautiful of all lyric poems and truly, as he himself puts it,

> a discovery of the Muses.

[1] See Alcman test. 16, where the text of Ptolemaeus as emended by Valesius runs, 'they say that the *Diving Women* of Alcman was found by the head of Tynnichus of Chalcis (when he died)'; the mss. have 'Tyronichus'.

Porphyry, *On Abstaining from Animal Food*

They say that Aeschylus on being asked by the Delphians to write a poem for Apollo answered that Tynnichus had already composed a most beautiful one: in comparison his would fare no better than modern statues by the side of ancient ones.

# LAMPRUS

## TESTIMONIA VITAE ATQUE ARTIS

**1** [Plut.] *Mus.* 31. 1142b (p. 126 Lasserre, vi 3. 26s. Ziegler)

τῶν γὰρ κατὰ τὴν αὑτοῦ ἡλικίαν φησὶ (sc. Ἀριστό-ξενος) Τελεσίᾳ τῷ Θηβαίῳ συμβῆναι νέῳ μὲν ὄντι τρα-φῆναι ἐν τῇ καλλίστῃ μουσικῇ καὶ μαθεῖν ἄλλα τε τῶν εὐδοκιμούντων καὶ δὴ καὶ τὰ Πινδάρου τά τε Διονυσίου τοῦ Θηβαίου καὶ τὰ Λάμπρου καὶ τὰ Πρατίνου καὶ τῶν λοιπῶν ὅσοι τῶν λυρικῶν ἄνδρες ἐγένοντο ποιηταὶ κρουμάτων ἀγαθοί.

**2** Athen. 1. 20e (i 45 Kaibel)

Σοφοκλῆς δὲ πρὸς τῷ καλὸς γεγενῆσθαι τὴν ὥραν ἦν καὶ ὀρχηστικὴν δεδιδαγμένος καὶ μουσικὴν ἔτι παῖς ὢν παρὰ Λάμπρῳ.

# LAMPRUS

## LIFE AND WORK

**1** 'Plutarch', *On Music*

Aristoxenus says that among his contemporaries Telesias[1] of Thebes was brought up in his youth on the most beautiful music and learned the works of the distinguished poets, in particular Pindar, Dionysius[2] of Thebes, Lamprus, Pratinas and all the other lyric poets who composed good music for the lyre.

[1] Unknown.  [2] Since he taught music to Epaminondas (Nepos, *Epam.* 2, who calls him 'as famous as Damon or Lamprus'), his work belongs to the second half of the 5th c.

**2** Athenaeus, *Scholars at Dinner*

Sophocles in addition to being a handsome youth had been taught dancing and music in his boyhood by Lamprus.[1]

[1] *C.* 480 B.C., since Sophocles was born *c.* 496? In Plato, *Menexenus* 236a Socrates speaks of Lamprus as a less than great music teacher. Since Phrynichus (test. 3 below) seems to portray Lamprus as a late 5th c. figure, it may have been the poet Lamprocles (see frr. 735–6 *P.M.G.*) who taught Sophocles.

# GREEK LYRIC

**3** Athen. 2. 44d (i 103 Kaibel)

ὑδροπότης δ᾽ ἦν καὶ Λάμπρος ὁ μουσικός, περὶ οὗ
Φρύνιχός φησι (fr. 74 K.-A.)·

λάρους[1] θρηνεῖν, ἐν οἷσι Λάμπρος ἐναπέθνησκεν
ἄνθρωπος ⟨ὢν⟩ ὑδατοπότης, μινυρὸς ὑπερσοφιστής,
Μουσῶν σκελετός, ἀηδόνων ἠπίαλος, ὕμνος Ἅιδου.

[1] καὶ νιγλάρους Bergk

# LAMPRUS

**3** Athenaeus, *Scholars at Dinner*

Lamprus the musician was another water-drinker: Phrynichus[1] says of him: sea-mews,[2] among which Lamprus died, lamented for him, a water-drinking fellow, a whimpering supersophist, mummy of the Muses, nightmare to nightingales, hymn for Hades.

[1] The Athenian comic poet.    [2] 'trills' in Bergk's emended text.

# PRATINAS

## TESTIMONIA VITAE ATQUE ARTIS

**1** *Sud.* Π 2230 (iv 191 Adler)

Πρατίνας, Πυρρωνίδου ἢ Ἐγκωμίου, Φλιάσιος, ποιητὴς τραγῳδίας· ἀντηγωνίζετο δὲ Αἰσχύλῳ τε καὶ Χοιρίλῳ ἐπὶ τῆς ο´ Ὀλυμπιάδος, καὶ πρῶτος ἔγραψε Σατύρους. ἐπιδεικνυμένου δὲ τούτου συνέβη τὰ ἴκρια ἐφ᾽ ὧν ἑστήκεσαν οἱ θεαταὶ πεσεῖν, καὶ ἐκ τούτου θέατρον ᾠκοδομήθη Ἀθηναίοις. καὶ δράματα μὲν ἐπεδείξατο ν´, ὧν Σατυρικὰ λβ´· ἐνίκησε δὲ ἅπαξ.

**2** Hypoth. i Aes. *Sept.* (M + P.Oxy. 2256 fr. 2) (ii 1 Smith)

ἐδιδάχθη ἐπὶ Θεαγενίδου ὀλυμπιάδι οη´. ἐνίκα Αἰσχύλος Λαΐῳ Οἰδίποδι Ἑπτὰ ἐπὶ Θήβας Σφιγγὶ σατυρικῇ, δεύτερος Ἀριστίας ταῖς τοῦ πατρὸς αὐτοῦ τραγῳδίαις Περσεῖ Ταντάλῳ < . . . > Παλαισταῖς σατύροις.

# PRATINAS

## LIFE AND WORK[1]

**1** *Suda,* Pratinas

Son of Pyrrhonides or of Encomius, of Phlius, tragic poet. He competed against Aeschylus and Choerilus in the 70th Olympiad (500/496 B.C.), and he was the first to write satyr-plays.[2] It was when he was putting on a play that the platform on which the spectators were standing collapsed, and as a result the Athenians built a theatre. He put on fifty plays, thirty-two of which were satyr-plays. He won one victory.[3]

[1] See also Lamprus test. 1. [2] So ps.-Acro on Hor. *A. P.* 216, where *Cratini* is emended to *Pratinae.* Dioscorides xxiii 4 (Gow-Page) = *A.P.* 7. 707. 4 speaks of Phliasian satyrs. Cf. also Tzetz. *De Poetis* 92. [3] For testimonia about his tragedies see Snell *T.G.F.* i 79 f.

**2** Introduction to Aeschylus, *Seven against Thebes*

It was produced in the archonship of Theagenides (468/7 B.C.) in the 78th Olympiad. Aeschylus was the winner with his *Laius, Oedipus, Seven against Thebes* and his satyr-play *Sphinx*; Aristias[1] was second with his father's tragedies, *Perseus, Tantalus, . . .* and the satyr-play, *The Wrestlers.*

[1] Son of Pratinas, who must have died before 467.

**3** Paus. 2. 13. 6 (i 138 Rocha-Pereira)

ἐνταῦθά ἐστι καὶ ᾿Αριστίου μνῆμα τοῦ Πρατίνου·
τούτῳ τῷ ᾿Αριστίᾳ σάτυροι καὶ Πρατίνᾳ τῷ πατρί εἰσι
πεποιημένοι πλὴν τῶν Αἰσχύλου δοκιμώτατοι.

**4** Athen. 1. 22a (i 48 Kaibel)

φασὶ δὲ καὶ ὅτι οἱ ἀρχαῖοι ποιηταί, Θέσπις, Πρατί-
νας, ⟦Κρατῖνος,⟧ Φρύνιχος, ὀρχησταὶ ἐκαλοῦντο διὰ τὸ
μὴ μόνον τὰ ἑαυτῶν δράματα ἀναφέρειν εἰς ὄρχησιν
τοῦ χοροῦ, ἀλλὰ καὶ ἔξω τῶν ἰδίων ποιημάτων διδά-
σκειν τοὺς βουλομένους ὀρχεῖσθαι.

### FRAGMENTA

**708** Athen. 14. 617b-f (iii 361s. Kaibel)

Πρατίνας δὲ ὁ Φλειάσιος αὐλητῶν καὶ χορευτῶν μισθοφόρων
κατεχόντων τὰς ὀρχήστρας ἀγανακτήσας (Wilamowitz: ἀγανα-
κτεῖν τινας cod. A) ἐπὶ τῷ τοὺς αὐλητὰς μὴ συναυλεῖν τοῖς χοροῖς
καθάπερ ἦν πάτριον ἀλλὰ τοὺς χοροὺς συνᾴδειν τοῖς αὐληταῖς· ὃν
οὖν εἶχεν κατὰ τῶν ταῦτα ποιούντων θυμὸν ὁ Πρατίνας ἐμφανίζει
διὰ τοῦδε τοῦ ὑπορχήματος·

τίς ὁ θόρυβος ὅδε; τί τάδε τὰ χορεύματα;
τίς ὕβρις ἔμολεν ἐπὶ Διονυσιάδα πολυπάταγα
     θυμέλαν;
ἐμὸς ἐμὸς ὁ Βρόμιος, ἐμὲ δεῖ κελαδεῖν, ἐμὲ δεῖ
     παταγεῖν
ἀν᾿ ὄρεα σύμενον μετὰ Ναϊάδων
5 οἷά τε κύκνον ἄγοντα ποικιλόπτερον μέλος.

# PRATINAS

**3** Pausanias, *Description of Greece*

Here[1] too is the memorial of Aristias, son of Pratinas. This Aristias and Pratinas his father composed the finest satyr-plays except for those of Aeschylus.

[1] In the agora of Phlius.

**4** Athenaeus, *Scholars at Dinner*

They say also that the ancient poets Thespis, Pratinas and Phrynichus were called 'dancers' because they not only made their plays dependent on the dancing of the chorus but quite apart from their own poetry they taught any who wanted to dance.

## FRAGMENTS

**708** Athenaeus, *Scholars at Dinner*

When hired pipers and dancers occupied the orchestras, Pratinas of Phlius was angry because the pipers were not accompanying the choruses, as was traditional, but the choruses were singing an accompaniment to the pipers; he reveals the indignation he felt against the offenders in the following hyporcheme[1]:

What is this din? What are these dance-steps? What outrage has come to the noisy altar of Dionysus? Mine, mine is Bromius[2]: it is for me to shout and stamp, racing over the mountains with the Naiads, singing a song of flashing wings like the

[1] Perhaps a 'dance-song' for the chorus of a satyr-play.
[2] Dionysus.

# GREEK LYRIC

τὰν ἀοιδὰν κατέστασε Πιερὶς βασίλειαν· ὁ δ' αὐλὸς
ὕστερον χορευέτω· καὶ γάρ ἐσθ' ὑπηρέτας.
κώμῳ μόνον θυραμάχοις τε πυγμαχίαισι νέων θέλοι
    παροίνων
ἔμμεναι στρατηλάτας.
10 παῖε τὸν φρυνεοῦ ποικίλαν πνοὰν ἔχοντα,
    φλέγε τὸν ὀλεσισιαλοκάλαμον
    λαλοβαρύοπα παραμελορυθμοβάταν
    ὑπαὶ τρυπάνῳ δέμας πεπλασμένον.
    ἢν ἰδού· ἄδε σοι δεξιᾶς καὶ ποδὸς διαρριφά·
15 θριαμβοδιθύραμβε κισσόχαιτ' ἄναξ,
    <ἄκου'> ἄκουε τὰν ἐμὰν Δώριον χορείαν.

6 Heringa, Bergk: κατεστα ἐπιερεις βασιλεια οὐδ' A, ὁ δ' pro οὐδ'
E      8 Bergk: κωμῶν μόνον A κώμων μόνων E      Wilamowitz:
θεαεῖ A θέα E      10 Girard: φρυναιου A      13 Page: θυπα A, θ'
ὑπαὶ Emperius      14 Bamberger: δεξιὰ A      16 suppl. Page

**709** Athen. 14. 632f–633a (iii 396 Kaibel)

διετήρησαν δὲ μάλιστα τῶν Ἑλλήνων Λακεδαιμόνιοι τὴν μου-
σικήν, πλείστῃ αὐτῇ χρώμενοι, καὶ συχνοὶ παρ' αὐτοῖς ἐγένοντο
μελῶν ποιηταί. τηροῦσιν δὲ καὶ νῦν τὰς ἀρχαίας ᾠδὰς ἐπιμελῶς
πολυμαθεῖς τε εἰς ταύτας εἰσὶ καὶ ἀκριβεῖς. ὅθεν καὶ Πρατίνας
φησί·

Λάκων ὁ τέττιξ εὔτυκος ἐς χορόν.

**710** Athen. 11. 461e (iii 5 Kaibel)

κατὰ τὸν Φλιάσιον ποιητὴν Πρατίναν·

οὐ γᾶν αὐλακισμέναν
    ἀρῶν ἀλλ' ἄσκαφον ματεύων,

κυλικηγορήσων ἔρχομαι.

322

# PRATINAS

swan. Song was made queen by the Pierian[3]: so let
the pipe dance in second place: he is the servant!
May he wish only to be commander-in-chief of revels
and the street-brawling boxing-matches of drunken
youths. Beat the one with the mottled toad-breath,
burn the spittle-wasting reed with its prattling
growl, striding across melody and rhythm, its body
fashioned under the auger! Look this way! Here
is how to fling out hand and foot! Thriambo-
dithyrambus, lord with ivy in your hair,[4] hear, hear
my Dorian[5] dance-song.[6]

[3] The Muse.      [4] Dionysus.      [5] Perhaps with reference to
Pratinas' birthplace in the Peloponnese.      [6] On the poem see
R. Seaford, *Maia* 29–30 (1977–78) 81–94.


**709** Athenaeus, *Scholars at Dinner*

The Spartans more than any other Greeks preserved
the art of music, making much use of it; lyric poets were
common among them. Even nowadays they preserve the
ancient songs carefully and are knowledgeable and strict
over them. That is why Pratinas says,

the Spartan, that cicada apt for the choral song.

**710** Athenaeus, *Scholars at Dinner*

In the words of the Phliasian poet Pratinas,

not ploughing furrowed ground but seeking undug
land,

I come to talk over our cups.

2 Scaliger: δρῶν codd.     Bergk: ἀλλὰ σκάφον codd. (σκύφον E)
Fiorillo: μαντεύων, μαστεύων codd.

**711**     ΔΥΜΑΙΝΑΙ Η ΚΑΡΥΑΤΙΔΕΣ

Athen. 9. 392f (ii 356 Kaibel)

Πρατίνας δ' ἐν Δυμαίναις (Toup: Δυμαναις codd., Δυσμαίναις Meineke) ἢ Καρυάτισιν

ἁδύφωνον

ἰδίως καλεῖ τὸν ὄρτυγα, πλὴν εἰ μή τι παρὰ τοῖς Φλιασίοις ἢ τοῖς Λάκωσι φωνήεντες ὡς καὶ οἱ πέρδικες.

**712** Athen. 14. 624f–625a (iii 378 Kaibel)

καὶ Πρατίνας δέ πού φησι·

(a)  μήτε σύντονον δίωκε
     μήτε τὰν ἀνειμέναν [[Ἰαστί]]
     μοῦσαν, ἀλλὰ τὰν μέσαν
     νεῶν ἄρουραν αἰόλιζε τῷ μέλει·

ἐν δὲ τοῖς ἑξῆς σαφέστερόν φησιν·

(b)                    πρέπει τοι
     πᾶσιν ἀοιδολαβράκταις
     Αἰολὶς ἁρμονία.

(a) 2–3 Toup, Valckenaer: ἰαστὶν οὖσαν codd. (ἰαστὶ οὖσαν E) ἰαστί del. Page        (b) 2 Bergk: ἀοιδὰ λαβρ. codd.

**713** [Plut.] *Mus.*

(i) 7. 1133e (p. 114 Lasserre, vi 3. 7 Ziegler)

ἄλλοι δὲ Κράτητος εἶναί φασι τὸν πολυκέφαλον νόμον, γενομένου μαθητοῦ Ὀλύμπου· ὁ δὲ Πρατίνας Ὀλύμπου φησὶν εἶναι τοῦ νεωτέρου τὸν νόμον τοῦτον.

# PRATINAS

DYMAENAE *or* CARYATIDS

Athenaeus, *Scholars at Dinner*

Pratinas in his *Dymaenae* or *Caryatids*[1] is peculiar in calling the quail

> sweet-voiced,

unless of course quails in Phlius or Sparta have a voice as partridges do.

[1] Alternative titles of a tragedy or satyr-play. Dymaenae are girls from Dyme in Laconia (see Alcman 4 fr. b; 11); the Caryatids were priestesses of Artemis at Caryae in Laconia.

**712** Athenaeus, *Scholars at Dinner*[1]

And Pratinas says somewhere,

(a) Do not pursue the tight-strung Muse nor the relaxed Muse either[2]: plough the middle of the field and Aeolise in your song;

and in the next lines he says more clearly,

(b) The Aeolian *harmonia* is appropriate for all singer-braggarts.

[1] The passage, derived from Heraclides, *On Music,* book 3, follows Lasus 702.      [2] I.e. high-pitched and low-pitched tuning; the Aeolian was between the extremes.

**713** 'Plutarch', *On Music*

(i) Others say that the Many-headed nome is the work of Crates, a pupil of Olympus, but Pratinas says it is by the younger Olympus.[1]

[1] See Olympus test. 3.

# GREEK LYRIC

(ii) 9. 1134c (p. 114 Lasserre, vi 3. 8 Ziegler)

ἄλλοι δὲ Ξενόδαμον ὑπορχημάτων ποιητὴν γεγονέναι φασὶ καὶ οὐ παιάνων, καθάπερ Πρατίνας, καὶ αὐτοῦ δὲ τοῦ Ξενοδάμου ἀπομνημονεύεται ᾆσμα ὅ ἐστι φανερῶς ὑπόρχημα.

(iii) 42. 1146bc (p. 131 Lasserre, vi 3. 35 Ziegler)

Τέρπανδρον δ' ἄν τις παραλάβοι τὸν τὴν γενομένην ποτὲ παρὰ Λακεδαιμονίοις στάσιν καταλύσαντα, καὶ Θαλήταν τὸν Κρῆτα, ὅν φασι κατά τι πυθόχρηστον Λακεδαιμονίους παραγενόμενον διὰ μουσικῆς ἰάσασθαι· ἀπαλλάξαι τε τοῦ κατασχόντος λιμοῦ τὴν Σπάρτην, καθάπερ φησὶ Πρατίνας.

# PRATINAS

(ii) Others, like Pratinas, say that Xenodamus[1] composed hyporchemes,[2] not paeans, and indeed a song of Xenodamus himself is recorded which is clearly a hyporcheme.

[1] See Thaletas test. 7.          [2] As Pratinas did: see fr. 708.

(iii) One might cite the cases of Terpander,[1] who put an end to the civil strife which had broken out in Sparta, and of the Cretan Thaletas,[2] who is said to have arrived in Sparta in accordance with an oracle and by means of his music to have cured them and delivered Sparta from the plague that gripped it, as Pratinas says.

[1] See Terpander test. 9.          [2] See Thaletas test. 4.

# CYDIAS

**714** Pl. *Charm.* 155de

   . . . τότε δή, ὦ γεννάδα, εἶδόν τε τὰ ἐντὸς τοῦ ἱματίου καὶ ἐφλε-
γόμην καὶ οὐκέτ' ἐν ἐμαυτοῦ ἦν καὶ ἐνόμισα σοφώτατον εἶναι τὸν
Κυδίαν τὰ ἐρωτικά, ὃς εἶπεν ἐπὶ καλοῦ λέγων παιδός, ἄλλῳ ὑποτι-
θέμενος, εὐλαβεῖσθαι

       μὴ κατέναντα λέοντος
νεβρὸς ἐλθὼν μοῖραν αἱρεῖσθαι κρεῶν·

αὐτὸς γάρ μοι ἐδόκουν ὑπὸ τοῦ τοιούτου θρέμματος ἑαλωκέναι.

2 νεβρὸν ἐλθόντα codd.    ἀθανατώσῃ θεία μοίρα cod. B

**715** = Stes. 271

**948** Schol. RV Ar. *Nub.* 967 (p. 185s. Holwerda)

   ἢ 'τηλέπορόν τι βόαμα' : καὶ τοῦτο μέλους ἀρχή. φασὶ δὲ μὴ
εὑρίσκεσθαι ὅτου ποτέ ἐστιν· ἐν γὰρ ἀποσπάσματι ἐν τῇ βιβλιο-
θήκῃ εὑρεῖν Ἀριστοφάνῃ (fr. 379 Slater). τινὲς δέ φασι Κυδίου
(Bernhardy: Κυδίδου codd.) τινὸς Ἑρμιονέως·

       τηλέπορόν τι βόαμα λύρας

cf. *Sud.* T 490 (iv 539 Adler)

---

[1] Given by the Just Argument as an example of a good old-
fashioned song; cf. Stes. 274 = Lamprocles 735.    [2] The mss.
give 'Cydidas', which Page retains, treating the fragment as
adespoton; see also 714 n. 1, W. J. W. Koster, *Mnemos.* 6 (1953) 63.

# CYDIAS[1]

**714** Plato, *Charmides*

Then, my noble friend, I saw what was inside his cloak[2] and I was on fire and no longer in control of myself, and I reckoned that the wisest man in matters of love was Cydias, who when speaking of a beautiful boy advised someone to look out

in case like a fawn you come up against a lion and are seized as his portion of flesh.[3]

For I felt that I was in the clutches of just such a creature.

[1] A lyre-player, bearded and balding, who leads a komos on a RF psykter dated *c.* 500 B.C. (B.M. E767: see Beazley *ARV* i 31) is labelled Cydias.   [2] Socrates describes his meeting with the handsome youth Charmides. See also Athen. 5. 187e.   [3] Or 'and meet the fate of flesh'.

**715** = Stes. 271

**948** Scholiast on Aristophanes, *Clouds* ('A far-travelling shout')[1]

This too is the beginning of a song. They say that its authorship is not established, since Aristophanes (sc. of Byzantium) found it as a fragment in the library (sc. of Alexandria). Some say it is the work of a certain Cydias[2] of Hermione:

A far-travelling shout of the lyre.

# SIMONIDES

## TESTIMONIA VITAE ATQUE ARTIS

**1** *Sud.* Σ 439 (iv 361 Adler)

Σιμωνίδης, Λεωπρεποῦς, Ἰουλιήτης τῆς ἐν Κέῳ τῇ νήσῳ πόλεως, λυρικός, μετὰ Στησίχορον τοῖς χρόνοις· ὃς ἐπεκλήθη Μελικέρτης διὰ τὸ ἡδύ. καὶ τὴν μνημονικὴν δὲ τέχνην εὗρεν οὗτος· προσεξεῦρε δὲ καὶ τὰ μακρὰ τῶν στοιχείων καὶ διπλᾶ καὶ τῇ λύρᾳ τὸν τρίτον φθόγγον. γέγονε δ' ἐπὶ τῆς πεντηκοστῆς ἕκτης ὀλυμπιάδος, οἱ δὲ ξβ' γεγράφασι. καὶ παρέτεινε μέχρι τῆς οη', βιοὺς ἔτη πθ'. καὶ γέγραπται αὐτῷ Δωρίδι διαλέκτῳ †ἡ Καμβύσου καὶ Δαρείου βασιλεία καὶ Ξέρξου ναυμαχία καὶ† ἡ ἐπ' Ἀρτεμισίῳ ναυμαχία, δι' ἐλεγείας· ἡ δ' ἐν Σαλαμῖνι μελικῶς· θρῆνοι, ἐγκώμια,

---

1 Some of this material is in the brief biography of P.Oxy. 1800 fr. i col. ii 36 ff. (*c.* 200 A.D.).   2 See Aelian, *V.H.* 2. 24 for an apophthegm of L.   3 Stes. was said to have died in the 56th Olympiad (Stes. test. 2); see also fr. 564.   4 Meli- means 'honey'.   5 See testt. 24–26.   6 I.e. the letters eta and omega, xi and psi; cf. Plut. *Qu. Conv.* 738 f., ix 3. 2, comment. Melamp. or Diom. on Dion. Thr. (i 3. 35 Hilgard), schol. Dion. Thr. (i 3. 185 Hilgard), *Anecd. Gr.* (de Villoison) ii 187.   7 A mistake: the lyre had seven strings from the 7th c.   8 The later dating was championed by L. A. Stella, 'Studi Simonidei', *R.F.C.*

# SIMONIDES

## BIOGRAPHY

**1** *Suda,* Simonides (1st notice)[1]

Son of Leoprepes[2]; from Iulis, a city on the island of Ceos; lyric poet, later than Stesichorus.[3] He was given the name Melicertes because of the sweetness of his poetry.[4] He invented the art of mnemonics[5]; he also invented the long vowels and double consonants[6] and the third note on the lyre.[7] He was born in the 56th Olympiad (556/552 B.C.) or according to some writers in the 62nd (532/528),[8] and he survived until the 78th (468/464), having lived 89 years. He composed in the Doric dialect 'The Reign of Cambyses and Darius', 'Sea-battle against Xerxes'[9] and 'The Sea-battle at Artemisium' in elegiacs; 'The Sea-battle at Salamis' in lyric metre,[10] and dirges,[11] eulogies,[12] epigrams, paeans[13] and

1946, 1–24, but is not generally accepted.    [9] Text corrupt: the source of the *Suda* may have said that S. composed during the reigns of Cambyses (530–522) and Darius (521–486) and that he wrote poems on the battles fought at Artemisium and Salamis (480) during the invasion of Xerxes.    [10] Since the Artemisium poem was in lyric metre (fr. 533), Bergk suggested that the Salamis poem was in elegiacs (fr. eleg. 1 and perhaps 2–3 West).    [11] See frr. 520–531.    [12] I.e. the epinicians, frr. 506–519; also 531.    [13] See fr. 519.

ἐπιγράμματα, παιᾶνες καὶ τραγῳδίαι καὶ ἄλλα. οὗτος
ὁ Σιμωνίδης μνημονικός τις ἦν, εἴπερ τις ἄλλος . . .

**2** Str. 10. 5. 6 (ii 418 Kramer)

Κέως δὲ τετράπολις μὲν ὑπῆρξε, λείπονται δὲ δύο,
ἥ τε Ἰουλὶς καὶ ἡ Καρθαία, εἰς ἃς συνεπολίσθησαν αἱ
λοιπαί, ἡ μὲν Ποιήεσσα εἰς τὴν Καρθαίαν, ἡ δὲ Κορη-
σία εἰς τὴν Ἰουλίδα. ἐκ δὲ τῆς Ἰουλίδος ὅ τε Σιμωνί-
δης ἦν ὁ μελοποιὸς καὶ Βακχυλίδης ἀδελφιδοῦς ἐκεί-
νου, καὶ μετὰ ταῦτα Ἐρασίστρατος ὁ ἰατρὸς καὶ τῶν ἐκ
τοῦ περιπάτου φιλοσόφων Ἀρίστων . . .

**3** Callim. fr. 222 (i 214 Pfeiffer)

οὐ γὰρ ἐργάτιν τρέφω
τὴν Μοῦσαν, ὡς ὁ Κεῖος Ὑλίχου νέπους.

tragedies and other works.[14] This Simonides had
an outstandingly good memory . . .[15]

[14] 'Plutarch', *On Music* 17 mentions his maiden-songs (parthenia)
and processionals (prosodia); he also composed dithyrambs (frr.
539, XXVII). See test. 33. [15] The entry goes on to compare
him in this respect with Apollonius of Tyana, the neopythagorean
teacher (1st c. A.D.).

## BIRTHPLACE AND FAMILY

**2** Strabo, *Geography*

Ceos[1] was a tetrapolis, but only two of the cities
remain, Iulis and Carthaea[2]; the other two,
Poeëessa and Coresia, were incorporated into
Carthaea and Iulis respectively. From Iulis came
Simonides the lyric poet and Bacchylides his
nephew,[3] and later Erasistratus the physician and
the peripatetic philosopher Ariston . . .

[1] Bacch. 17. 130 mentions the choruses of the island, Pind. *Paean* 4.
23 f. the poets. [2] See Stes. 200. [3] So *Suda* B 59; B.
was the son of S.'s sister.

**3** Callimachus, *Iambics*

For I do not bring up my muse a mercenary,[1] as
did the Cean descendant of Hylichus.[2]

[1] See test. 22. [2] S. belonged to the family of the Hylichidae.
The names Leoprepes (see test. 1) and Hylichus occur in inscrip-
tions from Ceos (*I.G.* XII 5. 609. 102 f., 5. 637).

**4** *Sud.* Σ 442 (iv 362 Adler)

Σιμωνίδης, Κεῖος, θυγατριδοῦς κατά τινας τοῦ προ-
τέρου, ὃς ἐπεκλήθη Μελικέρτης. γέγονε δὲ πρὸ τῶν
Πελοποννησιακῶν· καὶ γέγραφε Γενεαλογίαν ἐν βι-
βλίοις γ', Εὑρήματα ἐν βιβλίοις γ'.

**5** 'Simonides' XXVIII (*F.G.E.* p. 243)

ἦρχεν Ἀδείμαντος μὲν Ἀθηναίοις ὅτ᾽ ἐνίκα
   Ἀντιοχὶς φυλὴ δαιδάλεον τρίποδα·
Ξεινοφίλου δέ τις υἱὸς Ἀριστείδης ἐχορήγει
   πεντήκοντ᾽ ἀνδρῶν καλὰ μαθόντι χορῷ·
ἀμφὶ διδασκαλίῃ δὲ Σιμωνίδῃ ἕσπετο κῦδος
   ὀγδωκονταέτει παιδὶ Λεωπρέπεος.

# SIMONIDES

**4** *Suda,* Simonides (4th notice)

A Cean; according to some, son of the daughter of the earlier Simonides who was given the name Melicertes.[1] He was born before the Peloponnesian War. He wrote *Genealogy* in three books, *Discoveries* in three books.[2]

[1] Under the year 489/8 the *Parian Marble* 49 records a victory in Athens of 'Simonides, grandfather of the poet Simonides, himself a poet'; 'grandfather' cannot be correct.   [2] See *F.Gr.H.* i 158 f., S. Fogelmark, *Chrysaigis* 37 ff.

## CHRONOLOGY[1]

**5** Anonymous epigram[2]

Adimantus was archon in Athens[3] when the Antiochid tribe won the intricately-made tripod; one Aristides, son of Xenophilus, was *choregos* of the chorus of fifty men[4] who had learned well; and for their training glory came the way of Simonides, son of Leoprepes, at the age of eighty.[5]

[1] See also test. 1 with n. 3. It is not certain whether the Simonides addressed by Theognis (467 ff., 667 ff., 1349 f.) is the lyric poet.   [2] Probably from the Hellenistic period.   [3] In 477/6 B.C.   [4] I.e. a dithyrambic chorus.   [5] Cf. Plut. *an seni* 3. 785a, Val. Max. 8. 7. 13, *Marm. Par.* 54, Cyril *contr. Iul.* 1. 13 (who puts S.'s *floruit* rather than his birth in Ol. 56), Euseb. Ol. 55 (who makes the same mistake: the Olympic dating has been misaligned). C. Gallavotti, *Q.U.C.C.* 20 (1975) 165–71 argues that a fragmentary *horos* from the Acropolis commemorates S.'s victory.

**6** Euseb. *Chron.*

(a) Ol. 60 (p. 103b Helm): Simonides lyricus et Phocyl[l]ides clari habentur et Xenophanes . . .

(b) Ol. 73 (p. 108 Helm): Pindarus et Simonides lyrici poetae insignes habentur.

**7** Vit. Pind. Ambros. (i 2s. Drachmann)

ἐπέβαλλε δὲ τοῖς χρόνοις Σιμωνίδη νεώτερος πρεσβυτέρῳ. τῶν γοῦν αὐτῶν μέμνηνται ἀμφότεροι πράξεων· καὶ γὰρ Σιμωνίδης τὴν ἐν Σαλαμῖνι ναυμαχίαν γέγραφε, καὶ Πίνδαρος (fr. 272 Snell) μέμνηται τῆς Κάδμου βασιλείας.

**8** *Marm. Par.* Ep. 57 (*F.Gr.H.* ii B p. 1000)

ἀφ᾽ οὗ . . . Σιμωνίδης ὁ ποιητὴς ἐτελεύτησεν, βιοὺς ἔτη ⋀ΔΔΔΔ, ἔτη ΗΗΓ, ἄρχοντος ᾿Αθήνησι Θεαγενίδου.

**9** [Luc.] *Macr.* 26 (i 81 Macleod)

Σιμωνίδης δὲ ὁ Κεῖος (sc. ἔζησεν) ὑπὲρ τὰ ἐνενήκοντα (sc. ἔτη).

# SIMONIDES

**6** Eusebius, *Chronicle*

(a) Olympiad 60 (540/536 B.C.): Simonides the lyric poet and Phocylides are regarded as famous, and Xenophanes . . .

(b) Olympiad 73 (488/484 B.C.): Pindar and Simonides, the lyric poets, are regarded as distinguished.

**7** 'Ambrosian' Life of Pindar

Pindar's life overlapped that of Simonides as younger man's overlaps older man's. At least, they mention the same events, for Simonides wrote 'The Sea-battle at Salamis',[1] and Pindar mentions the reign of Cadmus.[2]

[1] See test. 1, fr. 536, eleg. 1.   [2] Son of Scythes and tyrant of Cos: see Hdt. 7. 163 f.

**8** *Parian Marble* (468/7 B.C.)

From the time when Simonides the poet died, having lived for ninety years, 205 years[1]; Theagenides was archon in Athens.

[1] Calculated inclusively from 264/3 B.C.

**9** 'Lucian', *On Longevity*

Simonides of Ceos lived for over ninety years.[1]

[1] Cicero, *On Old Age* 7. 23 says that S. continued to compose in his old age.

**10** Aristot. *Ath. Pol.* 18. 1 (p. 22 Oppermann)

ἦσαν δὲ κύριοι μὲν τῶν πραγμάτων διὰ τὰ ἀξιώ-
ματα καὶ διὰ τὰς ἡλικίας Ἵππαρχος καὶ Ἱππίας,
πρεσβύτερος δὲ ὢν ὁ Ἱππίας καὶ τῇ φύσει πολιτικὸς
καὶ ἔμφρων ἐπεστάτει τῆς ἀρχῆς. ὁ δὲ Ἵππαρχος παι-
διώδης καὶ ἐρωτικὸς καὶ φιλόμουσος ἦν (καὶ τοὺς περὶ
Ἀνακρέοντα καὶ Σιμωνίδην καὶ τοὺς ἄλλους ποιητὰς
οὗτος ἦν ὁ μεταπεμπόμενος) . . .

**11** 'Simonides' XXVII *F.G.E.* ( =*A.P.* 6. 213)

ἓξ ἐπὶ πεντήκοντα, Σιμωνίδη, ἤραο ταύρους
    καὶ τρίποδας πρὶν τόνδ' ἀνθέμεναι πίνακα,
τοσσάκι δ' ἱμερόεντα διδαξάμενος χορὸν ἀνδρῶν
    εὐδόξου Νίκας ἀγλαὸν ἅρμ' ἐπέβης.

**12** Plut. *Them.* 5. 6, 114c (i 1. 163 Ziegler)

. . . ὥς που καὶ πρὸς Σιμωνίδην τὸν Κεῖον εἰπεῖν,
αἰτούμενόν τι τῶν οὐ μετρίων παρ' αὐτοῦ στρατηγοῦν-
τος, ὡς οὔτ' ἐκεῖνος ἂν γένοιτο ποιητὴς ἀγαθὸς ᾄδων

# SIMONIDES

## LIFE[1]

**10** Aristotle, *Constitution of Athens*

Because of their rank and age Hipparchus and Hippias held power (sc. in Athens after the death of their father Pisistratus), but since Hippias was the elder and a natural politican and sensible he was in charge of the government; Hipparchus was frivolous, amorous and fond of the arts: it was he[2] who sent for Anacreon and Simonides and the other poets.[3]

[1] Phaedrus 4. 23 tells a story of shipwreck; for a miraculous preservation from drowning see LXXXIV, LXXXV *F.G.E.*      [2] Between 527 and 514 B.C. See also 'Plato', *Hipparchus* 228bc ( = Anacr. test. 6), Aelian, *V.H.* 8. 2. For the Pisistratids see I, XXVI *F.G.E.*, for Pisistratus fr. 607.      [3] E.g. Lasus of Hermione (see Lasus test. 2).

**11** Anonymous epigram[1]

Fifty-six bulls and tripods,[2] Simonides, did you win before setting up this tablet; fifty-six times after training the delightful chorus of men did you step aboard the glorious chariot of honoured Victory.[3]

[1] A late Hellenistic poem.      [2] The dithyrambic prizes for poet and tribe.      [3] Cf. Lasus test. 3.

**12** Plutarch, *Life of Themistocles*[1]

So once, when Simonides of Ceos made an improper request of him during his term as *strategos,* Themistocles answered, 'You would not have turned out to be a good poet if you sang out of tune,

[1] Continued at test. 27.

παρὰ μέλος, οὔτ᾽ αὐτὸς ἀστεῖος ἄρχων παρὰ νόμον
χαριζόμενος.

13 Theocr. 16. 42–47

ἄμναστοι δὲ τὰ πολλὰ καὶ ὄλβια τῆνα λιπόντες
δειλοῖς ἐν νεκύεσσι μακροὺς αἰῶνας ἔκειντο,
εἰ μὴ θεῖος ἀοιδὸς ὁ Κήιος αἰόλα φωνέων
βάρβιτον ἐς πολύχορδον ἐν ἀνδράσι θῆκ᾽ ὀνομα-
      στούς
ὁπλοτέροις· τιμᾶς δὲ καὶ ὠκέες ἔλλαχον ἵπποι,
οἵ σφισιν ἐξ ἱερῶν στεφανηφόροι ἦλθον ἀγώνων.

14 Plut. *aud. poet.* 15c (i 29s. Paton-Wegehaupt)

οὐ γὰρ ἅπτεται τὸ ἀπατηλὸν αὐτῆς ἀβελτέρων
κομιδῇ καὶ ἀνοήτων. διὸ καὶ Σιμωνίδης μὲν ἀπεκρί-
νατο πρὸς τὸν εἰπόντα 'τί δὴ μόνους οὐκ ἐξαπατᾷς
Θεσσαλούς;' 'ἀμαθέστεροι γάρ εἰσιν ἢ ὡς ὑπ᾽ ἐμοῦ
ἐξαπατᾶσθαι.'

15 *Vit. Aesch.* (p. 332 Page O.C.T., *T.G.F.* iii 33s.)

ἀπῆρεν δὲ ὡς Ἱέρωνα . . . κατὰ δὲ ἐνίους ἐν τῷ εἰς

nor I a fine magistrate if I gave favours against the law.'[2]

[2] So *Mor.* 185cd, 534e, 807b. For Them. see also test. 25.

**13** Theocritus (on the Thessalian patrons of S.)

And having left behind that great wealth they[1] would have lain forgotten among the wretched dead for long ages, had not a divine bard, the man of Ceos, sung his varied songs to the lyre with its many strings and made them famous among later generations. Honour was won also by their swift horses, which came from the holy contests wearing the garlands of victory.

[1] Antiochus, Aleuas, the Scopadae and the Creondae, rulers of Thessaly; the scholia on the passage are at frr. 528, 529. For S. in Thessaly see also 510, 511, 519 fr. 148, 521, 542, 632, and perhaps eleg. 6 and LXIX.

**14** Plutarch, *How the young man should study poetry*

For the deceptive element in it (sc. in poetry) makes no impression on complete fools and idiots. That explains Simonides' answer to the man who asked why the Thessalians were the only people he did not deceive: 'They are too ignorant to be deceived by me.'[1]

[1] Van Groningen, *Mnem.* 1 (1948) 1–7, took this to mean that S. did not use myth in his Thessalian poems.

**15** Anonymous life of Aeschylus

He went off to Hiero ... according to some

τοὺς ἐν Μαραθῶνι τεθνηκότας ἐλεγείῳ ἡσσηθεὶς Σιμω-
νίδῃ· τὸ γὰρ ἐλεγεῖον πολὺ τῆς περὶ τὸ συμπαθὲς
λεπτότητος μετέχειν θέλει, ὃ τοῦ Αἰσχύλου, ὡς ἔφα-
μεν, ἐστὶν ἀλλότριον.

**16** Diog. Laert. 2. 46 (i 76 Long)

καθά φησιν Ἀριστοτέλης ἐν τρίτῳ περὶ ποιητικῆς
(fr. 75 Rose), ἐφιλονείκει . . . Σιμωνίδῃ Τιμοκρέων.

**17** Plat. *Ep.* 2. 311a (v Burnet)

οἷον καὶ περὶ Ἱέρωνος ὅταν διαλέγωνται ἄνθρωποι
καὶ Παυσανίου τοῦ Λακεδαιμονίου, χαίρουσι τὴν Σιμω-
νίδου συνουσίαν παραφέροντες, ἅ τε ἔπραξεν καὶ εἶπεν
πρὸς αὐτούς.

**18** Paus. 1. 2. 3 (i 4 Rocha-Pereira)

συνῆσαν δὲ ἄρα καὶ τότε τοῖς βασιλεῦσι ποιηταὶ καὶ
πρότερον ἔτι καὶ Πολυκράτει Σάμου τυραννοῦντι Ἀνα-
κρέων παρῆν καὶ ἐς Συρακούσας πρὸς Ἱέρωνα Αἰσχύ-
λος καὶ Σιμωνίδης ἐστάλησαν.

---

[1] Euripides at the court of king Archelaus of Macedonia. [2] See also
Aelian *V.H.* 9. 1 (S. in his old age was attracted by Hiero's gifts), 4.
15, 12. 25, Plut. *de exil.* (S. went to Sicily before Aeschylus), Synes.
*Ep.* 49. For Hiero see also testt. 17, 23, fr. 580, eleg. 7, 'Sim.'
XXXIV, Xenophon, *Hiero* (an imaginary conversation between S.
and Hiero on despotism) and anecdotes of conversations between S.
and Hiero or Hiero's wife, e.g. test. 47(c). For a possible reference

# SIMONIDES

authorities because he was defeated by Simonides in the competition for the elegy on those who died at Marathon[1]; for the elegiac metre needs the delicate touch which rouses sympathy, and that, as we have said, is foreign to Aeschylus.

[1] See XX and XXI *F.G.E.*

**16** Diogenes Laertius, *Lives of the Philosophers*

Aristotle says in his third book *On Poetry* ... that Simonides was assailed by Timocreon.[1]

[1] See Timocr. test. 1, 'Sim.' XXXVII, eleg. 17, Timocr. 10 West.

**17** Plato, *Letters*

For example, when men talk about Hiero or about Pausanias the Spartan they enjoy bringing in their association with Simonides and what he did and said to them.[1]

[1] According to Plut. *Cons. Apoll.* 6. 105a he told Pausanias to remember that he was human. See also 'Sim.' XVII(a), Aelian *V.H.* 9. 41.

**18** Pausanias, *Description of Greece*

In those days, then, poets lived at the courts of kings,[1] and also earlier still Anacreon lived with Polycrates, tyrant of Samos, and Aeschylus and Simonides made their way to Hiero in Syracuse.[2]

in S. to the Sicilian village of Hyccara see K. Latte, *Eranos* 54 (1956) 65 n. 2.

# GREEK LYRIC

**19** Schol. Pind. *Ol.* 2. 29d (i 68s. Drachmann)

ὁ δὲ Δίδυμος τὸ ἀκριβέστερον τῆς ἱστορίας ἐκτίθε-
ται, μάρτυρα Τίμαιον (*F.Gr.H.* IIIB 566 F 93b) τὸν
συντάξαντα τὰ περὶ τῆς Σικελίας προφερόμενος. ἡ δὲ
ἱστορία οὕτως ἔχει· . . . καὶ οὕτω τὸν Θήρωνα, ὑπερ-
αγανακτήσαντα θυγατρὸς ἅμα καὶ γαμβροῦ, συρρῆξαι
πρὸς Ἱέρωνα πόλεμον παρὰ Γέλᾳ τῷ Σικελιωτικῷ
ποταμῷ . . . μή γε μὴν εἰς βλάβην, μηδὲ εἰς τέλος
προχωρῆσαι τὸν πόλεμον· φασὶ γὰρ τότε Σιμωνίδην
τὸν λυρικὸν περιτυχόντα διαλῦσαι τοῖς βασιλεῦσι τὴν
ἔχθραν.

**20** Pind. *Ol.* 2. 86ss.

σοφὸς ὁ πολλὰ εἰδὼς φυᾷ·
μαθόντες δὲ λάβροι
παγγλωσσίᾳ κόρακες ὣς ἄκραντα γαρύετον
Διὸς πρὸς ὄρνιχα θεῖον.

Schol. ad loc. (157a, i 99 Drachmann)

κόρακες· . . . αἰνίττεται Βακχυλίδην καὶ Σιμωνίδην,
ἑαυτὸν λέγων ἀετόν, κόρακας δὲ τοὺς ἀντιτέχνους.

**21** Callim. fr. 64. 1–14

οὐδ᾽ ἄν τοι Καμάρινα τόσον κακὸν ὁκκόσον ἀνδρός
κινηθεὶς ὁσίου τύμβος ἐπικρεμάσαι·
καὶ γ]ὰρ ἐμόν κοτε σῆμα, τό μοι πρὸ πόληος ἔχ[ευ]αν

---

[1] The citizens of Camarina in Sicily drained their lake in defiance
of an oracle, and their city was later captured.     [2] S. is the
speaker.

# SIMONIDES

**19** Scholiast on Pindar, *Olympian* 2. 15 (on Thero's past deeds)

Didymus[1] gives the more accurate version of the story, quoting as his authority Timaeus[2] who composed the history of Sicily. The story runs as follows ... So Thero, angry on account of his daughter and son-in-law (Polyzelus, brother of Hiero), made war against Hiero at Gela, the Sicilian river ... But no harm resulted and the war came to nothing; for they say that Simondes the lyric poet turned up and put an end to the kings' enmity.[3]

[1] Alexandrian scholar, 1st c. B.C.   [2] *C.* 356–260 B.C.   [3] For another version see the previous scholium (29c).

**20** Pindar, *Olympian* 2. 86 ff.

The wise man is he who knows many things by the gift of nature: those who learned, boisterous in their garrulity, utter (the pair of them) idle words like crows against the holy bird of Zeus.

Scholiast on the passage

He is making riddling reference to Bacchylides and Simonides, calling himself an eagle and his rivals crows.[1]

[1] It is not certain that this explanation is correct. See also test. 45.

**21** Callimachus, *Aetia*

Not even Camarina would be such a threatening disaster[1] as the removal of the tomb of a holy man: once my burial mound,[2] which the citizens of Acra-

Ζῆν'] 'Ακραγαντῖνοι Ξείνι[ο]ν ἁζόμενοι,
... κ]ατ' οὖν ἤρειψεν ἀνὴρ κακός, εἴ τιν' ἀκούει[ς
Φοίνικα πτόλιος σχέτλιον ἡγεμόνα·
πύργῳ δ' ἐγκατέλεξεν ἐμὴν λίθον οὐδὲ τὸ γράμμα
ᾐδέσθη τὸ λέγον τόν με Λεωπρέπεος
κεῖσθαι Κήϊον ἄνδρα τὸν ἱερόν, ὃς τὰ περισσά
καὶ] μνήμην πρῶτος ὃς ἐφρασάμην,
οὐδ' ὑμέας, Πολύδευκες, ὑπέτρεσεν, οἵ με μελάθρου
μέλλοντος πίπτειν ἐκτὸς ἔθεσθέ κοτε
δαιτυμόνων ἄπο μοῦνον, ὅτε Κραννώνιος αἰαῖ
ὤλισθεν μεγάλους οἶκος ἐπὶ Σκοπάδας.

**22** Ar. *Pax* 695ss.

Ἐρ.     πρῶτον δ' ὅ τι πράττει Σοφοκλέης ἀνήρετο.
Τρ.     εὐδαιμονεῖ· πάσχει δὲ θαυμαστόν.
Ἐρ.                                           τὸ τί;
Τρ.     ἐκ τοῦ Σοφοκλέους γίγνεται Σιμωνίδης.
Ἐρ.     Σιμωνίδης; πῶς;
Τρ.                              ὅτι γέρων ὢν καὶ σαπρὸς
         κέρδους ἕκατι κἂν ἐπὶ ῥιπὸς πλέοι.

---

[1] See also Arist. *Eth. Nic.* 4. 1, test. 47(d), fr. 515, Stob. 3. 10. 61. S. was called the first poet to compose for a fee; later tradition followed Xenophanes in attributing this to avarice.

# SIMONIDES

gas heaped up in front of their city out of reverence
for Zeus, god of strangers, was thrown down by an
evil man, Phoenix, the wicked general of the city —
you may have heard of him; and he built my tomb-
stone into a tower and showed no respect for the
inscription,[3] which declared that I, son of
Leoprepes, lay there, the holy man of Ceos, who
(knew?) rare things and was the first to devise a sys-
tem of memory; nor did he fear you, Polydeuces and
your brother, who once got me alone of the ban-
queters outside the hall which was about to collapse,
when alas! the house at Crannon fell upon the
mighty Scopads.

[3] Tzetzes, *chil.* 1. 639 ff. claims to give S.'s epitaph, a variation on
'Sim.' XXVII.

**22** Aristophanes, *Peace*

Hermes: She (Peace) first asked how Sophocles is
   doing.
Trygaeus: He's flourishing; but an amazing thing is
   happening to him.
H.: What's that?
T.: He's changing from Sophocles into Simonides.
H.: Simonides? What do you mean?
T.: Well, now that he's old and decayed, he'd even
   sail on a hurdle to make some money.

Schol. ad loc. (p. 107s. Holwerda)

ὁ Σιμωνίδης δοκεῖ πρῶτος σμικρολογίαν εἰσ-
ενεγκεῖν εἰς τὰ ᾄσματα καὶ γράψαι ᾆσμα μισθοῦ.
τοῦτο δὲ καὶ Πίνδαρος ἐν τοῖς Ἰσθμιονίκαις φησὶν
αἰνιττόμενος·

   ... ἁ Μοῖσα γὰρ οὐ φιλοκερδής
     πω τότ᾽ ἦν οὐδ᾽ ἐργάτις ... (2. 6).

τὸ μέντοι περὶ τῶν κιβωτῶν ἐπὶ Σιμωνίδου λεγόμενον,
ὅτι παρακειμένας εἶχε δύο, τὴν μὲν κενήν, τὴν δὲ με-
στήν, καὶ τὴν μὲν κενὴν χαρίτων ἔλεγεν εἶναι, τὴν δὲ
μεστὴν <ἀργυρίου>, γνώριμον ...· καὶ <...>
μέμνηται, ὅτι σμικρολόγος ἦν· ὅθεν Ξενοφάνης (fr. 21
West) κίμβικα αὐτὸν προσαγορεύει.

23 Athen. 14. 656de (iii 452 Kaibel)

ὄντως δ᾽ ἦν ὡς ἀληθῶς κίμβιξ ὁ Σιμωνίδης καὶ
αἰσχροκερδής, ὡς Χαμαιλέων φησιν (fr. 33 Wehrli, 41
Giordano). ἐν Συρακούσαις γοῦν τοῦ Ἱέρωνος ἀπο-
στέλλοντος αὐτῷ τὰ καθ᾽ ἡμέραν λαμπρῶς πωλῶν τὰ
πλείω ὁ Σιμωνίδης τῶν παρ᾽ ἐκείνου πεμπομένων
ἑαυτῷ μικρὸν μέρος ἀπετίθετο. ἐρομένου δέ τινος τὴν
αἰτίαν· ὅπως, εἶπεν, ἥ τε Ἱέρωνος μεγαλοπρέπεια
καταφανὴς ᾖ καὶ ἡ ἐμὴ κοσμιότης.

# SIMONIDES

Scholiast on the passage

Simonides seems to have been the first to intro-
duce money-grabbing into his songs and to write a
song for pay. This is what Pindar says in riddling
fashion in his *Isthmians* (2. 1 ff.): '. . . For then the
Muse was not yet fond of profit nor mercenary[1] . . .'
The story told of Simonides is well-known[2]: he had
two boxes by him, one empty, the other full, and
used to say that the empty one was the box of
favours, the full one the box of money . . . ; . . . men-
tions that he was a money-grabber; that is why
Xenophanes calls him a skinflint.

[1] The scholiast on Pindar's lines says that S. was the first to com-
pose epinicians for a fee and quotes Callim. fr. 222 ( = test.
3).      [2] See Plut. *de curios.* 10. 520a, schol. Theocr. arg. 16,
Stob. *Ecl.* 3. 10. 38, *Suda* Σ 440, Tzetz. *chil.* 8. 807 ff.

**23** Athenaeus, *Scholars at Dinner*[1]

Simonides really was a skinflint[2] and greedy for
money, as Chamaeleon says.[3] At any rate in Syra-
cuse when Hiero used to send him his daily provi-
sions Simonides would openly sell most of what was
sent and keep only a small portion for himself. Once
when he was asked the reason he replied, 'So that
all may see Hiero's magnificence and my modera-
tion.'

[1] The passage follows eleg. 7.      [2] Xenophanes' term: see test.
22.      [3] In his work *On Simonides* (test. 30).

**24** Plin. *N.H.* 7. 24. 89 (ii 31 Jan-Mayhoff)

ars postremo eius rei facta et inventa est a
Simonide melico, consummata a Metrodoro Scepsio,
ut nihil non isdem verbis redderetur auditum.

**25** Cic. *de Fin.* 2. 32. 104 (p. 79 Schiche)

primum in nostrane potestate est, quid memine-
rimus? Themistocles quidem, cum ei Simonides an
quis alius artem memoriae polliceretur, 'oblivionis',
inquit, 'mallem. nam memini etiam quae nolo,
oblivisci non possum quae volo.'

**26** Longin. *Rhet.* 718 (i 316 Spengel)

ἤδη δὲ καὶ Σιμωνίδης καὶ πλείους μετ᾽ ἐκεῖνον
μνήμης ⟦γνώμης⟧ ὁδοὺς προὐδίδαξαν, εἰδώλων παρά-
θεσιν καὶ τόπων εἰσηγούμενοι πρὸς τὸ μνημονεύειν
ἔχειν ὀνομάτων τε καὶ ῥημάτων· τὸ δέ ἐστιν οὐδὲν ἕτε-
ρον ἢ τῶν ὁμοίων πρὸς τὸ δοκοῦν καινὸν παραθεώρησις
καὶ συζυγία πρὸς ἄλλο.

# SIMONIDES

## MNEMONICS[1]

**24** Pliny, *Natural History*

Finally a technique of mnemonics was created by the lyric poet Simonides[2] and perfected by Metrodorus of Scepsis, which allowed anything once heard to be repeated in the identical words.

[1] See also testt. 1, 21, fr. 510 (Cic. and Quint.), eleg. 14.  [2] Cf. *Marm. Par.* 54, Aelian, *N.A.* 6. 10, Amm. Marc. 16. 5. 8, Philostrat. *Vit. Ap.* 1. 14.

**25** Cicero, *On the Chief Good and Evil*

In the first place, can we choose what we remember? When Themistocles was promised by Simonides — or was it someone else? — a technique of memory, he explained, 'I would prefer a technique of forgetting, for I remember what I would rather not remember and cannot forget what I would rather forget.'[1]

[1] Cf. *de Orat.* 2. 74. 299, 86. 351.

**26** Longinus, *Rhetoric*

Simonides and many after him have taught methods of remembering, advocating the comparison of images and places for the remembrance of names and events; but this is merely the comparative examination of what is similar and what seems new and its linking with something else.[1]

[1] Cf. Cic. *de Orat.* 2. 86. 357 ( = fr. 510 below).

**27** Plut. *Them.* 5. 7 (i 163 Ziegler)

πάλιν δέ ποτε τὸν Σιμωνίδην ἐπισκώπτων ἔλεγε
νοῦν οὐκ ἔχειν, Κορινθίους μὲν λοιδοροῦντα μεγάλην
οἰκοῦντας πόλιν, αὑτοῦ δὲ ποιούμενον εἰκόνας οὕτως
ὄντος αἰσχροῦ τὴν ὄψιν.

**28** [Plut.] *Mus.* 20. 1137ef (p. 119 Lasserre, vi 3. 16
Ziegler)

ἀπείχετο γὰρ καὶ οὗτος (sc. Παγκράτης) ὡς ἐπὶ τὸ
πολὺ τούτου (sc. τοῦ χρωματικοῦ γένους), ἐχρήσατο δ᾽
ἔν τισιν. οὐ δι᾽ ἄγνοιαν οὖν δηλονότι, ἀλλὰ διὰ τὴν
προαίρεσιν ἀπείχετο· ἐζήλου γοῦν, ὡς αὐτὸς ἔφη, τὸν
Πινδάρειόν τε καὶ Σιμωνίδειον τρόπον καὶ καθόλου τὸ
ἀρχαῖον καλούμενον ὑπὸ τῶν νῦν.

**29** Athen. 14. 625e (iii 380 Kaibel)

δεῖ δὲ τὴν ἁρμονίαν εἶδος ἔχειν ἤθους ἢ πάθους,
καθάπερ ἡ Λοκριστί· ταύτῃ γὰρ ἔνιοι τῶν γενομένων
κατὰ Σιμωνίδην καὶ Πίνδαρον ἐχρήσαντό ποτε, καὶ
πάλιν κατεφρονήθη.

---

[1] The passage is derived from Heraclides of Pontus, *On Music* iii.

# SIMONIDES

## PORTRAITS[1]

**27** Plutarch, *Themistocles*[2]

Then again Themistocles once made fun of Simonides by saying that he had no sense, in that he abused the Corinthians, who lived in a great city, but had likenesses made of himself, although his face was so ugly.

[1] See Richter, *Portraits of the Greeks* i 69, 73; *A.P.* 2. 44ff. refers to a statue of S. in the Zeuxippus gymnasium in Constantinople.
[2] The passage follows test. 12.

## MUSIC[1]

**28** 'Plutarch', *On Music*

Pancrates[2] too for the most part avoided the chromatic genus, but he used it in some works; so it was clearly not out of ignorance that he avoided it but as a matter of preference. Indeed, as he himself said, he tried to follow the style of Pindar and Simonides and in general what is now called the ancient style.

[1] See also Philod., *Mus.* 4. 26, 29.  [2] Unknown composer, perhaps of the 4th c. B.C.

**29** Athenaeus, *Scholars at Dinner*[1]

But a *harmonia* must have a definite character or feeling, as does the Locrian: this was once used by some who flourished in the time of Simonides and Pindar, but it fell into disrepute again.

**30** Athen. 13. 611a (iii 348 Kaibel)

. . . ὡς Χαμαιλέων φησὶν ἐν τῷ περὶ Σιμωνίδου . . .

**31** *Sud.* Π 72 (iv 9 Adler)

Παλαίφατος, Αἰγύπτιος ἢ Ἀθηναῖος, γραμματι-
κός. . . . Ὑποθέσεις εἰς Σιμωνίδην . . .

**32** *Sud.* Τ 1115 (iv 601 Adler)

Τρύφων, Ἀμμωνίου, Ἀλεξανδρεύς, γραμματικὸς
καὶ ποιητής, γεγονὼς κατὰ τοὺς Αὐγούστου χρόνους
καὶ πρότερον . . . Περὶ τῶν παρ᾽ Ὁμήρῳ διαλέκτων
καὶ Σιμωνίδῃ καὶ Πινδάρῳ καὶ Ἀλκμᾶνι καὶ τοῖς
ἄλλοις λυρικοῖς . . .

**33** Ar. *Av.* 917ss.

Ποι. μέλη πεπόηκ᾽ εἰς τὰς Νεφελοκοκκυγίας
τὰς ὑμετέρας κύκλιά τε πολλὰ καὶ καλὰ
καὶ παρθένεια καὶ κατὰ τὰ Σιμωνίδου.

# SIMONIDES

**30** Athenaeus, *Scholars at Dinner*

... as Chamaeleon says in his work *On Simonides*[2] ...

[1] See also P.Oxy. 2433, 2434 ( = fr. 608), fr. 650.      [2] Also quoted by Athen. at 456c–457a (for S.'s riddles, with apophthegms) and 656c-e (see test. 23, eleg. 7): frr. 31–33 Wehrli, 41–43 Giordano.

**31** *Suda*

Palaephatus[1]: an Egyptian or an Athenian, grammarian. Wrote ... *Introductions to Simonides*.

[1] Date unknown; perhaps *c.* 200 B.C.

**32** *Suda*

Tryphon: son of Ammonius, of Alexandria, grammarian and poet; lived in the time of Augustus and before; wrote ... *On the Dialects in Homer and in Simonides, Pindar, Alcman and the other lyric poets* ...

**33** Aristophanes, *Birds*

Poet: I have composed for your Cloudcuckooland many fine dithyrambs and maiden-songs and pieces after the manner of Simonides.

[1] See also Stes. test. 33.

355

Schol. ad loc. (p. 174 White)

καὶ κατὰ τὰ Σιμωνίδου· ἤτοι κατάτεχνα, ποικίλα, οἷον ὕμνους, παιᾶνας, προσόδια, καὶ τὰ λοιπὰ τούτοις παραπλήσια.

**34** Plat. *Prot.* 316d

ἐγὼ δὲ τὴν σοφιστικὴν τέχνην φημὶ μὲν εἶναι παλαιάν, τοὺς δὲ μεταχειριζομένους αὐτὴν τῶν παλαιῶν ἀνδρῶν, φοβουμένους τὸ ἐπαχθὲς αὐτῆς, πρόσχημα ποιεῖσθαι καὶ προκαλύπτεσθαι, τοὺς μὲν ποίησιν, οἷον Ὅμηρόν τε καὶ Ἡσίοδον καὶ Σιμωνίδην
. . .

**35** Plat. *Resp.* i 335e

μαχούμεθα ἄρα, ἦν δ' ἐγώ, κοινῇ ἐγώ τε καὶ σύ, ἐάν τις αὐτὸ φῇ ἢ Σιμωνίδην ἢ Βίαντα ἢ Πιττακὸν εἰρηκέναι ἤ τιν' ἄλλον τῶν σοφῶν τε καὶ μακαρίων ἀνδρῶν.

**36** *Anth. Pal.* 4. 1. 8 = Meleager i Gow-Page

καὶ νέον οἰνάνθης κλῆμα Σιμωνίδεω.

**37** Cat. 38. 7s.

paulum quidlibet allocutionis,
maestius lacrimis Simonideis.

356

Scholiast on the passage

'pieces after the manner of Simonides': i.e. artistic, elaborate, e.g. hymns, paeans, processionals and the other similar kinds.

## 34 Plato, *Protagoras*[1]

I declare[2] that sophistic skill is ancient, but that the men of ancient times who practised it, afraid of giving offence, hid it behind a screen: poetry, as in the case of Homer, Hesiod and Simonides . . .

[1] See also fr. 542.     [2] The speaker is the sophist Protagoras.

## 35 Plato, *Republic*[1]

'Then we will fight side by side, you and I,' I said, 'against anyone who alleges that Simonides or Bias or Pittacus or any other of the wise and blessed said this.'

[1] See also fr. 642(a).

## 36 *Palatine Anthology*: Meleager, *The Garland*[1]

. . . and the young vine-twig of Simonides.

[1] Introductory poem to M.'s collection of Greek epigrams in which he likens each poet's work to a flower.

## 37 Catullus, *Poems*

Send me some small scrap of comfort, sadder than Simonidean tears.

# GREEK LYRIC

**38** Hor. *Carm.* 2. 1. 37ss.

sed ne relictis, Musa procax, iocis
Ceae retractes munera neniae:
mecum Dionaeo sub antro
quaere modos leviore plectro.

**39** Dion. Hal. *Comp.* 23 (vi 114 Usener-Radermacher)

ἐποποιῶν μὲν οὖν ἔμοιγε κάλλιστα τουτονὶ δοκεῖ
τὸν χαρακτῆρα (sc. τὸν γλαφυρόν) ἐξεργάσασθαι
Ἡσίοδος, μελοποιῶν δὲ Σαπφὼ καὶ μετ’ αὐτὴν Ἀνα-
κρέων τε καὶ Σιμωνίδης . . .

**40** Dion. Hal. *Imit.* 2. 420 (vi 205 Usener-Radermacher)

Σιμωνίδου δὲ παρατήρει τὴν ἐκλογὴν τῶν ὀνομά-
των, τῆς συνθέσεως τὴν ἀκρίβειαν· πρὸς τούτοις, καθ’
ὃ βελτίων εὑρίσκεται καὶ Πινδάρου, τὸ οἰκτίζεσθαι μὴ.
μεγαλοπρεπῶς ἀλλὰ παθητικῶς.

**41** Quint. *Inst.* 10. 1. 64 (ii 580 Winterbottom)

Simonides, tenuis alioqui, sermone proprio et
iucunditate quadam commendari potest, praecipua
tamen eius in commovenda miseratione virtus, ut
quidam in hac eum parte omnibus eiusdem operis
auctoribus praeferant.

# SIMONIDES

**38** Horace, *Odes*[1]

But, wanton Muse, do not abandon jests and take up again the rites of Cean dirge: along with me in the cave of Dione[2] seek out tunes with lighter plectrum.

[1] See also Stes. test. 36.　　　[2] Venus.

**39** Dionysius of Halicarnassus, *On Literary Composition*

Among the epic poets Hesiod seems to me to have developed this style (i.e. the polished style) most excellently; among the lyric poets Sappho,[1] and after her Anacreon and Simonides.

[1] See Sa. 1.

**40** Dionysius of Halicarnassus, *On Imitation*[1]

Observe in Simonides his choice of words and his care in combining them; in addition — and here he is found to be better even than Pindar — observe how he expresses pity not by using the grand style but by appealing to the emotions.[2]

[1] See also Stes. test. 38, which follows immediately.　　　[2] Cf. test. 15.

**41** Quintilian, *Principles of Oratory*

Simonides has a simple style, but he can be commended for the aptness of his language and for a certain charm; his chief merit, however, lies in the power to excite pity, so much so that some prefer him in this respect to all other writers of the genre.

# GREEK LYRIC

**42** *Anth. Pal.* 9. 184. 5 = anon. xxxvi(a) 1198 *F.G.E.*

ἥ τε Σιμωνίδεω γλυκερὴ σελίς . . .

**43** *Anth. Pal.* 9. 571. 1s = anon. xxxvi(b) 1204s. *F.G.E.*

ἔπνεε τερπνά
ἡδυμελιφθόγγου Μοῦσα Σιμωνίδεω.

**44** εἰς τοὺς ἐννέα λυρικούς 15s. (Schol. Pind. i 11 Drach-mann)

ἠδὲ Σιμωνίδεω Κείου Δωριστὶ λαλοῦντος
τὸν πατέρ᾽ αἰνήσας ἴσθι Λεωπρέπεα.

**45** Schol. Pind. *Nem.* 4. 60b (iii 75 Drachmann)

δοκεῖ δὲ ταῦτα τείνειν εἰς Σιμωνίδην, ἐπεὶ ἐκεῖνος παρεκβάσεσι χρῆσθαι εἴωθε.

**46** Joh. Sic. in Hermog. *Id.* 2. 4 (20) (*Rhet. Gr.* vi 399 Walz)

ποιητικὴ γὰρ ἡ Ἰὰς καὶ ἡδεῖα ὡς τῶν ἄλλων οὐδεμία· διὸ καὶ τὰ Ἰωνικὰ ποιήματα ἐξαίρουσι ταῖς ἡδοναῖς, ὥσπερ τὰ Σιμωνίδου καὶ Μενελάου καί τινα τῶν Ὁμήρου Στησιχόρου τε καὶ ἄλλων πολλῶν.

# SIMONIDES

**42** *Palatine Anthology* (anon.)[1]

. . . and the sweet page of Simonides . . .

[1] A prayer to the nine lyric poets.

**43** *Palatine Anthology* (anon.): *On the Nine Lyric Poets*

The Muse of Simonides, singer of sweet song, breathed delight.

**44** *On the Nine Lyric Poets* (quoted by Scholiast on Pindar)

And if you speak of the father of Simonides the Cean, whose dialect was Dorian,[1] know that he was Leoprepes.

[1] In the choral poetry; cf. testt. 1, 46, fr. 514.

**45** Scholiast on Pindar ('The rule checks me from telling the long story in full . . . Struggle against conspiracy! Mightily we shall seem to reach our goal in splendour, superior to our enemies.')

This seems to be directed at Simonides, since he is accustomed to use digressions.[1]

[1] The comment is of doubtful value; cf. test. 20.

**46** John of Sicily on Hermogenes, *Kinds of Style* (on the Ionic dialect)

The Ionic is poetical and sweet, more so than any other; that is why Ionic poems excite with their delights, e.g. the poems of Simonides and Menelaus[1] and parts of Homer, Stesichorus and many others.

[1] Epic poet of uncertain date.

# GREEK LYRIC

## APOPHTHEGMATA

**47** (a) Mich. Psell. π. ἐνεργ. δαιμ. (*P.G.* cxxii 821)

. . . κατὰ τὸν Σιμωνίδην ὁ λόγος τῶν πραγμάτων
εἰκών ἐστιν.

(b) Plut. *de glor. Ath.* 3. 346f (ii 2. 125 Nachstädt)

πλὴν ὁ Σιμωνίδης τὴν μὲν ζωγραφίαν ποίησιν
σιωπῶσαν προσαγορεύει, τὴν δὲ ποίησιν ζωγραφίαν
λαλοῦσαν. ἃς γὰρ οἱ ζωγράφοι πράξεις ὡς γινομένας
δεικνύουσι, ταύτας οἱ λόγοι γεγενημένας διηγοῦνται
καὶ συγγράφουσιν.

(c) Cic. *N.D.* 1. 22. 60 (p. 23s. Ax)

roges me quid aut quale sit deus: auctore utar
Simonide, de quo cum quaesivisset hoc idem
tyrannus Hiero, deliberandi sibi unum diem postu-
lavit; cum idem ex eo postridie quaereret, biduum
petivit; cum saepius duplicaret numerum dierum
admiransque Hiero requireret cur ita faceret, 'quia
quanto diutius considero' inquit 'tanto mihi spes

362

# SIMONIDES

## APOPHTHEGMS

*Many wise sayings were attributed to Sim., and a collection of them may have existed (see fr. 653). His skill in repartee (εὐτραπέλων λόγων) is mentioned by Athenaeus at 8.352c, his composition of riddles at 10.456c (=Chamaeleon fr. 34 Wehrli, 42 Giordano). The following are the more notable apophthegms; see also frr. 645–648, P.M.G. p. 323.*

**47** (a) Michael Psellus, *On the Working of Demons*

... according to Simonides, the word is the image of the thing.

(b) Plutarch, *On the Glory of Athens*

But Simonides calls painting silent poetry and poetry painting that speaks[1]; for actions which painters represent as happening words set out and describe after they have happened.

[1] Cf. *Qu. Conv.* 9. 15. 2, 748a.

(c) Cicero, *On the Nature of the Gods*

If you ask me what god is or what he is like, I shall follow the example of Simonides: when the tyrant Hiero asked him this very question, he requested one day for deliberation; when Hiero put the question on the next day, he asked for two days; and when he doubled the number of days several times and an astonished Hiero asked why, he replied, 'Because the longer I think about it, the

videtur obscurior.' sed Simonidem arbitror (non enim poeta solum suavis verum etiam ceteroqui doctus sapiensque traditur), quia multa venirent in mentem acuta atque subtilia, dubitantem quid eorum esset verissimum desperasse omnem veritatem.

(d) Aristot. *Rhet*. 2. 16. 1391 a (p. 106 Ross)

ὅθεν καὶ τὸ Σιμωνίδου εἴρηται περὶ τῶν σοφῶν καὶ πλουσίων πρὸς τὴν γυναῖκα τὴν Ἱέρωνος ἐρομένην πότερον γενέσθαι κρεῖττον πλούσιον ἢ σοφόν· 'πλούσιον' εἰπεῖν· τοὺς σοφοὺς γὰρ ἔφη ὁρᾶν ἐπὶ ταῖς τῶν πλουσίων θύραις διατρίβοντας.

(e) Plut. *an seni* 786b (v 1. 28 Hubert)

... Σιμωνίδης ἔλεγε πρὸς τοὺς ἐγκαλοῦντας αὐτῷ φιλαργυρίαν, ὅτι τῶν ἄλλων διὰ τὸ γῆρας ἀπεστερημένος ἡδονῶν ὑπὸ μιᾶς ἔτι γηροβοσκεῖται τῆς ἀπὸ τοῦ κερδαίνειν.

(f) P. Hibeh 17

ἀνηλωμάτων· Σιμωνίδου· εὐδοκιμεῖ δ' αὐτοῦ πρὸς ἀλήθε[ι]αν καὶ τὸ πρὸς τὴν Ἱέρωνος γυναῖκα λεχθέν· ἐρωτηθε[ὶς] γὰρ εἰ πάντα γηράσκει 'ναί' ἔφη 'πλήγ γε κέρδους· τάχισ[τα] δὲ αἱ εὐεργεσίαι.' καὶ πρ[ὸ]ς τὸν πυνθανόμενον διὰ τί εἴη φειδωλὸς ἔφη διὰ τοῦτ' εἶναι φειδωλὸς ὅ[τ]ι μᾶλλον ἄχθοιτο τοῖς ἀνηλωμένοις ἢ τοῖς περιοῦσιν ...

fainter become my hopes of an answer.' Now Simonides was not only a delightful poet but is said to have been also a learned and wise man, and my belief is that since many intelligent and subtle ideas occurred to him, he hesitated over which was the truest and despaired of finding the whole truth.

### (d) Aristotle, *Rhetoric*

Hence the answer of Simonides about the wise and the wealthy when Hiero's wife asked him whether it was better to be wealthy or wise: 'Wealthy; for I see the wise spending their days at the doors of the wealthy.'[1]

[1] So Stob. *Ecl.* 4. 31. 32. Plato quotes the epigram, saying that the author, unnamed, was a liar (*Rep.* 6. 489c); cf. also Diog. Laert. 2. 69.

### (c) Plutarch, *Should Old Men Govern?*

When people accused Simonides of avarice, he answered that old age had robbed him of his other pleasures and that only one sustained him now — the pleasure of money-making.

### (f) Hibeh Papyrus (*c.* 250 B.C.)

On expenditure: Simonides: his reply to Hiero's wife is highly regarded for its truth: asked if all things grow old he answered, 'Yes, all except money-making; and kind deeds most quickly of all.' Asked by someone why he was frugal he replied that he was more upset by expenses than by a credit balance . . .

(g) Aristot. (fr. 92 Rose) ap. Stob. *Ecl.* 4. 29. 25 (v 711 Wachsmuth-Hense)

Σιμωνίδην δέ φασιν ἀποκρίνασθαι διερωτώμενον τίνες εὐγενεῖς τοὺς ἐκ πάλαι πλουσίων φάναι.

(h) Plut. *de garr.* 514f–515a (iii 311 Pohlenz-Sieveking)

ἐπὶ πᾶσι δὲ καὶ παρὰ ταῦτα πάντα δεῖ πρόχειρον ἔχειν καὶ μνημονεύειν τὸ Σιμωνίδειον, ὅτι λαλήσας μὲν πολλάκις μετενόησε σιωπήσας δ' οὐδέποτε.

(i) Stob. *Ecl.* 3. 2. 41 (iii 188 Wachsmuth-Hense)

Σιμωνίδου. Σιμωνίδης ὁ μελοποιὸς εἰπόντος τινὸς ὅτι πολλοὶ αὐτὸν αὐτῷ κακῶς λέγουσιν 'οὐ παύσῃ' ἔφη 'ποτὲ σὺ τοῖς ὠσί με βλασφημῶν;'

(j) *Gnom. Vat.* 514 Sternbach (*Wien. Stud.* 11, 1889, 227)

ὁ αὐτὸς (sc. Σιμωνίδης) ἐρωτηθεὶς πότερος κρείσσων, Ὅμηρος ἢ Ἡσίοδος, εἶπεν· Ἡσίοδον μὲν αἱ Μοῦσαι, Ὅμηρον δὲ αἱ Χάριτες ἐτέκνωσαν.

(k) *App. Vat.* 217 Sternbach

Σιμωνίδης τὸν Ἡσίοδον κηπουρὸν ἔλεγε, τὸν δὲ Ὅμηρον στεφανηπλόκον, τὸν μὲν ὡς φυτεύσαντα τὰς περὶ θεῶν καὶ ἡρώων μυθολογίας, τὸν δὲ ὡς ἐξ αὐτῶν συμπλέξαντα τὸν Ἰλιάδος καὶ Ὀδυσσείας στέφανον.

# SIMONIDES

(g) Aristotle in Stobaeus, *Anthology* (on nobility)

They say that when Simonides was asked who were the noble he answered, 'Those with ancestral wealth.'

(h) Plutarch, *Garrulity*

In all things and for all these reasons one ought to keep ready and bear in mind the saying of Simonides, that he had often felt sorry after speaking but never after keeping silent.[1]

[1] Cf. *Quaest. Conv.* 3. 644ef, Stob. *Ecl.* 3. 33. 12.

(i) Stobaeus, *Anthology* (on vice)

When someone told Simonides, the lyric poet, that he was hearing much unfavourable criticism of him, he replied, 'Please stop slandering me with your ears.'

(j) *Vatican Anthology of Gnomic Sayings*

Simonides on being asked who was the better, Homer or Hesiod, said, 'The Muses bore Hesiod, the Graces Homer.'

(k) *Vatican Appendix*

Simonides said Hesiod was a gardener, Homer a garland-maker: Hesiod planted the mythologies of gods and heroes, Homer plaited from them the garland of the *Iliad* and *Odyssey*.

# SIMONIDES

## FRAGMENTA

*Frr. 506–518 are from epinicians (see also 555), 519, 519A, 519B are papyrus scraps of epinicians, paeans and perhaps other choral lyric, 520–531 are from dirges, 532–536 are concerned with the poems on the battles of Artemisium and Salamis, 537–538 are from prayers, 539 is about a dithyramb, 540 is from the miscellaneous works; most of the*

---

## ΕΠΙΝΙΚΟΙ ΔΡΟΜΕΣΙ[1]

**506** Phot. *Lex.* s.v. περιαγειρόμενοι (ii 77 Naber, p. 413s. Porson)

ἐκ τούτου σύνηθες ἐγένετο κύκλῳ περιπορευομένους τοὺς ἀθλη-τὰς ἐπαγείρειν καὶ λαμβάνειν τὰ διδόμενα. ὅθεν Σιμωνίδης περὶ Ἀστύλου φησὶν οὕτως·

τίς δὴ τῶν νῦν τοσάδ᾽ ἢ πετάλοισι μύρτων
ἢ στεφάνοισι ῥόδων ἀνεδήσατο,
νικάς<αις> ἐν ἀγῶνι περικτιόνων;

cf. *Sud.* Σ 1054 (iv 90 Adler), Didym. ap. Miller *Mélanges* 403, Apostol. *Cent.* xiv 18 (ii 610 Leutsch-Schneidewin)

1 Page τοσάδε πετ. *Sud.*, Phot. τόσας δὴ πετ. Didym. 3 νίκας codd., suppl. Page

[1] vid. *Anecd. Oxon.* iii 254 Cramer, Choerob. in Theodos. i 139. 6 Hilgard

368

# SIMONIDES

## FRAGMENTS

*remainder cannot be classified: 541–543 are the longest pieces; 544–548 deal with the Argonauts, 549–579 deal with other mythological matter, 580 is from a propemptikon for Hiero, 581 refutes Cleobulus, 582–606 are book-quotations (in alphabetical order of author), 607–608 are from commentaries, 609–639 give isolated words (in alphabetical order), 640–644 give the content of various passages, 645–648 may be from the apophthegms (see test. 47), 649 deals with metres, 650–653 are labelled 'doubtful and spurious' by Page.*

### EPINICIANS FOR RUNNERS

**506** Photius, *Lexicon* (on περιαγειρόμενοι, 'going round collecting').

So it became customary for the athletes to go round and collect and accept what was offered. That is why Simonides speaks of Astylus[1] as follows:

Who among men of this day has so often crowned himself with leaves of myrtle or garlands of roses after winning in a contest of the neighbours[2]?

[1] Famous athlete from Croton, who won the stadion and diaulos at Olympia in 488 and again in 484 and 480, when he was proclaimed as from Syracuse; he also won the Olympic hoplite race in 480 and 476 (Paus. 6. 13. 1, Dion. Hal. 8. 77. 1, Diod. 11. 12, P.Oxy. 222 col. i).
[2] I.e. in local games.

# GREEK LYRIC

## &lt;ΕΠΙΝΙΚΟΙ ΠΑΛΗΙ&gt;

**507** Ar. *Nub.* 1355ss., 1362

Στρ.   πρῶτον μὲν αὐτὸν τὴν λύραν λαβόντ᾽ ἐγὼ ᾽κέλευσα
ᾆσαι Σιμωνίδου μέλος, τὸν Κριόν, ὡς ἐπέχθη.
ὁ δ᾽ εὐθέως ἀρχαῖον εἶν᾽ ἔφασκε τὸ κιθαρίζειν
ᾄδειν τε πίνονθ᾽ . . .
καὶ τὸν Σιμωνίδην ἔφασκ᾽ εἶναι κακὸν ποιητήν.

Scholl. RVE ad loc. (p. 238 Holwerda)

ἀρχὴ μέλους (ᾠδῆς RV) εἰς Κριὸν τὸν Αἰγινήτην, ἐπέξαθ᾽ ὁ Κριὸς οὐκ ἀεικέως. φαίνεται δὲ εὐδοκιμεῖν καὶ διαφανὴς εἶναι.

Scholl. EΘMRs

Σιμωνίδου ἐξ ἐπινίκου, ἐπέξαθ᾽ . . . ἀεικέως. ἦν δὲ παλαιστὴς Αἰγινήτης.

Schol. E

τῇ πρὸς τὸ ζῷον κοινωνίᾳ τῆς λέξεως συνέπλεξε τὰς †κοινωνίας† ὁ ποιητὴς λέγων

ἐπέξαθ᾽ ὁ Κριὸς οὐκ ἀεικέως
ἐλθὼν ἐς εὔδενδρον ἀγλαὸν Διὸς
τέμενος.

v. W. J. W. Koster, *Mnem.* 19 (1966) 395s.

2 Dobree: εἰς δένδρον codd.

# SIMONIDES

## EPINICIANS FOR WRESTLING

**507** Aristophanes, *Clouds*

Strepsiades (on his son): First I told him to take his lyre and sing Simonides' song about how Crius[1] was shorn; and he immediately said it was old-fashioned to play the lyre and sing while drinking ... and he said Simonides was a bad poet!

Scholiast on the passage

This is the beginning of a song on Crius of Aegina, 'Crius not surprisingly got himself shorn.' He seems to have been well-known and distinguished.

Another scholiast

From an epinician by Simonides, 'Crius not surprisingly got himself shorn.' He was a wrestler from Aegina ... The poet has given the man's name the associations of the animal in saying

Crius not surprisingly got himself shorn when he came to the glorious sanctuary of Zeus[2] with its fine trees.

[1] His name means Ram; cf. Hdt. 6. 50, 73, 85, 8. 92–93. The poem may have been composed soon after 491 B.C.: see D. L. Page, *J.H.S.* 71 (1951) 140 ff.    [2] At Nemea or Olympia.

# GREEK LYRIC

## ΕΠΙΝΙΚΟΙ ΠΕΝΤΑΘΛΟΙΣ

**508** Aristot. *H.A.* 5. 8. 542b (p. 161s. Dittmeyer)

ἡ δ' ἀλκυὼν τίκτει περὶ τροπὰς τὰς χειμερινάς. διὸ καὶ καλοῦνται, ὅταν εὐδιειναὶ γένωνται αἱ τροπαί, ἀλκυονίδες ἡμέραι ἑπτὰ μὲν πρὸ τροπῶν, ἑπτὰ δὲ μετὰ τροπάς, καθάπερ καὶ Σιμωνίδης ἐποίησεν·

> ὡς ὁπόταν
> χειμέριον κατὰ μῆνα πινύσκῃ
> Ζεὺς ἤματα τέσσερα καὶ δέκα,
> λαθάνεμον δέ μιν ὧραν
> 5 καλέουσιν ἐπιχθόνιοι
> ἱερὰν παιδοτρόφον ποικίλας
> ἀλκυόνος.

Phot. *Lex.* A 981 (i 105 Theodoridis)

ἀλκυονίδες ἡμέραι· περὶ τοῦ ἀριθμοῦ διαφέρονται. Σιμωνίδης γὰρ ἐν Πεντάθλοις ιδ' (Naber: ια' codd.) φησὶν αὐτὰς καὶ Ἀριστοτέλης ἐν τοῖς περὶ ζῴων.

cf. *Sud.*, Hesych. s.v. ἀλκ. ἡμ., Arsen. = Apostol. *Cent.* 2. 20, Eust. *Il.* 776. 34.

4 Schneidewin: τέ codd.

## <ΕΠΙΝΙΚΟΙ ΠΥΚΤΑΙΣ>

**509** Lucian. *pro imag.* 19 (iii 127 Macleod)

ἀλλὰ πῶς ἐπήνεσε ποιητὴς εὐδόκιμος τὸν Γλαῦκον, οὐδὲ Πολυδεύκεος βίαν φήσας ἀνατείνασθαι ἂν αὐτῷ ἐναντίας τὰς χεῖρας οὐδὲ σιδάρεον Ἀλκμάνας τέκος; ὁρᾷς ὁποίοις αὐτὸν θεοῖς εἴκασε; μᾶλλον δὲ καὶ αὐτῶν ἐκείνων ἀμείνω ἀπέφαινεν. καὶ οὔτε αὐτὸς ὁ

372

# SIMONIDES

### EPINICIANS FOR PENTATHLETES

**508** Aristotle, *History of Animals*

The halcyon breeds at the time of the winter solstice.
That is why when there is calm weather at the solstice the
seven days before it and seven after it are called halcyon
days, as Simonides said in his poem:

> as when in the winter month Zeus admonishes
> fourteen days, and mortals call it the holy season
> which forgets the winds, the season of child-rearing
> for the dappled halcyon.

Photius, *Lexicon* (on 'halcyon days')

They differ over the number of days: Simonides in his
*Pentathletes* says there are fourteen, as does Aristotle in
his account of animals.

### EPINICIANS FOR BOXERS

**509** Lucian, *In Defence of Portraits*

But think how a famous poet praised Glaucus[1] when he
said,

> Not even mighty Polydeuces would raise[2] his
> hands to fight him, nor Alcmena's iron son.[3]

Do you see with what gods he compared him? Or rather he
represented him as better than those gods! And Glaucus

---

[1] Glaucus of Carystus seems to have won the boys' boxing event at
Olympia in 520 B.C.; but see H. J. Rose, *C.R.* 47 (1933) 165 ff.,
J. Fontenrose, *C.S.C.A.* 1 (1968) 99 ff.     [2] Or 'would have
raised'.     [3] Heracles.

# GREEK LYRIC

Γλαῦκος ἠγανάκτησεν τοῖς ἐφόροις τῶν ἀθλητῶν θεοῖς ἀντεπαινούμενος οὔτε ἐκεῖνοι ἠμύναντο ἢ τὸν Γλαῦκον ἢ τὸν ποιητὴν ὡς ἀσεβοῦντα περὶ τὸν ἔπαινον, ἀλλὰ εὐδοκίμουν ἄμφω καὶ ἐτιμῶντο ὑπὸ τῶν Ἑλλήνων, ὁ μὲν ἐπὶ τῇ ἀλκῇ ὁ Γλαῦκος, ὁ δὲ ποιητὴς ἐπί τε τοῖς ἄλλοις καὶ ἐπ᾿ αὐτῷ τούτῳ μάλιστα τῷ ᾄσματι.

poetae verba ita restituit Page:

> οὐδὲ Πολυδεύκεος βία
> χεῖρας ἀντείναιτό κ᾿ ἐναντίον αὐτῷ,
> οὐδὲ σιδάρεον Ἀλμάνας τέκος.

**510** Cic. *de orat.* 2. 86. 351–3 (p. 253s. Kumaniecki)

'non sum tanto ego' inquit 'ingenio quanto Themistocles fuit, ut oblivionis artem quam memoriae malim; gratiamque habeo Simonidi illi Cio, quem primum ferunt artem memoriae protulisse. dicunt enim, eum cenaret Crannone in Thessalia Simonides apud Scopam, fortunatum hominem et nobilem, cecinissetque id carmen, quod in eum scripsisset, in quo multa ornandi causa poetarum more in Castorem scripta et Pollucem fuissent, nimis illum sordide Simonidi dixisse se dimidium eius ei, quod pactus esset, pro illo carmine daturum; reliquum a suis Tyndaridis, quos aeque laudasset, peteret, si ei videretur. paulo post esse ferunt nuntiatum Simonidi, ut prodiret; iuvenes stare ad ianuam duo quosdam, qui eum magno opere vocarent; surrexisse illum, prodisse, vidisse neminem. hoc interim spatio conclave ilud, ubi epularetur Scopas, concidisse; ea ruina ipsum cum cognatis oppressum suis interisse. quos cum humare vellent sui neque possent obtritos internoscere ullo modo, Simonides dicitur ex eo, quod meminisset quo eorum loco quisque cubuisset, demonstrator unius cuiusque sepeliendi fuisse. hac tum re admonitus invenisse fertur ordinem esse maxime, qui memoriae lumen adferret.'

# SIMONIDES

was not annoyed at being praised as the equal of the gods
who watch over athletes, nor did the gods punish either
Glaucus or the poet for impiety: in fact they both continued
to enjoy reputation and honour among the Greeks,
Glaucus for his strength, the poet for this song in particu-
lar.

**510** Cicero, *On the Orator*

'I am not such a genius as Themistocles,' he said, 'so as
to prefer an art of forgetting to an art of remembering, and
I am grateful to the famous Simonides of Ceos, who is said
to have been the first to devise an art of remembering. The
story goes that he was dining at Crannon in Thessaly at
the house of a prosperous nobleman called Scopas and had
sung the song[1] which he had composed for him, in which
by way of ornament he had inserted many references to
Castor and Pollux[2] as poets do; whereupon Scopas with
excessive meanness declared that he would pay him half of
the agreed fee for the song; if he thought fit, he could apply
for the other half to his Tyndaridae, since he had devoted
an equal share of the praise to them. Shortly afterwards,
they say, a message was brought to Simonides telling him
to go outside, since two young men were standing by the
door, urgently calling him out. He got up and went out but
saw no one; and in the meantime the hall where Scopas
was dining collapsed, crushing him and his relatives to
death. When their kinsmen wanted to bury them and
were quite unable to tell the bodies apart, Simonides, they
say, was able from his recollection of the place where each
had reclined at the table to identify them for individual
burial. It was this, they say, that prompted his discovery
that it is order above all that serves as an aid to clear
memory.'

---

[1] An epinician for a boxer: see Quintilian below.      [2] Poly-
deuces, famous as a boxer (see 509); he and Castor were sons of
Tyndareus.

Quint. *Inst*. 11. 2. 11–16 (ii 644s. Winterbottom)

artem autem memoriae primus ostendisse dicitur Simonides, cuius vulgata fabula est. cum pugili coronato carmen, quale componi victoribus solet, mercede pacta scripsisset, abnegatam ei pecuniae partem, quod more poetis frequentissimo degressus in laudes Castoris ac Pollucis exierat. quapropter partem ab his petere, quorum facta celebrasset, iubebatur. et persolverunt, ut traditum est. nam cum esset grande convivium in honorem eiusdem victoriae atque adhibitus ei cenae Simonides, nuntio est excitus, quod eum duo iuvenes equis advecti desiderare maiorem in modum dicebantur. et illos quidem non invenit, fuisse tamen gratos erga se deos exitu comperit. nam vix eo ultra limen egresso triclinium illud supra convivas corruit atque ita confudit ut non ora modo oppressorum sed membra etiam omnia requirentes ad sepulturam propinqui nulla nota possent discernere. tum Simonides dicitur memor ordine quo quisque discubuerat corpora suis reddidisse. est autem magna inter auctores dissensio Glaucone Carystio an Leocrati an Agatharcho an Scopae scriptum sit id carmen, et Pharsali fuerit haec domus, ut ipse quodam loco significare Simonides videtur utque Apollodorus (244 *F.Gr.H.* 67) et Eratosthenes (241 *F.Gr.H.* 34) et Euphorion (fr. 55 Scheidweiler) et Larissaeus Eurypylus tradiderunt, an Crannone, ut Apollas (266 *F.Gr.H.* 6) Callimach<i>us (suppl. Preller: A. et Callimachus Bentley), quem secutus Cicero hanc famam latius fudit. Scopam nobilem Thessalum perisse in eo convivio constat, adicitur sororis eius filius, putant et ortos plerosque ab alio Scopa, qui maior aetate fuerit. quam-

---

[1] See 509.    [2] See Page, *F.G.E.* p. 144.    [3] 2nd c. B.C. scholar of Alexandria and Pergamum.    [4] 3rd c. B.C. Alexandrian scholar.    [5] 3rd c. B.C. poet of Antioch.    [6] Unknown, but

# SIMONIDES

Quintilian, *Principles of Oratory*

Simonides is said to have been the first to reveal an art
of remembering. The story about him is well-known: when
for an agreed fee he had written for a garlanded boxer the
kind of song which is usually composed for victors, part of
the money was refused him because as poets commonly do
he had digressed and sung the praises of Castor and Pol-
lux; so he was told to seek the balance from those whose
deeds he had celebrated. And, as the story goes, they paid
their due: for when the victory was being marked by a
splendid banquet, to which Simonides had been invited, he
was summoned outside by a message that two young men
on horseback wanted him urgently; he failed to find the
young men, but the outcome showed him that the gods had
been grateful to him: he had scarcely crossed the threshold
to leave when the dining-hall collapsed on the banqueters,
causing such havoc among the victims that their kinsmen
who came to find them for burial completely failed to dis-
tinguish not only their faces but even their limbs. Then
Simonides is said to have recalled the order in which the
guests had been reclining and so to have restored the
bodies to their relatives.

There is, however, much disagreement among the
authorities as to whether the song was composed for
Glaucus of Carystus[1] or Leocrates[2] or Agatharchus or
Scopas, and whether the house was at Pharsalus, as
Simonides himself seems to indicate in a certain passage,
along with Apollodorus,[3] Eratosthenes,[4] Euphorion[5] and
Eurypylus of Larissa,[6] or at Crannon, as in Callimachus'
pupil Apollas,[7] whom Cicero followed when he gave wider
circulation to the story. All agree that Scopas, a nobleman
of Thessaly, died at the banquet, and his sister's son is also
said to have lost his life; and they believe that several des-
cendants of an elder Scopas died too. But in my view the

see Jacoby in *R.E.* s.v. Eurypylos 16.    [7] Presumably a 3rd c.
B.C. Alexandrian scholar; Bentley read 'Apollas and Callimachus'.

quam mihi totum de Tyndaridis fabulosum videtur, neque omnino huius rei meminit usquam poeta ipse, profecto non taciturus de tanta sua gloria.

<ΕΠΙΝΙΚΟΙ ΙΠΠΟΙΣ:> ΚΕΛΗΤΙ

**511** P.Oxy. 2431

fr. 1

Κέλητι
τοῖς Αἰατίου παισίν

(a)
    Οὐρανίδ]α Κρόνοιο παῖς ἐρικυδ[ής
        ] Αἰατίου γενεάν

5       ]ται καὶ χρυσοφ[όρ]μι[γξ
    Ἀπόλλων ἐκαταβόλο[ς
    σαμαίνει λιπαρά τε Πυθ[ώ
    τό] θ' ἱπποδρ[ομίας κῦδος . . .
    .] . σε . [ . ]υν[ . . . . . . ] . . [

(b) 3           ] . κολπο
           ]σπασ[ . ]αν

5    βασιλῆα [τ]ελεσφόρον
    ἀμφικ[τιό]νων ἔχρησαν
    Π]υρρίδαν · ἅμα δεγεν ̣ ο σὺν ὄλβω[ι
    Θεσσαλῶν καὶ παντὶ δάμωι

fr. 4    2 πο]λύφορβον, 4 ]νκρονον, 5 ]καλλιέρει

fr. 1(a) 3–7 suppl. Lobel    3 vel εὐρυόπ]α Lobel    8 suppl.
Gentili    (b) pro κολπο[ etiam κεληθ[ possis    5, 7 fin.
suppl. Lobel, 6, 7 init. Gentili    fr. 4. 2 suppl. Lobel

# SIMONIDES

whole business about the Tyndaridae is sheer fiction; and the poet nowhere mentions the affair, although he was not in the least likely to keep silent on a matter which brought him such glory.[8]

[8] See also test. 21, fr. 521 (Favorinus), Ovid, *Ibis* 511 f., Phaedrus 4. 26, Valerius Maximus 1. 8 ext. 7, Ael. Aristid. 50. 36, Aelian frr. 63 (= *Suda* Σ 441), 78, Alciphron 3. 32. 2, Libanius, *or. Artem.* 53; J. H. Molyneux, *Phoenix* 25 (1971) 197 ff., W. J. Slater, *Phoenix* 26 (1972) 232 ff.

## EPINICIANS FOR HORSE-RACING

**511** Oxyrhynchus papyrus (2nd c. A.D.)

*For the race-horse, for the sons of Aeatius*

fr. 1

(a) The glorious son[1] of Cronus, child of Uranus, (protects?) the race of Aeatius, and the far-shooting Apollo of the golden lyre and shining Pytho mark them out[2] and (the glory of) the horse-racing . . .

(b) . . . (bosom?) . . . they proclaimed the descendant of Pyrrhus[3] king with full authority over those who dwelt around; and at the same time . . . with happiness even for every people of the Thessalians.

fr. 4 . . . bountiful (earth) . . . Cronus . . . (he) obtained good omens . . .

[1] Zeus, giver of victory at Olympia or Nemea.    [2] By a victory at Delphi.    [3] Perhaps with reference to the royal house of Epirus, linked by kinship with the Aleuadae of Thessaly.

## ΤΕΘΡΙΠΠΟΙΣ

**512** Ar. *Eq.* 405s.

> ᾄσαιμι γὰρ τότ᾽ ἂν μόνον·
> > πῖνε πῖν᾽ ἐπὶ συμφοραῖς.

Schol. ad loc. (p. 102 Jones)

τότε γάρ, φησίν, ἐπάσαιμί σοι τὸ Σιμωνίδου μέλος· πῖνε πῖνε ἐν ταῖς συμφοραῖς. ἐκ τῶν Σιμωνίδου δὲ τοῦτο Τεθρίππων. τὸ δὲ συμφοραῖς, ἐπ᾽ ἐσθλοῖς· τῶν μέσων γὰρ ἡ συμφορά.

cf. *Sud.* Σ 1408 (ἐπὶ συμφορᾷ), Eust. *opusc.* xxv 40 (p. 279b Tafel)

**513** Ξενοκράτει ᾿Ακραγαντίνῳ

Schol. Pind. *Isthm.* 2 argum. (iii 212 Drachmann)

οὗτος δὲ ὁ Ξενοκράτης οὐ μόνον ῎Ισθμια νενίκηκεν ἵπποις ἀλλὰ καὶ Πύθια κδ᾽ Πυθιάδα, ὡς ᾿Αριστοτέλης ἀναγράφει (fr. 617 Rose). καὶ Σιμωνίδης δὲ ἐπαινῶν αὐτὸν ἀμφοτέρας αὐτοῦ τὰς νίκας κατατάσσει.

## <ΤΕΘΡΙΠΠΟΙΣ Η ΑΠΗΝΗΙ>

**514** ᾿Ορίλλᾳ ἡνιόχῳ

Athen. 7. 318f (ii 201 Kaibel)

Δωριεῖς δ᾽ αὐτὸν διὰ τοῦ ω καλοῦσι πώλυπον, ὡς ᾿Επίχαρμος (fr. 61 Kaibel). καὶ Σιμωνίδης δ᾽ ἔφη

# SIMONIDES

### FOR THE FOUR-HORSE CHARIOT

**512** Aristophanes, *Knights*

Chorus. For then my one song would be

Drink, drink for good fortune!

Scholiast on the passage

For then, says the chorus, I should sing at your expense the song of Simonides, 'Drink, drink for good fortune!' This is from the *Four-horse chariots* of Simonides. 'Good fortune' here; fortune (συμφορά) is a neutral word.

**513**            *For Xenocrates of Acragas*

Scholiast on Pindar, *Isthmian* 2

This Xenocrates was victorious with his horses not only at the Isthmian games but also at the Pythian games in the 24th Pythiad (490 B.C.),[1] as Aristotle records; and Simonides when singing his praises lists both his victories.

[1] Pindar *Pyth.* 6, written for this victory, does not mention the Isthmian success, which may therefore be later; *Ol.* 2. 49 f. (476 B.C.) mentions both victories.

### FOR THE FOUR-HORSE CHARIOT OR THE MULE-CAR

**514**            *For Orillas the charioteer*

Athenaeus, *Scholars at Dinner*

Dorians call the octopus 'pōlypos' with a long o, e.g. Epicharmus; so Simonides when he said

πώλυπον διζήμενος.

Ἀττικοὶ δὲ πουλύπουν.

Cod. Paris. suppl. gr. 676 (ed. L. Cohn, *Zu den Paroemiographen* p. 79)

ὁ Κάριος αἶνος· μέμνηται ταύτης Σιμωνίδης ἐπαινῶν τινα ἡνίοχον νικήσαντα ἐν Πελλήνῃ καὶ λαβόντα ἐπινίκιον χλαμύδα, ᾧ χρησάμενος ἀπηλλάγη τοῦ ῥίγους· χειμῶνος <1–2 vocc. illeg.> ἐν Πελλήνῃ ἐπετελεῖτο. φασὶ δὲ ὅτι ἁλιεὺς ἰδὼν ἐν χειμῶνι πολύποδα εἶπεν· εἰ μὴ κολυμβήσω, πεινήσω. τοῦτον οὖν εἶναι τὸν Κάριον αἶνον.

[Diogenian.] *praef. paroem.* (i 179 Leutsch-Schneidewin)

κέχρηται δὲ τῷ λόγῳ τούτῳ καὶ Τιμοκρέων ἐν μέλεσι (fr. 734), καὶ Σιμωνίδης δ᾽ αὐτοῦ μνημονεύει ἐν τῷ εἰς Ὀριλλαν ἐπινικίῳ.

<ΑΠΗΝΗΙ>

515    Ἀναξίλᾳ Ῥηγίνῳ

Aristot. *Rhet.* 3. 2. 1405b (p. 148 Ross)

καὶ ὁ Σιμωνίδης ὅτε μὲν ἐδίδου μισθὸν ὀλίγον αὐτῷ ὁ νικήσας τοῖς ὀρεῦσιν οὐκ ἤθελε ποιεῖν ὡς δυσχεραίνων εἰς ἡμιόνους ποιεῖν, ἐπεὶ δ᾽ ἱκανὸν ἔδωκεν ἐποίησε

χαίρετ᾽ ἀελλοπόδων θύγατρες ἵππων.

καίτοι καὶ τῶν ὄνων θυγατέρες ἦσαν.

cf. Heracl. Pont. *Pol.* 25 (*F.H.G.* ii 219)

---

[1] Heraclides Ponticus says the victory was won at Olympia by Anaxilas of Messana; the date was perhaps 480 B.C. (Dunbabin, *The Western Greeks* 398 n. 4). Athenaeus 1. 3e gives the victor's name

looking for an octopus.

Attic speakers say 'poulypous'.

Proverb (ed. Cohn)

The Carian fable: Simonides mentions this when sing-
ing the praises of a charioteer who had been victorious at
Pallene and had won as his prize a cloak which he used to
keep off the cold; for (the games) were held at Pallene in
winter. They say that a fisherman saw an octopus in the
winter and said, 'If I don't dive, I shall starve,' and that
this is the Carian fable.

'Diogenian', preface to *Proverbs*

Timocreon uses this story (viz. the Carian fable) in his
songs (fr. 734), and Simonides mentions it in his epinician
for Orillas.

### FOR THE MULE-CAR

**515**              *For Anaxilas of Rhegium*[1]

Aristotle, *Rhetoric*

When the victor in the mule-race offered Simonides
only a small fee, he refused to compose a poem, since he
took a poor view of writing in honour of mules; but on being
given an adequate fee he wrote

Greetings, daughters of storm-footed horses!

Yet they were daughters of the asses also.[2]

as Leophron (schol. Pindar Pyth. 2. 38 names Cleophron as the son
of Anaxilas).       [2] F. Mosino, *Q.U.C.C.* 28 (1978) 93 ff. notes
Aesop's fable, 285 Hausrath-Hunger.

# GREEK LYRIC

**516** Schol. V Ar. *Pac.* 117g (p. 27 Holwerda)

τὸ μεταμώνιος οἱ μὲν ἐξεδέξαντο ματαίως καὶ πρὸς οὐδὲν χρή-
σιμον, οἱ δέ φασιν ἰδίως μεταμώνιον τὸ αἰωρηθὲν (Holwerda: τὸν
ἑτέρωθεν cod.) μετέωρον σημαίνειν, πιστούμενοι τοῦτο παρὰ Σιμω-
νίδου οὕτως εἰπόντος·

κονία δὲ παρὰ τροχὸν μεταμώνιος ἠέρθη.

fort. ἠέρθη μεταμώνιος metri causa (Page)

**517** Plut. *virt. moral.* 6. 445c (iii 139 Pohlenz-Sieveking)

οἷον ὁ Πλάτων ἐξεικονίζει περὶ τὰ τῆς ψυχῆς ὑποζύγια, τοῦ
χείρονος πρὸς τὸ βέλτιον ζυγομαχοῦντος ἅμα καὶ τὸν ἡνίοχον
διαταράττοντος ἀντέχειν ὀπίσω καὶ κατατείνειν ὑπὸ σπουδῆς
ἀναγκαζόμενον ἀεί,

μὴ βάλῃ φοίνικας ἐκ χειρῶν ἱμάντας,

κατὰ Σιμωνίδην.

**518** Hdt. 5. 102. 3

καὶ πολλοὺς αὐτῶν οἱ Πέρσαι φονεύουσι, ἄλλους τε ὀνομαστούς,
ἐν δὲ δὴ καὶ Εὐαλκίδην στρατηγέοντα Ἐρετριέων, στεφανηφόρους
τε ἀγῶνας ἀναραιρηκότα καὶ ὑπὸ Σιμωνίδεω τοῦ Κηίου πολλὰ
αἰνεθέντα.

# SIMONIDES

**516** Scholiast on Aristophanes, *Peace* ('you will go to the crows μεταμώνιος')

Some have taken μεταμώνιος to mean 'pointlessly, for no useful purpose'; others say that the proper meaning is 'raised high in the air',[1] supporting their case by reference to Simonides, who said

and by the wheel the dust rose high in the air.

[1] Deriving it from ἄνεμος, 'wind'.

**517** Plutarch, *On Moral Virtue*

. . . just as Plato[1] uses the simile of the draught-horses of the soul, the worse horse struggling under the yoke against the better and disconcerting the charioteer, who must constantly hold him back and rein him in with all his strength,

lest he drop from his hands the crimson thongs,

as Simonides puts it.

[1] *Phaedrus* 253c–254e.

**518** Herodotus, *Histories*

The Persians killed many of the Ionians,[1] distinguished figures among them, including Eualcides, the Eretrian commander, who had been the winner at festivals where the victor is garlanded and had been highly[2] praised by Simonides of Ceos.

[1] In 498 B.C. during the Ionian Revolt.     [2] Or 'often'.

# GREEK LYRIC

## ΕΠΙΝΙΚΙΩΝ ΚΑΙ ΠΑΙΑΝΩΝ ΑΠΟΣΠΑΣΜΑΤΑ

**519** P.Oxy. 2430 (ed. et suppl. Lobel)

fr. 1 col. i schol. εὐαρᾶν τε πεφευγό[ (vid. Lobel ad loc.)

col. ii 2 εὔφρονα κωμ[ 3 τοδε σὸν θάητο[ν
4 ανθεων· 5s. καί τοι μιξοβόα[ πτυ]] χαί τε
Πίσ[α]ς ι [

fr. 4 col. ii 1 μακαρ[ 2 ερικτυπ[ 3 νικασε [
4 ευδειελο[ 6 ποίαιε[ 8 άεισαν· ι[

fr. 5(a) 4 ]μοιοκοραι

fr. 6(a) 5 ολβου[

fr. 7 2 ]δῖα [ 5 γλάυ[ 7 χρυσο[

fr. 8 2 ιερᾱ͞ι [ 3 μαντ[ 4 θυωδε [
5 φυγοντ[

fr. 9 2 Ζεὺς το [ 4 νος· Δελφω[ 5 φοιβος·
ινε [ 6 ἁγίων τε βωμ[

# SIMONIDES

## FRAGMENTS OF EPINICIANS AND PAEANS[1]

**519** Oxyrhynchus papyrus (*c.* 100 A.D.)

fr. 1 col. i (and having escaped from the well-fitted
...?)

col. ii ... cheerful (revel?) ... your wonderful ... (of
flowers?); and ... mingled with shouts ... and the
glens of Pisa[2] ...

---

[1] At least five unrelated texts are represented; for epinicians see
frr. 1, 4, 18, 53, 79, 85, 92, 96, 99, 120, 131; for paeans see 9, 23, 32,
35, 55, 61, 78.     [2] With reference to Olympia; cf. 589, 633.

---

fr. 4 col. ii ... blessed ... loud-sounding[1] ... (he) con-
quered ... sunny ... of what kind ... (they) sang ...

---

[1] Of Poseidon? From an epinician for an Isthmian victory?

---

fr. 5 (a) ... maiden(s) ...


fr. 6 (a) ... prosperity ...


fr. 7 ... illustrious (goddess? woman?) ... (Glaucus?)
... gold ...


fr. 8 ... holy ... oracle ... fragrant ... fleeing ...


fr. 9 ... Zeus ... (Delphi?) ... Phoebus ... and holy
altars ...

fr. 12  2 ]δαίδαλα . [

fr. 18  3 ]ω· στεφαν[        5 ]αδευξαο[

fr. 22  2 ]ομοτιμον (v.l. ἰσότιμον)        3 ] . ι Μοισᾶν[
4 Π]ηνειοῦ[

fr. 23  2 ]ξ ᾿Απολλο[ν

fr. 24  2 ]ιαφιεις

fr. 27  2 ]ονανδρω[

fr. 31  2 ]αρτεμ[

fr. 32        ]ντο Καρῶν ἀλκίμων . [

        ἀμ]φὶ ῥέεθρα καλὸν ἔστασαν [
        ] λειμῶνας· ἤδη γὰρ αἰδοῖ[αι
         ἐ]βάρυνον ὠ[δ]ῖνες· αὖσε
  5    νη]δύος ἀθαν[άτ]ας· ἧκε
        κλ]ῦθί μοι ασ . [ . . ]ωσ . .

schol. marg. sup. ]στρατος και αγαθ[ | ]αρεθηκαν ουνο . [ | ] . τα ωτα
ενοπη[ | ] . καθοπλιζομενων[

388

# SIMONIDES

fr. 12 . . . (cunningly-made?) . . .

fr. 18 . . . garland(s) . . . you prayed . . .

fr. 22 . . . of equal honour . . . Muses . . . Peneus[1] . . .

[1] River near Pieria, home of the Muses.

fr. 23 . . . Apollo! . . .

fr. 24 . . . letting go . . .

fr. 27 . . . men . . .

fr. 31 . . . (Artemis?) . . .

fr. 32 . . . (of) the valiant Carians . . . by the waters
. . . they set a fine . . . meadows; for already the
august birthpangs were heavy on her; she[1] cried out
. . . the immortal (womb?); he came[2] . . . (Hear?) me
. . .

Scholiast: (-stratus and Agath -?) . . . (they) set . . . the ears
. . . shout . . . of men arming. . . .

[1] Leto, mother of Apollo and Artemis? Or 'He (Apollo?) cried
out'.    [2] Or 'she sent forth'.

fr. 35    ] τροφ[         Π]άρνηθος [ἀ]πὸ ζα[θέας
        ] πε . [          ].δοις Ἀπολλον
                  ]οι᾽ Ἀθάνας
             ἐν]θάδ᾽ εὐμενεῖ φρενὶ [
    5         ]αίτιον οὐ πάρειτι ἔαρ · . [ ]ων χάριν [
           π]όνον ὑπομίμνομε[ν
            ]αν ὀρείδρομον Ἄρτεμιν [
           παρ]θενικάν · καὶ σέ, ἄναξ ἑκαβ[ε-
         ]λέτα ἱέμενοι ἐνοπὰν ἀγανοῖσιν [
   10        ] εὔφαμον ἀπὸ φρενὸς ὁμορρόθο[υ
             ]                  [

                 ] Ἀνδρίοις εἰς Πυθώ [
               ]μοι α[ἴ]σιον κελαδεῖ[[σ]] ἀμφι . [

schol. (e) 4 ]η εις δηλον[    (f) ]των αθηναιων παρ[

1 vel [ὑ]πὸ      5 v.l. παρεῖτι

fr. 37   4 ] . χαις ὀρίδρομο[

fr. 40   2 ]αδ᾽ εἶδεν ἀπείρ . [     3 ]μα πέφρικεν μ[

fr. 41      Ἀρ]τέμιδός τε βαθυ[
           ]όν τε τόξον     [
        ἄν]αξ ἀπὸ πασσάλο[υ
          ]εν οἴκωι Διὸς ἀθαν[ατ-
    5     σ]άματα κου[ρα(ι)]ς · αἴδ[

1 βαθρ[ possis     2 vel πασσαλόφιν

390

# SIMONIDES

fr. 35[1] ... nurse ... from[2] sacred Parnes ... Apollo!
... Athena ... here with gracious mind ... spring
does not pass; ... favour ... we submit to the bur-
den[3] ... Artemis the mountain-runner, the virgin;
and you, far-shooting lord, (we) uttering the cry ...
gentle ... an auspicious (cry?) with minds in agree-
ment ...

Scholiast: ... to Delos ... (of) the Athenians ...

### For the Andrians for Pytho[4]

... shouts an auspicious (song) about ...

[1] Probably the last verses of a paean written for the Athenians for
performance in Delos.     [2] Or 'under'.     [3] By singing in
honour of Artemis and Apollo?     [4] The title of another paean
to be performed at Delphi.

fr. 37 ... mountain-runner[1] ...

[1] Cf. fr. 35.

fr. 40 ... (he) saw the mainland ... shudders ...

fr. 41 Of Artemis ... deep ... and (Apollo's?) bow ...
lord, from the peg ... in the house of Zeus immortal
... notes[1] (for?) the maidens; and they ...

[1] Perhaps Apollo makes music, taking his lyre from the peg.

fr. 44   5   ] . ν ἱκᾱν[     6   ]θαλεα . [     8   ] . ν ἁδεῖ[α

fr. 46   2   ]ανεμοιο[

fr. 47   2   ὅτ᾽ ἐς Δᾱ[λον? (Page)

fr. 51   2   ]ᾱι · θοαισ . [

fr. 52   2   ]κελ[α]δε[     3   ]εος ἀκαμ[ατ-     5   δρο-
σοεν[     6   κυ]ναγέταν γ[     7   δ]έξατο γείτ[

fr. 53   8   ]ε τᾶς τ᾽ Ὀλυμπίας[     9   ]Δωρίων τ᾽
ἔοικα π[

fr. 55     π]τυχαὶ Λύκιον . [
          ]σα κάλλιστον υἱόν · ἰη[
          ]ξατε Δαλίων θύγατ[ρες
          ]σὺν εὐσεβεῖ ·     [
    5     ]ντ᾽ ἐν τᾶιδε γὰρ δικα[
          ]με πλαξιάλοι᾽ απα[
          ἔ]αρ μόληι · πότνια γ[λαυκ]ῶπι δ[
          ]αείδοντες ὀλβο[ . ] . [
          ] . οις ὕπο μενο[
    10    ]εφερον[

7 vel χρυσ]ῶπι

fr. 56   3   ]να <δονά>κων[

# SIMONIDES

fr. 44 . . . come . . . sweet . . .


fr. 46 . . . (of) wind . . .

fr. 47 . . . (when to Delos?) . . .

fr. 51 . . . swift . . .

fr. 52 . . . (shout?) . . . (unwearied?) . . . dewy . . . (huntsman?) . . . received his neighbour[1] . . .

[1] Or 'his neighbour received.'

fr. 53 . . . (Olympia?) . . . (Dorians I seem likely?) . . .


fr. 55 . . . the glens[1] . . . Lycian (Apollo), fairest son; oh joy![2] . . ., daughters of the Delians, with pious[3] . . .; for in this . . . sea-smiting . . . spring comes; (grey-eyed?) lady, (we?) singing . . . prosperous . . . under . . . carried . . .

[1] Perhaps of Mt. Cynthus on Delos, where Leto gave birth to Apollo.    [2] The distinctive cry of the paean, *iē*.    [3] Or 'sacred'.


fr. 56 . . . reeds . . .

fr. 57   1 β]ροτῶν κ[      2 ]ν βία · ει[

fr. 60   3 ]ων μυχ[      4 λι]παρόσκηπ[τρο- vel
-σκαπ[το-   5 ] μελλοντ[

schol. θ]αλασσια γ(ὰρ) η . [

fr. 61   2 ] · οὔτ᾽ ἄνευθεν αἰχμ[ᾶς   ]ουραν[    3
]παιάν .   4 ]δῶ[ν ᾽Α]πόλλωνα · τ[    6 ἄ]ναξ
πο[

fr. 62   1 ]πει φίλοι[   1s. ἡ| ρώων στρ[ατ-
3 ]σαμάντορ[   4 ]᾽Αθάναν αρ[

fr. 70   1 ]αν ἐς Δᾶλον[

fr. 73(b) 1   . . ] . ιν ᾱπειρω[   2 πορον   3 νι
πειθόμενα[ι

(c) 2 θυσιᾶων λ[    3 ὀλβιωτάτο[

fr. 76  2 ]ιμερω[

fr. 77  2 ]ἔαριτῖδας ο[
   ]στεφάνων[    ]λευκω[
   ]περὶ πάντ[    ]ρατον[    ]ατεσ[
   5 ]τε βρύων πο[λλ]οῖσι φέρων τ᾽ ἐπ[ιχ]ώρια π[
   ] . λα φύλλα β[ίαι] Ποτ[ιδ]ᾶνος ἐπλάθη δ[α
   ]μασίχθονο[ς

5 ἐπιχώρια Page

## SIMONIDES

fr. 57 ... mortals ... violence ...

fr. 60 (recess?) ... of the brilliant sceptre ... future ...

Scholiast: connected with the sea

fr. 61 neither apart from the spear ... heavenly ... Paean! ... Apollo ... lord ...

fr. 62 ... friends ... (of) heroes a host ... leader ... Athena ...

fr. 70 ... to Delos ...

fr. 73(b) ... mainland ... (channel?) ... obeying ... (c) ... (of) sacrifices ... most prosperous ...

fr. 76 ... (desire?) ...

fr. 77 ... (springtime?) ... garlands ... white ... around all ... abounding in many ... and bearing native leaves, (in spite of?) Poseidon the earth-subduer (he) approached ...

fr. 78 4 ]παιήων.    9 ]καλαῖς ἐν    10 ]ὕμνοις·
ιηιη

fr. 79 (a)(b)(c)

3                                ὅσ]τις δὲ βροτῶν
                                 ]νιτε ἔμμορ' ἐν
5              ]  [π]επρωμένον
               ἀ]θάνατον κα [ ]
               εὐθ]υμείτω χαμαι[
         ]πάμπα[ν . . . . ]  βαλών · πολέ[ων
     ἀνθρ]ώπων εὖχον[τ'] ἄγ[α]ν ἀποστάξαι
10           ]ων · ἀρέσθ[αι τε] κῦδος εὐωνύμου
          Νίκας ἐς ἄρ]μα [(βά)ντες]·
          ἐνὶ δ' οἶον ] εἴκει θ[εὰ δίφρ]ον ἐς μέγαν θορέν
               ]διμοισ[                    ]ῷ [

(d)            ]αρ ὕστατον[
               ]φάμαν · ζ[

11 schol. α βαντες    12 οἶον Page οἴωι Lobel

Cyrill. *lex.* (*Anecd. Par.* iv 186 Cramer) + cod. Lips. ed.
Reitzenstein *Gesch. Etym.* p. 309

Ἀπολλώνιος δὲ ὁ τοῦ Ἀρχιβίου φησὶν ὃ ἐνὶ εἴκει, τουτέστιν ἐνὶ
ὑποχωρεῖ. γέγονε δὲ κατ' ἀφαίρεσιν τοῦ ε καὶ συγκοπῇ τοῦ ει
διφθόγγου. ὁ γοῦν Σιμωνίδης παρετυμολογεῖ αὐτό, φησὶ γάρ·

ἐνὶ δ' οἴῳ εἴκει θεὰ μέγαν ἐς δίφρον.

οἴῳ[ ut vid. cod. Lips. ἐν δὲ οἰονείκει θεαὶ μ. εἰς δ. Cyrill. cod.
cf. *Anecd. Ox.* i 440 Cramer

# SIMONIDES

fr. 78 . . . Paean! . . . beautiful . . . with hymns: oh joy! oh joy![1]

[1] See fr. 55 n. 2.

fr. 79 . . . whosoever among mortals . . . obtains as his lot . . . fated . . . immortal . . . let him be of good cheer, having cast (jealousy?) utterly on the ground; of many men they pray (the envy?) may distil . . . and to win glory, stepping (into the chariot) of honoured Victory: for to one man only does the goddess grant to jump into her great carriage; . . . last . . . reputation . . .

Cyril, *Lexicon* (on νίκη, 'victory')

Apollonius, son of Archibius, says it comes from ὃ ἑνὶ εἴκει, i.e. 'what yields to one'; the form has arisen from the dropping of the ε and syncope of the diphthong ει.[1] Simonides plays on its etymology when he says, 'to one man only does the goddess yield into her great carriage.'

[1] Nonsense.

fr. 80 4 ]πάσας· καὶ γὰρ νῦν [    5 ]ν στεφάνων τυ-
ραν . [    6 ]ος ἀνὴρ γενέσθαι· καί[    8 ] . αἴχ[

fr. 84 1 ]ομιω . [    2 ἀμ]βρόταν [    4 ]μιν
ἀνήρ . [    5 ]ἀείδηι ὄντινα σ[    6 ]ς εὐέθειρα
κ . [    7 ]μετεραν . [    9 χρυ]σοκόμα θ[    10
]μεν· πίνων[    11 ]ρ[ . ] . ὕδωρ· τὸ δ[    12 ]σε
δ' ἐγὼ[

fr. 85 4s. σταδ]ιοδρο| [μ- ?

fr. 86 2 ]ὕμνεον    5 ]ὕδωρ Ἰλι[σ(σ)- ?

fr. 92

2              ]εσσι περιστ[[ε]]ίχοι δέ [
            ] ποταίνιον στάδιον τελέσσαις [
            ]ώνιος εὔφρων [ . . . . . . . ]μέλ[ο]ισαν [
5       ]μέλλοντος ὄλβου· τονδ' ε[ ]
        ]μα . [ ]χαίρων δ' ἀμφὶ πᾶχυν, ὥσθ' υἴωι μάτηρ ὀψι-
γόνωι πεφυ]λαγμένως ἔχω·
πολέων ]οναε[ . . . ]ν . [εἶ]δέ μιν β[ . . . . . . ]νος· εδε

schol. 5 ]ουτος π(ερι)στιχοι ωιτινι . . . | τωι ορριχιδαι    7 εχωπο-
λεων εχω· πολεω

fr. 93 1 ἐ]πεὶ δὲ[    1s. ἀπό]| προθεν    3 μελαμ-
φυλ[λ-

fr. 94 2 Κ]ρονιδαι[    3 ]ν τεκεμ[

398

# SIMONIDES

fr. 80 . . . all; for now . . . (of) garlands . . . to become a
( ) man . . . (spear?) . . .

fr. 84 . . . (Chromius?)[1] . . . immortal . . . a man . . .
sings, whomsoever . . . the lovely-haired[2] . . . (our?)
lord Apollo of the golden locks! . . . drinking the
water . . . and I . . .

[1] Pindar commemorated the chariot-victory of Chromius of Aetna
in the Pythian games at Sicyon in *Nemean* 9.  [2] Perhaps an
epithet of a goddess at Anacr. 418.

fr. 85 . . . (stadion-runner?) . . .

fr. 86 . . . they sang . . . (the water of the Ilissus?)[1] . . .

[1] The Athenian stream.

fr. 92 . . . and may    -onius, having completed a new
stadion, walk round . . . cheerfully . . . of concern . . .
future prosperity; and I (welcome?) him and rejoic-
ing hold my arm about him, as a mother about her
late-born son, protectingly . . . of many . . . saw him
. . .

Scholiast: may he walk round, to whom . . . to Orrhichidas
. . .

fr. 93 . . . and when . . . far off . . . dark-leaved . . .

fr. 94 . . . the son of Cronus . . . she bore . . .

399

fr. 96  3 στά]διόν τε νικα[      4 ] ̣ἀτιτάλλειν· π[
6 ] ̣θι μὴ πελάσεις (παλ- pap.)·      7 ]αν· οὖτ'
οἰνίζομε[

fr. 99  2 στά]διον γναμ̣[

fr. 114  2 ]ευ̣ρὺ φῦλ̣[      3 ] ̣ρ' ἀγγελία[ ?

fr. 115  1 ]Σικυωνι[

fr. 117 schol. κλεο[ ] ̣ ̣νικηι γενέσθα[ι Μ]ενδαίωι προστ ̣
[ Σ]ικυῶνι

fr. 118 schol. ἤτοι τοῦ βωμοῦ τῆς Ἑστ[ίας] περιφ[αι]νομένου ἢ
τοῦ [ταύ]τ̣η̣ς ἀγάλματος ... ποδάνε̣μον ...

fr. 119  2 ε]σφαλμέν[ -      3 ]αὐγᾶι πυρός (vid. S.L.G.
p. 157)      4 ]ν ἑπόμε[

fr. 120 (a)  2 ]σιν ἱππ ̣ ̣[

(b)  3 κέλη]τι Ἀθηναίωι λ̣[

4 ]κ̣αὶ σ' ἐπορνύνα[ι ?      5 ]πάρεδρε ἀθανα[
6 ]α̣ρων ἀγλαΐζ[

# SIMONIDES

fr. 96 ... and winning the stadion ... to rear ... lest you draw near; ... (neither by getting wine?) ...

fr. 99 ... turn round the stadion[1] ...

[1] To run the second lap of the diaulos?

fr. 114 ... (wide tribe?) ... (message?) ...

fr. 115 ... Sicyon ...

fr. 117 Scholiast: glory ... victory ... of Mende[1] ... Sicyon ...

[1] City on the Chalcidic promontory of Pallene.

fr. 118 Scholiast: either the altar of Hestia being sprinkled or her statue ... wind-swift ...

fr. 119 ... (tripped?) ... the gleam of the fire ... follow ...

fr. 120 ... horse ...

*For the race-horse, for Athenaeus of ...*

... and you ... (to arouse?) ..., you who sit beside ... immortal ... glorify ...

fr. 124 3 ]κρατον ἐν χερσὶ[      4 ]γεραίρειν γα[

fr. 131 2 ]ει ποδά[νεμ-      3 ]κυκλον μ[
4 ]ἐπ' Ἀλφείωι· λέγοι.[      5 ]ας τέτρα-
τον[ .]ηκ[
6 Ὀλυ]μπίαι μήδ[

fr. 134 1 ] .σ' Αἰγειδᾶν (v.l. -ειδαν)

fr. 135 1 ἀ]καδέα[ς (vid. *Pap.* . . . *Turner* p. 22)

fr. 136 2 ]δελφῖ .[

fr. 143 2 ]νῖδος ἁλικία[

fr. 148 1 ]πετραίω[

fr. 155 2 ]ς ἐξήλασε[

fr. 156 2 ]ἀριγνωτο .[      3 ] .ἀρετᾶς (v.l. ἀρετὰς)
ἀπολ. .[

fr. 157 2 ]ο θυώδεοι[      4 ]ς ὀλβιοτελε[

# SIMONIDES

fr. 124 ... in the hands ... to honour with a gift ...

fr. 131 ... wind-swift ... circle ... at the Alpheus[1];
(he) might tell ... fourth ... Olympia ...

[1] The river of Olympia.

fr. 134 ... of the Aegeid family ...

fr. 135 ... untroubled ...

fr. 136 ... dolphin ...

fr. 143 ... contemporaries of ...

fr. 148 ... rocky[1] ...

[1] Perhaps with reference to Poseidon, Thessalian 'god of the rocks',
or his games.

fr. 155 ... (he) drove out ...

fr. 156 ... easily-recognised ... excellence(s) ...

fr. 157 ... fragrant ... accomplisher of prosperity ...

# GREEK LYRIC

**519A** = S 319–386  P.Oxy. 2623 (ed. et suppl. Lobel)

fr. 1   4   φοιτᾷ̣ι γὰρ π̣[
       5   μάρ[ν]αντο· τ̣ [
           Ζευ[ξ]ίδαμος· ἐκ[
           κατόπισθε κλο[ν
           θρόνος ἀμφο̣[τερ-
           μι̣δαν θ' ὑπεδ̣.[
     10   .ον θεμίστων.[
           τοι δ' Ἱπποκρατι̣δ[α-    σκᾶ-
           π̣τρόν τεδεξ[
           στέφανος.[
           ..]ωνε.ιο̣υ[

fr. 2  1 παμφυλ[     2 λίμνασε[     4 .ε κλυτα.[
9 θοα[ ].οιν[  9s. θρα]‖ σὺς [..]ιλια.[  11 γεράνων[
12 Κ̣ηναίου Δ[ιὸς     13 ρον πλόν̣[     14 πόλιν
ἁλίας[    14s. ἐ]‖ ναντίον κ.[    16 κεῖθι καὶ μ.[
17 δοιαὶ γὰρ φατ̣[     18 σκοποί· πε[

17 vel αἰ| δοῖαι

fr. 4  2 ]κ φίλον[      3 ]ε θεοισιε[      5 ]..ς
τηλαυ[γ-

fr. 5  8 μελα[    14 χρόνος· ἱ̣δρυ̣[    15 μανύε-
τα̣[ι] βίος[    16 ὦ μάκαρ[ε]ς γον[    17 κατέ-
μαρψεν π̣[

# SIMONIDES

**519A** = S 319–386 Oxyrhynchus papyrus (early 2nd c. A.D.)

*The authorship of Simonides is almost certain (see fr. 14 and Lobel in Pap. ... Turner p. 21 f.). Frr. 21–22 seem to belong to epinicians.*

fr. 1 ... for (he goes?) ... (they) fought ... Zeuxi-damus[1]; ... behind (he) drove ... throne ... both ... and    -midas[2] ... judgements ...; and they ... Hippocratidas[3] ... and he received the sceptre ... garland ...

[1] Name found only in the Eurypontid royal house of Sparta; perhaps king Leotychidas' son, who died, old enough to be a father, before 469 B.C. (Hdt. 6. 71).    [2] Another Spartan?    [3] Another Eurypontid name (Hdt. 8. 131).

fr. 2 ... of mingled tribes[1] ... (lake?) ... famous ... (swift?) ... bold (man's name?) ... cranes ... Cenaean (Zeus?)[2] ... voyage ... city of the sea-goddess ... opposite ... there ... since two[3] watch-ers[4] ...

[1] Or 'Pamphylian' with reference to the Dorian tribe (or to the region on the south coast of Asia Minor).    [2] Worshipped at Cenaeum in N.W. Euboea.    [3] Or 'august'; the watchers are female.    [4] The poem has triadic structure (strophe and anti-strophe of 4 lines, epode of 7).

fr. 4 ... dear ... to the gods ... far-shining ...

fr. 5 ... (black?) ... time; ... establish- ... life is dis-closed ... Oh blessed children! ... (he, it) caught up with ...[1]

[1] Like fr. 2, from a triadic poem.

fr. 9  3 ]ακηδε[


fr. 10  1 Δι]όνυσ[ο]ς    2 ]ν ὕπν[ο]ν ·
3 ]φ . [ ] . ος ἀπὸ γλυκυ[    5 ]λωι πίνωμεν χα[
6 ]ανους ἁζομενοι[    8 ]ιαι . [περικ]αλλεα[
11 ἐ̣]ξ ἱερ[

1 vel Δι]ώ-    8 suppl. Bossi


fr. 14    ] . δεθε[
        ] . ς μεγα[
        ]θεῶν α[
        ]εοικοι[
    5 ]άτος · ἄπ[
        ]ωιπ[


fr. 16  4 ] . δολομ[    5 ]εν κάσιν[

4 δολομηχαν- vel δολομηδ- vel δολομητ-


fr. 19  3 ]χας ἠὺν . [    4 ]βωτιαν[ειρ-
5 ] . κισσον θ[    6 ] . αν ἀφικο[


fr. 21  1 μικτα δεν . . [    2 . ]νατωρ στεφ . [    5
    . [ . ]σθεὶς χάριν . [    6 πατέρος τ᾽ ἄπο ν[ . ]χ[
6s. Ἐ]‖ ριτίμου κασιγ[νητ] . [    8 ὁ μὲν σταδιο[

5 π[ρο]σθεὶς Bossi

fr. 9 . . . (untroubled?) . . .

fr. 10 . . . Dionysus . . . sleep . . . let us drink . . .
standing in awe of . . . (very beautiful?) . . . out of
holy . . .

fr. 14 . . . great . . . (of) the gods . . .[1]

[1] The scraps of the last two lines of the fragment provide a few
letters of the opening lines of 520 (Lobel, *Pap. . . . Turner* p. 21).

fr. 16 . . . crafty . . . brother[1] . . .

[1] Or 'sister'.

fr. 19 . . . brave . . . nurse of heroes[1] . . . (ivy?) . . .
arrived . . .

[1] Homeric epithet for a fruitful country; 'brave' is also epic.

fr. 21[1] . . . mixed . . . garland . . . (adding?) favour . . .
from his father, brother of Eritimus . . . he (won?)
the stadion . . .

[1] Frr. 21 and 22 may be related.

fr. 22 2 ]φορίαν γέρας μ[    3 ]ου· Πυθοῖ γάρ ποτ[(ε)
4 ] ₊ ₊ ο[ ] ₊ · αὐτὰρ ο[ ₊ ] ₊ [    5 ]εμ ₊ ι Κορι̣ν[θ-

2 στεφανα]φ- vel νικα]φ-    γέρας vel ἱερας

fr. 24 2 ]ων λίθω[    6 ἀ]νορεαν[

fr. 29 1 (ἀπ)αμ]βλύνει κ[

fr. 30 4 φωτι πα[    5 καὶ σὺ μὲ[ν    5s. ἐ]| λαύ-
νεις ₊ [    7 κνισον α[    8 παγκοίτᾳ ₊ [

fr. 32 1 ]κυνέαν δ[ ] ₊ ₊ [    2 ]το· ὡς ὅτε ₊ ₊ ₊ [

fr. 35 3 ]άβαλεπ[    5 ] ₊ δοξα· ε[

fr. 41 5 Ἄλκησ[τι- ?    6 ὁππότ[

fr. 43 5 ]εὐϊπ[π-

fr. 45 3 Τ]υνδαρ[    4 Ἡρ]ακλει[    5 ἀ]μφο-
τερ[    6 ]εν Ὑλλου[

# SIMONIDES

fr. 22[1] ... victory ... privilege[2] ...; for at Pytho once
...; but ... (Corinth?) ...

[1] May be related to 21: Pindar *Ol.* 13 commemorates the victory
of the Corinthian Xenophon, who won the stadion and pentathlon
at Olympia in 464 B.C.; his father had won the stadion at the Pythia,
and he seems to have had an uncle called Eritimus.   [2] Or
'holy'.

fr. 24 ... stone ... manliness ...

fr. 29 ... blunts ...

fr. 30 ... man[1] ...; and you drive ... savoury[2] ...
where all must sleep[3] ...

[1] Or 'light'.   [2] Of a sacrifice?   [3] Epithet for the world of
the dead.

fr. 32 ... helmet ...; as when[1] ...

[1] A simile.

fr. 35 ... threw ... glory ...

fr. 41 ... (Alcestis?) ... whenever ...

fr. 43 ... of the fine horses ...

fr. 45 ... (Tyndareus?) ... (Heracles?) ... both ...
Hyllus[1] ...

[1] Son of Heracles.

fr. 46 1 ] Ἀκέστορος· o[ ] ͺι . .    2 ]ταῦτα μαλ'
ἀμ[φοτ]έροις . [   3   ]ειρομεν·  με[  ]πογεζ[
5 ]ε διὲκ μεγάρ[οιο] θύραζε συν[  6 μελάμ]πυγον
Ἀλκ[μάν]ας θρασυ[    7 ]κεοντος . [ ]ρεσας . . [
8 ]ος ἁλιμοχθ[ ] . ῳ[

2 suppl. Page

fr. 48 1 ] . ας πάλ[ι]ν υἱ[    3 ]ς ἀκηδέας·    4 ]ν
φρασὶν ἐνθ . [   5 ]μηδάμ' Ἑλλανε[σ(-)    6
]τον ἀίδιον    9 ]α σὺν θεοῖς[    10 ]ων παρα-
δεγμε[ν-    12 ] πείθον    13 ] . . ν φοβε[
14 ] . [ . ]ε· αἶψα τ̣[

fr. 50 2 ]καί οἱ κελ . [    3 ]μετερας̣[    4 ἀν]θρώ-
πων κα . [

fr. 54 3 Κ]ολχ̣[ -

fr. 57 3 ]Ἀλκμ[    4 ] . ιππο̣[

fr. 59 1 ]ὄρνυσθ' α̣[

**519B** = S 387–442  P.Oxy. 2624 (ed. et suppl. Lobel)

fr. 1     ]οὐραν[οῦ . . . ] . [θα]λάσσας
       ]ος ῥιπὰν μελαίνας·
      ] . δ' ἐρήμα θνατῶν τε κα[ὶ
      ]α δαῖμον α[ἰ]γίκναμε

2 λαιλαπ]ος ?

fr. 46 ... (of) Acestor[1]; ... these things very much (to) both ... we ... out through the hall ... black-rumped bold (son of) Alcmena[2] ... toiling at sea ...

[1] I.e. Healer; of Apollo?  [2] Heracles, referred to elsewhere as 'black-rumped'; see Fraenkel on Aes. *Ag.* 115.

fr. 48 ... (again?) the son ... untroubled[1]; ... in their hearts ... by no means the Greeks ... everlasting ... with the help of the gods ... receiving from ... they urged ... fear-...; suddenly ...

[1] Lobel detected an overlap of the text with 519 fr. 135 (*Pap.* ... *Turner* p. 22).

fr. 50 ... and ... bid him ... (y)our ... (of) men ...

fr. 54 ... Colchis ...

fr. 57 ... (Alcmena?) ... horse ...

fr. 59 ... rush ...

**519B** = S 387–442 Oxyrhynchus papyrus (100–150 A.D.)

*Attribution to Simonides is likely enough but not certain; see notes to frr. 4, 9. M. van der Weiden, Z.P.E. 64 (1986) 15 ff. argues for Pindar's authorship.*

fr. 1 ... (of) sky ... (of) sea ... blast of black (hurricane?); ... empty both of men and (of gods)[1] ...,

[1] Or (of beasts).

5 ]μέμυκεν ἠδ' ἄναυδος ὕ[πν-
] κε[ῑ]νος ἄειδε περικλυτ[
] γ[ . . ] ος· ἄμμι δ' ἀλαθέω[ς
]ας θεὸς αὐτίκα σαμή[ια
ἐ]ναργέα θεσπεσίω . [
10 ὁ]ππότ' ἐγὼ μὲν ἐρε[
εὐ]αγέας θυσίας γλυκε[
] . τοι σπένδων

7 vel -θέω[ν    11 suppl. Page

fr. 4 5 ]κ' ἀϊδνὰ    6 ]ὕδωρ    7 ]θέσμιον·
8 ζ]ωὰ μεροπ[    9 ]ἀδειέα    11 ]ὀργὰν

fr. 8 5 τηλυ[γετ- ?

fr. 9(a) 2 ]κῦδος . [    4 ]ι διαμπε[ρε-    5 ] . . ν
ἀλόχω[    6 -έ]ι φύτλαι μ[    (b)2 εὐ]ρυεδοῦς[
4 ἀμβ]ρόσιον π[

(b) 4 suppl. Page

fr. 10 2 μαιομ[εν-    3 δίδου π[    4 ἀλκα . [

fr. 12 3 ἀ]χλυοεσ[σ-

fr. 13 4 Πτ]οιοδω[ρ-

fr. 24 2 ]πυρος[

goat-legged divinity[2]! ... keeps mouth[3] closed and uttering no sound ... (sleep?) ... he sang about famous ...; and to us ... truth ... the god at once ... clear notes ... divine[4] ..., whenever I ... undefiled sacrifices ... sweet ... pouring libation ...

[2] Pan.    [3] Or 'eyes'.    [4] Pindar is said to have heard from Pan in a dream the words of a song he had just composed and was about to perform (schol. Aristides iii 564 Dindorf). Should the story have been told rather of Simonides?

fr. 4 ... obscure ... water ... lawful[1] ... life of mortal ... (fearless?) ... temperament[2] ...

[1] Pindar uses the form τέθμιος, never θέσμιος.    [2] Or 'anger'.

fr. 8 ... (darling child?) ...

fr. 9 ... glory ... continuously ... wives ... generation ... broad-based[1] ... immortal ...

[1] Epithet of earth at 542. 24; not found elsewhere.

fr. 10 ... seeking ... give![1] ... (valour?) ...

[1] Or 'gave'.

fr. 12 ... misty ...

fr. 13 ... (Ptoeodorus?)[1]

[1] A relative of the Corinthian athlete Xenophon (Pindar, Ol. 13. 41); see 519A frr. 21, 22.

fr. 24 ... fire

fr. 28(a)(b) 1 ὠκ]υάλων[     3 ].κο.[ ]. ἀτρυγέτας
ἁλός·    4 ]κ᾽ ἀμαιμ[ακ]έταν πόντοιο    5s. ]ρι-
πὰν [ἀ]πιοδερ | κ-]    (d)(e) 2 δειν[ῶ]πας ἀνέ-
μω[ν    4 π]λωτῆρσι πείρατα ψ[    5 ]βίοτος
ναυτᾳ[    6 ...]ιων· οὐδὲ μ[    7 κ]υβερνατῆ-
ρε[ς ....]ενε[    8 ].ισι νεῶσ᾽ ά.[...,
.]πτο[    10 ]γεωμορίαις·    11 ].οντος ἔμ-
[π]εδον    12 ]στον· οὐ πό[λ]ισμα    13 οὐ]
πύ[ργος ο]ὐ δόμος εὔκτιτος

fr. 29 2 ]..[.]αν· Παλλάδα δ[    3 μ]ητιόεσσαν
ἀρη[γόνα    4 ]τισταν βασιληΐδ[    5 ]τᾷ. πίσυ-
νος στ.[    6 ]νιας θρασὺν[    7 ]νων δαμά-
λιξε[    8 -μα]χίας κρατερᾶς    11 ]δεξιτέρα[
14 ].πτολεμ[    17 ].θνατοι[    22 κ]υκλοδ[

8 πυγμα]χίας?

fr. 32 5 ψυχὰν γ.[    6 Μο[ισ]ᾷ[ν    7 λ[ε]υγαλέ[

fr. 47 1 οὐδὲ Μιδηϊα..[


fr. 48 1 ].ἀυτμὰν.[    2 ].αντ᾽ ἄφαρ.[
4 ]ερα δ᾽ αἰόλο[    5 ]ρατα λυσιμ[ελής
8 ]ξ χάεος.[

5 vel Λυσίμ[αχος

fr. 49 3 ]χρυσου[

fr. 52 3 ]ὕβρι.[

# SIMONIDES

fr. 28 ... sea-swift (ships) ... (of) the unharvested brine; ... the irresistible rush of the sea ... gently-glancing ... grim-eyed ... (of) winds ... seamen ... limits ... life ... sailor(s) ...; nor ... helmsmen ... to renew ... tilled lands; ... firmly ...; not a town, not a wall-tower, not a well-built house ...

fr. 29 ... Pallas, wise helper, ... royal ... trusting in ... bold ... he subdued ... (of) the stern fight[1] ... right hand ... war ... mortal ... circle ...

[1] Perhaps 'boxing'.

fr. 32 ... soul ... (of) the Muses ... wretched ...

fr. 47 ... nor Midean[1] ...

[1] Obscure; from Midas or Midea?

fr. 48 ... breath ... suddenly ... flashing ... limb-loosening[1] ... the void ...

[1] Or 'Lysimachus'; see 530.

fr. 49 ... gold ...

fr. 52 ... violence ...

fr. 53 1 ] ͜ ς αἶψα δ[  8 ] ιδος ὕψι φ[
10 λ]ιβάδας σταλά[σσ-  11 ]οντων ὄχον[
12 ]ων κουροτρό[φ-

fr. 56(a)(b) 2 ] ͜ φόρμιγγι  3 Φοί]βωι· Δάλου
4 ]ε μεσόχθονο[ς  5 ]μ ̣ [ ̣ ̣ ]ε' ἀγνᾶς [
(c) 4 ] ̣ ι ̣ ̣ ν δαιμον[  5 ] ̣ πόντου·[  6 γ]αιήοχε ̣ [

<ΘΡΗΝΟΙ>

**520** Plut. *cons. Apoll.* 11, 107ab (i 220 Paton-Wegehaupt)

. . . τὴν παρ' ἐνίοις κρατοῦσαν δόξαν ὡς ἄρα κρεῖττόν ἐστι τὸ τεθνάναι τοῦ ζῆν. ὁ γοῦν Σιμωνίδης ἀνθρώπων, φησίν, ὀλίγον . . .

ἀνθρώπων ὀλίγον μὲν
κάρτος ἄπρακτοι δὲ μεληδόνες,
αἰῶνι δ' ἐν παύρῳ πόνος ἀμφὶ πόνῳ·
ὁ δ' ἄφυκτος ὁμῶς ἐπικρέμαται θάνατος·
5 κείνου γὰρ ἴσον λάχον μέρος οἵ τ' ἀγαθοὶ
ὅστις τε κακός.

vv. 1–3 divisio incerta  3 δ' ἐν Pflugk, Schneidewin  δὲ codd.

**521** Stob. *Ecl.* 4. 41. 9 (v 930 Wachsmuth-Hense)

Σιμωνίδου Θρήνων·

ἄνθρωπος ἐὼν μή ποτε φάσῃς ὅ τι γίνεται αὔριον,
μηδ' ἄνδρα ἰδὼν ὄλβιον ὅσσον χρόνον ἔσσεται·
ὠκεῖα γὰρ οὐδὲ τανυπτερύγου μυίας
οὕτως ἁ μετάστασις.

416

# SIMONIDES

fr. 53 ... suddenly ... on high ... let(ting) drop streams ... chariot ... nurse of children[1] ...

[1] Epithet of a place or a goddess or peace?

fr. 56 ... lyre ... (to) Phoebus, (master) of Delos ... (and Delphi) at the earth's centre ... holy ... deity ... (of) the sea ... earth-shaker[1]! ...

[1] Poseidon.

## DIRGES

**520** Plutarch, *Letter of Consolation to Apollonius*

... the view, prevalent among some people, that it is better to be dead than alive. Simonides at any rate says,

Men's strength is slight, their plans impossible; within their brief lifetime toil upon toil; and death hangs inescapable over all alike: of death an equal portion is allotted to good men and to bad.[1]

[1] See 519A fr. 14.

**521** Stobaeus, *Extracts* (on the insecurity of man's prosperity)

From the Dirges of Simonides:

You are man: then never say what will happen tomorrow, nor, when you see a prosperous man, how long he will prosper; for not even the movement of a long-winged fly is so swift.

# GREEK LYRIC

4. 41. 62 (v 946 W.-H.)

Φαβωρίνου· ἄνθρωπος — ἔσσεται. ἀλλὰ μηδὲ οἶκον. ὥσπερ ἀμέλει ὁ ποιητὴς διεξέρχεται τὴν τῶν Σκοπαδῶν ἀθρόαν ἀπώλειαν.

cf. schol. Hom. *Il.* 7. 76 ap. P.Oxy. 1087 col. i 30 (Σιμωνίδης· v. 3)

1 Bergk: φήσης, φήσῃ, φῂς, φῆς, εἴπῃς codd.     αὔριον om. Stob. 9
2 ὄλβιον om. Stob. 9

**522** Stob. *Ecl.* 4. 51. 5 (v 1067 Wachsmuth-Hense)

Σιμωνίδου·

πάντα γὰρ μίαν ἱκνεῖται δασπλῆτα Χάρυβδιν,
αἱ μεγάλαι τ' ἀρεταὶ καὶ ὁ πλοῦτος.

1 fort. γὰρ <ἐς>, Page

**523** Stob. *Ecl.* 4. 34. 14 (v 829 Wachsmuth-Hense)

Σιμωνίδου Θρήνων·

†οὐδὲ γὰρ οἳ πρότερόν ποτ' ἐπέλοντο,
θεῶν δ' ἐξ ἀνάκτων ἐγένονθ' υἷες ἡμίθεοι,
ἄπονον οὐδ' ἄφθιτον οὐδ' ἀκίνδυνον βίον
ἐς γῆρας ἐξίκοντο τελέσαντες.†

**524** Stob. *Ecl.* 4. 51. 7 (v 1067 Wachsmuth-Hense)

Σιμωνίδου·

ὁ δ' αὖ θάνατος κίχε καὶ τὸν φυγόμαχον.

Bergk: ἔκιχε καὶ, ἔκιχε τε codd.     καὶ φυγαίχμαν ci. Garrod

418

# SIMONIDES

Favorinus[1]: 'You are man ... prosper.' And do not say it of a household either; just look how the poet describes the wholesale destruction of the Scopads.

[1] 2nd c. A.D. rhetorician, quoted by Stob. later in the same chapter.

**522** Stobaeus, *Extracts* (on death and its inevitability)

From Simonides:

for all things arrive at one single horrible Charybdis,[1] great excellences and wealth alike.

[1] The destructive whirlpool of Homer, *Od.* 12.

**523** Stobaeus, *Extracts* (that life is short, worthless and full of cares)

From the Dirges of Simonides:

for not even those who lived in olden days and were born the half-divine sons of the gods, our masters, reached old age without first passing a life of hardship, destruction and danger.

**524** Stobaeus, *Extracts* (on death and its inevitability)

From Simonides:

but Death overtakes even the man who runs from the battle.[1]

[1] Translated by Horace (mors et fugacem persequitur virum, *Carm.* 3. 2. 14). Oates, *Influence of Sim. upon Horace* 1–55 argues that Horace's poem is based on a poem by Sim.

# GREEK LYRIC

**525** = Semon. 42 West     Stob. *Ecl.* 2. 1. 10 (ii 5
Wachsmuth-Hense)

Σιμωνίδου·

ῥεῖα θεοὶ κλέπτουσιν ἀνθρώπων νόον.

**526** Theophil. Antioch. *ad Autolycum* 2. 8 (p. 36 Grant)

καὶ Σιμωνίδης·

οὔτις ἄνευ θεῶν
ἀρετὰν λάβεν, οὐ πόλις, οὐ βροτός.
θεὸς ὁ πάμμητις· ἀπή-
μαντον †δ᾽ οὐδέν ἐστιν ἐν αὐτοῖς.†

cf. Stob. *Ecl.* 1. 1. 10 (vv. 1–2)

4 δ᾽ del. Page     οὐδέν ἐστι θνατοῖς Bergk

**527** Theophil. Antioch. *ad Autolycum* 2. 37 (p. 94 Grant)

ὅτι μέλλει ἡ τοῦ θεοῦ κρίσις γενέσθαι καὶ τὰ κακὰ τοὺς
πονηροὺς αἰφνιδίως καταλαμβάνειν, καὶ τοῦτο ... ἐσήμανεν ... ὁ
Σιμωνίδης·

οὐκ ἔστιν κακὸν
ἀνεπιδόκητον ἀνθρώποις· ὀλίγῳ δὲ χρόνῳ
πάντα μεταρρίπτει θεός.

**528** Ael. Aristid. *Or.* 31. 2 (i 126s. Dindorf, ii 212 Keil)

ποῖος ταῦτα Σιμωνίδης θρηνήσει, τίς Πίνδαρος ποῖον μέλος ἢ
λόγον τοιοῦτον ἐξευρών; τίς χόρος ἄξιον φθέγξεται τοιούτου πά-
θους; ποία δὲ Δύσηρις Θετταλὴ τοιοῦτο πένθος ἐπένθησεν ἐπ᾽ Ἀν-
τιόχῳ τελευτήσαντι ὅσον νῦν μητρὶ τῇ τούτου πένθος πρόκειται;

# SIMONIDES

**525** Stobaeus, *Extracts* (on those who interpret divine things . . . )

From Simonides[1]:

the gods easily steal the wits of men.

[1] Attributed by Welcker and Wilamowitz to Semonides of Amorgos as an iambic line, perhaps rightly: see R. Renehan, *H.S.C.P.* 87 (1983) 8 f.

**526** Theophilus of Antioch, *To Autolycus*

And Simonides said,

No one ever attained excellence without the gods, no city, no mortal. The all-clever one is God: for mortals nothing is free from misery.

**527** Theophilus of Antioch, *To Autolycus*

That the judgement of God is fated to come and that evil will suddenly overtake the wicked[1] was indicated by . . . Simonides:

There is no evil which men cannot expect; and within a brief time god turns everything upside down.

[1] Sim.'s lines are not in fact relevant to divine judgement.

**528** Aelius Aristides, *Orations* (funeral speech for Eteoneus)

What Simonides will bewail this, what Pindar? What melody or suitable words will he devise? What chorus will utter a song worthy of such a misfortune? What Thessalian Dyseris made lament over the dead Antiochus to equal the grief brought now to this boy's mother?

Schol. Theocr. 16. 34s. (p. 327 Wendel)

πολλοὶ ἐν ᾽Αντιόχοιο δόμοις· ἀντὶ τοῦ ἄγαν πλούσιοι, ὥστε πολλοῖς παρέχειν τὴν τροφήν. ἀλλ᾽ οὐδὲν ἤνυσεν ὁ πλοῦτος αὐτῶν πρὸς τὴν νῦν δόξαν, εἰ μὴ ὑπὸ Σιμωνίδου ὑμνήθησαν. . . . ὁ δὲ ᾽Αντίοχος ᾽Εχεκρατίδου καὶ Δυσήριδος υἱὸς ἦν, ὥς φησι Σιμωνίδης.

**529** Schol. Theocr. 16. 36s. (p. 327s. Wendel)

οἱ δὲ Σκοπάδαι Κραννώνιοι τὸ γένος. Κραννὼν δὲ πόλις Θεσσαλίας, ὅθεν Σκόπας ὁ Κραννώνιος Κρέοντος καὶ ᾽Εχεκρατείας υἱός. καὶ Σιμωνίδης ἐν Θρήνοις.

ibid. 44 ὁ Κήιος· τὸν Σιμωνίδην φησί, παρόσον αὐτὸς τοῖς προειρημένοις ἐνδόξοις ἀνδράσι τῶν Θεσσαλῶν ἐπινικίους ἔγραψε καὶ θρήνους.

**530** Harp. s.v. Ταμύναι (i 286s. Dindorf)

Αἰσχίνης κατὰ Κτησιφῶντος (88). πόλις ἐστὶν ἐν Εὐβοίᾳ ἐν τῇ χώρᾳ τῇ ᾽Ερετριέων αἱ Ταμύναι, ἔνθα καὶ ἱερὸν ᾽Απόλλωνος, ὡς οἵ τε τὰ Εὐβοϊκὰ γράψαντες μαρτυροῦσι καὶ Σιμωνίδης ἐν τῷ εἰς Λυσίμαχον τὸν ᾽Ερετριέα θρήνῳ.

**531** Diodor. 11. 11. 6 (ii 240s. Vogel)

διόπερ οὐχ οἱ τῶν ἱστοριῶν συγγραφεῖς μόνοι ἀλλὰ πολλοὶ καὶ τῶν ποιητῶν καθύμνησαν αὐτῶν τὰς ἀνδραγαθίας· ὧν γέγονε καὶ Σιμωνίδης ὁ μελοποιὸς ἄξιον τῆς ἀρετῆς αὐτῶν ποιήσας ἐγκώμιον, ἐν ᾧ λέγει·

# SIMONIDES

Scholiast on Theocritus 16. 34 f.[1]

'Many (serfs) in the halls of Antiochus ...': i.e. they
(Antiochus and Aleuas) were extremely rich, so that they
provided sustenance for many; but their wealth would
have contributed nothing to their present fame, if they had
not been celebrated in song by Simonides.... Antiochus
was the son of Echecratidas and Dyseris, as Simonides
says.

[1] See test. 13.

**529** Scholiast on Theocritus 16. 36 f.[1]

The Scopads were a family of Crannon, a city of Thes-
saly to which belonged Scopas the Crannonian, son of
Creon and Echecrateia: cf. Simonides in his Dirges.

(On 16. 44) 'The man of Ceos': he means Simonides,
inasmuch as he composed epinicians and dirges for the dis-
tinguished Thessalians mentioned above.

[1] See test. 13.

**530** Harpocration, *Lexicon of the Ten Attic Orators*

Tamynae: mentioned by Aeschines in his speech
against Ctesiphon. It is a city of Euboea in the country of
the Eretrians, where there is a temple of Apollo, as we
learn from the authors of the *Euboica* and from Simonides
in his dirge for Lysimachus of Eretria.

**531** Diodorus Siculus, *World History*

Therefore not only the writers of the histories but also
many of the poets have celebrated the brave deeds of these
men (Leonidas and his Spartans); among them is the lyric
poet Simonides, who composed a eulogy befitting their
valour. In it he says,

τῶν ἐν Θερμοπύλαις θανόντων
εὐκλεὴς μὲν ἁ τύχα, καλὸς δ' ὁ πότμος,
βωμὸς δ' ὁ τάφος, πρὸ γόων δὲ μνᾶστις, ὁ δ' οἶκτος
  ἔπαινος·
ἐντάφιον δὲ τοιοῦτον εὐρὼς
5 οὔθ' ὁ πανδαμάτωρ ἀμαυρώσει χρόνος.
ἀνδρῶν ἀγαθῶν ὅδε σηκὸς οἰκέταν εὐδοξίαν
Ἑλλάδος εἵλετο· μαρτυρεῖ δὲ καὶ Λεωνίδας,
Σπάρτας βασιλεύς, ἀρετᾶς μέγαν λελοιπὼς
κόσμον ἀέναόν τε κλέος.

cf. Arsen. p. 342 Walz (Σιμωνίδης ὁ μελοποιός· vv. 1–9)

3 Eichstädt, Ilgen: προγόνων codd.   Jacobs: οἶτος codd.   4 τ.
οὔτ' εὐρὼς codd., οὔτ' del. Bergk       7 Hermann: εἵλατο codd.
καὶ Arsenius, om. Diodorus   8 ὁ Σπάρτας codd., ὁ del. Bergk

## Η ΕΠ' ΑΡΤΕΜΙΣΙΩΙ ΝΑΥΜΑΧΙΑ

**532** *Sud.* Σ 439 (iv 361 Adler) s.v. Σιμωνίδης

καὶ γέγραπται αὐτῷ Δωρίδι διαλέκτῳ †ἡ Καμβύσου καὶ
Δαρείου βασιλεία καὶ Ξέρξου ναυμαχία καὶ† ἡ ἐπ' Ἀρτεμισίῳ
ναυμαχία δι' ἐλεγείας, ἡ δ' ἐν Σαλαμῖνι μελικῶς.

**533** Prisc. *de metr. Ter.* 24 (iii 428 Keil)

Simonides et Alcman in iambico teste Heliodoro non
solum in fine ponunt spondeum sed etiam in aliis locis:
Simonides in ἐπ' Ἀρτεμισίῳ ναυμαχίᾳ in dimetro catalectico:

  (a) ἐβόμβησεν θαλάσσας,

424

# SIMONIDES

Of those who died at Thermopylae glorious is the
fortune, fair the fate; their tomb is an altar, for
lamentation they have remembrance, for pity
praise. Such a funeral-gift[1] neither mould nor all-
conquering time shall destroy. This precinct[2] of
noble men chose the glory of Greece as its inhabi-
tant; witness to this is Leonidas himself, king of
Sparta, who left behind a great adornment of valour
and imperishable glory.

[1] Or 'shroud'.     [2] Bowra, *G.L.P.*[2] 345–9 argued that the hymn
was composed for a ceremony of remembrance at a shrine in
Sparta; *contra*, A. J. Podlecki, *Historia* 17 (1968) 258 ff., M. L.
West, e.g. *C.Q.* 25 (1975) 309.

## THE SEA-BATTLE AT ARTEMISIUM

**532** *Suda,* Simonides (1st notice)[1]

He composed in the Doric dialect 'The Reign of Cam-
byses and Darius', 'Sea-battle against Xerxes' and 'The
Sea-battle at Artemisium' in elegiacs, 'The Sea-battle at
Salamis' in lyric metre...

[1] See test. 1 with nn. 9, 10: 533 shows that the Artemisium poem
was in lyric metre. Fr. 635 may belong here.

**533** Priscian, *On the Metres of Terence*

In their iambic lines Simonides and Alcman, according
to Heliodorus, place a spondee not only at the end but in
other positions also: Simonides in 'The Sea-battle at
Artemisium' in a catalectic dimeter placed a spondee in the
second position:

(a) the sea's (waves) roared.

# GREEK LYRIC

in secundo loco spondeum posuit. ἀντιστρέφει δὲ αὐτῷ·

    (b) ἀποτρέπουσι κῆρας.

Alcman autem (v. fr. 14) ... quarto loco spondeum posuit
... teste Heliodoro, qui ait Simonidem hoc frequenter
facere.

(a) sc. κύματα?   (b) -ουσει RV, -οισει A: -ουσα Ursinus, -οισα
Schneidewin, -οισι Bergk

### 534 Schol. Ap. Rhod. 1. 211–15c (p. 26 Wendel)

τὴν δὲ Ὠρείθυιαν Σιμωνίδης ἀπὸ Βριλησσοῦ (Naeke: βριλισσοῦ
L, Ἰλισσοῦ (e schol. d) H, om. P) φησιν ἁρπαγεῖσαν ἐπὶ τὴν Σαρ-
πηδονίαν πέτραν τῆς Θρᾴκης ἐνεχθῆναι.... ἡ δὲ Ὠρείθυια
Ἐρεχθέως θυγάτηρ, ἣν ἐξ Ἀττικῆς ἁρπάσας ὁ Βορέας ἤγαγεν εἰς
Θρᾴκην κἀκεῖσε συνελθὼν ἔτεκε Ζήτην καὶ Κάλαϊν, ὡς Σιμωνίδης
ἐν τῇ ναυμαχίᾳ.

### 535 Himer. or. 47. 14 (p. 194s. Colonna)

λύσει δὲ τῆς νεὼς ᾠδὴ τὰ πείσματα, ἣν ἱερὸς προσᾴδουσιν
Ἀθηναῖοι χορός, καλοῦντες ἐπὶ τὸ σκάφος τὸν ἄνεμον παρεῖναί τε
αὐτὸν καὶ τῇ θεωρίδι συμπέτεσθαι. ὁ δὲ ἐπιγνοὺς οἶμαι τὴν οἰκείαν
(cod. R: Κείαν cod. A) ᾠδήν ἣν Σιμωνίδης αὐτῷ προσῇσε μετὰ
τὴν <κατὰ> θάλατταν <μάχην> (em. Edmonds), ἀκολουθεῖ μὲν
εὐθὺς τοῖς μέλεσι, πολὺς δὲ πνεύσας κατὰ πρύμνης οὔριος ἐλαύνει
τὴν ὁλκάδα τῷ πνεύματι.

# SIMONIDES

In the antistrophe the corresponding line is

> (b) they turn aside the Death-goddesses.

Alcman[1] ... put a spondee in the fourth position (of a catalectic trimeter) ... according to Heliodorus, who says Simonides often does this.

[1] See fr. 14.

**534** Scholiast on Apollonius of Rhodes ('Zetes and Calais, sons of Boreas')

Simonides says that Orithyia was carried off from Brilessus[1] and taken to the Sarpedonian rock in Thrace.... Orithyia was daughter of Erechtheus, and Boreas carried her off from Attica, took her to Thrace, had intercourse with her there and fathered Zetes and Calais, as Simonides tells in 'The Sea-battle'.[2]

[1] Mountain north-east of Athens.    [2] For the help given to the Athenians by Boreas at the battle of Artemisium see Hdt. 7. 189.

**535** Himerius, *Oration* 47

The cables of the ship[1] will be untied by an ode, the ode which a holy chorus of Athenians chants, summoning the wind to the boat, bidding it be present and fly in company with the sacred vessel; and the wind, doubtless recognising its very own ode[2] which Simonides sang to it after the sea-battle, at once obeys the music and blowing hard astern drives the ship with its blast on a prosperous voyage.

[1] The vessel represented in the Panathenaic procession.
[2] 'The Cean ode', according to one ms.

# GREEK LYRIC

12. 32–33 (p. 98 Colonna)

νῦν γὰρ ποιητικῶς ἐθέλων καλέσαι τὸν ἄνεμον, εἶτα οὐκ ἔχων ποιητικὴν ἀφεῖναι φωνήν, ἐκ τῆς Κείας (Wernsdorf: οἰκείας codd.) μούσης προσειπεῖν ἐθέλω τὸν ἄνεμον. . . . ἁπαλὸς δ' ὑπὲρ κυμάτων χεόμενος πορφυρᾶ σχίζει περὶ τὴν πρῶραν τὰ κύματα.

cf. 10. 22 (p. 92 C.) καὶ σχίσαι Ζεφύρῳ πορφύροντα περὶ τὴν πρῶραν τὰ κύματα.


## Η ΕΝ ΣΑΛΑΜΙΝΙ ΝΑΥΜΑΧΙΑ

**536** *Sud.* Σ 439 (iv 361 Adler) s.v. Σιμωνίδης

καὶ γέγραπται αὐτῷ . . . , ἡ δ' ἐν Σαλαμῖνι (sc. ναυμαχία) μελικῶς.


## ΚΑΤΕΥΧΑΙ

**537** Schol. Hom. *Od.* 6. 164 (i 308 Dindorf)

λέγοι δ' ἂν πολὺν λαὸν οὐ τὸν ἴδιον στόλον ἀλλὰ τὸν Ἑλληνικόν, ὅτ' ἀφηγούμενος εἰς Δῆλον ἦλθε Μενέλαος σὺν Ὀδυσσεῖ ἐπὶ τὰς Ἀνίου θυγατέρας αἳ καὶ Οἰνότροποι ἐκαλοῦντο. ἡ δ' ἱστορία καὶ παρὰ Σιμωνίδῃ ἐν ταῖς Κατευχαῖς.

---

[1] Or 'Curses': the character of the work is not known.
[2] 'Turners into wine': these princesses of Delos could change what-

# SIMONIDES

*Oration* 12

For now I wish to summon the wind[1] in poetic fashion, but not having the ability to utter poetic words I wish to address the wind in accordance with the Cean Muse: ... and spreading gently over the waves it cleaves the surging waves around the prow.

[1] To blow favourably for Flavian's voyage.

## THE SEA-BATTLE AT SALAMIS

**536** *Suda,* Simonides (1st notice)

He composed ... 'The Sea-battle at Salamis' in lyric metre.[1]

[1] See test 1, n. 10: the poem was probably in elegiacs, not in lyric metre. For Plutarch's allusion to it and other possible references see fr. eleg. 1 (+2+3) below. See also Lobel, *Ox. Pap.* xxii 67.

## PRAYERS[1]

**537** Scholiast on Homer, *Odyssey* ('For I went once to Delos also, and a great company followed me.')

By 'a great company' Odysseus will mean not his own contingent but the Greek force on the occasion when Menelaus along with Odysseus led it to Delos to fetch the daughters of Anius, also called Oenotropi.[2] The story is also in Simonides in his *Prayers*.

ever they touched into grain, wine, or oil. Agamemnon on his way to Troy carried them off to provision his army, but they appealed to Dionysus and were changed into doves (Lycophron, *Alex.* 570 ff., Ov. *Met.* 13. 650 ff.).

# GREEK LYRIC

**538** Schol. Plut. ex *Etymol.* Luperci (v. Paton, *C.R.* 26, 1912, 9)

ἐκ τοῦ ζ' τῶν Λουπέρκου· . . . Σιμωνίδης ἐν Κατευχαῖς·

χρὴ κορυδαλλίσι
πάσῃσιν ἐμφῦναι λόφον.

cf. Plut. *de cap. ex inimicis util.* 10, *praec. ger. reip.* 14, *vit. Timol.* 37. 1, Apostol. *Cent.* xiii 94

1 -ίσι, -ῆσι, -οῖς codd. Plut., -αῖς schol.   2 -ησιν, -ησι, -αισι, -αις, πᾶσι codd. Plut., -αις schol.   λόφον ἐγγενέσθαι Plut.

## ΔΙΘΥΡΑΜΒΟΙ : ΜΕΜΝΩΝ

**539** Str. 15. 3. 2 (iii 248 Kramer)

λέγεται γὰρ δὴ (sc. τὰ Σοῦσα) καὶ κτίσμα Τιθωνοῦ τοῦ Μέμνονος πατρός . . . · ἡ δ' ἀκρόπολις ἐκαλεῖτο Μεμνόνιον . . . · ταφῆναι δὲ λέγεται Μέμνων περὶ Πάλτον τῆς Συρίας παρὰ Βαδᾶν ποταμόν, ὡς εἴρηκε Σιμωνίδης ἐν Μέμνονι διθυράμβῳ τῶν Δηλιακῶν.

## ΣΥΜΜΙΚΤΑ

**540** Schol. Ap. Rhod. 1. 763s. (p. 66 Wendel) (= Simon. genealog. 8 F 3 Jacoby, *F.Gr.H.* i 159)

Μινυήιος ὁ Ἰώλκιος· τὴν γὰρ Ἰωλκὸν Μινύαι ᾤκουν, ὥς φησι Σιμωνίδης ἐν Συμμίκτοις.

# SIMONIDES

**538** Scholiast on Plutarch

From book 6 of Lupercus[1]: ... Simonides in his *Prayers* has

Every lark must have its crest.[2]

[1] Grammarian of 3rd c. A.D.; wrote *On Genders*: Sim. used a fem. noun for 'lark'.  [2] Plutarch thrice attributes the saying to Sim.; exact reading uncertain.

## DITHYRAMBS[1]

**539**                               MEMNON

Strabo, *Geography*

For Susa[2] is said to have been founded by Tithonus, father of Memnon ...; and its acropolis was called Memnonion ...; Memnon is said to have been buried near Paltus in Syria by the river Badas, as Simonides says in his dithyramb *Memnon,* part of the *Deliaca.*[3]

[1] For Sim.'s 56 dithyrambic victories see epigr. xxvii ( = test. 11).  [2] Persian capital.   [3] Perhaps a collection of his poems composed for (and preserved in ?) Delos.

## MISCELLANEOUS WORKS

**540** Scholiast on Apollonius of Rhodes ('Phrixus the Minyan')

'Minyan' is Iolcian, for Iolcus[1] was inhabited by Minyans, as Simonides says in his *Miscellaneous Works.*

[1] Thessalian city from which the Argonauts sailed. The Minyans were a prehistoric tribe associated especially with Orchomenus in Boeotia.

## INCERTI LOCI

**541** P.Oxy. 2432

τό τ]ε καλὸν κρίνει τό τ᾿ αἰσχρόν· εἰ δέ
. . . κ]ακαγορεῖ τις ἄθυρον [σ]τόμα
περι]φέρ[ω]ν, ὁ μὲν καπνὸς ἀτελής, ὁ δέ[
χρυ]σὸς οὐ μιαίνετ[α]ι,
5 ἁ δ᾿] ἀλάθε[ι]α παγκρατής·
ἀλλ᾿] ὀλίγοις ἀρετὰν ἔδωκεν ἔ[χειν θεός
ἐς τ]έλος, οὐ γὰρ ἐλαφρὸν ἐσθλ[ὸν ἔμμεν·
ἢ γ]ὰρ ἀέκοντά νιν βιᾶται
κέρ]δος ἀμάχητον ἢ δολοπλ[όκου
10 με]γασθενὴς οἶστρος Ἀφροδίτ[ας
ἀρ]τίθαλοί τε φιλονικίαι.
ὧι δ]ὲ μὴ δι᾿ αἰῶνος ὁσίαν
πάρεστιν ἐλ]θεῖν κέλευθον,
           ]ος ἐς τὸ δυνατὸν.[
15         ]αγκυλαν[
      ε]ὐθὺς ἀπο[
        ]θέοντι· το[
      ] . ντρο[
20       ]α . [
      ] . ο[

suppl. Lobel praeter   2 κακ. Treu, Gentili   6 fin. Treu,
Bowra   11 Treu   12s. Page (sed 'θεῖν, 'vix ἐλθεῖν')
7 ἔμμεν vel ἔμμεναι

# SIMONIDES

**541** Oxyrhynchus papyrus (*c.* 1 A.D.)[1]

... distinguishes[2] between the noble and the base; and if someone defames him, carrying around a mouth unbarred, the smoke[3] is ineffectual, and the gold is not tarnished, and truth is all-powerful. But only to a few does god grant that they have virtue to the end; for it is not easy to be good[4]: either irresistible greed for profit or the powerful gadfly of wile-weaving Aphrodite or vigorous ambitions coerce a man against his will. But he who is unable to travel the path of righteousness throughout his life[5] ... as far as possible ... crooked[6] ... a just man ... at once ...

[1] Attributed to Simonides by most scholars because of similarity with 542; Lloyd-Jones (*C.R.* 11, 1961, 19) and Bowra (*Hermes* 91, 1963, 257 ff.) argued for Bacchylides.    [2] The subject of the verb may be the man whom Sim. finds acceptable.    [3] I.e. the malicious talk.    [4] So Pittacus: cf. 542.    [5] Lobel suggested that the sense of the next words was, 'still, if he is as good as he can be, (he) may be termed virtuous.'    [6] Perhaps '(avoiding the) crooked (path)'.

**542** Plat. *Protag.* 339a–346d

λέγει γάρ που Σιμωνίδης πρὸς Σκόπαν τοῦ Κρέοντος υἱὸν τοῦ
Θετταλοῦ ὅτι

1  ἄνδρ' ἀγαθὸν μὲν ἀλαθέως γενέσθαι
   χαλεπὸν χερσίν τε καὶ ποσὶ καὶ νόῳ
       τετράγωνον ἄνευ ψόγου τετυγμένον·

*desunt vii versus*

11  οὐδέ μοι ἐμμελέως τὸ Πιττάκειον
    νέμεται, καίτοι σοφοῦ παρὰ φωτὸς εἰ-
        ρημένον· χαλεπὸν φάτ' ἐσθλὸν ἔμμεναι.
    θεὸς ἂν μόνος τοῦτ' ἔχοι γέρας, ἄνδρα δ' οὐκ
15      ἔστι μὴ οὐ κακὸν ἔμμεναι,
    ὃν ἀμήχανος συμφορὰ καθέλῃ·
    πράξας γὰρ εὖ πᾶς ἀνὴρ ἀγαθός,
    κακὸς δ' εἰ κακῶς [
        [ἐπὶ πλεῖστον δὲ καὶ ἄριστοί εἰσιν
20      [οὓς ἂν οἱ θεοὶ φιλῶσιν.]

    τοὔνεκεν οὔ ποτ' ἐγὼ τὸ μὴ γενέσθαι
    δυνατὸν διζήμενος κενεὰν ἐς ἄ-
        πρακτον ἐλπίδα μοῖραν αἰῶνος βαλέω,
    πανάμωμον ἄνθρωπον, εὐρυεδέος ὅσοι
25      καρπὸν αἰνύμεθα χθονός·
    ἐπὶ δ' ὑμὶν εὑρὼν ἀπαγγελέω.
    πάντας δ' ἐπαίνημι καὶ φιλέω,

16 Bergk: ὃν ἂν codd.      17 Hermann: μὲν γὰρ codd.      24
εὐρυεδοῦς Plato, -οδοῦς Plut. codd. plerique      26 ἔπειθ' ὑμῖν (bis)
codd.: ἐπὶ δ' ὕμμιν Bergk

# SIMONIDES

**542** Plato, *Protagoras*[1]

For Simonides says somewhere to Scopas, son of the Thessalian Creon:

It is difficult for a man to be truly good, four-square in hands, in feet and in mind, fashioned without flaw....

Nor does that saying of Pittacus[2] ring true to me, although it was spoken by a wise man: he said that it was difficult to be good. Only a god could have that privilege: a man cannot avoid being bad,[3] when he is in the grip of irresistible misfortune. When his luck is good, any man is good; when it is bad he is bad; (and for the most part they are best whom the gods love).

And so I shall never throw away my span of life on an empty, vain hope in quest of the impossible, the completely blameless man among all of us who win the fruit of the wide earth. When I find one I shall tell you. No, I commend and love any man who

---

[1] Protagoras and Socrates discuss virtue by examining Sim.'s poem. Each claims to know it well: Prot. could quote it all if necessary, Socr. has studied it closely. In vv. 4–10, which are not quoted in the dialogue, Sim. will have named Scopas, perhaps complimenting him on the success he has achieved in life. The end of stanza two and the opening of stanza four are given in paraphrase only and are marked above by parentheses.     [2] Ruler of Mytilene (590–580 B.C.) and one of the Seven Sages.     [3] 'Good' and 'bad' carry their Homeric overtones of 'noble, successful, great' and the opposite.

ἑκὼν ὅστις ἔρδῃ
μηδὲν αἰσχρόν· ἀνάγκᾳ
30 δ᾽ οὐδὲ θεοὶ μάχονται.

[
[
[οὐκ εἰμὶ φιλόψογος, ἐπεὶ ἔμοιγε ἐξαρκεῖ
ὃς ἂν μὴ κακὸς ᾖ] μηδ᾽ ἄγαν ἀπάλαμνος εἰ-
35    δὼς γ᾽ ὀνησίπολιν δίκαν,
ὑγιὴς ἀνήρ· οὐδὲ μή μιν ἐγὼ
μωμήσομαι· τῶν γὰρ ἠλιθίων
ἀπείρων γενέθλα.
πάντα τοι καλά, τοῖσίν
40 τ᾽ αἰσχρὰ μὴ μέμεικται.

cf. Diog. Laert. 1. 76, *Sud.* Π 1658, Aristot. *Eth. Nic.* 1. 11. 1100b,
*Metaph.* A 2. 982b, Plut. *tranq. anim.* 10, *rat. am.* 14, *quaest. conv.*
9. 14. 2, Plat. *Legg.* 7. 818b, Stob. *Ecl.* 1. 4. 2c (v. etiam Page,
*P.M.G.* p. 283)

36 Bergk: οὐ μὴν ἐγὼ codd.


**543** D. H. *Comp.* 26 (vi 140ss. Radermacher)

ἐκ δὲ τῆς μελικῆς τὰ Σιμωνίδεια ταῦτα· γέγραπται δὲ κατὰ
διαστολὰς οὐχ ὧν Ἀριστοφάνης ἢ ἄλλος τις κατεσκεύασε κώλων
ἀλλ᾽ ὧν ὁ πεζὸς λόγος ἀπαιτεῖ. πρόσεχε δὴ τῷ μέλει καὶ ἀναγίνω-
σκε κατὰ διαστολάς, καὶ εὖ ἴσθ᾽ ὅτι λήσεταί σε ὁ ῥυθμὸς τῆς ᾠδῆς
καὶ οὐχ ἕξεις συμβαλεῖν οὔτε στροφὴν οὔτε ἀντίστροφον οὔτ᾽ ἐπῳ-
δόν, ἀλλὰ φανήσεταί σοι λόγος εἷς εἰρόμενος. ἔστι δὲ ἡ διὰ πελά-
γους φερομένη Δανάη τὰς ἑαυτῆς ἀποδυρομένη τύχας·

        ὅτε λάρνακι
ἐν δαιδαλέᾳ

of his own will does nothing shameful: against necessity not even the gods fight.

(... I am not a fault-finder: I am satisfied with the man who is not bad[4]) nor too shiftless, one who understands the justice that helps his city, a sound man. I shall not find fault with him; for the generation of fools is numberless. All things are fair in which the base is not mingled.

[4] Perhaps 'not bad in understanding' with e.g. νόον added in the text.

**543** Dionysius of Halicarnassus, *On Literary Composition*

From lyric poetry come the following lines of Simonides. They are written out not in the metrical divisions established by Aristophanes or someone else but in the divisions demanded by prose.[1] Pay attention to the song and read it according to divisions, and take my word for it that the poem's rhythm will escape you: you will be unable to make out strophe, antistrophe or epode and will think it rather one continuous piece of prose. It is Danae being carried over the sea and bewailing her fate[2]:

... When in the intricately-carved chest the

[1] The colometry given here is that of Page, *P.M.G.*; see also R. Führer, *Gott. Nachr.* 4 (1976) 111–64, M. L. West, *B.I.C.S.* 28 (1981) 30 ff. Metre and text are often uncertain.    [2] She and her infant son Perseus had been put to sea in a chest by her father Acrisius because of a prophecy that his grandson would kill him.

ἄνεμός τέ μιν πνέων
κινηθεῖσά τε λίμνα δείματι
5 ἔρειπεν, οὐκ ἀδιάντοισι παρειαῖς
ἀμφί τε Περσέι βάλλε φίλαν χέρα
εἶπέν τ᾽· ὦ τέκος, οἷον ἔχω πόνον·

σὺ δ᾽ ἀωτεῖς, γαλαθηνῷ
δ᾽ ἤτορι κνοώσσεις
10 ἐν ἀτερπέι δούρατι χαλκεογόμφῳ
νυκτί <τ᾽ ἀ>λαμπέι
κυανέῳ τε δνόφῳ σταλείς·
ἄχναν δ᾽ ὕπερθε τεᾶν κομᾶν
βαθεῖαν παριόντος
15 κύματος οὐκ ἀλέγεις, οὐδ᾽ ἀνέμου
φθόγγον, πορφυρέᾳ
κείμενος ἐν χλανίδι, πρόσωπον καλόν.
εἰ δέ τοι δεινὸν τό γε δεινὸν ἦν,
καί κεν ἐμῶν ῥημάτων
20 λεπτὸν ὑπεῖχες οὖας.

κέλομαι <δ᾽>, εὗδε βρέφος,
εὑδέτω δὲ πόντος, εὑδέτω <δ᾽> ἄμετρον κακόν·
μεταβουλία δέ τις φανείη,
Ζεῦ πάτερ, ἐκ σέο·
25 ὅττι δὲ θαρσαλέον ἔπος εὔχομαι
ἢ νόσφι δίκας,
σύγγνωθί μοι.

cf. Athen. 9. 396e (ὦ τέκος — κνώσσεις) = fr. 553

438

# SIMONIDES

blasts of wind and the troubled water prostrated her
in fear, with streaming cheeks she put her loving
arm about Perseus and said, 'My child, what suffer-
ing is mine! But you sleep, and with babyish heart
slumber in the dismal boat with its brazen bolts,
sent forth in the unlit night and dark blue murk.
You pay no attention to the deep spray above your
hair as the wave passes by nor to the sound of the
wind, lying in your purple blanket, a lovely face. If
this danger were danger to you, why, you would
turn your tiny ear to my words. Sleep, my baby,
I tell you; and let the sea sleep, and let our vast
trouble sleep. Let some change of heart appear from
you, father Zeus. If anything in my prayer is auda-
cious or unjust, pardon me.'

---

3 Schneidewin: τε μὴν PM    τ᾽ ἐμῆι V    4 Brunck: δὲ codd. δεί-
ματι VP    δεῖμα M    5 ἔρειπεν MV    ἔριπεν P Thiersch: οὖτ᾽
codd.    7 τέκος Athen.    τέκνον Dion.    8 Casaubon: οὐδ᾽ αυταις
ἐγαλαθηνωδει θει PV (ἀγαλαθηνώδει. . . .    M)    σὺ δ᾽ αὖτε εἰς γαλα-
θηνῶι δ᾽ ἦτορι Athen.    9 κνοώσσεις PV    κνώσσεις M, Athen.
10 -γόμφω δε codd.    11 Gentili: ν. λαμπεῖ codd.    12 Bergk:
ταδ᾽ εις codd.    ταθείς Schneidewin    13 Page: αὐλέαν PV
αὐλαίαν M    ὕπερθεν codd.    17 π. κ. MV    π. κ. πρόσωπον P
18 Sylburg: ἦι P    ἢ M    ἢ V    20 Stephanus: λεπτῶν codd.
21 suppl. Bergk    22 suppl. Thiersch    23 μαιτ βουλία P
μαιτ βουλίου M    ματαιοβουλία V    25 Mehlhorn: ὅτι δὴ codd.
26 Victorius: ηνοφι δίκας P    ἢν οφειδίας MV    κνόφι δίκας cod. Guelf.

# GREEK LYRIC

**544** *Et. Gen.* (p. 38 Calame) = *Et. Mag.* 597. 14

νάκος, νάκη· τὸ αἴγειον δέρμα· κωδία καὶ κώδιον τὸ προβάτειον. οὐκ ἄρα τὸ ἐν Κόλχοις νάκος ῥητέον· κακῶς οὖν Σιμωνίδης φησὶ

νάκης.

*Et. Gen.* : νάκος *Et. Mag.*

**545** Schol. Eur. *Med.* 19 (ii 144 Schwartz) (cod. B)

ὅτι δὲ καὶ ἐβασίλευσε (sc. Μήδεια) Κορίνθου ἱστοροῦσιν Εὔμηλος (fr. 3B Davies) καὶ Σιμωνίδης λέγων οὕτως·

ὁ δ' ἵκετ' ἐς Κόρινθον, οὐ Μαγνησίαν
ναῖ', ἀλόχῳ δὲ Κολχίδι ξυνέστιος
†θράνου† Λεχαίου τ' ἄνασσε.

cf. schol. ad v. 9

1 Hermann, Elmsley: οὐδὲ κάτ' εἰς Κ. cod.      2 Schwartz: ναῖεν
ἀλόχου cod.      Elmsley: συνάστεος cod.

**546** Schol. Eur. *Med.* 2 (ii 141 Schwartz)

τὰς Συμπληγάδας ὁ Σιμωνίδης

συνορμάδας

φησίν.

ita cod. B: συναρβώδας cod. A

**547** Schol. Pind. *Pyth.* 4. 451 (ii 160 Drachmann)

καὶ γὰρ καὶ παρὰ Σιμωνίδῃ ἐστὶν ἡ ἱστορία, ὅτι περὶ ἐσθῆτος ἠγωνίσαντο (sc. οἱ Ἀργοναῦται).

# SIMONIDES

**544** *Etymologicum Genuinum*

νάκος, νάκη: goatskin, whereas κωδία and κώδιον are sheepskin. So the fleece at Colchis[1] should not be called νάκος.[2] Simonides, then, is wrong to use νάκης,[3]

fleece.

[1] I.e. the 'golden fleece' sought by Jason.    [2] As e.g. by Pind. *Pyth.* 4. 68!    [3] Or νάκος; see also 576.

**545** Scholiast on Euripides, *Medea*

That Medea was also queen of Corinth we are told by Eumelus[1] and by Simonides, who says[2]

And he (Jason) came to Corinth — he did not dwell in Magnesia[3] — and sharing his hearth with his Colchian wife ruled over . . . and Lechaeum.[4]

[1] 8th c. Corinthian poet, wrote *Corinthian History*.    [2] Text very uncertain.    [3] Region near Iolcus.    [4] Harbour of Corinth.

**546** Scholiast on Euripides, *Medea*

Simonides calls the Symplegades[1]

the colliding rocks.

[1] The Clashing Rocks of the Bosporus.

**547** Scholiast on Pindar, *Pythian* 4. 253

Simonides too tells that the Argonauts competed[1] with a garment as the prize.

[1] In an athletic contest on Lemnos.

# GREEK LYRIC

**548** Argum. Eur. *Med.* (ii 137 Schwartz)

Φερεκύδης (fr. 113ab Jacoby) δὲ καὶ Σιμωνίδης φασὶν ὡς ἡ Μήδεια ἀνεψήσασα τὸν Ἰάσονα νέον ποιήσειε.

cf. schol. Ar. *Eq.* 1321

**549** Schol. Eur. *Or.* 46 (i 102 Schwartz)

φανερὸν ὅτι ἐν Ἄργει ἡ σκηνὴ τοῦ δράματος ὑπόκειται. Ὅμηρος δὲ ἐν Μυκήναις φησὶ τὰ βασίλεια Ἀγαμέμνονος, Στησίχορος δὲ (216) καὶ Σιμωνίδης ἐν Λακεδαίμονι.

**550** Plut. *vit. Thes.* 17. 4s. (i 1. 14 Ziegler)

τότε δὲ τοῦ Θησέως τὸν πατέρα θαρσύνοντος καὶ μεγαληγοροῦντος ὡς χειρώσεται τὸν Μινώταυρον ἔδωκεν ἕτερον ἱστίον λευκὸν τῷ κυβερνήτῃ κελεύσας ὑποστρέφοντα σῳζομένου τοῦ Θησέως ἐπάρασθαι τὸ λευκόν, εἰ δὲ μή, τῷ μέλανι πλεῖν καὶ ἀποσημαίνειν τὸ πάθος. ὁ δὲ Σιμωνίδης οὐ λευκόν φησιν εἶναι τὸ δοθὲν ὑπὸ τοῦ Αἰγέως ἀλλὰ

(a) φοινίκεον ἱστίον ὑγρῷ
    πεφυρμένον ἄνθεϊ πρίνου
    ἐριθαλέος,

καὶ τοῦτο τῆς σωτηρίας αὐτῶν ποιήσασθαι σημεῖον. ἐκυβέρνα δὲ τὴν ναῦν

(b) Ἀμαρσυάδας Φέρεκλος,

ὥς φησι Σιμωνίδης.

(a) 2 πρινὸς ἄνθει codd.: πρίνου Méziriac, transpos. Schneidewin 3 Bergk: -θάλλου codd.

**551** Schol. Soph. *Aj.* 740 (p. 64 Papageorgiu)

τί δ' ἐστὶ χρείας (τῆσδ' ὑπεσπανισμένον); οἷον τί σοι λείπει ὅπερ σπάνιόν ἐστι πρὸς τὴν χρείαν τὴν νῦν; ἐσπάνιζε δὲ τὸ ἄμεινον

442

# SIMONIDES

**548** Scholiast on Euripides, *Medea*

Pherecydes[1] and Simonides say that Medea boiled Jason and made him young again.

[1] Athenian genealogist, 5th c. B.C.

**549** Scholiast on Euripides, *Orestes*

It is clear that the play is set in Argos. But Homer puts Agamemnon's palace in Mycenae, Stesichorus (216) and Simonides in Sparta.

**550** Plutarch, *Life of Theseus*

But then Theseus cheered up his father and boasted that he would defeat the Minotaur; so his father gave the helmsman a second sail, white this time, telling him to hoist the white if he were returning with Theseus safe, otherwise to sail with the black and so indicate the disaster. But Simonides says that the sail given by Aegeus was not white but

(a) a crimson sail dyed with the moist flower of the sturdy holm-oak;

and this was to be the signal of their safe return. The ship's helmsman was

(b) Phereclus, son of Amarsyas,

according to Simonides.[1]

[1] Philochorus (fr. 111 Jacoby) said the helmsman was Nausithous of Salamis.

**551** Scholiast on Sophocles, *Ajax*

'What has been left lacking in this urgent business?' I.e., what is missing for you that is lacking in the present business? By 'lacking' is meant that it would have been

# GREEK LYRIC

εἶναι πρὸ ὀλίγου αὐτὸν παραγεγονέναι. καὶ ἐν Σιμωνίδῃ ἐπὶ τοῦ πρὸς Αἰγέα ἀγγέλου πεμφθέντος·

βιότου κέ σε μᾶλλον ὄνασα πρότερος ἐλθών.

Hermann: βιότω καί σε codd.

**551A** 'Apollod.' *Bibl.* 3 (v. A. Papadopulos-Kerameus, *Rh. Mus.* 46 (1891) 184, A. Lorenzoni, *Mus. Crit.* 15–17 (1980–82) 51 s.)

συστρατευσάμενος δὲ (sc. Θησεὺς) ἐπὶ 'Αμαζόνας Ἡρακλεῖ ἥρπασεν 'Αντιόπην, ὡς δέ τινες Μελανίππην, Σιμωνίδης (cod. -ίτης) δὲ Ἱππολύτην.

**552** Schol. Theocr. 1. 65/66a (p. 56 Wendel)

ἡ δὲ Αἴτνη ὄρος ἀπὸ Αἴτνης τῆς Οὐρανοῦ καὶ Γῆς, ὥς φησιν Ἄλκιμος ἐν τῷ περὶ Σικελίας (*F.Gr.H.* III B 560 fr. 5 Jacoby). Σιμωνίδης δὲ Αἴτνην φησὶ κρῖναι Ἥφαιστον καὶ Δήμητραν περὶ τῆς χώρας ἐρίσαντας.

**553** Athen. 9. 396e (ii 365 Kaibel)

Σιμωνίδης δ' ἐπὶ τοῦ Περσέως τὴν Δανάην ποιεῖ λέγουσαν· ὦ τέκος — γαλαθηνῷ δ' ἤτορι κνοώσσεις (543). καὶ ἐν ἄλλοις ἐπ' 'Αρχεμόρου εἴρηκεν·

<Εὐρυδίκας>
ἰοστεφάνου γλυκεῖαν ἐδάκρυσαν
ψυχὰν ἀποπνέοντα γαλαθηνὸν τέκος.

1 suppl. Bergk

444

better if he had arrived a little earlier.  Simonides says in the case of the messenger sent to Aegeus,[1]

I would have given you a benefit greater than life, if I had come sooner.[2]

[1] Now dead, after the black sail had indicated Theseus' death.
[2] Text uncertain.

**551A** 'Apollodorus', *Library*

Theseus, making a joint expedition with Heracles against the Amazons, carried off Antiope; some give her name as Melanippe, and Simonides says Hippolyte.

**552** Scholiast on Theocritus ('Thyrsis of Etna')

Etna is a mountain in Sicily, named after Etna, daughter of Heaven and Earth, according to Alcimus in his work on Sicily.  Simonides says that Etna decided between Hephaestus and Demeter when they quarrelled over possession of the land.

**553** Athenaeus, *Scholars at Dinner* (on γαλαθηνός, 'suckling')

Simonides makes Danae say of Perseus, 'My child, ... and with childish[1] heart you slumber' (543). In other lines he says of Archemorus,[2]

they wept for the suckling babe of violet-crowned Eurydice as he breathed out his sweet soul.

[1] Lit. 'suckling'.      [2] A. (or Opheltes) was infant son of Lycurgus, king of Nemea, and his wife Eurydice. He was killed by a snake while left unattended by his nurse Hypsipyle. The Nemean Games were established in his honour.

**554** Schol. Pind. *Ol.* 7. 42b (i 210s. Drachmann)

'Αστυδαμείας· ... ἦν δὲ Φύλαντος θυγάτηρ. τινὲς δὲ ἐξ
'Αντιγόνης αὐτῷ Τληπόλεμόν φασιν· ἐνταῦθα δὲ 'Αμύντορος αὐτήν
φησιν ὁ Πίνδαρος, Ἡσίοδος δὲ (fr. 232 M.-W.) καὶ Σιμωνίδης 'Ορ-
μένου.

**555** Athen. 11. 490ef (iii 81 Kaibel)

καὶ Σιμωνίδης δὲ τὰς Πλειάδας Πελειάδας εἴρηκεν ἐν τούτοις·

δίδωτι δ' εὖ παῖς Ἑρμᾶς ἐναγώνιος
Μαιάδος οὐρείας ἑλικοβλεφάρου·
ἔτικτε δ' Ἄτλας ἑπτὰ ἰοπλοκάμων φιλᾶν θυγατρῶν
τάνδ' ἔξοχον εἶδος, <ὅσ>αι καλέονται
5 Πελειάδες οὐράνιαι.

cf. schol. Pind. *Nem.* 2. 17c, schol. Lycophr. 219, Eust. *Od.* 1713. 3

1 Page: δευτες Athen.   2 scholl. Pind. et Lyc.: Μαίας εὐπλοκά-
μοιο παῖς Athen.   3 τίκτε ci. Wilamowitz   Musurus: ἐπιτα
Athen.   Schneidewin: -τέρων Athen.   4 Page: τάν γ' Athen.
suppl. Page: ἀγι Athen.

**556** Philodem. *Piet.* (p. 37 Gomperz)

Εὐριπίδης [(*Ion* 1), ... Σ]ιμωνίδης [δὲ τὸν] οὐρανὸν ἐ[πὶ τῶν]
ὤμων [ . . . . . . . . Ἡσίο]δ[ος δὲ (*Theog.* 517).

# SIMONIDES

**554** Scholiast on Pindar, *Ol.* 7. 24 f. ('on the mother's side the Rhodians are from Astydamia, so that they are of the family of Amyntor')[1]

Astydamia was daughter of Phylas; some say that Tlepolemus was his son by Antigone. Here Pindar calls Astydamia daughter of Amyntor, whereas Hesiod and Simonides make her daughter of Ormenus.

[1] Pindar makes Tlepolemus, founder of Rhodes, son of Heracles and Astydamia.

**555** Athenaeus, *Scholars at Dinner*

Simonides also calls the Pleiads Peleiades[1] in these lines:

and it[2] is deservedly given by Hermes, lord of contests, son of mountain[3] Maias of the lively eyes: Atlas fathered her, outstanding in beauty among his seven dear violet-haired daughters who are called the heavenly Peleiades.

[1] Doves.    [2] The victor's prize?    [3] The scholiast on Pindar ('the mountain Peleiades') says Sim. used the epithet since she bore Hermes on Mt. Cyllene.

**556** Philodemus, *Piety* (on Atlas)

Euripides (*Ion* 1), ... Simonides (represents him as holding) the sky on his shoulders, Hesiod (*Theog.* 517).

**557** 'Longinus' *de subl.* 15. 7 (p. 23 Russell)

ἄκρως δὲ καὶ ὁ Σοφοκλῆς ἐπὶ τοῦ θνήσκοντος Οἰδίπου καὶ ἑαυτὸν μετὰ διοσημείας τινὸς θάπτοντος πεφάντασται, καὶ κατὰ τὸν ἀπόπλουν τῶν Ἑλλήνων ἐπὶ τἀχιλλέως προφαινομένου τοῖς ἀναγομένοις ὑπὲρ τοῦ τάφου, ἣν οὐκ οἶδ᾽ εἴ τις ὄψιν ἐναργέστερον εἰδωλοποίησε Σιμωνίδου· πάντα δ᾽ ἀμήχανον παρατίθεσθαι.

**558** Schol. Ap. Rhod. 4. 814–15a (p. 293 Wendel)

ὅτι δὲ Ἀχιλλεὺς εἰς τὸ Ἠλύσιον πεδίον παραγενόμενος ἔγημε Μήδειαν πρῶτος Ἴβυκος (fr. 291) εἴρηκε, μεθ᾽ ὃν Σιμωνίδης.

**559** Schol. B Hom. *Il.* 10. 252 (iii 436 Dindorf)

Ὁμήρου εἰπόντος· ἐννεακαίδεκα μέν μοι ἰῆς ἐκ νηδύος ἦσαν (*Il.* 24. 496), Σιμωνίδης φησί·

> καὶ σὺ μὲν εἴκοσι παίδων
> μᾶτερ ἔλλαθι.

cf. Porphyr. *quaest. hom.* i 148 Schrader, schol. Theocr. 15. 139

incert. utrum ἔλλαθι an ἴλαθι cod.

**560** *Et. Mag. Gen.* 436, *Et. Sym.* 04/08, *Et. Mag. Auct.* 810 (p. 278s. Lasserre-Livadaras)

Ἀλέρα· Ἐλάρα

### Ἐλάρας γενεά·

οὕτως παρὰ Σιμωνίδῃ ἡ Ἐλάρα, Ἀλέρα δὲ παρὰ Πινδάρῳ, οἷον· Ἀλέρας υἱόν (fr. 294 Snell: cf. Paean XIIIb 3)

# SIMONIDES

**557** 'Longinus', *On Sublimity*

Sophocles too has excellently visualised the scene of
Oedipus dying and giving himself burial amid divine por-
tents,[1] and also that of Achilles at the time of the Greek
departure from Troy, when he appears above his tomb as
they are putting out to sea[2]; and yet I suspect that no one
represented that vision more vividly than Simonides —
but it is impossible to quote every example.

[1] *Oed. Col.* 1586 ff.      [2] Probably in his *Polyxena* (see Radt,
*T.G.F.* iv 403); Achilles' ghost demanded the sacrifice of Polyxena
(Ibyc. 307).

**558** Scholiast on Apollonius of Rhodes

Ibycus was the first to say that Achilles married Medea
when he reached the Elysian plain, and Simonides fol-
lowed him.

**559** Scholiast on Homer, *Iliad*

Homer said, 'I had nineteen sons born from one womb',[1]
but Simonides says,

and you, mother of twenty children,[2] be gracious.

[1] Priam, with reference to Hecuba.      [2] So Theocr. 15. 139.

**560** *Etymologicum Genuinum* +

Alera and Elara:

child of Elara[1]:

so in Simonides, but Alera in Pindar, 'son of Alera'.

[1] Tityus, called son of Earth by Homer (*Od.* 11. 576).

# GREEK LYRIC

**561** Schol. T Hom. *Il.* 13. 516 (iii 500 Erbse)

ἀκόντισε Δηΐφοβος· ὡς ἀντεραστὴς Ἑλένης, ὡς μαρτυρεῖ Ἴβυ-
κος (fr. 297) καὶ Σιμωνίδης.

cf. Eust. *Il.* 944. 43 (iii 507 van der Valk)

**562**                    ΕΥΡΩΠΑ

Ar. Byz. fr. 124 Slater

Σιμωνίδης δ᾽ ἐν τῇ Εὐρώπῃ τὸν ταῦρον ὁτὲ μὲν ταῦρον ὁτὲ δὲ
μῆλον ὁτὲ δὲ πρόβατον ὀνομάζει.

cf. Eust. *Il.* 877. 58, *Od.* 1649. 2

**563** Schol. BT Hom. *Il.* 9. 557s. (ii 518s. Erbse)

Ἴδας ὁ Ἀφαρέως μὲν παῖς κατ᾽ ἐπίκλησιν, γόνος δὲ Ποσειδῶ-
νος, Λακεδαιμόνιος δὲ τὸ γένος, ἐπιθυμήσας γάμου παραγίνεται εἰς
Ὀρτυγίαν τὴν ἐν τῇ Χαλκίδι καὶ ἐντεῦθεν ἁρπάζει τὴν Εὐηνοῦ
θυγατέρα Μάρπησσαν. ἔχων δὲ ἵππους Ποσειδῶνος ἠπείγετο. ὁ δὲ
Εὐηνὸς εἰς ἐπιζήτησιν ἐξῆλθε τῆς θυγατρός, ἐλθὼν δὲ κατὰ τὸν
Λυκόρμαν ποταμὸν τῆς Αἰτωλίας, μὴ καταλαβών, ἑαυτὸν εἰς τὸν
ποταμὸν καθῆκεν· ὅθεν ὁ Λυκόρμας Εὐηνὸς μετωνομάσθη. κατὰ
δὲ τὴν Ἀρήνην ἀπαντήσας Ἀπόλλων τῷ Ἴδᾳ λαμβάνεται τῆς
Μαρπήσσης. ὁ δὲ ἔτεινε τὸ τόξον καὶ διεφέρετο περὶ τοῦ γάμου·
οἷς κριτὴς ὁ Ζεὺς γενόμενος αἵρεσιν τοῦ γάμου ἐπὶ τῇ Μαρπήσσῃ
τίθεται. ἡ δὲ δείσασα μὴ ἐπὶ γήρᾳ καταλίπῃ αὐτὴν ὁ Ἀπόλλων αἱ-
ρεῖται τὸν Ἴδαν. οὕτως δὴ Σιμωνίδης τὴν ἱστορίαν περιείργασται
(<οὐ> π. Snell).

450

# SIMONIDES

**561** Scholiast on *Iliad*

'Deiphobus threw his javelin (at Idomeneus)': since he was his rival for the love of Helen, according to Ibycus and Simonides.[1]

[1] See Ibyc. 297.

**562**                              EUROPA

Aristophanes of Byzantium

Simonides in his *Europa* calls the bull sometimes ταῦρος ('bull'), sometimes μῆλον,[1] sometimes πρόβατον.[2]

[1] Usually of sheep or goats.    [2] Usually (in pl.) of cattle or flocks; in Attic prose and comedy almost always of sheep.

**563** Scholiast on *Iliad* ('Cleopatra, daughter of Marpessa and Idas')

Idas, known as the son of Aphareus but in fact child of Poseidon, a Spartan by race, wanted a wife and made his way to Ortygia in (Aetolian) Chalcis, where he carried off Marpessa, daughter of Euenus; and since he was driving horses of Poseidon he made good speed. Euenus left home to search for his daughter, but on reaching the river Lycormas in Aetolia without finding her sank down into the stream, which for this reason came to be known as the Eucnus. Near Arene[1] Apollo met Idas and seized Marpessa; Idas drew his bow, ready to fight for his bride, but Zeus became arbiter between them and gave Marpessa her choice: afraid that Apollo would abandon her in her old age, she chose Idas. This is Simonides' elaboration of the story.[2]

[1] In Messenia (Paus. 4. 2. 5).    [2] Or, with Snell's emendation, 'Thus Sim. told the story to good effect.' See also *Il.* 9. 555–64.

451

**564** Athen. 4. 172e (i 388 Kaibel)

ὅτι δὲ τὸ ποίημα τοῦτο (sc. Ἆθλα ἐπὶ Πελίᾳ) Στησιχόρου ἐστὶν ἱκανώτατος μάρτυς Σιμωνίδης ὁ ποιητής, ὃς περὶ τοῦ Μελεάγρου τὸν λόγον ποιούμενός φησιν·

ὃς δουρὶ πάντας
νίκασε νέους, δινάεντα βαλὼν
Ἄναυρον ὕπερ πολυβότρυος ἐξ Ἰωλκοῦ·
οὕτω γὰρ Ὅμηρος ἠδὲ Στασίχορος ἄεισε λαοῖς.

2 Ursinus: νικαῖς ενεους A

**565** Schol. A Hom. Il. 2. 872a (i 351 Erbse)

ὅτι ἐπὶ τοῦ Ἀμφιμάχου ἐστὶ τὸ ὃς καὶ χρυσὸν ἔχων, ὁ δὲ Σιμωνίδης ἐπὶ τοῦ Νάστου λέγει. καὶ ὅτι οὐ λέγει ὅπλα αὐτὸν ἔχειν χρυσᾶ, ὡς καὶ πάλιν ὁ Σιμωνίδης ἐξέλαβεν, ἀλλὰ κόσμον χρυσοῦν.

**566** Hsch. O 248 (ii 740 Latte)

Οἰκιάδης·

Σιμωνίδης. <Δεξαμενοῦ> καὶ Ἱππόνου πατὴρ <Οἰκεύς>.

suppl. Ruhnken

# SIMONIDES

**564** Athenaeus, *Scholars at Dinner*

That this poem (viz. *Funeral Games of Pelias*) is the
work of Stesichorus[1] is adequately attested by the poet
Simonides, who says in his account of Meleager,

... who defeated all the young men with his
spear, hurling it over the eddying Anaurus from
grape-rich Iolcus; for so Homer and Stesichorus
sang to the peoples.

[1] See 179. The authority for the statement is Seleucus, 1st c. A.D.
Alexandrian scholar.

**565** Scholiast on *Iliad* (the Carian leaders were 'Nastes
and Amphimachus ..., the one who went to war wearing
gold like a girl')

(The *diple*[1] is used) because the words 'the one ...
wearing gold' refer to Amphimachus, whereas Simonides
applies them to Nastes; also because Homer does not say
that he wears gold armour, as Simonides again has it, but
that he wears gold ornaments.

[1] Marginal mark used by grammarians.

**566** Hesychius, *Lexicon*

## Oeciades

(i.e. 'son of Oeceus'), Simonides. Oeceus was father of Dex-
amenus[1] and Hipponous.

[1] Ruler of Olenus in Achaea; played host to Heracles, who saved his
daughter from marriage to the Centaur Eurytion.

**567** Tzetz. *chil.* 1. 312ss. (p. 14s. Leone)

ὡς γράφει που περὶ αὐτοῦ (sc. Ὀρφέως) καὶ Σιμωνίδης οὕτω·

τοῦ καὶ ἀπειρέσιοι
πωτῶντ᾽ ὄρνιθες ὑπὲρ κεφαλᾶς,
ἀνὰ δ᾽ ἰχθύες ὀρθοὶ
κυανέου ᾽ξ ὕδατος ἅλ-
5    λοντο καλᾷ σὺν ἀοιδᾷ.

2 Kiessling: πωτῶντ᾽ codd.    4 -έου ἐξ codd.

**568** Schol. Pl. *Resp.* 337a (p. 192 Greene) (σαρδάνιον)

Σιμωνίδης δὲ ἀπὸ Τάλω τοῦ χαλκοῦ ὃν Ἥφαιστος ἐδημιούργησε Μίνῳ φύλακα τῆς νήσου ποιήσασθαι. ἔμψυχον ὂν τοὺς πελάζοντας, φησί, κατακαῖον ἀνῄρει. ὅθεν ἀπὸ τοῦ σεσηρέναι διὰ τὴν φλόγα τὸν σαρδάνιόν φησι λεχθῆναι γέλωτα. ὁμοίως καὶ Σοφοκλῆς ἐν Δαιδάλῳ (fr. 160 Radt).

cf. *Sud.* Σ 124 (iv 327 Adler) = Phot. s.v., Zenob. *Cent.* 5. 85

**569** Schol. Hes. *Theog.* 313 (p. 60s. Di Gregorio)

... τὴν ὕδραν ..., ἣν Ἀλκαῖος μὲν (443) ἐννεακέφαλόν φησι, Σιμωνίδης δὲ πεντηκοντακέφαλον.

Serv. in Verg. *Aen.* 7. 658 (ii 177 Thilo-Hagen)

'centum angues' secundum Simonidem, ut diximus supra (v. 6. 575, ii 80 T.-H.); nam alii dicunt novem fuisse.

# SIMONIDES

**567** Tzetzes, *Chiliads*

... as Simonides writes somewhere about Orpheus:

Over his head flew numberless birds, and fish leaped straight up from the dark-blue water at his beautiful song.[1]

[1] Perhaps from a description of his voyage with the Argonauts.

**568** Scholiast on Plato, *Republic* ('he laughed very sardonically')

According to Simonides the origin of the expression is the story of Talos, the bronze figure which Hephaestus crafted for Minos to establish as guardian of the island. It was alive, he says, and destroyed those who approached by burning them up. This was the origin, he says, of the term 'sardonic laughter', because they grimaced (σεσηρέναι) in the flames.[1] Similarly Sophocles in his *Daedalus*.

[1] The *Suda* ( = Photius, *Lexicon*) and Zenobius, *Proverbs* say unconvincingly and with differing detail that Sim. introduced into his poem both of the ancient derivations, that from 'Sardinia' as well as that from σεσηρέναι; see Pearson on Soph. fr. 160.

**569** Scholiast on Hesiod, *Theogony*

The Hydra is called nine-headed by Alcaeus (443), fifty-headed by Simonides.

Servius on Virgil, *Aeneid* (on the Hydra)

One hundred snakes as in Simonides, as we said above[1]; others say there were nine.

[1] At *Aen.* 6. 575 Servius spoke of Sim.'s fifty-headed Hydra.

# GREEK LYRIC

**570** Str. 15. 1. 57 (iii 222 Kramer)

περὶ δὲ τῶν χιλιετῶν Ὑπερβορέων τὰ αὐτὰ λέγει (sc. Μεγασθένης) Σιμωνίδῃ καὶ Πινδάρῳ (v. *Pyth.* 10. 41) καὶ ἄλλοις μυθολόγοις.

**571** Plut. *de exil.* 8 (iii 519 Pohlenz-Sieveking)

ἂν γὰρ τούτων τις μνημονεύῃ . . . , αἱρήσεται καὶ νῆσον οἰκεῖν φυγὰς γενόμενος Γύαρον ἢ Κίναρον . . . , οὐκ ἀθυμῶν οὐδ' ὀδυρόμενος οὐδὲ λέγων ἐκεῖνα τὰ τῶν παρὰ Σιμωνίδῃ γυναικῶν,

ἴσχει δέ με πορφυρέας ἁλὸς ἀμφιταρασσομένας ὀρυμαγδός.

**572** Aristot. *Rhet.* 1. 6. 1363a (p. 33 Roemer)

διὸ λελοιδορῆσθαι ὑπέλαβον Κορίνθιοι ὑπὸ Σιμωνίδου ποιήσαντος· Κορινθίοις δ' οὐ μέμφεται τὸ Ἴλιον.

Schol. ad loc. (*Comment. in Ar. graec.* 21. 2, p. 294s. Rabe = *Anecd. Par.* i 284s. Cramer)

οἶδας μὲν ὃ δηλοῦται. μάταιος δὲ ἦν ὁ οὕτως αὐτὸ ἐξηγησάμενος, ὅτι οὐ μέμφεται τὸ Ἴλιον τοῖς Κορινθίοις, οὐδὲ γὰρ συνεμάχησαν τοῖς Ἕλλησιν οἱ Κορίνθιοι κατὰ τῶν Τρώων. καὶ γὰρ τοῖς Ἀχαιοῖς Εὐχήνωρ Κορίνθιος υἱὸς Πολυΐδου τοῦ μάντεως ἐπεκούρησε· καί φησιν Ὅμηρος (*Il.* 13. 663s.). ὃ γοῦν ὁ Σιμωνίδης λέγει τοῦτό ἐστιν, ὅτι Κορινθίοις οὐ μέμφεται τὸ Ἴλιον ὡς τάχα πολεμήσασιν αὐτοῖς διὰ τοῦ Εὐχήνορος, ὡς εἰρήκαμεν, ἀλλ' ἑτέρωθεν καὶ εὐχαριστεῖ αὐτοῖς μᾶλλον ὡς συμμαχήσασι τῇ Ἰλίῳ διὰ Γλαύκου τοῦ εἰς Βελλεροφόντην τὸν Κορίνθιον τὸ γένος ἀναφέροντος τοῦ Γλαύκου τοῦ Σισύφου, ὃς ἀνεγνώρισε Διομήδην. κάλλιστα δὲ τὴν θεωρίαν ταύτην ἐξαπλοῖ ὁ λυρικὸς Πίνδαρος ἐν τῷ εἰς Ξενοφῶντα Κορίνθιον σταδιοδρόμον ἐπινίκῳ, ὅτε λέγει (*Ol.* 13. 55–62). οὕτω

# SIMONIDES

**570** Strabo, *Geography*

Of the Hyperboreans who live a thousand years Megasthenes[1] says the same as Simonides, Pindar and other mythologers.

[1] Historian of India, *c.* 350–290 B.C.

**571** Plutarch, *Exile*

If a man keeps this in mind . . . , he will choose to live in exile even on an island like Gyaros or Cinaros . . . , without despairing or lamenting or saying with the women in Simonides,

I am held fast by the crash of the surging sea seething all around.

**572** Aristotle, *Rhetoric*

That is why the Corinthians took Simonides' words, 'Troy finds no fault with the Corinthians,' as an insult.

Scholiast on the passage

You know what is meant. It was a fool who explained the passage by saying, 'Troy does not find fault with the Corinthians, because the Corinthians did not fight with the Greeks against the Trojans.' For Euchenor of Corinth, son of the seer Polyidus, fought as ally of the Achaeans (*Il.* 13. 663 f.).[1] What Simonides means is that Troy finds no fault with the Corinthians for fighting against it in the person of Euchenor — see above — but on the contrary is actually grateful to them for fighting as allies of Troy in the person of Glaucus, who traced his lineage to Corinthian Bellerophon, son of Glaucus, son of Sisyphus, the Glaucus who recognised Diomedes.[2] This view is best explained by the lyric poet Pindar in his epinician for the Corinthian

[1] See also *Il.* 2. 570.    [2] *Il.* 6. 119 ff.

457

# GREEK LYRIC

δὲ καὶ Σιμωνίδης ἐποίησε·

> Κορινθίοις δ᾽ οὐ μανίει
> οὐδ᾽ αὖ Δαναοί,

τὸ Ἴλιον δηλαδή.

cf. schol. Pind. *Ol.* 13. 78 (i 374 Drachmann), Plut. *vit. Dion.* 1 (ii 1. 93 Ziegler)

1 -οις δ᾽ οὐ Ar., schol. Ar.: -οισιν οὐ schol. Pind. μέμφεται pro μανίει Ar. 2 ci. Page post Boeckh: οὐδὲ Δαναοῖς schol. Ar. et Pind.

## 573 Iulian. *Ep.* 24 (p. 236 Bidez-Cumont)

Σιμωνίδῃ δὲ ἄρα τῷ μελικῷ πρὸς τὴν Ἀπόλλωνος εὐφημίαν ἀρκεῖ τὸν θεὸν

> Ἕκατον

προειπόντι καὶ καθάπερ ἀντ᾽ ἄλλου τινὸς ἱεροῦ γνωρίσματος αὐτοῦ τὴν ἐπωνυμίαν κοσμῆσαι διότι τὸν Πυθῶνα, τὸν δράκοντα, βέλεσιν ἑκατὸν ὥς φησιν ἐχειρώσατο, καὶ μᾶλλον αὐτὸν Ἕκατον ἢ Πύθιον χαίρειν προσαγορευόμενον, οἷον ὁλοκλήρου τινὸς ἐπωνυμίας συμβόλῳ προσφωνούμενον.

cf. Tzetz. in Hom. *Il.* (p. 117. 17 Hermann), Eust. *Il.* 52. 11 (i 84 van der Valk)

## 574 Himer. *Or.* 47. 1 (p. 189s. Colonna)

... ἡδέως μὲν ἂν πείσας καὶ αὐτοὺς τοὺς λόγους λύραν μοι γενέσθαι καὶ ποίησιν, ἵνα τι κατὰ σοῦ νεανιεύσωμαι, ὁποῖον Σιμωνίδης ἢ Πίνδαρος κατὰ Διονύσου καὶ Ἀπόλλωνος.

## 575 Schol. Ap. Rhod. 3. 26 (p. 216 Wendel)

Ἀπολλώνιος μὲν Ἀφροδίτης τὸν Ἔρωτα γενεαλογεῖ, ... Σιμωνίδης δὲ Ἀφροδίτης καὶ Ἄρεως·

# SIMONIDES

Xenophon, the stadion-runner, when he says (*Ol.* 13. 55–62)[3]; similarly Simonides wrote of Troy,

and it is not angry with the Corinthians, nor are the Danaans.

[3] P. says that Corinthians fought well on both sides, Glaucus for the Trojans.


## 573 Julian, *Letters*

Simonides the lyric poet thinks it sufficient for his praise of Apollo to call the god Ἕκατος,

### Far-shooter,

and to adorn him with this title rather than any other sacred mark because, as he says, he killed the snake Python with a hundred (ἑκατόν) arrows and takes more pleasure in being called Ἕκατος than 'Pythian', as if he were being so addressed by the token of a perfect name.[1]

[1] Julian is writing about the perfect quality of the number 100.

## 574 Himerius, *Orations*[1]

I should gladly have persuaded the words themselves to be my lyre and poetry, so that I might sing of you with youthful abandon, as did Simonides or Pindar of Dionysus and Apollo.

[1] See Anacr. 380 for a longer quotation.

## 575 Scholiast on Apollonius of Rhodes[1]

Apollonius makes Eros child of Aphrodite, ... Simonides makes him child of Aphrodite and Ares:

[1] See also Sapph. 198, Ibyc. 324.

# GREEK LYRIC

σχέτλιε παῖ δολομήδεος Ἀφροδίτας,
τὸν Ἄρη †δολομηχάνῳ† τέκεν

cf. schol. Theocr. 13. 1–2 (p. 258 Wendel), Serv. in Verg. *Aen.* 1. 664
(i 190s. Thilo-Hagen)

1 Rickmann: -μηδες, -μητες codd.      2 κακομαχάνῳ ci. Bergk, θρα-
συμαχάνῳ Wilamowitz, δολομάχανον Davies, Marzullo

**576** Schol. Eur. *Med.* 5 (ii 142 Schwartz)

δέρας· τὸ δέρμα. τοῦτο οἱ μὲν ὁλόχρυσον εἶναί φασιν, οἱ δὲ
πορφυροῦν. καὶ Σιμωνίδης ἐν τῷ εἰς Ποσειδῶνα ὕμνῳ ἀπὸ τῶν ἐν
τῇ θαλάττῃ πορφυρῶν κεχρῶσθαι αὐτὸ λέγει.

Schol. Ap. Rhod. 4. 176–7 (p. 271 Wendel)

πολλοὶ δὲ χρυσοῦν τὸ δέρας εἰρήκασιν, οἷς Ἀπολλώνιος ἠκολού-
θησεν. ὁ δὲ Σιμωνίδης ποτὲ μὲν λευκόν, ποτὲ δὲ πορφυροῦν.

Tzetz. *chil.* 1. 433s. (p. 20 Leone)

Ἀτρέως δ' ἐν τοῖς θρέμμασιν ἦν τι χρυσοῦν ἀρνίον,
ὁ Σιμωνίδης πορφυροῦν εἶναι δὲ τοῦτο λέγει.

**577** Plut. *Pyth. orac.* 17 (iii 43 Pohlenz-Sieveking)

Μουσῶν γὰρ ἦν ἱερὸν ἐνταῦθα παρὰ τὴν ἀναπνοὴν τοῦ νάματος
ὅθεν ἐχρῶντο πρός τε τὰς λοιβὰς <καὶ τὰς χέρνιβας> τῷ ὕδατι
τούτῳ, ὥς φησι Σιμωνίδης·

(a) ἔνθα χερνίβεσσιν ἀρύεται τὸ Μοισᾶν
καλλικόμων ὑπένερθεν ἁγνὸν ὕδωρ.

μικρῷ δὲ περιεργότερον αὖθις ὁ Σιμωνίδης τὴν Κλειὼ προσειπών·

(b) ἁγνᾶν ἐπίσκοπε χερνίβων,

(a) Turnebus: εἰρύεται codd.      Bergk: τε Μουσᾶν codd.
(b) 1 Schneidewin: -σκοπον codd.

460

# SIMONIDES

you cruel child of guileful Aphrodite, whom she bore to ... Ares.[2]

[2] Mss. give 'guile-contriving Ares', which some scholars retain; others emend to 'evil-contriving' or 'bold in contriving', others to 'whom she bore, a guile-contriving son, to Ares'.

## 576 Scholiast on Euripides, *Medea* (on the golden fleece)

δέρας = δέρμα, animal skin. Some call it all-gold, others purple. Simonides in his hymn to Poseidon says it was dyed with the sea-purple.

### Scholiast on Apollonius of Rhodes

Many have called the skin golden, and Apollonius followed them. Simonides sometimes calls it white, sometimes purple.

### Tzetzes, *Chiliads*

Among the flocks of Atreus was a golden lamb, but Simonides says it was purple.[1]

[1] Tz. may have misapplied the description.

## 577 Plutarch, *The oracles at Delphi no longer given in verse*

For there was a shrine of the Muses here[1] where the spring wells up, and that is why they used this water for libations and lustrations, as Simonides says:

(a) where the holy water of the lovely-haired Muses is drawn from below for lustration.

Again Simonides with a little more elaboration says, addressing Clio,

(b) Overseer of the holy lustration-water, golden-

[1] South of Apollo's temple.

# GREEK LYRIC

φησί,

> πολύλλιστον <ἅ τ'> ἀρυόν-
> τεσσι, χρυσόπεπλε <Κλειοῖ,
> παρέχεις> εὐῶδες ἀμβροσίων
> 5 ἐκ μυχῶν ἐραννὸν ὕδωρ,
> λοιβᾶν . . .

οὐκ ὀρθῶς οὖν Εὔδοξος ἐπίστευσε τοῖς Στυγὸς ὕδωρ τοῦτο καλεῖσθαι πεφήνασι.

2 πολύλλιστον codd.    ἅ τ' add. Bergk    2s. Emperius: ἀραιόν τέ ἐστιν codd.    3 Hiller: ἀχρυσόπεπλον codd.    3s. suppl. Page    6 ci. Page: λαβόν codd.

## 578 Himer. *Or.* 62. 7 (p. 226 Colonna)

διὸ δὴ καὶ Σιμωνίδῃ πείθομαι ὅπερ ἐκεῖνος ἐν μέλεσι περὶ Μουσῶν ἀνύμνησε. φησὶ γὰρ δήπου τοῦτο ἐκεῖνος· ἀεὶ μὲν αἱ Μοῦσαι χορεύουσι καὶ φίλον ἐστὶ ταῖς θεαῖς ἐν ᾠδαῖς τε εἶναι καὶ κρούμασιν. ἐπειδὰν δὲ ἴδωσι τὸν Ἀπόλλωνα τῆς χορείας ἡγεῖσθαι ἀρχόμενον, τότε πλέον ἢ πρότερον τὸ μέλος ἐκτείνασαι ἠχόν τινα παναρμόνιον καθ' Ἑλικῶνος ἐκπέμπουσιν.

## 579 Clem. Alex. *Strom.* 4. 7. 48 (ii 270 Stählin)

εἰκότως οὖν Σιμωνίδης γράφει·

> ἐστί τις λόγος
> τὰν Ἀρετὰν ναίειν δυσαμβάτοισ' ἐπὶ πέτραις,
> †νῦν δέ μιν θοαν† χῶρον ἁγνὸν ἀμφέπειν·
> οὐδὲ πάντων βλεφάροισι θνατῶν
> 5 ἔσοπτος, ᾧ μὴ δακέθυμος ἱδρὼς
> ἔνδοθεν μόλῃ,
> ἵκῃ τ' ἐς ἄκρον ἀνδρείας.

cf. Theodoret. *gr. aff. cur.* 12. 46 (p. 311 Raeder) (v. 2)

robed Clio, who give the water-drawers from the
ambrosial cave the fragrant lovely water sought
with many prayers, . . . libations[2] . . .

So Eudoxus[3] was wrong to believe those who declare that
it is the water of the Styx that is so called.

[2] Reading uncertain.        [3] 4th c. mathematician and
geographer.

**578** Himerius, *Orations*

That is why I believe what Simonides said in his songs
in praise of the Muses. His words were along these lines:
the Muses are always dancing, and the goddesses love to
busy themselves with songs and strings. But when they
see Apollo beginning to lead the dance, they put their heart
into their singing even more than before and send down
from Helicon an all-harmonious sound.

**579** Clement of Alexandria, *Miscellanies*

So Simonides writes with good reason,

There is a tale that Arete (Excellence, Virtue) dwells
on unclimbable rocks and (close to the gods?) tends a
holy place; she may not be seen by the eyes of all
mortals, but only by him on whom distressing sweat
comes from within, the one who reaches the peak of
manliness.[1]

[1] Based on Hesiod, *Works and Days* 289 ff.

2 δυσβάτοις Theod.    3 ἐγγὺς δέ μιν θεῶν tent. Page post Wake-
field (θεῶν)    4 Ilgen: βλεφάροις codd.    7 ἀνδρείᾳ ci.
Wilamowitz

**580** Himer. *Or.* 31. 2 (p. 135 Colonna)

ἐπεὶ καὶ Σιμωνίδης ὁ Κεῖος Ἱέρων<α> (suppl. Wilamowitz)
πέμπων ἐκ Σικελίας ἐπ᾽ ἄλλης γῆς ἥπτετο μὲν λύρας, ἥπτετο δὲ
δάκρυα μίξας τοῖς κρούμασιν.

**581** Diog. Laert. 1. 89s. (i 39s. Long)

οὗτος (sc. Κλεόβουλος) ἐποίησεν ᾄσματα καὶ γρίφους εἰς ἔπη
τρισχίλια. καὶ τὸ ἐπίγραμμά τινες τὸ ἐπὶ Μίδᾳ τοῦτόν φασι ποιῆ-
σαι·

χαλκῆ παρθένος εἰμί, Μίδα δ᾽ ἐπὶ σήματι κεῖμαι.
ἔστ᾽ ἂν ὕδωρ τε νάῃ καὶ δένδρεα μακρὰ τεθήλῃ,
ἠέλιός τ᾽ ἀνιὼν λάμπῃ λαμπρά τε σελήνη,
καὶ ποταμοί γε ῥέωσιν, ἀνακλύζῃ δὲ θάλασσα,
αὐτοῦ τῇδε μένουσα πολυκλαύτῳ ἐπὶ τύμβῳ,
ἀγγελέω παριοῦσι Μίδας ὅτι τῇδε τέθαπται.

φέρουσι δὲ μαρτύριον Σιμωνίδου ᾆσμα ὅπου φησί·

τίς κεν αἰνήσειε νόῳ πίσυνος Λίνδου ναέταν Κλεό-
βουλον,
ἀεναοῖς ποταμοῖς ἄνθεσί τ᾽ εἰαρινοῖς
ἀελίου τε φλογὶ χρυσέας τε σελάνας
καὶ θαλασσαίαισι δίναις ἀντιθέντα μένος στάλας;
5 ἅπαντα γάρ ἐστι θεῶν ἥσσω· λίθον δὲ
καὶ βρότεοι παλάμαι θραύοντι· μωροῦ
φωτὸς ἅδε βουλά.

3 Hermann: χρυσᾶς codd.    4 ἀντιθέντα Schneidewin, Mehl-
horn, ἀντία θέντα Bergk    6 Hermann: βρότειοι codd.

**582** Ael. Aristid. *Or.* 3. 97 ( = 46. 143 Dindorf) (i 324 Lenz-
Behr)

... σιωπῆς ἀκίνδυνον γέρας, ὥς τις τῶν Κείων ἔφη ποιητής.

# SIMONIDES

**580** Himerius, *Orations* (propemptic speech for Ampelius, proconsul of Asia)

For Simonides of Ceos also, when seeing off Hiero from Sicily to another land,[1] touched the lyre and mingled tears with his notes as he touched it.

[1] Presumably Sim. wrote a propemptic ode for him.

**581** Diogenes Laertius, *Lives of the Philosophers*

Cleobulus[1] composed songs and riddles, three thousand hexameters in all. Some say that it was he who wrote the epigram on Midas: 'I am a maiden of bronze, and I stand on the tomb of Midas. As long as water flows and tall trees grow, and the rising sun gives light or the bright moon, and rivers flow and the sea boils, here I shall remain on this sad tomb and tell passers-by that Midas is buried here.' They adduce as evidence a song of Simonides where he says,

What man who can trust his wits would commend Cleobulus, dweller in Lindus, who against ever-flowing rivers, spring flowers, the flame of the sun or the golden moon or the eddies of the sea set the might of a statue? All things are less than the gods. Stone is broken even by mortal hands. That was the judgement of a fool.

[1] Tyrant of Lindus on Rhodes *c.* 600 B.C., sometimes regarded as one of the Seven Sages.

**582** Aelius Aristides, *Orations*

... the danger-free reward of silence, as one of the Ceans, a poet, puts it.

# GREEK LYRIC

Schol. ad loc. (iii 501 Dindorf)

τὸ δὲ σιωπῆς ἀκίνδυνον γέρας ἐκ Σιμωνίδους ἐστὶ τοῦ Κ<ε>ίου.

Plut. reg. et imp. apophth. 207c (ii 107 Nachstädt)

ἔστι καὶ σιγᾶς ἀκίνδυνον γέρας,

ubi σιγῆς codd.

cf. Stob. Ecl. 3. 33. 5 (ἔστι καὶ τὸ σιγᾶν ἀ. γ.), I.G. xiv 2136 (εστι δε και σιγαν α. γ.), Sopat. Rhet. Gr. viii 119 Walz, Clem. Alex. Paedag. 2. 7. 58, Strom. 2. 15. 68, Iulian. Or. 1. 3 B, Liban. Declam. 15. 4, Phil. Vit. Mos. 1. 52, Apostol. Cent. vii 97, Arsen. p. 242 Walz

**583** Athen. 9. 374d (ii 318 Kaibel)

Σιμωνίδης

ἱμερόφων' ἄλεκτωρ

ἔφη.

ἡμερο- Ursinus    Edmonds: ἀλέκτωρ codd.

**584** Athen. 12. 512c (iii 131 Kaibel)

καὶ οἱ φρονιμώτατοι δέ, φησίν (sc. Ἡρακλείδης ὁ Ποντικός, fr. 55 Wehrli), καὶ μεγίστην δόξαν ἐπὶ σοφίᾳ ἔχοντες μέγιστον ἀγαθὸν τὴν ἡδονὴν εἶναι νομίζουσιν, Σιμωνίδης μὲν οὑτωσὶ λέγων·

τίς γὰρ ἁδονᾶς ἄτερ θνα-
τῶν βίος ποθεινὸς ἢ ποί-
α τυραννίς;
τᾶς ἄτερ οὐδὲ θεῶν ζηλωτὸς αἰών.

4 Kaibel: τᾶς δ' codd.

466

# SIMONIDES

Scholiast on the passage

'the danger-free reward of silence' is from Simonides of Ceos.

Plutarch, *Sayings of kings and commanders* (Augustus to the philosopher Athenodorus)

Silence too brings a danger-free reward.[1]

[1] Much quoted by later writers and adapted by Horace (est et fideli tuta silentio/merces, *Carm.* 3. 2. 25 f.: see also Sim. 524).

**583** Athenaeus, *Scholars at Dinner*

Simonides said,

Lovely-voiced cock!

**584** Athenaeus, *Scholars at Dinner*

Even the most sensible men, says Heraclides,[1] those who have the highest reputation for wisdom, reckon pleasure to be the greatest good, Simonides, for example, saying,

What human life is desirable without pleasure, or what lordly power? Without it not even the life of the gods is enviable.

[1] Her. of Pontus, 4th c. B.C. philosopher, in his work *On Pleasure*.

**585** Athen. 13. 604ab (iii 332 Kaibel)

καὶ πρὸς τόδε ἠμείφθη ὁ Ἐρετριεύς· . . . οὐκ εὖ εἴρηκε Φρύνιχος
(fr. 13 Snell) πορφυρέας εἰπὼν τὰς γνάθους τοῦ καλοῦ· . . . γελά-
σας ἐπὶ τῷ Ἐρετριεῖ Σοφοκλῆς· οὐδὲ τόδε σοι ἀρέσκει ἄρα, ὦ ξένε,
τὸ Σιμωνίδειον, κάρτα δοκέον τοῖς Ἕλλησιν εὖ εἰρῆσθαι·

πορφυρέου ἀπὸ στόματος
ἱεῖσα φωνὰν παρθένος

δ' ἀπὸ ci. Schneidewin, ἀπὸ del. Naeke

**586** *Et. Mag.* 813. 5

χλωρηῒς ἀηδών (*Od.* 19. 518)· ἀπὸ τοῦ χρώματος. ἢ διότι ἐν
ἔαρι φαίνεται ὅτε πάντα χλωρά. οἱ δὲ τὴν χλωροῖς ἡδομένην. ἀλη-
θὲς δὲ τὸ πρῶτον· τοιαύτην γὰρ τὴν πτέρωσιν ἔχει. καὶ Σιμωνί-
δης·

εὖτ' ἀηδόνες πολυκώτιλοι
χλωραύχενες εἰαριναί

cf. schol. Hom. *Od.* 19. 518, Eust. *Od.* 1875. 41

**587** Hdn. π. μον. λέξ. α 12 (ii 919 Lentz)

οὐδὲν εἰς -υρ λῆγον οὐδέτερον μονοσύλλαβον ἀλλὰ μόνον τὸ
πῦρ. ὅπερ Σιμωνίδης καὶ ἕνεκα μέτρου δισυλλάβως ἀπεφήνατο·

τοῦτο γὰρ μάλιστα φῆρες ἐστύγεον πύυρ.

# SIMONIDES

**585** Athenaeus, *Scholars at Dinner*[1]

The Eretrian replied, '. . . Phrynichus[2] did not do well to use the word "crimson" of the handsome boy's cheeks. . . .' With a smile at the Eretrian Sophocles said, 'Then, stranger, you do not like these words of Simonides, although the Greeks in general think very highly of them:

the girl, sending forth words from her crimson lips . . .

[1] Part of an extract from the *Visits* of Ion of Chios, 5th c. tragedian: Sophocles converses with an Eretrian schoolmaster.    [2] Early 5th c. tragedian.

**586** *Etymologicum Magnum*

'green nightingale' (*Od.* 19. 518): 'green' because of its colour, or because it appears in spring when everything is green; according to some, because it enjoys greenery. The first explanation is correct, for its plumage is green[1]: so Simonides,

when the nightingales, babbling, green-necked,[2] birds of spring, . . .

[1] Brown in fact; 'green' may not be the appropriate translation of the words χλωρός, χλωρηίς: see e.g. D'Arcy Thompson, *Glossary of Greek Birds* 17, E. Irwin, *Colour Terms in Greek Poetry* 68 ff.
[2] Irwin suggests 'with throbbing throat'.

**587** Herodian, *On Anomalous Words*

There is no neuter monosyllabic word ending in -υρ except πῦρ, 'fire'. Simonides made it disyllabic (πύυρ) for the sake of the metre[1]:

for this, fire, is what the beasts[2] hated most.

[1] Presumably the long syllable of πῦρ was sung on two notes, as perhaps with κνοώσσεις at 543. 9: West, *Z.P.E.* 37 (1980) 153 ff.
[2] The Centaurs?

# GREEK LYRIC

**588** Hsch. N 172 (ii 700 Latte)

Νεαιρῆϊσιν ἵπποις· ταῖς (Latte: τὸν cod.) ἀπὸ †Νεαίρας†. καὶ Σιμωνίδης·

νέαιραν γνάθον.

ναιαιραν cod.

**589** Himer. *Or.* 39. 1 (p. 159 Colonna)

Ἠλεῖοί ποτε τῆς Σιμωνίδου λύρας λαβόμενοι, ὅτε ἐπὶ τὴν Πίσαν ἔσπευδεν ὕμνῳ κοσμῆσαι τὸν Δία, δημοσίᾳ φωνῇ τὴν Διὸς πόλιν πρὸ Διὸς ᾄδειν ἐκέλευον.

**590** Plut. *vit. Arat.* 45. 7 (iii 1. 309 Ziegler)

καὶ γὰρ εἰ δεινὸν ἄνδρας ὁμοφύλους καὶ συγγενεῖς οὕτω μεταχειρίσασθαι δι᾽ ὀργήν, ἀλλ᾽

ἐν δ᾽ ἀνάγκαισι γλυκὺ γίνεται
καὶ σκληρόν,

κατὰ Σιμωνίδην, ὥσπερ ἀλγοῦντι τῷ θυμῷ καὶ φλεγμαίνοντι θεραπείαν καὶ ἀναπλήρωσιν προσφερόντων.

tent. Page post Bergk: ἐν ἀνάγκαις γ. γ. οὐ σκληρόν codd.

**591** Plut. *quomodo adul. ab amico internosc.* 2 (i 98 Paton-Wegehaupt)

ἔτι δ᾽ ὥσπερ ὁ Σιμωνίδης τὴν ἱπποτροφίαν φησὶν οὐ Ζακύνθῳ (Vulcobius: λακύθῳ codd.) ὀπαδεῖν ἀλλ᾽ ἀρούραισι πυροφόροις, οὕτως τὴν κολακείαν ὁρῶμεν οὐ πένησιν οὐδ᾽ ἀδόξοις οὐδ᾽ ἀδυνάτοις ἀκολουθοῦσαν ἀλλ᾽ οἴκων τε καὶ πραγμάτων μεγάλων ὀλίσθημα καὶ νόσημα γινομένην, unde Schneidewin

ἱπποτροφία γὰρ οὐ Ζακύνθῳ
ἀλλ᾽ ἀρούραισι πυροφόροις ὀπαδεῖ.

470

# SIMONIDES

**588** Hesychius, *Lexicon*

Νεαιρῆϊσιν ἵπποις : mares from (Neaera?).[1] Simonides has
νέαιραν γνάθον,

## youthful cheek.[2]

[1] A corrupt place-name? Or 'young fillies'?     [2] Or 'lower jaw'
(LSJ)?

**589** Himerius, *Orations*

Once when Simonides was hurrying to Pisa[1] to honour
Zeus with a hymn the Eleans took hold of his lyre and with
one voice told him to sing of the city of Zeus instead of
Zeus.

[1] Olympia: see 519 fr. 1 col. ii 6, 633.

**590** Plutarch, *Life of Aratus*

Certainly it is a terrible thing so to treat men of the
same race and blood out of anger; still, as Simonides says,

in times of necessity even harshness is sweet,

when men, as it were, tend and satisfy the spirit that is
sick and fevered.

**591** Plutarch, *How to tell a flatterer from a friend*

Moreover, just as Simonides says,

horse-rearing goes not with Zacynthus but with
wheat-bearing fields,

so we see flattery not following after the poor or obscure or
powerless but becoming a pitfall and pestilence to great
houses and great undertakings.

**592** Plut. *quomodo adul. ab amico internosc.* 24 (i 130 Paton-Wegehaupt)

τὸν δὲ κρείττονα τρέμει καὶ δέδοικεν, οὐ μὰ Δία παρὰ Λύδιον ἅρμα πεζὸς οἰχνεύων (Pind. fr. 206 Snell), ἀλλὰ

παρὰ χρυσὸν ἐφθόν,

ὥς φησι Σιμωνίδης,

ἀκήρατον οὐδὲ μόλυβδον ἔχων.

**593** Plut. *quomodo quis sent. prof. virt.* 8 (i 158 Paton-Wegehaupt)

ὥσπερ γὰρ ἄνθεσιν ὁμιλεῖν ὁ Σιμωνίδης φησὶ τὴν μέλιτταν

ξανθὸν μέλι μηδομέναν, . . .

*Anecd. Oxon.* iii 173 Cramer

καλῶ δέ σε . . . μέλιτταν Μούσης οὐκ ἀπό τινων θύμων καὶ δριμυτάτων ἀνθέων ξανθὸν μέλι μηδομένην, ὥς φησιν ὁ Σιμωνίδης, ἀλλ᾽ ἀπὸ τῶν ἄνω λειμώνων ἐργαζομένην τὸ μέλι τὸ σόν.

cf. Plut. *de audiendo* 8, *de amore prolis* 2, Plat. *Ion* 534ab

**594** Plut. *an seni sit gerenda resp.* 1 (v 1. 21s. Hubert)

πολιτεία δὲ δημοκρατικὴ καὶ νόμιμος ἀνδρὸς εἰθισμένου παρέχειν αὑτὸν οὐχ ἧττον ἀρχόμενον ὠφελίμως ἢ ἄρχοντα καλὸν ἐντάφιον ὡς ἀληθῶς τὴν ἀπὸ βίου δόξαν τῷ θανάτῳ προστίθησι. τοῦτο γὰρ

ἔσχατον δύεται κατὰ γᾶς,

ὥς φησι Σιμωνίδης.

# SIMONIDES

**592** Plutarch, *How to tell a flatterer from a friend*

He trembles in fear of the better man, not 'walking on foot beside a Lydian chariot'[1] but, as Simonides puts it,

possessing not even lead to compare with refined, unalloyed gold.

[1] Pindar fr. 206.

**593** Plutarch, *How to perceive one's progress in virtue*

For just as Simonides says of the bee that she consorts with flowers

contriving her yellow honey,[1] . . .

*Anecdota Oxoniensia*

I call you . . . the bee of the Muse, not contriving her yellow honey, as Simonides puts it, from thymes and pungent flowers, but creating your honey from the upper meadows.

[1] Sim. may have compared the poet or the Muse with the bee: see Bergk *ad loc.*, Oates, *Influence of Sim. upon Horace* 98 ff.

**594** Plutarch, *Should old men govern?*

But when a man has habitually been ready to be ruled no less than to rule for the good of the community, a government that is democratic and lawful grants him on his death a truly fine funeral-gift,[1] the fame he won by his life. This gift, as Simonides says,

is last to sink under the earth.

[1] Cf. 531. 4. G. Burzacchini, *Q.U.C.C.* 25 (1977) 31 ff. argues that Sim.'s line belongs to the Thermopylae poem.

# GREEK LYRIC

**595** Plut. *quaest. conv.* 8. 3. 4 (iv 270 Hubert)

νηνεμία γὰρ ἠχῶδες καὶ γαλήνη καὶ τοὐναντίον, ὡς Σιμωνίδης φησίν·

οὐδὲ γὰρ ἐννοσίφυλλος ἀήτα
τότ' ὦρτ' ἀνέμων, ἅτις κ' ἀπεκώλυε
κιδναμένα μελιαδέα γάρυν
ἀραρεῖν ἀκοαῖσι βροτῶν.

2 Page: κατεκώλυε codd.     3 Wyttenbach: σκιδ- codd.

**596** Schol. Ap. Rhod. 4. 1212–14 (p. 310 Wendel)

Ἐφύρα ἡ Κόρινθος ἀπὸ Ἐφύρας τῆς Ἐπιμηθέως θυγατρός. Σιμωνίδης (P: Εὔμηλος L: Εὔμηλος δὲ καὶ Σιμωνίδης ci. Schneidewin) δὲ ἀπὸ Ἐφύρας τῆς Ὠκεανοῦ καὶ Τηθύος, γυναικὸς δὲ γενομένης Ἐπιμηθέως.

**597** Schol. Ar. *Av.* 1410 (p. 256 White)

τινὲς παρὰ τὸ Ἀλκαίου (345) καὶ παρὰ τὸ Σιμωνίδου·

ἄγγελε κλυτὰ ἔαρος ἁδυόδμου,
κυανέα χελιδοῖ.

cf. schol. ad 1301 (p. 239 White)

1 κλητὰ codd. ΓΕ

**598** Schol. Eur. *Or.* 235 (i 122 Schwartz)

Σιμωνίδης·

τὸ δοκεῖν καὶ τὰν ἀλάθειαν βιᾶται.

cf. schol. ad 782, Plat. *Resp.* 2. 365c

**599** Schol. A Hom. *Il.* 2. 2b (i 175 Erbse)

νήδυμος· . . . οἱ δὲ μεθ' Ὅμηρον καὶ χωρὶς τοῦ ν λέγουσι. καὶ

474

# SIMONIDES

**595** Plutarch, *Table-Talk*

For in windless calm conditions sound carries, and the opposite is true; as Simonides says,

for then arose no leaf-shaking blast of the winds, which might have spread abroad and prevented the honey-sweet voice from fastening on the ears of mortals.


**596** Scholiast on Apollonius of Rhodes

Ephyra is Corinth, named after Ephyra, daughter of Epimetheus; but Simonides[1] makes her daughter of Oceanus and Tethys, and wife of Epimetheus.

[1] 'Eumelus' in one ms.; perhaps 'Eum. and Sim.'.

**597** Scholiast on Aristophanes, *Birds* 1410

Some say that the passage is a parody of Alcaeus' lines (345) and of Simonides'

famous messenger of sweet-scented spring, blue-black swallow!


**598** Scholiast on Euripides, *Orestes* ('appearance is stronger, even if it is far from the truth')

Simonides says,

appearance does violence even to the truth.

**599** Scholiast on *Iliad* (νήδυμος ὕπνος, 'sweet sleep')

Homer's successors use also the form ἥδυμος without the

# GREEK LYRIC

Ἀντίμαχος (fr. 94 Wyss)· ἐπεί ῥά οἱ ἤδυμος ἐλθών. καὶ Σιμωνί-
δης·

> οὗτος δέ τοι ἤδυμον ὕπνον ἔχων

cf. Eust. *Il.* 163. 32 (i 252 van der Valk)

**600** Schol. B Hom. *Il.* 21. 126 (v 149 Erbse)

καὶ ἔστιν ἡ φρὶξ κινουμένου τοῦ πνεύματος ἀρχή. Σιμωνίδης δὲ
αὐτὴν καὶ δεῖξαι πειρώμενος οὕτως ἔφη·

> εἶσ' ἅλα στίζουσα πνοιά

cf. Porphyr. *quaest. hom.* (p. 40s. Sodano)

Bergk: ἐς cod.

**601** Schol. BT Hom. *Il.* 24. 5 (v 512 Erbse)

πανδαμάτωρ· Σιμωνίδης δὲ

> δαμασίφωτα

τὸν ὕπνον καλεῖ.

cf. Eust. *Il.* 1336. 7

**602** Schol. Pind. *Ol.* 9. 74b (i 285 Drachmann)

δοκεῖ δὲ τοῦτο πρὸς τὸ Σιμωνίδειον εἰρῆσθαι· ἐπεὶ ἐκεῖνος
ἐλασσωθεὶς ὑπὸ Πινδάρου λοιδορίας ἔγραψε κατὰ τοῦ κρίναντος
Ἀγαθωνίδου (Drachmann: ἀγαθῶν εἰδέου cod.), ἐπειδὴ ἐκεῖνος
εἶπεν·

> ἐξελέγχει νέος οἶνος οὔπω
> <τὸ> πέρυσι δῶρον ἀμπέλου·
> †ὁ δὲ μῦθος· ὁ δὲ κενεόφρων· κούρων δέ,†

διὰ τοῦτο ὁ Πίνδαρος ἐπαινεῖ παλαιὸν οἶνον.

1 Gerhard: ὁ νέος cod.    2 suppl. Gerhard, Boeckh    3 κού-
ρων δ' ὅδε μῦθος κενεόφρων tent. Page

# SIMONIDES

$\nu$,[1] e.g. Antimachus (fr. 94 Wyss) and Simonides:

> but he, possessing sweet sleep . . .

[1] See Kirk on *Il.* 2. 1–2.

**600** Scholiast on *Iliad*

φρίξ, 'ripple', is the beginning of a rising wind. Simonides in an attempt to represent it said,

> the breeze comes stippling the sea.

**601** Scholiast on *Iliad* ('all-subduing sleep')

Simonides calls sleep

> man-subduing.[1]

[1] Eustathius describes Sim.'s epithet as shabby (σμικροπρεπῶς).

**602** Scholiast on Pindar, *Ol.* 9. 48 f. ('praise an old wine but the flowers of new songs')

This seems to be directed against the lines of Simonides: when he had been judged inferior to Pindar, he wrote abuse of the Agathonides who had pronounced the verdict, when he said,

> 'New wine does not yet bring to the test last year's gift of the vine': that is an empty-headed saying of children.[1]

That is why Pindar praises an old wine.

[1] Reading and interpretation uncertain, but Sim. seems to say that a one-year-old wine does indicate the quality of the vintage; perhaps his point was that new song also is good.

**603** Schol. Soph. *Aj.* 377 (p. 36 Papageorgiu)

ἐπ' ἐξειργασμένοις· ἐπὶ τετελεσμένοις καὶ ἴασιν οὐκ ἔχουσιν, κατὰ τὸ Σιμωνίδου·

τὸ γὰρ γεγενημένον οὐκέτ' ἄρεκτον ἔσται.

cf. *Sud.* T 564, Plut. *consol. Apoll.* 26

**604** Sext. Emp. *adv. math.* xi 49 (ii 386 Mutschmann)

Σιμωνίδης μὲν γὰρ ὁ μελοποιός φησι μηδὲ καλᾶς σοφίας εἶναι χάριν εἰ μή τις ἔχοι σεμνὴν ὑγείαν, unde Schneidewin, Bergk

οὐδὲ καλᾶς σοφίας ἐστὶν χάρις
εἰ μή τις ἔχει σεμνὰν ὑγίειαν.

**605** Theodorus Metochita *misc. philos. et hist.* (p. 90 Mueller-Kiessling)

μόνος ἄλιος ἐν οὐρανῷ,

φησὶ Σιμωνίδης.

Schneidewin: οὐρανοῖς codd.    ἐν fort. delendum (Bergk)

**606** Tzetz. in Hes. *Op.* 372 (ii 236s. *Poet. Min. Gr.*)

κωτίλη γὰρ ἡ χελιδὼν διὰ τὸ λάλος εἶναι παρά τε Ἀνακρέοντι (453) καὶ Σιμωνίδῃ καλεῖται.

cf. cod. Laur. xxxii 16

**607** P. Berol. 13875, ed. Zuntz, *C.R.* 49 (1935) 4–7

οὐδὲ πελέκεις οὐδὲ σηρήν (Pind. fr. 339 Snell)· ταῦτα πρὸς Σιμωνίδην, ἐπεὶ ἐκεῖνος ἐν ἑνὶ [ἄ]ισματι ἐπόησεν

σειρῆνα

# SIMONIDES

**603** Scholiast on Sophocles, *Ajax* ('Why grieve over what is fully accomplished?')

I.e. over what is finished and allows no cure; in the words of Simonides,

for what has once happened will never be undone.

**604** Sextus Empiricus, *Against the Ethicists*

Simonides the lyric poet says,

There is no pleasure even in beautiful wisdom,[1] unless a man has holy health.

[1] Perhaps with reference to poetic skill.

**605** Theodorus the Metochite, *Miscellany*

The sun is alone in the sky,

says Simonides.

---

**606** Tzetzes on Hesiod, *Works and Days*

In Anacreon (453) and Simonides the swallow is called

chatterbox

because it is garrulous.

**607** Berlin papyrus (2nd c. A.D.) (commentary on Pindar)

'neither axes nor Siren': this is in answer to Simonides, since in one song he called Pisistratus

Siren.[1]

[1] For 'his seductive eloquence' (Zuntz): Pindar may have meant that neither the executioners' axes nor the eloquence of Pis. could terrify his opponent.

τὸν Πεισίστρατον. ἐν ἄλλοις δὲ ἄισμασι καὶ τὸν

$$πελεκυφ[ό]ραν$$

ἵππον ὀνομάζε[ι, τ]ὸν χελιδόνα ἐπίσημον ἔχοντα· χελιδόνας γὰρ
ἵππους [ἔστιζον.

**608** P.Oxy. 2434

fr. 1(a)(b) + 2

```
. . . φησι κωκυτὸν [            ]τούτωι ὁ Σιμω[νίδης ἂν
σημαί]νοι τὸ περὶ τοῦ [ ̣ ]ου[     ] ̣ ν εὐλόγως η παρ ̣ ̣ [
]τον ἐθρήνουν ἐπιο ̣ [       ] ἔοικεν δαιμονι ̣ [          ]
      ἑτοῖμοι στ ̣ενά[ζ]ε[ιν     γ]ὰρ τὸ ὅλον συνημμ[έν- ἂν]
γένοιτο ῥῆσις περὶ το[        ] . . . τὴν σφαζομέν[ην
      ] ̣ ν
      τὸν λαὸν αὔει ̣ [        ]ν ̣ ιτ᾽ ἐπὶ τὸ ἐναν[τίο]ν
[ . . . . . . ]ι ἐξαλλαγῆι. μητρὶ δὲ ὑπ᾽ οὐδενὸς ἂν ἡττηθείη ἡ λύπη,
ἀναιρουμένων δὲ τῶν παί[δων ἑ]τοῖμον στενάζειν. φέρεται [δὲ καὶ
ἄλλη γραφή· ἐμοὶ δὲ τίς ἄμφατις (ἔστι)· πάνυ σαφὴς ἀπὸ
τῆς προκειμ[ένης] ἐξηγήσεως. παρατηρεῖν δε ̣ [ῖ ὅτι ἠθικῶ]ς πέ-
πλασται ὁ λόγος αυ[
      ] γὰρ ἐν Μυκάναισι δ᾽ αυ[        ]τασευε κωκυτὸν
ηκο[        ]πειν· οἱ δέ γε κωκύοντες [    ἔ]πρασσον ὅτι οὐχὶ
ἀναίρε[σις φα]ύλη ἀλλὰ ἐπὶ τιμῆι τοῦ δαιμ[ονίο]υ· τοῦτο δὲ αὐτὸ
ἠθικῶς ἀπήγ[γειλ]εν τῆ[ι] ἀναφωνήσει χρησά[μενος     ] ̣ α[ ]το
τίς ἄμφατις ἔσται.
      ]Κ ̣ ̣ [ ̣ ] ̣ [        ] ̣ ε ̣ οι βαρεῖα λαί[λαψ
```

fr. 6. 5 ε]ὐρυχορ[

omnia suppl. vel tent. Lobel

# SIMONIDES

In other songs he speaks of

> the axe-bearing horse,

the one with the swallow[2] as its mark: they used to brand
swallow-marks on horses.

[2] The rambling commentator (Didymus?) takes the swallow and
the double axe to be the same mark.

**608** Oxyrhynchus papyrus (late 2nd c. A.D.) (commentary
on Simonides)

fr. 1 + 2 . . . says 'wailing' . . . : by this Simonides might
(be indicating) the matter of . . . reasonably . . . they
mourned . . . it seemed good (to the deity?) . . .

'(they) certain to groan' . . . for the sense (of . . . ?)
taken together would be a speech about . . . the one being
slain[1] . . .

'(she?) calls on the people'[2] . . . by a change to the
opposite.[3] And no one could outdo a mother in her grief,
and when one's children are being killed 'groaning' is 'cer-
tain'. Another reading is found: and for me what . . .[4] is
there?' The reading is quite comprehensible in the light of
the present explanation. One must note that the sentence
has been given an expressive form . . .

'for . . . in Mycenae . . . -ed wailing . . .': the wailers
were (so?) acting because it is not a trivial killing but done
to honour a deity. This too he has described expressively
by using the exclamation, 'and for me what . . .[4] will there
be?'

'. . . grievous hurricane . . .'

fr. 6.5 . . . 'spacious' . . .

[1] Feminine: probably of Iphigenia in view of 'Mycenae' below.
[2] Perhaps 'the army'.     [3] 'Something was conveyed in terms of
its opposite' (Lobel).     [4] An obscure noun.

# GREEK LYRIC

**609** Schol. Pind. *Ol.* 13. 31b (i 364 Drachmann)

ἐν δὲ Μοῖσ' ἀδύπνοος· ἀντὶ τοῦ μουσικοί εἰσι· παρόσον καὶ ποιηταὶ διασημότατοι ἐν Κορίνθῳ ἐγένοντο, ὧν ἦν καὶ Αἴσων, οὗ μέμνηται Σιμωνίδης.

Αἴγων cod. C: Ἀρίων ci. Wilamowitz, Κιναίσων Bergk

**610** Steph. Byz. s.v. Ἄκανθος (i 57 Meineke)

τὸ ἐθνικὸν τῆς Ἀκάνθου Ἀκάνθιος, ἐξ οὗ καὶ παροιμία Ἀκάνθιος τέττιξ ἐπὶ τῶν ἀφώνων· τοιοῦτοι γὰρ οἱ τῆς χώρας τέττιγες, ὡς Σιμωνίδης.

cf. Hdn. i 119 Lentz, Diogenian. *cent.* i 22, Apostol. *cent.* i 100a, xvi 32

**611** Phot. *Lex.* (p. 96 Reitzenstein)

ἀμύνεσθαι· . . . Σιμωνίδης δὲ ἀντὶ τοῦ χάριτας ἀποδιδόναι.

cf. *Sud.* A 1676, Zonar. *Lex.* (p. 160 Tittmann), Ar. Byz. fr. 33 Slater

**612** Schol. T Hom. *Il.* 15. 625–6a (iv 130 Erbse)

κῦμα . . . ἀνεμοτρεφές· . . . καὶ Σιμωνίδης

ἀνεμοτρεφέων πυλάων

εἴρηκεν.

cf. Eust. 1034. 2 (iii 774 van der Valk) (Σιμ. . . . πύλας ἀνεμοτρεφέας λέγει, τὰς εὐτόνους δηλαδή.)

**613** *Anecd. Par.* (i 166 Cramer) (Anon. περὶ Ἱππομάχου)

ἀλλ' ἄκουσον τὸ τοῦ Κρωβύλου· Ἀθηναῖος ἦν, τοῖς δὲ πολίταις ποτὲ τοῖς αὐτοῦ συνεβούλευε μὴ προσέχειν τῷ Μακεδόνι Φιλίππῳ προισχομένῳ τὰ εἰρηνικά. . . .· εἴ γε βούλεσθε μὴ ληρεῖν ἀλλὰ τοὺς Ἕλληνας ἐλευθερῶσαι καὶ κτήσασθαι πάλιν αὖ τὴν πατρῴαν ἡγεμονίαν,

ἀπροφασίστως δουλεύοντα,

κατὰ τὸν Σιμωνίδην, . . .

# SIMONIDES

**609** Scholiast on Pindar, *Ol.* 13. 22 ('among the Corinthians is the sweet-breathed Muse')

I.e. they are musical; for there were very distinguished poets in Corinth, among them Aeson,[1] whom Simonides mentions.

[1] Unknown. Editors suggest Arion or Cinaethon.

**610** Stephanus of Byzantium (on Acanthus)

The ethnic adjective is Acanthian, whence the proverb 'Acanthian cicada' used of silent people; for the cicadas of that land are silent, according to Simonides.

**611** Photius, *Lexicon*

ἀμύνεσθαι: Simonides uses it in the sense of 'repay favours'.[1]

[1] Usually 'defend oneself, take vengeance'.

**612** Scholiast on *Iliad* ('a wind-fed wave')

Simonides speaks of

wind-fed gates.[1]

[1] Cf. Homer's 'wind-fed spear' (*Il.* 11. 256), made from a tree toughened by the wind.

**613** *Anecdota Parisiensia* (Anon., *On Hippomachus*)

Listen to the words of Crobylus, an Athenian who was once advising his fellow-citizens to pay no attention to Philip of Macedon's offer of peace: '. . . if you are ready to stop talking nonsense and to free the Greeks and regain your traditional leadership — all

inexcusably in slavery,

as Simonides puts it . . .'

**614** Athen. 3. 99b (i 227 Kaibel)

οἶδα δ' ὅτι καὶ Σιμωνίδης που ὁ ποιητὴς

ἀρίσταρχον

εἶπε τὸν Δία.

**615** Men. Rh. π. ἐπιδεικτικῶν 1. 2 (p. 6 Russell-Wilson)

πεπλασμένοι δὲ (sc. ὕμνοι), ὅταν αὐτοὶ σωματοποιῶμεν καὶ
θεὸν καὶ γονὰς θεῶν ἢ δαιμόνων, ὥσπερ Σιμωνίδης <τὴν>

Αὔριον

δαίμονα κέκληκε, καὶ ἕτεροι Ὄκνον καὶ ἕτεροι ἕτερόν τινα.

**616** Plut. *vit. Ages.* 1 (iii 2. 194 Ziegler)

διὸ καί φασιν ὑπὸ τοῦ Σιμωνίδου τὴν Σπάρτην προσηγορεῦσθαι

δαμασίμβροτον,

ὡς μάλιστα διὰ τῶν ἐθῶν τοὺς πολίτας τοῖς νόμοις πειθηνίους καὶ
χειροήθεις ποιοῦσαν ὥσπερ ἵππους εὐθὺς ἐξ ἀρχῆς δαμαζομένους.

**617** Schol. T Hom. *Il.* 15. 713b (iv 148 Erbse)

μελάνδετα· ... τὴν δὲ λαβὴν

δεσμὸν

καλεῖ ὁ Σιμωνίδης.

**618** *Et. Gen.* (p. 13 Calame) = *Et. Mag. Gen.* (p. 164 Lasserre-
Livadaras), *Et. Sym.* (p. 140, 210 Sell)

εἰριπόνοι δμωαί·

Edmonds: αἰριπόλιοι sim. (bis) codd.          cf. *Sud.* Ει 204 (ii 534
Adler) εἰροπόνος

# SIMONIDES

**614** Athenaeus, *Scholars at Dinner* (on remarkable compound words)

I know that even the poet Simonides somewhere called Zeus

### best-ruling.[1]

[1] So Bacch. 13. 58.

**615** Menander the rhetorician, *Declamations*

Fictitious hymns are when we ourselves personify a god or the children of gods or deities, as when Simonides calls

### Tomorrow

a deity ('daemon') and others Hesitation and so on.

**616** Plutarch, *Life of Agesilaus*

That is why they say Sparta was called

### breaker-in of men

by Simonides, since Sparta above all made her citizens obedient to the laws and manageable by means of her customs, like horses that are broken in right from the beginning.

**617** Scholiast on *Iliad* ('black-bound swords')

Simonides uses δεσμός ('binding')[1] for

### hilt.

[1] The 'binding' may have been a leather thong wound round the hilt to give a good grip: Lorimer, *Homer and the Monuments* 276.

**618** *Etymologicum Genuinum* +

### wool-working slave-women:

Σιμωνίδης ἐκ τοῦ εἰριοπόνοι, συγκοπῇ τοῦ ο. οὕτως Ἡρωδιανὸς περὶ Παθῶν (ii 251 Lentz).

**619** Schol. Aes. *Cho.* 325 (i 23 Smith)

ἡ γνάθος συνήθης, ὡς ὁ κρημνὸς λέγει Πίνδαρος καὶ

$$\mathring{\eta} \; \mathring{\eta}\chi\grave{\omega}$$

Σιμωνίδης.

**620** Schol. ABT Hom. *Il.* 4. 79 (i 459 Erbse)

τὸ

$$\theta\acute{\alpha}\mu\beta o\varsigma$$

δὲ οὐδετέρως παρ' Ὁμήρῳ, Σιμωνίδης δὲ ἀρσενικῶς.

**621** Himer. *Or.* 27. 30 (p. 126 Colonna)

καὶ Σιμωνίδῃ καὶ Βακχυλίδῃ (fr. 43) ἡ Ἰουλὶς (Wernsdorf: ἡ πόλις cod. Rom., πόλεις cod. Nap.) ἐσπούδασται.

**622** Schol. A Hom. *Il.* 9. 586a (ii 525 Erbse)

κεδνότατοι· ὅτι σωφρονέστατοι. ὁ δὲ Σιμωνίδης

$$\kappa\epsilon\delta\nu o\grave{\upsilon}\varsigma$$

τοὺς φίλους.

**623** Schol. T Hom. *Il.* 24. 228b (v 559s. Erbse)

Ἀρίσταρχος δέ φησι τὴν

$$\kappa\iota\beta\omega\tau\grave{o}\nu$$

λέξιν νεωτέραν εἶναι· ἀγνοεῖ δὲ ὅτι καὶ Σιμωνίδης καὶ Ἑκαταῖος (fr. 368 Müller) μέμνηται αὐτῆς.

so Simonides with εἰριπόνοι, from εἰριοπόνοι with syncope of the o. So Herodian, *On Inflexions.*

**619** Scholiast on Aeschylus

ἡ γνάθος ('jaw') is usual; so Pindar says ὁ κρημνός ('bank') and Simonides ἡ ἠχώ,[1]

sound.

[1] Rather than Doric ἀχώ? Or rather than ὁ ἦχος?

**620** Scholiast on *Iliad* ('amazement held them')

The word θάμβος,

amazement,

is neuter in Homer, masculine in Simonides.

**621** Himerius, *Orations*

Simonides and Bacchylides speak of Iulis[1] with respect.

[1] Their native city; see Stes. 270 n. 1.

**622** Scholiast on *Iliad* ('most cherished and dear')

κεδνότατοι ('most cherished'): note that it means 'most wise'; but Simonides calls friends κεδνούς,

cherished.

**623** Scholiast on *Iliad* (φωριαμῶν, 'coffers')

Aristarchus says κιβωτός,

chest,

is a modern term: he does not know that both Simonides and Hecataeus use it.

**624** *Anecd. Oxon.* (i 424 Cramer)

τὰ εἰς -τος δισύλλαβα ἀπαρασχημάτιστα ἔχοντα ἐν τῇ πρὸ
τέλους τὸ ρ βαρύνεται· κύρτος, Μύρτος ἡ πόλις,

κίρτος·

παρὰ Σιμωνίδῃ ἡ χρῆσις.

cf. Hdn. (i 216 Lentz)

σκίρτος ci. Hecker

**625** = eleg. 2   *Et. Gen.* (p. 42 Calame), *Et. Mag.* 692. 25

πρῶρα· σὺν τῷ ι. ... εὕρηται κατὰ διάστασιν, ὡς παρὰ τῷ
ποιητῇ· κυανοπρῴρους, καὶ παρὰ Σιμωνίδῃ·

κυανοπρῴϊραν.

τὸ δὲ πρῴρα οἱ μὲν διὰ τοῦ ι λέγουσιν ὡς ἀπὸ τοῦ πρῶρα κατὰ διά-
στασιν τοῦ ι πρῴρα· ὁ δὲ Ἡρωδιανὸς (ii 410 Lentz) διὰ τῆς ει
διφθόγγου γράφει πρὸς τὸν χαρακτῆρα τῶν διὰ τοῦ ειρα.

**626** *Et. Gen.* (p. 14 Calame) = *Et. Gen. Mag.* (p. 406s.
Lasserre-Livadaras)

ἀμιθρῆσαι (Callim. fr. 314)· Σιμωνίδης τὸν ἀριθμὸν ἄμιθρον
εἶπεν καθ᾽ ὑπερβιβασμόν (ὑπέρθεσιν *Et. Mag.*), οἷον·

†κύματ᾽† ἄμιθρον.

... οὕτως Ἡρωδιανὸς περὶ Παθῶν (ii 387 Lentz) καὶ Μεθόδιος.

κυμάτων ἄμιθρον ci. Bergk

**627** Plut. *vit. Them.* 1. 4 (I i 157s. Ziegler)

ὅτι μέντοι τοῦ Λυκομιδῶν γένους μετεῖχε δῆλόν ἐστι. τὸ γὰρ
Φλυῆσι τελεστήριον, ὅπερ ἦν Λυκομιδῶν κοινόν, ἐμπρησθὲν ὑπὸ
τῶν βαρβάρων αὐτὸς ἐπεσκεύασε καὶ γραφαῖς ἐκόσμησεν, ὡς
Σιμωνίδης ἱστόρηκεν.

# SIMONIDES

**624** *Anecdota Oxoniensia*

Disyllables in -τος which do not change their form and have ρ in the penultimate syllable take the acute accent on that syllable: κύρτος ('lobster-pot'), the city Μύρτος (Myrtus), κίρτος,[1] used by Simonides.

[1] Meaning unknown; Hecker conjectured σκίρτος, 'frisky'.

**625** = eleg. 2   *Etymologicum Genuinum +*

πρῴρα ('prow'): with the letter ι. . . . It is found with the vowels separate, as in Homer's κυανοπρῴρους[1] and in Simonides' κυανοπρῴϊραν,

## blue-prowed.[2]

Some write πρῴϊρα with the ι as if from πρῶρα with separation of the ι, but Herodian spells it with the diphthong ει on the pattern of words in -ειρα.

[1] Not in our Homer: see e.g. *Il*. 15. 693, *Od*. 3. 299.   [2] Perhaps from the Salamis poem (536, eleg. 1).

**626** *Etymologicum Genuinum*

ἀμιθρῆσαι ('to count'): Simonides said ἄμιθρον instead of ἀριθμόν ('number') by metathesis:

## the number (of the waves?).

. . . So Herodian, *On Inflexions* and Methodius.

**627** Plutarch, *Life of Themistocles*

However, it is clear that Themistocles belonged to the Lycomid family[1]; for when the initiation-place at Phlya, the common property of the Lycomids, was burned down by the Persians, it was he who restored it and decorated it with paintings, as Simonides has related.[2]

[1] Ancient Athenian family.   [2] In a dedicatory epigram?

# GREEK LYRIC

**628** Plut. *vit. Lycurg.* 1 (iii 2. 2 Ziegler)

οὐ μὴν ἀλλὰ καίπερ οὕτως πεπλανημένης τῆς ἱστορίας πειρα-
σόμεθα τοῖς βραχυτάτας ἔχουσιν ἀντιλογίας ἢ γνωριμωτάτους μάρ-
τυρας ἑπόμενοι τῶν γεγραμμένων περὶ τοῦ ἀνδρὸς ἀποδοῦναι τὴν
διήγησιν. < . . . > ἐπεὶ καὶ Σιμωνίδης ὁ ποιητὴς οὐκ Εὐνόμου λέγει
τὸν Λυκοῦργον πατρὸς ἀλλὰ Πρυτάνιδος καὶ τὸν Λυκοῦργον καὶ τὸν
Εὔνομον. οἱ πλεῖστοι σχεδὸν οὐχ οὕτω γενεαλογοῦσιν, ἀλλὰ . . .

cf. schol. Plat. *Resp.* 599d (p. 271 Greene), Dion. Hal. *Ant.* 2. 49

**629** Schol. Theocr. 12. 27–33bc (p. 255s. Wendel)

Νισαῖοι Μεγαρῆες ἀριστεύοντες ἐρετμοῖς · (1) ναυτικοὶ γάρ εἰσι.
μαρτυρεῖ δὲ αὐτοῖς <καὶ> Σιμωνίδης <τὴν> ναυτικήν. (2) καὶ
Σιμωνίδης ἐπαινεῖ τοὺς Μεγαρεῖς.

**630** Schol. Marc. Dion. Thrac. 7 (p. 346 Hilgard)

ἐὰν εἰς σύμφωνον λήγῃ συλλαβή, τὸ ζ τῆς ἑξῆς ἀρκτικὸν οὐκ
ἔσται, εἰ μὴ βάρβαρος εἴη λέξις, οἷον Ἀριοβαρζάνης, ἢ σύνθεσις, ὡς
τὸ

### μελάνζοφος

παρὰ Σιμωνίδῃ.

cf. *Et. Mag.* 370. 20

**631** Athen. 11. 498e (iii 99 Kaibel)

Σιμωνίδης δὲ

### οὐατόεντα σκύφον

ἔφη.

cf. Eust. *Il.* 870. 6, *Od.* 1775. 19

fort. e dact. hexam., σκύφον οὐατόεντα

490

# SIMONIDES

**628** Plutarch, *Life of Lycurgus*

Nevertheless, although the history of those times is so confused, I shall try to base my account of the man on those writings which are least contradicted and use the most distinguished authorities.... For example, the poet Simonides[1] says that Lycurgus was not the son of Eunomus, but that both Lycurgus and Eunomus were sons of Prytanis.[2] Most authorities give a different genealogy ...

[1] See L. Piccirilli, *R.F.I.C.* 106 (1978) 272 ff.       [2] The scholiast on Plato adds that Sim. made Lycurgus uncle of king Charilaus.

**629** Scholiasts on Theocritus ('Nisaean Megarians, masters of the oar')

(1) Because they are seafarers. Simonides bears witness to their naval skill. (2) Simonides too praises the Megarians.[1]

[1] Perhaps in his poem on Salamis (fr. 536, eleg. 1).

**630** Scholiast on Dionysius of Thrace

If a syllable ends with a consonant, the letter $\zeta$ will not begin the next syllable, unless the word is foreign, like Ariobarzanes, or a compound like Simonides' μελάν-ζοφος,

black-dark.

**631** Athenaeus, *Scholars at Dinner*

Simonides said

the eared[1] bowl.

[1] I.e. with handles.

491

**632** Str. 9. 5. 20 (ii 322s. Kramer)

διὰ δὲ τὸ ἀναμὶξ οἰκεῖν Σιμωνίδης Περραιβοὺς καὶ Λαπίθας κα-
λεῖ τοὺς Πελασγιώτας ἅπαντας, τοὺς τὰ ἑῷα κατέχοντας τὰ περὶ
Γυρτῶνα καὶ τὰς ἐκβολὰς τοῦ Πηνειοῦ καὶ Ὄσσαν καὶ Πήλιον καὶ
τὰ περὶ Δημητριάδα καὶ τὰ ἐν τῷ πεδίῳ, Λάρισαν Κραννῶνα Σκο-
τοῦσσαν Μόψιον Ἄτρακα καὶ τὰ περὶ τὴν Νεσσωνίδα λίμνην καὶ
<τὴν> Βοιβηίδα.

**633** Schol. Pind. *Ol.* 1. 28a (i 27 Drachmann)

τὸ

## Πίσας

δὲ συσταλτέον διὰ τὸ ἀντίστροφον. οὕτω δὲ οἱ περὶ Πίνδαρον καὶ
Σιμωνίδην.

**634** Athen. 5. 210ab (i 465 Kaibel)

οὕτως γὰρ καὶ Πολέμων ὁ περιηγητὴς εἶπεν ἐν γ' τῶν πρὸς
Ἀδαῖον καὶ Ἀντίγονον (fr. 58 Preller) ἐξηγούμενος διάθεσιν ἐν
Φλιοῦντι κατὰ τὴν πολεμάρχειον στοὰν γεγραμμένην ὑπὸ Σίλλα-
κος τοῦ Ῥηγίνου, οὗ μνημονεύουσιν Ἐπίχαρμος (fr. 163 Kaibel)
καὶ Σιμωνίδης.

**635** Schol. Ap. Rhod. 1. 583–84a (p. 50s. Wendel)

νῆσος γὰρ ἡ Σκίαθος τῆς Θεσσαλίας ἐγγὺς Εὐβοίας, ἧς καὶ
Σιμωνίδης μέμνηται.

# SIMONIDES

**632** Strabo, *Geography*

Because the Perrhaebians and Lapiths lived intermingled, Simonides applies the names to all the Pelasgiots, those living in the east around Gyrton, the mouths of the Peneus, Ossa, Pelion and the district of Demetrias, and in the towns of the plain, Larissa, Crannon, Scotussa, Mopsium, Atrax, and the area round lakes Nessonis and Boebeis.

**633** Scholiast on Pindar, *Ol.* 1. 18

The strophic correspondence shows that the first syllable of

Pisa[1]

must be scanned as short. This is the practice of Pindar and Simonides.

[1] See 519 fr. 1 col. ii 6, 589.

**634** Athenaeus, *Scholars at Dinner*

Polemon the geographer[1] said so too in book 3 of his work *To Adaeus and Antigonus,* where he describes the subject of a painting in the polemarch's stoa at Phlius: the painter was Sillax of Rhegium, who is mentioned by Epicharmus and Simonides.

[1] *Floruit c.* 190 B.C.

**635** Scholiast on Apollonius of Rhodes ('sea-girt Sciathos')

Sciathos is an island in Thessaly near Euboea; Simonides mentions it.[1]

[1] Almost certainly in his poem on Artemisium, fr. 532.

**636** Choerob. in Theodos. (i 267 Hilgard) (=*Anecd. Gr.* Bekker iii 1424 = Hdn. i 18, ii 627 Lentz)

σπανίως γὰρ εὕρηται ἐν χρήσει ἡ εἰς ν κατάληξις, ὡς παρὰ Σιμωνίδῃ·

τριγλώχιν ὀιστός,

καὶ παρὰ Καλλιμάχῳ (fr. 1. 36 Pfeiffer)

**637** *Et. Gen.* (p. 45 Calame)

υἱός· ἔστι ὕῑς, ὕιος ὡς ὄφις, ὄφιος· εἴρηται ἡ εὐθεῖα παρὰ Σιμωνίδῃ, συναιρέσει τοῦ ι καὶ υ εἰς τὴν υι δίφθογγον,

<υἷς>,

ὕιος προπαροξυτόνως· ἐξ Ἰλίου υἷος ἄποινα (*Il.* 2. 230). ἡ δοτικὴ ὕϊ· Νηληΐῳ υἷϊ (*Il.* 2. 20). ὁ δὲ Ἡρωδιανός, ὅ ἐστιν ὕῑς διὰ τῆς υι διφθόγγου· τούτου ἡ γενικὴ ὕιος καὶ κατὰ συναίρεσιν υἱός. κατὰ δὲ τὴν εὐθεῖαν οὐ πάσχει συναίρεσιν, ἐπειδὴ οὐδέποτε μετὰ τῆς υ διφθόγγου εὑρίσκεται ἐπιφερομένου συμφώνου, οἷον ἄρπυια, μυῖα.

**638** *Et. Gud.* (645. 43 Sturz)

φύξιμος ὀδμή·

ἡ φυγὴν ἐμποιοῦσα. Σιμωνίδης ὁ Κήιος ἀπὸ τῆς Κέου (ὁ Τήιος ἀπὸ τῆς Τέω cod.).

**639** Hdn. *de soloec.* ap. *Anecd. Gr.* Boissonade iii 250, p. 302 Nauck

γίνεται τοίνυν περὶ τὰ πρόσωπα σφάλματα ... οἷον

ὡς δὴ ἐγὼ γελᾷ

παρὰ τῷ λυρικῷ Σιμωνίδῃ. τὸ γὰρ ἐγὼ πρώτου ἐστὶ προσώπου, τὸ γελᾷ(ι) codd. AC: -ῶ BD

# SIMONIDES

**636** Choeroboscus on Theodosius (on τριγλώχις, τριγλώχιν)

The form ending with ν is rarely found; Simonides has it:

> three-barbed arrow,

as does Callimachus.

**637** *Etymologicum Genuinum*

υἱός· there exists ὓϊς, genitive ὓϊος, as ὄφις, ὄφιος. The nominative is used by Simonides,

> son,

with coalescing of the ι and υ to give the diphthong υι, ὓϊος being so accented. Cf. υἷος (gen.) (*Il.* 2. 230), υἷι (dat.) (*Il.* 2. 20). But Herodian says that it is ὓϊς because of the diphthong υι: its genitive is ὓϊος and with coalescing υἱός; but in the nominative there is no coalescing, since the υ diphthong with a consonant following is never found: cf. ἅρπυια, μυῖα.[1]

---

[1] Difficult: perhaps a text of Sim. had nom. υἷς, but Herodian preferred the disyllabic form ὓϊς on the grounds that υἷς was an impossible form; see schol. *Il.* 5. 266, however.

**638** *Etymologicum Gudianum*

φύξιμος ὀδμή,

> loathsome smell,

one that causes flight: Simonides of Ceos.

**639** Herodian, *On Solecism*

> he laughs, as I do.

Mistakes are made over persons ..., e.g. 'as I laughs' in the lyric poet Simonides; for 'I' is first person, 'laughs' is

# GREEK LYRIC

δὲ γελᾷ τρίτου.

**640** Amm. Marc. 14. 6. 7 (i 13 Seyfarth)

ut enim Simonides lyricus docet, beate perfecta ratione
victuro ante alia patriam esse convenit gloriosam.

**641** Myth. Vat. (iii 206 Mai)

neque verum est, inquiunt, animam deserere corpus,
cum potius corpus animam deserat. hinc et Simonides
poeta et Statius itidem in viii (*Theb.* 8. 738s.),

> odi artus fragilemque hunc corporis usum,
> desertorem animi.

**642** (a) Plat. *Resp.* 1. 331 de

οὐκ ἄρα οὗτος ὅρος ἐστὶν δικαιοσύνης, ἀληθῆ τε λέγειν καὶ ἃ ἂν
λάβῃ τις ἀποδιδόναι; — πάνυ μὲν οὖν, ἔφη, ὦ Σώκρατες, ὑπολα-
βὼν ὁ Πολέμαρχος, εἴπερ γέ τι χρὴ Σιμωνίδῃ πείθεσθαι.... —
λέγε δή, εἶπον ἐγώ, σὺ ὁ τοῦ λόγου κληρονόμος, τί φῂς τὸν Σιμωνί-
δην λέγοντα ὀρθῶς λέγειν περὶ δικαιοσύνης; — ὅτι, ἦ δ᾽ ὅς, τὸ τὰ
ὀφειλόμενα ἑκάστῳ ἀποδιδόναι δίκαιόν ἐστι. τοῦτο λέγων δοκεῖ
ἔμοιγε καλῶς λέγειν. — ἀλλὰ μέντοι, ἦν δ᾽ ἐγώ, Σιμωνίδῃ γε οὐ
ῥᾴδιον ἀπιστεῖν· σοφὸς γὰρ καὶ θεῖος ἀνήρ.

(b) Procl. in Hes. *Op.* 709–10 (p. 217 Pertusi) ( = Plut. *com-
ment. in Hes.* vii 85 Bernardakis)

Σιμωνίδης γοῦν ταύτην εἶναι δικαιοσύνην ὡρίσατο, τοὺς φίλους
εὖ ποιεῖν, τοὺς <δ᾽> ἐχθροὺς κακῶς.

496

# SIMONIDES

third.[1]

[1] A misinterpretation of the text '(he), as I, laughs'.

**640** Ammianus Marcellinus, *History*

For as the lyric poet Simonides[1] tells us, if a man is going to live happily and in accordance with perfect reason, he must above all else have a fatherland that is glorious.

[1] Euripides, rather (fr. 756 *P.M.G.*): see D. M. Lewis, *C.R.* 82 (1968) 267.

**641** Anonymous mythographer

Nor is it true, they say, that the soul leaves the body, since it is rather the body that leaves the soul; whence the poet Simonides,[1] and to the same effect Statius in book 8 (of his *Thebaid*), 'I hate these limbs of mine and this fragile and useless body that deserts the soul.'

[1] Quotation not preserved.

**642** (a) Plato, *Republic*

'This, then, to speak the truth and to return what one takes, is not the definition of justice.' 'Oh yes it is, Socrates,' said Polemarchus, taking over the conversation, 'at least if we must believe Simonides.' ... 'Tell me, then, you the inheritor of the argument,' said I, 'what do you say is Simonides' correct statement about justice?' 'That to give each his due is just. I think these words of his are well spoken.' 'Certainly,' said I, 'it is not easy to disbelieve Simonides; for he is a wise man and divinely inspired.'

(b) Proclus on Hesiod, *Works and Days*

Simonides at any rate gave this as the definition of justice — to do good to one's friends, harm to one's enemies.

# GREEK LYRIC

**643** Plut. *vit. Thes.* 10 (i 1. 8 Ziegler)

οἱ δὲ Μεγαρόθεν συγγραφεῖς, ὁμόσε τῇ φήμῃ βαδίζοντες καὶ τῷ πολλῷ χρόνῳ, κατὰ Σιμωνίδην, πολεμοῦντες, οὔθ᾿ ὑβριστὴν οὔτε λῃστὴν γεγονέναι τὸν Σκείρωνά φασιν.

cf. *de Is. et Osir.* 23, Aristot. *Pol.* 2. 1264a

**644** Schol. Eur. *Rhes.* 5 (ii 326 Schwartz)

οἱ ἀρχαῖοι εἰς τρεῖς φυλακὰς νέμουσι τὴν νύκτα. Ὅμηρος . . . (*Od.* 14. 483). Στησίχορος δὲ (268) καὶ Σιμωνίδης πενταφύλακόν φασιν [[ὑποτίθεσθαι τὴν νύκτα]].

Schwartz: στησι (superscr. χρ) δὲ ὁ σιμ. π. φησιν ὑ. τ. ν. cod. A Στησίχορον δὲ ὁ Σιμ. π. φησιν ὑ. τ. ν. Vater

**645** Aristot. *Phys.* 4. 13. 222b 16 (ed. Ross)

ἐν δὲ τῷ χρόνῳ πάντα γίγνεται καὶ φθείρεται. διὸ καὶ οἱ μὲν σοφώτατον ἔλεγον, ὁ δὲ Πυθαγόρειος Πάρων ἀμαθέστατον, ὅτι καὶ ἐπιλανθάνονται ἐν τούτῳ, λέγων ὀρθότερον.

Simplicius ad loc. (*comment. in Ar. graec.* ix 754 Diels)

Σιμωνίδης μὲν γὰρ σοφώτατον, ὅτι γίνονται ἐπιστήμονες ὑπὸ χρόνου. Πάρων δὲ ὁ Πυθαγόρειος ἀμαθέστατον, ὅτι ἐπιλανθάνονται ὑπὸ χρόνου. οὗτος δὲ ἔοικεν εἶναι οὗ καὶ Εὔδημος ἀνωνύμως ἐμνήσθη, λέγων ἐν Ὀλυμπίᾳ Σιμωνίδου τὸν χρόνον ἐπαινοῦντος ὡς

# SIMONIDES

**643** Plutarch, *Life of Theseus*

But the writers from Megara fly in the face of the traditional story and, as Simonides puts it,

> war against the length of time,

in denying that Sciron was either a violent man or a robber.

**644** Scholiast on Euripides, *Rhesus* ('the fourth watch of the night')

The ancients divide the night into three watches, e.g. Homer (*Od.* 14 483); but Stesichorus (268) and Simonides[1] speak of

> night with its five watches.[2]

[1] See Stes. 268 n. 1.    [2] So Euripides in *Rhesus* 562.

*Fragments 645–648 may be from apophthegms (see test. 47).*

**645** Aristotle, *Physics*

In time all things come into existence and are destroyed. That is why some called time the wisest of things; but the Pythagorean Paron called it the most stupid, because men also forget in time, which is more correct.

Simplicius on the passage

It was Simonides who called it the wisest, since men become knowledgeable thanks to time; but Paron the Pythagorean called it the most stupid, because men also forget thanks to time. This Paron seems to be the man of whom Eudemus spoke without giving his name when he told how at Olympia Simonides praised time as being

# GREEK LYRIC

σοφώτατον, εἴπερ ἐν αὐτῷ αἱ μαθήσεις γίνονται καὶ αἱ ἀναμνήσεις,
παρόντα τινὰ τῶν σοφῶν εἰπεῖν· τί δέ, ὦ Σιμωνίδη, οὐκ ἐπιλανθα-
νόμεθα μέντοι ἐν τῷ χρόνῳ; καὶ μήποτε καὶ παρὰ Ἀριστοτέλει ἐν
τῷ 'ὁ δὲ Πυθαγόρειος Παρων', τὸ Παρων οὐκ εἶναι ὄνομα κύριον
ἀλλὰ μετοχήν.

similia Themistius, Philoponus

**646** Theon *Progymn.* 33 (*Rhet. Gr.* i 215 Walz)

βλαβερῶς παραινεῖ Σιμωνίδης παίζειν ἐν τῷ βίῳ καὶ περὶ
μηδὲν ἁπλῶς σπουδάζειν.

**647** Athen. 2. 40a (i 92 Kaibel)

Σιμωνίδης τὴν αὐτὴν ἀρχὴν τίθησιν οἴνου καὶ μουσικῆς.

**648** Plut. *consol. Apoll.* 17 (i 229 Paton-Wegehaupt)

τὰ γὰρ χίλια καὶ τὰ μύρια κατὰ Σιμωνίδην ἔτη στιγμή τίς ἐστιν
ἀόριστος, μᾶλλον δὲ μόριόν τι βραχύτατον στιγμῆς.

cf. ibid. 31, *de lib. educ.* 17

**649** (a) Aphth. ( = 'Mar. Vict.', vi 73 Keil) (de dactylico
metro)

trimetrus autem acatalectus, qui e tribus, ut:

cui non dictus Hylas puer;

hoc hemiepes dicitur, quo Simonides frequenter usus est.

# SIMONIDES

wisest,[1] since in time learning and reminiscence occur; but a philosopher who was present said, 'What, Simonides? Don't we forget in time?' And perhaps when Aristotle spoke of 'The Pythagorean Paron', he was using Paron not as a proper name but as a participle (παρών, 'being present').

[1] In a hymn to Zeus (589) or an epinician?

**646** Theon, *Preliminary Exercises in Rhetoric*

Simonides' advice is harmful, that we should play throughout our lives and take nothing quite seriously.

**647** Athenaeus, *Scholars at Dinner*

Simonides says that wine and music have the same origin.

**648** Plutarch, *Letter of Consolation to Apollonius*

For according to Simonides a thousand or ten thousand years are an undeterminable point, or rather the tiniest part of a point.


## METRE

**649** (a) Aphthonius, *On all the metres* (on dactylic metres)[1]

The trimeter acatalectic has three dactyls[2]:

$$-- \mid -\cup\cup \mid -\cup\cup.$$

It is called the hemiepes, and it was frequently used by Simonides.

[1] See West, *Greek Metre* 69 ff.    [2] Or the equivalent.

pentametrus acatalectus, qui e quinque, ut:

> Phoebus me docuit iuga Pieridum sequi;

et hoc simonidium dicitur.

cf. Serv. *cent. metr.* iv 460s. Keil

(b) = Ibyc. 345 (b)

[(c) 'Censorin.' *fragm. de musica* (vi 607 Keil)

mox Archilochus et Simonides trimetrum iambicum <et> choriacum catalecticum tetrametron composuerunt.]

(d) Serv. *cent. metr.* (iv 462) (de anapaesticis)

simonidium constat trimetro hypercatalectico, ut est hoc:

> tuba terribili procul aere sonat, clipeum quate miles.

(e) = fr. 533 (fin.)

(f) Heph. *Poem.* 4. 4 (p. 67 Consbruch)

ἐπῳδικὰ μὲν οὖν ἐστιν, ἐν οἷς ὁμοίοις ἀνόμοιόν τι ἐπιφέρεται, ὡς τά γε πλεῖστα Πινδάρου καὶ Σιμωνίδου πεποίηται.

(g) Ox. Pap. 220 (v. Heph. p. 404 Consbruch)

col. v . . . μετὰ ταῦτα [δὲ ζητῶν τόν τε] Αἰσχύ[λον εὖρον τού-τ]ωι [κεχρημένον καὶ ἔτι πρότερο]ν τούτου τὸν Ἀλκμᾶνα καὶ [τὸν Σιμω]νίδη . . .

suppl. Wilamowitz post Grenfell, Hunt

# SIMONIDES

The pentameter acatalectic has five[3]:

$$-- \mid -\cup\cup \mid -\cup\cup \mid -\cup\cup \mid -\cup-.$$

This too is called simonidean.

[3] Or the equivalent.

(b) = Ibycus 345 (b)

[(c) 'Censorinus', *On Music*

Soon[1] Archilochus and Simonides composed the iambic trimeter and choriac (i.e. trochaic) tetrameter catalectic.

[1] I.e. soon after Homer, Hesiod and the early elegiac poets; but the passage refers to Semonides of Amorgos, not Simonides of Ceos.]

(d) Servius, *Hundred Metres* (on anapaests)

The simonidean consists of a trimeter hypercatalectic:

$$\cup\cup-\cup\cup- \mid \cup\cup-\cup\cup- \mid \cup\cup-\cup\cup- \mid -$$

(e) = fr. 533 (fin.)

(f) Hephaestion, *On Poetry*

Now epodic songs are those in which like stanzas are followed by an unlike one,[1] as in most of the poems of Pindar and Simonides.

[1] Strophe and antistrophe followed by epode in triadic structure.

(g) Oxyrhynchus papyrus (early 2nd c. A.D.) (anon. metrician)

Later in my researches I discovered that Aeschylus used this metre[1] and, still earlier, Alcman and Simonides.

[1] Not identifiable.

503

**650** *Et. Gud.* (ap. Reitzenstein, *Gesch. Etym.* p. 161)

Σελεύκου· Ἰλεύς· ὁ Αἴαντος πατήρ· ἐτυμολογεῖται ὑφ' Ἡσιόδου (fr. 235 M.-W.). ταῦτα παρατίθεται ἐν δ' Σιμωνίδου.

**651** = Carm. Conv. 890 Schol. Plat. *Gorg.* 451e (p. 133 Greene) (1)

τὸ σκολιὸν τοῦτο οἱ μὲν Σιμωνίδου φασίν, οἱ δὲ Ἐπιχάρμου (v. fr. 262 Kaibel). ἔστι δὲ τοιοῦτον·

ὑγιαίνειν μὲν ἄριστον ἀνδρὶ θνητῷ,
δεύτερον δὲ φυὰν καλὸν γενέσθαι,
τὸ δὲ τρίτον πλουτεῖν ἀδόλως,
τέταρτον δὲ ἡβᾶν μετὰ τῶν φίλων.

cf. Plat. *Legg.* 1. 631c, 2. 661a, schol. Arist. *Rhet.* 1394b 13 (*comment.* xxi 2. 301 Rabe), Clem. Alex. *strom.* 4. 5. 23, schol. Lucian. *de lapsu* 6, Theodoret. *gr. aff. cur.* 11. 14, Stob. iv 39. 9, Apostol. *cent.* 17. 48d

**652** 'Ambigitur etiam de sequentibus (i)–(v)' (Page)

# SIMONIDES

**650** *Etymologicum Gudianum*

From Seleucus[1]: Ileus[2]: father of Ajax; the origin of his name is given by Hesiod (fr. 235 M.-W.). Seleucus quotes this in book 4 of his *Simonides*.

[1] Seleucus Homericus of Alexandria, commentator on Greek poetry, 1st c. A.D.    [2] Son of Apollo and father of Locrian Ajax.

**651** = Drinking song 890    Scholiast on Plato[1]

Some say this scolion is by Simonides, others by Epicharmus.[2] It runs as follows:

To be healthy is best for mortal man, second is to be handsome in body, third is to be wealthy without trickery, fourth, to be young with one's friends.

[1] Plato spoke of 'the composer of the scolion', the comic poet Anaxandrides of 'the man who devised the scolion, whoever he was' (Athen. 15. 694ef). Clement of Alexandria attributed it to Simonides and Aristotle, Stobaeus to an unknown Sclerias. It is given with the Attic scolia in Athen. loc. cit.    [2] A line of his runs, 'and for a man to be healthy is best, as it seems to us.'

**652** Page lists the following items which have been ascribed to Simonides or are of little value: (i) Pind. fr. 333 (dub.) Snell    (ii) Bacch. fr. 60 (dub.) Snell[1]    (iii) Pind. fr. 52n Snell (= Paean xiii)    (iv) P.Oxy. 220 col. v init. = fr. 649 (g) above, P. Univ. Giss. 40 col. ii init., al., P. Varsov. (1935) 7    (v) Sim. eleg. 8 (dub.) West, Sim. fr. 227 Bergk, Apul. *apolog.* 9, Sim. fr. 242 (Bergk) = Simmias fr. 12 Powell, Pap. Strasb. *inv. gr.* 1406–9.[1]

[1] See *Ox. Pap.* xxv (1959) p. 45 n. 2.

# GREEK LYRIC

## ΑΤΑΚΤΟΙ ΛΟΓΟΙ

**653** Aristot. *Metaph.* N 3. 1091a. 5 (ed. Ross)

πάντα δὴ ταῦτα ἄλογα, καὶ μάχεται αὐτὰ ἑαυτοῖς καὶ τοῖς εὐ-
λόγοις, καὶ ἔοικεν ἐν αὐτοῖς εἶναι ὁ Σιμωνίδου μακρὸς λόγος.
γίγνεται γὰρ ὁ μακρὸς λόγος ὥσπερ ὁ τῶν δούλων ὅταν μηθὲν ὑγιὲς
λέγωσιν.

Alex. Aphrodis. ad loc. (*comment. in Ar. graec.* i 818 Hay-
duck)

ὁ Σιμωνίδης ἐν τοῖς λόγοις οὓς ἀτάκτους ἐπιγράφει μιμεῖται
καὶ λέγει οὓς εἰκός ἐστι λόγους λέγειν δούλους ἐπταικότας πρὸς
δεσπότας ἐξετάζοντας αὐτοὺς τίνος ἕνεκα ταῦτα ἐπταίκασι· καὶ
ποιεῖ αὐτοὺς ἀπολογουμένους λέγειν πάνυ μακρὰ καὶ πολλά, οὐδὲν
δὲ ὑγιὲς ἢ πιθανόν, ἀλλὰ πᾶν τὸ ἐπιφερόμενον ἐναντίον τῷ προ-
φρασθέντι· τοιοῦτον γὰρ ὡς εἰκὸς τὸ βάρβαρον καὶ παιδείας ἄμοι-
ρον.

## ΕΛΕΓΕΙΑΙ

## Η ΕΝ ΣΑΛΑΜΙΝΙ ΝΑΥΜΑΧΙΑ

**eleg. 1** Plut. *vit. Them.* 15. 4 (1. 1. 176 Ziegler)

οἱ δὲ ἄλλοι τοῖς βαρβάροις ἐξισούμενοι τὸ πλῆθος ἐν στενῷ κατὰ
μέρος προσφερομένους καὶ περιπίπτοντας ἀλλήλοις ἐτρέψαντο,
μέχρι δείλης ἀντισχόντας, ὥσπερ εἴρηκε Σιμωνίδης, τὴν καλὴν
ἐκείνην καὶ περιβόητον ἀράμενοι νίκην, ἧς οὔθ' Ἕλλησιν οὔτε βαρ-
βάροις ἐνάλιον ἔργον εἴργασται λαμπρότερον.

# SIMONIDES

## MISCELLANEOUS STORIES

**653** Aristotle, *Metaphysics*

This is all absurd, in conflict both with itself and with common sense, like Simonides' 'long story', the kind that slaves tell when they have no sound excuse to offer.

Alexander of Aphrodisias on the passage

Simonides in the stories which he entitles 'miscellaneous'[1] represents and reproduces the stories which slaves are likely to tell when they have blundered and their masters are investigating the reason: he recounts their long rambling excuses which have nothing sound or convincing about them and nothing whatever to do with the case. Speech of this kind, it would seem, is the mark of the uneducated foreigner.

[1] 'Irregular', 'prose'? Meaning uncertain; perhaps an anthology of apophthegms is meant (Wilamowitz).

---

## ELEGIACS

### THE SEA-BATTLE AT SALAMIS[1]

**eleg. 1** Plutarch, *Life of Themistocles*

The rest of the Greeks, their inferior numbers compensated by the narrowness of the strait, which forced the Barbarians to attack only by detachments and made them collide with each other, routed them although they resisted till afternoon, as Simonides says, and won that splendid, famous victory, the most brilliant naval exploit ever carried out by Greeks or Barbarians.

[1] See testt. 1, 7, fr. 536.

# GREEK LYRIC

**eleg. 2** = fr. 625

**eleg. 3** Habron (?) ap. P.Oxy. 1087 ii 39s. (ii 224 Erbse)

τὸ λᾶος, ἀφ' οὗ φη(σι) Σιμωνίδης

ξύλα κα[ὶ] λάους ἐπιβάλλων.

### CONVIVIALIA

**eleg. 4** Athen. 10. 447a (ii 471 Kaibel)

σὺ δὲ πιὼν μὴ φοβηθῇς ὡς εἰς τοὐπίσω μέλλων καταπεσεῖσθαι·
τοῦτο γὰρ παθεῖν οὐ δύνανται οἱ τὸν κατὰ Σιμωνίδην πίνοντες οἶ-
νον,

ἀμύντορα δυσφροσυνάων.

**eleg. 5** Athen. 1 (epit.) 32b (i 74s. Kaibel)

ἦν ἄρ' ἔπος τόδ' ἀληθές, ὅτ' οὐ μόνον ὕδατος αἶσαν
ἀλλά τι καὶ λέσχης οἶνος ἔχειν ἐθέλει.

(Callim. fr. 178. 15s. Pfeiffer)

οὐ γὰρ ἀπόβλητον Διονύσιον οὐδὲ γίγαρτον,

ὁ Κεῖός φησι ποιητής.

Schweighäuser: οὐδὲ γὰρ codd.

**eleg. 6** ( = LXXXVIII *F.G.E.*) Athen. 3. 125c (i 286 Kaibel)

Καλλίστρατος ἐν ζ' Συμμίκτων (*F.Gr.H.* 348 F 3) φησὶν ὡς
ἑστιώμενος παρά τισι Σιμωνίδης ὁ ποιητὴς ʻκραταιοῦ καύματος
ὥρᾳʼ καὶ τῶν οἰνοχόων τοῖς ἄλλοις μισγόντων εἰς τὸ ποτὸν χιόνος,

# SIMONIDES

**eleg. 2** = fr. 625

**eleg. 3** Habron (?) in scholiast on *Iliad* 7. 76 (μάρτυρος)

λᾶος[1], 'stone', used by Simonides:

> (he), hurling logs and stones.

[1] Given as an example of a 'paronymous' noun, the nominative of which (e.g. μάρτυρος, λᾶος) is the same as the genitive of a cognate form (μάρτυς, λᾶας); see also Stes. 214.


## DRINKING SONGS

**eleg. 4** Athenaeus, *Scholars at Dinner*

But when you have drunk, have no fear that you are likely to fall on your back; for that cannot happen to those who drink the wine which Simonides calls

> the repeller of worries.

**eleg. 5** Athenaeus, *Scholars at Dinner*

'Then this is a true saying, that wine demands not only its portion of water but also its portion of conversation' (Callimachus).

> For nothing that belongs to Dionysus should be thrown away, not even a grape-pip,

says the poet of Ceos.

**eleg. 6** ( = LXXXVIII *F.G.E.*) Athenaeus, *Scholars at Dinner*

Callistratus[1] in book 7 of his *Miscellanies* says that when the poet Simonides was dining with friends 'in the season of mighty heat' and the wine-bearers mixed snow in

[1] 2nd c. B.C. scholar, pupil of Aristophanes of Byzantium.

509

# GREEK LYRIC

αὐτῷ δὲ οὔ, ἀπεσχεδίασε τόδε τὸ ἐπίγραμμα·

    τήν ῥά ποτ' Οὐλύμποιο περὶ πλευρὰς ἐκάλυψεν
       ὠκὺς ἀπὸ Θρήκης ὀρνύμενος Βορέης,
    ἀνδρῶν δ' ἀχλαίνων ἔδακεν φρένας, αὐτὰρ ἐκάμφθη
       ζωὴ Πιερίην γῆν ἐπιεσσαμένη,
5 ἔν τις ἐμοὶ καὶ τῆς χείτω μέρος· οὐ γὰρ ἔοικεν
       θερμὴν βαστάζειν ἀνδρὶ φίλῳ πρόποσιν.

5 West: χεέτω codd.

**eleg. 7** Athen. 14. 656c (iii 452 Kaibel)

περὶ δὲ λαγῶν Χαμαιλέων φησὶν ἐν τῷ περὶ Σιμωνίδου (fr. 33 Wehrli, 41 Giordano) ὡς δειπνῶν παρὰ τῷ Ἱέρωνι ὁ Σιμωνίδης, οὐ παρατεθέντος αὐτῷ ἐπὶ τὴν τράπεζαν καθάπερ καὶ τοῖς ἄλλοις λαγωοῦ, ἀλλ' ὕστερον μεταδιδόντος τοῦ Ἱέρωνος, ἀπεσχεδίασεν·

    οὐδὲ γὰρ <οὐδ'> εὐρύς περ ἐὼν ἐξίκετο δεῦρο.

οὐδ' ap. Eust. Od. 1821. 37, qui affert Il. 14. 33s. (οὐδὲ γὰρ οὐδ' εὐρύς περ ἐὼν ἐδυνήσατο πάσας | αἰγιαλὸς νῆας χαδέειν)

**eleg. 8** Stob. Ecl. 4. 34. 28 (v 834s. Wachsmuth-Hense)

Σιμωνίδου·

    ἓν δὲ τὸ κάλλιστον Χῖος ἔειπεν ἀνήρ·
    'οἵη περ φύλλων γενεή, τοίη δὲ καὶ ἀνδρῶν'·
    παῦροί μιν θνητῶν οὔασι δεξάμενοι
    στέρνοις ἐγκατέθεντο· πάρεστι γὰρ ἐλπὶς ἑκάστῳ
5    ἀνδρῶν, ἥ τε νέων στήθεσιν ἐμφύεται.

---

[1] Attributed by Bergk and others to Semonides of Amorgos, perhaps rightly; but see West, *Studies* 179 f., H. Lloyd-Jones, *Females of the Species* 96 f.    [2] Homer, *Il.* 6. 146.

the drink of the others but not in his, he improvised this epigram[2]:

Of that with which Boreas, rushing swiftly from Thrace, once covered the sides of Olympus, so that it gnawed the hearts of cloakless men but was humbled when clad alive in Pierian soil[3] — of that let someone pour me my share; for it is not right to raise a hot drink to toast one's friend.

[2] Sim.'s riddles are mentioned by Athenaeus 10. 456c.    [3] Buried for preservation?

**eleg. 7** Athenaeus, *Scholars at Dinner*

With regard to hares Chamaeleon says in his work *On Simonides* that when the poet was dining with Hiero, hare was served to the others but not to him; and when Hiero later offered him some, he improvised this line:

'for even although it was wide, it did not reach me here.'[1]

[1] Eustathius noted the parody of *Il.* 14. 33, 'for even although it was wide, the beach could not hold all the ships.'

**eleg. 8** Stobaeus, *Extracts* (that life is short, worthless and full of cares)

From Simonides[1]:

and this was the best thing the man of Chios[2] ever said: 'As the generation of leaves, so is that of men.' Few mortals having heard it with their ears have deposited it within their breasts. For hope is present with each man, hope which grows in the

# GREEK LYRIC

θνητῶν δ' ὄφρά τις ἄνθος ἔχῃ πολυήρατον ἥβης,
  κοῦφον ἔχων θυμὸν πόλλ' ἀτέλεστα νοεῖ·
οὔτε γὰρ ἐλπίδ' ἔχει γηρασέμεν οὔτε θανεῖσθαι,
  οὐδ', ὑγιὴς ὅταν ᾖ, φροντίδ' ἔχει καμάτου.
10 νήπιοι, οἷς ταύτῃ κεῖται νόος, οὐδὲ ἴσασιν
  ὡς χρόνος ἔσθ' ἥβης καὶ βιότου ὀλίγος
θνητοῖς. ἀλλὰ σὺ ταῦτα μαθὼν βιότου ποτὶ τέρμα
  ψυχῇ τῶν ἀγαθῶν τλῆθι χαριζόμενος.

cf. 'Plut.' vit. Hom. 2. 2 Ὅμηρον τοίνυν Πίνδαρος μὲν ἔφη Χῖόν τε καὶ
Σμυρναῖον γενέσθαι, Σιμωνίδης δὲ Χῖον, . . .

3 μὴν Hermann

**eleg. 9** Ar. *Pax* 736ss.

  εἰ δ' οὖν εἰκός τινα τιμῆσαι, θύγατερ Διός, ὅστις ἄριστος
  κωμῳδοδιδάσκαλος ἀνθρώπων καὶ κλεινότατος γεγένηται,
  ἄξιος εἶναί φησ' εὐλογίας μεγάλης ὁ διδάσκαλος ἡμῶν.

Schol. (V) (p. 114 Holwerda)

  παρὰ τὰ Σιμωνίδου ἐκ τῶν ἐλεγείων·

  εἰ δ' ἄρα τιμῆσαι, θύγατερ Διός, ὅστις ἄριστος,
    δῆμος 'Αθηναίων ἐξετέλεσσε μόνος.

2 Hartung: ἐξετέλεσα cod.

**eleg. 10** Plut. *de Herod. malign.* 42. 872de (V 2. 2. 50 Häsler)

  ἀλλὰ Κορινθίους γε καὶ τάξιν ἣν ἐμάχοντο τοῖς βαρβάροις καὶ
τέλος ἡλίκον ὑπῆρξεν αὐτοῖς ἀπὸ τοῦ Πλαταιᾶσιν ἀγῶνος ἔξεστι

512

# SIMONIDES

hearts of the young. As long as a mortal has the lovely flower of youth, he ponders with light heart many impossibles; for he neither expects to grow old or die, nor when he is healthy does he worry about illness. Fools, to think like that and not realise that mortals' time for youth and life is brief: you must take note of this, and since you are near the end of your life endure, indulging yourself with good things.

*Frr. 9–16 may be from epigrams rather than from elegiac poems. See also test. 15.*

**eleg. 9** Aristophanes, *Peace*

Now if it is right, daughter of Zeus, to honour the best and most famous comic poet in the world, then our poet claims that he deserves great praise.

Scholiast on the passage

This is adapted from Simonides, from his elegiacs:

but if it is right,[1] daughter of Zeus,[2] to honour the best, it was the people of Athens that performed it alone.[3]

[1] Supplying εἰκός (as in Aristophanes) from the previous couplet; text and interpretation uncertain.  [2] The Muse?  [3] With reference to Marathon or Salamis? See A. J. Podlecki, *Historia* 17 (1968) 269 ff.

**eleg. 10** Plutarch, *On the Malice of Herodotus*

As for the Corinthians, the position they occupied while fighting the Barbarians and the consequences the battle

Σιμωνίδου πυθέσθαι γράφοντος ἐν τούτοις·

μέσσοις δ' οἵ τ' Ἐφύρην πολυπίδακα ναιετάοντες,
    παντοίης ἀρετῆς ἴδριες ἐν πολέμῳ,
οἵ τε πόλιν Γλαύκοιο Κορίνθιον ἄστυ νέμοντες·

**eleg. 11** pergit Plut.

οἳ

κάλλιστον μάρτυν ἔθεντο πόνων,
χρυσοῦ τιμήεντος ἐν αἰθέρι· καί σφιν ἀέξει
    αὐτῶν τ' εὐρεῖαν κληδόνα καὶ πατέρων.

ταῦτα γὰρ οὐ χορὸν ἐν Κορίνθῳ διδάσκων, οὐδ' ᾆσμα ποιῶν εἰς τὴν
πόλιν, ἄλλως δὲ τὰς πράξεις ἐκείνας ἐλεγεῖα γράφων ἱστόρηκεν.

**eleg. 12** Apoll. Soph. (p. 117 Bekker)

ξενοδόκος, ξενοδόχος, ὁ τοὺς ξένους ὑποδεχόμενος. ὁ δὲ Πίνδα-
ρος (fr. 311 Snell) 'ξεινοδόκησέν τε δαίμων' ἀντὶ τοῦ ἐμαρτύρησε.
καὶ ἐν τῇ Ὀδυσσείᾳ (18. 64) 'ξεινοδόκος μὲν ἐγώ' ἔδοξέ τισι λέ-
γειν <    >. φησὶ γοῦν Σιμωνίδης·

ξεινοδόκων †δ'† ἄριστος ὁ χρυσὸς ἐν αἰθέρι λάμπων,

ἀντὶ τοῦ μαρτύρων.

cf. *Et. Gen.* (p. 38 Calame), *Et. Mag.* 610. 43, *Et. Gud.* 414. 35,
Zonar. 1415, Hsch. ξ 32, 48 (ii 725 Latte)

ξεινοδοκῶν *Et. Gen.* cod. B        γὰρ ἄριστος Bergk        ὁ om. *Et.*
λαμπρός Apoll.

of Plataea had for them, we may learn all this from Simonides, who writes:

and in the centre the men who dwell in Ephyra[1] with its many springs, skilled in all manner of excellence in war, and those who inhabit the Corinthian city of Glaucus[2];

[1] See fr. 596.    [2] Founder of Corinth; see fr. 572.

**eleg. 11** Plutarch (continued)

who

established for themselves the finest witness of their struggle, a witness of precious gold in the sky,[1] which increases the wide glory of both them and their fathers.

He gave this account not when training a chorus in Corinth nor when composing an ode for the city but simply when putting those exploits into elegiacs.

[1] The sun.

**eleg. 12** Apollonius the Sophist

ξεινοδόκος, ξενοδόχος : 'he who welcomes strangers'; but Pindar (fr. 311 Snell) has 'and the god welcomed' (ξεινοδόκη-σεν) in the sense of 'bore witness', and in the *Odyssey* (18. 64) 'I am the host' (ξεινοδόκος) has been taken by some to mean 'I am the witness'. Simonides at any rate says,

best of witnesses is the gold,[1] shining in the sky,

where ξεινοδόκων ('hosts') has the sense of 'witnesses'.

[1] Cf. eleg. 11.

# GREEK LYRIC

**eleg. 13** = LXXXIX *F.G.E.*    Stob. 1. 8. 22 (i 97 Wachs-muth-Hense) (περὶ χρόνου οὐσίας καὶ μερῶν καὶ πόσων εἴη αἴτιος)

Σιμωνίδου ἐπιγραμμάτων·

ὅ τοι Χρόνος ὀξὺς ὀδόντας,
καὶ πάντα ψήχει καὶ τὰ βιαιότατα.

2 Pierson: ψύχει, ψύχῃ codd.    πάντα καταψήχει Bergk    κἂπ πάντα ψήχει ci. West

**eleg. 14** Ael. Aristid. *Or.* 28. 59s. (ii 160s. Keil)

ἀλλὰ τήν γε τοῦ Σιμωνίδου σωφροσύνην οἶσθα. . . . οὗτος τοίνυν ἀνὴρ φανεῖταί σοι καὶ αὐτὸς μειρακιευόμενος καὶ τὸ λεγόμενον δὴ τοῦτο ἐπὶ γήραος οὐδῷ γευόμενος τῆς ἀλαζονείας· ἐτόλμησε γοῦν εἰπεῖν·

μνήμην δ᾽ οὔτινά φημι Σιμωνίδῃ ἰσοφαρίζειν.

ταυτὶ γὰρ οὐχ ἕτερος δήπου περὶ τοῦ Σιμωνίδου λέγει, ἀλλ᾽ αὐτὸς εἰς ἑαυτὸν πεποίηκεν· ἵνα δὲ μὴ δόξῃ νέος ὢν ἔτι καὶ ὡραϊζόμενος λέγειν ταῦτα, προστίθησιν·

ὀγδωκονταέτει παιδὶ Λεωπρέπεος,

ὥσπερ ἐνδεικνύμενος καὶ λέγων ὅτι ταῦτα ἐγὼ περὶ ἐμαυτοῦ φρονῶ καὶ λέγω καὶ ἀνακηρύττω ὀγδοηκοντούτης ὤν, ὥστε οὐ μειρακιεύομαι ἀλλὰ τἀληθὲς εἴρηκα.

1 μνήμην cod. Q: μνήμη cett.

**eleg. 15** Plut. *an seni sit gerenda resp.* 1 (v 1. 23 Hubert)

τὸ γὰρ

πόλις ἄνδρα διδάσκει

κατὰ Σιμωνίδην ἀληθές ἐστιν ἐπὶ τῶν χρόνον ἐχόντων μεταδιδαχθῆναι καὶ μεταμαθεῖν μάθημα διὰ πολλῶν ἀγώνων καὶ πραγμάτων μόλις ἐκπονούμενον.

516

# SIMONIDES

**eleg. 13** Stobaeus, *Anthology* (on the nature, parts and effects of time)

From the epigrams of Simonides:

Time is sharp-toothed, and he grinds up all things, even the mightiest.

**eleg. 14** Aelius Aristides, *Orations*

But you know, of course, the moderation of Simonides.... Now even he will give you the clear impression of behaving like a youngster and although 'on the threshold of old age', as the saying goes, of indulging in braggadocio; at any rate he could say,

and I declare that in power of memory no one rivals Simonides.

This is not someone else speaking about Simonides: he wrote it about himself, and so as not to give the impression of saying it while still in the bloom of his youth he adds,

eighty years old, the son of Leoprepes,[1]

as if to say with all clarity, 'This is my view and my statement and my proclamation about myself at the age of eighty: I am not behaving like a youngster but have spoken the truth.'

[1] This line recurs at XXVIII 6.

**eleg. 15** Plutarch, *Should old men govern?*

For Simonides' saying,

the city is teacher of the man,

is true for those who still have time to be taught a new lesson and learn a new subject which can be mastered only with difficulty after much toil and trouble.

# GREEK LYRIC

**eleg. 16** ( = LXXV *F.G.E.*)    *A.P.* 7. 511

τοῦ αὐτοῦ = Σιμωνίδου·

σῆμα καταφθιμένοιο Μεγακλέος εὖτ᾽ ἂν ἴδωμαι,
οἰκτίρω σε, τάλαν Καλλία, οἷ᾽ ἔπαθες.


**eleg. 17** *A.P.* 13. 30

Σιμωνίδου. ἑξάμετρος, καὶ οὗτος τροχαϊκὸς τετράμετρος κατὰ μετάθεσιν τῆς λέξεως·

Μοῦσά μοι ᾽Αλκμήνης καλλισφύρου υἱὸν ἄειδε·
υἱὸν ᾽Αλκμήνης ἄειδε Μοῦσά μοι καλλισφύρου.

1, 2 καλλίσφυρον cod.

518

# SIMONIDES

**eleg. 16** ( = LXXV *F.G.E.*)    *Palatine Anthology*

By Simonides:

Whenever I see the tomb of dead Megacles, I pity you, poor Callias, for your loss.

**eleg. 17** *Palatine Anthology*

By Simonides: a hexameter followed by a trochaic tetrameter formed by rearrangement of the words:

Muse, sing for me of the son[1] of fair-ankled Alcmena. Of the fair-ankled son of Alcmena sing, Muse, for me.

[1] Heracles. See Timocreon fr. 10 West.

## EPIGRAMS

*The following epigrams are those included by Page in Epigrammata Graeca and Further Greek Epigrams under the heading 'Simonides', and the numeration is his. 'Epigram' in this context has its literal meaning of 'inscription' (ἐπί-γραμμα): the poems are intended for inscription on a gravestone or to accompany a dedication or a monument. Since inscriptions of the age of Sim. never bear the poet's name, there is no certainty that Sim. was the author of any of them; VI and perhaps XXII (a) and (b) have the strongest claim to authenticity; an ascription to Sim. in e.g. Palatine Anthology is worthless. I–IV are dated before the Persian Wars; I–II are ascribed to Sim. V–XXIV deal with events of the Wars; V–XIX are ascribed to Sim. XXV–XL deal with people and events of Sim.'s lifetime; XXV–XXXVII (except for XXVIb) are ascribed to him. XLI–XLIV are miscellaneous epigrams ascribed to him. XLV–LVIII, although ascribed to him, deal with events after his death, and the remainder, although bearing his name, are also*

# GREEK LYRIC

## ΕΠΙΓΡΑΜΜΑΤΑ

I Heph. *Ench.* 4. 6 (p. 14s. Consbruch) (1–2) + lapis ed.
Meritt, *Hesperia* 5 (1936) 355 (2 Ἁρμόδιο[ς, 4) = *S.E.G.* x
320 = 430 Hansen

πᾶν μέτρον εἰς τελείαν περατοῦται λέξιν· ὅθεν ἐπίληπτά ἐστι
τὰ τοιαῦτα Σιμωνίδου ἐκ τῶν ἐπιγραμμάτων·

ἦ μέγ' Ἀθηναίοισι φόως γένεθ', ἡνίκ' Ἀριστο-
    γείτων Ἵππαρχον κτεῖνε καὶ Ἁρμόδιος·
[                                              ]
[          ἰσόνομον πα]τρίδα γῆν ἐθέτην.

4 ἰσόνομον suppl. Peek, ἐν ἐλευθερίαι Friedländer

II *A. Plan.* 26

Σιμωνίδου·

Δίρφυος ἐδμήθημεν ὑπὸ πτυχί, σῆμα δ' ἐφ' ἡμῖν
    ἐγγύθεν Εὐρίπου δημοσίᾳ κέχυται·
οὐκ ἀδίκως, ἐρατὴν γὰρ ἀπωλέσαμεν νεότητα
    τρηχεῖαν πολέμου δεξάμενοι νεφέλην.

# SIMONIDES

*likely to be spurious. A collection of 'Simonidean' epigrams, the Sylloge Simonidea, was in circulation by c. 100 B.C., when Meleager drew on it for his Garland, and may have been begun by 250 B.C.; see F.G.E. pp. 119–123.*

**I** Hephaestion, *Handbook on Metres*

Every line ends with a complete word; so lines like those of Simonides from his epigrams are reprehensible[1]:

Truly a great light dawned for the Athenians when Aristogiton and Harmodius killed Hipparchus.

Inscribed base from Athenian agora (477/6 B.C.)[2]

... Harmodius ... (the pair) made their native land (democratic?).[3]

[1] Since the word Aristo-giton is split between hexameter and pentameter. [2] The two couplets will have formed the inscription on the base of the bronze monument of Harmodius and Aristogiton sculpted in 477/6 by Critias and Nesiotes to replace the earlier group (c. 508/7) by Antenor, which was carried off by the Persians. [3] Or 'free'.

**II** *Planudean Anthology*

By Simonides:

We were laid low in a glen of Dirphys,[1] and the mound has been piled up over us near the Euripus at public expense; not without justice, for we lost our lovely youth when we awaited the harsh cloud of war.[2]

[1] Mountain in Euboea, north-east of Chalcis. [2] Perhaps the epitaph for the Euboeans or the Athenians killed when Athens defeated Chalcis in 507/6 B.C. (Hdt. 5. 74–77); see also III.

# GREEK LYRIC

**III** Hdt. 5. 77. 2–4 = *I.G.* 1² 394 ( = Suppl. 334a) = 1. 334 + 373. 69 = 179 Hansen

τῆς δὲ αὐτῆς ταύτης ἡμέρης οἱ Ἀθηναῖοι διαβάντες ἐς τὴν Εὔ-
βοιαν συμβάλλουσι καὶ τοῖσι Χαλκιδεῦσι, νικήσαντες δὲ καὶ τούτους
τετρακισχιλίους κληρούχους ἐπὶ τῶν ἱπποβοτέων τῇ χώρῃ λεί-
πουσι· οἱ δὲ ἱπποβόται ἐκαλέοντο οἱ παχέες τῶν Χαλκιδέων. ὅσους
δὲ καὶ τούτων ἐζώγρησαν, ἅμα τοῖσι Βοιωτῶν ἐζωγρημένοισι εἶχον
ἐν φυλακῇ ἐν πέδαις δήσαντες· χρόνῳ δὲ ἔλυσάν σφεας δίμνεως
ἀποτιμησάμενοι. τὰς δὲ πέδας αὐτῶν, ἐν τῇσι ἐδεδέατο, ἀνεκρέμα-
σαν ἐς τὴν ἀκρόπολιν, αἵ περ ἔτι καὶ ἐς ἐμὲ ἦσαν περιεοῦσαι, κρε-
μάμεναι ἐκ τειχέων περιπεφλευσμένων πυρὶ ὑπὸ τοῦ Μήδου, ἀντίον
δὲ τοῦ μεγάρου τοῦ πρὸς ἑσπέρην τετραμμένου. καὶ τῶν λύτρων
τὴν δεκάτην ἀνέθηκαν ποιησάμενοι τέθριππον χάλκεον· τὸ δὲ ἀρι-
στερῆς χειρὸς ἕστηκε πρῶτα ἐσιόντι ἐς τὰ προπύλαια τὰ ἐν τῇ
ἀκροπόλι· ἐπιγέγραπται δὲ οἱ τάδε·

desμῷ ἐν †ἀχλυόεντι† σιδηρέῳ ἔσβεσαν ὕβριν
παῖδες Ἀθηναίων ἔργμασιν ἐν πολέμου
ἔθνεα Βοιωτῶν καὶ Χαλκιδέων δαμάσαντες·
τῶν ἵππους δεκάτην Παλλάδι τάσδ' ἔθεσαν.

cf. P.Oxy. 2535, Diodor. 10. 24. 3, Ael. Aristid. *or.* 28. 64, *A.P.* 6. 343 (ἄδηλον)

ἀχνυνθέντι Hdt. codd. AB, *A.P.*, ἀχνυνθέντι Hdt. cod. C, ἀχλυόεντι Hdt. cett., Diodor.: ἀχνυόεντι Hecker

**IV** Hdt. 4. 88

Δαρεῖος δὲ μετὰ ταῦτα ἡσθεὶς τῇ σχεδίῃ τὸν ἀρχιτέκτονα αὐτῆς
Μανδροκλέα τὸν Σάμιον ἐδωρήσατο πᾶσι δέκα. ἀπ' ὧν δὴ Μανδρο-
κλέης ἀπαρχήν, ζῷα γραψάμενος πᾶσαν τὴν ζεῦξιν τοῦ Βοσπόρου

---

[1] On his expedition against Scythia, c. 514/513 B.C.　　[2] Over the Bosporus.

522

# SIMONIDES

**III** Herodotus, *Histories*

On the same day[1] the Athenians crossed to Euboea and joined battle with the Chalcidians also, and on defeating them too left four thousand landed settlers on the estates of the 'horse-owners', as the wealthy Chalcidians were called. All whom they captured they kept under guard in chains along with the Boeotian prisoners, but eventually they let them go free for an assessed ransom of two hundred drachmas each. The chains in which they had been bound they hung up on the Acropolis, where they still were in my time, hanging on walls scorched by the Persians opposite the west-facing shrine. Moreover, they spent a tenth of the ransom-money on the dedication of a bronze four-horse chariot, which stands first on the left as one enters the Propylaea on the Acropolis.[2] The inscription on it is as follows:

In (painful?) iron chains the sons of the Athenians quenched the pride of the nations of Boeotia and Chalcis, subduing them in war's work; with a tenth part of the ransom they dedicated these mares to Pallas.[3]

[1] After the defeat of the Boeotians in 507/6 B.C.; see also II.
[2] See Paus. 1. 28. 2.    [3] Found also on two fragmentary bases from the Acropolis, dated to late 6th c. and mid-5th c. (when Pericles must have replaced the original monument), and in Diodorus, Aristides and *Palatine Anthology*; in all except the earlier inscription the line-order is 3, 2, 1, 4. No ancient source attests Sim.'s authorship.

**IV** Herodotus, *Histories*

Darius,[1] delighted by the pontoon,[2] rewarded its builder, the Samian Mandrocles, with no fewer than ten gifts. Mandrocles used part of these to have a painting done showing the whole business of bridging the Bosporus

523

καὶ βασιλέα τε Δαρεῖον ἐν προεδρίῃ κατήμενον καὶ τὸν στρατὸν αὐ-
τοῦ διαβαίνοντα, ταῦτα γραψάμενος ἀνέθηκε ἐς τὸ Ἥραιον ἐπιγρά-
ψας τάδε·

Βόσπορον ἰχθυόεντα γεφυρώσας ἀνέθηκε
    Μανδροκλέης Ἥρῃ μνημόσυνον σχεδίης,
αὑτῷ μὲν στέφανον περιθείς, Σαμίοισι δὲ κῦδος,
    Δαρείου βασιλέος ἐκτελέσας κατὰ νοῦν.

cf. *A.P.* 6. 341 (vv. 1–3)

2 Μανδροκρέων *A.P.*        3 τῷ μὲν δὴ *A.P.*

**V** *A. Plan.* 232

Σιμωνίδου·

τὸν τραγόπουν ἐμὲ Πᾶνα, τὸν Ἀρκάδα, τὸν κατὰ Μή-
        δων,
    τὸν μετ' Ἀθηναίων στήσατο Μιλτιάδης.

**VI** Hdt. 7. 228. 3–4

Λακεδαιμονίοισι μὲν δὴ τοῦτο, τῷ δὲ μάντι τόδε·

μνῆμα τόδε κλεινοῖο Μεγιστία, ὅν ποτε Μῆδοι
    Σπερχειὸν ποταμὸν κτεῖναν ἀμειψάμενοι,
μάντιος, ὃς τότε Κῆρας ἐπερχομένας σάφα εἰδώς
    οὐκ ἔτλη Σπάρτης ἡγεμόνας προλιπεῖν.

and king Darius sitting on his throne and his army crossing over; this painting he dedicated in the temple of Hera, inscribing it as follows:

Having bridged the fishy Bosporus Mandrocles dedicated to Hera a memorial of his pontoon. He won a crown for himself and glory for the Samians by completing it to the liking of king Darius.[3]

[3] Also in *Palatine Anthology* (anon.).

**V** *Planudean Anthology*

By Simonides:

I, goat-footed Pan, the Arcadian, enemy of the Medes, ally of the Athenians, was set up by Miltiades.[1]

[1] For Pan's help to Athens in 490 B.C. see Hdt. 6. 105; Sozomenus 2. 5 and Nicephorus 8. 33 speak of a statue of Pan in Constantinople dedicated after the Persian Wars by Pausanias (an error for Miltiades?).

**VI** Herodotus, *Histories*

This then (XXIIb) is the inscription for the Spartans; the inscription for the seer[1] is as follows:

This is the tomb of glorious Megistias, whom once the Medes killed when they crossed the river Sperchius[2]: he was a seer, who recognised clearly that the Spirits of Death were approaching then, but could not bring himself to desert Sparta's leaders.[3]

[1] Megistias of Acarnania: see Hdt. 7. 219, 221.   [2] Just north of Thermopylae.   [3] Also in *Palatine Anthology* (anon.).

# GREEK LYRIC

... τὸ δὲ τοῦ μάντιος Μεγιστίεω (sc. ἐπίγραμμα) Σιμωνίδης ὁ
Λεωπρέπεός ἐστι κατὰ ξεινίην ὁ ἐπιγράψας.

cf. *A.P.* 7. 677 (anon.)

1 κλειτοῖο Hdt. codd. DRSV

**VII** *A.P.* 7. 301, Plan.

τοῦ αὐτοῦ = Σιμωνίδου·

εὐκλέας αἶα κέκευθε, Λεωνίδα, οἳ μετὰ σεῖο
τῇδ᾽ ἔθανον, Σπάρτης εὐρυχόρου βασιλεῦ,
πλείστων δὴ τόξων τε καὶ ὠκυπόδων σθένος ἵππων
Μηδείων ἀνδρῶν δεξάμενοι πολέμῳ.

**VIII** *A.P.* 7. 253, Plan.

Σιμωνίδου·

εἰ τὸ καλῶς θνήσκειν ἀρετῆς μέρος ἐστὶ μέγιστον,
ἡμῖν ἐκ πάντων τοῦτ᾽ ἀπένειμε Τύχη·
Ἑλλάδι γὰρ σπεύδοντες ἐλευθερίην περιθεῖναι
κείμεθ᾽ ἀγηράντῳ χρώμενοι εὐλογίῃ.

cf. schol. Aristid. (iii 154s. Dindorf)

**IX** *A.P.* 7. 251, Plan.

τοῦ αὐτοῦ = Σιμωνίδου·

ἄσβεστον κλέος οἵδε φίλῃ περὶ πατρίδι θέντες
κυάνεον θανάτου ἀμφεβάλοντο νέφος·
οὐδὲ τεθνᾶσι θανόντες, ἐπεί σφ᾽ ἀρετὴ καθύπερθε
κυδαίνουσ᾽ ἀνάγει δώματος ἐξ Ἀίδεω.

---

[1] Like VIII, referred by the lemmatist to Thermopylae, but probably the epitaph of the Spartans at Plataea.

# SIMONIDES

... The inscription for the seer Megistias was put there by
Simonides, the son of Leoprepes, for friendship's sake.

**VII** *Palatine Anthology*

By Simonides:

Glorious the men whom the earth covers, those
who died here with you, Leonidas, king of wide
Sparta, after awaiting in battle the might of the
many bows and swift-footed horses of the Medes.[1]

[1] Probably a Hellenistic composition; the epitaph for the Spartan
grave at Thermopylae is XXII(b).

**VIII** *Palatine Anthology*

By Simonides:

If the greatest part of virtue is to die nobly, then
Fortune granted it to us above all others; for we
strove to crown Greece with freedom and lie here in
possession of unaging praise.[1]

[1] Said by the lemmatist to refer to Thermopylae, but more probably
the epitaph of the Athenians at Plataea. Pausanias 9. 2. 4 says the
tombs of the Spartans and Athenians there carried epitaphs by
Sim.; see also IX.

**IX** *Palatine Anthology*

By Simonides:

These men set imperishable fame about their
dear country, and threw around themselves the
dark cloud of death. They died but are not dead:
their valour gives them glory above and brings them
up from the house of Hades.[1]

# GREEK LYRIC

**X** Plut. *de Herod. malign.* 39. 870f (V 2. 2. 46 Häsler)

αὐτός γε μὴν ὁ Ἀδείμαντος, ᾧ πλεῖστα λοιδορούμενος Ἡρόδοτος διατελεῖ καὶ λέγων μοῦνον ἀσπαίρειν τῶν στρατηγῶν, ὡς φευξόμενον ἀπ' Ἀρτεμισίου καὶ μὴ περιμενοῦντα, σκόπει τίνα δόξαν εἶχεν·

οὗτος Ἀδειμάντου κείνου τάφος, ὃν διὰ πᾶσα
Ἑλλὰς ἐλευθερίας ἀμφέθετο στέφανον.

(871a) οὔτε γὰρ τελευτήσαντι τοιαύτην εἰκὸς ἦν ἀνδρὶ δειλῷ καὶ προδότῃ γενέσθαι τιμήν . . .

cf. *A.P.* 7. 347, Favorin. (ps.-Dio Prus.) *or.* 37. 19 (Σιμωνίδῃ)

1 κλεινοῦ ci. Page     οὗ διὰ βουλὰς *A.P.*, Favorin.


**XI** Plut. *de Herod. malign.* 39. 870e (V 2. 2. 45 Häsler) = *I.G.* 1² 927 (1 ]ονποκεναιομεσαστυϙορινθο[ , 2 ]ντος[) = 131 Hansen

ἐν δὲ Σαλαμῖνι παρὰ τὴν πόλιν ἔδωκαν αὐτοῖς θάψαι τε τοὺς ἀποθανόντας ὡς ἄνδρας ἀγαθοὺς γενομένους καὶ ἐπιγράψαι τόδε τὸ ἐλεγεῖον·

ὦ ξεῖν', εὔυδρόν ποκ' ἐναίομες ἄστυ Κορίνθου,
νῦν δ' ἅμ' Αἴαντος νᾶσος ἔχει Σαλαμίς·
ἐνθάδε Φοινίσσας νᾶας καὶ Πέρσας ἑλόντες
καὶ Μήδους ἱαρὰν Ἑλλάδα ῥυσάμεθα.

cf. Favorin. (ps.-Dio Prus.) *or.* 37. 18 (Σιμωνίδῃ)

1 ξεῖν' Favorin. cod. M     ξένε Plut., Favorin. codd. UB     2 Bergk: δ' ἀνάματος Plut.     δὲ μετ' Αἴαντος Favorin.     3 ἐνθάδε Plut.     ῥεῖα δὲ Favorin.     Boegehold: νῆας, ναῦς codd.     4 Boegehold: ἱερὰν codd.     Jacobs: ῥυόμεθα Plut.     ἱδρυσάμεθα Favorin.

528

# SIMONIDES

**X** Plutarch, *On the Malice of Herodotus*

As for Adimantus[1] himself, on whom Herodotus is forever pouring abuse,[2] in particular when he says that he was the only commander who protested, since he wanted to flee from Artemisium instead of staying to fight,[3] just look at the reputation he enjoyed later:

This is the tomb of that[4] Adimantus, thanks to whom all Greece put on the garland of freedom.[5]

It was not likely that he should be so honoured after his death if he had been a coward and traitor . . .

[1] Commander of the Corinthians at Artemisium and Salamis.
[2] 8. 5, 59, 61, 94.  [3] 8. 5; cf. 8. 94 (on Salamis).  [4] Or 'famous'.  [5] Also in *Palatine Anthology* (anon.) and Favorinus, who ascribes it to Sim.

**XI** Plutarch, *On the Malice of Herodotus*

And on Salamis near the city the Athenians allowed the Corinthians to bury their dead since they had displayed courage and to inscribe the following elegiac poem:

Stranger, once we lived in the well-watered[1] city of Corinth, but now Salamis, the island of Ajax, holds us; here we destroyed Phoenician ships and Persians and Medes and saved holy Greece.[2]

[1] With reference to its fountains.  [2] Quoted also by Favorinus, who attributes it to Sim.; the original stone has parts of the first two lines and may well have had all four: see A. L. Boegehold, *G.R.B.S.* 6 (1965) 179 ff.

# GREEK LYRIC

**XII** Plut. *de Herod. malign.* 39. 870e (V 2. 2. 45 Häsler)

τὸ δ' ἐν Ἰσθμῷ κενοτάφιον ἐπιγραφὴν ἔχει ταύτην·

ἀκμᾶς ἑστακυῖαν ἐπὶ ξυροῦ Ἑλλάδα πᾶσαν
    ταῖς αὐτῶν ψυχαῖς κείμεθα ῥυσάμενοι
[δουλοσύνης· Πέρσαις δὲ περὶ φρεσὶ πήματα πάντα
    ἥψαμεν, ἀργαλέης μνήματα ναυμαχίης.
5 ὀστέα δ' ἡμὶν ἔχει Σαλαμίς, πατρὶς δὲ Κόρινθος
    ἀντ' εὐεργεσίης μνῆμ' ἐπέθηκε τόδε.]

cf. *A.P.* 7. 250 (Σιμωνίδου) (vv. 1–2), Plan., schol. Aristid. (iii 136 Dindorf (vv. 1–2), Ael. Aristid. *or.* 28. 66 (ii 163 Keil) (vv 1–6)

**XIII** Plut. *de Herod. malign.* 39. 870f (V 2. 2. 46 Häsler)

Διοδώρου δέ τινος τῶν Κορινθίων τριηράρχων ἐν ἱερῷ Λητοῦς ἀναθήμασι κειμένοις καὶ τοῦτ' ἐπιγέγραπται·

ταῦτ' ἀπὸ δυσμενέων Μήδων ναῦται Διοδώρου
    ὅπλ' ἀνέθεν Λατοῖ, μνάματα ναυμαχίας.

cf. *A.P.* 6. 215 (τοῦ αὐτοῦ = Σιμωνίδου)

1 δυσαμένων *A.P.*          2 Blomfield: ἀνέθεντο codd.

**XIV** Schol. Pind. *Ol.* 13. 32b (i 364s. Drachmann)

... Θεόπομπος δέ φησι (*F.Gr.H.* 115 F 285 Jacoby) καὶ τὰς γυναῖκας αὐτῶν (sc. τῶν Κορινθίων) εὔξασθαι τῇ Ἀφροδίτῃ ἔρωτα ἐμπεσεῖν τοῖς ἀνδράσιν αὐτῶν μάχεσθαι ὑπὲρ τῆς Ἑλλάδος τοῖς Μήδοις, εἰσελθούσας εἰς τὸ ἱερὸν τῆς Ἀφροδίτης ...· εἶναι δὲ καὶ νῦν ἀναγεγραμμένον ἐλεγεῖον εἰσιόντι εἰς τὸν ναὸν ἀριστερᾶς χειρός·

# SIMONIDES

**XII** Plutarch, *On the Malice of Herodotus*

The cenotaph at the Isthmus carries this inscription:

All Greece stood on the razor's edge: we lie here, having rescued it with our own lives [from slavery; on the Persians' hearts we fastened all manner of woe, a reminder of a grievous sea-battle. Salamis holds our bones, but our native land Corinth set this monument over us in return for our good deed].[1]

[1] Vv. 3–6 are given only by Aristides and are probably a later addition; but 1 2 are scarcely complete in themselves.

**XIII** Plutarch, *On the Malice of Herodotus*

And this is the inscription on offerings dedicated in the temple of Leto by a Diodorus, one of the Corinthian captains:

These weapons, taken from the hostile Medes, the sailors of Diodorus dedicated to Leto as a memorial of the sea-battle.[1]

[1] Salamis. Epigram ascribed to Sim. in *Palatine Anthology*.

**XIV** Scholiast on Pindar, *Ol.* 13. 23 ('in Corinth Ares flourishes in the deadly spears of the young men')

Theopompus[1] says that the Corinthian wives too went into Aphrodite's temple and prayed to her that their men be smitten with a passion for fighting the Medes on behalf of Greece . . .; even now, he says, there is an inscribed elegiac poem on the left as one enters the temple:

[1] Historian from Chios, 4th c. B.C.

# GREEK LYRIC

αἵδ᾽ ὑπὲρ Ἑλλάνων τε καὶ ἀγχεμάχων πολιατᾶν
ἔστασαν εὐχόμεναι Κύπριδι δαιμόνια·
οὐ γὰρ τοξοφόροισιν ἐβούλετο δῖ᾽ Ἀφροδίτα
Μήδοις Ἑλλάνων ἀκρόπολιν δόμεναι.

cf. Plut. *de Herod. malign*. 39. 871ab (vv. 1–4, Σιμωνίδης), Athen.
13. 573c-e (vv. 1–4, Σιμωνίδης)

1 ἰθυμάχων Plut., εὐθυμάχων Athen.      2 ἐστάθεν seu ἐστ- Plut.,
Athen.      εὐξάμεναι Plut., εὔχεσθαι Athen.      δαιμόνια ( = δαιμονίας
εὐχάς) Bernardakis: δαιμόνιαι codd.      3 ἐμήδετο Plut., ἐμήσατο
Athen.      4 Πέρσαις Athen.      προδόμεν Plut., Athen.

**XV** Plut. *vit. Aristid*. 19. 7 (1. 1. 276 Ziegler)

καὶ τὸν βωμὸν οὐκ ἂν ἐπέγραψαν οὕτως, εἰ μόναι τρεῖς πόλεις
ἠγωνίσαντο τῶν ἄλλων ἀτρέμα καθεζομένων·

τόνδε ποθ᾽ Ἕλληνες Νίκης κράτει, ἔργῳ Ἄρηος,
Πέρσας ἐξελάσαντες ἐλευθέρᾳ Ἑλλάδι κοινόν
ἱδρύσαντο Διὸς βωμὸν Ἐλευθερίου.

cf. *de Herod. malign*. 42. 873b, *A.P.* 6. 50, Plan., (Σιμωνίδου), ubi v. 2
invenias εὐτόλμῳ ψυχῆς λήματι πειθόμενοι

1 Ν. κ. Plut.: ῥώμη χερὸς *A.P.*, Plan.      2 ἐλεύθερον Plut. codd.
UA, *A.P.*, Plan.      κόσμον *A.P.*, Plan.

**XVI** *I.G.* vii 53 = *S.E.G.* xiii 312 (v. A. Wilhelm ap.
G. Pfohl, *Die griechische Elegie* 311ss.)

τὸ ἐπίγραμμα τῶν ἐν τῷ Περσικῷ πολέμῳ ἀποθανόντων καὶ
κειμένων ἐνταῦθα ἡρώων, ἀπολόμενον δὲ τῷ χρόνῳ, Ἑλλάδιος ὁ
ἀρχιερεὺς ἐπιγραφῆναι ἐποίησεν εἰς τιμὴν τῶν κειμένων καὶ τῆς
πόλεως. Σιμωνίδης ἐποίει.

---

[1] Helladius probably used a literary source for his text. The monu-

# SIMONIDES

These women stand making an inspired prayer to
Cypris for the Greeks and their close-fighting
fellow-countrymen; for the goddess Aphrodite was
unwilling to hand over to the bowmen Medes the
acropolis of the Greeks.[2]

[2] I.e. Corinth. Athenaeus' account is drawn from the essay *On Pin-
dar* by Chamaeleon, who cites Theopompus and book 7 of Timaeus
as his authorities; in his version, the women were the temple-
slaves of Aphrodite, the dedication was a painting, and Sim. wrote
the epigram. Plutarch, *On the Malice of Herodotus* says the women
were Corinthian wives, bronze statues were dedicated, and Sim.
composed the epigram.

## XV Plutarch, *Life of Aristides*

And they would not have put the following inscription
on the altar if only three cities had fought while the others
sat quietly by[1]:

Once the Greeks, having driven out the Persians
by the might of Victory and the work of Ares,[2] set up
this altar of Zeus, giver of freedom, an altar common
to a free Greece.[3]

[1] At Plataea; Hdt. 9. 59 ff., 85, says only Spartans, Tegeans and
Athenians fought in the final engagement.    [2] *Palatine
Anthology* adds a pentameter, omitted in Plutarch, 'obeying the
bold pride of their spirit', and ascribes the epigram to Sim.
[3] Cf. Paus. 9. 2. 5, Strabo 9. 2. 31.

## XVI Inscribed stone from Megara (4th c. A.D. or later)

Since the epigram for the heroes who died in the Per-
sian war and lie here had been destroyed by time, Hella-
dius the high priest had it inscribed in honour of the dead
and the city.[1] Simonides was the author.[2]

ment is likely to have been a cenotaph, but see Paus. 1. 43. 3.
[2] Doubtful, as usual, but see fr. 629.

Ἑλλάδι καὶ Μεγαρεῦσιν ἐλεύθερον ἆμαρ ἀέξειν
  ἱέμενοι θανάτου μοῖραν ἐδεξάμεθα,
τοὶ μὲν ὑπ' Εὐβοίαι καὶ Παλίωι, ἔνθα καλεῖται
  ἁγνᾶς Ἀρτέμιδος τοξοφόρου τέμενος,
5 τοὶ δ' ἐν ὄρει Μυκάλας, τοὶ δ' ἔμπροσθεν Σαλαμῖνος
  <                                              >
τοὶ δὲ καὶ ἐν πεδίωι Βοιωτίωι, οἵτινες ἔτλαν
  χεῖρας ἐπ' ἀνθρώπους ἱππομάχους ἱέναι.
ἀστοὶ δ' ἄμμι τόδε <ξυνὸν> γέρας ὀμφαλῶι ἀμφίς
10    Νισαίων ἔπορον λαοδόκωι 'ν ἀγορᾶι.

μέχρις ἐφ' ἡμῶν δὲ ἡ πόλις ταῦρον ἐναγίζει (-εν lapis).

9 suppl. Wade-Gery        10 Wade-Gery: λαοδοκων lapis

XVII (a) Thuc. 1. 132. 2

. . . ἐπὶ τὸν τρίποδά ποτε τὸν ἐν Δελφοῖς, ὃν ἀνέθεσαν οἱ Ἕλλη-
νες ἀπὸ τῶν Μήδων ἀκροθίνιον, ἠξίωσεν ἐπιγράψασθαι αὐτὸς ἰδίᾳ
τὸ ἐλεγεῖον τόδε·

Ἑλλάνων ἀρχαγός, ἐπεὶ στρατὸν ὤλεσε Μήδων,
  Παυσανίας Φοίβωι μνᾶμ' ἀνέθηκε τόδε.

τὸ μὲν οὖν ἐλεγεῖον οἱ Λακεδαιμόνιοι ἐξεκόλαψαν εὐθὺς τότε ἀπὸ
τοῦ τρίποδος τόδε καὶ ἐπέγραψαν ὀνομαστὶ τὰς πόλεις ὅσαι ξυγκα-
θελοῦσαι τὸν βάρβαρον ἔστησαν τὸ ἀνάθημα.

cf. 'Dem.' in Neaer. 97, Aristodem. (F.Gr.H. 104 F 4 Jacoby), Plut.
de Herod. malign. 42. 873c, Apostol. cent. vii 9d, Sud. Π 820, A.P. 6.
197 (Σιμωνίδου), Paus. 3. 8. 2 (Σιμωνίδης), Nep. Paus. 1. 3, Ael. Aris-
tid. 3. 199

# SIMONIDES

While striving to foster the day of freedom for Greece and the Megarians, we received the portion of death, some under Euboea and Pelion, where stands the sanctuary of the holy archer Artemis,[3] others at the mountain of Mycale,[4] others before Salamis . . .[5], others again in the Boeotian plain, those who had courage to lay hands on the cavalry warriors.[6] The citizens granted us this privilege in common about the navel of the Nisaeans[7] in their agora where the people throng.

Up to our own day the city has consecrated a bull.

[3] At Artemisium.   [4] Site of the naval battle of 479 B.C.
[5] The stone-cutter has omitted a pentameter line.   [6] At Plataea; Hdt. 9. 69 reports that the Theban cavalry killed 600 Megarians and Phliasians.   [7] Nisus was mythical king of Megara.

**XVII** (a) Thucydides, *History*

. . . Pausanias[1] had once thought fit to inscribe on his own authority the following elegiac couplet on the tripod at Delphi which the Greeks dedicated from the spoils of the Medes:

When Pausanias, commander of the Greeks, had destroyed the army of the Medes, he set up this memorial to Phoebus.

The Spartans had at once erased this couplet from the tripod and inscribed on it the names of all the cities which had set up the dedication after jointly destroying the Barbarians.[2]

[1] Commander of the Greeks at Plataea.   [2] The names may still be seen on the snake-column, now in the Hippodrome of Constantinople.

(b) Diod. Sic. 11. 33. 2 (ii 272 Vogel)

οἱ δ᾽ Ἕλληνες ἐκ τῶν λαφύρων δεκάτην ἐξελόμενοι κατεσκεύα-
σαν χρυσοῦν τρίποδα καὶ ἀνέθηκαν εἰς Δελφοὺς χαριστήριον τῷ
θεῷ, ἐπιγράψαντες ἐλεγεῖον τόδε·

Ἑλλάδος εὐρυχόρου σωτῆρες τόνδ᾽ ἀνέθηκαν
    δουλοσύνης στυγερᾶς ῥυσάμενοι πόλιας.

**XVIII** *A.P.* 7. 257, Plan. (ἄδηλον, Plan. ἀδέσποτον)

παῖδες Ἀθηναίων Περσῶν στρατὸν ἐξολέσαντες
    ἤρκεσαν ἀργαλέην πατρίδι δουλοσύνην.

cf. schol. Aristid. (iii 154 Dindorf: τοῦ αὐτοῦ = Σιμωνίδου; iii 136 Dindorf)

1 ἐξελάσαντες schol. 136 cod. unus

**XIX** *A.P.* 6. 2, Plan.

Σιμωνίδου·

τόξα τάδε πτολέμοιο πεπαυμένα δακρυόεντος
    νηῷ Ἀθηναίης κεῖται ὑπωρόφια,
πολλάκι δὴ στονόεντα κατὰ κλόνον ἐν δαῒ φωτῶν
    Περσῶν ἱππομάχων αἵματι λουσάμενα.

**XIX** (a) Plut. *de Herod. malign.* 36. 869c (V 2. 2. 41s. Häsler)

ὅτι δ᾽ οὐκ ἐπαινέσαι βουληθεὶς Δημόκριτον ἀλλ᾽ ἐπ᾽ αἰσχύνη
Ναξίων συνέθηκε τὸ ψεῦδος δῆλός ἐστι τῷ παραλιπεῖν ὅλως καὶ

# SIMONIDES

(b) Diodorus Siculus, *World History*

The Greeks set aside a tenth part of the spoils[1] and made a gold tripod, which they dedicated at Delphi as a thank-offering to the god, inscribing this elegiac couplet on it:

The saviours of spacious Greece dedicated this tripod, having rescued their cities from hateful slavery.

[1] After Plataea, but the memorial was for the whole war.

## XVIII *Palatine Anthology* (anon.)

The sons of the Athenians destroyed the army of the Persians and warded off painful slavery from their native land.[1]

[1] Ascribed to Sim. by scholiast on Aristides.

## XIX *Palatine Anthology*

By Simonides:

These bows, at rest from tearful war, lie beneath the roof of Athena's temple; often in the grievous turmoil amid the fighting of warriors they bathed in the blood of Persian cavalrymen.[1]

[1] The style suggests a Hellenistic literary exercise.

## XIX (a) Plutarch, *On the Malice of Herodotus*

It is clear that it was not from any wish to praise Democritus that he fabricated his lie[1] but in order to disgrace the Naxians, for he has suppressed completely the success

[1] Hdt. 8. 46. 3 says the Naxians sent four ships to Salamis to fight on the Persian side, but Democritus, one of the captains, persuaded them to join the Greeks.

537

# GREEK LYRIC

παρασιωπῆσαι τὸ Δημοκρίτου κατόρθωμα καὶ τὴν ἀριστείαν, ἣν
ἐπιγράμματι Σιμωνίδης ἐδήλωσε·

Δημόκριτος τρίτος ἦρξε μάχης, ὅτε πὰρ Σαλαμῖνα
    Ἕλληνες Μήδοις σύμβαλον ἐν πελάγει·
πέντε δὲ νῆας ἕλεν δήων, ἕκτην δ' ὑπὸ χειρός
    ῥύσατο βαρβαρικῆς Δωρίδ' ἁλισκομένην.

3s Turnebus: χεῖρα . . . βαρβαρικὴν codd.

**XX** *S.E.G.* x 404 + Meritt, *The Aegean and the Near East:
Studies . . . H. Goldman* (1956) 268ff. = 2 Hansen

(a) ἀνδρῶν τῶνδ' ἀρετῆ[ς ἔσται κλέ]ος ἄφθι[τον] αἰεί
    [ . . . . . . . . . ]ν[ . ]ρ . [ . . . . . . . ] νέμωσι θεοί·
    ἔσχον γὰρ πεζοί τε [καὶ] ὠκυπόρων ἐπὶ νηῶν
    Ἑλλά[δα μ]ὴ πᾶσαν δούλιον ἦμαρ ἰδεῖν.

(b) ἦν ἄρα τοῖσζ' ἀδάμ[αντος ὑπέρβιον ἦτορ,] ὅτ'
        αἰχμήν
    στῆσαν πρόσθε πυλῶν ἀν[
    ἀγχίαλον πρῆσαι ῥ[        c.xviii litt.        ]ο
    ἄστυ, βίαι Περσῶν κλινάμενο[ι προμάχους.

(a) 1 suppl. Peek        (b) 1 suppl. Page post Wilhelm
2s. ἀντία δ' ἱεμένους | ἀ. π. ῥύσαντ' ἐρικυδὲς Ἀθηνᾶς e.g. Page
4 suppl. Page

538

of Democritus and his display of valour which Simonides set out in an epigram[2]:

Democritus was the third[3] to begin battle when the Greeks clashed at sea with the Medes off Salamis; he captured five enemy ships and rescued a sixth, a Dorian vessel, from capture at barbarian hands.

[2] Rather, a short elegiac poem, perhaps composed by a Naxian (Page).    [3] After Athens and Aegina (Hdt. 8. 84. 2).

**XX** Inscriptions on an Athenian monument base (soon after 479 B.C.?)[1]

(a) The fame of the valour of these men[2] will be undying always, (so long as) the gods apportion (glory to brave men); for both on foot and on swift-sailing ships they kept all Greece from seeing the day of slavery.[3]

(b) These men[2] must have had (a stout heart of adamant), when they took up arms before the gates (and checked men eager) to burn (Athena's glorious) seaside city, forcibly turning back the champions of the Persians.[4]

[1] (b) was added after (a); a fragment of a 4th c. B.C. copy of (a) is also known.    [2] The monument must have given the names of the dead.    [3] Probably composed to commemorate Salamis (including the land-fighting on Psyttalia).    [4] Seemingly an epigram for the Marathon dead, added to the Salamis monument after the original Marathon monument was destroyed by the Persians in 480.

# GREEK LYRIC

**XXI** Lycurg. *in Leocr*. 109 (p. 71 Durrbach)

τοιγαροῦν ἐπὶ τοῖς ἠρίοις (Wurm: ὁρίοις τοῦ βίου codd.) μαρ-
τύριά ἐστιν ἰδεῖν τῆς ἀρετῆς αὐτῶν ἀναγεγραμμένα ἀληθῆ πρὸς
ἅπαντας τοὺς Ἕλληνας, ἐκείνοις μὲν (XXIIb), τοῖς δ' ὑμετέροις
προγόνοις·

> Ἑλλήνων προμαχοῦντες Ἀθηναῖοι Μαραθῶνι
> χρυσοφόρων Μήδων ἐστόρεσαν δύναμιν.

cf. Ael. Aristid. *or*. 28. 63, schol. Aristid. *or*. 46. 118 (p. 289 From-
mel), *Sud*. Π 3079

2 ἔκτειναν Μήδων ἐννέα μυριάδας Aristid.    ἔκτειναν Μ. εἴκοσι μ.
schol., *Sud*.

**XXII** Hdt. 7. 228

θαφθεῖσι δέ σφι αὐτοῦ ταύτῃ τῇ περ ἔπεσον καὶ τοῖσι πρότερον
τελευτήσασι ἢ <τοὺς> ὑπὸ Λεωνίδεω ἀποπεμφθέντας οἴχεσθαι
ἐπιγέγραπται γράμματα λέγοντα τάδε·

(a) μυριάσιν ποτὲ τῇδε τριηκοσίαις ἐμάχοντο
    ἐκ Πελοποννήσου χιλιάδες τέτορες.

ταῦτα μὲν δὴ τοῖσι πᾶσι ἐπιγέγραπται, τοῖσι δὲ Σπαρτιήτῃσι ἰδίη·

(b) ὦ ξεῖν', ἀγγέλλειν Λακεδαιμονίοις ὅτι τῇδε
    κείμεθα, τοῖς κείνων ῥήμασι πειθόμενοι.

540

# SIMONIDES

**XXI** Lycurgus, *Against Leocrates*

So on their tombs there is inscribed true testimony of their valour for all the Greeks to see: for the Spartans (XXII b), for your ancestors:

Fighting to defend the Greeks the Athenians laid low at Marathon the might of the gold-apparelled Medes.[1]

[1] Probably inscribed together with a list of the fallen on a stele on the grave-mound at Marathon. Aristides, scholiast on Aristides, and the *Suda* give a different pentameter: '(the Athenians at Marathon) killed ninety thousand (or 'two hundred thousand') of the Medes.' The *Suda* reports that the couplet was on the painting of Marathon in the Stoa Poikile in Athens. No ancient authority ascribes it to Sim.

**XXII** Herodotus, *Histories* (on the fighting at Thermopylae)

They were buried where they fell, as were those who died before the departure of those whom Leonidas sent away, and over them are inscriptions worded as follows:

(a) Here four thousand from the Peloponnese once fought against three million.[1]

That is the inscription for the whole army; the Spartans have their own:

[1] Attributed to Sim. in *Palatine Anthology*.

(b) Stranger, report to the Spartans that we lie here, obedient to their words.[2]

[2] Much quoted by later writers; ascribed to Sim. in *Palatine Anthology* and by Cicero, who translated it (*T.D.* 1. 42).

Λακεδαιμονίοισι μὲν δὴ τοῦτο, τῷ δὲ μάντι τόδε· (VI). ἐπι-
γράμμασι μέν νυν καὶ στήλησι, ἔξω ἢ τὸ τοῦ μάντιος ἐπίγραμμα,
Ἀμφικτύονές εἰσί σφεας οἱ ἐπικοσμήσαντες, τὸ δὲ τοῦ μάντιος
Μεγιστίεω Σιμωνίδης ὁ Λεωπρέπεός ἐστι κατὰ ξεινίην ὁ ἐπιγρά-
ψας.

(a) cf. Diod. Sic. 11. 33. 2, Ael. Aristid. 28. 65, A.P. 7. 248 (Σιμωνί-
δου), Plan., Sud. Λ 272

1 διηκοσίαις, διακ-, Diod.          2 -νάσου Hdt. cod. B, A.P.

(b) cf. Lycurg. in Leocr. 109 (v. XXI supra), Diod. Sic. 11. 33. 2, Str.
9. 4. 16, A.P. 7. 249 (Σιμωνίδου), Plan, Sud. Λ 272, Cic. T.D. 1. 42
(Simonides)

1 ἄγγειλον Lycurg., Diod., A.P.     ἄγγελλε Sud.     ὦ ξέν' ἀπάγγειλον
Str.     2 ῥ. π. Hdt., A.P., Plan., Sud.     πειθόμενοι νομίμοις
Lycurg., Diod., Str.

**XXIII** Str. 9. 4. 2 (ii 284 Kramer)

ὁ δ' Ὁποῦς ἐστι μητρόπολις, καθάπερ καὶ τὸ ἐπίγραμμα δηλοῖ
τὸ ἐπὶ τῇ πρώτῃ τῶν πέντε στηλῶν τῶν περὶ Θερμοπύλας ἐπιγε-
γραμμένον πρὸς τῷ πολυανδρίῳ·

τούσδε ποθεῖ φθιμένους ὑπὲρ Ἑλλάδος ἀντία Μήδων
μητρόπολις Λοκρῶν εὐθυνόμων Ὀπόεις.

1 Meineke: ποτὲ codd.

**XXIV** Plut. vit. Themist. 8. 4s. (1. 1. 166s. Ziegler)

ἔχει δὲ (sc. Ἀρτεμίσιον) ναὸν οὐ μέγαν Ἀρτέμιδος ἐπίκλησιν
Προσηῴας, καὶ δένδρα περὶ αὐτὸν πέφυκε καὶ στῆλαι κύκλῳ λίθου
λευκοῦ πεπήγασιν· ... ἐν μιᾷ δὲ τῶν στηλῶν ἐλεγεῖον ἦν τόδε
γεγραμμένον·

παντοδαπῶν ἀνδρῶν γενεὰς Ἀσίας ἀπὸ χώρας
παῖδες Ἀθηναίων τῷδέ ποτ' ἐν πελάγει
ναυμαχίᾳ δαμάσαντες, ἐπεὶ στρατὸς ὤλετο Μήδων
σήματα ταῦτ' ἔθεσαν παρθένῳ Ἀρτέμιδι.

cf. de Herod. malign. 34. 867f

That is the Spartan inscription; the inscription for the seer is as follows (VI). The inscriptions and stelae, with the exception of the seer's inscription, were put there in their honour by the Amphictions[3]; the inscription for the seer Megistias was put there by Simonides, the son of Leoprepes, for friendship's sake.

[3] Members of the league based on the temple of Demeter at Anthela (near Thermopylae).

**XXIII** Strabo, *Geography* (on the Locrians)

Opus is their mother-city, as is shown by the inscription on the first of the five stelae at Thermopylae near the heroes' grave:

These men who died for Greece against the Medes are mourned by Opus, mother-city of the Locrians of the upright laws.

**XXIV** Plutarch, *Life of Themistocles*

Artemisium has a smallish temple of Artemis of the East; around it trees grow and stelae of white stone stand in a circle; ... on one of the stelae these elegiac couplets were inscribed:

The sons of the Athenians once subdued in a sea-battle[1] on these waters tribes of all manner of men from the land of Asia, and after the host of the Medes perished dedicated these tokens to the virgin Artemis.

[1] See frr. 532–5.

**XXV** A. *Plan.* 24

τοῦ αὐτοῦ ( = Σιμωνίδου)

Μίλωνος τόδ' ἄγαλμα καλοῦ καλόν, ὅς ποτε Πίσῃ
ἑπτάκι νικήσας ἐς γόνατ' οὐκ ἔπεσεν.

**XXVI** (a) Thuc. 6. 59. 3

Ἱππόκλου γοῦν τοῦ Λαμψακηνοῦ τυράννου Αἰαντίδῃ τῷ παιδὶ
τὴν θυγατέρα ἑαυτοῦ μετὰ ταῦτα Ἀρχεδίκην Ἀθηναῖος ὢν Λαμ-
ψακηνῷ ἔδωκεν, αἰσθανόμενος αὐτοὺς μέγα παρὰ βασιλεῖ Δαρείῳ
δύνασθαι. καὶ αὐτῆς σῆμα ἐν Λαμψάκῳ ἐστὶν ἐπίγραμμα ἔχον
τόδε·

ἀνδρὸς ἀριστεύσαντος ἐν Ἑλλάδι τῶν ἐφ' ἑαυτοῦ
Ἱππίου Ἀρχεδίκην ἥδε κέκευθε κόνις,
ἣ πατρός τε καὶ ἀνδρὸς ἀδελφῶν τ' οὖσα τυράννων
παίδων τ' οὐκ ἤρθη νοῦν ἐς ἀτασθαλίην.

cf. Ar. *Rhet.* 1. 9. 20, 1367b (v. 3, τὸ τοῦ Σιμωνίδου)

**XXVI** (b) Thuc. 6. 54. 6s. = *I.G.* i² 761 = 305 Hansen

τὰ δὲ ἄλλα αὐτὴ ἡ πόλις τοῖς πρὶν κειμένοις νόμοις ἐχρῆτο,
πλὴν καθ' ὅσον αἰεί τινα ἐπεμέλοντο σφῶν αὐτῶν ἐν ταῖς ἀρχαῖς
εἶναι. καὶ ἄλλοι τε αὐτῶν ἦρξαν τὴν ἐνιαύσιον Ἀθηναίοις ἀρχὴν
καὶ Πεισίστρατος ὁ Ἱππίου τοῦ τυραννεύσαντος υἱός, τοῦ πάππου
ἔχων τοὔνομα, ὃς τῶν δώδεκα θεῶν βωμὸν τὸν ἐν τῇ ἀγορᾷ ἄρχων

# SIMONIDES

## XXV *Planudean Anthology*

By Simonides:

This is the handsome statue of handsome Milo,
who once won seven times by the water of Pisa[1]
without falling to his knees.

[1] Pausanias 6. 14. 5 says he won six wrestling victories at Olympia,
but *Palatine Anthology* 11. 316 records a crown awarded when no
opponent appeared. His career is dated *c.* 540 to *c.* 510.

## XXVI (a) Thucydides, *History*

At any rate after that Hippias[1] gave his daughter
Archedice in marriage to Aeantides, son of Hippoclus, the
tyrant of Lampsacus — an Athenian to a Lampsacene! —
since he saw that the family had great influence with King
Darius. Her tomb is in Lampsacus with this inscription:

This dust covers Archedice, daughter of Hippias,
the foremost man in Greece of his day; although her
father, her husband, her brothers[2] and her sons
were tyrants, she did not lift up her heart to arro-
gance.[3]

[1] Tyrant of Athens, 527–510 B.C.   [2] One brother was archon
in Athens: see XXVI (b).   [3] Aristotle ascribes the epitaph to
Sim.

## XXVI (b) Thucydides, *History* (on the Pisistratids)

In other respects the city itself enjoyed the laws that
had previously been established, except that they always
made sure that one of their own family was in office.
Among those of them who held the annual archonship at
Athens was Pisistratus, son of Hippias who held the
tyranny, with the same name as his grandfather: when he
was archon,[1] he dedicated the altar of the twelve gods in

[1] Almost certainly in 522/1 B.C.

ἀνέθηκε καὶ τὸν τοῦ Ἀπόλλωνος ἐν Πυθίου. . . . τοῦ δ' ἐν Πυθίου
ἔτι καὶ νῦν δῆλόν ἐστιν ἀμυδροῖς γράμμασι λέγον τάδε ·

μνῆμα τόδ' ἧς ἀρχῆς Πεισίστρατος Ἱππίου υἱός
θῆκεν Ἀπόλλωνος Πυθίου ἐν τεμένει.

## XXVII A.P. 6. 213

ἀνάθημα τοῦ αὐτοῦ ( = Σιμωνίδου)

ἓξ ἐπὶ πεντήκοντα, Σιμωνίδη, ἤραο ταύρους
    καὶ τρίποδας πρὶν τόνδ' ἀνθέμεναι πίνακα,
τοσσάκι δ' ἱμερόεντα διδαξάμενος χορὸν ἀνδρῶν
    εὐδόξου Νίκας ἀγλαὸν ἅρμ' ἐπέβης.

cf. Tzetz. *chil.* 1. 639–42, 4. 486

## XXVIII Syrian. in Hermog. (i 86 Rabe)

πάσης γὰρ ἐπιστήμων ἀνὴρ ποιητικῆς τε καὶ μουσικῆς ὑπῆρχεν
(sc. ὁ Σιμωνίδης), ὡς ἐκ νεότητος μέχρις ὀγδοήκοντα ἐτῶν νικᾶν
ἐν τοῖς ἀγῶσιν Ἀθήνησιν, ὡς καὶ τὸ ἐπίγραμμα δηλοῖ ·

ἦρχεν Ἀδείμαντος μὲν Ἀθηναίοις ὅτ' ἐνίκα
    Ἀντιοχὶς φυλὴ δαιδάλεον τρίποδα ·
Ξεινοφίλου δέ τις υἱὸς Ἀριστείδης ἐχορήγει
    πεντήκοντ' ἀνδρῶν καλὰ μαθόντι χορῷ ·
5 ἀμφὶ διδασκαλίῃ δὲ Σιμωνίδῃ ἕσπετο κῦδος
    ὀγδωκονταέτει παιδὶ Λεωπρέπεος.

φασὶ δὲ αὐτὸν μετὰ τὴν νίκην πλεῦσαι πρὸς Ἱέρωνα καὶ μετ'
ὀλίγον ἐν Σικελίᾳ τελευτῆσαι.

cf. Plut. *an seni* 3. 785a, Val. Max. 8. 7. 13, schol. Tzetz. *chil.* 1. 624
(p. 552s. Leone)

the agora and that of Apollo in the Pythian precinct.... The inscription on the altar in the Pythion is still visible in dim lettering[2] with the following wording:

This memorial of his archonship was dedicated by Pisistratus, son of Hippias, in the sanctuary of Pythian Apollo.[3]

[2] The paint must have faded.

[3] Parts of the altar and inscription survive.

## XXVII *Palatine Anthology*

Dedication by Simonides[1]:

Fifty-six bulls and tripods, Simonides, did you win before setting up this tablet; fifty-six times after training the delightful chorus of men did you step aboard the glorious chariot of honoured Victory.

[1] See test. 11. Tzetzes also ascribes his version of the lines to Sim.

## XXVIII Syrianus on Hermogenes, *On Kinds of Style*

For Simonides was knowledgeable in all poetry and music, so that he won victories in the Athenian contests from his youth to the age of eighty, as the inscription shows[1]:

Adimantus was archon in Athens when the Antiochid tribe won the intricately-made tripod; one Aristides, son of Xenophilus, was *choregos* of the chorus of fifty men who had learned well; and for their training glory came the way of Simonides, son of Leoprepes, at the age of eighty.[2]

They say that after the victory he sailed to Hiero and died soon after in Sicily.

[1] See test. 5.

[2] The last line recurs at eleg. 14. 2.

# GREEK LYRIC

**XXIX** Paus. 6. 9. 9 (ii 98s. Rocha-Pereira)

παρὰ δὲ τοῦ Γέλωνος τὸ ἅρμα ἀνάκειται Φίλων, τέχνη τοῦ Αἰ-
γινήτου Γλαυκίου. τούτῳ τῷ Φίλωνι Σιμωνίδης ὁ Λεωπρέπους
ἐλεγεῖον δεξιώτατον ἐποίησε·

> πατρὶς μὲν Κόρκυρα, Φίλων δ' ὄνομ', εἰμὶ δὲ Γλαύκου
> υἱός, καὶ νικῶ πὺξ δύ' Ὀλυμπιάδας.

**XXX** A. Plan. 2

Σιμωνίδου·

> γνῶθι Θεόγνητον προσιδὼν τὸν Ὀλυμπιονίκαν
> παῖδα, παλαισμοσύνης δεξιὸν ἡνίοχον,
> κάλλιστον μὲν ἰδεῖν, ἀθλεῖν δ' οὐ χείρονα μορφῆς,
> ὃς πατέρων ἀγαθῶν ἐστεφάνωσε πόλιν.

1 Schneidewin: Θεόκριτον cod.

**XXXI** A. Plan. 23

Σιμωνίδου·

> — εἶπον τίς, τίνος ἐσσί, τίνος πατρίδος, τί δ' ἐνίκης;
> — Κασμύλος, Εὐαγόρου, Πύθια πύξ, Ῥόδιος.

1 Bergk: δὲ νικῆς cod.

# SIMONIDES

**XXIX** Pausanias, *Description of Greece* (on Olympia)

Next to Gelo's chariot is dedicated the statue of Philo, the work of Glaucias of Aegina.[1] For this statue Simonides son of Leoprepes composed a very clever couplet:

My native land is Corcyra, my name is Philo, I am the son of Glaucus, and I won two boxing victories at Olympia.[2]

[1] Early 5th c. B.C.     [2] In 492 and 488 B.C.


**XXX** *Planudean Anthology*

By Simonides:

Learn when you look that this is Theognetus, boy winner at Olympia,[1] skilled driver of the chariot of wrestling, most handsome to look at and no less impressive as athlete, the boy who garlanded the city of his excellent fathers.

[1] Probably in 476 B.C. (see P.Oxy. 222. 15). Paus. 6. 9. 1 says the statue was by Ptolichus of Aegina, the boy's home. Pindar celebrated his nephew's wrestling victory at Delphi (*Pyth.* 8).


**XXXI** *Planudean Anthology*

By Simonides:

— Give your name, father's name, native city and victory.
— Casmylus, Euagoras, Rhodes, Pythian boxing.[1]

[1] Pindar celebrated his victory in Isthmian boxing (frr. 2, 3).

# GREEK LYRIC

**XXXII** *A.P.* 9. 757, Plan. (Σιμωνίδου)

Ἰφίων τόδ᾽ ἔγραψε Κορίνθιος · οὐκ ἔνι μῶμος
χερσίν, ἐπεὶ δόξας ἔργα πολὺ προφέρει.

cf. *A.P.* 13. 17 Ἰφίων ἔγραψεν ἑᾷ χερί, τόν ποκα ὕδωρ | ἔθρεψε Πειράνας
ἄπο.

1 ἔπι Bergk

**XXXIII** (a) *A. Plan.* 84

οὐκ ἀδαὴς ἔγραψε Κίμων τάδε · παντὶ δ᾽ ἐπ᾽ ἔργῳ
μῶμος, ὃν οὐδ᾽ ἥρως Δαίδαλος ἐξέφυγεν.

(b) *A.P.* 9. 758, Plan. (Σιμωνίδου)

Κίμων ἔγραψε τὴν θύραν τὴν δεξιάν,
τὴν δ᾽ ἐξιόντων δεξιὰν Διονύσιος.

**XXXIV** Schol. Pind. *Pyth.* 1. 152b (ii 26 Drachmann)

φασὶ δὲ τὸν Γέλωνα τοὺς ἀδελφοὺς φιλοφρονούμενον ἀναθεῖναι
τῷ θεῷ χρυσοῦς τρίποδας ἐπιγράψαντα ταῦτα ·

φημὶ Γέλων᾽, Ἱέρωνα, Πολύζηλον, Θρασύβουλον,
παῖδας Δεινομένευς, τοὺς τρίποδας θέμεναι

2 τὸν τρίποδ᾽ ἀνθέμεναι *A.P.*, *Sud.*

# SIMONIDES

**XXXII** *Palatine Anthology*

Iphion of Corinth[1] painted this; there is no fault to be found in his hands: his works far surpass his reputation.

[1] *C.* 500 B.C.: see next poem. The *Anthology* (13. 17) has another of his 'advertisements': 'Iphion painted this with his own hand: water from Pirene once nourished him', i.e. he is Corinthian.

**XXXIII** (a) *Planudean Anthology*

Cimon[1] who painted these is not unskilled; yet fault may be found in any work: even the hero Daedalus did not escape it.

[1] *C.* 500 B.C.; see Pliny *N.H.* 35. 56. The lines may be an answer to the previous poem.

(b) *Palatine Anthology*[1]

Cimon painted the right-hand door, Dionysius the right-hand door as one leaves.

[1] Ascribed to Sim. by *Planudean Anthology*.

**XXXIV** Scholiast on Pindar, *Pyth.* 1. 79

They say that Gelo out of kindness to his brothers dedicated gold tripods to the god[1] with the following inscription:

I say that Gelo, Hiero, Polyzelus and Thrasybulus, the sons of Dinomenes, dedicated the tripods after defeating the barbarian tribes,[2] and gave the

[1] Apollo at Delphi.    [2] Gelo defeated the Carthaginians at Himera in 480, Hiero the Etruscans at Cumae in 474.

βάρβαρα νικήσαντας ἔθνη, πολλὴν δὲ παρασχεῖν
σύμμαχον Ἕλλησιν χεῖρ' ἐς ἐλευθερίην.

cf. A.P. 6. 214 (Σιμωνίδου), Sud. Δ 71

3s. ἐξ ἑκατὸν λιτρῶν καὶ πεντήκοντα ταλάντων | δαρετίου χρυσοῦ τὰς
δεκάτας δεκάταν A.P., Sud.

**XXXV** A.P. 13. 14

Σιμωνίδου ·

Ἀργεῖος Δάνδις σταδιόδρομος ἐνθάδε κεῖται
νίκαις ἱππόβοτον πατρίδ' ἐπευκλεΐσας
Ὀλυμπίᾳ δίς, ἐν δὲ Πυθῶνι τρία,
δύω δ' ἐν Ἰσθμῷ, πεντεκαίδεκ' ἐν Νεμέᾳ.
τὰς δ' ἄλλας νίκας οὐκ εὐμαρές ἐστ' ἀριθμῆσαι.

**XXXVI** A.P. 13. 26

Σιμωνίδου ἐπιτύμβιον ·

μνήσομαι, οὐ γὰρ ἔοικεν ἀνώνυμον ἐνθάδ' Ἀρχεναύτεω
κεῖσθαι θανοῦσαν ἀγλαὰν ἄκοιτιν
Ξανθίππην, Περιάνδρου ἀπέκγονον, ὅς ποθ' ὑψιπύργου
σήμαινε λαοῖς τέρμ' ἔχων Κορίνθου.

Greeks a strong helping hand in the cause of freedom.[3]

[3] The poem is probably a Hellenistic literary exercise; the inscriptions for Gelo's dedication and (in part) for Hiero's survive (*S.I.G.* 34, 35c). *Palatine Anthology* ('Sim.') and *Suda* give a different second couplet: '(tripods) of a hundred litres and fifty talents of daretian gold, a tithe of the tithe'; see Page's discussion (*F.G.E.* 247 ff.).

**XXXV** *Palatine Anthology*

By Simonides:

Dandis of Argos, the stadion-runner, lies here after glorifying with his victories his horse-breeding land, twice at Olympia,[1] three times at Pytho, twice at the Isthmus, fifteen times in Nemea. His other victories it is not easy to count.

[1] In 476 and 472 (P.Oxy. 222. 8, 20): cf. Diod. Sic. 11. 53. 1.

**XXXVI** *Palatine Anthology*

An epitaph by Simonides:

I shall mention her[1]: for it is not fitting that the glorious wife of Archenautes lie here unnamed in death, Xanthippe, great-grandchild of Periander[2] who once gave orders to the people of high-towered Corinth where he held sway.

[1] The stele speaks.     [2] Tyrant of Corinth, *c.* 625–585 B.C.

# GREEK LYRIC

**XXXVII** *A.P.* 7. 348, Plan.

Σιμωνίδου τοῦ Κηίου·

πολλὰ πιὼν καὶ πολλὰ φαγὼν καὶ πολλὰ κάκ' εἰπὼν
ἀνθρώπους κεῖμαι Τιμοκρέων Ῥόδιος.

cf. Athen. 10. 415f

**XXXVIII** Ael. Aristid. *or.* 28. 63 (ii 162 Keil)

ἀρά σοι καὶ τὰ τοιάδε δόξει ἀλαζόνειά τις εἶναι· (XXI), καὶ

ἀμφί τε Βυζάντειαν ὅσοι θάνον ἰχθυόεσσαν
ῥυόμενοι χώραν ἄνδρες ἀρηΐθοοι.

1 Bergk: Βυζάντιον codd.

**XXXIX** Athen. 12. 536ab (ii 181s. Kaibel)

Νύμφις δ' ὁ Ἡρακλεώτης ἐν ἕκτῳ τῶν περὶ τῆς πατρίδος
(*F.Gr.H.* 432 F 9) 'Παυσανίας' φησίν 'ὁ περὶ Πλαταιὰς νικήσας
Μαρδόνιον, τὰ τῆς Σπάρτης ἐξελθὼν νόμιμα καὶ εἰς ὑπερηφανίαν
ἐπιδοὺς περὶ Βυζάντιον διατρίβων τὸν χαλκοῦν κρατῆρα τὸν ἀνα-
κείμενον τοῖς θεοῖς τοῖς ἐπὶ τοῦ στόματος ἱδρυμένοις, ὃν ἔτι καὶ νῦν
εἶναι συμβαίνει, ἐτόλμησεν ἐπιγράψαι ὡς αὐτὸς ἀναθείη, ὑποθεὶς
τόδε τὸ ἐπίγραμμα, διὰ τὴν τρυφὴν καὶ ὑπερηφανίαν ἐπιλαθόμενος
αὑτοῦ·

μνᾶμ' ἀρετᾶς ἀνέθηκε Ποσειδάωνι ἄνακτι
Παυσανίας ἄρχων Ἑλλάδος εὐρυχόρου
πόντου ἐπ' Εὐξείνου, Λακεδαιμόνιος γένος, υἱός
Κλεομβρότου, ἀρχαίας Ἡρακλέος γενεᾶς.'

554

# SIMONIDES

**XXXVII** *Palatine Anthology*

By Simonides of Ceos:

After much drinking, much eating and much slandering[1] of men I lie here, Timocreon of Rhodes.[2]

[1] E.g. fr. 727 on Themistocles.    [2] A mock epitaph, attributed to Sim. by the Corrector in *Anthology*; see also Sim. eleg. 17 with Timocr. 10 West.

**XXXVIII** Aelius Aristides, *Orations*

You will surely not regard lines like these as braggadocio of a sort: (XXI) and

and all who died to save the land of Byzantium,[1] rich in fish, men swift for Ares.

[1] Occasion unknown.

**XXXIX** Athenaeus, *Scholars at Dinner*

Nymphis[1] of Heraclea says in book 6 of his *History of Heraclea,* 'Pausanias, victor over Mardonius at Plataea, went beyond all bounds of Spartan convention and became excessively arrogant; while at Byzantium[2] he had the insolence to inscribe as his own dedication the bronze mixing-bowl dedicated to the gods whose shrines are at the entrance to the Black Sea[3]; the bowl still exists, and this was the inscription he added, forgetting himself in his wanton arrogance:

This memorial of his valour was dedicated to lord Poseidon at the Black Sea by Pausanias, commander of spacious Greece, a Spartan by birth, son of Cleombrotus, of the ancient family of Heracles.'

[1] Historian of 3rd c. B.C.    [2] Pausanias captured the city when commanding an allied Greek fleet in 478 B.C.    [3] See Hdt. 4. 81. 3.

# GREEK LYRIC

**XL** Aeschin. *in Ctes.* 183ss. (p. 256s. Blass)

ἦσάν τινες, ὦ ἄνδρες Ἀθηναῖοι, κατὰ τοὺς τότε καιρούς, οἳ
πολὺν πόνον ὑπομείναντες καὶ μεγάλους κινδύνους ἐπὶ τῷ Στρυ-
μόνι ποταμῷ ἐνίκων μαχόμενοι Μήδους· οὗτοι δεῦρο ἀφικόμενοι τὸν
δῆμον ᾔτησαν δωρεάν, καὶ ἔδωκεν αὐτοῖς ὁ δῆμος τιμὰς μεγάλας,
ὡς τότ' ἐδόκει, τρεῖς λιθίνους Ἑρμᾶς στῆσαι ἐν τῇ στοᾷ τῇ τῶν
Ἑρμῶν, ἐφ' ᾧτε μὴ ἐπιγράφειν τὸ ὄνομα τὸ ἑαυτῶν, ἵνα μὴ τῶν
στρατηγῶν ἀλλὰ τοῦ δήμου δοκῇ εἶναι τὸ ἐπίγραμμα. ὅτι δ' ἀληθῆ
λέγω, ἐξ αὐτῶν τῶν ποιημάτων γνώσεσθε. ἐπιγέγραπται γὰρ ἐπὶ
τῷ μὲν πρώτῳ τῶν Ἑρμῶν·

(b) ἦν ἄρα κἀκεῖνοι ταλακάρδιοι, οἵ ποτε Μήδων
    παισὶν ἐπ' Ἠϊόνι Στρυμόνος ἀμφὶ ῥοάς
λιμόν τ' αἴθωνα κρυερόν τ' ἐπάγοντες Ἄρηα
    πρῶτοι δυσμενέων εὗρον ἀμηχανίην.

τῷ δὲ δευτέρῳ·

(c) ἡγεμόνεσσι δὲ μισθὸν Ἀθηναῖοι τάδ' ἔδωκαν
    ἀντ' εὐεργεσίης καὶ μεγάλων ἀγαθῶν·
μᾶλλόν τις τάδ' ἰδὼν καὶ ἐπεσσομένων ἐθελήσει
    ἀμφὶ περὶ ξυνοῖς πράγμασι δῆριν ἔχειν.

(b) 3 κρυερόν Plut.: κρατερόν Aeschin.    (c) 2 μεγάλων ἀγαθῶν
Plut.: μεγάλης ἀρετῆς Aeschin.    4 ἀμφὶ ξυνοῖσι πράγμασι μόχθον
ἔχειν Aeschin.

# SIMONIDES

**XL** Aeschines, *Against Ctesiphon*

In those days, gentlemen, there were some who endured much hardship and great dangers at the river Strymon before defeating the Medes in battle.[1] When they returned here to Athens they asked the people for a reward, and the people granted them what was then regarded as high honour, the right to set up three stone Herms in the Stoa of the Herms, on condition that they did not inscribe their own names on them, lest the inscription seem to belong to the generals rather than to the people. You will learn the truth of my words from the poems themselves: on the first of the Herms is written:

(b)[2] They too were of steadfast heart who once at Eion on the waters of the Strymon subjected the sons of the Medes to fiery hunger and chilling Ares and were the first to discover the helplessness of the enemy.

On the second:

(c) And to their leaders the Athenians granted these as reward for their good services and great benefits. A man of future generations who sees these will be the more willing to engage in battle for the common good.

[1] In 475 B.C. Cimon with a Greek army captured Eion from the Persians (Hdt. 7. 107, Thuc. 1. 98, Diod. 11. 60). Plutarch, *Cimon* quotes the verses; see also Demosthenes, *Lept.* 112.  [2] Plutarch also gives the verses in this order, but the sequence should clearly be (a) (b) (c).

# GREEK LYRIC

ἐπὶ δὲ τῷ τρίτῳ ἐπιγέγραπται Ἑρμῇ·

(a) ἔκ ποτε τῆσδε πόληος ἅμ᾽ Ἀτρεΐδῃσι Μενεσθεύς
    ἡγεῖτο ζαθέον Τρωϊκὸν ἐς πεδίον,
ὅν ποθ᾽ Ὅμηρος ἔφη Δαναῶν πύκα θωρηκτάων
    κοσμητῆρα μάχης ἔξοχον ὄντα μολεῖν.
5 οὕτως οὐδὲν ἀεικὲς Ἀθηναίοισι καλεῖσθαι
    κοσμηταῖς πολέμου τ᾽ ἀμφὶ καὶ ἠνορέης.

cf. Plut. *vit. Cim.* 7, Dem. *Lept.* 112

(a) 3 π. χαλκοχιτώνων Aeschin.    4 ὄντα Plut.: ἄνδρα
Aeschin.    6 κοσμητὰς Aeschin.


## XLI Aristot. *Rhet.* 1. 7. 1365a (p. 41 Roemer)

ὅθεν καὶ τὸ ἐπίγραμμα τῷ Ὀλυμπιονίκῃ·

πρόσθε μὲν ἀμφ᾽ ὤμοισιν ἔχων τραχεῖαν ἄσιλλαν
    ἰχθῦς ἐξ Ἄργους εἰς Τεγέαν ἔφερον.

cf. 1. 9. 1367b, Ar. Byz. fr. 5 Slater (παρὰ Σιμωνίδῃ)

1 πρόσθεν μὲν τρ. ἔχ. ὤμ. ἄσ. priore Aristot. loco cod. A in mg. γρ


## XLII A. *Plan.* 3

τοῦ αὐτοῦ ( = Σιμωνίδου)

Ἴσθμια καὶ Πυθοῖ Διοφῶν ὁ Φίλωνος ἐνίκα
    ἅλμα ποδωκείην δίσκον ἄκοντα πάλην.

# SIMONIDES

On the third Herm is written:

(a) Once from this city Menestheus went as leader with the sons of Atreus to the holy plain of Troy; Homer once said[3] that as marshal in battle he was outstanding among the stout-corsleted Danaans. So it is not unseemly that Athenians be called marshals in war and manliness.

[3] *Il.* 2. 553 f.

**XLI** Aristotle, *Rhetoric*

Hence the inscription for the Olympic victor:

Once I used to carry a painful yoke on my shoulders and take fish from Argos to Tegea, (but now . . . )[1]

[1] The missing couplet(s) must have spoken of the Olympic victory. Aristotle, *Rhet.* 1. 9 implies that Sim. was not the author, but Aristophanes of Byzantium said he was.

**XLII** *Planudean Anthology*

By Simonides[1]:

At the Isthmian and Pythian games Diophon son of Philo won jump, foot-race, discus, javelin, wrestling.[2]

[1] Perhaps a Hellenistic literary exercise.   [2] The events of the pentathlon, but see Page *F.G.E.* 260 ff.

# GREEK LYRIC

**XLIII** *A.P.* 13. 19

Σιμωνίδου·

ἄνθηκεν τόδ' ἄγαλμα Κορίνθιος, ὅσπερ ἐνίκα
ἐν Δελφοῖς ποτε, Νικολάδας,
καὶ Παναθηναίοις στεφάνους λάβε πέντ' ἐπ' ἀέθλοις
†ἑξήκοντα ἀμφιφορεῖς† ἐλαίου·
5 Ἰσθμῷ δ' ἐν ζαθέᾳ τρὶς ἐπισχερὼ †οὐδ' ἐγένοντο
ἀκτίνων τομίδων ποταθμοι†·
καὶ Νεμέᾳ τρὶς ἐνίκησεν καὶ τετράκις ἄλλα
Πελλάνα, δύο δ' ἐν Λυκαίῳ,
καὶ †Νεμέαι† καὶ ἐν Αἰγίνᾳ κρατερᾷ τ' Ἐπιδαύρῳ
10 καὶ Θήβᾳ Μεγάρων τε δάμῳ·
ἐν δὲ Φλειοῦντι στάδιον τά τε πέντε κρατήσας
ηὔφρανεν μεγάλαν Κόρινθον.

2 ποσί Bergk  4 ἑξ. κάδους Blinkenberg  ἑξῆντ' ἀμ. Merkel-
bach  5s. οἶδεν ἑλόντα | ἀκτὰ Pflugk  Ποντομέδοντος ἄθλον
(vel ἄθλα) Jacobs  9 Τεγέᾳ Brunck  10 Θήβαις Bergk
Θήβας Wilamowitz  11 Hermann: σταδίω cod.

**XLIV** Trypho, *Trop.* ( = 'Greg. Cor.' *Trop.* 5, *Rhet. Gr.* viii
768 Walz) + P. Vindob. 29332 (ed. West, *C.Q.* 15, 1965,
239)

ἔνιοι δὲ καὶ ἐν ταῖς συλλαβαῖς ὑπερβατὰ πεποιήκασιν, ὡς καὶ
Σιμωνίδης ἐν ἐπιγράμμασιν· (deest epigramma)·  λοθε . ες
υπερβ[ . . ] . . . . [ἐνταῦθα τ]οῦ Δήμητρος τὴν τ[ε]λευταίαν [ὑπερ-
έβιβασε·] τὸ γὰρ ἑξῆς οὕτω[ς ἀπ]οδίδοται· [ Ἑρμῆν τόνδ]ε
ἀνέθηκεν Δη[μή]τριος, ὄρθια [δ' οὐκ ἐν προθ]ύροις Δήμητρος
ο . . [ . ] . . κ . ιμαθ . [

post προθύροις, ἀντὶ τοῦ οὐκ ὄρθια δέ codd.

# SIMONIDES

**XLIII** *Palatine Anthology*

By Simonides:

This statue was dedicated by Nicolaidas of Corinth, who once[1] was victor at Delphi and at the Panathenaic games won the award[2] in the pentathlon, sixty amphoras of oil; and at the holy Isthmus thrice in succession (the shore of Pontomedon knows that he took the prize?)[3]; he won thrice at Nemea and four times also at Pallene, twice at Lycaeus[4] and at (Tegea?) and in Aegina and strong Epidaurus and at Thebes and the town of Megara; and by his victory at Phlius in the stadion and pentathlon he gladdened great Corinth.

[1] Or 'in running'.    [2] Literally 'garlands'; interpretation uncertain.    [3] Text uncertain: Pontomedon is Poseidon, 'ruler of the sea'.    [4] In Arcadia.

**XLIV** Tryphon, *Figures of Speech*

Some have composed hyperbata (transpositions) of syllables, for instance Simonides in his epigrams[1]: ... hyperbaton ... (here he has transposed) the last syllable of Δή-μητρος ('of Demeter'), for the normal sequence would be

Demetrius dedicated this Herm, but the erect not in the porch of Demeter ...[2]

[1] The quotation is missing.    [2] All obscure. Headlam before publication of the papyrus suggested that the text might be Ἑρμῆν τόνδ' ἀνέθη- Δημήτριος Ὀρθιάδου -κεν | ἐν προθύροις with the last syllable of ἀνέθηκεν detached: 'Demetrius dedicated this Herm in the porch of Orthiades'; West suggests a couplet on the following lines: Ἑρμῆν τόνδ' ἀνέθηκε Σύρος Δημήτριος, οὐκ εὖ· | ὄρθια δ' οὐ Δήμητρ' ἔπρεπεν ἐν προθύροις ('Syrian Demetrius dedicated this Herm, but inappropriately: the erect was not fitting for Demeter in the porch'); he assumes that Tryphon mistook Δήμητρ(ι) for a genitive with the last syllable lost. See Page, *F.G.E.* 264 ff.

**XLV** Diod. Sic. 11. 62. 3 (ii 311 Vogel)

ὁ δὲ δῆμος τῶν Ἀθηναίων δεκάτην ἐξελόμενος ἐκ τῶν λαφύρων
ἀνέθηκε τῷ θεῷ καὶ τὴν ἐπιγραφὴν ἐπὶ τὸ κατασκευασθὲν ἀνάθημα
ἐπέγραψε τήνδε·

ἐξ οὗ τ' Εὐρώπην Ἀσίας δίχα πόντος ἔνειμεν
καὶ πόλιας θνητῶν θοῦρος Ἄρης ἐπέχει,
οὐδέν πω τοιοῦτον ἐπιχθονίων γένετ' ἀνδρῶν
ἔργον ἐν ἠπείρῳ καὶ κατὰ πόντον ἅμα·
5  οἵδε γὰρ ἐν Κύπρῳ Μήδους πολλοὺς ὀλέσαντες
Φοινίκων ἑκατὸν ναῦς ἕλον ἐν πελάγει
ἀνδρῶν πληθούσας· μέγα δ' ἔστενεν Ἀσὶς ὑπ'
αὐτῶν
πληγεῖσ' ἀμφοτέραις χερσὶ κράτει πολέμου.

cf. Ael. Aristid. 3. 140, 141, 28. 64, schol. Aristid. (iii 209 Dindorf)
(Σιμωνίδης), A.P. 7. 296 (Σιμωνίδης), Apostol. *cent.* vii 57a (Σιμωνί-
δου)

1 τ' Aristid.    γ' A.P., Diod.    ἔνειμε(ν) A.P., Diod.    ἔκρινε Aris-
tid.    2 πόλιας θν. Aristid.    πολέας θν. Diod.    πόλεμον λαῶν
A.P.    ἐπέχει Diod.    ἐφέπει A.P., Aristid.    3 οὐδέν (vel
οὐδέ) πω τοιοῦτον Diod.    οὐδενί πω κάλλιον Aristid.    οὐδάμα πω
καλλίων A.P.    4 ἅμα A.P., Diod.    ὁμοῦ Aristid.    5 Κύπρῳ
A.P., Diod.    γαίῃ Aristid.    Μήδους Diod.    Μήδων A.P.,
Aristid.    7 αὐτῶν Aristid.    αὐτῷ Diod.

**XLVI** A.P. 7. 258, Plan.

Σιμωνίδου·

οἵδε παρ' Εὐρυμέδοντά ποτ' ἀγλαὸν ὤλεσαν ἥβην
μαρνάμενοι Μήδων τοξοφόρων προμάχοις
αἰχμηταί, πεζοί τε καὶ ὠκυπόρων ἐπὶ νηῶν,
κάλλιστον δ' ἀρετῆς μνῆμ' ἔλιπον φθίμενοι.

1 -μέδοντί Plan.    ἀγλαὰν A.P.    3 αἰχμηταῖς A.P.

# SIMONIDES

**XLV** Diodorus Siculus, *World History*

The people of Athens took a tenth part of the booty[1]
and dedicated it to the god; on the dedication they put the
following inscription:

Since the time when the sea first separated
Europe from Asia[2] and wild Ares controlled the
cities of mortals, no such deed of earthly men was
ever carried out on land and sea at the same time:
these men destroyed many Medes on Cyprus and
then on the sea captured a hundred ships of the
Phoenicians with their full complement of men; and
Asia groaned loudly when struck with both hands
by them with the strength of war.[3]

[1] Diodorus connects the inscription with Cimon's victory over the
Persians at Eurymedon (468 B.C.), but he confused Eurymedon with
the Cyprus campaign (449 B.C.), to which the poem refers.
[2] V. 1 also of a late 5th c. B.C. inscription from Lycia (Hansen
177).       [3] Ascribed to Sim. by scholiast on Aristides, *Palatine
Anthology* and Apostolius; Sim. may have died in 468 or soon after.

**XLVI** *Palatine Anthology*

By Simonides:

These men once lost their splendid youth at the
Eurymedon,[1] spearmen fighting the vanguard of the
Median archers both on foot and on swift-sailing
ships, and when they died they left the finest
memorial of their valour.

[1] Where Cimon defeated the Persians (468 B.C.).

# GREEK LYRIC

**XLVII** *A.P.* 7. 443

Σιμωνίδου·

τῶνδέ ποτ' ἐν στέρνοισι τανυγλώχινας ὀιστούς
λοῦσεν φοινίσσᾳ θοῦρος "Αρης ψακάδι·
ἀντὶ δ' ἀκοντοδόκων ἀνδρῶν μνημεῖα θανόντων
ἄψυχ' ἐμψύχων ἅδε κέκευθε κόνις.

1 Meineke: ποτε στ. cod.

**XLVIII** Paus. 10. 27. 4 (iii 154 Rocha-Pereira)

κάθηται δὲ <καὶ> ἐπὶ ὄνου παιδίον μικρόν. κατὰ τοῦτο τῆς
γραφῆς καὶ ἐλεγεῖόν ἐστι Σιμωνίδου·

γράψε Πολύγνωτος, Θάσιος γένος, Ἀγλαοφῶντος
υἱός, περθομένην Ἰλίου ἀκρόπολιν.

cf. *A.P.* 9. 700 (Σιμωνίδου), Plut. *def. orac.* 47. 436b, schol. Plat.
*Gorg.* 448b, Hsch. Θ 121 Latte

1 γράψεν Ἀρίγνωτος *A.P.*

**XLIX** *A.P.* 7. 254, Plan. ( = *I.G.* i² 946 = 4 Hansen)

Σιμωνίδου·

χαίρετ' ἀριστῆες πολέμου μέγα κῦδος ἔχοντες,
κοῦροι Ἀθαναίων ἔξοχοι ἱπποσύνᾳ,
οἵ ποτε καλλιχόρου περὶ πατρίδος ὠλέσαθ' ἥβαν
πλείστοις Ἑλλάνων ἀντία μαρνάμενοι.

2 Kalinka: Ἀθην- *A.P.*, Plan.    ἱπποσύναι lapis, -νη *A.P.*, Plan.
3 ἥβην *A.P.*, Plan.

564

# SIMONIDES

**XLVII** *Palatine Anthology*

By Simonides:

Once in the breasts of these men wild Ares
washed his long-barbed arrows in crimson drops;
and in place of men who died, javelin-struck, this
dust covers memorials, lifeless in place of living.[1]

[1] A Hellenistic product, guessed by the lemmatist to refer like
XLVI to Eurymedon.

**XLVIII** Pausanias, *Description of Greece* (on Polygnotus'
painting in the Cnidian Hall at Delphi)

A little boy is sitting on the donkey. In this part of the
painting is an elegiac couplet by Simonides[1]:

Polygnotus[2] of Thasos, son of Aglaophon, painted
the sack of the acropolis of Troy.

[1] Attributed to Sim. by *Palatine Anthology* also.     [2] *Floruit c.*
475–445 B.C.

**XLIX** *Palatine Anthology*

By Simonides:

Farewell, noble warriors who enjoy great glory,
sons of the Athenians, outstanding in horseman-
ship, who once lost your youth for your native land
with its fair dancing-places, fighting against the
greater part of the Greeks.[1]

[1] The Spartan League defeated Athens and her allies at Tanagra in
457 B.C. (Thuc. 1. 107 f.). A few letters of the poem were identified
on a fragmentary stone.

**L** *A.P.* 13. 11

Σιμωνίδου·

- τίς εἰκόνα τάνδ' ἀνέθηκεν ; – Δωριεὺς ὁ Θούριος.
- οὐ Ῥόδιος γένος ἦν ; – ναί, πρὶν φυγεῖν γε πατρίδα,
δεινᾷ γε χειρὶ πολλὰ ῥέξας ἔργα καὶ βίαια.

2, 3 γε Bergk: τε cod.     3 Jacobs: πόλλ' ἔρξας cod.

**LI** *A.P.* 7. 20, Plan.

Σιμωνίδου (Corrector ἀδέσποτον)

ἐσβέσθης, γηραιὲ Σοφόκλεες, ἄνθος ἀοιδῶν,
οἰνωπὸν Βάκχου βότρυν ἐρεπτόμενος.

**LII** Heph. *Poem.* 4 (pp. 60, 65 Consbruch)

τοιοῦτόν ἐστι καὶ τὸ Σιμωνίδειον ἐπίγραμμα·

Πύθια δίς, Νεμέᾳ δίς, Ὀλυμπίᾳ ἐστεφανώθην,
οὐ πλάτεϊ νικῶν σώματος ἀλλὰ τέχνᾳ,
Ἀριστόδαμος Θράσυος Ἀλεῖος πάλᾳ.

cf. Paus. 6. 3. 4

1 Πύθια Brunck: Ἴσθμια Heph.     3 Scaliger: -δάμας, -δημος Heph.
Wilamowitz: θρασὺς Heph. Θράσιδος Paus. ἅλιος Heph.

# SIMONIDES

**L** *Palatine Anthology*

By Simonides:

— Who dedicated this portrait? — Dorieus of Thurii.[1] — Was he not a Rhodian? — Yes, before he fled his native land after doing many violent deeds with his formidable right hand.

[1] Winner of the Olympic pancration in 432, 428 and 424, he tried unsuccessfully to overthrow Athenian control in Rhodes, fled to Thurii in south Italy, fought as naval commander against Athens, was spared when captured by Athenians in 407, and was executed by Sparta *c.* 395; see Paus. 6. 7.

**LI** *Palatine Anthology*

By Simonides[1]:

Your flame was extinguished, aged Sophocles, flower of poets, when you fed on the wine-coloured cluster of Bacchus.[2]

[1] The Corrector says 'author unknown'.  [2] He was said to have died (in 406 B.C.) by choking on a grape.

**LII** Hephaestion, *On Poetry* (on irregular metres)

The Simonidean inscription is of this kind[1]:

I was garlanded twice at the Pythian games, twice at Nemea, and at Olympia,[2] victor not by my breadth of body but by my skill, Aristodemus, son of Thrasys, of Elis, in the wrestling.

[1] Elegiac couplet + iambic trimeter.  [2] In 388 B.C.; Paus. 6. 3. 4 notes the statue and its inscription.

# GREEK LYRIC

**LIII** *A.P.* 7. 512, Plan.

τοῦ αὐτοῦ = Σιμωνίδου (Corrector)

τῶνδε δι᾽ ἀνθρώπων ἀρετὰν οὐχ ἵκετο καπνός
αἰθέρα δαιομένας εὐρυχόρου Τεγέας,
οἳ βούλοντο πόλιν μὲν ἐλευθερίᾳ τεθαλυῖαν
παισὶ λιπεῖν, αὐτοὶ δ᾽ ἐν προμάχοισι θανεῖν.

2 Hiller: δαιομένης *A.P.*      Schneidewin: Τεγέης *A.P.*

**LIV** *A.P.* 7. 442, Plan.

Σιμωνίδου·

εὐθυμάχων ἀνδρῶν μνησώμεθα, τῶν ὅδε τύμβος,
οἳ θάνον εὔμηλον ῥυόμενοι Τεγέαν,
αἰχμηταὶ πρὸ πόληος, ἵνα σφίσι μὴ καθέληται
Ἑλλὰς ἀποφθιμένη κρατὸς ἐλευθερίαν.

4 Bergk: ἀποφθιμένου *A.P.*, ἀποφθιμένοις κάρτος ἐλευθερίας Plan.

**LV** *Syll.* Σπ (*A.P.* app. 77)

Σιμωνίδου·

δῆμος Ἀθηναίων σε, Νεοπτόλεμ᾽, εἰκόνι τῆδε
τίμησ᾽ εὐνοίης εὐσεβίης θ᾽ ἕνεκα.

568

# SIMONIDES

**LIII** *Palatine Anthology*

By Simonides:

Thanks to the valour of these men the smoke of burning Tegea with its wide dancing-places did not reach the sky: they chose to leave to their children a city flourishing in freedom and to die themselves in the vanguard.[1]

[1] Occasion uncertain: suggestions are Plataea (479 B.C.), fighting against Sparta *c.* 473–470, Mantinea (362 B.C.).

**LIV** *Palatine Anthology*

By Simonides:

Let us remember the fair-fighting men, whose tomb this is, who died to save Tegea, rich in sheep, spearmen in defence of their city, lest they should see Greece perish and have freedom removed from her head.[1]

[1] Text uncertain, occasion unknown (see LIII n. 1): perhaps Plataea.

**LV** Palatine Anthology (appendix)

By Simonides:

The people of Athens honoured you with this statue, Neoptolemus,[1] for your kindness and piety.

[1] Wealthy philanthropist, mid-4th c. B.C.

# GREEK LYRIC

**LVI** *A. Plan.* 204

Σιμωνίδου·

Πραξιτέλης ὃν ἔπασχε διηκρίβωσεν Ἔρωτα
  ἐξ ἰδίης ἕλκων ἀρχέτυπον κραδίης,
Φρύνη μισθὸν ἐμεῖο διδοὺς ἐμέ· φίλτρα δὲ τίκτω
  οὐκέτι τοξεύων ἀλλ᾽ ἀτενιζόμενος.

cf. Athen. 13. 591a

3 τίκτω Plan.  βάλλω Athen.  4 τοξεύων Plan.  διστεύων Athen.

**LVII** *A. Plan.* 60, Syll. Σπ

Σιμωνίδου·

τίς ἅδε; — Βάκχα. — τίς δέ νιν ξέσε; — Σκόπας.
  — τίς δ᾽ ἐξέμηνε, Βάκχος ἢ Σκόπας; — Σκόπας.

**LVIII** ( = anon. LVIII B, Gow-Page *H.E.*) *A. Plan.* 82

Σιμωνίδου·

τὸν ἐν Ῥόδῳ κολοσσὸν ἑπτάκις δέκα
Χάρης ἐποίει πηχέων ὁ Λίνδιος.

cf. Str. 14. 2. 5, Constant. Porphyrog. *de admin. imp.* 21

1 ἑπτάκις Str.: ὀκτάκις Plan.  2 Χάρης Str.: Λάχης Plan., Constant.

**LIX** ( = 'Sim.' II, Gow-Page *H.E.*) *A.P.* 6. 217

ἀνάθημα τοῦ αὐτοῦ ( = Σιμωνίδου)·

χειμερίην νιφετοῖο κατήλυσιν ἡνίκ᾽ ἀλύξας
  Γάλλος ἐρημαίην ἦλυθ᾽ ὑπὸ σπιλάδα

2 ἦλθεν Sud.

# SIMONIDES

**LVI** *Planudean Anthology*

By Simonides:

Praxiteles made an accurate portrayal of the Love he was enduring[1] by finding his model in his own heart, giving me[2] to Phryne[3] as payment for me; and I bring love to birth not by shooting arrows now but by being gazed at.

[1] His statue of Eros (mid-4th c. B.C.).    [2] The statue.    [3] The courtesan from whom his Aphrodite was modelled (Athenaeus; see also Paus. 1. 20. 1).

**LVII** *Planudean Anthology*

By Simonides:

Who is this? — A Bacchant. — Who sculpted her? — Scopas.[1] — And who drove her mad, Bacchus or Scopas? — Scopas.

[1] 4th c. B.C. sculptor.

**LVIII** *Planudean Anthology*

By Simonides:

The Colossus in Rhodes, seventy cubits high,[1] was made by Chares of Lindus.[2]

[1] About 120 feet: so Strabo; the *Anthology* has 'eighty cubits'.
[2] Early 3rd c. B.C.

**LIX** *Palatine Anthology*

By Simonides:

A Gallus[1] sought shelter from a wintry snowfall and went beneath a lonely rock. He had just wiped

[1] A castrated worshipper of Cybele (Rhea), the name 'Gallus' not before 3rd c. B.C.

571

ὑετὸν ἄρτι κόμης ἀπεμόρξατο, τοῦ δὲ κατ' ἴχνος
βουφάγος εἰς κοίλην ἀτραπὸν ἷκτο λέων·
5 αὐτὰρ ὁ πεπταμένῃ μέγα τύμπανον ὃ σχέθε χειρί
ἤραξεν, καναχῇ δ' ἴαχεν ἄντρον ἅπαν·
οὐδ' ἔτλη Κυβέλης ἱερὸν βρόμον ὑλονόμος θήρ
μεῖναι, ἀν' ὑλῆεν δ' ὠκὺς ἔθυνεν ὄρος
δείσας ἡμιγύναικα θεῆς λάτριν, ὃς τάδε Ῥείᾳ
10   ἐνδυτὰ καὶ ξανθοὺς ἐκρέμασεν πλοκάμους.

cf. Sud. K 1050 (1–2), A 3019, B 473 (3–4), H 482 (5–6), Λ 147, O
541 (9–10), E 1196 (10)

5 ὃ σχέθε Corr. marg.   ἔσχεθε Corr. text. ἔσχεν A.P. ἔσχετο
Sud.      9 τάδ' ὄρεια Sud.

**LX**  ( = 'Sim.' I, Gow-Page H.E.) A.P. 5. 159, Plan.

Σιμωνίδου·

Βοίδιον ηὐλητρὶς καὶ Πυθιάς, αἵ ποτ' ἐρασταί,
  σοί, Κύπρι, τὰς ζώνας τάς τε γραφὰς ἔθεσαν.
ἔμπορε καὶ φορτηγέ, τὸ σὸν βαλλάντιον οἶδεν
  καὶ πόθεν αἱ ζῶναι καὶ πόθεν οἱ πίνακες.

**LXI** A.P. 6. 52, Plan.

Σιμωνίδου·

οὕτω μοι, μελία ταναά, ποτὶ κίονα μακρόν
  ἧσο πανομφαίῳ Ζηνὶ μένουσ' ἱερά·
ἤδη γὰρ χαλκός τε γέρων αὐτά τε τέτρυσαι
  πυκνὰ κραδαινομένα δαΐῳ ἐν πολέμῳ.

cf. Sud. H 597, M 504, T 70 (1–2), T 418 (3)

1 μοι A.P. a. c.   τοι p.c.   3 Schneidewin: αὐτή A.P., Plan., Sud.
4 δηΐῳ A.P. a.c., Plan.

the snow from his hair when on his trail an ox-eating lion came to the cave-mouth; with the flat of his hand he struck the great timbrel he was carrying, and the whole cave rang with the din: the forest beast could not abide the holy booming of Cybele and raced quickly up the forested mountain, afraid of the goddess' half-woman servant — who hung up[2] for Rhea these garments and yellow locks.

[2] As a dedication.

## LX *Palatine Anthology*

By Simonides:

Boidion the pipe-player and Pythias, lovely women once, dedicated to you, Cypris, these girdles and paintings. Trader and merchant, your purse knows where the girdles and pictures came from.[1]

[1] The pair were hetaerae. Probably a 3rd c. B.C. poem.

## LXI *Palatine Anthology*

By Simonides:

Rest so, my long ash-spear, against the tall pillar, and remain sacred to Zeus, god of all omens; for your bronze tip is old now, and you yourself are worn from much brandishing in destructive battle.[1]

[1] Probably a 3rd c. B.C. poem.

**LXII** A.P. 6. 212

Σιμωνίδου·

εὔχεό τοι δώροισι, Κύτων, θεὸν ὧδε χαρῆναι
Λητοΐδην, ἀγορῆς καλλιχόρου πρύτανιν,
ὥσπερ ὑπὸ ξείνων τε καὶ οἳ ναίουσι Κόρινθον
αἶνον ἔχεις, χαρίτων δέσποτα, τοῖς στεφάνοις.

1 Κύλων Bergk

**LXIII** Diog. Laert. 4. 45 (i 187 Long)

γεγόνασι δὲ καὶ ἄλλοι τρεῖς Ἀρκεσίλαοι· . . . ἕτερος ἀγαλμα-
τοποιός, εἰς ὃν καὶ Σιμωνίδης ἐποίησεν ἐπίγραμμα τουτί·

Ἀρτέμιδος τόδ᾽ ἄγαλμα. διηκόσιαι δ᾽ ἄρ᾽ ὁ μισθός
δραχμαὶ ταὶ Πάριαι, τῶν ἐπίσημα τράγος.
ἀσκητῶς δ᾽ ἐποίησεν Ἀθηναίης παλάμῃσιν
Ἄξιος Ἀρκεσίλας, υἱὸς Ἀριστοδίκου.

1 δ᾽ ἄρ᾽ cod. F: γὰρ codd. CPB     2 Heyne: ἐπίσημ᾽ ἄρατος
codd.     3 Bergk: ἀσκητὸς codd. BP, -τῆς cod. F

**LXIV** A.P. 13. 20

Σιμωνίδου·

πατρίδα κυδαίνων ἱερὴν πόλιν Ὦπις Ἀθηνᾶς
†τέκνον μελαίνης γῆς χαρίεντας† αὐλούς
τούσδε σὺν Ἡφαίστῳ τελέσας ἀνέθηκ᾽ Ἀφροδίτῃ
καλοῦ δαμασθεὶς ἱμέρῳ Βρύσωνος.

1 Bergk: Ἀθανᾶς A.P.     2 τ. Μελαίνης καὶ Χάρητος Hartung

# SIMONIDES

**LXII** *Palatine Anthology*

By Simonides:

Pray, Cyton, that the god, Leto's son, lord of the agora[1] with its fine dancing-places, find in your gifts pleasure as great as the praise you enjoy from strangers and the inhabitants of Corinth, master of the joys of victory, for your crowns.[2]

[1] Probably at Corinth, where Apollo had a statue in the agora (Paus. 2. 2. 8).   [2] Interpretation uncertain, but Cyton seems to have been a victorious Corinthian athlete who made a dedication to Apollo. The poem may be of 3rd c. B.C. or later.

**LXIII** Diogenes Laertius, *Lives of the Philosophers*

There have been three others called Arcesilaus: ... the third was a sculptor, on whom Simonides composed the following inscription:

This is a statue of Artemis, its cost two hundred Parian drachmae with the goat stamped on them. It was skilfully made through the craftsmanship of Athena by Arcesilaus of Axus,[1] son of Aristodicus.[2]

[1] In central Crete; but the reading is disputed.   [2] Perhaps a poem of 2nd c. B.C. or later.

**LXIV** *Palatine Anthology*

By Simonides:

Bringing glory to his native land, Athena's holy city, Opis (child of Melaena and Chares?) dedicated to Aphrodite these pipes which he made with the help of Hephaestus, overwhelmed by love for handsome Bryson.[1]

[1] Perhaps a 3rd c. B.C. poem.

**LXV** ( = 'Sim.' V, Gow-Page *H.E.*) *A.P.* 7. 431, Plan.

ἄδηλον, οἱ δὲ Σιμωνίδου·

οἵδε τριακόσιοι, Σπάρτα πατρί, τοῖς συναρίθμοις
  Ἰναχίδαις Θυρέαν ἀμφὶ μαχεσσάμενοι,
αὐχένας οὐ στρέψαντες, ὅπᾳ ποδὸς ἴχνια πρᾶτον
  ἁρμόσαμεν, ταύτᾳ καὶ λίπομεν βιοτάν·
5 ἄρσενι δ' Ὀθρυάδαο φόνῳ κεκαλυμμένον ὅπλον
  καρύσσει 'Θυρέα, Ζεῦ, Λακεδαιμονίων.'
αἰ δέ τις Ἀργείων ἔφυγεν μόρον, ἦς ἀπ' Ἀδράστου·
  Σπάρτᾳ δ' οὐ τὸ θανεῖν ἀλλὰ φυγεῖν θάνατος.

1 Bergk: τριηκ- *A.P.*, Plan.    2 Ἰναχίδας *A.P.*    3 ἴχνος
ἄπρατον *A.P.*, ἴχνια πρῶτον Plan.

**LXVI** ( = 'Sim.' III, Gow-Page *H.E.*) *A.P.* 7. 24, Plan.

Σιμωνίδου·

ἡμερὶ πανθέλκτειρα μεθυτρόφε μῆτερ ὀπώρης,
  οὔλης ἢ σκολιὸν πλέγμα φύεις ἕλικος,
Τηίου ἡβήσειας Ἀνακρείοντος ἐπ' ἄκρῃ
  στήλῃ καὶ λεπτῷ χώματι τοῦδε τάφου,
5 ὡς ὁ φιλάκρητός τε καὶ οἰνοβαρὴς φιλόκωμος
  παννύχιος κρούων τὴν φιλόπαιδα χέλυν
κἠν χθονὶ πεπτηὼς κεφαλῆς ἐφύπερθε φέροιτο
  ἀγλαὸν ὡραίων βότρυν ἀπ' ἀκρεμόνων,
καί μιν ἀεὶ τέγγοι νοτερὴ δρόσος, ἧς ὁ γεραιός
10  λαρότερον μαλακῶν ἔπνεεν ἐκ στομάτων.

cf. *Sud.* H 304 (1–2), Λ 126, Γ 192 (9–10)

2 Küster: φύσεις *A.P.*, Plan., φύης *Sud.*    8 Lascaris: ὡραῖον
*A.P.*, Plan.    9 μιν Plan., *Sud.*    φιν *A.P.* (P), σφιν (Corr.)

---

1 Probably Hellenistic, like LXVII and the others in *A.P.* 7. 23–33.

# SIMONIDES

LXV *Palatine Anthology*

Author unknown, but some say by Simonides:

We three hundred, o Sparta our native land, fought over Thyrea[1] against as many Inachids.[2] We never looked behind but laid down our lives where we first planted our feet; and the shield, covered with the male[3] blood of Othryadas, proclaims, 'Thyrea, Zeus, belongs to Sparta.' If any Argive escaped death, then he was a descendant of Adrastus[4]; for Sparta it is not dying but fleeing that is death.

[1] C. 546 B.C. 300 Spartans fought 300 Argives for the disputed town of Thyrea; after the battle only two Argives survived and one Spartan, Othryadas, who built a trophy and inscribed it with his blood (Hdt. 1. 82). [2] Argives: Inachus was mythical founder of Argos. [3] I.e. valiant. [4] Mythical Argive king who fled from Thebes, sole survivor of the Seven.

LXVI *Palatine Anthology*

By Simonides:

Vine, all-enchanting, nourishing mother of the vintage, who send forth a twisting tangle of curly tendrils, may you thrive over the gravestone top and the shallow earth of this, the tomb of Teian Anacreon, so that he, the wine-lover, the inebriate revel-lover, who struck all night long his boy-lover lyre, may even when lying in the ground have over his head splendid grape-clusters hanging in season from your branches; and may he always be moistened by your dripping dew, less sweet, however, than the song the old man breathed from his soft lips.[1]

**LXVII** ( = 'Sim.' IV, Gow-Page *H.E.*) *A.P.* 7. 25, Plan.

τοῦ αὐτοῦ = Σιμωνίδου·

οὗτος Ἀνακρείοντα τὸν ἄφθιτον εἵνεκα Μουσέων
  ὑμνοπόλον πάτρης τύμβος ἔδεκτο Τέω,
ὃς Χαρίτων πνείοντα μέλη, πνείοντα δ' Ἐρώτων
  τὸν γλυκὺν ἐς παίδων ἵμερον ἡρμόσατο·
5 μοῦνον δ' εἰν Ἀχέροντι βαρύνεται οὐχ ὅτι λείπων
  ἠέλιον Λήθης ἐνθάδ' ἔκυρσε δόμων,
ἀλλ' ὅτι τὸν χαρίεντα μετ' ἠιθέοισι Μεγιστέα
  καὶ τὸν Σμερδίεω Θρῆκα λέλοιπε πόθον.
μολπῆς δ' οὐ λήγει μελιτερπέος, ἀλλ' ἔτ' ἐκεῖνον
10  βάρβιτον οὐδὲ θανὼν εὔνασεν εἰν Ἀίδῃ.

cf. *Sud.* M 1205 (9)

5 Bothe: μοῦνος *A.P.*, Plan.     9 Porson: λῆγεν *Sud.*, λήθει *A.P.*, Plan.

**LXVIII** *A.P.* 7. 496

Σιμωνίδου·

ἠερίη Γεράνεια, κακὸν λέπας, ὤφελες Ἴστρον
  τῆλε καὶ ἐκ Σκυθέων μακρὸν ὁρᾶν Τάναϊν,
μηδὲ πέλας ναίειν Σκειρωνικὸν οἶδμα θαλάσσης
  ἄγκεα νειφομένης ἀμφὶ Μολουριάδος·
5 νῦν δ' ὁ μὲν ἐν πόντῳ κρυερὸς νέκυς, οἱ δὲ βαρεῖαν
  ναυτιλίην κενεοὶ τῇδε βοῶσι τάφοι.

1 Salmasius: ὤφελεν cod.     2 ἐκ: ἐς Heringa     4 Salmasius: ἀγνέα . . . Μεθουριάδος cod.

578

# SIMONIDES

**LXVII** *Palatine Anthology*

By Simonides:

This tomb received Anacreon, whom the Muses made deathless, the singer of his native Teos, who tuned his lyre for songs of the sweet love of boys, songs with the scent of the Graces and Loves. One thing alone distresses him in Acheron: not that he left the sun behind and found there the halls of Lethe, but that he has left behind Megisteus, graceful among the youths, and Smerdies, his Thracian passion. But he does not cease from his honey-sweet song: even after death he still has not put to sleep in Hades that lyre of his.

**LXVIII** *Palatine Anthology*

By Simonides:

Lofty Gerania,[1] evil crag, if only you were far off in Scythia and overlooked the Ister or the long Tanais[2] instead of dwelling nearby in the Scironian sea-swell[3] round the glens of snowy Molourias[4]: now he is in the sea, a cold corpse,[5] while the empty tomb cries aloud here of his grievous voyage.[6]

---

[1] Mountain range west of Megara. [2] The Danube and Don. [3] The robber Sciron threw his victims from the cliff where Gerania meets the Saronic gulf. [4] Another cliff in the area (schol. Pind. *Isthm.* prooem., Paus. 1. 44. 7); but ms. 'Methourias' may be correct, since there were small islands called Methouriades nearby. [5] Wrecked off Gerania. [6] Perhaps a Hellenistic literary exercise.

# GREEK LYRIC

**LXIX** Pollux 5. 47 (i 274 Bethe)

ἦ σεῦ καὶ φθιμένας λεύκ' ὀστέα τῷδ' ἐνὶ τύμβῳ
ἴσκω ἔτι τρομέειν θῆρας, ἄγρωσσα Λυκάς·
τὰν δ' ἀρετὰν οἶδεν μέγα Πήλιον ἅ τ' ἀρίδηλος
Ὄσσα Κιθαιρῶνός τ' οἰονόμοι σκοπιαί.

1 H. Stephanus: ἦς αὖ, εἰς αὖ codd.

**LXX** *A.P.* 7. 515, Plan.

Σιμωνίδου·

αἰαῖ νοῦσε βαρεῖα, τί δὴ ψυχαῖσι μεγαίρεις
ἀνθρώπων ἐρατῇ πὰρ νεότητι μένειν;
ἦ καὶ Τίμαρχον γλυκερῆς αἰῶνος ἄμερσας
ἠίθεον, πρὶν ἰδεῖν κουριδίην ἄλοχον.

2 Jacobs: ἀρεταὶ *A.P.*, ἐρατᾷ Plan.

**LXXI** *A.P.* 7. 514

Σιμωνίδου·

Αἰδὼς καὶ Κλεόδημον ἐπὶ προχοῇσι Θεαίρου
ἀενάου στονόεντ' ἤγαγεν εἰς θάνατον
Θρηικίῳ κύρσαντα λόχῳ· πατρὸς δὲ κλεεννόν
Διφίλου αἰχμητὴς υἱὸς ἔθηκ' ὄνομα.

# SIMONIDES

**LXIX** Pollux, *Vocabulary*

Simonides made even the Thessalian Lycas famous by composing this inscription for the dog's tomb:

Although you are dead, huntress Lycas, I fancy that the beasts still tremble at your white bones in this tomb: your valour is known to high Pelion and far-seen Ossa and the peaks of Cithaeron with their lonely pastures.[1]

[1] Perhaps a 3rd c. B.C. poem.


**LXX** *Palatine Anthology*

By Simonides:

Alas, cruel disease, why do you begrudge men's souls their sojourn with lovely youth? You robbed Timarchus too of his sweet life, a young man, before ever he looked on a wedded wife.[1]

[1] Perhaps composed *c.* 3rd c. B.C.


**LXXI** *Palatine Anthology*

By Simonides:

Honour brought Cleodemus too to a lamentable death at the mouth of the ever-flowing Theaerus[1] when he met with a Thracian ambush: the spearman son made famous the name of his father Diphilus.

[1] Perhaps the Thracian Tearus of Hdt. 4. 89–91.

# GREEK LYRIC

**LXXII** *A.P.* 7. 510, Plan.

τοῦ αὐτοῦ = Σιμωνίδου

σῶμα μὲν ἀλλοδαπὴ κεύθει κόνις, ἐν δέ σε πόντῳ,
Κλείσθενες, Εὐξείνῳ μοῖρ᾽ ἔκιχεν θανάτου
πλαζόμενον· γλυκεροῦ δὲ μελίφρονος οἴκαδε νόστου
ἤμπλακες, οὐδ᾽ ἵκευ Χῖον ἐπ᾽ ἀμφιρύτην.

1 σῶμα Plan.: σῆμα A.P.    4 ἤμβροτες Plan.

**LXXIII** *A.P.* 7. 300, Plan.

Σιμωνίδου·

ἐνθάδε Πυθώνακτα κασίγνητόν τε κέκευθε
γαῖ᾽ ἐρατῆς ἥβης πρὶν τέλος ἄκρον ἰδεῖν.
μνῆμα δ᾽ ἀποφθιμένοισι πατὴρ Μεγάριστος ἔθηκεν
ἀθάνατον θνητοῖς παισὶ χαριζόμενος.

1 κασίγνητόν A.P. Corr. marg.: -την Corr. in textu, κασιγνήτην Plan.
3 Grotius: μέγ᾽ ἄριστος A.P., μέγ᾽ ἄριστον Plan.

**LXXIV** *A.P.* 7. 513, Plan.

τοῦ αὐτοῦ = Σιμωνίδου·

φῆ ποτε Πρωτόμαχος, πατρὸς περὶ χεῖρας ἔχοντος,
ἡνίκ᾽ ἀφ᾽ ἱμερτὴν ἔπνεεν ἡλικίην,
'ὦ Τιμηνορίδη, παιδὸς φίλου οὔποτε λήσῃ
οὔτ᾽ ἀρετὴν ποθέων οὔτε σαοφροσύνην.'

1 Hecker: Πρόμαχος A.P., Τίμαρχος Plan.    3 λήξεις Hecker

**LXXV** = eleg. 16

# SIMONIDES

**LXXII** *Palatine Anthology*

By Simonides:

Foreign dust covers your body, Cleisthenes, for the fate of death caught you in the Black Sea, wandering off course; you were cheated of your sweet honeyed homecoming and never reached sea-girt Chios.

**LXXIII** *Palatine Anthology*

By Simonides:

Here the earth covers Pythonax and his brother,[1] before they saw the full term of lovely youth. Their father Megaristus set the monument over the dead, an immortal gift to his mortal children.

[1] Or 'sister': text uncertain.

**LXXIV** *Palatine Anthology*

By Simonides:

Once Protomachus, breathing away his lovely youth in his father's arms, said, 'Son of Timenor, you will never forget your dead son but will long for his virtue and modesty'.

**LXXV** = eleg. 16

# GREEK LYRIC

**LXXVI** (a) *A.P.* 7. 270, Plan.

Σιμωνίδου·

τούσδε ποτ᾽ ἐκ Σπάρτας ἀκροθίνια Φοίβῳ ἄγοντας
ἓν πέλαγος, μία νύξ, ἓν σκάφος ἐκτέρισεν.

1 Φοῖβ᾽ ἀγαγόντας A.P.

(b) *A.P.* 7. 650b

Σιμωνίδου·

τούσδ᾽ ἀπὸ Τυρρηνῶν ἀκροθίνια Φοίβῳ ἄγοντας
ἓν πέλαγος, μία ναῦς, εἷς τάφος ἐκτέρισεν.

**LXXVII** *A.P.* 7. 302, Plan.

Σιμωνίδου·

τῶν αὑτοῦ τις ἕκαστος ἀπολλυμένων ἀνιᾶται,
Νικοδίκου δὲ φίλοι καὶ πόλις ἥδε γ᾽ ὅλη.

2 Salmasius: Νικόδικον A.P., Plan.      γ᾽ ὅλη Fettes: πόλη P, πολλὴ Corr. A.P., om. Plan.

**LXXVIII** *A.P.* 7. 254b

Σιμωνίδου·

Κρὴς γενεὰν Βρόταχος Γορτύνιος ἐνθάδε κεῖμαι,
οὐ κατὰ τοῦτ᾽ ἐλθὼν ἀλλὰ κατ᾽ ἐμπορίην.

**LXXIX** *A.P.* 10. 105, Plan.

Σιμωνίδου A.P., ἄδηλον Plan.

χαίρει τις, Θεόδωρος ἐπεὶ θάνον· ἄλλος ἐπ᾽ αὐτῷ
χαιρήσει. θανάτῳ πάντες ὀφειλόμεθα.

# SIMONIDES

**LXXVI** *Palatine Anthology*

By Simonides:

(a) Once as these men were bringing spoils from Sparta for Phoebus[1] one sea, one night, one boat gave them burial.

[1] For Apollo at Delphi.

(b) As these men were bringing spoils from the Etruscans[1] for Phoebus one sea, one ship, one tomb gave them burial.[2]

[1] After the battle of Cumae (474 B.C.)? See XXXIV.    [2] An imitation of (a)?

**LXXVII** *Palatine Anthology*

By Simonides:

Each man mourns his own dead; but Nicodicus is mourned both by his friends and by the whole of this city.

**LXXVIII** *Palatine Anthology*

By Simonides:

I, Brotachus of Gortyn, a Cretan by birth, lie here; I came not for this but for trade.

**LXXIX** *Palatine Anthology*

By Simonides[1]:

Some man rejoices now that I, Theodorus, am dead; and some other will rejoice over *his* death. All of us are owed to death.

[1] 'Author unknown', acc. to Planudes.

# GREEK LYRIC

**LXXX** ( = Alexander I, *F.G.E.*) *A.P.* 7. 507a, Plan.

Σιμωνίδου *A.P.*, Ἀλεξάνδρου Plan.

ἄνθρωπ᾽, οὐ Κροίσου λεύσσεις τάφον· ἀλλὰ γὰρ
  ἀνδρός
χερνήτεω μικρὸς τύμβος, ἐμοὶ δ᾽ ἱκανός.

**LXXXI** *A.P.* 7. 507b

Σιμωνίδου·

οὐκ ἐπιδὼν νυμφεῖα λέχη κατέβην τὸν ἄφυκτον
Γόργιππος ξανθῆς Φερσεφόνης θάλαμον.

2 Salmasius: θάλαμος *A.P.*

**LXXXII** *A.P.* 7. 509

τοῦ αὐτοῦ = Σιμωνίδου

σῆμα Θεόγνιδός εἰμι Σινωπέος, ᾧ μ᾽ ἐπέθηκεν
Γλαῦκος ἑταιρείης ἀντὶ πολυχρονίου.

**LXXXIII** (a) *A.P.* 7. 344, Plan.

Σιμωνίδου·

θηρῶν μὲν κάρτιστος ἐγώ, θνατῶν δ᾽ ὃν ἐγὼ νῦν
φρουρῶ τῷδε τάφῳ λάινος ἐμβεβαώς.

(b) *A.P.* 7. 344b, Plan.

Καλλιμάχου Corr. *A.P.*, τοῦ αὐτοῦ = Σιμωνίδου Plan.

ἀλλ᾽ εἰ μὴ θυμόν γε Λέων ἐμὸν ὡς ὄνομ᾽ εἶχεν,
οὐκ ἂν ἐγὼ τύμβῳ τῷδ᾽ ἐπέθηκα πόδας.

(a) 2 Meineke: λαίνῳ *A.P.*, Plan.          (b) 1 ἐμὸν οὔνομά τ᾽ εἶχεν *A.P.*

586

# SIMONIDES

**LXXX** *Palatine Anthology*

By Simonides[1]:

Sir, it is not Croesus' grave that you see; a poor man needs only a small tomb, and it is big enough for me.

[1] Ascribed by Planudes to Alexander, Aetolian poet in 3rd c. B.C. Alexandria; joined in the *Anthology* to LXXXI.

**LXXXI** *Palatine Anthology*

By Simonides:

Before ever I looked on my marriage bed I, Gorgippus, went down to the chamber of yellow-haired Persephone from which there is no escape.

**LXXXII** *Palatine Anthology*

By Simonides:

I am the tomb of Theognis of Sinope. Glaucus placed me over him for the sake of a companionship of many years.

**LXXXIII** *Palatine Anthology*

By Simonides[1]:

I am the mightiest of beasts, and mightiest of men was he whom I now guard, standing in stone over his tomb.[2] If Leon ('lion') had not had my nature as he has my name, I should not have set foot on this tomb.

[1] The couplets are given as separate epigrams in the *Anthology* and by Planudes; Plan. ascribes both to Sim., the *Anthology* ascribes the first to Sim., the second to Callimachus. It is not certain that they should be united.     [2] Hdt. 7. 225. 2 speaks of a stone lion which commemorated Leonidas at Thermopylae.

**LXXXIV** *A.P.* 7. 516, Plan.

τοῦ αὐτοῦ = Σιμωνίδου

οἱ μὲν ἐμὲ κτείναντες ὁμοίων ἀντιτύχοιεν,
  Ζεῦ ξένι', οἱ δ' ὑπὸ γᾶν θέντες ὄναιντο βίου.

2 βίον *A.P.* (P)

**LXXXV** *A.P.* 7. 77

Σιμωνίδου·

οὗτος ὁ τοῦ Κείοιο Σιμωνίδου ἐστὶ σαωτήρ,
  ὃς καὶ τεθνηὼς ζῶντι παρέσχε χάριν.

cf. schol. Arist. iii 533 Dindorf (Σιμωνίδης), Tzetz. *chil.* 1. 63s. (Σιμωνίδης)

1 ὁ Κίου schol., ὁ Κείου Tzetz.     Σιμωνίδεω schol., Tzetz.     2 ζ. π. schol., Tzetz.     ζῶντ' ἀπέδωκε *A.P.*

**LXXXVI** *A.P.* 7. 177

Σιμωνίδου·

σᾶμα τόδε Σπίνθηρι πατὴρ ἐπέθηκε θανόντι.

**LXXXVII** *Syll.* Σπ (quinta post indicem in *A.P.* pagina)

Σιμωνίδου·

588

# SIMONIDES

**LXXXIV** *Palatine Anthology*

By Simonides:

May those who killed me, Zeus, god of strangers, meet the same fate; and may those who gave me burial have enjoyment of life.[1]

[1] The lemmatist says, 'Sim. found a corpse on a certain island, gave it burial and set this inscription over it.' See LXXXV.

**LXXXV** *Palatine Anthology*

By Simonides:

This man is the saviour of Simonides of Ceos: although dead, he paid his debt of gratitude to the living.[1]

[1] See LXXXIV: 'The ghost of the buried man appeared to Sim. and told him not to sail. His fellow-travellers did not take the advice, but he alone stayed behind and was saved (from drowning). He put this couplet on the tomb': so the lemmatist; ascribed to Sim. also by scholiast on Aristides and Tzetzes. For the story see also Cic. *de div.* 1. 27. 56, Val. Max. 1. 7 ext. 3, ps.-Liban., *Narr.* 13 (viii 42 Foerster).

**LXXXVI** *Palatine Anthology*

By Simonides:

This tomb was set over dead Spinther by his father.[1]

[1] Perhaps an early inscription (6th c. B.C.?) in a single hexameter.

**LXXXVII** *Palatine Anthology* (appendix)

By Simonides:

Κρὴς Ἄλκων Διδ<ύμου> Φοίβῳ στέφος Ἴσθμι᾽ ἑλὼν πύξ.

suppl. Bergk


**LXXXVIII** = eleg. 6

**LXXXIX** = eleg. 13

**165** Bergk = 74 Diehl    Hdn. π. μον. λέξ. β΄ 45 (ii 950 Lentz)

> ἦν γὰρ ἐγὼ Ἀττικοὶ λέγουσι καὶ ἦν ἐκεῖνος· καὶ πληθυντικῶς Σιμωνίδης ἐπὶ πρώτου προσώπου, ὡς καὶ ἐν ἐπιγράμμασιν·

> > ἦν ἑκατὸν φιάλαι δίχθα σφισίν·

ἀντὶ γὰρ τοῦ ἦμεν ἦν.

Ludwich: δίχα cod.


**166** Bergk    Schol. Pind. *Nem.* 7. 1a (iii 117 Drachmann)

> Ἀριστόδημος δὲ ὁ Ἀριστάρχου μαθητὴς βέλτιον οὕτω φησίν· ὀψέ ποτε τῷ Θεαρίωνι καὶ παρὰ τὴν ἡλικίαν ἤδη προήκοντι εὐξαμένῳ τῇ θεῷ Σωγένην τεκνωθῆναι, καὶ τὴν τοῦ παιδὸς αὐτοῦ γέννησιν οἶον Εἰλειθυίας εἶναι χάριν. διὰ τὴν ἰδιότητα οὖν τῆς γενέσεως τοῦ ἀθλητοῦ πρὸς τὴν θεὸν ταύτην ἐπήρεισε τὸν λόγον. ἐπιστοῦτο δὲ τοῦτο ἐξ ἐπιγράμματος Σιμωνίδου.

Alcon of Crete, son of Didymus, dedicates his wreath to Phoebus, having won the boxing at the Isthmian games.[1]

[1] Like LXXXVI, perhaps a complete 6th c. B.C. inscription.

**LXXXVIII** = eleg. 6

**LXXXIX** = eleg. 13

**165** Bergk = 74 Diehl    Herodian, *On Anomalous Words* (on ἦν)

Attic writers say ἦν ἐγώ, 'I was', and ἦν ἐκεῖνος, 'he was'; and Simonides uses it for the first person plural, as in his inscriptions:

we were a hundred cups belonging to them separately,

where ἦν stands for ἦμεν, 'we were'.[1]

[1] Nonsense: the words mean 'there were a hundred cups ...'; the continuation may have been 'but now we have been melted down and are ...'

**166** Bergk    Scholiast on Pindar, Nemean 7[1] ('Eileithyia')

Aristodemus, the pupil of Aristarchus, gives a better explanation: Sogenes was born when his father Thearion was advanced in years and had made a prayer to the goddess, and the boy's birth was as it were a favour on the part of Eileithyia. Because of the peculiar circumstances of the athlete's birth it was this goddess whom Pindar addressed. Aristodemus' view was supported by an epigram of Simonides.

[1] Composed in honour of Sogenes of Aegina, winner of the boys' pentathlon at Nemea; date uncertain, but perhaps 485 or 467.

# COMPARATIVE NUMERATION

The numeration of the present edition is that of the margin of *P.M.G.* The numbers given in the second column below are the internal numbers for Stesichorus, Ibycus etc., in *P.M.G.*

## STESICHORUS

| Loeb/*P.M.G.* (margin) | *P.M.G.* (Stes.) | Bergk | Diehl |
|---|---|---|---|
| 178 | 1 | 1 | 1 |
| 179 | 2 | 2–3 | 2–3 |
| 180 | 3 | 4 | — |
| 181 | 4 | 7 | 5 |
| 182 | 5 | 9 | 6a |
| 183 | 6 | 10 | 6b |
| 184 | 7 | 5 | 4 |
| 184A | — | — | — |
| 185 | 8 | 8 | 6 |
| 186 | 9 | 6 | 4a |
| 187 | 10 | 29 | 10 |
| 188 | 11 | 30 | 10d |
| 189 | 12 | 31 | 10e |
| 190 | 13 | 28 | 10c |
| 191 | 14 | 27 | 10b |
| 192 | 15 | 32 | 11 |
| 193 | 16 | — | — |
| 194 | 17 | 16 | 8 |

# STESICHORUS

| Loeb/*P.M.G.* (margin) | *P.M.G.* (Stes.) | Bergk | Diehl |
|---|---|---|---|
| 195 | 18 | 15 | — |
| 196 | 19 | 23 | — |
| 197 | 20 | 21 | 9c |
| 198 | 21 | 19 | 9a |
| 199 | 22 | 24 | 9e |
| 200 | 23 | 18 | 9 |
| 201 | 24 | 25 | 9f |
| 202 | 25 | 20 | 9b |
| 203 | 26 | 18 adnot. | — |
| 204 | 27 | 22 | 9d |
| 205 | 28 | p. 212 | — |
| 206 | 29 | 11 | — |
| 207 | 30 | 12 | 6c |
| 208 | 31 | 33 | — |
| 209 | 32 | — | — |
| 210 | 33 | 35 | 12 |
| 211 | 34 | 36 | 13 |
| 212 | 35 | 37 | 14 |
| 213 | 36 | 34 | — |
| 214 | 37 | — | 14e |
| 215 | 38 | 38 | 14a |
| 216 | 39 | 39 | 14b |
| 217 | 40 | (40) | (14c) |
| 218 | 41 | 41 | 14d |
| 219 | 42 | 42 | 15 |
| 220 | 43 | 13 | — |
| 221 | 44 | 14 | 7 |
| 222 | 45 | — | — |
| 222A | — | — | — |
| 222B | — | — | — |
| 223 | 46 | 26 | 17 |
| 224 | 47 | 69 | — |
| 225 | 48 | 70 | — |
| 226 | 49 | 84 | — |
| 227 | 50 | 61 | — |

## COMPARATIVE NUMERATION

| Loeb/*P.M.G.* (margin) | *P.M.G.* (Stes.) | Bergk | Diehl |
|---|---|---|---|
| 228 | 51 | 17 | 8a |
| 229 | 52 | 57 | 26a |
| 230 | 53 | 58 | 26b |
| 231 | 54 | 59 | 26c |
| 232 | 55 | 50 | 22 |
| 233 | 56 | (62) | (26d) |
| 234 | 57 | 72 | — |
| 235 | 58 | 49 | 21 |
| 236 | 59 | 68 | — |
| 237 | 60 | 64 | — |
| 238 | 61 | 54 | — |
| 239 | 62 | 60 | — |
| 240 | 63 | 45 | 18 |
| 241 | 64 | 46 | — |
| 242 | 65 | 48 | 20 |
| 243 | 66 | 53 | 19 |
| 244 | 67 | 51 | 23 |
| 245 | 68 | 52 | 24 |
| 246 | 69 | 74 | — |
| 247 | 70 | 75 | — |
| 248 | 71 | 56 | — |
| 249 | 72 | 76 | — |
| 250 | 73 | 77 | — |
| 251 | 74 | 78 | — |
| 252 | 75 | 81 | — |
| 253 | 76 | 82 | — |
| 254 | 77 | 83 | — |
| 255 | 78 | 85 | — |
| 256 | 79 | 86 | — |
| 257 | 80 | 47 | — |
| 258 | 81 | 79 | — |
| 259 | 82 | 87 | — |
| 260 | 83 | 88 | — |
| 261 | 84 | 89 | — |
| 262 | 85 | 91 | — |

# STESICHORUS

| Loeb/*P.M.G.* (margin) | *P.M.G.* (Stes.) | Bergk | Diehl |
|---|---|---|---|
| 263 | 86 | 90 | — |
| 264 | 87 | 92 | — |
| 265 | 88 | 93 | — |
| 266 | 89 | 95 | — |
| 267 | 90 | 94 | — |
| 268 | 91 | 55 | — |
| 269 | 92 | 67 | — |
| 270 | 93 | 65 | — |
| 271 | 94 | 73 | — |
| 272 | 95 | 80 | — |
| 273 | 96 | — | — |
| 274 | 97 | — | — |
| 274A | — | — | — |
| 275 | 98 | — | — |
| 276 | 99 | — | — |
| 277 | 100 | 43 | 15a |
| 278 | 101 | 44 | 16 |
| 279 | 102 | 63 | — |
| 280 | 103 | 66 | — |
| 281 | 104 | — | — |

N.B. The papyrus fragments published in *S.L.G.* have been inserted as follows:

> S 7–87 (*Geryoneis*) after fr. 180
> S 88–132 (*Sack of Troy*?) and
> S 133–147 (*Wooden Horse*) after fr. 205
> S 148–150 (*Eriphyle*) after fr. 194

The Lille Papyrus (*Thebaid*?) is fr. 222A,
P.Oxy. 3876 is fr. 222B

* * * * * * * * * * * * *

## COMPARATIVE NUMERATION

| Bergk | Loeb/*P.M.G.* (margin) | Bergk | Loeb/*P.M.G.* (margin) |
|---|---|---|---|
| 1 | 178 | 36 | 211 |
| 2 | 179(a) | 37 | 212 |
| 3 | 179(b) | 38 | 215 |
| 4 | 180 | 39 | 216 |
| 5 | 184 | 40 | (217) |
| 6 | 186 | 41 | 218 |
| 7 | 181 | 42 | 219 |
| 8 | 185 | 43 | 277 |
| 9 | 182 | 44 | 278 |
| 10 | 183 | 45 | 240 |
| 11 | 206 | 46 | 241 |
| 12 | 207 | 47 | 257 |
| 13 | 220 | 48 | 242 |
| 14 | 221 | 49 | 235 |
| 15 | 195 | 50 | 232 |
| 16 | 194 | 51 | 244 |
| 17 | 228 | 52 | 245 |
| 18 | 200 + 203 | 53 | 243 |
| 19 | 198 | 54 | 238 |
| 20 | 202 | 55 | 268 |
| 21 | 197 | 56 | 248 |
| 22 | 204 | 57 | 229 |
| 23 | 196 | 58 | 230 |
| 24 | 199 | 59 | 231 |
| 25 | 201 | 60 | 239 |
| 26 | 223 | 61 | 227 |
| 27 | 191 | 62 | (233) |
| 28 | 190 | 63 | 279 |
| 29 | 187 | 64 | 237 |
| 30 | 188 | 65 | 270 |
| 31 | 189 | 66 | 280 |
| 32 | 192 | 67 | 269 |
| 33 | 208 | 68 | 236 |
| 34 | 213 | 69 | 224 |
| 35 | 210 | 70 | 225 |

# STESICHORUS

| Bergk | Loeb/*P.M.G.* (margin) | Bergk | Loeb/*P.M.G.* (margin) |
|---|---|---|---|
| 71 | test.18 | 84 | 226 |
| 72 | 234 | 85 | 255 |
| 73 | 271 | 86 | 256 |
| 74 | 246 | 87 | 259 |
| 75 | 247 | 88 | 260 |
| 76 | 249 | 89 | 261 |
| 77 | 250 | 90 | 263 |
| 78 | 251 | 91 | 262 |
| 79 | 258 | 92 | 264 |
| 80 | 272 | 93 | 265 |
| 81 | 252 | 94 | 267 |
| 82 | 253 | 95 | 266 |
| 83 | 254 | | |

\* \* \* \* \* \* \* \* \* \* \* \* \*

| Diehl | Loeb/*P.M.G.* (margin) | Diehl | Loeb/*P.M.G.* (margin) |
|---|---|---|---|
| 1 | 178 | 9c | 197 |
| 2 | 179(a) | 9d | 204 |
| 3 | 179(b) | 9e | 199 |
| 4 | 184 | 9f | 201 |
| 4a | 186 | 10 | 187 |
| 5 | 181 | 10a | adesp.1014 |
| 6 | 185 | 10b | 191 |
| 6a | 182 | 10c | 190 |
| 6b | 183 | 10d | 188 |
| 6c | 207 | 10e | 189 |
| 7 | 221 | 11 | 192 |
| 8 | 194 | 12 | 210 |
| 8a | 228 | 13 | 211 |
| 9 | 200 | 14 | 212 |
| 9a | 198 | 14a | 215 |
| 9b | 202 | 14b | 216 |

## COMPARATIVE NUMERATION

| Diehl | Loeb/*P.M.G.* (margin) | Diehl | Loeb/*P.M.G.* (margin) |
|---|---|---|---|
| 14c | (217) | 21 | 235 |
| 14d | 218 | 22 | 232 |
| 14e | 214 | 23 | 244 |
| 15 | 219 | 24 | 245 |
| 15a | 277 | 25 | adesp.947 |
| 16 | 278 | 26 | adesp.938(e) |
| 17 | 223 | 26a | 229 |
| 18 | 240 | 26b | 230 |
| 19 | 243 | 26c | 231 |
| 20 | 242 | 26d | (233) |

\* \* \* \* \* \* \* \* \* \* \* \* \*

### IBYCUS

| Loeb/*P.M.G.* (margin) | *P.M.G.* (Ibyc.) | Bergk | Diehl |
|---|---|---|---|
| 282 | 1 | — | 3,4,5 |
| 283 | 2 | 21 | 1 |
| 284 | 3 | 44 | 1 adnot. |
| 285 | 4 | 16 | 2 |
| 286 | 5 | 1 | 6 |
| 287 | 6 | 2 | 7 |
| 288 | 7 | 5 | 8 |
| 289 | 8 | 30 | — |
| 290 | 9 | 13–14 | 27–28 |
| 291 | 10 | 37 | — |
| 292 | 11 | 49 | — |
| 293 | 12 | 12 | 26 |
| 294 | 13 | 38 | — |
| 295 | 14 | 34a | — |
| 296 | 15 | 35 | — |
| 297 | 16 | 34b | — |
| 298 | 17 | — | — |

# IBYCUS

| Loeb/*P.M.G.* (margin) | *P.M.G.* (Ibyc.) | Bergk | Diehl |
|---|---|---|---|
| 299 | 18 | 45 | — |
| 300 | 19 | 46 | — |
| 301 | 20 | 39 | — |
| 302 | 21 | 15 | 15 |
| 303 | 22 | 9,7 | 16,11 |
| 304 | 23 | 41 | — |
| 305 | 24 | 11 | — |
| 306 | 25 | 10a | 17 |
| 307 | 26 | 36 | — |
| 308 | 27 | 48 | — |
| 309 | 28 | 32 | — |
| 310 | 29 | 24 | 22 |
| 311 | 30 | 26 | 19 |
| 312 | 31 | 17 | 20 |
| 313 | 32 | 27 | 23 |
| 314 | 33 | 3 | 12 |
| 315 | 34 | 6 | 13 |
| 316 | 35 | 10b | 14 |
| 317 | 36 | 8,4 | 9,10 |
| 318 | 37 | 18,19 | 24,25 |
| 319 | 38 | 29 | 29 |
| 320 | 39 | 20 | 18 |
| 321 | 40 | 22 | 21 |
| 322 | 41 | 47 | — |
| 323 | 42 | 23 | — |
| 324 | 43 | 31 | — |
| 325 | 44 | 33 | — |
| 326 | 45 | 51 | — |
| 327 | 46 | 50 | — |
| 328 | 47 | 52 | — |
| 329 | 48 | 54 | — |
| 330 | 49 | — | 30 |
| 331 | 50 | 42,43 | — |
| 332 | 51 | 55 | — |
| 333 | 52 | 56 | — |

# COMPARATIVE NUMERATION

| Loeb/*P.M.G.* (margin) | *P.M.G.* (Ibyc.) | Bergk | Diehl |
|---|---|---|---|
| 334 | 53 | 57 | — |
| 335 | 54 | 53 | — |
| 336 | 55 | 58 | — |
| 337 | 56 | 59 | — |
| 338 | 57 | 60 | — |
| 339 | 58 | 61 | — |
| 340 | 59 | 62 | — |
| 341 | 60 | — | — |
| 342 | 61 | 25 | — |
| 343 | 62 | — | — |
| 344 | 63 | 40 | — |
| 345 | 64 | — | — |

N.B. The papyrus fragments published in *S.L.G.* have been numbered as follows:

S 151 = fr. 282(a)            S 220–257 = fr. 282B
S 152–165 = fr. 282(b)(c)     S 258 = fr. 327A
S 166–219 = fr. 282A          P.Oxy. 3538 = fr. 282C

\* \* \* \* \* \* \* \* \* \* \* \* \*

| Bergk | Loeb/*P.M.G.* (margin) | Bergk | Loeb/*P.M.G.* (margin) |
|---|---|---|---|
| 1 | 286 | 11 | 305 |
| 2 | 287 | 12 | 293 |
| 3 | 314 | 13 | 290 |
| 4 | 317(b) | 14 | 290 |
| 5 | 288 | 15 | 302 |
| 6 | 315 | 16 | 285 |
| 7 | 303(b) | 17 | 312 |
| 8 | 317(a) | 18 | 318(a) |
| 9 | 303(a) | 19 | 318(b) |
| 10(a) | 306 | 20 | 320 |
| 10(b) | 316 | 21 | 283 |

# IBYCUS

| Bergk | Loeb/*P.M.G.* (margin) | Bergk | Loeb/*P.M.G.* (margin) |
|-------|------------------------|-------|------------------------|
| 22    | 321                    | 42    | 331                    |
| 23    | 323                    | 43    | 331                    |
| 24    | 310                    | 44    | 284                    |
| 25    | 342                    | 45    | 299                    |
| 26    | 311                    | 46    | 300                    |
| 27    | 313                    | 47    | 322                    |
| 28    | S223(b)                | 48    | 308                    |
| 29    | 319                    | 49    | 292                    |
| 30    | 289                    | 50    | 327                    |
| 31    | 324                    | 51    | 326                    |
| 32    | 309                    | 52    | 328                    |
| 33    | 325                    | 53    | 335                    |
| 34(a) | 295                    | 54    | 329                    |
| 34(b) | 297                    | 55    | 332                    |
| 35    | 296                    | 56    | 333                    |
| 36    | 307                    | 57    | 334                    |
| 37    | 291                    | 58    | 336                    |
| 38    | 294                    | 59    | 337                    |
| 39    | 301                    | 60    | 338                    |
| 40    | 344                    | 61    | 339                    |
| 41    | 304                    | 62    | 340                    |

\* \* \* \* \* \* \* \* \* \* \* \* \* \*

| Diehl | Loeb/*P.M.G.* (margin) | Diehl | Loeb/*P.M.G.* (margin) |
|-------|------------------------|-------|------------------------|
| 1     | 283                    | 9     | 317(a)                 |
| 2     | 285                    | 10    | 317(b)                 |
| 3     | 282(b)                 | 11    | 303(b)                 |
| 4     | 282(b)                 | 12    | 314                    |
| 5     | 282(b)                 | 13    | 315                    |
| 6     | 286                    | 14    | 316                    |
| 7     | 287                    | 15    | 302                    |
| 8     | 288                    | 16    | 303(a)                 |

## COMPARATIVE NUMERATION

| Diehl | Loeb/*P.M.G.* (margin) | Diehl | Loeb/*P.M.G.* (margin) |
|-------|------------------------|-------|------------------------|
| 17 | 306 | 24 | 318(a) |
| 18 | 320 | 25 | 318(b) |
| 19 | 311 | 26 | 293 |
| 20 | 312 | 27 | 290 |
| 21 | 321 | 28 | 290 |
| 22 | 310 | 29 | 319 |
| 23 | 313 | 30 | 330 |

* * * * * * * * * * * * *

### LASUS

| Loeb/*P.M.G.* (margin) | *P.M.G.* (Lasus) | Bergk | Diehl |
|------------------------|------------------|-------|-------|
| 702 | 1 | 1 | 1 |
| 703 | 2 | 3 | — |
| 704 | 3 | 1 adnot. | — |
| 705 | 4 | — | — |
| 706 | 5 | 2 | — |
| 706A | — | 4 | — |

### PRATINAS

| Loeb/*P.M.G.* (margin) | *P.M.G.* (Prat.) | Bergk | Diehl |
|------------------------|------------------|-------|-------|
| 708 | 1 | 1 | 1 |
| 709 | 2 | 2 | 2 |
| 710 | 3 | 3 | 3 |
| 711 | 4 | 4 | — |
| 712 | 5 | 5 | 4 |
| 713 | 6 | — | — |

# SIMONIDES

## SIMONIDES
### LYRIC FRAGMENTS

| Loeb/*P.M.G.* (margin) | *P.M.G.* (Sim.) | Bergk | Diehl |
|---|---|---|---|
| 506 | 1 | 10 | 21 |
| 507 | 2 | 13 | 22 |
| 508 | 3 | 12 | 20 |
| 509 | 4 | 8 | 23 |
| 510 | 5 | p.389 adnot. | — |
| 511 | 6 | — | — |
| 512 | 7 | 14 | 14 |
| 513 | 8 | 6 | — |
| 514 | 9 | 11 | 15 |
| 515 | 10 | 7 | 19 |
| 516 | 11 | 16 | 16 |
| 517 | 12 | 17 | 17 |
| 518 | 13 | 9 | — |
| 519 | 14 | — | — |
| 519A | — | — | — |
| 519B | — | — | — |
| 520 | 15 | 39 | 9 |
| 521 | 16 | 32 | 6 |
| 522 | 17 | 38 | 8 |
| 523 | 18 | 36 | 7 |
| 524 | 19 | 65 | 12 |
| 525 | 20 | 42 | Semon.27 |
| 526 | 21 | 61 | 10 |
| 527 | 22 | 62 | 11 |
| 528 | 23 | 34 | — |
| 529 | 24 | 33 | — |
| 530 | 25 | 35 | — |
| 531 | 26 | 4 | 5 |
| 532 | 27 | — | — |
| 533(a) | 28(a) | 1 | 1 |
| 533(b) | 28(b) | 2 | 2 |

## COMPARATIVE NUMERATION

| Loeb/*P.M.G.* (margin) | *P.M.G.* (Sim.) | Bergk | Diehl |
|---|---|---|---|
| 534 | 29 | 3 | — |
| 535 | 30 | 25 | — |
| 536 | 31 | — | — |
| 537 | 32 | 24 | — |
| 538 | 33 | 68 | 3 |
| 539 | 34 | 27 | — |
| 540 | 35 | — | — |
| 541 | 36 | — | — |
| 542 | 37 | 5 | 4 |
| 543 | 38 | 37 | 13 |
| 544 | 39 | 21 adnot. | — |
| 545 | 40 | 48 | 31 |
| 546 | 41 | 22 | — |
| 547 | 42 | 205 | — |
| 548 | 43 | 204 | — |
| 549 | 44 | 207 | — |
| 550(a) | 45(a) | 54 | 33 |
| 550(b) | 45(b) | 56 | — |
| 551 | 46 | 55 | 34 |
| 551A | — | — | — |
| 552 | 47 | 200b | — |
| 553 | 48 | 52 | 29 |
| 554 | 49 | 219b | — |
| 555 | 50 | 18 | 30 |
| 556 | 51 | 202b | — |
| 557 | 52 | 209 | — |
| 558 | 53 | 213 | — |
| 559 | 54 | 49 | 35 |
| 560 | 55 | 234 | — |
| 561 | 56 | 208 | — |
| 562 | 57 | 28 | — |
| 563 | 58 | 216 | — |
| 564 | 59 | 53 | 32 |
| 565 | 60 | 214 | — |
| 566 | 61 | 245 | — |
| 567 | 62 | 40 | 27 |

# SIMONIDES

| Loeb/*P.M.G.* (margin) | *P.M.G.* (Sim.) | Bergk | Diehl |
|---|---|---|---|
| 568 | 63 | 202a | — |
| 569 | 64 | 203 | — |
| 570 | 65 | 197 | — |
| 571 | 66 | 51 | 13Aa |
| 572 | 67 | 50 | 36 |
| 573 | 68 | 26a | — |
| 574 | 69 | 210a | — |
| 575 | 70 | 43 | 24 |
| 576 | 71 | 21+200a | — |
| 577(a) | 72(a) | 44 | 26 |
| 577(b) | 72(b) | 45 | 25 |
| 578 | 73 | 201 | — |
| 579 | 74 | 58 | 37 |
| 580 | 75 | — | 61 |
| 581 | 76 | 57 | 48 |
| 582 | 77 | 66 | 38 |
| 583 | 78 | 80b | 47 |
| 584 | 79 | 71 | 57 |
| 585 | 80 | 72 | 44 |
| 586 | 81 | 73 | 45 |
| 587 | 82 | 59 | 58 |
| 588 | 83 | 244 | — |
| 589 | 84 | 20 | — |
| 590 | 85 | 226 | — |
| 591 | 86 | 15 | 18 |
| 592 | 87 | 64 | 50 |
| 593 | 88 | 47 | 43 |
| 594 | 89 | 63 | 59 |
| 595 | 90 | 41 | 40 |
| 596 | 91 | 206 | — |
| 597 | 92 | 74 | 46 |
| 598 | 93 | 76 | 55 |
| 599 | 94 | 79 | 60 |
| 600 | 95 | 78 | 41 |
| 601 | 96 | 232 | — |
| 602 | 97 | 75 | 49 |

## COMPARATIVE NUMERATION

| Loeb/*P.M.G.* (margin) | *P.M.G.* (Sim.) | Bergk | Diehl |
|---|---|---|---|
| 603 | 98 | 69 | 54 |
| 604 | 99 | 70 | 56 |
| 605 | 100 | 77 | 52 |
| 606 | 101 | 243 | — |
| 607 | 102 | — | — |
| 608 | 103 | — | — |
| 609 | 104 | 215 | — |
| 610 | 105 | 220 | — |
| 611 | 106 | 229 | — |
| 612 | 107 | 230 | — |
| 613 | 108 | 211 | — |
| 614 | 109 | 231 | — |
| 615 | 110 | 210b | — |
| 616 | 111 | 218 | — |
| 617 | 112 | 233 | — |
| 618 | 113 | 235 | — |
| 619 | 114 | 236 | — |
| 620 | 115 | 237 | — |
| 621 | 116 | 223 | — |
| 622 | 117 | 238 | — |
| 623 | 118 | 239 | — |
| 624 | 119 | 240 | — |
| 625 | 120 | 241 | — |
| 626 | 121 | 228 | — |
| 627 | 122 | 222 | — |
| 628 | 123 | 217 | — |
| 629 | 124 | 199 | — |
| 630 | 125 | — | — |
| 631 | 126 | 246 | — |
| 632 | 127 | 198 | — |
| 633 | 128 | 247 | — |
| 634 | 129 | 194 | — |
| 635 | 130 | 212 | — |
| 636 | 131 | 248 | — |
| 637 | 132 | 249 | — |
| 638 | 133 | 250 | — |

## SIMONIDES

| Loeb/*P.M.G.* (margin) | *P.M.G.* (Sim.) | Bergk | Diehl |
|---|---|---|---|
| 639 | 134 | 224 | — |
| 640 | 135 | 225 | — |
| 641 | 136 | 195 | — |
| 642 | 137 | 191 | — |
| 643 | 138 | 193 | — |
| 644 | 139 | 219a | — |
| 645 | 140 | 19 | — |
| 646 | 141 | 192 | — |
| 647 | 142 | 221 | — |
| 648 | 143 | 196 | — |
| 649 | 144 | — | — |
| 650 | 145 | — | — |
| 651 | 146 | 190a | — |
| 652 | 147 | — | — |
| 653 | 148 | 189 | — |

N.B. The papyrus fragments published in *S.L.G.* have been numbered as follows:

> S 319–386 = fr. 519A
> S 387–442 = fr. 519B

\*\*\*\*\*\*\*\*\*\*\*\*\*\*

### ELEGIAC FRAGMENTS

| Loeb/West *I.E.G.* | Bergk | Diehl |
|---|---|---|
| 1 | 83 | — |
| 2 | 241 | — |
| 3 | — | 66a |
| 4 | 86 | 73 |
| 5 | 88(3) | 72 |
| 6 | 167 | 67 |
| 7 | 171 | 68 |
| 8 | 85 | Semon.29 |
| 9 | 81 | 62 |

## COMPARATIVE NUMERATION

| Loeb/West *I.E.G.* | Bergk | Diehl |
|---|---|---|
| 10 | 84.1–3 | 64.1–3 |
| 11 | 84.4–6 | 64.4–6 |
| 12 | 84.7 | 51 |
| 13 | 176 | 75 |
| 14 | 146 | 78 |
| 15 | 67 | 53 |
| 16 | 113 | 84 |
| 17 | 170 | 162 |

* * * * * * * * * * * * *

### EPIGRAMS

| Loeb/*F.G.E.* | Bergk | Diehl |
|---|---|---|
| I | 131 | 76 |
| II | 89 | 87 |
| III | 132 | 100 |
| IV | — | — |
| V | 133 | 143 |
| VI | 94 | 83 |
| VII | 95 | 120 |
| VIII | 100 | 118 |
| IX | 99 | 121 |
| X | 98 | 94 |
| XI | 96 | 90 |
| XII | 97 | 95 |
| XIII | 134 | 108 |
| XIV | 137 | 104 |
| XV | 140 | 107 |
| XVI | 107 | 96 |
| XVII | 138 | 105 |
| XVIII | 101 | 119 |
| XIX | 143 | 144 |
| XIX(a) | 136 | 65 |

# SIMONIDES

| Loeb/*F.G.E.* | Bergk | Diehl |
|---|---|---|
| XX | — | 88ab |
| XXI | 90 | 88 |
| XXII(a) | 91 | 91 |
| XXII(b) | 92 | 92 |
| XXIII | 93 | 93 |
| XXIV | 135 | 109 |
| XXV | 156 | 153 |
| XXVI(a) | 111 | 85 |
| XXVI(b) | — | — |
| XXVII | 145 | 79 |
| XXVIII | 147 | 77 |
| XXIX | 152 | 148 |
| XXX | 149 | 111 |
| XXXI | 154 | 149 |
| XXXII | 161 | 154 |
| XXXIII | 162 | 163 |
| XXXIV | 141 | 106 |
| XXXV | 125 | 98 |
| XXXVI | 112 | 86 |
| XXXVII | 169 | 99 |
| XXXVIII | 104 | 89 |
| XXXIX | p.516 | — |
| XL | p.518 | — |
| XLI | 163 | 110 |
| XLII | 153 | 151 |
| XLIII | 155 | 147 |
| XLIV | 159 | 113 |
| XLV | 142 | 103 |
| XLVI | 105 | 115 |
| XLVII | 106 | 116 |
| XLVIII | 160 | 112 |
| XLIX | 108 | 117 |
| L | 187 | 166 |
| LI | 180 | 127 |
| LII | 188 | 152 |
| LIII | 102 | 122 |

## COMPARATIVE NUMERATION

| Loeb/*F.G.E.* | Bergk | Diehl |
|---|---|---|
| LIV | 103 | 123 |
| LV | 186 | 155 |
| LVI | (ed.2) p.323 | (ed.1) p.95 |
| LVII | 185A | 164 |
| LVIII | 185B | 165 |
| LIX | 179 | 158 |
| LX | 178 | 157 |
| LXI | 144 | 145 |
| LXII | 164 | 146 |
| LXIII | 157 | 114 |
| LXIV | 151 | 159 |
| LXV | 182 | 124 |
| LXVI | 183 | 125 |
| LXVII | 184 | 126 |
| LXVIII | 114 | 80 |
| LXIX | 130 | 142 |
| LXX | 117 | 130 |
| LXXI | 120 | 136 |
| LXXII | 119 | 135 |
| LXXIII | 123 | 134 |
| LXXIV | 115 | 128 |
| LXXV | 113 | 84 |
| LXXVI | 109 | 97 |
| LXXVII | 121 | 137 |
| LXXVIII | 127 | 138 |
| LXXIX | 122 | 139 |
| LXXX | 124A | 140 |
| LXXXI | 124B | 131 |
| LXXXII | 118 | 132 |
| LXXXIII | 110 | 141 |
| LXXXIV | 128 | 81 |
| LXXXV | 129 | 82 |
| LXXXVI | 126 | 133 |
| LXXXVII | 158 | 150 |
| LXXXVIII | 167 | 67 |
| LXXXIX | 176 | 75 |

* * * * * * * * * * * * *

# SIMONIDES

| Bergk | Loeb | Bergk | Loeb |
|-------|------|-------|------|
| 1 | 533(a) | 36 | 523 |
| 2 | 533(b) | 37 | 543 |
| 3 | 534 | 38 | 522 |
| 4 | 531 | 39 | 520 |
| 5 | 542 | 40 | 567 |
| 6 | 513 | 41 | 595 |
| 7 | 515 | 42 | 525 |
| 8 | 509 | 43 | 575 |
| 9 | 518 | 44 | 577(a) |
| 10 | 506 | 45 | 577(b) |
| 11 | 514 | 46 | (adesp.947) |
| 12 | 508 | 47 | 593 |
| 13 | 507 | 48 | 545 |
| 14 | 512 | 49 | 559 |
| 15 | 591 | 50 | 572 |
| 16 | 516 | 51 | 571 |
| 17 | 517 | 52 | 553 |
| 18 | 555 | 53 | 564 |
| 19 | 645 | 54 | 550(a) |
| 20 | 589 | 55 | 551 |
| 21 | 576 + 544 | 56 | 550(b) |
| 22 | 546 | 57 | 581 |
| 23 | (adesp.1005) | 58 | 579 |
| 24 | 537 | 59 | 587 |
| 25 | 535 | 60 | — |
| 26A | 573 | 61 | 526 |
| 26B | (adesp.950) | 62 | 527 |
| 27 | 539 | 63 | 594 |
| 28 | 562 | 64 | 592 |
| 29 | (Pind. fr.107a) | 65 | 524 |
| 30 | (Pind. fr.107a) | 66 | 582 |
| 31 | (Pind. fr.107b) | 67 | eleg.15 |
| 32 | 521 | 68 | 538 |
| 33 | 529 | 69 | 603 |
| 34 | 528 | 70 | 604 |
| 35 | 530 | 71 | 584 |

# COMPARATIVE NUMERATION

| Bergk | Loeb | Bergk | Loeb |
|-------|------|-------|------|
| 72 | 585 | 107 | XVI |
| 73 | 586 | 108 | XLIX |
| 74 | 597 | 109 | LXXVI |
| 75 | 602 | 110 | LXXXIII |
| 76 | 598 | 111 | XXVI(a) |
| 77 | 605 | 112 | XXXVI |
| 78 | 600 | 113 | eleg.16 = LXXV |
| 79 | 599 | 114 | LXVIII |
| 80A | 519 fr. 79 | 115 | LXXIV |
| 80B | 583 | 116 | (Simmias fr.21 P.) |
| 81 | eleg.9 | 117 | LXX |
| 82 | (anon. CXXVI v.9) | 118 | LXXXII |
| 83 | 536=eleg.1 | 119 | LXXII |
| 84 | eleg.10,11,12 | 120 | LXXI |
| 85 | eleg.8 | 121 | LXXVII |
| 86 | eleg.4 | 122 | LXXIX |
| 87 | (adesp. eleg.21) | 123 | LXXIII |
| 88 | eleg.5 | 124A | LXXX |
| 89 | II | 124B | LXXXI |
| 90 | XXI | 125 | XXXV |
| 91 | XXII(a) | 126 | LXXXVI |
| 92 | XXII(b) | 127 | LXXVIII |
| 93 | XXIII | 128 | LXXXIV |
| 94 | VI | 129 | LXXXV |
| 95 | VII | 130 | LXIX |
| 96 | XI | 131 | I |
| 97 | XII | 132 | III |
| 98 | X | 133 | V |
| 99 | IX | 134 | XIII |
| 100 | VIII | 135 | XXIV |
| 101 | XVIII | 136 | XIX(a) |
| 102 | LIII | 137 | XIV |
| 103 | LIV | 138 | XVII(a) |
| 104 | XXXVIII | 139 | XVII(b) |
| 105 | XLVI | 140 | XV |
| 106 | XLVII | 141 | XXXIV |

| Bergk | Loeb | Bergk | Loeb |
|-------|------|-------|------|
| 142 | XLV | 178 | LX |
| 143 | XIX | 179 | LIX |
| 144 | LXI | 180 | LI |
| 145 | XXVII | 181 | ('Anacreon' XVI) |
| 146 | eleg.14 | 182 | LXV |
| 147 | XXVIII | 183 | LXVI |
| 148 | (Antigenes I) | 184 | LXVII |
| 149 | XXX | 185A | LVII |
| 150 | ('Anacreon' XV) | 185B | LVIII |
| 151 | LXIV | 186 | LV |
| 152 | XXIX | 187 | L |
| 153 | XLII | 188 | LII |
| 154 | XXXI | 189 | 653 |
| 155 | XLIII | 190A | 651 |
| 156 | XXV | 190B | test.47(a) |
| 157 | LXIII | 191 | 642 |
| 158 | LXXXVII | 192 | 646 |
| 159 | XLIV | 193 | 643 |
| 160 | XLVIII | 194 | 634 |
| 161 | XXXII | 195 | 641 |
| 162 | XXXIII | 196 | 648 |
| 163 | XLI | 197 | 570 |
| 164 | LXII | 198 | 632 |
| 165 | after LXXXIX | 199 | 629 |
| 166 | after LXXXIX | 200A | 576 |
| 167 | eleg.6 = LXXXVIII | 200B | 552 |
| 168 | — | 201 | 578 |
| 169 | XXXVII | 202A | 568 |
| 170 | eleg.17 | 202B | 556 |
| 171 | eleg.7 | 203 | 569 |
| 172 | — | 204 | 548 |
| 173 | — | 205 | 547 |
| 174 | — | 206 | 596 |
| 175 | (adesp. eleg.22) | 207 | 549 |
| 176 | eleg.13 = LXXXIX | 208 | 561 |
| 177 | — | 209 | 557 |

## COMPARATIVE NUMERATION

| Bergk | Loeb | Bergk | Loeb |
|-------|------|-------|------|
| 210A | 574 | 230 | 612 |
| 210B | 615 | 231 | 614 |
| 211 | 613 | 232 | 601 |
| 212 | 635 | 233 | 617 |
| 213 | 558 | 234 | 560 |
| 214 | 565 | 235 | 618 |
| 215 | 609 | 236 | 619 |
| 216 | 563 | 237 | 620 |
| 217 | 628 | 238 | 622 |
| 218 | 616 | 239 | 623 |
| 219A | 644 | 240 | 624 |
| 219B | 554 | 241 | 625=eleg.2 |
| 220 | 610 | 242 | (Simmias fr.12P.) |
| 221 | 647 | 243 | 606 |
| 222 | 627 | 244 | 588 |
| 223 | 621 | 245 | 566 |
| 224 | 639 | 246 | 631 |
| 225 | 640 | 247 | 633 |
| 226 | 590 | 248 | 636 |
| 227 | — | 249 | 637 |
| 228 | 626 | 250 | 638 |
| 229 | 611 | | |

\* \* \* \* \* \* \* \* \* \* \* \* \* \*

| Diehl | Loeb | Diehl | Loeb |
|-------|------|-------|------|
| 1 | 533(a) | 11 | 527 |
| 2 | 533(b) | 12 | 524 |
| 3 | 538 | 13 | 543 |
| 4 | 542 | 13Aa | 571 |
| 5 | 531 | 13a | Bacch.60 |
| 6 | 521 | 13b | Bacch.61 |
| 7 | 523 | 14 | 512 |
| 8 | 522 | 15 | 514 |
| 9 | 520 | 16 | 516 |
| 10 | 526 | 17 | 517 |

# SIMONIDES

| Diehl | Loeb | Diehl | Loeb |
|-------|------|-------|------|
| 18 | 591 | 54 | 603 |
| 19 | 515 | 55 | 598 |
| 20 | 508 | 56 | 604 |
| 21 | 506 | 57 | 584 |
| 22 | 507 | 58 | 587 |
| 23 | 509 | 59 | 594 |
| 24 | 575 | 60 | 599 |
| 25 | 577(b) | 61 | 580 |
| 26 | 577(a) | 62 | eleg.9 |
| 27 | 567 | 63 | (anon. CXXVI v.9) |
| 28 | 571 | 64 | eleg.10,11 |
| 29 | 553 | 65 | XIX |
| 30 | 555 | 66 | (adesp. eleg.21) |
| 31 | 545 | 66a | eleg.3 |
| 32 | 564 | 67 | eleg.6 = LXXXVIII |
| 33 | 550(a) | 68 | eleg.7 |
| 34 | 551 | 69 | — |
| 35 | 559 | 70 | — |
| 36 | 572 | 71 | — |
| 37 | 579 | 72 | eleg.5 |
| 38 | 582 | 73 | eleg.4 |
| 39 | 519 fr. 79 | 74 | after LXXXIX |
| 40 | 595 | 75 | eleg.13 = LXXXIX |
| 41 | 600 | 76 | I |
| 42 | (adesp. 1005) | 77 | XXVIII |
| 43 | 593 | 78 | eleg.14 |
| 44 | 585 | 79 | XXVII |
| 45 | 586 | 80 | LXVIII |
| 46 | 597 | 81 | LXXXIV |
| 47 | 583 | 82 | LXXXV |
| 48 | 581 | 83 | VI |
| 49 | 602 | 84 | eleg.16 = LXXV |
| 50 | 592 | 85 | XXVI(a) |
| 51 | eleg.12 | 86 | XXXVI |
| 52 | 605 | 87 | II |
| 53 | eleg.15 | 88 | XXI |

## COMPARATIVE NUMERATION

| Diehl | Loeb | Diehl | Loeb |
|-------|------|-------|------|
| 88ab | XX | 124 | LXV |
| 89 | XXXVIII | 125 | LXVI |
| 90 | XI | 126 | LXVII |
| 91 | XXII(a) | 127 | LI |
| 92 | XXII(b) | 128 | LXXIV |
| 93 | XXIII | 129 | (Simmias fr. 21 P.) |
| 94 | X | 130 | LXX |
| 95 | XII | 131 | LXXXI |
| 96 | XVI | 132 | LXXXII |
| 97 | LXXVI | 133 | LXXXVI |
| 98 | XXXV | 134 | LXXXIII |
| 99 | XXXVII | 135 | LXXII |
| 100 | III | 136 | LXXI |
| 101 | ('Anacreon' XV) | 137 | LXXVII |
| 102 | XVII(b) | 138 | LXXVIII |
| 103 | XLV | 139 | LXXIX |
| 104 | XIV | 140 | LXXX |
| 105 | XVII | 141 | LXXXIII |
| 106 | XXXIV | 142 | LXIX |
| 107 | XV | 143 | V |
| 108 | XIII | 144 | XIX |
| 109 | XXIV | 145 | LXI |
| 110 | XLI | 146 | LXII |
| 111 | XXX | 147 | XLIII |
| 112 | XLVIII | 148 | XXIX |
| 113 | XLIV | 149 | XXXI |
| 114 | LXIII | 150 | LXXXVII |
| 115 | XLVI | 151 | XLII |
| 116 | XLVII | 152 | LII |
| 117 | XLIX | 153 | XXV |
| 118 | VIII | 154 | XXXII |
| 119 | XVIII | 155 | LV |
| 120 | VII | 156 | ('Anacreon' XVI) |
| 121 | IX | 157 | LX |
| 122 | LIII | 158 | LIX |
| 123 | LIV | 159 | LXIV |

# SIMONIDES

\* \* \* \* \* \* \* \* \* \* \* \* \*

# INDEX OF AUTHORS AND SOURCES

# INDEX OF AUTHORS AND SOURCES

# INDEX OF AUTHORS AND SOURCES

# INDEX OF AUTHORS AND SOURCES

# INDEX OF AUTHORS AND SOURCES

624

# INDEX OF AUTHORS AND SOURCES

# INDEX OF AUTHORS AND SOURCES

627

# INDEX OF AUTHORS AND SOURCES

629

# INDEX OF AUTHORS AND SOURCES

# GENERAL INDEX

Acamas, son of Theseus and
Phaedra: 97

Acanthus, city of Chalcidice:
483

Acarnania, district of N.W.
Greece: 525

Acestor (Healer) ( = Apollo?):
411

Achaeans, the Greeks: 109,
113, 135, 223, 457

Acheron, river of Hades; used of
the world of Hades: 579

Achilles, son of Peleus and
Thetis: 41, 43, 117, 119, 121,
131, 151, 163, 185, 223, 243,
259, 449

Acragas (Agrigentum), city of
S.W. Sicily: 13, 345, 381

Acrisius, mythical king of
Argos: 141, 437

Acropolis of Athens: 523

Actaeon, killed by his hounds
after he saw Artemis
bathing: 165

Adimantus, archon in 477/6
B.C.: 335, 547

Adimantus, Corinthian
commander at Salamis: 529

Admetus, king of Pherae in
Thessaly: 63

Adrastus of Argos, leader of
Seven against Thebes: 99,
141, 223, 225, 577

Aea, land of the Golden Fleece:
249

Aeaces, father of Polycrates,
tyrant of Samos: 208

Aeacus, son of Zeus and Aegina,
father of Peleus and
grandfather of Achilles: 117

Aeantides of Lampsacus, son-
in-law of Hippias: 545

Aeatius, sons praised by
Simonides: 379

Aegean Sea: 223

Aegeus, king of Athens, father
of Theseus: 403, 443, 445

Aegialeus, son of Adrastus:
223, 225

Aegina, island in Saronic Gulf:
371, 539, 549, 561

Aegisthus, cousin of
Agamemnon, seducer of
Clytemnestra: 27, 133, 157,
213

Aeneas, Trojan hero, ancestor
of Romans: 106, 107

Aeolian Islands, N. of Sicily:
147, 155

Aeolian Sea, the
Mediterranean N. of Sicily:
183

Aeolian tuning in music: 307,
325

Aeolus, ruler of winds: 147,
151, 153, 154

631

# GENERAL INDEX

# GENERAL INDEX

Antenor, Athenian sculptor, *fl. c.* 540–500 B.C.: 521

Anthela, place near Thermopylae, centre of Amphictionic League: 543

Antigone, mother of Tlepolemus: 447

Antiochid tribe at Athens: 335, 547

Antiochus, ruler of Thessaly: 341, 421, 423

Antiope, Amazon: 445

Antiphates, son of Melampus: 159

Antissa, city of Lesbos: 193

Aphareus, brother of Tyndareus and father of Idas: 159, 451

Aphidna, town of N.E. Attica: 91

Aphrodite, goddess of love and beauty: 113, 115, 157, 231, 247, 251, 263, 279, 433, 461, 531, 571, 575; *see also* Cypris, Dione

Apodeixeis, Arcadian Festival: 205

Apollo, god of music, prophecy etc.: 59, 103, 115, 131, 137, 155, 157, 163, 169, 205, 207, 243, 259, 261, 291, 313, 379, 389, 391, 393, 395, 423, 451, 459, 461, 463, 505, 547, 551, 575, 585; *see also* Paean, Phoebus

Apollonius of Tyana, neopythagorean sage, 1st c. A.D.: 333

Arabus, eponymous hero of Arabia: 165

Arcadia, mountainous region of central Peloponnese: 2, 29, 81, 89, 201, 205, 525, 561

Arcesilaus, sculptor: 575

Archedice, daughter of Hippias: 545

Archelaus, king of Macedonia *c.* 413–399 B.C.: 342

Archemorus, infant son of Lycurgus, king of Nemea: 445

Archenautes, husband of Xanthippe: 553

Arcisius, grandfather of Odysseus: 267

Arene, place in Messenia: 451

Ares, god of war: 99, 123, 167, 277, 279, 461, 531, 533, 555, 557, 563, 565; *see also* Enyalius

Arete (Excellence, Virtue): 463

Arethusa, spring in Syracuse: 279

Argonauts, heroes who sailed with Jason to fetch the Golden Fleece: 4, 8, 369, 430, 441

Argos, city of E. Peloponnese: 27, 91, 93, 131, 141, 161, 201, 203, 205, 207, 221, 223, 261, 443, 553, 559, 577

Argyrippa, Arpi, city of E. Italy: 261

Aristaeus, god or hero, protector of cattle and fruit-trees; father of Actaeon by Autonoe: 265

Aristides, Athenian statesman, commander at Plataea: 533

Aristides, son of Xenophilus, Athenian *choregos* in 477/6 B.C.: 335, 547

Aristodemus of Elis, wrestler: 567

Aristodicus, father of Arcesilaus: 575

633

# GENERAL INDEX

# GENERAL INDEX

# GENERAL INDEX

640

# GENERAL INDEX

festival: 205

Gyrton, place in N.E. Thessaly: 493

Hades, god of dead in lower world; also the lower world itself: 67, 85, 113, 121, 149, 163, 253, 317, 527, 579; *see also* Clymenus

Harmodius, killer of Hipparchus in 514 B.C.: 521

Harpagus ('snatcher'), horse of Dioscuri: 61

Harpies, winged females who snatched away people and things: 259

Heaven (Ouranos): 279, 445

Hecate, chthonian goddess: 129

Hector, Trojan warrior, son of Priam: 157, 243, 261

Hecuba, wife of Priam: 103, 449

Helen, wife of Menelaus: 4, 8, 25, 29, 41, 43, 89–97, 103, 105, 107, 113, 115, 125, 157, 221, 259, 261, 263, 451

Helianax, brother of Stesichorus: 29

Helicon, mountain of Boeotia, haunt of Muses: 207, 223, 463

Helius: *see* Sun

Helladius, priest of Megara, 4th c. A.D.?: 532, 533

Hephaestus, lame god of fire and the smithy: 85, 87, 163, 265, 279, 445, 455, 575

Hera, wife of Zeus: 61, 167, 525

Heraclea, city on the Black Sea coast of Bithynia: 555

Heracles, hero, son of Zeus (or Amphitryon) and Alcmena: 4, 8, 27, 65–81, 121, 123, 153, 161, 173, 181, 201, 225,

233, 255, 263, 265, 373, 409, 411, 445, 447, 453, 519, 555

Hermes (Hermaon), young god, messenger of Zeus: 61, 165, 447

Hermione, city of S.E. Argolis: 9, 193, 297–311, 329

Hermione, daughter of Helen and Menelaus: 113, 261

Hermione, Syracusan name for Persephone: 113

Hesperides, 'western' goddesses who guarded a tree of golden apples: 65, 235

Hesperus, the evening star: 283

Hestia, goddess of the hearth: 401

Hicanus, killer of Stesichorus?: 43

Hicetaon, brother of Priam: 123

Hiero, tyrant of Syracuse 478–467/6 B.C.: 13, 341, 343, 349, 363, 365, 369, 465, 511, 547, 551

Himera, city on N. coast of Sicily, home of Stesichorus; also two rivers nearby: 2, 5, 7, 29, 32, 33, 37, 39, 41, 43, 45, 47, 51, 89, 91, 107, 161, 165, 181, 193, 197, 291, 551

Hipparchus, astronomer, c. 190–after 126 B.C.: 183

Hipparchus, son of Pisistratus; murdered 514 B.C.: 9, 12, 299, 339, 521

Hippias, son of Pisistratus, tyrant of Athens 527–510 B.C.: 339, 545, 547

Hippoclus, tyrant of Lampsacus, late 6th c. B.C.: 545

Hippocratidas (of Sparta?): 405

Hippolyta, queen of Amazons:

641

# GENERAL INDEX

Laodice, daughter of Priam: 107

Laodice, earlier name of Electra: 27

Lapiths, Thessalian tribe: 493

Larissa, principal city of Thessaly: 135, 493

Lechaeum, harbour of Corinth: 441

Leda, daughter of Thestius and wife of Tyndareus: 267

Lemnos, island in N.E. Aegean: 299, 441

Leocrates, athlete?: 377

Leon, commemorated by 'Simonides': 587

Leonidas, king of Sparta 490–480 B.C., leader of resistance at Thermopylae: 425, 527, 541, 587

Leontichus, lover of Rhadine: 195

Leontini, city of E. Sicily: 7, 237

Leonymus of Croton, general, 6th c. B.C.: 41, 43

Leophron, victor in mule-cart race?: 383

Leoprepes, father of Simonides: 331, 333, 335, 347, 361, 517, 527, 543, 547, 549

Leotychidas, king of Sparta: 405

Lesbos, largest island off Asia Minor: 1, 19, 21, 177

Lethe (Forgetfulness) in Hades: 579

Leto, Lato, mother of Apollo and Artemis: 259, 389, 393, 531, 575

Leucas, cliff on S.W. Leucas in Ionian Sea: 193

Leucippus, brother of Tyndareus: 159; cf. 175

Libya = Africa; nymph, ancestor of Cadmus: 285

Libyan Sea, the S. Mediterranean between Carthage and Egypt: 181

Lindus, city of rhodes: 465, 571

Linus, mythical musician: 47

Lipara, city in the Aeolian Islands: 147

Locri Epizephyrii, Dorian city in the toe of Italy: 2, 3, 35, 39, 41

Locrian tuning in music: 353

Locris, region of central Greece, east and west of Phocis: 135, 543

Love: see Eros

Lycaeus, place in Arcadia: 561

Lycaon, son of Priam; killed by Achilles: 185

Lycas, hound: 581

Lycia, country in S.W. Asia Minor: 103, 393, 563

Lycomidae, Athenian family: 489

Lycormas, Aetolian river: 451

Lycurgus, king of Nemea: 445

Lycurgus, king of Thrace, hostile to Dionysus: 163

Lycurgus, son of Pronax, brother of Adrastus' wife: 99

Lycurgus, Spartan lawgiver: 289, 491

Lydia, kingdom of W. Asia Minor: 473

Lydian tuning in music: 203

Lysimachus of Eretria: 415, 423

Macar, legendary first settler of Lesbos: 177

Maeonia, ancient name for Lydia: 53

643

# GENERAL INDEX

Magna Graecia, the Greek
cities of S. Italy: 27

Magnesia, mountainous region
of Thessaly E. of Iolcus: 441

Maia, Maias, mother of
Hermes: 447

Maidens (Parthenoi) =
Nymphs?: 255

Mamercus, Mamertinus,
brother of Stesichorus: 29,
37

Mandrocles of Samos, engineer,
*fl. c.* 514/13 B.C.: 523, 525

Mantinea, city of Arcadia: 569

Marathon, eponymous hero of
Marathon: 269

Marathon, village of N.E.
Attica where Athenians
defeated Persians in 490
B.C.: 12, 343, 513, 539, 541

Mardonius, Persian
commander at Plataea: 555

Marpessa, wife of Idas: 451

Mars, planet: 175

Marsyas, Phrygian silenus and
piper flayed by Apollo: 207

Matauria, Mataurus,
Metauron, city in S. Italy: 2,
29, 35

Medea of Colchis, wife of Jason:
249, 259, 441, 443, 449

Medes: *see* Persians

Medusa, daughter of Priam:
107

Megacles, mourned by
Simonides: 519

Megara, coastal city between
Corinth and Athens: 165,
491, 499, 533, 535, 561, 579

Megara, wife of Heracles: 161

Megaristus, father of Pythonax:
583

Megisteus, young companion of
Anacreon: 579

Megistias, Acarnanian seer
killed at Thermopylae: 525,
543

Melampus, mythical seer: 159

Melampus of Cephallenia,
cithara-singer, Pythian
victor in 586 B.C.: 201

Melanippe, Amazon: 445

Meleager, mythical prince of
Calydon: 4, 8, 51, 63, 135,
147, 259, 453

Melicertes, nickname of
Simonides: 331, 335

Memnon, son of Tithonus and
Dawn, leader of Ethiopians,
Trojan allies: 149, 151, 431

Mende, city of Pallene: 401

Menelaus, king of Sparta: 8, 89,
91, 107, 115, 125, 157, 259,
261, 263, 429

Menestheus, leader of
Athenians at Troy: 559

Menoites, herdsman of Hades:
67

Messana (mod. Messina), city
of N.E. Sicily facing
Rhegium: 6, 211, 382

Messene, city of Messenia in
S.W. Peloponnese: 1, 207,
451

Metapont(i)um, Greek city in S.
Italy: 261

Methouriades, islands in
Saronic Gulf: 579

Methymna, city of Lesbos: 17,
19, 23

Metion, son of Erechtheus: 269

Midas, king of Phrygia 736–696
B.C.: 415, 465

Midea, city E. of Argos,
birthplace of Alcmena: 415

# GENERAL INDEX

# GENERAL INDEX

647

# GENERAL INDEX

# GENERAL INDEX